THE HEBREW GOSPEL AND THE DEVELOPMENT
OF THE SYNOPTIC TRADITION

The Hebrew Gospel and the Development of the Synoptic Tradition

James R. Edwards

WILLIAM B. EERDMANS PUBLISHING COMPANY
GRAND RAPIDS, MICHIGAN / CAMBRIDGE, U.K.

Published 2009 by

Wm. B. Eerdmans Publishing Co.

2140 Oak Industrial Drive N.E., Grand Rapids, Michigan 49505 /

P.O. Box 163, Cambridge CB3 9PU U.K.

Printed in the United States of America

14 13 12 11 10 09   7 6 5 4 3 2 1

Library of Congress Cataloging-in-Publication Data

Edwards, James R.

The Hebrew Gospel and the development of the synoptic tradition /
James R. Edwards.

p.   cm.

Includes bibliographical references.

ISBN 978-0-8028-6234-1 (pbk.: alk. paper)

1. Bible. N.T. Gospels — Criticism, interpretation, etc.

2. Bible. N.T. Gospels. Hebrew — Versions.   3. Synoptic problem.

4. Two source hypothesis (Synoptics criticism)

5. Q hypothesis (Synoptics criticism)   I. Title.

BS2555.52.E39   2009

226'.066 — dc22

2009026538

www.eerdmans.com

With grateful appreciation to

Bill and Peggy Welch

whose endowment of

the Bruner-Welch Chair of Theology at Whitworth University

helped make this book possible

Contents

PREFACE xi

ABBREVIATIONS xiv

Introduction **xviii**

Genesis of a Thesis xviii

A Panorama of Modern Research on the Hebrew Gospel xxiii

1. References to a "Hebrew Gospel" in Early Christianity **1**

Papias 2

Irenaeus 10

Pantaenus 12

Clement of Alexandria 12

Hegesippus 15

Hippolytus 16

Origen 17

Eusebius 18

Ephrem the Syrian 23

Didymus of Alexandria 23

Epiphanius 26

John Chrysostom 28

Jerome   28

Theodoret of Cyrrhus   38

Marius Mercator   38

Philip Sidetes   39

Venerable Bede   40

Scholia in Codex Sinaiticus   40

Islamic Hadith   42

Summary   43

2. **Quotations from the Hebrew Gospel in Early Christianity**   **44**

Ignatius   45

Origen   55

Eusebius   62

Epiphanius   65

Jerome   76

3. **Taking Stock of the Hebrew Gospel in Early Christianity**   **97**

1. The Hebrew Gospel Was Widespread and
   Widely Known in Early Christianity   102

2. The Hebrew Gospel Was Endowed with Unusual
   Authority in Early Christianity   105

3. The Hebrew Gospel Is Not a Compilation
   of the Synoptic Gospels, but Repeatedly and
   Distinctly Similar to Luke   107

4. The Hebrew Gospel Was Most Plausibly a
   Source of the Gospel of Luke   112

5. The Relation of the Hebrew Gospel to Other
   "Jewish Christian Gospels"   118

4. **Semitisms in the Gospel of Luke**   **125**

Luke's Semitic Vocabulary   126

The Nature of Semitisms   127

Semitisms Characteristic of the Gospel of Luke   131

Summary of Evidence 141

Luke's Prologue 148

5. **The *Hebrew* Gospel** **154**

The Task 155

The Septuagint Hypothesis 156

The Aramaic Hypothesis 162

The Use of Hebrew and Aramaic among Jews
    in First-Century Palestine 166

The Probability of a *Christian* Text like the
    Hebrew Gospel being Written in Hebrew 174

Luke's Use of a Hebrew Source 182

6. **The Neglect of the Hebrew Gospel in Christian Tradition** **187**

Why Is There No Extant Copy of Hebrew Matthew? 189

Resistance to a Hebrew Ancestor in the Family 194

7. ***Adieu* to "Q"** **209**

The Challenge 211

The Genesis of "Q" 212

Is There a Precedent for "Q" in Early Christianity? 224

"Q" and Luke 233

Adieu to "Q" 240

8. **The Hebrew Gospel and the Gospel of Matthew** **243**

Matthean Posteriority 245

The Authorship of Canonical Matthew 252

EPILOGUE: Summary Theses 259

APPENDIX I: References to the Hebrew Gospel
    in the First Nine Centuries 263

APPENDIX II: Semitisms in the Gospel of Luke 292

APPENDIX III: Luke 6:5 (D) 333

Contents

SELECTED BIBLIOGRAPHY   336

INDEX OF MODERN AUTHORS   342

INDEX OF SUBJECTS   346

INDEX OF SCRIPTURE REFERENCES   348

INDEX OF OTHER ANCIENT WRITINGS   356

Preface

Pursuit of the Hebrew Gospel invites — indeed summons — one into many different and important subdisciplines of NT studies: Synoptic studies, patristics, philology, the use of Hebrew in Second Temple Judaism, and post-Enlightenment Gospels research, particularly of nineteenth-century Germany. The dividends with which each of these subdisciplines has rewarded me have sustained this study over many years. When asked if he did not tire of chiseling stone, Michelangelo is reputed to have said that each blow of the hammer put strength *into* him. I have had a similar experience in the writing of this book. Whenever a particular passion is alloyed to an equally particular work a strong metal is forged, and I have experienced that happy alchemy in the writing of this book. I provide a brief narrative of this alchemy in the Introduction. Here I only wish to add that the felicity of this *oeuvre* has been equally enjoyable and stimulating in the teaching of my students and in conversations with colleagues. Their interest — even enthusiasm — in the subject of the Hebrew Gospel has added a unique synergy from the conception to the completion of this endeavor.

The following hints will aid the reader in understanding references and translations in the work. In bibliographical material and in all references to both ancient and modern works I have followed *The SBL Handbook of Style*.[1]

---

1. *The SBL Handbook of Style for Ancient Near Eastern, Biblical, and Early Christian Studies,* ed. P. Alexander, J. Kutsko, J. Ernest, S. Decker-Lucke, and D. Petersen (Peabody: Hendrickson Publishers, 1999).

The list of Abbreviations immediately after this Preface supplies complete information for all abbreviations in footnotes, except for well-known abbreviations of books of the Bible. The Selected Bibliography at the end of the book supplies complete references to the chief sources relevant to study of the Hebrew Gospel, many of which are frequently cited in this book. Whenever a source in the Selected Bibliography is cited in footnotes, I include only the author's name, the title of the work, and page number. Whenever a source is cited that is not listed in the Selected Bibliography, I include a full bibliographical reference.

References and quotations of the Hebrew Gospel, cited mainly in the first three chapters, are scattered far and wide in the church fathers and early Christian texts. For the most part, these sources were written in Greek or Latin and can be found in either the Patrologia Graeca or Patrologia Latina. Some of the texts have not, to the best of my knowledge, been translated into English, and many of those that have still exist only in antiquated English translations scattered in obscure books. I have therefore sought to give each text a clear and faithful rendering in modern English; hence, unless otherwise noted, all translations are my own. For readers interested in consulting the originals and/or checking my English translation, the original Greek or Latin texts are cited in full in the footnotes. For the sake of convenience, all known references to the Hebrew Gospel are gathered in Appendix I, complete with original citations, English translation, and page references in parentheses where each citation is discussed in the text of this book.

With respect to modern scholarship, I not infrequently quote non-English sources in their original languages in footnotes. In the body of the book, however, I have attempted to keep the English free from foreign languages and provide translations of non-English sources. Since many of these sources are not translated into English, translations in the body of the book are also my own, unless otherwise noted. Finally, BibleWorks 7 has been especially helpful to me in several procedures related to this work.

The writing of a book is inevitably and necessarily a solitary activity, but the conception of this book and the process of its development were assisted by a number of people to whom I am both indebted and grateful. Several individuals were helpful to me in their willingness to discuss, read, and advise me on individual chapters of this book, including Quinn Fox, Ron Huggins, Robert MacLennan, Lee McDonald, Scott Starbuck, Gary and Myra Watts, and Keith Wyma. Two students, Amy Whisenand and

David Sittser, provided valuable assistance in my spring 2008 Greek class, allowing me valuable hours to continue the writing of the manuscript, and Amy also ably and accurately proofread all the Greek in Appendix II. I benefited from conversations and correspondence with Eduard Schweizer and Martin Hengel over a number of years regarding this project. I am particularly grateful to Martin Hengel, Ulrich Mauser, Thomas Gillespie, and Darrell Guder for recommending it to the Center of Theological Inquiry in Princeton, where much of the writing of the manuscript was completed in fall 2007. While there, I was aided and encouraged by Will Storrar, Director of CTI, and his able staff, and by both the counsel and enthusiasm of the Members of CTI for this project. Lloyd Moote of the Institute of Advanced Studies in Princeton was a delightful *Gesprächspartner* and mentor on a variety of points raised in the course of writing. Several people have gone more than the second mile in their consistent engagement and advocacy over the long gestation of this book. Among these are Shane Berg and Ross Wagner, both of Princeton Seminary, whose questions, insights, and suggestions, especially in relation to Semitisms in the Gospel of Luke, have been unfailingly helpful. Also among these are my wife Janie and two of my colleagues at Whitworth, Jerry Sittser and Adam Neder, all three of whom have read every word of the manuscript and whose interest and counsel — grammatically, historically, and theologically — have improved my work in countless ways.

Finally, with profound gratitude and yet deep sadness I mention again the names of Ulrich Mauser and Martin Hengel, whose deaths in June 2008 and July 2009 respectively have been a great loss to me personally. Conversations with Ulrich in the late 1990s were seminal in the conception of this project, and the combination of his erudition and mature theological convictions was of inestimable help and encouragement as he carefully read the entire manuscript except for the Introduction before his sudden death. On several visits to the home of Martin and Marianne Hengel in the past decade I enjoyed warm hospitality and spirited conversation regarding my research into an early Hebrew source behond Luke. Hengel's intimate knowledge of Jewish and patristic sources and his willingness to challenge scholarly trends have often lighted my way. Of these two mentors, I can only echo the words of Hebrews 11: *in Dominio morientes, adhuc loquuntur.*

JAMES R. EDWARDS
Spokane, July 6, 2009

Abbreviations

AB	Anchor Bible
ABD	*Anchor Bible Dictionary*. Ed. D. N. Friedman. 6 vols. New York, 1992.
AJT	*American Journal of Theology*
ANF	*Ante-Nicene Fathers*
ANRW	*Aufstieg und Niedergang der römischen Welt: Geschichte und Kultur Roms im Spiegel der neueren Forschung*. Ed. H. Temporini and W. Hanse. Berlin, 1972-
Ant.	Josephus, *Antiquities of the Jews*
2 Apoc. Jas.	*Second Apocalypse of James* from Nag Hammadi
1 Apol.	Justin Martyr, *First Apology*
Apol. Hier.	Rufinus, *Apologia adversus Hieronymum (Defense against Jerome)*
BAR	*Biblical Archaeological Review*
BDAG	Danker, F. W., W. Bauer, W. F. Arndt, and F. W. Gingrich. *Greek-English Lexicon of the New Testament and Other Early Christian Literature*. 3rd ed. Chicago, 2000
BDF	Blass, F., A. Debrunner, and R. W. Funk. *A Greek Grammar of the New Testament and Other Early Christian Literature*. Chicago, 1961
BETL	Bibliotheca ephemeridum theologicarum lovaniensium
bGit.	Tractate *Gittin, Babylonian Talmud*
BR	*Biblical Research*
bŠabb.	Tractate *Shabbat*, Babylonian Talmud
bSanh.	Tractate *Sanhedrin*, Babylonian Talmud
bSotah	Tractate *Sotah*, Babylonian Talmud

BZNW	Beihefte zur Zeitschrift für die neutestamentliche Wissenschaft
C. Ap.	Josephus, *Contra Apionem (Against Apion)*
CCSL	Corpus Christianorum: Series latina, Turnhout, 1953-
Cels.	Origen, *Against Celsus*
Chron. Brev.	Nicephorus, *Chronographia Brevis Quae Scripturae Canonica*
Civ.	Augustine, *De civitate Dei (The City of God)*
1, 2 Clem.	*1, 2 Clement*
Comm. Eccl. IV	Didymus the Blind, *Commentary on Ecclesiastes*
Comm. Eph.	Jerome, *Commentary on Ephesians*
Comm. Ezech.	Jerome, *Commentary on Ezechiel*
Comm. Isa.	Jerome, *Commentary on Isaiah*
Comm. Jo.	Origen/Jerome, *Commentary on John*
Comm. Matt.	Origen/Jerome, *Commentary on Matthew*
Comm. Mich.	Jerome, *Commentary on Micah*
Conf.	Philo, *De confusione linguarum (On the Confusion of Tongues)*
Dial.	Justin Martyr, *Dialogue with Trypho*
DSS	Dead Sea Scrolls
ed.	Edited
EDNT	*Exegetical Dictionary of the New Testament.* Edited by H. Balz and G. Schneider. 3 vols. Grand Rapids: Eerdmans, 1990-1993
Epist.	Jerome, *Epistulae (Letters)*
ETL	*Ephemerides theologicae Lovanienses*
Exp.	*The Expositor*
ExpT	*The Expository Times*
Gen. Rab.	*Genesis Rabbah*
Gos. Eb.	*Gospel of the Ebionites*
Haer. fab.	Theodoret of Cyrrhus, *Haereticarum fabularum (Of Heretical Fables)*
Haer.	Irenaeus, *Against Heresies*
Hist. eccl.	Eusebius's *Ecclesiastical History*
Hist. pass. Dom.	*Historia passionis Domini (History of the Lord's Passion)*
HNT	Handbuch zum Neuen Testament
Hom. Jer.	Origen, *Homilies on Jeremiah*
Hom. Luc.	Origen, *Homilies on Luke*
Hom. Matt.	John Chrysostom, *Homilies on Matthew*
IDB	*Interpreter's Dictionary of the Bible.* Ed. G. A. Buttrick. 4 vols. Nashville, 1962

J.W.	Josephus, *The Jewish War*
JBL	*Journal of Biblical Literature*
JJS	*Journal of Jewish Studies*
JSNT	*Journal for the Study of the New Testament*
JSOTSup	Journal for the Study of the Old Testament: Supplement Series
JSP	*Journal for the Study of the Pseudepigrapha*
JTS	*Journal of Theological Studies*
LCL	Loeb Classical Library
Libr. Isa.	Hugo of St. Cher, *The Book of Isaiah*
LXX	Septuagint, Greek translation of Hebrew OT
Marc.	Tertullian, *Adversus Marcionem (Against Marcion)*
MT	Masoretic Text of the Hebrew OT
NGS	New Gospel Series
NIGTC	New International Greek Testament Commentary
NovT	*Novum Testamentum*
NovTSup	Supplements to Novum Testamentum
NS	New Series
NT	New Testament
NTS	*New Testament Studies*
Or. Bas.	*Oratio in laudem Basilii (Orations in Honor of Basil)*
OT	Old Testament
Panarion	Epiphanius, *Panarion (Refutation of All Heresies)*
Pap.	Papyrus
Pelag.	Jerome, *Adversus Pelagianos (Against the Pelagians)*
PG	Patrologia graeca. 163 vols. Ed. J. P. Migne, 1857-1886
Phil.	Polycarp, *Philippians*
PL	Patrologia latina. 217 vols. Ed. J. P. Migne. Paris, 1844-1864
Praef.	*Praefatio (Preface)*
Princ.	Origen, *De principiis (First Principles)*
Proem.	*Proemium (Preface)*
PSB	*Princeton Seminary Bulletin*
RB	*Revue biblique*
Rev.	Revised
RGG	*Religion in Geschichte und Gegenwart.* Ed. K. Galling. 7 vols. Tübingen, 1957-1965.
SBEC	Studies in the Bible and Early Christianity
SBLTCS	Society of Biblical Literature Text-Critical Studies
SBT	Studies in Biblical Theology
SJOT	*Scandinavian Journal of the Old Testament*
Smyrn.	Ignatius, *To the Smyrnaeans*

SNTA	Studiorum Novi Testamenti Auxilia
ST	*Studia theologica*
Str-B	Strack, H. L., and P. Billerbeck, *Kommentar zum Neuen Testament aus Talmud und Midrasch.* 6 vols. Munich, 1922-1961.
Strom.	Clement of Alexandria, *Stromata (Miscellanies)*
SUNT	Studien zur Umwelt des Neuen Testaments
TDNT	*Theological Dictionary of the New Testament.* 10 vols. Ed. G. Kittel and G. Friedrich. Grand Rapids, 1964-1976
TDOT	*Theological Dictionary of the Old Testament.* 8 vols. Ed. G. J. Botterweck and H. Ringgren. Trans. J. T. Willis, G. W. Bromiley, and D. E. Green. Grand Rapids, 1974-
Theoph.	Eusebius, *Theophania (Divine Manifestation)*
Thom. Cont.	*The Book of Thomas the Contender* from Nag Hammadi
ThStKr	*Theologische Studien und Kritiken*
TLG	*Thesaurus linguae graecae*
Tract. Ps.	Jerome, *Tractatus in Psalmos (Tractate on the Psalms)*
Trans.	Translated
TU	Texte und Untersuchungen
TWNT	*Theologische Wörterbuch zum Neuen Testament.* 9 vols. Ed. G. Kittel and G. Friedrich. Stuttgart, 1932-1979
TZ	*Theologische Zeitschrift*
VC	*Vigiliae christianae*
Vir. ill.	Jerome, *De Viris Illustribus (On Illustrious Men)*
Vit. Mos.	Philo, *De vita Mosis (Life of Moses)*
VTSup	Supplements to Vetus Testamentum
WMANT	Wissenschaftliche Monographien zum Alten und Neuen Testament.
WUNT	Wissenschaftliche Untersuchungen zum Neuen Testament
ZNW	*Zeitschrift für die neutestamentliche Wissenschaft*
ZTK	*Zeitschrift für Theologie und Kirche*

Introduction

The Genesis of a Thesis

This book offers a new paradigm, at least in part, for the resolution of the Synoptic problem. Hans-Herbert Stoldt speaks of the critical analysis of the sources of the Gospels as "one of the most difficult research problems in the history of ideas. . . . one can truly say that no other enterprise in the history of ideas has been subjected to anywhere near the same degree of scholarly scrutiny."[1] Although the Synoptic problem has become a heavy industry of NT scholarship, it is not the exclusive property of scholars. The earliest record of the post-apostolic church already indicates an awareness of the challenges posed by having four evangelical accounts of the life of Jesus and by their possible relationships to one another. The Synoptic problem is part of the legacy of the church and of ordinary Christians. It is a problem I recognized as a junior in high school when I first read through the Gospels, and those who knew and still remember me from those years will assure you that at the time I was not a scholar. Why, on the one hand, are the NT Gospels so similar, and even repetitive; and, on the other hand, how can their distinctive differences be accounted for? This puzzle confronts virtually every thoughtful reader of the New Testament, and any help that can be rendered in understanding and resolving the Synoptic problem is a service to the church as well as to the academy.

---

1. *History and Criticism of the Marcan Hypothesis* (Macon: Mercer University Press/Edinburgh: T. & T. Clark, 1980), 1.

The specific genesis of this study began in the early years of my college teaching. As I lectured on the Synoptic problem in my course in New Testament I found myself simply repeating what I had learned as a student. Nothing in my formulation or resolution of the problem was the result of personal research or conviction. I respected the professors under whom I had studied, and my esteem for them was one reason why I had not investigated the problem personally.

I believed — and still believe — that internal evidence allows us to be reasonably certain about Markan priority, i.e., that the Gospel of Mark was utilized as a chief source for the Gospels of both Matthew and Luke. But I was at the same time vaguely discontent with the other tenet of the Two-Source Hypothesis, that a hypothetical source consisting of sayings of Jesus, code-named "Q," also belonged in the literary pedigree of Matthew and Luke. My misgivings about "Q" were prompted by two data that failed to comply with the hypothesis. The first is that the presence of material common to Matthew and Luke can be explained in other ways than by positing a second and hypothetical source. Second, and more important, to my knowledge there was no source of sayings known to the fathers that conformed to the proposed "Q" document. This latter observation was not simply an unruly datum, but one that actually argued against the "Q" hypothesis. Had a compendium of the sayings of Jesus compiled by the early church existed, it is virtually impossible to imagine that it would not be mentioned by the fathers. One may suppose that such misgivings gave birth to the present volume, but that is not the case. Though relatively easy to define, the Synoptic problem is immensely complex. An entire school of the Western intellectual tradition has hurled itself against its heights without having reached the summit. One of the distinguishing characteristics of *homo sapiens* is a tolerance for intellectual contradictions — and on this issue my tolerance had fairly wide margins, if simply by necessity. I abided something about which I had misgivings because I did not possess the expertise to critique it properly. It may be that other scholars share my predicament on this point.

I might still be living with reservations about "Q" had it not been for the first study program in Israel that I led, in 1986. *Eretz Israel* rekindled — or perhaps kindled for the first time — a desire to achieve greater mastery of biblical Hebrew. I rejuvenated my Hebrew in order to read the OT with greater facility, but one of the unanticipated consequences of this rejuvenation was a different perspective on the *New* Testament. In no NT book did

Hebrew make a greater difference than in my reading of the Third Gospel. In the ancient world, a scribe or author would often rub the writing off an old parchment in order to reclaim the surface for a new text. The result was called a palimpsest. A complete erasure of the first hand would practically destroy a parchment, so palimpsests were treated more kindly and invariably retain the faint but visible ligatures of the original lettering beneath the most recent text. Reading the Greek NT with a knowledge of biblical Hebrew is like reading a palimpsest. The Hebrew thought world, like a subtext, often lies faintly beneath the Greek surface. But in the Gospel of Luke — or at least in parts of it — the subtext became much more visible. The Hebrew words seem to have been erased less completely than elsewhere in the Gospels. They are more evident, intrusive, and inescapable. Like rocks and coral reefs, they lay barely submerged beneath Luke's Greek. Nor did Luke seem to make an effort to tame or camouflage the Hebraisms. Their primitive and alien dignity seem to be consciously retained without Hellenizing or harmonizing to Lukan style. They give every appearance of coming from a *source* that the author valued and attempted to preserve.

At the time I did not know that my discovery concurred with that of other scholars. In the past century and a half, scholars have repeatedly recognized an inordinately high number of Semitisms in the Third Gospel. This abnormality is remarkable in itself and is made more so by the probability that Luke is the only author in the NT who was a Gentile rather than a Jew. The awareness of Luke's distinctive Semitisms fermented within me long before I made a conscious decision to investigate the phenomenon in earnest. In the summer of 1998 I made my first academic reconnaissance of the project by spending several weeks examining the topic at Speer Library in Princeton, during which I was ably assisted by the research abilities of my son-in-law, Shane Berg. By the end of that time the contours of my hypothesis were evident — as was the immense amount of work that would be needed to evince it. A decade of work followed in which the thesis, or parts of it, was vetted with colleagues, proposed in journal articles, and eventually transposed into chapters of this book. Conversations with colleagues on the topic evoked within me the same hopes and fears I faced as a mountaineer before attempting an ascent. This would be a first ascent, however, that had been frequently but unsuccessfully attempted. Many friends and colleagues encouraged me that my thesis promised a feasible route to the summit. Others were dubious. One of my most respected scholarly mentors gently suggested that the Hebrew Gospel could be a trap. An acquaintance, less well known, told me that if I published my thesis it would be the end of my scholarly career. Without having willed it, I stood at a classic existential fork in the road: should I give up and admit the unlikelihood of succeeding where others had failed, or should I forsake the safety of *Haus und Hof* for the upward call of the summit? This book is evidence of my decision. Thanks to a generous invitation to pursue the project as a Member at the Center of Theological Inquiry in Princeton, I returned to Speer Library in the fall of 2007, where I completed *The Hebrew Gospel and the Development of the Synoptic Tradition.*

The thesis, *in nuce,* is that the high concentration of Semitisms in Special Luke — those portions of Luke that are not shared in common with Matthew and/or Mark — can be accounted for on the assumption that they derive from the original Hebrew Gospel. Several lines of corroborative evidence converge in support of this thesis. For one, the Semitisms in Special Luke are prolific and undisguised. An exact and comprehensive account of them is attempted in Appendix II, which shows that there is a nearly 400% increase of Semitisms in Special Luke over Semitisms in the portions of Luke shared in common with Matthew and/or Mark. This striking contrast in Lukan styles begs for explanation; and the inference to the best explanation is that the Semitisms in Special Luke derive from a Hebrew source. This hypothesis seems, by far, the strongest explanation of the otherwise puzzling fact that Luke — a non-Jew who otherwise wrote sophisticated Greek — allowed those portions of his Gospel that are not shared in common with Matthew and/or Mark to be distinctly punctuated by Semitisms.

A second and equally striking line of evidence comes from the patristic era. Of the two dozen fathers and early Christian sources that mention the Hebrew Gospel, ten preserve *quotations* from it. Some of the sources, such as Ignatius of Antioch or Sedulius Scottus, preserve single quotations, others like Origen or Epiphanius preserve several, and Jerome preserves twenty-two. All told, some fourscore quotations from the Hebrew Gospel — a fairly sizeable amount of material — are preserved from the patristic era. When these quotations are compared with the Synoptic Gospels they exhibit a decidedly stronger correspondence with the Gospel of Luke, and particularly with those portions of Luke that are not shared with Matthew and/or Mark, than with either Matthew or Mark. Thus, the comparative data from the patristic era rather indisputably corroborate evidence of Semitic influence in Special Luke. The Semitisms in Special Luke most plausibly derive from the same source as the quotations from the fathers — the Hebrew Gospel. This hypothesis is further supported by the prologue to the Third Gospel, in which Luke professes to having utilized eyewitness sources in the composition of his Gospel. According to the fathers, the Hebrew Gospel was composed by such an eyewitness, the apostle Matthew. These three remarkable data all converge in support of the thesis that Luke's Semitisms derive from his use of an original Hebrew Gospel.

This book is dedicated to exploring the various ramifications of this hypothesis. Indeed, I hope to offer sufficient evidence to transform a hypothesis into a viable theory of the development of the Synoptic tradition. The first three chapters document and discuss all known references to the Hebrew Gospel in the first nine centuries of the Christian era. In Chapters Two and Three I attempt to show that when the fathers actually *quote* from the Hebrew Gospel the quotations correlate more distinctly and repeatedly with Special Luke than with either Matthew or Mark. The fourth chapter shifts from a survey of the patristic tradition to a detailed discussion of Lukan Semitisms in which the above thesis is argued on the dual basis of philological evidence in Luke and the testimony of the prologue. The second half of the book considers questions of further relevance to the thesis. Chapter Five is devoted to the controversial question whether Luke's "Semitisms" are, in fact, only "Septuagintisms," i.e., not genuine Semitisms at all but merely imitations of Septuagint Greek, Aramaisms, or, as I argue, the result of reliance on a *Hebrew* Gospel of Matthew. The next chapter investigates reasons for the neglect of the Hebrew Gospel, particularly in twentieth-century scholarship. The lack of an extant copy of the Hebrew Gospel and an anti-Jewish resistance to a Hebrew source in the Greek Christian family tree are the two most important factors, in my opinion, for that neglect. Chapter Seven explores the controversial question of "Q." I investigate Schleiermacher's original proposal of the theory and factors that favored its adoption in nineteenth-century Germany. The "Q" hypothesis is further evaluated in terms of its ability to explain material in Luke not accounted for by Mark or by the Hebrew Gospel, and I conclude with a negative judgment regarding Q's continued viability as a hypothesis. The eighth and final chapter considers the relation between canonical Greek Matthew and the Hebrew Gospel. An Epilogue of twenty-three conclusions recapitulates the summary theses of the book.

A Panorama of Modern Research on the Hebrew Gospel

In the course of developing and articulating the above thesis I have repeatedly encountered a stock response to "the Hebrew Gospel." An initial pause is often followed by slightly apologetic questions: "I didn't know there was a Hebrew Gospel." "Is there a copy of it?" "Why have I not heard more about it?" Rather than releasing intellectual energy, mention of the Hebrew Gospel often afflicts one — particularly if one is a scholar — with self-doubt.

The ever-increasing particularization in NT studies is one of the reasons for ignorance of the Hebrew Gospel. Specialization inevitably results in a restricted field of vision, and knowledge of nineteenth-century scholarship is often a casualty of that restricted vision. Our chief witnesses to the Hebrew Gospel come from the patristic era, and nineteenth-century NT scholarship was, on the whole, remarkably well informed about that era. The nineteenth century, in fact, witnessed something of a "quest" for the Hebrew Gospel, less exalted to be sure than the quest for the historical Jesus, but a quest nonetheless. The rigor of nineteenth-century patristic scholarship has in general not been sustained in twentieth-century NT scholarship, and its abatement has inevitably resulted in diminished contact with the Hebrew Gospel.

The large number of scholars who participated in the quest for the Hebrew Gospel and the sustained rigor with which they pursued it comprise a remarkable tradition of NT scholarship. No less remarkable, perhaps, is that the scope and gains of this tradition are largely unknown to modern scholarship. The investigation that I set forth in this book pioneers new territory and reaches new conclusions with regard to the Hebrew Gospel, but it cannot be properly understood or evaluated without an appreciation of the history of scholarship behind it.

The first fifty years of the quest could be graphed by an initial high point of optimism, followed by slow decline to skepticism. The first modern scholar to shine a light into the darkness of the Hebrew Gospel was Gotthold Ephraim Lessing, who in 1778 published a series of sixty-eight hypotheses in which he argued for an original Hebrew Gospel as the source of all three Synoptic Evangelists, each of whom employed it according to his authorial intentions.[2] In assembling his theses, Lessing de-

---

2. G. E. Lessing, "New Hypothesis on the Evangelists as Merely Human Historians." The purpose of the following survey is to provide a panorama of scholarship on the Hebrew Gospel extending from Lessing to the present. The purpose is to provide a flow of names and

pended on fragmentary work on the Hebrew Gospel of Johannes Ernst Grabe, Johann Albert Fabricius, and Richard Simon earlier in the eighteenth century. In 1805, Johann Gottfried Eichhorn,[3] like Lessing, attributed similarities among the Synoptics to an original Hebrew Gospel. But Eichhorn believed that differences among the Synoptics derived from a series of now lost intermediate documents. In the year following Eichhorn's *Introduction,* his student Weber published an entire book[4] in which he maintained that the Hebrew Gospel was a biography of Jesus dependent on Palestinian sources. Additionally, Weber maintained 1) the extreme antiquity of the Hebrew Gospel, 2) its derivation from the earliest days of Christianity, and 3) and its high esteem in the church. In reaction to this and in order to defend the apostolicity of canonical Matthew, the Roman Catholic scholar Johann Hug published an *Einleitung in die Schriften des Neuen Testaments* in 1821 in which argued for the Greek rather than Hebrew provenance of canonical Matthew. Hug believed that Hebrew Matthew was simply the Jewish Christian *Gospel of the Ebionites* associated with Matthew. It, along with the work cited by Papias, was unrelated to canonical Greek Matthew, although Hug regarded some sayings from the Hebrew Gospel quoted by the fathers as possibly genuine. At roughly the same time, Johann Gieseler[5] argued that a living oral tradition was the source behind all four canonical Gospels, whereas the Hebrew Gospel was an arbitrary Jewish-Christian Gospel produced about the time of Hadrian early in the second century in opposition to the emerging canonical Gospels. In a series a studies between 1817 and 1832[6] Schleiermacher argued that the Hebrew Gospel was not a *Gospel* per se, but an aggregate of sayings and bits of tradition that was incorporated into canonical Matthew.[7] At the same

---

trends rather than detailed source information. Footnotes are thus reduced to a minimum. A bibliography of the seminal scholars in the following survey can be found in the Selected Bibliography.

3. *Einleitung in das Neue Testament.*

4. *Neue Untersuchung über Alter und Ansehen des Hebräerevangeliums,* 1806.

5. *Historisch-kritischer Versuch über Entstehung der schriftlichen Evangelien,* 1818.

6. *Versuch über Lucas,* 1817; "Über die Zeugnisse des Papias von unseren beiden ersten Evangelien," 1832.

7. The theory of a λόγια source of Jesus' sayings, preserved by the apostles and included in the Gospel of Matthew, became a staple in nineteenth-century scholarship, and particularly Protestant scholarship. D. Gla, *Die Originalsprache des Matthäusevangeliums,* 5-6, lists Lachmann, Weisse, Reuss, Baumgarten-Crusius, Meyer, Köstlin, Réville, Scholten, and B. Weiss as adhering to this theory in one form or another.

time, Hermann Olshausen[8] regarded both canonical Matthew and the Hebrew Gospel as free reworkings of an original Hebrew Matthew. In
Olshausen's view, however, the Hebrew Gospel was produced for Hebrew-
speaking Jewish Christians and contained extraneous and foreign material. The plummet of initial optimism regarding the Hebrew Gospel
reached a nadir in Matthias Schneckenburger's 1834 study of the Gospel of
Matthew.[9] Schneckenburger cast doubts on the apostolic authorship of
canonical Greek Matthew by identifying the Hebrew Gospel with Schleiermacher's sayings source, a redaction of which, in Schneckenburger's opinion, lay behind canonical Matthew. Although Schneckenburger's hypothesis found neither adherents nor defenders, his work concluded fifty years
of scholarly investigation into the Hebrew Gospel, during which the star of
the Hebrew Gospel fell from a valuable memoir of the apostolic age to the
status of a second-century fabrication that perpetrated separatist Jewish
Christian ideas and that was repeatedly but erroneously identified with canonical Greek Matthew.

The initial wave of interest in the Hebrew Gospel suffered a sobering
critique in the incisive work of Karl August Credner in 1832.[10] In a
historical-critical study, Credner concluded that the title "the Hebrew
Gospel" was applied by the fathers to three different documents: 1) the
Gospel of the Ebionites mentioned by Epiphanius, 2) another Greek Gospel
that the fathers believed was a falsification of canonical Matthew, and
3) the *Gospel of the Nazarenes* mentioned by Jerome. For Credner, "the Hebrew Gospel" *per se* did not exist. "The Hebrew Gospel" was not a specific
document, but simply the transmission of the gospel tradition by Jewish
Christian circles. Credner's skepticism would be prophetic, for whenever
scholars uncritically assumed a generic relationship between the Hebrew
Gospel and canonical Greek Matthew, his skeptical conclusions would be
re-invoked.

Although a decade-long sabbatical followed Credner, too much historical evidence existed to warrant his conclusion that the Hebrew Gospel never
existed. The middle third of the nineteenth century released a volley of
scholarship on the Hebrew Gospel, most of which reduced it to an inferior
second-century replica of canonical Matthew. Nevertheless, too much philo-

---

8. *Nachweis der Aechtheit sämtlichen Neutestamentlichen Schriften*, 1832.
9. *Über den Ursprung des ersten Evangeliums.*
10. *Beiträge zur Einleitung in die biblischen Schriften.*

logical evidence existed to deny Credner's conclusion that it was not related to the Gospel of Matthew. It remained for the Tübingen School to give the Hebrew Gospel a facelift. F. C. A. Schwegler,[11] a student of F. C. Baur, again asserted that the Hebrew Gospel lay behind the canonical Gospels (although he dated all four Gospels late in the second century). But Schwegler further asserted that the entire gospel tradition, which was rooted in a mistaken Jewish Christian view of Christianity represented in the Hebrew Gospel, was superseded by Pauline Christianity. F. C. Baur[12] swept up and orchestrated Schwegler's schema into the larger movement of the Tübingen School, over which he presided. In the attempt to apply Hegelian dialect to the development of the early Christianity, the Tübingen School saw the Hebrew Gospel as the chief witness to the early (but inferior) Jewish Christian interpretation of Christianity, which was necessarily superseded by a mature Pauline interpretation of Christianity. Like Credner, the Tübingen School did not regard the Hebrew Gospel as a specific Gospel or document but rather as an epithet for a *Jewish tradition of interpretation.*

Inevitably, the tradition itself of a Hebrew Gospel fell under attack. In an 1848 article in *Theologische Studien und Kritiken* (the same journal in which Schleiermacher published his famous essay on Papias), Frank argued that the patristic witness to the Hebrew Gospel — and particularly the witness of Jerome — rested on nothing more than flawed oral tradition and ecclesiastical memory and was therefore unreliable. Frank's disparagement of the patristic witness to the Hebrew Gospel consigned it to the category of apocryphal literature. His critique was echoed by Franz Delitzsch,[13] a convert to Christianity from Judaism, who likewise denied the existence of a Hebrew Gospel, ascribing it to a misunderstanding on the part of Jerome to passages in Matthew that resembled it. In reaction, H. W. Thiersch, Johann Ebrard, and Friedrich Bleek offered more positive assessments of the Hebrew Gospel between 1845 and 1850, by returning to the traditional assumption that the Hebrew Gospel was, in one form or another, the prototype of the Gospel of Matthew. In reaction to these more moderate assessments, however, G. H. A. Ewald in 1854 mounted a fierce attack on the Hebrew Gospel, calling it a *Bastardwerk* that belonged to the dregs of the gospel tradition.

11. *Das nachapostolische Zeitalter,* 1846.
12. *Kritische Untersuchungen über die Evangelien,* 1847.
13. *Zeitschrift für lutherische Theologie und Kirche,* 1850.

The Hebrew Gospel was thus unremittingly reduced to an inferior second-century Gospel replica — usually in Aramaic — of canonical Greek Matthew. This school of opinion was represented by Anger,[14] Weizsäcker,[15] D. F. Strauss,[16] Keim,[17] Volkmar,[18] H. J. Holtzmann,[19] and many others.[20] E. G. E. Reuss[21] offered a lone but unseconded vote for the antiquity and Hebrew language of the Hebrew Gospel. The tide of opinion could not be reversed. But even in the skeptical judgment that the Hebrew Gospel was a later and inferior replica of canonical Matthew, scholars continued to associate the Hebrew Gospel with the Gospel of Matthew. This mistaken assumption led to further problems, however, for the incompatibility of the Hebrew Gospel with canonical Greek Matthew were manifest. To my knowledge, with the exception of C. G. Wilke,[22] no scholar in the first seventy-five years of work on the Hebrew Gospel considered a possible relationship of the Hebrew Gospel with the Gospel of Luke rather than canonical Matthew. But Wilke only hinted at the possibility of such a relationship in his long (nearly 700 pages) and turgid book, and it made no mark on the discussion.

Two Roman Catholic scholars likewise produced books on the Hebrew Gospel that reaffirmed its ties with the Gospel of Matthew. Johann Sepp[23] attributed the Hebrew Gospel to Jewish schismatics and heretics exiled from Jerusalem. The fragments of the Hebrew Gospel preserved in the fathers were, in Sepp's view, second-century expansions ("the leaven of heresy") of canonical Greek Matthew. Nearly two decades later D. Gla[24] took

---

14. *Leipziger Universitätsprogramm,* 1862.

15. *Untersuchungen über die evangelische Geschichte,* 1864.

16. *Leben Jesu für das deutsche Volk,* 1864.

17. *Geschichte Jesu von Nazara,* 1867.

18. *Die Religion Jesus,* 1857; *Ursprung unserer Evangelien,* 1866.

19. *Die synoptischen Evangelien, ihr Ursprung und geschichtlicher Charakter,* 1863.

20. In his review of early nineteenth-century scholarship on the Hebrew Gospel, D. Gla, *Die Originalsprache des Matthäusevangeliums,* 5, lists the names of a dozen additional scholars (Schubert, Paulus, Theile, Fritzsche, Grawitz, Schott, Ungarelli, Harless, Roberts, Grau, Böhl, and Michelhaus) who followed the position that the Hebrew Gospel was a later translation of canonical Matthew into Hebrew.

21. *Geschichte der Schriften des Neuen Testaments,* 1874.

22. *Der Urevangelist,* 1838.

23. *Das Hebräer-Evangelium oder die Markus- und Matthäusfrage und ihre friedliche Lösung,* 1870.

24. *Die Originalsprache des Matthäusevangeliums,* 1887.

the opposite view, that the Hebrew Gospel was the *Vorlage* of canonical Greek Matthew. Gla based his position solely on patristic testimony rather than on internal evidence. In doing so, he followed an expiring methodology, for late nineteenth- and twentieth-century methodologies would rely on internal evidence over patristic testimony in Synoptic hypotheses.

Seventy-five years of intensive study had left the Hebrew Gospel in a cycle of untested assumptions and a netherworld of skepticism. In the latter part of the nineteenth century, however, three scholars broke the cycle and breathed life into the near-lifeless Gospel. The first was Adolf Hilgenfeld, who in 1854[25] initially followed the prevailing consensus in imagining the Hebrew Gospel to be a second-century Aramaic translation of original canonical Greek Matthew. He repented of this conclusion, however, and in a subsequent work[26] became the first to subject the extant patristic evidence of the Hebrew Gospel to rigorous scientific scrutiny and to attempt a reconstruction of the original Hebrew Gospel on the basis of it. He recognized the incompatibilities between the Hebrew Gospel and canonical Greek Matthew, but he asserted that they were evidence of the earlier and more original status of the Hebrew Gospel. For Hilgenfeld, the Hebrew Gospel formed the "Archimedes point" of the entire gospel tradition, which scholars until then had sought in vain to find in the Gospel of Mark.

Hilgenfeld was followed and surpassed by E. B. Nicholson,[27] an English scholar. In an attempt to safeguard the apostolicity of canonical Matthew, Nicholson returned to the old assumption that the apostle Matthew composed Greek Matthew. But Nicholson was the first to take seriously the strong correlations of the Hebrew Gospel with the Gospel of Luke rather than with canonical Greek Matthew. He hypothesized that the apostle Matthew wrote *two* versions of his Gospel, similar to Luke's two-part composition of the Third Gospel and the Book of Acts. According to Nicholson, the apostle Matthew composed the first Gospel in Greek and a subsequent version in Hebrew. Matthew's Hebrew sequel was then utilized by Luke in the composition of his Gospel. Nicholson's work on the Hebrew Gospel was the most careful, scientific, and comprehensive to date and remains today, along with the works of R. Handmann and A. F. J. Klijn, one of the three most important books written on the Hebrew Gospel.

25. *Die Evangelien nach ihrer Entstehung.*
26. *Novum Testamentum extra Canonem Receptum*², 1866.
27. *The Gospel according to the Hebrews,* 1879.

The third book in the trilogy produced on the Hebrew Gospel in the late nineteenth century came from the hand of Rudolf Handmann,[28] a student of Adolf von Harnack. Handmann understood the history of research on the Hebrew Gospel better than any of his predecessors, and his recognition of their errors spared him from repeating them. Handmann succeeded in severing several Gordian knots that had bound investigation of the Hebrew Gospel. First and foremost, in contrast to Hilgenfeld and Nicholson, he resolved *not* to equate the Hebrew Gospel with canonical Greek Matthew. Handmann also weighed and differentiated the testimony of the fathers to the Hebrew Gospel, assigning first rank to Eusebius and Jerome. Handmann's positive estimation of patristic witnesses, and particularly Jerome, would be an exception to the general skepticism with regard to patristic testimony in the late nineteenth and twentieth centuries. Finally, Handmann recognized the similarities of the quotations from the Hebrew Gospel with the Third Gospel and saw in the Jewish-Christian character of the quotations evidence of an *earlier* tradition appropriated by Luke, and also to some extent by Matthew.

Unfortunately, the breakthroughs achieved by Hilgenfeld, Nicholson, and Handmann went unrecognized at the time. Virtually all introductions to the NT produced in the late nineteenth century continued to maintain a relationship between the Hebrew Gospel and the Gospel of Matthew. The majority position remained that of Gieseler at the beginning of the century, that the Hebrew Gospel was an inferior second-century replica (probably in Aramaic) of canonical Greek Matthew. This position was maintained at the end of the nineteenth century by A. Resch,[29] who found the only remaining remnants of the Hebrew Gospel in the fragments of the *Gospel of the Nazarenes* quoted by Jerome, and in the *Gospel of the Ebionites* quoted by Epiphanius, both of which Resch believed descended from a Semitic translation of canonical Matthew. Finally, the two Titans of nineteenth-century patristic scholarship weighed in on the Hebrew Gospel, although with opposite assessments. In his magisterial four-volume history of early Christian literature,[30] Adolf von Harnack assigned a late date, 200 or later, to the Hebrew Gospel and the *Gospel of the Ebionites*. On the other hand, Theodor Zahn's equally magisterial four-volume history of

---

28. *Das Hebräer-Evangelium*, 1888.
29. *Agrapha. Aussercanonische Evangelienfragmente*, 1889.
30. *Geschichte der altchristlichen Literatur bis Eusebius*[2], 1896.

the development of the NT canon[31] maintained that the Hebrew Gospel was a loose version of an original Hebrew Matthew, which in time became the source of canonical Greek Matthew.

Several salient characteristics and trends emerged in the nineteenth-century quest for the Hebrew Gospel. First and most obviously, the nineteenth-century quest was overwhelmingly concentrated in German scholarship. Likewise, it was determined to find or even force a relationship between the Hebrew Gospel and canonical Greek Matthew. Third, that determination was inevitably frustrated — and the frustration resulted in a precipitous decline of interest in the Hebrew Gospel in twentieth-century NT scholarship. The plethora of scholars and the intensity of engagement with the Hebrew Gospel in the nineteenth century had produced neither consensus nor progress in resolving questions associated with its provenance or relationship to the canonical Gospels. Only a handful of names would persist with the quest after the turn of the century, and after 1940 the Hebrew Gospel succumbed to ennui and virtual abandonment.

In the early 1920s the French Dominican savant M.-J. Lagrange devoted attention to the Hebrew Gospel in his *Évangile selon Saint Luc* and in two important articles in *Revue biblique,* the prestigious journal he founded in 1892 and in which he published 160 articles over the next 46 years. Lagrange devoted the same acumen to the exegesis of the patristic fragments of the Hebrew Gospel that he devoted to his exegesis of the NT. He may not have been permitted by the Catholic authorities of his day to publish his sincere judgment of the Hebrew Gospel.[32] He was certain, however, that it was an original and independent work, not one derived from canonical Greek Matthew. Although Lagrange stated that the Hebrew Gospel was composed after Matthew and Luke, he recognized that Epiphanius's quotations of the Hebrew Gospel corresponded as closely with Luke as with Matthew, and he at least considered the possibility that the quotations of the Hebrew Gospel *could* have been the source of parts of Luke.

In the 1930s Alfred Schmidtke[33] and Hans Waitz[34] published influential works on the Hebrew Gospel, although with contrasting methods and

---

31. *Geschichte des neutestamentlichen Kanons,* 1892.
32. See Chapter Three, p. 115, n. 61.
33. "Zum Hebräerevangelium," *ZNW* (1936) 24-44.
34. *Neue Untersuchungen über die sogen. judenchristlichen Evangelien,* 1937.

conclusions. Where Lagrange was exegetical, Schmidtke and Waitz were assertive and dogmatic. Schmidtke resuscitated the division of the Hebrew Gospel into various Jewish Christian traditions first proposed by Credner (and followed by Resch). Schmidtke saw the Hebrew Gospel as a Greek document essentially identical with the *Gospel of the Ebionites* mentioned by Epiphanius. The *Gospel of the Nazarenes,* on the other hand, was essentially a targum of canonical Greek Matthew composed in Berea. It was mistaken by Papias — and even worse, by Jerome — as an original Hebrew Gospel written by the apostle Matthew. Both documents were produced in the second century. Schmidtke thus returned to the familiar nineteenth-century consensus that the Hebrew Gospel was a late and inferior replica of canonical Greek Matthew. His style is polemical and characterized by sweeping pronouncements. Schmidtke is strong on conclusion and weak on evidence, and his stance vis-à-vis the patristic witnesses, particularly Jerome, is antagonistic and caustic. Waitz follows Schmidtke's lead, but further divides the "Hebrew Gospel" into three Jewish Christian gospel traditions: 1) the *Gospel of the Nazarenes,* composed in Greek, 2) the heretical *Gospel of the Ebionites,* and 3) the Hebrew Gospel, which was a later reworking or recension of the *Gospel of the Ebionites.* Although less polemical than Schmidtke, Waitz too affects a summary tone, resting his case more on pronouncement than on evidence.

The division of the Hebrew Gospel into various Jewish Christian gospel traditions (usually three) set the course for discussions of the Hebrew Gospel in the twentieth century. It has been followed by Vielhauer and Strecker in Schneemelcher's *New Testament Apocrypha;* by J. K. Elliott in his 2004 *Apocryphal New Testament;* by D. Lührmann in his *Apokryph gewordenen Evangelien* of the same year; and most importantly, by A. F. J. Klijn in his 1992 *Jewish-Christian Gospel Tradition.* Along with Nicholson's and Handmann's studies, Klijn's is one of the three most erudite studies of the Hebrew Gospels to appear. Like Waitz, Klijn divides the Jewish-Christian gospel tradition into three branches, a Greek *Gospel of the Ebionites,* an Aramaic *Gospel of the Nazarenes,* and a *Gospel according to the Hebrews,* which he attributes to Egyptian Christians in the mid-second century. Also like Schmidtke and Waitz, Klijn is skeptical of the patristic witness, and generally unsympathetic toward the Hebrew Gospel. All three view the Hebrew Gospel as late and derivative, a product of a form of Christianity that was destined to wither and die. In their perspective — and their perspective dominated the twentieth century — the Hebrew

Gospel does not contribute to the understanding of the NT, but is rather something to be dispensed with.

The general abandonment of interest in the Hebrew Gospel in the twentieth century, and certainly the skepticism about its antiquity, its independence of the Synoptic tradition, and its original Hebrew character, are sufficient to explain why many modern scholars doubt its existence or significance for NT studies. To conclude the survey on this note, however, would do an injustice to a tradition within the foregoing tradition, a tradition that sees a more positive and promising role for the Hebrew Gospel in NT studies. It is this remnant tradition, as it were, that I wish to claim and develop in this book.

The blurry beginnings of the tradition emerge already in Lessing's original 1778 proposal that a genuine Hebrew Gospel lies behind the NT canonical gospel tradition. This proposal gains a degree of precision in Wilke's recognition in 1838 that the Hebrew Gospel exhibits a pronounced correlation with the Gospel of Luke. In 1889 Rudolf Handmann brought the picture into greater focus in positing that the Hebrew Gospel was not a later compilation of the Synoptics but an earlier independent Palestinian Christian Gospel which, along with the Gospel of Mark, influenced the formation of Luke and Matthew. In 1905, in a text-critical study of the then recently discovered Etchmiadzin version of the woman caught in adultery, B. W. Bacon[35] gave solid philological grounds for concluding that the Third Evangelist had before him the Greek form of the pericope (which he intentionally excluded from his Gospel), which originally derived from the Hebrew Gospel. More precise and important was J. Vernon Bartlet's 1911 article on "The Source of St. Luke's Gospel," in which he argued that a single source of unusual Semitic character (which he thought was a conflation of several earlier sources) played a primary role in the composition of Luke, both supplying the balance of material in the Third Gospel that was not found in Mark and also influencing the form in which Mark's material was represented in Luke. Although less specific than Bartlet, Roderic Dunkerley later concurred that the Hebrew Gospel was not dependent on the Synoptics but was one of the sources of the Synoptics.[36] In his 1931 *Das Evangelium des Lukas. Aus seinen Quellen erklärt*, Adolf Schlatter ascribed the material in Luke not shared in common with Matthew and/or Mark to

---

35. "Papias and the Gospel According to the Hebrews," *Exp.* 11 (1905), 161-77.
36. "According to the Hebrews," 1928.

"the New Narrator," one of Jesus' first followers who wrote a Hebrew Gospel narrative that was alluded to in Luke's prologue. Schlatter's position was later adopted, with modification, by Joachim Jeremias in his *Eucharistic Words of Jesus*. In 1937, the Jewish scholar Hugh Schonfield[37] independently arrived at Bartlet's essential thesis that when Luke changes the order of Mark or substitutes material different from or in addition to Mark he is following a Hebrew testimony-type source. In 1940, in a prophetic article that, true to its genre, was received without honor, Pierson Parker[38] first set forth the mature theory to which I devote this book, that the *Gospel according to the Hebrews* is not Matthean, but is rather the source of the non-Markan portions of Luke. Eduard Schweizer[39] independently arrived at a similar position a decade later when he argued that Special Luke derived from a Hebraic-type Gospel that was represented in the Hebrew Gospel. This genealogical line extending from Lessing to the mid-nineteenth century is, to be sure, neither unbroken nor uniform. But it represents an alternative to the repetitive crests and troughs that have epitomized two centuries of work on the Hebrew Gospel. Moreover, the remnant tradition is agreed that the Hebrew Gospel, which was widely attested and honored in early Christianity, shows distinct similarities with Luke and provides a plausible explanation for Lukan Semitisms.

In a swing of the dialectical pendulum, interest in the Hebrew Gospel has recently showed signs of recovery from its plunge in the second half of the twentieth century. In general, the renewed interest has not followed the skepticism that prevailed through most of the century. Rather, a growing number of scholars have shown interest in reclaiming the independence and priority of the Hebrew Gospel to the Synoptic tradition and its influence upon it. This approach received fresh stimulus in the 1970s and 1980s from Robert Lindsey[40] and David Flusser,[41] who recognized that the Gospel of Luke, in particular, translates naturally back into Hebrew and that a hypothetical Hebrew source appears to lie behind both Luke and Matthew. In the 1990s Philippe Rolland[42] similarly concluded that an original Hebrew docu-

37. *According to the Hebrews*, 1937.
38. "A Proto-Lukan Basis for the Gospel according to the Hebrews," *JBL* 59 (1940), 471-78.
39. "Eine hebraisierende Sonderquelle des Lukas?" *TZ* 6/3 (1950), 161-85.
40. *Hebrew Translation of the Gospel of Mark*, 1969.
41. *Jesus*, 1969; *Entdeckungen im Neuen Testament*, 1987.
42. *L'Origine et la Date des Évangiles*, 1994.

ment was a base document for Luke. More recently, in publishing the *editio princeps* of a recently discovered Middle Egyptian dialect of a Coptic text of the Gospel of Matthew, Hans-Martin Schenke[43] finds a text form that is suggestive of Epiphanius's quotations of the Hebrew Gospel of Matthew used by the Ebionites, which Schenke correctly affirms was independent of canonical Greek Matthew. More importantly, on the basis of both patristic evidence and a text-critical study of Ignatius's *To the Smyrnaeans*, C.-B. Amphoux[44] asserts that the Hebrew Gospel constitutes one of the sources of the Third Gospel. Finally, in a larger study of the apostolic fathers, P. F. Beatrice[45] seeks to demonstrate that the whole NT gospel tradition can be traced back to two major sources — the *Gospel of the Hebrews* and the Gospel of Mark.

The present book builds on this positive assessment of the Hebrew Gospel. My purpose is not to attempt a literary reconstruction of the Hebrew Gospel, except to affirm that it was a gospel narrative that included material extending from the baptism of Jesus through the resurrection. Nor is my purpose to attempt a sociological description of the various Jewish Christian communities that transmitted the Hebrew Gospel. I attempt something more fundamental. I see myself rather like a person attempting to free a stream that has been dammed and diverted into channels and tributaries and lagoons so that it may return to its natural streambed and reach its proper goal. The natural course of the Hebrew Gospel has been discerned in a general way by the foregoing remnant tradition, though none of its voices fully succeed in restoring its vital current. In the present volume I offer a solution to the Synoptic problem that liberates the stream of gospel tradition from obstructing dams and diversions, allowing it to follow the two constraints of nature: the gravity of the ancient sources and the terrain of internal evidence in the Synoptics. These natural constraints demonstrate that the Gospel of Mark and the Hebrew Gospel are sufficient to account for the composition of the Third Gospel, that there is no evidence that the so-called "Q" source existed and no need to posit it or any mere compendium of Jesus sayings as a formative component of either Luke or Matthew, and that canonical Matthew exhibits multiple and consistent signs of being the final and consummate Gospel in the Synoptic tradition.

43. *Das Matthäus-Evangelium im mittelägyptischen Dialekt des Koptischen (Codex Schøyen)*, 2001. Further on Coptic Matthew, see C. Evans, "The Jewish Christian Gospel Tradition," 270-76.

44. "L'Évangile selon les Hébreux. Sources de L'Évangile de Luc," 1995.

45. "The 'Gospel according to the Hebrews' in the Apostolic Fathers," 2006.

CHAPTER ONE

References to a "Hebrew Gospel" in Early Christianity

In defining and investigating the Synoptic Problem, modern scholarship has by and large favored literary evidence and hypotheses over historical testimony from the church fathers. Since Schleiermacher, approaches to the problem have limited themselves almost exclusively to internal evidence among Matthew, Mark, and Luke. Little reference has typically been devoted to the evidence of the church fathers relating to the formation of the gospel tradition.[1] Several reasons contribute to this neglect of the early tradition, among which are the elevation of Scripture over tradition in Protestantism, a bias against Roman Catholic scholarship and dogma that has characterized some streams of Protestant scholarship, and a predisposition in favor of Greek over Hebrew origins of the Christian tradition. Some of these issues will be raised in subsequent chapters of this book, but it is neither my primary nor present purpose to investigate the causes of the neglect of early church tradition. Rather, I wish to seek to document a fact insufficiently known and acknowledged, namely, that there is an extensive and diverse testimony in the early centuries of Christianity to an early "Hebrew Gospel," which was apparently the first Gospel in the Christian tradition and which was attributed by a number of fathers to the apostle Matthew. The purpose of this chapter and the next two is to survey and

---

1. In the late nineteenth century, D. Gla, *Die Originalsprache des Matthäusevangeliums*, 80, lamented "bis zu welchem Grade die Voreingenommenheit gegen das kirchliche Altertum und der Glaube an die Untrüglichkeit subjektiver Kritik den richtigen Blick zu trüben vermögen."

discuss every known reference to this Hebrew Gospel in early church tradition. In subsequent chapters I will seek to demonstrate influence of the Hebrew Gospel on the development of the Synoptic tradition.

Papias (c. 60-130)

In the second century, six fathers mention the Hebrew Gospel, the earliest of which, according to Eusebius, was Papias, bishop of Hierapolis. Papias's five treatises entitled "Of the Interpretation of the Sayings of the Lord" are no longer extant, but they were preserved by Irenaeus no more than seventy-five years later and are, in turn, quoted from Irenaeus by Eusebius in the *Ecclesiastical History*. Eusebius expresses an unfavorable opinion of Papias's millenarianism and gullibility regarding oral tradition.[2] Given Eusebius's bias, we may be confident that, had he also distrusted Papias's testimony regarding the formation of the Gospels, he would have avoided it.[3] But he ranks Papias, along with Clement of Rome, Ignatius, and Polycarp, as an indispensable link in the chain of apostolic witnesses and second only to an eyewitness authority regarding the formation of the Gospels.[4] That significance was due to Papias's proximity to the generation of the apostles and his determination to acquaint himself with apostolic memory of both kerygma and Scripture. Papias's life overlapped the life of John the Apostle by thirty to forty years, and his bishopric in Hierapolis lay only a hundred miles distant from Ephesus, where John is reputed to have lived his last years.

Eusebius grounds the authority of Papias's testimony in his personal links to the apostles, and especially to John. "If anyone came who had followed the presbyters," attests Papias, "I inquired into the words of the presbyters, what Andrew or Peter or Philip or Thomas or James or John or Matthew, or any other of the Lord's disciples had said, and what Aristion and the presbyter John say."[5] The use of παρακολουθεῖν, a term we shall

---

2. See *Hist. eccl.* 3.39.9-10.

3. Bernard Orchard reinforces this point by noting that 3.39 is the only chapter in the *Ecclesiastical History* in which two protagonists of the orthodox tradition, Papias and Irenaeus, are called into question by Eusebius (B. Orchard and H. Riley, *The Order of the Synoptics: Why Three Synoptic Gospels?* 171).

4. *Hist. eccl.* 3.37.4; 3.38.1; 3.39.1-3. Also D. Gla, *Die Originalsprache des Matthäusevangeliums*, 13-28.

5. καὶ παρηκολουθηκώς τις τοῖς πρεσβυτέροις ἔλθοι, τοὺς τῶν πρεσβυτέρων ἀνέκρινον

2

consider in Chapter Four in relation to Luke 1:3, is a *terminus technicus* for investigating a matter and preserving a received teaching.[6] Papias refers to what the apostles *said* (εἶπεν), but to what Aristion and John the Elder *say* (λέγουσιν). This change in verb tenses implies that Papias was a contemporary of Aristion and John the Elder, only one generation removed from the apostles. This is corroborated in *Ecclesiastical History* 3.39.7 and 14, where Eusebius says that Papias confessed to having received the words of the apostles from their followers. Of course, if John the Elder was in fact John the Apostle[7] — although this seems unlikely — then Papias's testimony comes directly from the apostolic fountainhead. It is in any case very early, within living memory of the apostolic age.

Eusebius records Papias's relevant testimony: "Matthew organized the oracles (of Jesus) in the Hebrew language, and each interpreted them as he was able."[8] This testimony does not specifically identify the Hebrew work of Matthew as the Hebrew Gospel, but it is reasonable to equate the two.[9] Papias's primary intent seems to have been to emphasize the Hebrew composition of the work. Nevertheless, since Schleiermacher's celebrated treatment of this text (discussed in Chapter Seven), the emphasis on Hebrew has been eclipsed by the meaning of τὰ λόγια, which needs to be discussed here. Τὰ λόγια, signifying a body of material, perhaps "oracles," is usually understood as a compilation of sayings of Jesus; often it is brought into connection with the hypothetical "Q" source. But the term almost cer-

---

λόγους, τί Ἀνδρέας ἢ τί Πέτρος εἶπεν ἢ τί Φίλιππος ἢ τί Θωμᾶς ἢ Ἰάκωβος ἢ τί Ἰωάννης ἢ Ματθαῖος ἢ τις ἕτερος τῶν τοῦ κυρίου μαθητῶν ἅ τε Ἀριστίων καὶ ὁ πρεσβύτερος Ἰωάννης, τοῦ κυρίου μαθηταί, λέγουσιν (*Hist. eccl.* 3.39.4). B. Orchard, *The Order of the Synoptics,* 176, also notes the historical significance of Eusebius's switch from past to present tense.

6. G. Schneider, παρακολουθέω, *EDNT* 1.52.

7. So B. Orchard, *The Order of the Synoptics,* 179-84.

8. Ματθαῖος μὲν οὖν Ἑβραΐδι διαλέκτῳ τὰ λόγια συνετάξατο, ἡρμήνευσεν δ' αὐτὰ ὡς ἦν δυνατὸς ἕκαστος (*Hist. eccl.* 3.39.16).

9. A. S. Barnes, "The Gospel according to the Hebrews," 361, observes: "Is it possible seriously to maintain that there were two separate documents, each of them written at Jerusalem during the Apostolic age and in the Hebrew tongue, each of them assigned to the Apostle Matthew, and each of them dealing in some way with the Gospel story? Or are we not rather forced to the conclusion that these two documents, whose descriptions are so strangely similar, must really be identical, and that the lost Gospel according to the Hebrews, in its earliest and uninterpolated state, was indeed none other than the Book of the Logia, the Discourses of Christ, drawn up by St Matthew at Jerusalem about A.D. 40, and carried with them into exile by the fugitive Christians when they left Jerusalem for ever, a little before its final destruction in the year 71?"

tainly refers to an organic whole, a volume, rather than a selection of sayings.[10] The use of the term in early Christian literature confirms this sense. It occurs four times in the NT, twice in the sense of summarizing the OT revelation of God (Acts 7:38; Rom 3:2), once in the sense of the gifts of divine proclamation (i.e., prophecy, teaching, admonition, 1 Pet 4:11), and once summarizing the essentials of the Christian proclamation of salvation (Heb 5:12). In *1 and 2 Clement* τὰ λόγια appears with reference to the revealed word of God (*1 Clem.* 13:6) or in the sense of "gospel" (*2 Clem.* 13:3) or of the holy Scriptures of the Old and New Testaments (*1 Clem.* 53:1). In his Preface to *Against Heresies* and again in *Against Heresies* 1.8.1, Irenaeus employs τὰ λόγια as a designation for the revelation of God in the canonical Gospels. In his *Commentary on Matthew* 5:19; 19:13, Origen uses τὰ λόγια likewise, and in his *Homilies on Jeremiah* 10:1 he uses it with reference to the entire OT. The most illuminating use of τὰ λόγια is found in Polycarp, a contemporary of Papias, who uses the term for a complete Gospel containing the cross, resurrection, and last judgment.[11] All these texts employ τὰ λόγια with reference to a more or less body of revelation as opposed to a specialized collection of sayings.[12]

Papias himself provides the most important evidence for understanding τὰ λόγια in the sense of "Gospel." Immediately before his testimony to Matthew's Hebrew Gospel, Papias speaks of "ordering the material" of Mark. This material is specifically identified as both the *words and deeds* of Jesus.[13] The words he uses of the ordering of the material are συντάσσω and λόγια, the exact words he uses immediately following in describing Matthew's Hebrew Gospel. The terms refer to Mark's produc-

10. J. Kürzinger, "Papias von Hierapolis. Zu Titel und Art seines Werkes," in *Papias von Hierapolis und die Evangelien des Neuen Testaments* (Regensburg: F. Pustet, 1983) 69-89; C. E. Hill, "What Papias Said about John (and Luke): A 'New' Papian Fragment," *JTS* NS 49 (1998) 623.

11. ὃς ἂν μεθοδεύῃ τὰ λόγια τοῦ κυρίου πρὸς τὰς ἰδίας ἐπιθυμίας (Polycarp, *Phil.* 1.7: "whoever perverts the account of the Lord for his own ends"). See P. F. Beatrice, "The Gospel According to the Hebrews," 182: "It seems to me quite reasonable to claim that Polycarp is speaking here about the Aramaic *Gospel of the Hebrews,* and that the two texts of Papias and Polycarp shed light on each other reciprocally."

12. D. Gla, *Die Originalsprache des Matthäusevangeliums,* 29-35; G. Kittel, λόγιον, *TWNT* 4.140-45; W. L. Schmidt, דבר, *TDOT* 3.11125, demonstrate that τὰ λόγια should not be restricted to a collection of sayings. Rather, it signifies a summary historical presentation of divine revelation or essential account of both word and event.

13. τὰ ὑπὸ τοῦ κυρίου ἢ λεχθέντα ἢ πραχθέντα (*Hist. eccl.* 3.39.15).

ing a Gospel and should be understood likewise with respect to Matthew in the same context.

Evidence elsewhere in Eusebius lends further support to this conclusion. Immediately before Matthew's λόγια, Eusebius speaks of "the words of the Lord given by Aristion."[14] Eusebius uses a different Greek word for the "words" (λόγοι) of Aristion than he does in referring to Matthew's works (τὰ λόγια), as described by Papias. It seems possible, perhaps even proper, to understand the λόγοι of Aristion in terms of "a collection of sayings." But Matthew's λόγια must be a Gospel, since Eusebius earlier refers to this same work as Matthew's "recollections" or "memoirs."[15] This is a technical term for "Gospel" in Eusebius, who uses the same word (ὑπόμνημα) to refer to the Gospel of Mark (*Ecclesiastical History* 2.15.1) and elsewhere to "Gospels" in general.[16] Throughout his discussion of Matthew's literary achievements in *Ecclesiastical History* 3.24.5-13 and 6.14.5-7, Eusebius speaks only of a Gospel, not of a collection of sayings.[17] C. E. Hill observes astutely that in describing evangelical literature, Eusebius employs no fewer than ten terms that also appear in Luke's prologue. It seems highly likely that the *apologia* of Luke 1:1-3 was consciously employed by Papias as a model for his own descriptions of the Gospels.[18]

Συντάσσω was just mentioned in relation to τὰ λόγια, but it deserves further attention. The term means to compose and organize an account, even to publish a book.[19] Josephus depicts his writing of *The Jewish War*

14. Ἀριστίωνος . . . τῶν τοῦ κυρίου λόγων (*Hist. eccl.* 3.39.14).

15. ὑπομνήματα (*Hist. eccl.* 3.24.5)

16. See *Hist. eccl.* 1.9.3; 9.5.1; 9.7.1. Origen, *Cels.* 1.9.3, also uses ὑπόμνημα of "Gospel," whereas Justin favors ἀπομνημόνευμα (*1 Apol.* 66.3; *Dial.* 100.4). T. Zahn, *Geschichte des neutestamentlichen Kanons,* 1/2.471-76, saw Justin's term as the most appropriate way to give pagans with a literary education a correct impression of the Gospels. On the two terms, see M. Hengel, *The Four Gospels and the One Gospel of Jesus Christ,* 4.211-12; C. H. Roberts, *Cambridge History of the Bible,* ed. P. Ackroyd and C. F. Evans (Cambridge: University Press, 1970) 1.54-55.

17. R. Kraft, "Para-mania: Beside, Before, and Beyond Bible Studies," *JBL* 126 (2007), 11-12, suggests that λόγια may be plural because they could not all be gathered into a single volume.

18. C. E. Hill, "What Papias Said about John (and Luke). A 'New' Papian Fragment," 593. ἀνατάξασθαι (cf. τάξις, σύνταξις, *Hist. eccl.* 3.39.15); διήγησις (3.24.7); πραγμάτων (cf. πεπραγμένα, πράξεις, πραχθέντα, 3.24.8, 10, 11, 12, 13; 3.39.15); παραδίδωμι (3.24.11, 12); ἀκριβῶς (3.39.15); παρακολουθέω (3.39.4, 15).

19. Liddell and Scott, *Greek-English Lexicon,* 1725. "We may safely assume . . . that the passage refers to the entire Gospel," A. F. J. Klijn, *Jewish-Christian Gospel Tradition,* 11.

with this word.[20] In the Septuagint of Exodus, Leviticus, and Numbers συντάσσω is used some seventy times in virtually the same form as a *terminus technicus* for bringing a task to completion in accordance with God's commandments to Moses. If this specialized use influenced Papias, we should think of his literary achievement as a complete account rather than a partial collection of sayings.

With reference to Papias's use of ἡρμήνευσεν, Hengel is correct that it refers to the *translating* of an original Hebrew text into Greek as opposed to "mere rhetorical 'interpretation.'"[21] The Latin version of the Papias quotation preserved by Rufinus and dating to perhaps 400 also implies a translation from Hebrew into Greek.[22] These multiple lines of reasoning all lead to the conclusion that τὰ λόγια means a form of Gospel. Thus, although Papias's reference to Matthew's λόγια does not specifically refer to the Hebrew Gospel, a wealth of factors argue that it should be understood as such in *Ecclesiastical History* 3.39.16.

According to A. F. J. Klijn, three questions must be answered if the Papias testimony is to be satisfactorily explained. First, why does the Hebrew Matthew mentioned by Papias differ so remarkably from Greek canonical Matthew? Second, what is the meaning of τὰ λόγια, a collection of sayings or an entire Gospel? Third, who was responsible for the various translations of it?[23] The theory I propose answers each question satisfactorily. The first question posed by Klijn is premature at this point of the study, but allow me to state a position that I shall shortly stake out more thoroughly, namely that the Papias note refers not to canonical Matthew but to the original Hebrew Matthew, which antedated the Synoptic tradition. Papias thus cannot have meant to equate Hebrew Matthew and canonical Greek Matthew. The extensive evidence already considered in favor of τὰ λόγια meaning a "written account," "memoir," or "Gospel" is a sufficient answer to the second question. The answer to Klijn's final ques-

---

20. *J.W.* 1.3.

21. *The Four Gospels and the One Gospel of Jesus Christ,* 71. In Chapter Seven I discuss Schleiermacher's epic misunderstanding of ἡρμήνευσε as "Erklärungen" ("explanatory notes") rather than "Übersetzung" ("translation").

22. Rufinus translates the Papias quotation as follows: Matthaeus quidem scripsit Hebraeo sermone, interpretatus est autem ea quae scripsit unusquisque, sicut potuit. See D. Lührmann, *Die apokryph gewordenen Evangelien,* 245, n. 70, for further patristic evidence of the translation of Hebrew Matthew into Greek.

23. *Jewish-Christian Gospel Tradition,* 10-11.

tion must await the discussion in Chapter Four, but I shall anticipate it here simply by saying that Hebrew Matthew appears to be one of the sources referred to in the prologue of Luke (1:1-4), which Luke used in the composition of the Third Gospel.

Eusebius records a second though less celebrated testimony of Papias to a "Hebrew Gospel" at the end of Book 3 of the *Ecclesiastical History*. "The same writer [Papias] has used testimonies from the First Epistle of John and likewise from Peter, and he has also set forth another account about a woman who was accused before the Lord of many sins, which is found in the Gospel according to the Hebrews."[24] Eusebius places this citation immediately after Papias's testimonies to Mark and Matthew, which implies that the Hebrew Gospel, like Mark and Matthew, was itself a Gospel and not a mere collection of sayings. Dietrich Gla doubts that the Hebrew Gospel mentioned in 3.39.17 and the Hebrew λόγια of 3.39.16 refer to the same document. Greater verbal linkage between the two documents would be expected, according to Gla, if Eusebius intended them to be equated.[25] This objection is ill-founded. Eusebius doubtlessly mentions the story of the woman accused of many sins precisely because it occurs in the Hebrew Gospel just mentioned. Nevertheless, the point of 3.39.17 is not to emphasize the Hebrew Gospel *per se,* but rather the story of the woman accused of many sins found in that Gospel. Eusebius does not expressly say that Papias got the story from the Hebrew Gospel (compare Hegesippus's extracts from the Hebrew Gospel in *Hist. eccl.* 4.22.8), but only that the story also exists in the Hebrew Gospel. The placement of the two stories adjacent to each other justifies the assumption that the Hebrew Gospel of 3.39.17 is the same document as Hebrew Matthew in 3.39.16.

Ecclesiastical History 3.39.17 is often taken as a reference to the story of the woman caught in adultery in John 7:53–8:12.[26] Rufinus, the translator

---

24. κέχρηται δ' ὁ αὐτὸς [ὁ Παπίας] μαρτυρίαις ἀπὸ τῆς Ἰωάννου προτέρας ἐπιστολῆς καὶ ἀπὸ τῆς Πέτρου ὁμοίως, ἐκτέθειται δὲ καὶ ἄλλην ἱστορίαν περὶ γυναικὸς ἐπὶ πολλαῖς ἁμαρτίαις διαβληθείσης ἐπὶ τοῦ κυρίου, ἣν τὸ καθ' Ἑβραίους εὐαγγέλιον περιέχει (*Hist. eccl.* 3.39.17).

25. *Die Originalsprache des Matthäusevangeliums,* 25.

26. Both E. B. Nicholson, *The Gospel according to the Hebrews,* 54, and R. Handmann, *Das Hebräer-Evangelium,* 94, make the reasonable suggestion that the account, though originally independent of the Fourth Gospel, was eventually placed in the Gospel of John because of a confusion in *Hist. eccl.* 3.39.14 of John the Presbyter with *John the Apostle.*

of Jerome, understood it so. B. W. Bacon likewise argues energetically that the passage recalls the Johannine version of the adulteress and even more the pruned version of the same story in the Etchmiadzin Codex, both of which derive from the Hebrew Gospel. Bacon further argues that the Hebrew Gospel supplied the *Urtext* of Luke 21:34-38, which contained the story of the adulteress between what is now Luke 21:37 and 21:38.[27] There is particularly strong evidence for Bacon's second point. Not only does family 13 in the extant manuscript tradition place the story of the adulteress at the end of Luke 21, but Appendix II reveals several Semitisms in Luke 21:34-38 (pp. 325-26 below). Both of these observations argue in favor of a Hebrew origin of the material.

It cannot be concluded for certain, however, that Papias and John 8 refer to the same event. The woman in John 8 is referred to as a "woman caught in the act of adultery,"[28] whereas Papias refers to a woman "accused of many sins."[29] On a formal lexical level, Papias's description is closer to the description of the woman in Luke 7:36-50 who was forgiven by Jesus of "many sins."[30] Moreover, although the adulteress of John 8 was known by certain Latin church fathers — including Ambrosius, Faustus of Mileve, Rufinus, Jerome, Pacian of Barcelona, and Augustine — no Greek church father prior to the twelfth century comments on it.[31] That Papias's woman of "many sins" is not the same woman as the adulteress in John 8 is further suggested by the fact that Eusebius does not attribute the story of the sinful woman to the Gospel of John but rather to "the Gospel according to the Hebrews."

---

27. B. W. Bacon, "Papias and the Gospel According to the Hebrews," *Exp.* 11 (1905), 171-77.

28. γυναῖκα ἐπὶ μοιχείᾳ κατειλημμένην (John 8:3).

29. ἐπὶ πολλαῖς ἁμαρτίαις διαβληθείσης (*Hist. eccl.* 3.39.17).

30. ἀφέωνται αἱ ἁμαρτίαι αὐτῆς αἱ πολλαί (Luke 7:47). D. Lührmann, *Die apokryph gewordenen Evangelien*, 212, concludes: "Mit Recht wird allgemein ausgeschlossen, dass Euseb hier Lk 7,36-50 im Sinne hat." So too A. Resch, *Agrapha. Aussercanonische Evangelienfragmente*, 341-42. M.-J. Lagrange, "L'Évangile selon les Hébreux," 173-74, argues, however, that Eusebius's reference to "another" story sets the Papias account sufficiently apart from the well-known accounts in John 8 and Luke 7.

31. D. Lührmann, *Die apokryph gewordenen Evangelien*, 194. On the pericope of the adulteress, see B. M. Metzger, *A Textual Commentary on the Greek New Testament*[2] (Stuttgart: Deutsche Bibelgesellschaft/United Bible Societies, 1994), 187-89, who declares: "The evidence for the non-Johannine origin of the pericope of the adulteress is overwhelming . . . the Committee was unanimous that the pericope was originally no part of the Fourth Gospel."

Didymus of Alexandria was familiar with a version of the story that agrees with Papias in calling the woman a sinner rather than an adulteress.

> A woman was condemned by the Jews for a sin and sent to the customary place to be stoned. When the Savior saw her and realized they were ready to stone her, he said to those who were about to throw the stones, "Whoever has not sinned, let him take up a stone and throw it. Whoever imagines himself not to have sinned, let that person take a stone and make sport with her." No one dared to do so. They knew themselves well enough, and they also knew full well that they would have to give account for themselves to others, so they dared not commit an offense against her.[32]

Didymus does not specifically identify the story as coming from the Hebrew Gospel, although (as we shall see later in this chapter) he was familiar with the Gospel. He prefaces this particular story by saying that it is found ἔν τισιν εὐαγγελίοις — "in certain Gospels" — which suggests Gospels other than the canonical Gospels. The Didymus narrative bears a number of similarities with the pericope of the adulteress in John 8:3-11, although a definite relationship between the two texts is again uncertain, for Didymus does not identify the woman as an "adulteress," as does John; and in John the story is set in the context of a *Streitgespräch* — a controversy — which is absent in Didymus.

Whether *Ecclesiastical History* 3.39.17 and John 8 refer to the same event cannot be decided with certainty. What can be said with greater certainty is that the story, whatever its history of transmission, appears originally to have derived from the Hebrew Gospel.[33] Moreover, the story at-

---

32. φέρομεν οὖν ἔν τισιν εὐαγγελίοις· γυνὴ κατεκρίθη ὑπὸ τῶν Ἰουδαίων ἐπὶ ἁμαρτίᾳ καὶ ἀπεστέλλετο λιθοβοληθῆναι εἰς τὸν τόπον, ὅπου εἰώθει γίνεσθαι. ὁ σωτήρ, ἑωρακὼς αὐτὴν καὶ θεωρήσας ὅτι ἕτοιμοί εἰσιν πρὸς τὸ λιθοβολῆσαι αὐτήν, τοῖς μέλλουσιν αὐτὴν καταβαλεῖν λίθοις εἶπεν· ὃς οὐκ ἥμαρτεν, αἱρέτω λίθον καὶ βαλέτω αὐτόν. εἴ τις σύνοιδεν ἑαυτῷ τὸ μὴ ἡμαρτηκέναι, λαβὼν λίθον παισάτω αὐτήν. καὶ οὐδεὶς ἐτόλμησεν. ἐπιστήσαντες ἑαυτοῖς καὶ γνόντες, ὅτι καὶ αὐτοὶ ὑπεύθυνοί εἰσίν τισιν, οὐκ ἐτόλμησαν καταπαῖσαι ἐκείνην (*Comm. Eccl.* 4.223.6-13, cited from D. Lührmann, *Die apokryph gewordenen Evangelien*, 199). See Didymus's *Commentary on Ecclesiastes* (J. Kramer and B. Krebber, *Didymos der Blinde. Kommentar zum Ecclesiastes* 4 [PTA 16; Bonn: R. Habelt, 1972], 88; see also A. F. J. Klijn, *Jewish-Christian Gospel Tradition*, 118).

33. A. F. J. Klijn, *Jewish-Christian Gospel Tradition*, 116-19, affirms that the story "was present in some Jewish-Christian Gospel or other, maybe the Gospel of the Hebrews." Even

tributed to the Hebrew Gospel in *Ecclesiastical History* 3.39.17 and the story arguably from the Hebrew Gospel in Didymus both exhibit links with Luke. Both textually and stylistically the adulteress passage in John also has affinities, in particular, with the ending of Luke 21. And, as noted above, several important ancient textual traditions associate *de muliere adultera* with the Third Gospel.[34]

Irenaeus (c. 130-200)

Irenaeus reports that "Matthew published among the Hebrews a written Gospel also in their own language, while Peter and Paul were preaching and founding the church in Rome."[35] He again writes that the Ebionites "use the Gospel according to Matthew only and repudiate the apostle Paul, maintaining that he was an apostate from the law."[36] The Hebrew Gospel is not mentioned in the second quotation, but Eusebius mentions the Gospel in a very similar statement. Presumably drawing on Irenaeus, Eusebius writes that "[The Ebionites] thought that the letters of the apostle [Paul] ought to be wholly rejected and called him an apostate from the law. They used only the Gospel called According to the Hebrews and made little account of the remaining [Gospels?]."[37] In a further reference from Eusebius we read, "the memoirs of Symmachus are still extant, by which, in adhering to the Gospel according to Matthew, he seems to hold to the above-

---

Lührmann, *Die apokryph gewordenen Evangelien*, 191-215, who rejects an origin in the Hebrew Gospel finds 1) that Didymus cites the story not from John's Gospel but from certain apocryphal Gospels, 2) that Didymus's account shares similarities with the Papias citation in *Hist. eccl.* 3.39.17 and may well be identical with it, 3) that Didymus clearly differentiates between canonical and apocryphal Gospels, and 4) that the Hebrew Gospel, though not canonical, is held in an especially positive category.

34. C.-B. Amphoux, "L'Évangile selon les Hébreux," 72-73.

35. ὁ μὲν δὴ Ματθαῖος ἐν τοῖς Ἑβραίοις τῇ ἰδίᾳ αὐτῶν διαλέκτῳ καὶ γραφὴν ἐξήνεγκεν εὐαγγελίου, τοῦ Πέτρου καὶ τοῦ Παύλου ἐν Ῥώμῃ εὐαγγελιζομένων καὶ θεμελιούντων τὴν ἐκκλησίαν (Eusebius, *Hist. eccl.* 5.8.2; Irenaeus, *Haer.* 3.1.1).

36. Solo autem eo quod est secundum Matthaeum evangelio utuntur (Ebionaei) et apostolum Paulum recusant apostatam eum legis dicentes (*Haer.* 1.26.2). In 3.11.7 Irenaeus repeats that "the Ebionites use only the Gospel of Matthew." For another reference to the Ebionite rejection of the Apostle Paul, see *Haer.* 3.15.1.

37. οὗτοι δὲ τοῦ μὲν ἀποστόλου πάμπαν τὰς ἐπιστολὰς ἀρνητέας ἡγοῦντο εἶναι δεῖν, ἀποστάτην ἀποκαλοῦντες αὐτὸν τοῦ νόμου, εὐαγγελίῳ δὲ μόνῳ τῷ καθ' Ἑβραίους λεγομένῳ χρώμενοι, τῶν λοιπῶν σμικρὸν ἐποιοῦντο λόγον (*Hist. eccl.* 3.27.4).

mentioned heresy [i.e., the Ebionites]."[38] With reference to the Ebionites, therefore, Eusebius refers interchangeably to "the Gospel according to Matthew" and "The Gospel of the Hebrews." Since the Ebionites were widely reputed to use only the Hebrew Gospel, it seems justified to take both references to imply the Hebrew Gospel that was attributed to Matthew — and that Eusebius assumes the same of his predecessor Irenaeus.

In *Against All Heresies* 1.26.1 Irenaeus writes that the Ebionites used only the Hebrew Gospel of Matthew; indeed, Irenaeus "believed that all heretical sects used one Gospel only."[39] Like many patristic references to the Hebrew Gospel, Irenaeus's statements are sometimes dismissed as the parroting of earlier unreliable testimony or as outright lies.[40] In this instance such skepticism is unfounded. Irenaeus nowhere quotes Papias with reference to the Hebrew Gospel, and his report appears independent of Papias in several important respects. For instance, he treats all four Gospels in their canonical order, whereas Papias treats the Gospels in the order of Mark, Matthew, and John, omitting Luke. Moreover, in Irenaeus, "Hebrew Matthew" is not simply τὰ λόγια, as Papias reports, but a "written Gospel." "Irenaeus himself does not seem to have been wholly dependent on Papias," writes Schonfield. "He has two statements on the subject [of Hebrew Matthew] in his work *Against Heresies,* and neither of them can be said to reflect Papias at all."[41] Nor is there any mention in Papias of the rejection of Paul as an apostate from the law or of the Ebionites, as there is in

---

38. The Symmachus here mentioned is the translator of the LXX. Inexplicably, J. E. L. Oulton's translation in LCL speaks of Symmachus's "opposition to the Gospel of Matthew." This translation violates both lexicography and context. Eusebius's text reads: καὶ ὑπομνήματα δὲ τοῦ Συμμάχου εἰς ἔτι νῦν φέρεται, ἐν οἷς δοκεῖ πρὸς τὸ κατὰ Ματθαῖον ἀποτεινόμενος εὐαγγέλιον τὴν δεδηλωμένην αἵρεσιν κρατύνειν (*Hist. eccl.* 6.17.1). Ἀποτείνω does not mean "oppose," but rather "stretch out," "extend," and by inference "refer to." Eusebius implies that Symmachus's *adherence* to the Gospel of Matthew put him in the camp of the Ebionites.

39. A. F. J. Klijn, *Jewish-Christian Gospel Tradition,* 4.

40. So E. Schwartz, *Gesammelte Schriften* 5 (Berlin: W. de Gruyter, 1963) 175-76, who speaks of Irenaeus's "refined untruthfulness" in this regard. Schwartz's elegant allegation may have been prompted by Harnack's assertion that Irenaeus's statements about the Hebrew Gospel exceeded his knowledge of it (see M.-J. Lagrange, "L'Évangile selon les Hébreux," 171).

41. Hugh J. Schonfield, *According to the Hebrews,* 246. D. Gla, *Die Originalsprache des Matthäusevangeliums,* 66, warns against overestimating Irenaeus's reliance on Papias, since Irenaeus 1) does not once testify to be Papias's disciple, and 2) quotes Papias only once (*Haer.* 5.33.4).

Irenaeus. Irenaeus's testimony provides a number of new data with reference to the Hebrew Gospel. It probably depends on tradition current in Rome in his day, for he expressly mentions the Hebrew Gospel in relationship to the preaching of Peter and Paul in Rome.[42]

Pantaenus († c. 190)

A third name associated with the Hebrew Gospel in the second century is Pantaenus. A Stoic philosopher who was converted to the Christian faith, Pantaenus was a teacher of Clement of Alexandria and head of the catechetical school in Alexandria until his death at the close of the second century. According to Eusebius, the Gospel according to Matthew had been taken to India by the apostle Bartholomew. This Gospel, Eusebius further notes, was written "in Hebrew script" (Ἑβραίων γράμμασι) and was preserved in India until the visit of Pantaenus, who died at the close of the second century.[43] Hippolytus, a later contemporary of Pantaenus, confirms this tradition, although the authenticity of the source of the tradition "On the Twelve Apostles" is disputed.[44] Jerome repeats this testimony of Eusebius, adding that Pantaenus brought Hebrew Matthew with him on his return from India to Alexandria.[45]

Clement of Alexandria (c. 150-215)

A fourth second-century witness to the Hebrew Gospel comes from Clement of Alexandria, who twice in the *Stromata* quotes from the *Gospel to the*

---

42. In Eusebius, *Hist. eccl.* 5.8.2, and Irenaeus, *Haer.* 3.1.1, note the appended genitive absolute, "while Peter and Paul were preaching in Rome." So too C. J. Thornton, *Der Zeuge des Zeugen* (WUNT 56; Tübingen: Mohr/Siebeck 1991), 10-54; M. Hengel, *The Four Gospels and the One Gospel of Jesus Christ*, 35-38.

43. ὁ Πάνταινος, καὶ εἰς Ἰνδοὺς ἐλθεῖν λέγεται, . . . οἷς Βαρθολομαῖον τῶν ἀποστόλων ἕνα κηρῦξαι αὐτοῖς τε Ἑβραίων γράμμασι τὴν τοῦ Ματθαίου καταλεῖψαι γραφήν (*Hist. eccl.* 5.10.3).

44. Βαρθολομαῖος δὲ Ἰνδοῖς, οἷς καὶ τὸ κατὰ Ματθαῖον εὐαγγέλιον ἐκδεδωκώς (Hippolytus, *De duodecim Apostolis*).

45. Ubi repperit Bartholomeum de duodecim apostolis adventum Domini Iesu iuxta Matthaei Evangelium praedicasse, quod Hebraicis litteris scriptum, revertens Alexandriam secum detulit (*Vir. ill.* 36.2).

Hebrews. The first quotation reads: "And in the Gospel according to the Hebrews it is written, 'The one who wonders will reign, and reigning he will rest.'"[46] Later, in *Stromata* 3.9.63, Clement cites the so-called *Gospel of the Egyptians* without naming it. His ascription of the quotation here to the Hebrew Gospel seems to indicate that the latter's circulation and authority were more widely recognized.[47] Immediately before *Stromata* 3.9.63 Clement cites another saying from a document he calls "The Traditions of Matthew." "And in 'The Traditions,' Matthew exhorts, 'Marvel at what is before you,' for this is the first step in gaining further knowledge."[48] The distinction between "The Traditions of Matthew" and the Hebrew Gospel seems to imply that they are two separate documents, a conclusion for which further evidence will be adduced later in this chapter and in Chapter Three. The two quotations were probably brought together by Clement because of the common theme of "wonder."

A fuller quotation of the same passage helps interpret this otherwise enigmatic text.[49] In Book 5 of the *Stromata* Clement writes, "Equal to these words [from the *Timaeus* immediately preceding] are the following: 'The one who seeks will not cease until he finds; and having found he will be amazed, and being amazed he will reign, and reigning he will rest.'"[50] This

46. κἂν τῷ καθ᾽ Ἑβραίους εὐαγγελίῳ ὁ θαυμάσας βασιλεύσει γέγραπται καὶ ὁ βασιλεύσας ἀναπαήσεται (*Strom.* 2.9.45).

47. R. Handmann, *Das Hebräer-Evangelium*, 26.

48. καὶ Ματθίας ἐν ταῖς Παραδόσεσι παραινῶν "θαύμασον τὰ παρόντα," βαθμὸν τοῦτον πρῶτον τῆς ἐπέκεινα γνώσεως ὑποτιθέμενος (*Strom.* 2.9.45)

49. Harnack, *Geschichte der altchristlichen Literatur*², 1/1.7, credits Theodor Zahn with being the first to note the connection between the two quotations.

50. Ἴσον γὰρ τούτοις ἐκεῖνα δύναται. οὐ παύσεται ὁ ζητῶν, ἕως ἂν εὕρῃ· εὑρὼν δὲ θαμβηθήσεται, θαμβηθεὶς δὲ βασιλεύσει, βασιλεύσας δὲ ἐπαναπαήσεται (*Strom.* 5.14.96). This saying is also preserved in a fragment from Oxyrhynchus 654, as reconstructed by H. G. E. White, *The Sayings of Jesus from Oxyrhynchus*, 5-8:

λέγει Ἰη[σοῦ]ς
μὴ παυσάσθω ὁ ζη[τῶν τοῦ ζητεῖν ἕως ἂν]
εὕρῃ, καὶ ὅταν εὕρῃ [θαμβηθήσεταί καὶ θαμ]
βηθεὶς βασιλεύσει, κα[ὶ βασιλεύσας ἀναπα]
ήσεται.

A variant of the saying appears also to be reproduced in *Gos. Thom.* 2: "Jesus said, 'He who seeks must not stop seeking until he finds; and when he finds, he will be bewildered; and if he is bewildered, he will marvel, and will be king over All'" (trans. B. M. Metzger, *Synopsis Quattuor Evangeliorum*⁵, ed. K. Aland [Stuttgart: Württembergische Bibelanstalt, 1968]

text is not specifically credited to the Hebrew Gospel, but its quotation without introduction suggests that it was both known and accepted as part of general Christian tradition.[51] In the Hebrew Gospel, Clement found a sorites of five admonitions: seeking, finding, marveling, reigning, resting. The substance of this longer version of the saying agrees with sayings of Jesus throughout the Synoptics. Seeking and finding obviously conform to Luke 11:9-10 and Matt 7:7-8 ("Ask and it will be given to you; seek and you will find; knock and it will be opened to you"), as well as to Matt 6:33 ("Seek first the kingdom of God"). The prevailing use of wonderment (θαυμ-) in the Gospels is reserved for astonishment and disbelief that befalls beholders of Jesus' miracles, but the sense of awe and wonderment does comport with the parable of the Hidden Treasure (Matt 13:44; also Matt 15:31; Mark 7:37; 16:5; Luke 5:9; John 5:20). Finally, the state of rest is echoed in Matt 11:28-29. In the version of the saying in *Stromata* 2, Clement quotes only the last three members of the sorites, marveling, reigning, and resting, which were relevant to the Platonic pursuit of the virtue of wisdom that he was addressing. This was probably not the extent of the saying known to Clement, however. I concur with H. G. E. White's judgment that "it seems in the highest degree probable that Clement's shorter version [in 2.9.45] is a modification — made by himself — of the longer form [in 5.14.96], and that the longer form is the true citation from the Hebrew gospel."[52] The saying preserved by Clement can scarcely be a compilation from the Gospels, since three-fifths of it is absent from the Gospels. The sayings preserved by Clement certainly derive, just as he attests, from the Hebrew Gospel. [53]

Clement cannot give unequivocal support to the Hebrew Gospel because it is not one of the four canonical Gospels. Furthermore, it is invoked by Gnostics, whom Clement, in his prodigious learning, endeavors to vanquish. His citation of the Hebrew Gospel is nevertheless noteworthy in several respects. On the one hand, citing the saying with the authoritative

---

517). A. F. J. Klijn, *Jewish-Christian Gospel Tradition*, 50, notes further similarities of the saying under consideration with *Thom. Cont.* 145.12-14 and *2 Apoc. Jas.* 56:2-6.

51. A. F. J. Klijn, *Jewish-Christian Gospel Tradition*, 6.

52. H. G. E. White, *The Sayings of Jesus from Oxyrhynchus*, 7.

53. H. G. E. White, *The Sayings of Jesus from Oxyrhynchus*, 7: "Coupling, then, the conclusion that the Sayings are extracts with the identity of Saying I and Clement's citation from the *Gospel according to the Hebrews*, we reach the important conclusion — which, I believe, is universally admitted, that Saying I is quoted from the *Gospel according to the Hebrews*."

formula γέγραπται, "it is written," signals Clement's deference to the tradition preserved in the Hebrew Gospel.[54] Moreover, both citations about wondering and rest are intended to show the superiority of Christian revelation to Plato's *Theaetetus* and *Timaeus,* which Clement cites immediately before. For Clement to counter a luminary such as Plato with a citation of the Hebrew Gospel is a remarkable testimony to its stature in the second century. The simple reference to the Hebrew Gospel as ἐκεῖνα further attests to its reputation at the same time.[55] Finally, preservation of the Hebrew Gospel in Oxyrhynchus in Middle Egypt evinces the breadth of its dissemination in early Christianity.

Hegesippus (late second century)

The final name associated with the Hebrew Gospel in the second century is Hegesippus, who made extracts "from the Gospel according to the Hebrews and from the Syriac, and especially from the Hebrew language."[56] Whether Eusebius, who preserves this reference, intends readers to understand two Gospels — one in Hebrew and one in Syriac — or only a single Hebrew Gospel with extracts from a Syriac document, is not entirely clear.[57] The syntax of the statement suggests that the Hebrew and Syriac were two separate documents.[58] The Syriac document may be the same as,

54. B. M. Metzger, *The Canon of the New Testament, 132.*

55. M.-J. Lagrange, "L'Évangile selon les Hébreux," 172, draws attention to evidence of a Semitic original behind Clement's quotation.

56. ἔκ τε τοῦ καθ' Ἑβραίους εὐαγγελίου καὶ τοῦ Συριακοῦ καὶ ἰδίως ἐκ τῆς Ἑβραΐδος διαλέκτου (Eusebius, *Hist. eccl.* 4.22.8). This passage is quoted verbatim a thousand years later by the fourteenth-century priest of Hagia Sophia in Constantinople, Nicephorus Callistus Xanthopulus, in his *Historia ecclesiastica* 4.7 (PG 145.992).

57. R. Handmann, *Das Hebräer-Evangelium,* 31-34, follows E. B. Nicholson, *The Gospel according to the Hebrews,* 6, in assuming that a scribal insertion of καί (εὐαγγελίου καὶ τοῦ Συριακου) has mistakenly made two documents out of one. R. Dunkerley, "The Gospel according to the Hebrews," *ExpT* 39 (1927-1928), 489, likewise argues for a single document on the basis of textual emendations. The text in question is certain, however, and there is no evidence of textual emendations. A. F. J. Klijn advances the mystifying assumption in *Jewish-Christian Gospel Tradition,* 12, that the Hebrew Gospel was written in Greek. D. Gla, *Die Originalsprache des Matthäusevangeliums,* 111, n. 1, investigates the matter thoroughly and finds all suggestions wanting, concluding that Hegesippus must have intended the Hebrew Gospel alone.

58. So Vielhauer and Strecker, *New Testament Apocrypha,* 1.138, who understand the

or similar to, the "Chaldean and Syriac" document that Jerome will mention in *Against the Pelagians* 3.2. Two centuries after Hegesippus, Jerome spoke of the Hebrew Gospel as a "fountainhead distributed into different channels,"[59] and it may be that Hegesippus is the first to note the fragmentation of the original Hebrew Gospel into different versions and traditions.

It is probable that the distinction between Hebrew and Syriac derives from Hegesippus himself and not from Eusebius, who lived two centuries later and probably knew neither Hebrew nor Syriac. Eusebius notes that Hegesippus had converted to Christianity from Judaism and was particularly (ἰδίως) adept at Hebrew. He knew the difference between Hebrew and Syriac, in other words, and this makes him an important witness to the Hebrew Gospel. In the words of R. Handmann, "It is therefore obvious that in addition to the other gospels [Hegesippus] used the one written in his mother tongue and with which he was best acquainted; for this reason he must always remain for us an important witness for the antiquity and status of this gospel."[60]

Hippolytus (c. 170–c. 236)

Hippolytus, the most important third-century theologian of the Roman church, sharply disagreed with the Monarchian inclinations of Zephyrinus and Callistus, both bishops of Rome, and allowed himself to be named a rival bishop in their stead. Because of his schismatic tendencies and because he was the last prominent Roman theologian to write in Greek, details of Hippolytus's life have been lost and the transmission of his writings has suffered gravely. Among the writings that have been attributed to him is "On the Twelve Apostles," a brief listing of names of the Twelve, where they preached, and how they died. Its authenticity has been doubted because it is not listed in Jerome's bibliography of Hippolytus (*Vir. ill.* 61) or in an inscription of Hippolytus's writings on a Roman statue recovered in 1551. On the other hand, Hippolytus's familiarity with the Hebrew Gospel would hardly be surprising, for few Western fathers possessed greater familiarity

---

wording to mean two Gospels, "both from the Gospel according to the Hebrews and from the Syriac (Gospel)."

59. *Praefatio in Quattuor Evangeliorum.*
60. *Das Hebräer-Evangelium,* 34.

with Judaism. In his exegetical works he relies on rabbinic methods of argument, and his denunciations of opponents are reinforced with OT tradition. The discovery of the Dead Sea Scrolls confirms the detail and accuracy of his knowledge of the Essenes — knowledge that can only have come from close contact with Jewish communities.[61] Indeed, the exact title of the work ascribed to Hippolytus *(De duodecim apostolis)* is mentioned by Jerome in reference to the apostle Bartholomew in *Illustrious Men* 36.2 (see n. 45 above). It is thus not improbable that the source of Jerome's note on Bartholomew comes from Hippolytus's "On the Twelve Apostles."

The text of Hippolytus reads: "Matthew, having written the Gospel in Hebrew, published it in Jerusalem, and slept in Hierae of Parthia."[62] The Greek spelling of "Jerusalem" is a transliteration of Hebrew and thus argues for the antiquity of the text.[63] New in the text is the identification of Jerusalem as the place of publication of the Hebrew Gospel. If the text is authentic, its omission from lists of Hippolytus's major works could be due to its brevity and relative unimportance.

Origen (185-254)

The tradition of a Hebrew Gospel was continued in the third century by Origen, whose reputation as a textual critic and exegete was unsurpassed in the ancient church. Origen's work concentrates overwhelmingly on the four canonical Gospels, but on occasion he refers (and not disapprovingly) to noncanonical Gospels. Among these are the *Gospel of Peter,* the *Protoevangelium of James,* and the *Gospel of the Hebrews.* He refers to the last sometimes without further comment[64] and sometimes with a qualifying phrase such as "if one receives it."[65] These parenthetical qualifications, which also appear in Eusebius, imply that the Hebrew Gospel cannot be cited with the same authority as canonical texts. Despite these reservations, Origen's references to the Hebrew Gospel indicate its widespread

---

61. W. H. C. Frend, *The Rise of Christianity* (Philadelphia: Fortress Press, 1984) 340-46.

62. Ματθαῖος δὲ, τὸ εὐαγγέλιον Ἑβραϊστὶ γράψας, δέδωκεν ἐν Ἰερουσαλήμ, καὶ ἐκοιμήθη ἐν Ἱερέει τῆς Παρθείας (*De Duodecim Apostolis;* PL 10.952).

63. On the spelling of Ἰερουσαλήμ, see pp. 136-38 below.

64. *Comm. Jo.* 2.12; *Comm. Matt.* 16.12.

65. *Hom. Jer.* 15:4; *Comm. Matt.* 15:14. Origen cites *Enoch* and the *Prayer of Joseph* with similar equivocations; M.-J. Lagrange, "L'Évangile selon les Hébreux," *RB* 31 (1922), 173.

recognition in the early church and its enduring status in the emergent canon. According to Eusebius, Origen followed the fourfold canonical order in discussing the origins of the Gospels in his *Commentaries on the Gospel according to Matthew.* The First Gospel, says Origen, "was written by Matthew, who once had been a tax collector but later became an apostle of Jesus Christ, having published it for believers from Judaism, composed in Hebrew script."[66] Origen thus attributes the Gospel of Matthew to Jesus' disciple who had been a tax collector and who wrote in Hebrew letters or script (γράμασσιν Ἑβραϊκοῖς) for the benefit of converts from Judaism. Origen's testimony that Matthew "published" the Hebrew Gospel is important here. The Greek word ἐκδεδωκότα carries the sense of producing a formal and complete work as opposed to a partial or provisional work.[67] Origen's reference to "the Hebrew script" of Matthew is very close to Pantaenus's wording (Ἑβραίων γράμμασι) and may well derive from the latter, who was Origen's predecessor (once-removed) at the catechetical school in Alexandria.[68]

Eusebius (c. 260–c. 340)

The existence of a Hebrew Gospel is acknowledged by Eusebius throughout the *Ecclesiastical History,* which he composed early in the fourth century. He reminds his readers that the Gospel according to the Hebrews (τὸ καθ' Ἑβραίους εὐαγγέλιον) was always and everywhere preferred by Jewish converts to Christianity.[69] Among those who accepted the Hebrew Gospel — indeed, who used little else — were the Ebionites, who "use only the said Gospel according to the Hebrews."[70] In contrast to burgeoning Gentile Christianity, such Jewish converts — and particularly the

---

66. πρῶτον μὲν γέγραπται τὸ κατὰ τόν ποτε τελώνην ὕστερον δὲ ἀπόστολον Ἰησοῦ Χριστοῦ Ματθαῖον, ἐκδεδωκότα αὐτὸ τοῖς ἀπὸ Ἰουδαϊσμοῦ πιστεύσασιν, γράμμασιν Ἑβραϊκοῖς συντεταγμένον (*Hist. eccl.* 6.25.4).

67. C. E. Hill, "What Papias Said about John (and Luke)," 602. Hippolytus uses the same word of the Hebrew Gospel in *De duodecim Apostolis.*

68. Pantaenus, the learned head of the catechetical school in Alexandria, taught Clement of Alexandria, who in turn was the teacher of Origen (*Hist. eccl.* 6.6.1).

69. *Hist. eccl.* 3.25.5; also in *Theoph.* 4.12 Eusebius refers to "the Gospel that is among the Jews in the Hebrew language."

70. εὐαγγελίῳ δὲ μόνῳ τῷ καθ' Ἑβραίους λεγομένῳ χρώμενοι (*Hist. eccl.* 3.27.4).

Ebionites — either preferred the Hebrew Gospel to the canonical Gospels or used it exclusively. In the canonical debates of the Gentile church, the canonical Gospels were "recognized," whereas the Hebrew Gospel was "disputed," but among the Ebionites the reverse seems to have been truer: the *Gospel of the Hebrews* was "recognized" and the canonical Gospels were either "disputed" or "rejected." In Book 3 of *Ecclesiastical History*, Eusebius notes that the apostles Matthew and John both wrote down their recollections (ὑπομνήματα). Matthew, says Eusebius, first began preaching to Hebrews (πρότερον Ἑβραίοις κηρύξας), but when he found it necessary to leave and go elsewhere, he committed the gospel he was preaching into his native tongue (πατρίῳ γλώττῃ γραφῇ παραδοὺς τὸ κατ᾽ αὐτὸν εὐαγγέλιον) as a substitute for his personal presence and preaching.[71] Eusebius does not here expressly say that Matthew wrote in Hebrew, but writing what he had preached to "Hebrews" clearly implies such. In citing the Hebrew Gospel Eusebius may be referring to a document he has personally seen, for in a fragment from the *Theophany,* he speaks of "the Gospel written in Hebrew characters that has come to us."[72] Lagrange understands "has come to us" here to mean that Eusebius received the Hebrew Gospel into his library in Caesarea.[73]

Eusebius's summary of the canonical status of various texts in circulation at the beginning of the fourth century is critical for a proper assessment of the Hebrew Gospel. He follows Origen's earlier threefold classification of Recognized Books (ὁμολογούμενα), Disputed Books (ἀντιλεγόμενα), and Rejected Books (νόθα). The summary occurs in *Ecclesiastical History* 3.25 and is worth quoting at length since it is preserves the most "authorized" report of the emerging NT canon — and the Hebrew Gospel in relation to it — in the early fourth century.

> At this point it seems reasonable to summarize the writings of the New Testament which have been quoted. In the first place should be put the holy tetrad of the Gospels. To them follows the writing of the Acts of the Apostles. After this should be reckoned the Epistles of Paul. Following

71. Ματθαῖός τε γὰρ πρότερον Ἑβραίοις κηρύξας, ὡς ἤμελλεν καὶ ἐφ᾽ ἑτέρους ἰέναι, πατρίῳ γλώττῃ γραφῇ παραδοὺς τὸ κατ᾽ αὐτὸν εὐαγγέλιον, τὸ λεῖπον τῇ αὐτοῦ παρουσίᾳ τούτοις ἀφ᾽ ὧν ἐστέλλετο, διὰ τῆς γραφῆς ἀπεπλήρου (*Hist. eccl.* 3.24.5-6).

72. Ἐπεὶ δὲ τὸ εἰς ἡμᾶς ἧκον Ἑβραϊκοῖς χαρακτῆρσιν εὐαγγέλιον (*Theoph.* 4.22; PG 24.685).

73. M.-J. Lagrange, "L'Évangile selon les Hébreux," 177.

them the Epistle of John called the first, and in the same way should be recognized the Epistle of Peter. In addition to these should be put, if it seem desirable, the Revelation of John, the arguments concerning which we will expound at the proper time. Those belong to the Recognized Books.

Of the Disputed Books which are nevertheless known to most are the Epistle of James, that of Jude, the second Epistle of Peter, and the so-called second and third Epistles of John, which may be the work of the Evangelist or of some other of the same name. Among the books which are not genuine (νόθα) must be reckoned the Acts of Paul, the work entitled the Shepherd, the Apocalypse of Peter, and in addition to them the letter called Barnabas and the so-called Teachings of the Apostles. And in addition, as I said, the Revelation of John, if this view prevail. For, as I said, some reject it, but others count it among the Recognized Books. Some have also counted the Gospel according to the Hebrews in which those of the Hebrews who have accepted Christ take a special pleasure.

These would all belong to the Disputed Books, but we have nevertheless been obliged to make a list of them, distinguishing between those writings which, according to the tradition of the Church, are true, genuine, and recognized, and those which differ from them in that they are not canonical but disputed, yet nevertheless are known to most of the writers of the Church, in order that we might know them and the writings which are put forward by heretics under the name of the apostles containing Gospels such as those of Peter, and Thomas, and Matthias, and some others besides, or Acts such as those of Andrew and John and the other apostles. To none of these has any who belonged to the succession of the orthodox ever thought it right to refer in his writings. . . . They ought, therefore, to be reckoned not even among spurious books (νόθα) but shunned as altogether wicked and impious.[74]

This summary begins with clear designations of canonical books, and ends with equally clear rejections of "wicked and impious" forgeries. The qualifications and ambiguities in the central discussion of Disputed Books obscure the discussion, however, making it difficult to know whether Eusebius understands a half-dozen books as belonging to the disputed or rejected categories. In this murky mid-section the *Gospel according to the*

---

74. According to Kirsopp Lake's translation in LCL.

Hebrews is mentioned. Some take Eusebius's description to imply that the Gospel belonged to the Rejected Books,[75] but this was almost certainly not his intent. He refers to it not in connection with the category of Rejected Books (i.e., *Acts of Paul, Shepherd of Hermas, Apocalypse of Peter, Epistle of Barnabas,* and the "Teachings of the Apostles" [=*Didache*]), but rather in connection with the Book of Revelation. Twice Eusebius mentions Revelation, both times with the qualification "if it seems" (εἰ φανείη). His equivocation betrays a degree of uncertainty about Revelation, but it also seems calculated not to offend the spectrum of opinion that his readers hold about the canonical status of Revelation.

Then, along with Revelation, "some have *also* counted the Gospel according to the Hebrews. . . ." Eusebius's ambiguity again seems calculated not to declare himself too firmly on a subject about which his readers' opinions are diverse and passionate. Much is less than clear in *Ecclesiastical History* 3.25, but it does seem clear that Eusebius places the *Gospel of the Hebrews* and the Book of Revelation in the same category. Both enjoy wide recognition (Eusebius twice notes that the documents specified in this summary are "known to most").[76] The designation of Rejected Books as νόθα ("illegitimate," "bastard") is an important clue to Eusebius's judgment of them. Their lack of ecclesiastical paternity, i.e., that they neither derive from nor transmit authorized tradition, makes them suspicious in the eyes of Eusebius and of the churches as a whole.[77] That the *Gospel of the Hebrews* is not explicitly included in the rejected category but mentioned in correlation with the Book of Revelation strongly suggests that it, like the Revelation, fell into the Disputed Books of Eusebius's taxonomy.[78]

Parenthetically, Eusebius's classification of the Hebrew Gospel in the "disputed" category is echoed in the *Chronographia Brevis* of Nicephorus.

---

75. See the discussion in B. M. Metzger, *The Canon of the New Testament,* 203-5.

76. On the recognition and acceptance of the *Gospel of the Hebrews* in the ancient church, see C.-B. Amphoux, "L'Évangile selon les Hebreux. Sources de L'Évangile de Luc," 67-77.

77. Also noted by G. Dorival, "Un Groupe Judéo-Chrétien Méconnu: les Hébreux," 9.

78. Zahn, *Geschichte des neutestamentlichen Kanons* 2/2.643-48, and Harnack, *Geschichte der altchristlichen Literatur bis Eusebius* 1/1.7, rightly understand Eusebius to assign the Hebrew Gospel to the "disputed" (ἀντιλεγόμενον) category. Likewise, note the conclusion of M.-J. Lagrange, "L'Évangile selon les Hébreux," 175: "The Hebrew Gospel was far from being considered heretical, and although it was not considered equal to the Four Gospels, it was accorded an honorable place among the books of the church."

In his early ninth-century catalog of canonical books, Nicephorus, bishop of Constantinople (806-15), lists four books as disputed (ἀντιλέγονται): the Revelation of John, the *Apocalypse of Peter,* the *Epistle of Barnabas,* and the *Gospel of the Hebrews.* Nicephorus thus reminds us that a full five centuries after Eusebius the Hebrew Gospel was still a single identifiable entity and still held in favorable repute.[79] Incidentally, Nicephorus is the only church father to report the length of the *Gospel of the Hebrews* as 2200 lines.[80]

Before leaving Eusebius we may further consider the relation of the Hebrew Gospel to the Gospel attributed to "Matthias." The latter, along with the Gospels of Peter and Thomas and the Acts of Andrew and John, is rejected by Eusebius as heretical and is thus clearly a different document from the *Gospel of the Hebrews.* As we saw in *Ecclesiastical History* 3.25, Eusebius is undecided about the Hebrew Gospel, but there is no indecision in his judgment of the *Gospel of Matthias,* which, he says, has never at any time been accorded apostolic status and should be rejected as spurious. Nor can the *Gospel of Matthias* be canonical Matthew since Eusebius holds the First Gospel in high esteem and nowhere calls it heretical. The *Gospel of Matthias* is also probably unrelated to the only other "Matthias" mentioned by Eusebius (the names are spelled the same), the apostle chosen as Judas's successor.[81] Rather, the Gospel attributed to Matthias must be the same document known to Clement of Alexandria and Hippolytus as "The Traditions of Matthew." In *Stromata* 2.9.45, Clement quotes a saying about a wonder attributed to Jesus as it appears in both "The Traditions of Matthew," and "The Gospel of the Hebrews." Hippolytus likewise distinguishes between "The Gospel of the Hebrews" and "The Traditions of Matthew," and, like Clement, rejects the latter, attributing it to the Gnostic heretic Basilides.[82]

---

79. Note the judgment of M.-J. Lagrange, "L'Évangile selon les Hébreux," 180, on the significance of Nicephorus's *Chronographia Brevis,* "L'importance de cette attestation est vraiment impressionnante. Cet évangile [des Hébreux] existait donc alors en grec et il était assez connu pour qu'on puisse en déterminer exactement l'étendue, trois cents lignes de moins que le Mt. canonique; ou bien il faut dire que c'est une affirmation en l'air!"

80. By comparison, Matthew, 2500 lines; Mark, 2000 lines; Luke, 2600 lines; John, 2300 lines.

81. *Hist. eccl.* 1.12.3; 2.1.1; 3.29.4; 3.39.9-10.

82. See B. M. Metzger, *The Canon of the New Testament,* 132; A. Harnack, *Geschichte der altchristlichen Literatur,* 1.157.

Ephrem the Syrian (c. 306-73)

A younger contemporary of Eusebius, Ephrem the Syrian, also records the tradition of an original Hebrew Gospel in his *Commentary on Tatian's Diatessaron,* preserved only in Latin. Commenting on the authorship of the four canonical Gospels, Ephrem says that "Matthew wrote his Gospel in Hebrew, and it was then translated into Greek."[83] Ephrem's theological interests lay with pre-Nicene Christian traditions and especially with early Jewish traditions.[84] He did not know Greek and wrote exclusively in Syriac. He obviously knew how to recognize Hebrew, and especially the difference between Hebrew and Aramaic, the latter of which was a sister language to his native Syriac. Ephrem follows Hegesippus in preserving a record that the Hebrew Gospel appeared in two versions. He is also the first witness to a long tradition of an original Hebrew Gospel in Syria. "For upwards of a thousand years in Syrian-speaking countries it was believed that Matthew's Gospel was written originally in Hebrew."[85]

Didymus of Alexandria (c. 310-98)

In 1941 a trove of hitherto unknown texts of noncanonical Christian papyrus codices was discovered twelve miles south of Cairo. Among these texts were the works of Didymus of Alexandria, also known as Didymus the blind. One of the Didymus documents contains an exposition of Ps 34:1 (LXX 33:1) in which he seeks to explain why the Bible sometimes refers to the same person by two different names. One example of this is the two names given to Matthew/Levi. In reference to this name change, Didymus writes:

> There are many such name changes. Matthew appears in the [Gospel] according to Luke under the name of Levi. He is not the same person,

---

83. Matthaeus hebraice scripsit id (i.e., evangelium), et deinde translatum est in graecum. Epiphanius knows a tradition linking the Diatessaron and the Gospel of the Hebrews: "It is said that from [Tatian] comes the Diatessaron, which is also called the Gospel according to the Hebrews" (*Pan.* 46.1). It is difficult to know what relationship, if any, Ephraem and Epiphanius share on this datum.

84. F. Rilliet, "Ephrem the Syrian," *Encyclopaedia of the Early Church,* ed. A. Di Berardino (New York: Oxford University Press, 1992), 1.276.

85. H. Schonfield, *According to the Hebrews,* 246.

but rather the Matthew who was appointed [apostle] in place of Judas; he and Levi are the same person under two different names. This is made apparent in the Hebrew Gospel.[86]

Two observations are noteworthy about this text. The first is the unstated though controlling assumption behind Didymus's exegesis, namely, that a canonical Gospel is defended on the basis of noncanonical text. The noncanonical text is the Hebrew Gospel, to which Didymus in this instance attributes an authority *over* the canonical Gospels. We shall see a further instance in the next chapter of the use of the Hebrew Gospel in order to resolve a difficulty in a canonical text. No church council or church father, of course, had ever or would ever officially sanction the Hebrew Gospel with canonical authority. Nevertheless, the Didymus text is an unspoken yet eloquent reminder that even in the third century and as far away as Egypt the status of the Hebrew Gospel was such that it was enlisted to resolve exegetical difficulties in canonical texts.[87]

The second observation is more complex, but no less revealing. Didymus's unconventional interpretation rejects the commonsense solution that the Matthew of Matt 9:9 and the Levi of Mark 2:14 and Luke 5:27, 29 are one and the same person. Without warning — and seemingly without warrant — Didymus asserts that the Levi of Mark and Luke is identical rather with the Matthias of Acts 1:23, 26, who was chosen to replace Judas after his defection from the company of the apostles. In Didymus's interpretation, the Levi of Mark and Luke was not an apostle during the Lord's earthly lifetime. He first became an apostle after the resurrection of Jesus, at which time he took the name Matthias. The post-resurrection apostolic cohort thus had two apostles with virtually the same names: a Matthew, who had been called by Jesus (Matt 9:9) and was an apostle

---

86. καὶ πολλαὶ γέ εἰσιν τοιαῦται ὁμωνυμίαι. τὸν Ματθαῖον δοκεῖ ἐν τῷ κατὰ Λουκᾶν Λευὶν ὀνομάζειν. οὐκ ἔστιν δὲ αὐτός, ἀλλὰ ὁ κατασταθεὶς ἀντὶ τοῦ Ἰούδα ὁ Ματθίας καὶ ὁ Λευίς εἷς διώνυμός εἰσιν ἐν τῷ καθ' Ἑβραίους εὐαγγελίῳ τοῦτο φαίνεται (from S. Brock, "A New Testimonium to the 'Gospel according to the Hebrews,'" *NTS* 18 [1971], 220; D. Lührmann, *Die apokryph gewordenen Evangelien*, 184). In the original manuscript διώνυμός ἐστιν has been altered to διώνυμός εἰσιν. The change to the plural verb has led some textual editors to emend the text to διώνυμοί εἰσιν.

87. So too G. Dorival, "Un Groupe Judéo-Chrétien Méconnu: Les Hébreux," 11-21, who further argues for the significance of the existence of a Hebrew-Christian community in Egypt and its use of the Hebrew Gospel.

throughout Jesus' ministry, and a Matthias, who was named to the apostolic guild after the defection and death of Judas Iscariot and the resurrection of Jesus.

But why would Didymus propose such a strained interpretation of an otherwise easily resolved problem? On the basis of the Synoptic Gospels alone, he should not — perhaps could not — have come to such a conclusion. Moreover, it is unexpected of Didymus, a staunch supporter of both Nicene orthodoxy and the authority of Scripture, to contravene the plain sense of Scripture by such an unlikely interpretation. The most plausible explanation is that he found in the Hebrew Gospel a version of the story similar to Mark 2:13-17 and Luke 5:27-32 with the name "Matthias" substituted for "Levi." On the basis of this *authority* he posited the identity of Levi and Matthias.

A separate text from Oxyrhynchus (papyrus 1224) seems to support this conjecture. Its reconstruction reads:

> When the scribes and Pharisees and priests saw [Jesus] they were indignant because he was reclining in the midst of sinners. But when Jesus heard this, he said, "It is not the well who need a physician. . . ."[88]

This passage is similar to Mark 2:16-17 and Luke 5:30-31, both of which conclude the Levi story, but it is dissimilar to the parallel passage in Matt 9:11 that follows the call of Matthew the tax collector. This noncanonical text associated with the Hebrew Gospel appears to preserve a tradition of a call of a tax collector named "Matthias," which otherwise agrees with the call of Levi in both Mark and Luke.

One further association of Matthias, rather than Levi, as the tax collector in question occurs in a quotation from Clement of Alexandria. Clement introduces his account of Luke 19:1-10 by adding parenthetically that Zacchaeus was known by some as "Matthias."[89] Over a century ago Theodor Zahn surmised that "Clement apparently knew a complete parallel story to Luke 19:1-10 in a non-canonical gospel."[90] This seems probable — and it seems equally probable that the tradition of which Zahn speaks was represented by the Hebrew Gospel, in which the Matthias associated

---

88. Cited from D. Lührmann, *Die apokryph gewordenen Evangelien*, 186.
89. Ζακχαῖον τοίνυν, οἱ δὲ Ματθίαν φασίν (*Strom.* 4.35.2).
90. *Geschichte des neutestamentlichen Kanons*, 2/2.752.

with Luke 19:1-10 should also be associated with the tax collector of Mark 2 and Luke 5.[91] Dieter Lührmann concludes that "The Didymus text strengthens the impression that the Hebrew Gospel should be considered a Gospel containing Jesus narratives similar to the narratives in the Synoptic Gospels. . . . The Hebrew Gospel contained not simply sayings of Jesus, but to this Gospel must also be ascribed narratives."[92] Lührmann's conclusion can only be corrected in one respect: the tradition represented by the Hebrew Gospel does not generally cohere with the Synoptics, but rather specifically with the stories of Levi and Zacchaeus in *Luke.*

Epiphanius (c. 315-403)

Later in the fourth century Epiphanius, bishop of Salamis, confirmed the existence of an original Hebrew Gospel. Eight important quotations of Epiphanius from the Hebrew Gospel will be considered in the next chapter. At this point we are only interested in his description of the document. In eight instances he ascribes its authorship to the apostle Matthew, in five of which he identifies its language as Hebrew.[93] He mentions the Hebrew Gospel only in relation to the sects of the Nazarenes and the Ebionites. A lone reference to the former reads: "[the Nazarenes] have the Gospel according to Matthew complete in Hebrew. For it is still distinctly preserved among them, as it was originally written, in Hebrew script."[94] Epiphanius's other references to the Hebrew Gospel occur in relationship to the Ebionites. Along with the Cerinthians and Merinthians, says Epiphanius, the Ebionites used only the Gospel of Matthew. "They call it, however, According to the Hebrews, which it truly is, for only Matthew put the exposition and proclamation of the gospel in the Hebrew and in Hebrew script in

---

91. For a fuller defense of this hypothesis, see D. Lührmann, *Die apokryph gewordenen Evangelien,* 180-91. Lührmann's conjecture is cautiously endorsed by S. Brock, "A New Testimonium to the 'Gospel according to the Hebrews,'" 222: "It may be suggested — and the speculative nature of this should at once be stressed — that the Gospel according to the Hebrews contained a single reference to a publican, but one which contained elements of the Lukan doublet in Luke xix as well."

92. D. Lührmann, *Die apokryph gewordenen Evangelien,* 190.

93. *Pan.* 29.9.4; 30.3.7; 30.6.9; 30.13.1, 2; 30.14.2, 3; 51.5.3.

94. ἔχουσι δὲ τὸ κατὰ Ματθαῖον εὐαγγέλιον πληρέστατον Ἑβραϊστί. παρ' αὐτοῖς γὰρ σαφῶς τοῦτο, καθὼς ἐξ ἀρχῆς ἐγράφη, Ἑβραϊκοῖς γράμμασιν ἔτι σῴζεται (*Pan.* 29.9.4).

the New Testament."[95] It seems unwarranted to conclude with some scholars that Epiphanius is referring to several distinct and self-contained Hebrew Gospel traditions.[96] Rather, especially in relation to what Hegesippus, Ephrem, and Jerome say on the matter, it seems reasonable to understand Epiphanius to be referring to an original Hebrew Gospel that was later altered — or "mutilated," as he says — in accordance with the interests of different Jewish Christian sects. The (mis)use of the Hebrew Gospel by such groups in the fourth and early fifth centuries may, in fact, account for the proliferation of references to it and the heightened polemic against it, especially in Epiphanius and Jerome. Epiphanius does not appear to have had firsthand knowledge "whether [the Nazarenes] have removed the genealogy from Abraham to Christ,"[97] but he seems to have had a copy before him of the Hebrew Gospel used by the Ebionites, from which the Matthean genealogy was removed and other changes were made that he deplored.[98] We do not know whether Epiphanius knew Hebrew as well as Hegesippus, Origen, Ephrem, and Jerome — the four fathers whom we know read Hebrew. Nevertheless, Epiphanius could both recognize and read at least some Hebrew, for in *Panarion* 30.31.1 he correctly cites the Hebrew word גלמי = Γολμή of Ps 139:16. According to Epiphanius, the Hebrew base-text of Matthew could be found in the Jewish treasuries in Tiberias, along with Hebrew translations of the Gospel of John and the Book of Acts, all of which was "described to [Epiphanius] in detail . . . by Jews who have been converted to Christ and who read [the Hebrew Gospel] there."[99]

---

95. καλοῦσι δὲ αὐτὸ κατὰ Ἑβραίους, ὡς τὰ ἀληθῆ ἔστιν εἰπεῖν, ὅτι Ματθαῖος μόνος Ἑβραϊστὶ καὶ Ἑβραϊκοῖς γράμμασιν ἐν τῇ καινῇ διαθήκῃ ἐποιήσατο τὴν τοῦ εὐαγγελίου ἔκθεσίν τε καὶ κήρυγμα (*Pan.* 30.3.7). Epiphanius again refers to Matthew's writing "in the Hebrew script" (Ἑβραϊκοῖς γράμμασιν) in *Pan.* 51.5.3. Further, see *Pan.* 30.6.9; 30.13.2.

96. So Vielhauer and Strecker, "Jewish Christian Gospels," 139-41.

97. ἔχουσι δὲ τὸ κατὰ Ματθαῖον εὐαγγέλιον πληρέστατον Ἑβραϊστί. παρ᾽ αὐτοῖς γὰρ σαφῶς τουτο, καθὼς ἐξ ἀρχῆς ἐγράφη, Ἑβραϊκοῖς γράμμασιν ἔτι σῴζεται. οὐκ οἶδα δὲ εἰ καὶ τὰς γενεαλογίας τὰς ἀπὸ τοῦ Ἀβραὰμ ἄχρι Χριστοῦ περιεῖλον (*Pan.* 29.9.4).

98. παρακόψαντες γὰρ τὰς παρὰ τῷ Ματθαίῳ γενεαλογίας (*Pan.* 30.14.3).

99. ὡς καὶ ἀπὸ τούτου τοὺς ἀναγνόντας Ἰουδαίους τοὺς ἡμῖν ὑφηγησαμένους εἰς Χριστὸν πεπιστευκέναι (*Pan.* 30.3.8-9).

John Chrysostom (c. 347-407)

Born in Antioch and influenced by the "Antiochene school" of exegesis, Chrysostom defended the gospel against both Jewish opposition and the renaissance of classical paganism under Julian the Apostate, Porphyry, and others. A gifted orator (hence the epithet "Chrysostom" = "golden mouth"), Chrysostom was appointed against his will bishop of Constantinople in 398. Attempts to reform the city, combined with his outspoken (and sometimes tactless) honesty and tendency toward asceticism, resulted in nine mercurial years as bishop in which he was alternatively deposed by the emperor and recalled by popular demand. His final deposition in 407 resulted in death by exhaustion on a forced march.

In his *Homilies on Matthew*, Chrysostom includes notes on the occasions for the writing of the Gospels of Luke and John, to which he appends this note on Matthew: "And of Matthew it is said, when Jews who believed approached him and asked him to reduce his spoken words into writing for them, he brought forth the Gospel in the language of the Hebrews."[100] According to Chrysostom, the impetus for the composition of Hebrew Matthew was a *request* from Jewish Christians. Otherwise, Chrysostom seems indebted to the similar and earlier testimony of Eusebius that

> Matthew had first preached to Hebrews, and when he was on the point of going to others he transmitted in writing in his native language the Gospel according to himself, and thus supplied by writing the lack of his own presence to those from whom he was sent.[101]

Jerome (c. 345-419)

The most numerous, specific, and contested references to the Hebrew Gospel come from the pen of Jerome. He preserves at least twenty-four references to and quotations from the Hebrew Gospel,[102] which can be divided into three general categories. The first is a series of passing refer-

---

100. λέγεται δὲ καὶ Ματθαῖος, τῶν ἐξ Ἰουδαίων πιστευσάντων προσελθόντων αὐτῷ καὶ παρακαλεσάντων, ἅπερ εἶπε διὰ ῥημάτων, ταῦτα ἀφεῖναι συνθεῖναι διὰ γραμμάτων αὐτοῖς, καὶ τῇ τῶν Ἑβραίων φωνῇ συνθεῖναιτὸ εὐαγγέλιον (*Hom. Matt.* 1.3).

101. *Hist. eccl.* 3.24.6 (K. Lake's translation in LCL).

102. In *Geschichte der altchristlichen Literatur*, 2/1.8-10, Harnack lists only nineteen.

ences to the Hebrew Gospel without further description.[103] Some of these references attribute its use specifically to the sect of the Nazarenes.[104] These frequent but unelaborated references indicate that the Hebrew Gospel was sufficiently well-known to be assumed as a point of reference for Jerome's readers.

A second group of references emphasizes the Hebrew character of the Gospel, often with the added note that the *Urtext* was composed by the apostle Matthew.[105] Some of these references simply introduce the Gospel as "written in Hebrew letters"[106] or composed "in the Hebrew speech."[107] Others mention that the apostle Matthew wrote the Gospel in Hebrew in order to bear witness to Jews or to minister to Jewish converts.

> The first Evangelist was Matthew, a tax-collector, surnamed Levi, who edited a Gospel in Judea in the Hebrew language chiefly for the sake of Jews who believed in Jesus but were serving in vain the shadow of the law after the true gospel had come.[108]

This testimony repeats data related to the Hebrew Gospel from earlier fathers, but its place of composition in Judea is new in Jerome.

Similar to the above, but more comprehensive, is the testimony in *Illustrious Men* 3:

> Matthew, also known as Levi, a tax-collector who became an apostle, was the first in Judea to compose a Gospel of Christ in Hebrew letters and words, on whose account those of the circumcision believed, although it is not certain who later translated the Gospel into Greek. Indeed, the Hebrew itself was diligently brought out by Pamphilus the

---

103. E.g., *Comm. Matt.* 6:11, "In evangelio quod appellatur secundum Hebraeos." Also *Comm. Matt.* 27:16; 27:51; *Comm. Eph.* 5:4.

104. *Comm. Matt.* 23:35, "In euangelio quo utuntur Nazaraeni." Also *Comm. Isa. praef.* (18); *Comm. Isa.* 11:1; *Comm. Isa.* 40:9; *Comm. Ezech.* 16:13; *Comm. Ezech.* 18:7.

105. *Epist.* 20.5 *ad Dam.*, "Denique Matthaeus, qui evangelium Hebraeo sermone conscripsit."

106. *Epist.* 120.8 *ad Hedy.*

107. *Comm. Isa.* (11:2).

108. Primus omnium Mattheus est publicanus cognomento Levi, qui evangelium in Judaea hebreo sermone edidit, ob eorum vel maxime causam qui in Iesum crediderant ex Iudaeis et nequaquam legis umbra succedente evangelii veritatem servabant (*Comm. Matt.* Praefatio).

Martyr and is still to this day in the library of Caesarea. I have actually had opportunity to have the volume described to me by people who use it, the Nazarenes of Beroea, a city in Syria. It should be noted that wherever the Evangelist, whether by his own person or by the Lord our Savior, quotes testimonies from the Old Testament he does not follow the authority of the translators of the Septuagint, but rather the Hebrew, from which these two forms exist: "Out of Egypt I have called my son," and "For he shall be called a Nazarene."[109]

This is Jerome's complete note on Matthew, the third figure treated in *Illustrious Men*. Remarkably, Jerome says nothing of Matthew's call to discipleship, his place in the apostolic company, or his relationship to canonical Greek Matthew. This is not a biographical sketch, as we should expect, but rather a bibliographical note about the author of the Hebrew Gospel — its composition, transmission, translation, and use. One-third of Jerome's second chapter on James is also devoted to the Hebrew Gospel. The prominence of the Hebrew Gospel in the important early chapters of *Illustrious Men* testifies to its significance for Jerome.

The first sentence of the note on Matthew resembles information in Eusebius.[110] Jerome may have derived the data from Eusebius, although we cannot be certain, since such information was widely current in the early church. R. Handmann accuses Jerome of making pronouncements about the Hebrew Gospel of which he has no knowledge and even of "an intentional deception" in implying that Hebrew Matthew and the Hebrew Gospel were one and the same document.[111] This accusation could only be true if Jerome's claim in *Illustrious Men* 2 to have translated the Hebrew Gospel into Greek and Latin is an outright lie. It is worth asking how

---

109. Matthaeus qui et Levi, ex publicano apostolus, primus in Iudaea, propter eos qui ex circumcisione crediderunt, Evangelium Christi Hebraeis litteris verbisque composuit, quod quis postea in Graecum transtulit, non satis certum est. Porro ipsum Hebraicum habetur usque hodie in Caesariensi bibliotheca, quam Pamphilus martyr studiosissime confecit. Mihi quoque a Nazaraeis qui in Beroea, urbe Syriae, hoc volumine utuntur, describendi facultas fuit. In quo animadvertendum quo ubicumque evangelista, sive ex persona sua sive ex Domini Salvatoris veteris scripturae testimoniis abutitur, non sequatur Septuaginta translatorum auctoritatem, sed Hebraicam. E quibus illa duo sunt: "Ex Aegypto vocavi Filium meum," et "Quoniam Nazaraeus vocabitur" (*Vir. ill.* 3).

110. Ματθαῖός τε γὰρ πρότερον Ἑβραίοις κηρύξας . . . πατρίῳ γλώττῃ γραφῇ παραδοὺς τὸ κατ' αὐτὸν εὐαγγέλιον (*Hist. eccl.* 3.24.5-6).

111. R. Handmann, *Das Hebräer-Evangelium*, 62.

Jerome could successfully perpetrate a lie for a period of no fewer than thirty years about a document that was available at the library of Caesarea and known to Pamphilus, the Nazarenes, and many others. A document in the library of Caesarea would appear to be as public as an ancient document could have been. It is difficult to imagine why Jerome would champion a document about which he was massively ignorant and that was never considered canonical. Jerome's various testimonies to the Hebrew Gospel are not entirely consistent, but they should not be attributed to fabrications and deceptions.

It seems more plausible that "Jerome knew the [Hebrew] Gospel from personal experience,"[112] and that his various testimonies reflect different impressions of the text over a long period of time. As Jerome indicates in the note on Matthew, the Hebrew Gospel had been translated before him into Greek. Moreover, the Hebrew Gospel was not merely a Hebrew transliteration, but genuine "Hebrew letters and words." Its composition in Hebrew rather than Aramaic is further supported by the fact that Jerome uses the same word for the language of the Hebrew Gospel as for the original language of the OT. Jerome ascribes its translation, perhaps even a recension of it, to studious preparation on the part of Pamphilus the Martyr. The implication of the third sentence of the Matthew note seems to be that the volume in the library of Caesarea, which is presumably the one Jerome testifies in *Illustrious Men* 2 to having translated into Greek and Latin, is also known to the Beroeans of Syria, who use it as a living text.[113]

The most puzzling statement of Jerome belonging to his second category of texts occurs in *Against the Pelagians*.

---

112. S. von Sychowski, *Hieronymus als Litterarhistoriker. Eine Quellenkritische Untersuchung der Schrift des. H. Hieronymus "De Viris Illustribus"* (Münster: Heinrich Schöningh, 1894), 81.

113. Vielhauer and Strecker dismiss the testimony of Jerome in *Vir. ill.* 3 by saying that "The conclusion is inevitable that it was not the Nazaraeans who communicated to [Jerome] his knowledge of this gospel" (*New Testament Apocrypha*, 1.143). This judgment is based on a faulty translation of the text on the part of Vielhauer and Strecker. Jerome's statement "Mihi quoque a Nazaraeis qui in Beroea, urbe Syriae, hoc volumine utuntur, describendi facultas fuit" does not say, as Vielhauer and Strecker maintain, that "The Nazaraeans in Beroea, a city of Syria, who use this book, also permitted me to copy it," but rather, as I have translated it, "I have actually had opportunity to have the volume described to me by people who use it, the Nazarenes of Beroea, a city in Syria." Jerome makes no mention of having been permitted by the Nazaraeans to copy their text.

In the Gospel according to the Hebrews, which is written in the Chaldean and Syrian language, but in Hebrew characters, and which is used to this day by the Nazarenes, which is of apostolic tradition, or as many assert "according to Matthew," which also is found in the library in Caesarea.[114]

The difficulty in this statement is Jerome's apparent description of the Hebrew Gospel as a Hebrew transliteration of a text written in both "Chaldean and Syriac." The use of *sermone* in the singular suggests that by "Chaldean and Syriac" Jerome means one language rather than two different languages. "Hebrew characters" could, of course, apply to either Hebrew or Aramaic. But which? Philo uses "Chaldean" repeatedly with reference to *Hebrew,* and it is thus possible that "Chaldean" means Hebrew here.[115] But this seems doubtful, for in Jerome's preface to his commentary on Tobit he differentiates between "lingua Chaldaeorum" (= Aramaic) and "sermoni Hebraico" (= Hebrew).[116] On the whole, it appears that Jerome here intends a Syriac (or perhaps another Babylonian dialect) transliterated into Hebrew, or perhaps simply Aramaic.[117]

Vielhauer and Strecker maintain that all along Jerome has used an "inexact, popular designation" to refer to an Aramaic text of various Synoptic

114. In Euangelio iuxta Hebraeos, quod Chaldaico quidem Syroque sermone, sed Hebraicis litteris scriptum est, quo utuntur usque hodie Nazareni, secundum apostolos, siue, ut plerique autumant, iuxta Matthaeum, quod et in Caesariensi habetur bibliotheca (*Pelag.* 3.2). The phrase "secundum apostolos, siue, ut plerique autumant, iuxta Matthaeum" is problematic. Majority opinion renders it "[the Gospel] according to the Apostles," but if Jerome intended a separate document we should expect "iuxta apostolos" (in conformity with "iuxta Hebraeos" and "iuxta Matthaeum" in the same sentence) rather than "secundum apostolos." I am inclined to take "secundum apostolos" as a parenthetical reference to the Hebrew Gospel, i.e., that the latter derives from *apostolic tradition.* The meaning seems to be that the *Gospel according to the Hebrews* is apostolic, or better known as the Gospel of Matthew.

115. In *Vit. Mos.* 2.26, 31, 38, 40 (2x), Philo refers five times to the translation of the LXX from "Chaldean," which can only mean from *Hebrew.*

116. *Praefatio in Librum Tobiae,* PL 29.25.

117. H. F. D. Sparks ("Jerome as Biblical Scholar," in *The Cambridge History of the Bible,* ed. P. R. Ackroyd and C. F. Evans [Cambridge: Cambridge University Press, 1970], 512) suggests that "the Syrian tongue" refers not to Aramaic or Syriac, but rather to *the place where Jerome learned Hebrew.* It is indeed the case that Jerome learned Hebrew in Syria, and in other instances "the Syrian tongue" may intend Hebrew, but in the present quotation it seems to intend a language other than Hebrew, since it would have been redundant for Jerome to add that he wrote *Hebrew* in Hebrew characters.

and Matthean texts (and their variants) that probably circulated among the Nazarene sect under the title of "The Gospel according to the Twelve Apostles."[118] This suggestion imputes something quite at variance from the plain sense of the vast majority of Jerome's references to the Hebrew Gospel. Jerome's testimony in *Against the Pelagians* to a Hebrew transliteration of Syriac is an exception among his more than two dozen references to the Hebrew Gospel. *Against the Pelagians* was written about 415, late in Jerome's life and only four years before his death. This final reference to the Hebrew Gospel should perhaps best be understood as evidence that early in the fifth century Jerome was aware of the use of the Hebrew Gospel in a different form or version by the sect of the Nazarenes. By the late patristic period the Hebrew Gospel evidently circulated among various Jewish Christian sects in one or more translations and/or recensions. Already in the nineteenth century Adolf Hilgenfeld recognized this "delta effect" at work on the Hebrew Gospel. Hilgenfeld saw the *Gospel of the Ebionites* as a later recension and corruption of an older and ostensibly original Hebrew Gospel.[119]

In his "Preface to the Four Gospels, Addressed to Pope Damasus in 383," Jerome himself alludes to such a fragmentation of the Hebrew Gospel into "various channels."

> I will now speak of the New Testament, which was undoubtedly composed in Greek, with the exception of the Apostle Matthew, who was the first in Judea to produce a Gospel of Christ in Hebrew letters. We must confess that as we have it in our language it is marked by discrepancies, and now that the stream is distributed into different channels we must go back to the fountainhead.[120]

---

118. *New Testament Apocrypha*, 1.146, 148. Schmidtke (as cited by M.-J. Lagrange, "L'Évangile selon les Hébreux," 164) likewise maintains that by "Hebrew" Jerome all along means Aramaic.

119. *Novum Testamentum extra Canonem Receptum*², 6-12; also M.-J. Lagrange, "L'Évangile selon les Hébreux," 162. Similarly Theodor Zahn, *Geschichte des neutestament-lichen Kanons*, 1/2.776-77, held that the Hebrew Gospel known to later church tradition was an expansion of an original Aramaic Gospel that was a *Vorlage* of canonical Greek Matthew.

120. De novo nunc loquor Testamento: quod Graecum esse non dubium est, excepto apostolo Matthaeo, qui primus in Judaea Evangelium Christi Hebraicis litteris edidit. Hoc certe cum in nostro sermone discordat, et diversos rivulorum tramites ducit: uno de fonte quaerendum est *(Praefatio in Quattuor Evangelia)*. A. Harnack, *Geschichte der altchristlichen Literatur*, 1.6, correctly notes the adulterated recensions of the Hebrew Gospel that are associated with the names of Cerinthus and Carpocrates, but there is no evidence in support of

Jerome's description in *Against the Pelagians* 3.2 of the rendering of the original Hebrew Gospel into other Middle Eastern languages seems to be an example of the fragmenting of the "fountainhead" into "different channels."

Finally, it is important to note that in *Against the Pelagians* 3.2 Jerome identifies the Hebrew Gospel ("euangelio iuxta Hebraeos") as the Gospel of Matthew ("iuxta Matthaeum"). Here Jerome is not simply ascribing the Hebrew Gospel to the apostle Matthew — an ascription that is ubiquitous in the patristic tradition — but equating it with a particular *Gospel* identified with Matthew. In the discussion of Epiphanius in the next chapter we shall again see multiple identifications of the Hebrew Gospel with the Gospel of Matthew. But like Epiphanius, Jerome does not correlate this Hebrew Gospel of Matthew with canonical Greek Matthew. Both Epiphanius and Jerome imply an entirely separate Hebrew document (which in *Against the Pelagians* 3.2 is said to have been later translated into either Aramaic or Syriac). I shall discuss the possible relation of this document to canonical Greek Matthew in the final chapter of this book. For now it is important to recognize that Jerome, along with Epiphanius, implies the continued existence in the early church of a different and presumably earlier Hebrew Gospel attributed to Matthew in addition to canonical Greek Matthew. This Hebrew Gospel was a genuine Hebrew text composed originally by the apostle Matthew, translations and recensions of which still resided in the library of Caesarea in his day, one version of which was used by the sect of the Nazarenes.

In a third set of statements about the Hebrew Gospel, Jerome testifies in four instances that he translated it into Greek and/or Latin. Shortly after 390 in his *Commentary on Micah* 7:5-7, Jerome mentions "the Gospel according to the Hebrews that we have recently translated."[121] In *Illustrious*

---

his assertion that the recensions began as early as Papias in the second century. In *Comm. Matt.* 2.5, Jerome attributes later corruptions to copyists' errors: "Librariorum hic error est; putamus enim ab euangelista primum editum. . . ."

121. Credideritque evangelio, quod secundum Hebraeos editum nuper transtulimus. The skepticism of Vielhauer and Strecker (*New Testament Apocrypha*, 1.142) about the veracity of Jerome's testimony here is unwarranted. They contend that Origen's two quotations of the same passage noted by Jerome (but without mentioning that it was in Hebrew) should be taken to mean that Jerome must have known the passage already in a Greek translation. Surely this is an unrealistic expectation. Anyone with a thorough mastery of languages — and in Origen's case it was not only Greek and Hebrew, as evinced by the *Hexapla*, but probably also Latin, Aramaic, and Syriac — is unlikely to draw attention to every foreign quotation.

Men 2, written perhaps a year or two later in 392-93, Jerome again testifies to having translated the Hebrew Gospel. "The Gospel that is called 'According to the Hebrews' was recently translated by me into the Greek and Latin."[122] Nearly a decade later, in about 398, in his *Commentary on Matthew,* Jerome gives a third testimony to the same effect, "In the Gospel used by the Nazarenes and Ebionites that we recently translated from the Hebrew language into Greek and that is called by many the authentic Matthew."[123] In this last and most explicit statement, Jerome expressly states that he (and others?) translated into Greek the text of "authentic Matthew," i.e., the original Hebrew Matthew that was used by both the Nazarene and Ebionite sects.

A fourth and final reference to Jerome's translation of the Hebrew Gospel is found in his note on Ignatius in *Illustrious Men* 16. In the introduction Jerome identifies Ignatius as a native of Syrian Antioch, third bishop of the church at Antioch after the apostle Peter, whom Emperor Trajan had condemned to death by combat with beasts in Rome. On his way in chains to Rome, probably in A.D. 107, Ignatius "arrived in Smyrna where Polycarp, who had heard John [the apostle], was bishop." There, Ignatius wrote letters to four churches at Ephesus, Magnesia, Tralles, and Rome; and having left Smyrna he wrote another three letters to Philadelphia, Smyrna, and Polycarp in Smyrna, all on the Asian mainland. Having described these circumstances, Jerome quotes Ignatius, noting first that the reference comes "from the Gospel that recently was translated by me." Jerome does not specifically mention the Hebrew Gospel, but his wording is identical to *Illustrious Men* 2 and his *Commentary on Micah* 7:6 where he does mention the Hebrew Gospel. Also, in the preface to his *Commentary on Isaiah* Jerome explicitly identifies the above passage with the *Gospel according to the Hebrews*.[124] In that Gospel, Jerome continues,

---

122. Evangelium quoque, quod appellatur secundum Hebraeos et a me nuper in Graecum Latinumque sermonem translatum est (*Vir. ill.* 2). With reference to the foregoing footnote, the words that immediately follow the quotation ("quo et Origenes saepe utitur") indicate that Origen in fact knew the *Hebrew* Gospel, not Greek and Latin translations of it.

123. In euangelio quo utuntur Nazareni et Hebionitae quod nuper in graecum de hebraeo sermone transtulimus et quod uocatur a plerisque Mathei authenticum (*Comm. Matt.* 12:13).

124. Cum enim apostolis eum putarent spiritum vel iuxta evangelium, quod Hebraeorum lectitant Nazaraei "Incorporale daemonium" (*Comm. Isa. Praef.* 18).

there is found a testimony about the person of Christ, saying, "I have truly seen him in the flesh after the resurrection, and I believe that he is." And when he came to Peter and those with Peter he said to them, "Behold, touch me and see, for I am not a disembodied demon." And immediately they touched him and believed.[125]

A full discussion of this important passage, which is unmistakably related to Luke 24:39, is reserved for the next chapter. For now I wish simply to note that this is Jerome's fourth attestation to having translated the Hebrew Gospel into Greek and/or Latin. Indeed, his desire to remind readers of this fact seems to explain the otherwise artless introduction of Ignatius in *Illustrious Men* 16. We shall see in the next chapter that Ignatius uses the dominical saying in this quotation as the cornerstone of his letter to Smyrna, but Jerome makes no theological use of it here. Instead, he moves swiftly to the journey of Ignatius to Rome and his fate there *ad bestias*.

The numerous references and citations in this chapter and the next attest to Jerome's intense interest in the Hebrew Gospel. Indeed, two of his contemporaries found his estimation of the Hebrew Gospel unduly excessive. In the decade of the 420s, Julian the Pelagian, in his controversy with Augustine, wrote that Jerome's trust in the antiquity and authority of the Hebrew Gospel rendered it a virtual "fifth Gospel, which he says has been translated by himself."[126] Similarly, Theodore of Mopsuestia, a contemporary of Jerome, is reported by Photius, the ninth-century Patriarch of Constantinople, to have said that Jerome "fabricated an additional fifth gospel, pretending that he had found it in the bookcases of Eusebius of Palestine."[127] No further word about the Hebrew Gospel is given by either Julian and Theodore, but it seems apparent that in an era when the fourfold Gospel tradition needed to be defended against a plethora of Gnostic and het-

---

125. commendans illi [Polycarpo] Antiochensem Ecclesiam, in qua et de Evangelio, quod nuper a me translatum est, super persona Christi ponit testimonium, dicens, Ego vero et post resurrectionem in carne eum vidi, et credo quia sit. Et quando venit ad Petrum et ad eos, qui cum Petro erant, dixit eis: Ecce palpate me et videte, quia non sum daemonium incorporale. Et statim tetigerunt eum et crediderunt (*Vir. ill.* 16).

126. Cum ille in Dialogo illo . . . etiam quinti Evangelii, quod a se translatum dicit, testimonio nitatur." Cited from E. B. Nicholson, *The Gospel according to the Hebrews*, 22.

127. τοῦτον (i.e., Jerome) δὲ πέμπτον εὐαγγέλιον προσαναπλάσαι λέγει (i.e., Theodore), ἐν ταῖς Εὐσεβίου τοῦ Παλαιστίνου βιβλιοθήκαις ὑπολαττόμενον εὑρεῖν (Photius, *Bibl.* 177; also cited in Nicholson, *The Gospel According to the Hebrews*, 22).

erodox Gospels, Jerome's high estimation of the Hebrew Gospel left him open to the criticism of at least two contemporaries.

Before leaving Jerome, I mention a final text that also bears a close relationship to the Third Gospel and plausibly also derives from the Hebrew Gospel. In a letter to Hedybia, Jerome writes that many Jews came to faith when Jesus prayed from the cross, "Father, forgive them, for they do not know what they are doing."[128] Like many citations from the Hebrew Gospel, this prayer for forgiveness is found in the canonical Gospels only in Luke (23:34). Jerome does not mention the Hebrew Gospel as the source of the story, but three late (ninth-fourteenth-century) texts that appear to quote the passage from Jerome do. In a ninth-century *Commentary on Isaiah,* Haimo of Halberstadt writes: "As it is said in the Gospel of the Nazarenes: at that voice of the Lord many thousands of the Jews who were standing around the cross believed."[129] The same testimony is repeated in the thirteenth century by Hugo of St. Cher: "And he prayed for the transgressors (Luke 24): Father, forgive them, because, etc. At that voice many thousands of the Jews who were standing around the cross believed, according to the Gospel of the Nazarenes."[130] Finally, the anonymous fourteenth-century *History of the Passion of the Lord* expands the story: "Father, forgive them, because they do not know what they do. And take heed of what is said in the Gospel of the Nazarenes that at this important prayer of Christ eight thousand were converted to the faith at a later date."[131] These three early medieval sources are beyond the purview of this study, but all three appear to derive from Jerome, who was fond of quoting from the Hebrew Gospel used by the Nazarenes.

---

128. *Epist.* 120.8-9, *ad Hedybiam.*

129. Sicut in Evangelio Nazaraeorum habetur, ad hanc vocem Domini multa milia Iudaeorum astantium circa crucem crediderunt (Haimo Halberstensis, *Comm. Isa.* 53:13).

130. Et pro transgressoribus rogavit. Luc 24 e. Pater, ignosce illis, quia etc. Ad hanc vocem secundum Evangelium Nazaraeorum multa milia Judaeorum astantium circa crucem crediderunt (Hugo of St. Cher, *Libr. Isa.*).

131. Pater ignosce eis. Non enim sciunt quid faciunt. Et nota quod in ewangelio Nazaraeorum legitur quod ad virtuam istam Christi oracionem VIII milia converse sunt postea ad fidem (*Hist. pass. Dom.* 55r). All three of the above passages are quoted from A. F. J. Klijn, *Jewish-Christian Gospel Tradition,* 129-31.

Theodoret of Cyrrhus (393–c. 460)

Theodoret was born in Antioch of Syria in 393 and in 423 became bishop of Cyrrhus, near Antioch. A personal friend and defender of Nestorius, Theodoret became (along with Nestorius) the object of Cyril of Alexandria's anathemas at the Council of Ephesus in 431. Theodoret died about 460, having apparently abandoned his Nestorian views — although a century later the Second Council of Constantinople (553) continued to name him, along with Theodore of Mopsuestia and Ibas of Edessa, as a Nestorian sympathizer.

Only a remnant of Theodoret's considerable theological legacy has survived. In addition to his christological writings, Theodoret attempted to carry forward the work of Eusebius in writing a history of the church to his day, and also the work of Epiphanius as a heresy hunter. Theodoret's name appears in relation to the Hebrew Gospel with regard to the latter. In a five-volume work entitled *Haereticarum Fabularum*, Theodoret condemns the Ebionites as those "who alone accept the Gospel according to the Hebrews, and regard the Apostle [Paul] as apostate."[132] Theodoret's testimony may echo Eusebius's *Ecclesiastical History* 3.27.4 rather than express his own personal acquaintance with the Hebrew Gospel.[133] Whatever the source, however, Theodoret's statement indicates the enduring legacy of the Hebrew Gospel in the fifth century.

Marius Mercator (early fifth century)

A Latin writer who was probably from Italy[134] and a friend and disciple of Augustine, Marius Mercator, commented on the above text of Theodoret and on a reference to the Hebrew Gospel in Jerome. Although the words of Marius were collected and edited in the third person about a century after his death in 450, his testimony to the Hebrew Gospel was written in Con-

---

132. μόνον δὲ τὸ καθ᾽ Ἑβραίους εὐαγγέλιον δέχονται, τὸν δὲ ἀπόστολον ἀποστάτην καλοῦσι (*Haer. Fab. Comp.* 2.1). A subsequent passage notes of the Ebionites: εὐαγγελίῳ δὲ τῷ κατὰ Ματθαῖον κέχρηνται μόνῳ (ibid.).

133. Both mention that the Ebionites accept only the Hebrew Gospel and consider the apostle Paul apostate; see M.-J. Lagrange, "L'Évangile selon les Hébreux," 180.

134. Marius is often supposed to be of African origin, but that may be a mistake due to his association with Augustine, who was a North African.

stantinople between 425 and 430. In connection with Nestorius's rejection
of the oneness of the divine and human natures in the person of Christ,
Marius recalls the error of Ebion, who taught that Jesus was a man born of
Joseph and Mary who, although exceeding others in virtue and innocence,
lived and taught the Mosaic law alone. "The followers of Ebion" — and
here Marius quotes Theodoret of Cyrrhus — "receive only the Gospel according to the Hebrews, they call the Apostle (Paul) an apostate . . . they
make use of the Gospel according to Matthew alone."[135] Later in the expose on the Ebionites Marius quotes verbatim Jerome's reference to the
Hebrew Gospel in his *Commentary on Matthew* 12:13. Marius's knowledge
of the Hebrew Gospel appears to be wholly dependent on Jerome and
Theodoret. His references to the Hebrew Gospel are, like those of his
sources, nonpejorative, but the aspersions that fall upon the Ebionites inevitably tarnish the reputation of the Hebrew Gospel as well.

Philip Sidetes (early fifth century)

Another early fifth-century historian, whose work also survives only in
fragmentary form, was Philip Sidetes, a native of Side in Pamphylia. A
friend of John Chrysostom, Philip wrote a 36-volume *Christian History*
(*Χριστιανικὴ Ἱστορία*), which apparently was a historical miscellany en-
compassing the creation of the world until 430, the date of Philip's death.
The following reference to the Hebrew Gospel is found in Philip's *History*:
"The Gospel according to the Hebrews and the Gospel attributed to Peter
and Thomas were wholly repudiated (by the ancients) who asserted that
they were jointly written by heretics."[136] Philip's reference indicates that
the Hebrew Gospel was known of in Constantinople in the fifth century,
but his claim that it was heretical is an anomaly in the extant patristic tradition. He is correct that the Gospels of *Peter* and *Thomas* were rejected by
the early church, but he is the only father to place the Hebrew Gospel in
the rejected category of texts.

135. Solum hi [the Ebionites] Evangelium secundum Hebraeos recipient, Apostolum
vero apostatam vocant . . . Evangelio autem secundum Matthaeium solo utuntur (Marius
Mercator, *De haeresi et libris Nestorii* 4.2; PL 48.1127-28).

136. τὸ δὲ καθ᾽ Ἑβραίους εὐαγγέλιον καὶ τὸ λεγόμενον Πέτρου καὶ Θωμᾶ τελείως
ἀπέβαλλον [the ancients] αἱρετικῶν ταῦτα συγγράμματα λέγοντες (cited from Lagrange,
"L'Évangile selon les Hébreux," 181).

Venerable Bede (c. 673-735)

A single reference to the Hebrew Gospel appears in Bede's commentary on Luke 1:1-4.

> Here it must be noted that the Gospel according to the Hebrews, as it is called, is not to be reckoned among apocryphal but among ecclesiastical histories; for it seemed good even to the translator of Holy Scripture himself, Jerome, to cite many testimonies from it, and to translate it into the Latin and Greek language.[137]

Having quoted Luke's "magnificent prologue," Bede quickly denounces the superstitions of Basilides and Apelles and the many pseudonymous Gospels circulating under the names of the twelve apostles. Among the latter he mentions the Gospels of *Thomas* and *Bartholomew*. Bede then declares that the *Gospel according to the Hebrews*, by contrast, belongs not to detestable counterfeits, but to "ecclesiastical histories," by which he means the orthodox tradition. To be sure, it is not sacred Scripture, but Jerome's approbation assures its status as orthodox rather than heterodox. The reference indicates that Bede knew of the Hebrew Gospel through Jerome, and perhaps only through him. Bede was supremely informed about the history of church tradition, however, and it seems reasonable to understand his reference to the Hebrew Gospel and to Jerome's approval of it as typical of the church at large.

Scholia in Codex Sinaiticus

In the margins of Codex Sinaiticus are four scholia that attribute textual emendations to "the Jewish [Gospel]" (τὸ ἰουδαϊκόν). They appear at Matt 4:5; 16:7; 18:22; and 26:74.[138] That "the Jewish [Gospel]" refers to the Hebrew Gospel is made probable by the fact that in the third and longest scholion the editor, Constantin Tischendorf, preserves a Greek reading

---

137. Inter quae notandum quod dicitur euangelium iuxta Hebraeos non inter apocriphas sed inter ecclesiasticas numerandum historias. Nam et ipsi sacrae scripturae interpreti Hieronimo pleraque ex eo testimonia usurpare, et ipsum in Latinum Graecumque visum est transferre sermonem (*In Lucae Evangelium Expositio* 1.1-4; CCSL 120.19-20).

138. A. Harnack, *Geschichte der altchristlichen Literatur,* 1/1.10.

that Jerome preserves in Latin and attributes to the "Gospel according to the Hebrews."[139] Other factors link the scholia specifically to the Gospel of Luke. The first scholion, on Matt 4:5, reads "The Jewish Gospel does not have 'into the Holy City,' but 'in Jerusalem.'"[140] The spelling of "Jerusalem" follows the uniquely Lukan Hebraic spelling of the word (Ἱερουσαλήμ) rather than the normal Greek rendering of Matthew (Ἱεροσόλυμα). In Chapter Three below evidence will be given for the provenance of the Lukan spelling of "Jerusalem" from the Hebrew Gospel. Likewise, the occurrence of ἑξῆς ("following," "later") in the third scholion also agrees with the same word in Luke, which in the NT occurs only in Luke-Acts.[141]

The scholia may have been added at Caesarea, for Sinaiticus was corrected by a group of editors working there at the time of Pamphilus. It is tempting to imagine that the scholia derived from the hand of Pamphilus himself, the librarian at Caesarea venerated by Eusebius and Jerome. A colophon at the end of the books of Esdras and Esther refers to the "very ancient manuscript that had been corrected by the hand of the holy martyr Pamphilus."[142] This is the same Pamphilus who, according to Jerome, "diligently gathered" fragments of the Hebrew Gospel.[143] Like the additions to Esdras and Esther, it is quite plausible that the scholia to Matthew also derive from the hand of Pamphilus.

Thirteen scholia are also found in margins of Matthew in codices 4, 273, 566, 899, and 1424, each introduced or identified as coming from τὸ ἰουδαϊκόν ("The Jewish [Gospel]"). Each supplies a word or short phrase of little consequence.[144] The codices in which the scholia appear are late, dating from the ninth or tenth to thirteenth centuries. None of the scholia is associated with the name of a church father or related to other quotations of the Hebrew Gospel preserved in the fathers. Virtually nothing is

---

139. Scholium to Matt. 18:22 of Codex Sinaiticus, τὸ ἰουδαϊκὸν ἑξῆς ἔχει μετὰ τὸ ἑβδομηκοντάκις ἑπτά· καὶ γὰρ ἐν τοῖς προφήταις μετὰ τὸ χρισθῆναι αὐτοὺς ἐν πνεύματι ἁγίῳ εὑρίσκετο ἐν αὐτοῖς λόγος ἁμαρτίας. Jerome, *Pelag.* 3.2, In Euangelio iuxta Hebraeos . . . Etenim in Prophetis quoque, postquam uncti sunt Spiritu sancto, inuentus est sermo peccati.

140. τὸ Ἰουδαϊκὸν οὐκ ἔχει εἰς τὴν ἁγίαν πόλιν, ἀλλ' ἐν Ἱερουσαλήμ.

141. (καθ)εξῆς, Luke 1:3; 7:11; 8:1; 9:37; Acts 3:24; 11:4; 18:23; 21:1; 25:17; 27:18.

142. See B. M. Metzger, *Text of the New Testament*, 46.

143. Jerome, *Vir. ill.* 3.2. See pp. 29-30 above.

144. Scholars sometimes refer to the source of these scholia as "The Zion Gospel." See the complete lot of scholia in J. K. Elliott, *The Apocryphal New Testament*, 13-14. The scholia are further discussed in A. F. J. Klijn, *Jewish-Christian Gospel Tradition*, 25, 34-36, 107-15.

known of their provenance and placement in the margins of the manuscripts except that the copies in which they appear date to the medieval period. Given these uncertainties and their late dating, I have discounted them from further consideration in relation to the Hebrew Gospel.[145]

Islamic Hadith (ninth and tenth centuries [?])

Finally, knowledge of the Hebrew Gospel extended beyond the Christian tradition and into the Islamic Hadith. "Khadija then accompanied [Muhammed] to her cousin Waraqa ibn Naufal ibn Asad ibn ʿabdul ʿUzza, who, during the Pre-Islamic Period became a Christian and used to write the writing with Hebrew letters. He would write from the Gospel in Hebrew as much as Allah wished him to write."[146] Sayings in the Hadith are not only undated but difficult to date precisely. For Muslims, however, *hadith* connote eyewitness testimony, and predominantly in oral form. By definition, therefore, *hadith* connote early tradition. This particular *hadith* likely comes from the early years of Muhammad's work on the Qur'an or at least from the early Islamic period because there is no anti-Jewish or anti-Christian polemic in the saying, which tends to characterize later Islamic references to "the People of the Book." The reference to "the Gospel in Hebrew" without further identification suggests a well-known document, and reference to it as "the writing" seems to signify its authoritative status. This extraneous reference, coupled with the reference to the Hebrew Gospel in The *Chronographia Brevis* of Nicephorus, expands the attestation to the Hebrew Gospel from Ignatius and Papias in the late first century and early second century well into the Byzantine and Islamic worlds.

---

145. A. Schmidtke ("Die das Ἰουδαϊκόν berücksichtigenden textkritischen Scholien zum Matthäustext der Ausgabe Zion," in *Texte und Untersuchungen zur Geschichte der altchristlichen Literatur,* vol. 3/7, ed. A. Harnack and C. Schmidt [Leipzig: J. C. Hinrichs, 1911], 21-31, 39-40), followed by M. R. James, *The Apocryphal New Testament,* 6-7, believes the marginal additions date from 370-500 and were written in Jerusalem. This is a speculative conclusion for which there is little evidence. It is of course possible that the scholia derive in some form from the Hebrew Gospel, but in their present form they do not show any particular relationship to the citations from the Hebrew Gospel in the church fathers. The present state of the scholia seems to date to the Middle Ages (so D. Lührmann, *Die apokryph gewordenen Evangelien,* 252-53).

146. Sahih al-Bukhari 1.3.

Summary

The purpose of this opening chapter has been to give an overview of the testimony to the Hebrew Gospel in the patristic era, specific quotations from which will be discussed in the next chapter. As noted at the outset of this chapter, there is an extensive and diverse testimony in the early centuries of Christianity to an early Hebrew Gospel. Seventeen church fathers attest to the Hebrew Gospel. In addition, the Hebrew Gospel is also either mentioned or alluded to in scholia to Codex Sinaiticus, in the Islamic Hadith, and by the Byzantine Patriarch Nicephorus. In subsequent chapters additional attestations will be cited from Pope Damasus, Sedulius Scottus, and *Shabbat* 116 in the Babylonian Talmud. The combined testimony to the Hebrew Gospel in the early centuries of Christianity amounts to more than two dozen witnesses. Of these witnesses, a dozen attribute it specifically to the apostle Matthew[147] and eleven specify that it was written in Hebrew.[148] The geographical locations of these witnesses range from Lyons and Rome in the west to Alexandria and North Africa in the south, India in the east, and Jerusalem and Constantinople in between. These points do not exhaust the extent of a map of the world in late antiquity, but they come close to most of its borders. Perhaps more important than persons and places is the actual reputation of the Hebrew Gospel in the early church. Although the Hebrew Gospel does not appear in the canonical lists of either Origen or Eusebius, it occupied the "disputed" category of a select six or eight books throughout early Christianity and is cited more frequently and positively alongside canonical texts than any non-canonical document of which I am aware. The Hebrew Gospel was widely known and, in general, highly esteemed in early Christianity. The examination of its content in the following chapters will not only demonstrate that esteem but present extensive data for its influence on the Synoptic tradition, and in particular on the Gospel of Luke.

---

147. Papias, Irenaeus, Pantaenus, Clement, Hippolytus, Origen, Eusebius, Ephrem the Syrian, Didymus, Epiphanius, John Chrysostom, and Jerome.

148. Papias, Pantaenus, Hesesippus, Hippolytus, Origen, Eusebius, Ephrem the Syrian, Epiphanius, John Chrysostom, Jerome, and Islamic Hadith.

CHAPTER TWO

Quotations from the Hebrew Gospel in Early Christianity

Chapter One provided an overview of what Christian writers (and one Islamic text) said about the Hebrew Gospel in the first nine centuries of the Christian era. In this chapter I wish to turn from statements *about* the Hebrew Gospel to *quotations* from it. Attention now shifts from the existence of the Hebrew Gospel and its general profile to its *content* — insofar as the content can be known from patristic citations. The majority of patristic references surveyed in Chapter One does not actually quote from the Hebrew Gospel. Specific quotations from the Hebrew Gospel occur only in Ignatius of Antioch, Clement of Alexandria, Origen, Didymus of Alexandria, Eusebius, Epiphanius, Jerome, Sedulius Scottus, and perhaps the Talmud. This chapter is devoted to discussing these quotations in the chronological order of their authors, beginning with Ignatius and ending with Jerome. The only exceptions will be Clement and Didymus, whose quotations were sufficiently discussed in Chapter One, and a final text from the Talmud, which will be considered in Chapter Seven.

Although fewer fathers are discussed in this chapter than in the last, the mass of material is greater, and the analysis of the various quotations is more complex. Since the Hebrew Gospel is no longer extant, the trustworthiness of the various fathers who transmit material from the Hebrew Gospel must necessarily be discussed and evaluated. This will be particularly required of Epiphanius and Jerome, who preserve the greatest number of quotations from the Hebrew Gospel — and whose credibility has not been uncontested. Beyond the question of the reliability of the patristic sources, however, lies the heart of the matter, namely, the possible relationship of the extant material quoted from the Hebrew Gospel to the Synoptic Gospels themselves. The comparison of Hebrew Gospel quotations with Synoptic texts requires careful lexical analysis. In several instances judgments must be made with generous margins of uncertainty. Nevertheless, the mass of material from the Hebrew Gospel is large enough to reveal a pattern of correspondence with the Gospel of Luke that appreciably exceeds its correspondence with either Matthew or Mark.

Ignatius (c. 35–c. 107)

The earliest ostensible quotation of the Hebrew Gospel occurs in Ignatius's *Letter to the Smyrnaeans* 3.1-2.

> For I know and believe that he was in the flesh even after the resurrection. And when he [Jesus] came to those with Peter, he said to them, "Take, touch me and see that I am not a disembodied ghost." And immediately they touched him and believed.[1]

Ignatius is silent about the source of the quotation, attributing it neither to the Hebrew Gospel nor to any other source. The quotation is also cited by Origen, Eusebius, and Jerome. Origen attributes it to a tractate circulating in Peter's name rather than to the Hebrew Gospel.[2] Eusebius cites it in his *Ecclesiastical History,* but other than attributing it to Ignatius admits igno-

---

1. ἐγὼ γὰρ καὶ μετὰ τὴν ἀνάστασιν ἐν σαρκὶ αὐτὸν οἶδα καὶ πιστεύω ὄντα. καὶ ὅτε πρὸς τοὺς περὶ Πέτρον ἦλθεν, ἔφη αὐτοῖς· λάβετε, ψηλαφήσατέ με καὶ ἴδετε, ὅτι οὐκ εἰμὶ δαιμόνιον ἀσώματον. καὶ εὐθὺς αὐτοῦ ἥψαντο καὶ ἐπίστευσαν (Ign. *Smyrn.* 3.1-2).

2. The source of Origen's version remains an unsolved mystery. It may be that the presence of Peter's name in *Smyrn.* 3.2 caused Origen to associate it with a tractate circulating in Peter's name rather than Matthew's. The title of the work he cites, *Petri doctrina,* could conceivably be either *The Gospel of Peter* or *The Kerygma of Peter,* but the saying "I am not a bodiless demon" appears in neither work. The fact that Origen associates the saying with a heretofore unknown work suggests that the saying was more widely known and disseminated than the work to which he attributes it. I am not inclined to associate the Hebrew Gospel with either of the above works bearing the name of Peter, primarily because both are typified by fanciful and embellished legends, which do not typify (so far as we know) the Hebrew Gospel (see H. Waitz, "Neue Untersuchungen über die sog. judenchristlichen Evangelien," *ZNW* 36 [1937], 69). On the source of Origen's quotation, see W. Schneemelcher, "The Kerygma Petri," in *New Testament Apocrypha,* 2.36-37; P. F. Beatrice, "The Gospel According to the Hebrews," 149-50.

rance of its source.[3] The explicit connection of *Smyrn.* 3.1-2 with the Hebrew Gospel first comes from Jerome, who in his chapter on Ignatius in *Illustrious Men* 16 quotes the passage in question, noting that it is a testimony about the person of Christ "from the Gospel that has recently been translated by me." "The Gospel" that Jerome refers to here can only be the Gospel that on four occasions he testifies to having translated from Hebrew into Greek and/or Latin.[4]

This dominical saying echoes the command of the resurrected Jesus to the bewildered disciples in Luke 24:39: "Touch me and see, for a ghost does not have flesh and bones as you see me having." This saying — written no later than 107 when Ignatius met his death in Rome *ad bestias* — occurs neither in Matthew nor in Mark, but only in Luke.[5] Since the saying is shared by Ignatius and Luke, it is possible — and often assumed — that Ignatius quotes it from Luke. Several reasons, however, suggest that Ignatius is quoting not from Luke but rather from a source earlier than and independent of Luke. Most importantly, although there are allusions to the canonical Gospels in Ignatius, he never quotes directly from them, and "explicit references to Luke's Gospel never appear in Ignatius, and nowhere in his letters does he reveal his knowledge and use of Luke."[6] There is thus no evidence that Ignatius quoted explicitly and verbatim from any Gospel, including the Third Gospel.

Two prominent differences between the saying as it appears in *Smyrn.* 3.1-2 and in Luke 24:39 also appear to rule out a direct quotation of Luke 24:39 by Ignatius. These differences even make a paraphrase from memory

---

3. "[Ignatius] wrote to the Smyrnaeans quoting words from a source I do not know" (*Hist. eccl.* 3.36.11). Apart from two minor changes (γάρ and ἦλθεν in *Smyrn.* 3.1-2 become δέ and ἐλήλυθεν), Eusebius agrees verbatim with Ignatius.

4. *Comm. Mich.* (7:6); *Comm. Matt.* 12:13; *Vir. ill.* 2; *Vir. ill.* 16.

5. λάβετε, ψηλαφήσατέ με καὶ ἴδετε (Ign. *Smyrn.* 3.2); ψηλαφήσατέ με καὶ ἴδετε (Luke 24:39). C.-B. Amphoux, "L'Évangile selon les Hébreux. Sources de L'Évangile de Luc," 68, rightly notes that "les deux plus anciennes mentions de ce livre semblent le rattacher à la tradition de *Luc* plutot qu'à celle de *Matthieu.*"

6. P. F. Beatrice, "The 'Gospel According to the Hebrews' in the Apostolic Fathers," 148. For a full discussion of citations from Luke up to the time of Irenaeus, see A. Gregory, *The Reception of Luke and Acts in the Period before Irenaeus: Looking for Luke in the Second Century* (WUNT 2/169; Tübingen: Mohr Siebeck, 2003), 69-75, 113. E. B. Nicholson, *The Gospel According to the Hebrews*, 72, further notes "that of Ignatius's 12 references to a Matthean text there is not one which is an unmistakeably exact quotation, while the words used differ several times very markedly from our Matthew."

seem unlikely. The first is the presence of three imperatives in *Smyrn.* 3.2, "Take, touch, and see," whereas in Luke 24:39 there are only two imperatives, "Touch and see." Nothing in the Lukan version suggests "Take" (λάβετε), and its presence in Ignatius can scarcely be attributed to Luke. The initial imperative "Take" has a Eucharistic ring to it (Matt 26:26; Mark 14:22), suggesting perhaps that the Ignatian version of the saying was preserved in the early Eucharistic liturgy. Jerome's Latin version of the saying replaces the imperative "Take" *(accipite)* with "Behold" *(ecce).* Jerome thus prefaces the Lukan wording with an exclamation rather than with a genuine imperative. In any case, the novelty of λάβετε (or *ecce* in Jerome) suggests a source other than Luke.

The second reason to doubt that Ignatius quoted Luke is the substitution of Ignatius's "I am not a bodiless demon" for Luke's "a ghost does not have flesh and bones as you see me having." Linguistically speaking, "bodiless demon" is a defensible Semitism and not a Greek abstraction that could not have been uttered by Jesus, as some critics claim (see further below). "A bodiless demon" can mean virtually the same thing as "a ghost without flesh and bones," but the two expressions are sufficiently different to make their confusion unlikely. It is unlikely that anyone familiar with Luke's version of the saying would paraphrase it in the words of Ignatius. This again suggests different sources for the two versions of the saying. Dunkerley observes that, particularly in reference to Jesus, "bodiless demon" is an expression that Luke would be inclined to soften to "spirit," rather than the reverse. "Bodiless demon" is the *lectio difficilior* and thus probably the earlier form of the expression.[7] Most critical scholars conclude that *Smyrn.* 3.1-2 is not a quotation of Luke but a tradition of the saying from an independent source.[8]

---

7. R. Dunkerley, "The Gospel according to the Hebrews," 494.

8. See E. Dobschütz, *Das Kerygma Petri kritisch untersucht* (Leipzig: J. C. Hinrichs, 1893), 82-84; H. Koester, *Synoptische Überlieferung bei den apostolischen Vätern* (TU 65; Berlin: Akademie, 1957), 45-46; H. Paulsen, *Studien zur Theologie des Ignatius von Antiochien* (FKDG 29; Göttingen: Vandenhoeck & Ruprecht, 1979), 39-41, 141; idem, *Die Briefe des Ignatius von Antiochia und der Brief des Polykarp von Smyrna* (HNT 18; Tübingen: Mohr Siebeck, 1985), 92-93; W. R. Schoedel, *Ignatius of Antioch: A Commentary on the Letters of Ignatius of Antioch* (Philadelphia: Fortress, 1985), 225; M. Bockmuehl, "Syrian Memories of Peter: Ignatius, Justin and Serapion," in *The Image of the Judaeo-Christians in Ancient Jewish and Christian Literature,* ed. P. J. Tomson and D. Lamberts-Petry (WUNT 158; Tübingen: Mohr Siebeck, 2003), 124-46.

As noted above, Origen, Eusebius, and Jerome preserve quotations of the saying, each of which conforms to the Ignatian version over against the Lukan version. This further argues in favor of a non-Lukan source for the saying, for had it been known to derive from Luke, at least one of these fathers would be expected to have "corrected" it to the Lukan version. Eusebius's ignorance of the source of the Ignatian version is further evidence of a source other than Luke, for Eusebius certainly knew the Lukan version of the saying. His admission of ignorance can only mean that he did not know what *other* source Ignatius relied on for the saying.

In the Preface to *First Principles,* Origen preserves the kernel of the Ignatian saying thus:

> But if any would produce to us from that book which is called "The Doctrine of Peter" the passage where the Savior is represented as saying to the disciples "I am not a bodiless demon," he must be answered in the first place that that book is not reckoned among the books of the church.[9]

Origen probably knew the longer version of the saying preserved in Ignatius and Eusebius, but he limits the citation to the "bodiless demon" statement, presumably because it alone was relevant to the form and nature of the Father, Son, and Holy Spirit to which he devotes the Preface of *First Principles.* The Greek original of *First Principles* has been lost, but the Latin translation of "I am not a bodiless demon" *(non sum daemonium incorporeum)* perfectly renders Ignatius's οὐκ εἰμὶ δαιμόνιον ἀσώματον, which was presumably Origen's original Greek wording.

The fourth version of the saying, and the most important next to Ignatius, comes in Jerome's discussion of Ignatius in *Illustrious Men* 16, which was quoted in the last chapter. To repeat what was said there, Jerome identifies Ignatius as a native of Syrian Antioch, third bishop of the church at Antioch after the apostle Peter, whom the emperor Trajan had condemned to mortal combat with beasts in Rome. On his way in chains to Rome, probably in A.D. 107, Ignatius "arrived in Smyrna where Polycarp,

---

9. Si vero qui velit nobis proferre ex illo libello, qui Petri Docrina appellatur, ubi salvator videtur ad discipulos dicere: Non sum daemonium incorporeum, primo respondendum est ei quoniam liber ipse inter libros ecclesiasticos non habetur (*Princ. Praefatio* 8. English translation by J. K. Elliott, *The Apocryphal New Testament,* 24).

who had heard John [the Apostle], was bishop." There, Ignatius wrote letters to the churches at Ephesus, Magnesia, Tralles, and Rome, and having left Smyrna he wrote another three letters back to Philadelphia, Smyrna, and Polycarp in Smyrna, all cities on the Asian mainland. Having so introduced the passage, Jerome quotes a reference from Ignatius, noting first that it comes "from the Gospel that recently was translated by me." Jerome does not further specify the Gospel, but his wording, which is identical to the relevant wording in *Illustrious Men* 2 and his *Commentary on Micah* 7:6, surely refers to the Hebrew Gospel. This is further verified by a reference to the same text in the preface to Jerome's *Commentary on Isaiah,* where he explicitly identifies the passage as coming from the *Gospel according to the Hebrews.*[10] In this Gospel, Jerome continues,

> there is found a testimony about the person of Christ, saying, "I have truly seen him in the flesh after the resurrection, and I believe that he is. And when he came to Peter and those with Peter he said to them, Behold, touch me and see, for I am not a disembodied demon." And immediately they touched him and believed.[11]

From Theodor Zahn onward critics have cast aspersions on Jerome's testimony in *Illustrious Men* 16.[12] These criticisms were renewed by Vielhauer and Strecker, who reject Jerome's testimony because of "solid

---

10. Cum enim apostoli eum putarent spiritum vel iuxta evangelium, quod Hebraeorum lectitant Nazaraei "Incorporale daemonium" (*Comm. Isa. Praef.* 18).

11. Commendans illi [Polycarpo] Antiochensem Ecclesiam, in qua et de Evangelio, quod nuper a me translatum est, super persona Christi ponit testimonium, dicens, "Ego vero et post resurrectionem in carne eum vidi, et credo quia sit. Et quando venit at Petrum et ad eos, qui cum Petro erant, dixit eis: Ecce palpate me et videte, quia non sum daemonium incorporale. Et statim tetigerunt eum et crediderunt (*Vir. ill.* 16). R. Handmann, *Das Hebräer-Evangelium,* 51, affirms, on the basis of Jerome's testimony, that Ignatius was indeed citing the Hebrew Gospel: "Erinnern wir uns endlich daran, dass Ignatius zu einer Zeit schrieb, wo der n.t. Kanon sich noch nicht fixirt hatte, wo also das judenchristliche Evangelium neben den andern Evangelien bestehen und auch in kirchlichen Kreisen Geltung finden konnte, so werden wir nach der Erwägung der Gründe und Gegengründe dem Hieronymus glauben dürfen, dass Ignatius das H.E. benützt hat, wenn wir es auch nicht sicher beweisen können."

12. *Geschichte des neutestamentlichen Kanons,* 1/2.920-24. None has reviled Jerome as harshly as has A. Schmidtke, "Zum Hebräerevangelium," 24-44, accusing him of "massenhaften Irrungen und Wirrungen" (30).

mistakes" on his part.[13] Vielhauer and Strecker claim that "the passage cited from Ignatius stands not in his epistle to Polycarp but in that to the Smyrnaeans."[14] The passage indeed appears in Ignatius's letter to Smyrna, but to reject Jerome's testimony on the basis of this point is pedantic. Smyrna was the home of Polycarp, and Jerome's wording seems to indicate that he was thinking of the city and bishop together.[15] Eusebius, who quotes the same passage, also conflates Smyrna and Polycarp in relation to the quotation.[16] Given the fact that Polycarp lived in Smyrna and that Ignatius wrote letters to both Polycarp and Smyrna — and furthermore that Jerome's introduction of the passage is not unambiguous — it is caviling to accuse Jerome of a "solid mistake" on this point.

Like Eusebius (and to a lesser extent Origen), Jerome's citation of the dominical saying follows the wording and syntax of Ignatius's Greek original rather than Luke 24:39. Two changes in Jerome, moreover, continue to exercise scholarly discussion. First and most important, Jerome explicitly ascribes the whole testimony of *Smyrn.* 3.1-2 to the Hebrew Gospel. This is a major difference from the quotations of the text in Ignatius, Origen, and Eusebius, and, not surprisingly, it is considered Jerome's second "solid mistake." According to Vielhauer and Strecker, "Jerome understands the first sentence ('and I have also seen him in the flesh after the resurrection,' etc.) as part of the fragment said to be quoted by Ignatius, whereas it is actually an avowal on the part of Ignatius."[17] Vielhauer and Strecker here assert that the preface of the dominical saying in Ignatius is a reference to Ignatius himself, which Jerome mistook for a *prior* witness.

This allegation seems both incautious and inattentive to the subtlety of the Ignatian text. A plain reading of the Ignatian text — which is also followed by Eusebius — indeed suggests that the introduction ("For I know and believe that he was in the flesh even after the resurrection") is a testimony of Ignatius, whereas the following dominical saying obviously belongs to Jesus. But this reading could be misleading, because Ignatius typically weaves earlier sources into his letters without identifying them as such. Ignatius saw himself as a broker of the apostolic tradi-

13. *New Testament Apocrypha*, 1.143-45.

14. *New Testament Apocrypha*, 1.143.

15. Cumque [Ignatius] navigans Smyrnam venisset, ubi Polycarpus, auditor Johannis, episcopus erat . . . (*Vir. ill.* 16).

16. *Hist. eccl.* 3.36.10-11.

17. *New Testament Apocrypha*, 1.143-44.

tion which, particularly in its oral form, was a living witness. Not unlike the author of the Fourth Gospel, Ignatius allowed the apostolic tradition to permeate and infuse his thinking and writing so that its external sources were absorbed in his own voice, resulting in a seamless, univocal testimony. This blending of sources with his own testimony is true even of the dominical saying, which is cited without identification. All this is to say that Jerome's understanding is defensible: the whole of *Symrn.* 3.1-2 — and not simply the dominical saying — could be a quotation from an undeclared source.

The crucial question, of course, is why Jerome would explicitly attribute the whole extract of *Smyrn.* 3.1-2 to the Hebrew Gospel when the sources on which he ostensibly relies are mute (Ignatius) or agnostic (Eusebius) or attribute the saying to a different source (Origen). The answer to this question depends in part on a final anomaly in Jerome's version of the saying, namely, his replacement of Ignatius's "I know" (οἶδα) with "I saw" *(vidi)*. Both Ignatius and Eusebius record, "I myself *know* (οἶδα) him after the resurrection and I believe that he exists," whereas Jerome writes, "I myself *saw (vidi)* him after the resurrection, and I believe that he exists."[18] Any believer could presumably say he or she "knew" Christ after the resurrection, but only an eyewitness would say he or she "saw" Christ after the resurrection. Jerome obviously cannot be claiming to have seen the physically resurrected body of Christ, and he clearly knew that Ignatius, who belonged to the postapostolic generation, had not witnessed the Lord's physical resurrection state either.

Why, then, would Jerome write *vidi*? Some scholars assume a mistranslation on his part. This assumption should be entertained only as a last resort. Jerome's competence in Latin was so extraordinary that he had dreams of being rejected from heaven because of his love for the Latin classics, and especially Cicero. He also was the early church's most accomplished translator of Greek and Hebrew texts into Latin. It is true that Jerome worked in haste, but it seems quite unlikely that he would make a most elementary error of mistaking οἶδα for *vidi*. Nicholson suggests that by adding *vidi* "Jerome was consciously or unconsciously correcting

---

18. A. F. J. Klijn, *Jewish-Christian Gospel Tradition*, 123, claims that Eusebius mistook οἶδα in Ignatius for εἶδον, and thus it is "an established fact" that Jerome's *vidi* came from Eusebius. Klijn is in error here. Eusebius's quotation in *Hist. eccl.* 3.36.11 is verbatim with Ignatius *Smyrn.* 3.3 and does not contain εἶδον. R. Handmann, *Das Hebräer-Evangelium*, 83-84, conversely, attributes the error to a memory lapse of Jerome, but this is entirely conjectural.

Ignatius's quotation by the Gospel according to the Hebrews."[19] There is, in fact, slight textual evidence in favor of this suggestion. If two later manuscripts of Ignatius are to be trusted, Jerome may have been correct in his translation *vidi*. The corrector of codex *Laurentianus* 70,7 (Tr) of Eusebius's *Ecclesiastical History* 3.36.11 reads εἶδον, and the Anglo-Latin version of the epistles of Ignatius — a translation that is generally acknowledged to be preferred in cases of questionable readings because of its fidelity to the Greek original — also reads *vidi*.[20] These three extant readings in the manuscript tradition of "I saw" instead of "I know" make it reasonable to assume that Jerome's reading is not a blunder. He very well could have relied on a different and perhaps earlier version of the saying quoted also by Ignatius and Eusebius.[21]

In their discussion of *Illustrious Men* 16, Vielhauer and Strecker level yet a third and more substantial charge against Jerome, which if true could compromise the dominical saying as a testimony to the Hebrew Gospel. This is the use in *Smyrn.* 3.1-2 of "bodiless demon" (δαιμόνιον ἀσώματον), which Vielhauer and Strecker regard as proving that the Ignatius quotation did not come from a Semitic original because "neither in Hebrew nor in Aramaic is there an equivalent for the Greek ἀσώματος."[22]

But here again Vielhauer and Strecker are in error. The idea of disembodiment can in fact be rendered in Hebrew. Indeed, there is even an extant rabbinic etiological tradition explaining how disembodied spirits came into existence. The Hebrew phrase רוח בלא גוף — literally, a "non-enclosed spirit" or "non-embodied spirit" — was used by the rabbis to mean "bodiless spirit," or "spirit without a body." According to the rabbis, angels and demons remained disembodied because God's attention was diverted from the completion of their bodily creation by the

---

19. E. B. Nicholson, *The Gospel According to the Hebrews*, 73.

20. For a discussion of both manuscripts, see P. F. Beatrice, "The Gospel According to the Hebrews," 156-58. Beatrice concludes: "In conclusion we can say with peace of mind that Jerome correctly translated with *vidi* the Greek verb εἶδον: this is the original word of Ignatius's text which Jerome could still read in his manuscript of Eusebius's *Church History*, and which can be recovered today only thanks to Jerome, to the medieval Latin translation of Ignatius's letters and to the late Byzantine correction found in a codex of Eusebius (Tr)."

21. The supposition of two different extant texts is strengthened by the fact that Jerome, writing in 392, translated the text of Eusebius by *vidi*, whereas Rufinus, writing eleven years later in 403, translated the same text by *scio*. See P. F. Beatrice, "The Gospel According to the Hebrews," 156.

22. *New Testament Apocrypha*, 1.153 (also 144).

need to sanctify the Sabbath.[23] R. Handmann, in fact, is probably correct in noting that "bodiless *demon* . . . corresponds better to the earlier Jewish perspective than does πνεῦμα, which belongs to the Greek world of thought."[24] We should expect to hear an objection from Origen and/or Jerome, both of whom knew Hebrew, if "bodiless demon" were a Semitic solecism. But we have seen that Origen cites the phrase "I am not a bodiless demon *(daemonium incorporeum)*" without any hint of objection — although he interprets it somewhat differently from the rabbis. For Origen *incorporeum* (= ἀσώματος) designates a bodily existence of the resurrected Jesus midway between the "gross and visible" bodies that humans have and the insubstantial wraith-like forms that Greek philosophers ascribe to demons. Ἀσώματος thus refers to Jesus' unique resurrected body, "a solid and palpable body," — although not a solely *human* body.[25] Like Origen, Jerome also saw nothing amiss in a "bodiless demon," for he expressly notes that the *spiritus* in Luke 24:38-39 corresponds precisely with the *incorporale daemonium* of the Hebrew Gospel.[26] Rather than seeing a contradiction in the two expressions, in other words, Jerome saw them as essentially synonymous. That neither Origen nor Jerome found ἀσώματος unsemitic is of particular significance because both were celebrated among the fathers for their proficiency in Hebrew. To assert that "bodiless demon" is a barbarism in Semitic vernacular is unsubstantiated.

This brings to a conclusion the discussion of the various charges leveled against Jerome's version of the Ignatian saying. The propriety of Jerome's quotation can be ably defended; indeed, a fair and critical reading

---

23. A third-century rabbinic tradition states: "The Shedim [שֵׁדִים = demons] are the souls that God created, and as he was considering the creation of their bodies he sanctified the Sabbath (which he had created in the meantime) and did not complete the creation of their bodies, in order to teach you a lesson in the Shedim, that when a person has a thing of value or a pearl in his hand on the Sabbath day of rest, and when it gets dark and someone says to him, 'Throw it away,' then the One who spoke and created the world was occupied with the creation of the world, and he created their souls and as he was considering creating their bodies as well he sanctified the Sabbath and thus did not create their bodies" (*Gen. Rab.* 7 [6a], quoted from Str-B 4/1.506). A wealth of material on demons in Str-B 4/1.501-35 ("Zur altjüdischen Dämonologie") and in *TWNT* 2.10-14 describes the Jewish conception of angels and especially demons, both of whom were created without physical bodies.

24. *Das Hebräer-Evangelium,* 85.

25. *Princ.* Praefatio 8.

26. *Comm. Isa.* 18, Prol. So too P. F. Beatrice, *Gospel According to the Hebrews,* 156.

inclines us to do so.[27] According to *Illustrious Men* 16, Jerome understands *Smyrn.* 3.1-2 to be a quotation from the Hebrew Gospel in which the apostle Matthew (presumably) claims to have seen the resurrected Lord Jesus, to have believed in him, and to have heard him say in the presence of Peter, "Take, touch me and see, that I am not a bodiless demon."

Returning now to the text of Ignatius himself, he uses the personal testimony and the saying of the resurrected Lord to chastise unbelievers for denying the physical passion of Jesus on the cross. In *Smyrn.* 2.1, immediately before the text under consideration, he describes unbelievers as "bodiless and demonic" (ἀσώματοι καὶ δαιμονικοί). In contrast to them (and in an unmistakable wordplay) Ignatius cites the resurrected Jesus, who expressly refutes the "demonic and bodiless" docetists by declaring, "Take, touch me and see that I am not a bodiless demon" (ὅτι οὐκ εἰμὶ δαιμόνιον ἀσώματον). The wording of the quotation is not alien to either Hebrew or Aramaic but is a thoroughly Hebraic idea, indeed a personal testimony, presumably of the apostle Matthew, to the resurrected Lord Jesus Christ, employed by Ignatius for maximum effect against the heresy of Docetism.

The letter to Smyrna, like Ignatius's letters as a whole, protests vigorously against heretical teachers, particularly *Docetic* teachers who denied the complete incarnation of Jesus Christ. The phrase "in the flesh" (ἐν σαρκί) appears with redundant regularity in the letter to Smyrna with reference to the earthly manifestation of Jesus. We noted earlier that Ignatius never quotes directly from the canonical Gospels. He *does* quote from the Hebrew Gospel in *Smyrn.* 3:2, however, and in such a way that it becomes the hermeneutical key to the epistle. The quotation refutes a rampant heresy of Ignatius's day with a dominical saying that claimed the highest degree of authority in the early church. According to Jerome's interpretation,

27. See the exoneration of Jerome in P. F. Beatrice, "The Gospel According to the Hebrews," 161: "In conclusion, we have to acknowledge that Jerome told the truth, and his testimony on the Judaeo-Christian Gospel tradition, still too often hastily criticized and rejected because it is deemed confused and unreliable, should instead be accepted, if not with absolute confidence, at least with less suspicion. Lapses of memory, which Jerome himself might not always have been able to avoid, are one thing, whereas quite another thing would be the repeated and insistent false declaration about his personal activity as translator of this text." For further support of Jerome's essential veracity, see P. L. Schmidt, "'Und es war geschrieben auf Hebräisch, Griechisch und Lateinisch': Hieronymus, das Hebräerevangelium und seine mittelalterliche Rezeption," *Filologia mediolatina* 5 (1998), 49-93.

Ignatius enhances the authority of the Jesus-saying by placing it within the context of the first person testimony of the apostle Matthew. Ignatius himself does not identify the speaker of *Smyrn.* 3.1 as the apostle Matthew, but by implication Jerome clearly does.

To summarize, four reputable witnesses in the early church — Ignatius, Origen, Eusebius, and Jerome — cite a text that bears an unmistakable correlation to Luke 24:39. None of the four, however, ascribes it to Luke. The most complete witness to the citation comes from Jerome, who ascribes it to the Hebrew Gospel, and by implication to the apostle Matthew. Jerome will not be alone in preserving a putative first person testimony of the apostle Matthew in the Hebrew Gospel. Further examples will be seen not only in Jerome, but also in Didymus and Epiphanius. The source of all these statements appears to be the personal memoirs of the narrator, who can be deduced to the apostle Matthew.[28] Thus, already in Ignatius's day the Hebrew Gospel of Matthew was recognized as an authority preserving an authentic saying of the resurrected Lord,[29] which, as we have seen, corresponds with the Gospel of Luke but does not apparently derive from it.[30]

Origen (185-254)

Origen refers to the Hebrew Gospel five times, three of which give quotations from it.[31] These may not have been Origen's only references to the

---

28. See P. F. Beatrice, "The Gospel According to the Hebrews," 160-61. Beatrice cites W. R. Inge, M.-J. Lagrange, A. Baumstark, J. Waitz, G. Quispel, and J. Daniélou, who likewise attribute Ignatius's quotation to the Hebrew Gospel — and by implication to the apostle Matthew (163).

29. C.-B. Amphoux, "L'Évangile selon les Hébreux," 71.

30. The statement in Mark 16:12 that Jesus appeared to the disciples ἐν ἑτέρᾳ μορφῇ ("in another form") might conceivably come from the Hebrew Gospel rather than from the Gospel of Luke, however, for Luke attributes the disciples' misperception of the risen Jesus to a problem with *their* vision rather than to a change in Jesus' form.

31. *Comm. Jo.* 2.12; *Comm. Matt.* 15.14; 16.12; *Hom. Jer.* 15.4; Eusebius, *Hist. eccl.* 6.25.4. G. Dorival, "Un Groupe Judéo-Chrétien Méconnu: Les Hébreux," 21-26, suggests that the reference to "the Hebrews" immediately in *Hist. eccl.* 6.25.1-2 should also be taken as a reference to Hebrew Christians. He argues that the canon advanced by Origen in *Hist. eccl.* 6.25.1-2 does not conform to the MT but rather to a rabbinic canon probably in use by Hebrew Christians in Egypt. Dorival's argument is weakened by the fact that the context of *Hist. eccl.*

Hebrew Gospel, however, for Jerome says Origen frequently made use of the Hebrew Gospel.[32]

The Holy Spirit as Mother

Two of Origen's three quotations are slightly different versions of the same quotation. The longer of the two versions is preserved in his *Commentary on John* (1:3):

> Whoever accepts the Gospel according to the Hebrews, where the Savior himself says, "Just now my mother, the Holy Spirit, took me by a lock of hair and lifted me up to great Mount Tabor," raises a new question how the Holy Spirit coming through the Word is able to be the mother of Christ.[33]

A shorter version of the same appears in Origen's *Homilies on Jeremiah* (15:4): "If anyone receives the [word], 'Just now my mother, the Holy Spirit, took me and bore me to great Mount Tabor,' etc., he can see his mother."[34] The reference to the Holy Spirit as "mother" may initially seem apocryphal and/or Gnostic. If this were the case, however, it is unlikely that Origen and Jerome, both of whom were decidedly anti-Gnostic, would each cite this passage *twice*. In both passages cited by Origen the speaker is Jesus, who reports being seized by the Holy Spirit and transported to Mount Tabor, where he is ostensibly transfigured.[35] Although most scholars suspect

---

6.25.1-2 clearly refers to the Hebrew OT and not to Hebrew Christian believers. Further, Origen's canonical proposals are among the earliest in the Christian tradition. It is hardly surprising that they would vary slightly (and the variations are very slight in Origen's list) from the church's later canon, which in Origen's day was not established.

32. *Vir. ill.* 2.11.

33. ἐὰν δὲ προσιῆταί τις τὸ καθ᾽ Ἑβραίους εὐαγγέλιον, ἔνθα αὐτὸς ὁ σωτὴρ φησίν; Ἄρτι ἔλαβέ με ἡ μήτηρ μου, τὸ ἅγιον πνεῦμα, ἐν μιᾷ τῶν τριχῶν μου καὶ ἀπήνεγκέ με εἰς τὸ ὄρος τὸ μέγα Θαβώρ, ἐπαπορήσει πῶς μήτηρ Χριστοῦ τὸ διὰ τοῦ λόγου γεγενημένον πνεῦμα ἅγιον εἶναι δύναται. ταῦτα δὲ καὶ τούτῳ οὐ χαλεπὸν ἑρμηνεῦσαι (*Comm. Jo. 2.12.87*).

34. εἰ δέ τις παραδέχεται τὸ Ἄρτι ἔλαβέ με ἡ μήτηρ μου, τὸ ἅγιον πνεῦμα, καὶ ἀπήνεγκέ με εἰς τὸ ὄρος τὸ μέγα Θαβώρ. καὶ τὰ ἑξῆς, δύναται αὐτοῦ ἰδεῖν τὴν μητέρα (*Hom. Jer. 15.4*).

35. So too A. Hilgenfeld, *Novum Testamentum extra Canonem Receptum*[2], 16. E. B. Nicholson, *The Gospel According to the Hebrews*, 75-76, however, suspects the episode to refer to the temptation, the "lifted up" being softened to "led up" in later tradition.

that this account was originally related to Jesus' temptation, the reference to "lifted up" seems to me more suited to the transfiguration. Handmann sees no reason to doubt that Jesus, like Elijah and Moses, experienced such prophetic-ecstatic phenomena as described here; indeed, in this concrete and rudimentary narrative he sees evidence of such an "objective event."[36]

Origen's longer first quotation bears an obvious similarity to Ezek 8:3, where the Spirit seizes Ezekiel by the hair and transports him to the holy sanctuary in Jerusalem.[37] Apart from a similar passage in Bel and the Dragon 5:36, this is the only passage in biblical tradition where the Spirit seizes anyone by the hair.[38] In Jerome's citations of this passage (see below), he explains the unusual reference to the maternity of the Holy Spirit on the basis of the Hebrew word for "spirit," רוח.[39] This observation hints at a Hebrew provenance of the saying, since "spirit" is feminine in Hebrew but neuter in Greek. The Holy Spirit is also assigned unique agency in the conception of Jesus in Matt 1:18 and Luke 1:35. Several passages in Hellenistic Jewish traditions are familiar with the maternity of the Holy Spirit.[40] Origen is not offended by such imagery, but interprets it metaphorically along the lines of Jesus' saying that "Whoever does the will of my Father in heaven is my brother, sister, and mother" (Matt 12:50//Mark 3:35//Luke 8:21). Whoever does the will of the heavenly Father, states Origen, has the Holy Spirit for his mother.[41] In his *Commentary on Micah*, Jerome will interpret the same quotation metaphorically in relation to the Song of Songs, namely, the word of God as the spouse of the Christian's soul. Klijn, however, is suspicious of the attempt to interpret the maternity of the Holy

36. R. Handmann, *Das Hebräer-Evangelium*, 72.

37. καὶ ἐξέτεινεν ὁμοίωμα χειρὸς καὶ ἀνέλαβέν με τῆς κορυφῆς μου καὶ ἀνέλαβέν με πνεῦμα ἀνὰ μέσον τῆς γῆς καὶ ἀνὰ μέσον τοῦ οὐρανοῦ καὶ ἤγαγέν με εἰς Ἱερουσαλημ (Ezek 8:3 LXX).

38. In Bel and the Dragon 5:36 an angel takes Habakkuk τῆς κόμης αὐτοῦ τῆς κεφαλῆς. Further references to seizures and transportations by the Spirit occur in Acts 8:39-40; 1 Kgs 18:12; 2 Kgs 2:16; and 2 Bar. 6:3.

39. *Comm. Isa.* 40:9-11; *Comm. Ezech.* 16:13. Also noted by M.-J. Lagrange, "L'Évangile selon les Hébreux," 173. A. Schmidtke, "Zum Hebräerevangelium," 41-42, is overly speculative in supposing without argument or evidence that the maternity of the Spirit was suggested by ἡ μήτηρ μου in Matt 12:47, which was then remembered and preserved by James, and which eventually made its way into the baptism narrative as a counterpart to the paternity of God.

40. A. F. J. Klijn, *Jewish-Christian Gospel Tradition*, 54-55.

41. *Comm. Jo.* 2.12.88.

Spirit along such lines. He suggests, perhaps not unreasonably, that Origen's attempt to justify the maternity of the Spirit may have been encouraged or even demanded by its wide acceptance in the church of his day.[42]

This same text is thrice quoted by Jerome in Latin, once in his *Commentary on Micah*,[43] again in his *Commentary on Isaiah*,[44] and finally in his *Commentary on* Ezekiel.[45] All five versions of the saying by Origen and Jerome preserve the first person testimony of Christ to his seizure by the maternal Holy Spirit. Minor variations in the three citations are probably due to mnemonic recall on the parts of Origen and Jerome.

The reference to the Spirit as "mother" has no exact parallel in the Gospels. The Holy Spirit plays a more prominent role in Luke, however, than it does in the other Synoptics. The envelopment of Jesus by the Spirit is expressly stated in Luke 1:35, and in Jesus' inaugural sermon in Nazareth he quotes Isa 61:1 ("The Spirit of the Lord is upon me," Luke 4:18) with reference to himself. Both of these texts are unique to Luke.

A Coptic fragment of a quotation from the Hebrew Gospel bears a possible relation to the text cited by Origen and Jerome. The fragment comes from a sermon of Cyril of Jerusalem (c. 315-86), who places the following words in the mouth of a monk who espoused the "Ebionite heresy":

> It is written in the [Gospel] according to the Hebrews that when Christ
> wished to come upon the earth to men the Good Father called a mighty
> power in the heavens which was called Michael and committed Christ

---

42. A. F. J. Klijn, *Jewish-Christian Gospel Tradition*, 7-8.

43. Sed qui legerit Canticum canticorum, et sponsum animae, Dei sermonem intellexerit, credideritque Evangelio, quod secundum Hebraeos editum nuper transtulimus, in quo ex persona Salvatoris dicitur: "Modo tulit me mater mea, Sanctus Spiritus in uno capillorum meorum" ("But whoever makes the Song of Songs the spouse of his soul will come to know the word of God and believe the Gospel, the Hebrew edition of which we recently translated, in which it is said of the person of the Savior, 'My mother, the Holy Spirit, once took me by a lock of hair,'" *Comm. Mich.* 7:7).

44. Sed et in Evangelio quod iuxta Hebraeos scriptum Nazaraei lectitant, Dominus loquitur: "Modo me tulit mater mea, Sanctus Spiritus" ("But in the Gospel written according to the Hebrews the Nazarenes read, the Lord says, 'My mother, the Holy Spirit, once took me,'" *Comm. Isa.* 40:9).

45. In Evangelio quoque Hebraeorum, quod lectitant Nazaraei, Salvator inducitur loquens: "Modo me arripuit mater mea, Spiritus Sanctus" ("Also in the Gospel of the Hebrews that the Nazarenes read, the Savior introduces the saying, 'My mother, the Holy Spirit, once seized me,'" *Comm. Ezech.* 16:13).

to the care thereof. And the power came down into the world, and it was called Mary, and [Christ] was in her womb for seven months.[46]

The monk held that there were five Gospels — the four canonical Gospels plus the *Gospel of the Hebrews.* To this, Cyril retorts, "Where in the four Gospels is it said that the Holy Virgin Mary and the Mother of God is a force?"[47] Whether this text from Cyril is actually related to the above quotations from Origen and Jerome is difficult to say.[48] In the Cyril quotation, "mother" has lost the unusual association with the Holy Spirit in favor of its more predictable association with Mary, and this, it seems, lessens the likelihood of its association with the Hebrew Gospel. It is not crucial for the present discussion, however, to pass a final judgment on the matter. What is important is that in the fourth century in Cyril's diocese the Hebrew Gospel was, at least in some quarters, highly esteemed. Indeed, it was a virtual fifth Gospel. B. W. Bacon characterizes it as a "quasi Gospel" in many circles of Christianity,[49] widely enough known to serve as a counterpoint for a homily by an archbishop of Jerusalem.

The Rich Man

Origen preserves a second and lengthier quotation from the Hebrew Gospel in his commentary on the rich man in Matt 19:16-22, in which he speculates why the parallel accounts in Mark 10:17-22 and Luke 18:18-23 omit the commandment to "love your neighbor as yourself."

---

46. V. Burch, "The Gospel According to the Hebrews: Some New Matter Chiefly from Coptic Sources," 310-15.

47. V. Burch, "The Gospel According to the Hebrews: Some New Matter Chiefly from Coptic Sources," 311.

48. Burch, "The Gospel According to the Hebrews: Some New Matter Chiefly from Coptic Sources," undertakes a *Wirkungsgeschichte* of the purported text from the Hebrew Gospel, attempting a reconstruction of its supposed influence on subsequent texts, including Christ's cry of dereliction from the cross in *Gos. Pet.* 5:19, "My power, my power, you have forsaken me." The influences proposed by Burch are speculative, however. A. Schmidtke, "Zum Hebräerevangelium," 37-38, is probably justified in his skepticism of them: "In Wahrheit hat der Heilige Geist mit dem Erzengel Michael auch nicht das mindeste gemein."

49. "Papias and the Gospel According to the Hebrews," 168.

It is written in that Gospel, which is called "According to the Hebrews" (if it pleases one to receive it, not as an authority, but as an example of the proposed question): "Another rich man," it says, "inquired, 'Master, what good must I do to live?'" He said to him, "Man, do the law and prophets." He responded to him, "I have done (so)." He said to him, "Go, sell all you possess and distribute it among the poor, and come, follow me." The rich man began to scratch his head in displeasure. The Lord said to him, "How can you say, 'I have done the law and prophets,' since it is written in the law: Love your neighbor as yourself; and behold, your many brothers, who are sons of Abraham, are covered in dung, dying from hunger, while your house is filled with many good things, and not one of the good things goes out to them." And [Jesus] turned to Simon, his disciple sitting with him, "Simon, son of John, it is easier for a camel to go through the eye of a needle, than for a rich man to enter the kingdom of heaven."[50]

Origen cites the Hebrew Gospel here to resolve a conflict that he finds in the version of the rich man in Matt 16:19-22. How could Jesus require the rich man to dispense with his wealth after the latter had confessed to keeping all the commandments, including the commandment to love one's neighbor? Conversely, how could the rich man profess to have kept all the commandments when wealth is contrary to the commandment to love

---

50. Scriptum est in evangelio quodam, quod dicitur secundum Hebraeos (sit tamen placet suscipere illud, non ad auctoritatem, sed ad manifestationem propositae quaestionis): Dixit, "inquit ad eum alter divitum: magister, quid bonum faciens vivam? dixit ei: homo, legem et prophetas fac. respondit ad eum: feci. dixit ei: vade, vende omnia quae possides et divide pauperibus, et veni, sequere me. coepit autem dives scalpere caput suum, et non placuit ei. et dixit ad eum Dominus, "Quomodo dicis 'legem feci et prophetas'? quoniam scriptum est in lege: diliges proximum tuum sicut teipsum, et ecce multi fratres tui filii Abrahae amicti sunt stercore, morientes prae fame, et domus tua plena est multis bonis, et non egreditur omnino aliquid ex ea ad eos. et conversus dixit Simoni discipulo suo sedenti apud se: Simon, fili Jonae, facilius est camelum intrare per foramen acus quam divitem in regnum coelorum" (*Comm. Matt.* 15:14). The fact that this citation exists only in a Latin translation of a lost Greek original has caused some scholars to doubt its authenticity. G. Dorival, "Un Groupe Judéo-Chrétien Méconnu: Les Hébreux," 16-19, defends its authenticity by noting that Origen does not introduce the passage from the Hebrew Gospel as an authority, but only as an illustration, similar to the way he introduces it in his *Commentary on John* and *Homilies on Jeremiah*. More importantly, the commentary that follows the quotation exhibits Origen's style and manner.

one's neighbor? Origen argues that the commandment to "love your neighbor as yourself" is a redundancy — and hence a later interpolation — made unnecessary by the commandment to "Go, sell all you possess and distribute it among the poor, and come, follow me," which contains the substance of the commandment to "love your neighbor as yourself." The Hebrew Gospel, in Origen's judgment, preserves the most original version of the story, the one without the commandment to "love your neighbor as yourself." Despite Origen's opening disclaimer that the Hebrew Gospel is not an authority, his exegesis in fact invests it with authority over canonical Matthew. Luke and Mark both reflect the Hebrew Gospel, and in this instance are also preferred over Matthew's account of the rich man.

The specific question of the rich man as preserved in the Hebrew Gospel is similar to its rendition in the Synoptic accounts, and particularly to Matt 19:17 (also *Clementine Homilies* 18.3, 17), in which the rich man also asks, "What good *thing* should I do?" Nicholson and Handmann suspect that the *"other"* rich man of the Hebrew Gospel version recalls Matthew's preference for *pairs* and that there were originally two rich men in the story.[51] It is not certain, however, that the "other" rich man is the second of two; it could simply be "another" in a rapid sequence of events (e.g., Luke 9:57-62//Matt 8:18-22).

The remainder of the story, however, is reminiscent of the parable of the Rich Man and Lazarus in Luke 16:19-31. Indeed, the Hebrew Gospel actually associates Jesus' rich interlocutor with the rich man in the parable.[52] Furthermore, a series of references in the Hebrew Gospel recall the graphic words and imagery of Luke 16:19-31. These include "the law and prophets,"[53] "son of Abraham," "a house filled with many good things," the displeasure of the rich man and the despicable poverty of the poor "brother," and the motif of final judgment. The detail of Simon *sitting* by Jesus recalls the Jewish custom of students learning from rabbis by sitting at their feet (e.g., Acts

---

51. Two brothers (4:18); two demoniacs (8:28); two blind men (9:27; 20:30); two disciples (21:1-2). E. B. Nicholson, *The Gospel According to the Hebrews,* 49; R. Handmann, *Das Hebräer-Evangelium,* 90.

52. Both P. Parker, "A Proto-Lukan Basis for the Gospel According to the Hebrews," 472, and J. Jeremias, *Unknown Sayings of Jesus²* (London: SPCK, 1964), 47, note the relationship with Luke's parable of the Rich Man and Lazarus.

53. According to Tertullian, *Marc.* 4.4, Marcion expunged this phrase from Luke because of its Jewishness. On Jewish elements in the account of the Hebrew Gospel, see C. Evans, "Jewish Chistian Gospel Tradition," 249-50.

22:3; *J. W.* 1.6.5). Other details recall Lukan style in general. The use of "son (or daughter) of Abraham" as a grounds for compassion is especially Lukan (13:16; 19:9), as is the use of "live" in the sense of "eternal life" (Luke 10:28). The command to the rich man to "Sell all you possess and distribute it among the poor, and come, follow me" is nearer in wording to Luke than to either Matthew or Mark. The absolute use of "the Lord" in narrative seems to have been common in the Hebrew Gospel and appears more frequently in Special Luke than in sections paralleled by Matthew and/or Mark.[54] Likewise, only in Luke (12:14; 22:58, 60) is "Man" used as a form of address.

All three Synoptics read that "it is easier for a camel to go through the eye of a needle than for a rich man to enter the kingdom of *God,*" whereas the Hebrew Gospel reads, ". . . kingdom of *heaven.*" The latter is a Hebraism intended to avoid using the name of God. Peter is called "Simon" in the Hebrew Gospel, which will also be the case in Jerome's quotation from the Hebrew Gospel in *Against the Pelagians* 3.2.[55] Handmann sees in these concrete particulars "signs of more original and less refined historical narrative."[56] Thus, not only does the passage exhibit several Hebraisms, but its content, imagery, and wording bear a distinct relationship with the parable of the Rich Man and Lazarus in Luke 16:19-31.

Eusebius

In two passages in the *Theophania* Eusebius refers to what appears to be the Hebrew Gospel.

Theophania 4.12

The first is extant only in Syriac, the English translation of which reads:

---

54. On the previous two points, see B. W. Bacon, "Papias and the Gospel According to the Hebrews," 174. Sixty percent of the appearances of κύριος in Luke appear in Special Luke.

55. A. F. J. Klijn, *Jewish-Christian Gospel Tradition,* 59, suggests that the Greek form of the name of Simon's father, Ἰωνᾶ, is a Septuagintism, since the Hebrew יונא cannot be found in Jewish sources before the fourth century. This is unpersuasive, for the spelling of "Jonah" in the MT is not יונא but יונה (8x in Jonah, elsewhere only 2 Kgs 14:25), which the LXX renders Ἰωνᾶ. Ἰωνᾶ thus does not appear to be a Septuagintism, but the normal rendering of יונה.

56. R. Handmann, *Das Hebräer-Evangelium,* 92.

> The cause therefore of the divisions of souls that take place in houses Christ himself taught, as we have found in a place in the Gospel existing among the Jews in the Hebrew language, in which it is said: "I will choose for myself the best which my Father in heaven has given me."[57]

The theme of dividing households against themselves is reminiscent of Matt 10:34-36//Luke 12:51-53. Matthew speaks of these divisions in terms of "peace" and "swords," whereas Luke describes them less graphically simply as "divisions" (διαμερισμός, διαμερίζω), which seems to reflect the character of the Syriac. The reference to God as "heavenly Father" is typically Matthean, occurring some twenty times in the First Gospel. But the theme of "choosing" and the quotation as a whole show a special affinity with Luke. The Hebrew Gospel again exhibits unusual agreement with a text unique to Luke. "I will choose for myself the best which my Father in heaven has given me" seems to be a first person rendition of Jesus' choosing of the Twelve, as recorded only in Luke 6:13. The idea is not simply that Jesus chooses the good but that he receives the good that God gives and therefore chooses it.[58] When Luke 6:13 is transposed from the third person to the first person, the result is very close to the above quotation, similar for example to John 6:37, "Everything that the Father gives to me will come to me, and the one who comes to me I will surely not reject."

Theophania 4.22

The second quotation from Eusebius's *Theophania* is longer:

> For the Gospel that has come to us in Hebrew characters does not bring condemnation on the man who hid [the money], but on the man who lived dissolutely. For he had three servants: the one who squandered the wealth of the master with prostitutes and flute-players, the one who greatly increased the principal sum, and the one who hid the talent. One of them was praised; another was merely rebuked; the other was locked

---

57. Cited from A. Harnack, *Geschichte der altchristlichen Literatur bis Eusebius,* 7; and J. K. Elliott, *The Apocryphal New Testament,* 11. For translational details related to the Syriac, see A. F. J. Klijn, *Jewish-Christian Gospel Tradition,* 63-64.

58. See R. Handmann, *Das Hebräer-Evangelium,* 97.

up in prison. As for the last condemnation of the servant who earned nothing, I wonder if Matthew repeated it not with him in mind but rather with reference to the servant who caroused with the drunks.[59]

This passage is vaguely related to the parable of the Talents variously preserved in Matthew 25:14-30 and Luke 19:11-27. The *Gospel of Thomas* 41 seems to preserve a similar saying, or perhaps a summary of the parable. The Lukan and Matthean versions of the parable exhibit patent differences, however. Luke's parable seems to be a combination of a parable about the lending of talents and another about a rebellious city. Matthew's is more coherent, omitting the motif of the rebellious city and limiting the parable to the talents alone. The version from the Hebrew Gospel likewise limits the parable to the giving of talents, and in this respect it corresponds with Matthew. But unlike either Matthew or Luke the responses of the three servants in the Hebrew Gospel differ distinctly in kind, and not merely in degree, as they do in Matthew and Luke. The Hebrew Gospel is leaner and less elaborate than Matthew and Luke, and quite plausibly represents "the earliest, simplest, and most natural form of the parable."[60] Eusebius may also have regarded the version of the Hebrew Gospel as the more primitive, for he recounts it without qualification and explains Matthean differences in the parable on the basis of the version in the Hebrew Gospel.

It would be difficult, if not impossible, to reconstruct the original parable of Jesus from these diverse and often conflicting versions. Fortunately, even the unreconstructed evidence allows us to draw two conclusions relevant to the Hebrew Gospel. First, *Theophania* 4.22 preserves yet another tradition in common with Matthew and Luke, but not with Mark. Second and more precisely, a host of terminology and phraseology in the quotation is special or unique to Luke. The Greek terms ἐφίστημι, ζάω, ἑξῆς,

---

59. ἐπὶ δὲ τὸ εἰς ἡμᾶς ἧκον ἑβραϊκοῖς χαρακτῆρσιν εὐαγγέλιον τὴν ἀπειλὴν οὐ κατὰ τοῦ ἀποκρύψαντος ἐπῆγεν, ἀλλὰ κατὰ τοῦ ἀσώτως ἐζηκότος· τρεῖς γὰρ δούλους περιεῖχε, τὸν μὲν καταφαγόντα τὴν ὕπαρξιν τοῦ δεσπότου μετὰ πορνῶν καὶ αὐλητρίδων, τὸν δὲ πολλαπλασιάσαντα τὴν ἐργασίαν, τὸν δὲ κατακρύψαντα τὸ τάλαντον· εἶτα τὸν μὲν ἀποδεχθῆναι, τὸν δὲ μεμφθῆναι μόνον, τὸν δὲ συγκλεισθῆναι δεσμωτηρίῳ· ἐφίστημι μήποτε κατὰ τὸν Ματθαῖον, μετὰ τὴν συμπλήρωσιν τοῦ λόγου τοῦ κατὰ τοῦ μηδὲν ἐργασαμένου, ἡ ἑξῆς ἐπιλεγομένη ἀπειλή, οὐ περὶ αὐτοῦ ἀλλὰ περὶ τοῦ προτέρου κατ' ἐπανάληψιν λέλεκται τοῦ ἐσθίοντος καὶ πίνοντος μετὰ τῶν μεθυόντων (Eusebius, *Theoph.* 4.22).

60. R. Handmann, *Das Hebräer-Evangelium*, 103.

συμπληροῦν, ἐργασία, ἀπειλή, ὕπαρξις, δεσπότης, and ἀποδέχομαι are all characteristic of or unique to Luke-Acts among the Gospels. The designation of the profligate servant who "lives dissolutely" (ἀσώτως ἐζηκότος) occurs only in Luke's parable of the Prodigal Son (15:13). The longer description of the dissolute servant as one "who squandered the wealth of the master with prostitutes" is reminiscent of the D reading of Luke 15:30.[61] The dissolute servant in the Hebrew Gospel citation is a mirror image of the prodigal younger son in Luke 15:13, 30. Both lexically and thematically, Eusebius's quotation of the Hebrew Gospel in *Theophania* 4.22 bears an unmistakable relationship to the Gospel of Luke, and particularly to the parable of the Prodigal Son.

Epiphanius (c. 315-403)

Epiphanius, bishop of Salamis, preserves eight references to the Hebrew Gospel. Although fewer in number than Jerome's references and quotations, they are of greater value because they are longer and afford greater comparison with the Synoptic narratives. All eight occur in *Panarion* 30, the chapter in which Epiphanius treats the "Ebionite" heresy.[62] Epiphanius associates the Hebrew Gospel with the Ebionite sect, and hence the Hebrew Gospel in Epiphanius is often referred to by modern scholars as "the Gospel of the Ebionites."[63] This is a scholarly neologism, however, which comes neither from Epiphanius nor from any other church father. Epiphanius never refers to the gospel as "the Gospel of the Ebionites," but always simply as a "Hebrew Gospel," which he further describes as a corruption of the Gospel of Matthew.[64]

Epiphanius's eight quotations make no reference to the Gospel of John, Acts, or the NT Epistles. All eight are related only to the Synoptic Gospels. These quotations confirm the same two conclusions that have

61. τὸν μὲν καταφαγόντα τὴν ὕπαρξιν τοῦ δεσπότου μετὰ πορνῶν; ὁ καταφαγών σου τὸν βίον μετὰ πορνῶν.

62. On the Ebionites, see Chapter Three, p. 121, n. 80.

63. A. F. J. Klijn and G. J. Reinink, *Patristic Evidence for Jewish-Christian Sects,* 24-25, fail to offer substantive evidence or argumentation for their conclusion that the Hebrew Gospel is not "the Gospel of the Ebionites."

64. Eusebius, *Hist. eccl.* 3.27.4, also refers to the Gospel used by the Ebionites as the Hebrew Gospel.

emerged from previous quotations of the Hebrew Gospel: first, they correspond predominantly with Luke as opposed to Matthew or the Synoptic tradition in general; and second, as Epiphanius claims, they are not abridgements or harmonies of the Synoptic tradition in general, but quotations from an original Hebrew Gospel authored by the apostle Matthew.[65]

Panarion 30.13.2-3

The first seven passages occur in quick succession in *Panarion* 30, with the eighth and final quotation further on in the chapter. The first quotation reads:

> In what they [i.e., the Ebionites] then call the Gospel according to Matthew, which however is not complete but forged and mutilated — they call it the Hebrew Gospel — it is reported: "There appeared a certain man by the name of Jesus, about thirty years of age, who chose us. And having come to Capernaum, he entered the house of Simon who was called Peter, and having opened his mouth, said, 'As I passed beside the Lake of Tiberias, I chose John and James the sons of Zebedee, and Simon and Andrew and Thaddaeus and Simon the Zealot and Judas the Iscariot, and you, Matthew, I called while you were sitting at the tax table, and you followed me. You therefore I desire to be twelve apostles for a witness to Israel.'"[66]

65. For a detailed linguistic analysis of all the Greek texts in *Pan.* 30 in which the Hebrew Gospel is mentioned, see J. R. Edwards, "The *Gospel of the Ebionites* and the Gospel of Luke," 568-86. In response to my article, A. Gregory, "Prior or Posterior? The *Gospel of the Ebionites* and the Gospel of Luke," 344-60, seems to concede 1) that all but two of the excerpts of the *Gospel of the Ebionites* that are found in Epiphanius are more closely related to Luke than to any other Gospel, and 2) that the Lukan parallels usually appear in Luke's single tradition (349). Gregory dismisses the weight of this evidence, however, and in a chain of reasoning that is neither entirely clear nor compelling concludes that the Hebrew Gospel was a compilation from Luke and the other Synoptic Gospels.

66. ἐν τῷ γοῦν παρ' αὐτοῖς εὐαγγελίῳ κατὰ Ματθαῖον ὀνομαζομένῳ, οὐχ ὅλῳ δὲ πληρεστάτῳ, ἀλλὰ νενοθευμένῳ καὶ ἠκρωτηριασμένῳ (Ἑβραϊκὸν δὲ τοῦτο καλοῦσιν) ἐμφέρεται ὅτι "ἐγένετό τις ἀνὴρ ὀνόματι Ἰησοῦς, καὶ αὐτὸς ὡς ἐτῶν τριάκοντα, ὃς ἐξελέξατο ἡμᾶς. καὶ ἐλθὼν εἰς Καφαρναοὺμ εἰσῆλθεν εἰς τὴν οἰκίαν Σίμωνος τοῦ ἐπικληθέντος Πέτρου καὶ ἀνοίξας τὸ στόμα αὐτοῦ εἶπεν· παρερχόμενος παρὰ τὴν λίμνην Τιβεριάδος ἐξελεξάμην Ἰωάννην καὶ Ἰάκωβον, υἱοὺς Ζεβεδαίου, καὶ Σίμωνα καὶ Ἀνδρέαν καὶ Θαδδαῖον καὶ Σίμωνα τὸν ζηλωτὴν καὶ Ἰούδαν τὸν Ἰσκαριώτην, καὶ σὲ τὸν Ματθαῖον

This passage is conclusively linked to the Gospel of Luke in six particulars. First, mention of Jesus being "about thirty years of age" parallels Luke 3:23, who alone of the Evangelists mentions Jesus' age. Second, reference to "the Lake of Tiberias" is exclusive to Luke. The word for "lake" is not θάλασσα, the word commonly used to describe the Sea of Galilee in Matthew (13x), Mark (16x), and John (9x), but λίμνη, which is unique to Luke (5x) among the Gospels. Third, mention of entering the house of Simon (εἰσῆλθεν εἰς τὴν οἰκίαν Σίμωνος) is verbatim with Luke 4:38 rather than Matthew's and Mark's wording of the same episode. Fourth, the further clarification of Simon's name as "Peter" more closely corresponds to Luke 6:14 than to the wording of either Matt 10:2 or Mark 3:16. A fifth distinctive linkage with Luke occurs in the apostolic list: the reference to "Simon the Zealot" is unique to Luke (6:15), and the order of "John and James," as opposed to "James and John," is found in the apostolic lists in the NT only in Acts 1:13, again from Luke. Sixth, the phrase "there appeared a certain man by the name of Jesus" is practically verbatim with Luke 1:5.[67] Finally, the source of this passage purports to be an eyewitness testimony of the apostle Matthew, who here, as in *Smyrn.* 3.1-2, speaks in the first person.

In three further instances *Panarion* 30.13.2-3 is at least suggestive of Luke as opposed to either Matthew or Luke. "Who chose us" (ἐξελέξατο) agrees with the same verb in Luke 6:13. Ἐκλέγομαι is characteristic of Luke, who uses it four times in the Gospel (6:13; 9:35; 10:42; 14:7) and another seven times in Acts, whereas the verb occurs only once in Mark and is absent in Matthew. Again, mention of Jesus' arrival in Capernaum (ἐλθὼν εἰς Καφαρναούμ) closely resembles Luke 4:31 (κατῆλθεν εἰς Καφαρναούμ), but is dissimilar from the wording in the dozen passages elsewhere in the four Gospels that note the same episode. Lastly, in "You therefore I desire to be twelve" (βούλομαι εἶναι δεκαδύο), the first word is clearly Lukan (βούλομαι: Luke 2x, Acts 14x, Matt 2x, Mark 1x, John 1x). Although δεκαδύο does not occur in the NT, δέκα alone is characteristically Lukan (Luke 12x, Matt 3x, Mark 1x, John 0x), as is the preceding infinitive.[68]

καθεζόμενον ἐπὶ τοῦ τελωνίου ἐκάλεσα καὶ ἠκολούθησάς μοι. ὑμᾶς οὖν βούλομαι εἶναι δεκαδύο ἀποστόλους εἰς μαρτύριον τοῦ Ἰσραήλ (*Pan.* 30.13.2-3).

67. Luke 1:5: ἐγένετο . . . τις ὀνόματι Ζαχαρίας; Epiphanius: ἐγένετό τις ἀνὴρ ὀνόματι.

68. D. Bertrand's cursory reference to only three points of correspondence with Luke (the age of Jesus, the choosing of the apostles, and Simon the Zealot) in "L'*Evangile des Ebionites.* Une Harmonie Evangelique Anterieure au *Diatessaron,*" 554, understates the significant agreement between *Pan.* 30.13.2-3 and Luke.

In only three minor instances does the above text appear to favor Matthew over Luke: in the mention of Judas as Ἰσκαριώτης (Matt 10:4) as opposed to Ἰσκαριώθ (Luke 6:16), in the phrase καὶ ἀνοίξας τὸ στόμα αὐτοῦ (so Matt 5:2; 17:27; but see Luke 1:64), and in Matthew's sitting at his tax table (Matt 9:9). In the last, however, Epiphanius's syntax is Lukan as opposed to Matthean. These minor exceptions notwithstanding, the above text corresponds soundly with the Third Gospel.[69]

Panarion 30.13.4-6

The above quotation is immediately followed by two more pertaining to John the Baptist, the first about John himself and the second about his baptism of Jesus. Combined, they read:

> And John came baptizing, and Pharisees went out to him, and they and all Jerusalem were baptized. And John had clothing made of camel hair and a leather belt around his waist; and his food, it is said, was wild honey, the taste of which was that of manna, as a cake dipped in oil. Thus they were resolved to pervert the word of truth to a lie, and they replace grasshoppers with a honey cake. The beginning of their Gospel has this, "In the days when Herod was king of Judea <when Caiaphas was high priest>, <a certain> John <by name> came baptizing a baptism of repentance in the Jordan River. John, it was said, was of the line of Aaron the priest, a child of Zechariah and Elisabeth, and all were going out to him."[70]

---

69. The conclusion of A. F. J. Klijn, *Jewish-Christian Gospel Tradition,* 66, that "a slight preference for Luke emerges" in *Pan.* 30.13.1-2 scarcely does justice to its overwhelming correspondence with Luke.

70. καὶ "ἐγένετο Ἰωάννης βαπτίζων, καὶ ἐξῆλθον πρὸς αὐτὸν φαρισσαῖοι καὶ ἐβαπτίσθησαν καὶ πᾶσα Ἱεροσόλυμα. καὶ εἶχεν ὁ Ἰωάννης ἔνδυμα ἀπὸ τριχῶν καμήλου καὶ ζώνην δερματίνην περὶ τὴν ὀσφὺν αὐτοῦ. καὶ τὸ βρῶμα αὐτοῦ, φησί, μέλι ἄγριον, οὗ ἡ γεῦσις ἡ τοῦ μάννα, ὡς ἐγκρὶς ἐν ἐλαίῳ." ἵνα δῆθεν μεταστρέψωσι τὸν τῆς ἀληθείας λόγον εἰς ψεῦδος καὶ ἀντὶ ἀκρίδων ποιήσωσιν ἐγκρίδα ἐν μέλιτι. ἡ δὲ ἀρχὴ τοῦ παρ' αὐτοῖς εὐαγγελίου ἔχει ὅτι "ἐγένετο ἐν ταῖς ἡμέραις Ἡρῴδου βασιλέως τῆς Ἰουδαίας <ἐπὶ ἀρχιερέως Καϊάφα>, ἦλθεν <τις> Ἰωάννης <ὀνόματι> βαπτίζων βάπτισμα μετανοίας ἐν τῷ Ἰορδάνῃ ποταμῷ, ὃς ἐλέγετο εἶναι ἐκ γένους Ἀαρὼν τοῦ ἱερέως παῖς Ζαχαρίου καὶ Ἐλισάβετ, καὶ ἐξήρχοντο πρὸς αὐτόν πάντες" (*Pan.* 30.13.4-6).

The agreement of *Panarion* 30.13.4 with Matt 3:4 may at first glance appear to link it with the First Gospel.[71] The roughly dozen words of agreement are less conclusive than they appear, however, for Matt 3:4 is nearly verbatim with Mark 1:5-6. *Panarion* 30.13.4 thus corresponds more properly with the double tradition of Matthew and Mark. The remainder of the above passage (30.13.5-6), however, corresponds with Luke — and only Luke. Epiphanius records that the *Gospel of the Ebionites* began with the words ἐγένετο ἐν ταῖς ἡμέραις Ἡρῴδου βασιλέως τῆς Ἰουδαίας. This eight-word phrase, which is found nowhere in either Matthew or Mark, is verbatim with Luke's infancy narrative in 1:5.[72] The statement that John appeared when "Caiaphas was high priest" is practically verbatim with Luke 3:2. Likewise, the reference to John's descent from the line of Aaron reflects Luke 1:5, as do the names of his parents, Zechariah and Elisabeth. Although John's diet is not honey cakes in any of the Gospels, it may also bear a relationship to Luke. The wording preserved by Epiphanius, ἡ γεῦσις . . . ὡς ἐγκρὶς ἐν ἐλαίῳ, reproduces the description of the manna in Exod 16:31 (LXX), τὸ δὲ γεῦμα αὐτοῦ ὡς ἐγκρὶς ἐν μέλιτι (cf. also Num 11:8). One possible explanation for the alteration of the Baptist's diet in the *Gospel of the Ebionites* might relate to the Aaronic priesthood, which is instructed in Lev 8:26 to eat cakes dipped in oil. Only in Luke 1:5 is John's descent linked to the line of Aaron. In sum, we have a text that corresponds generally with Matthew and Mark, but in many particulars with Luke. The material in agreement with Matthew and Mark is more or less evangelical "public domain," whereas the several distinct correspondences to Luke anchor the quotation genetically to the Third Evangelist.

Panarion 30.13.7-8

A fourth citation from Epiphanius, again with reference to John the Baptist, occurs immediately following the above quotation.

---

71. So D. Bertrand, "L'*Evangile des Ebionites*: Une Harmonie Evangelique Anterieure au *Diatessaron*," 555.

72. H. Schonfield, *According to the Hebrews*, 232, is one of the few scholars to recognize this manifest parallel between Luke and the Hebrew Gospel, as well as the parallel in Jesus' age of 30 years.

After many things had been said, it continues, "When the people had been baptized, Jesus also came and was baptized by John. And as he arose from the water, the heavens were opened, and he saw the Holy Spirit of God in the form of a dove descending and entering into him. And a voice came from heaven, saying 'You are my beloved Son, in you I am pleased'; and again, 'Today I have begotten you.' And immediately a great light shone on the place. When John saw it, it is recorded that he said to [Jesus], 'Who are you, Lord?' And again a voice from heaven came to him, 'This is my beloved Son, on whom my pleasure rests.' And then, it is reported, John fell before him saying, 'I beg you, Lord, to baptize me.' But he prevented it saying, 'Let it be, for in this way it is necessary for all things to be fulfilled.'"[73]

This is one of two passages in the Hebrew Gospel cited by Epiphanius that appears to be a harmony of the Synoptics, though with less material from Mark than from Matthew and Luke. But again the correspondences with Luke are numerous. The reference to Jesus being baptized with the people relates solely to Luke 3:21, as does the reference to the "Holy Spirit" (Luke 3:22) in the form of a dove. Hilgenfeld quotes Irenaeus (followed by Hippolytus), Epiphanius, and Theodoret, all of whom attest that the Cerinthians believed that the Spirit "descended into him [Jesus] in the shape of a dove." The Cerinthians were known to use Hebrew Matthew.[74] The first expression of the voice from heaven addresses Jesus in the second person singular in accordance with the texts of Luke and Mark, as opposed to Matthew's version where Jesus is referred to in the third person singular. Also, the voice ἐκ τοῦ οὐρανοῦ, which only in Luke is singular (ἐξ οὐρονοῦ, as opposed to plural in Matthew and Mark, ἐκ τῶν οὐρανῶν), agrees more closely with Luke. Epiphanius's reference to the "opening"

---

73. καὶ μετὰ τὸ εἰπεῖν πολλὰ ἐπιφέρει ὅτι "τοῦ λαοῦ βαπτισθέντος ἦλθεν καὶ Ἰησοῦς καὶ ἐβαπτίσθη ὑπὸ τοῦ Ἰωάννου. καὶ ὡς ἀνῆλθεν ἀπὸ τοῦ ὕδατος, ἠνοίγησαν οἱ οὐρανοὶ καὶ εἶδεν τὸ πνεῦμα ὁ ἅγιον ἐν εἴδει περιστερᾶς, κατελθούσης καὶ εἰσελθούσης εἰς αὐτόν. καὶ φωνὴ ἐκ τοῦ οὐρανοῦ λέγουσα· σύ μου εἶ ὁ υἱὸς ὁ ἀγαπητός, ἐν σοὶ ηὐδόκησα, καὶ πάλιν· ἐγὼ σήμερον γεγέννηκά σε. καὶ εὐθὺς περιέλαμψε τὸν τόπον φῶς μέγα. ὃ ἰδών, φησίν, ὁ Ἰωάννης λέγει αὐτῷ· σὺ τίς εἶ, κύριε; καὶ πάλιν φωνὴ ἐξ οὐρανοῦ πρὸς αὐτόν· οὗτός ἐστιν ὁ υἱός μου ὁ ἀγαπητός, ἐφ' ὃν ηὐδόκησα. καὶ τότε, φησίν, ὁ Ἰωάννης προσπεσὼν αὐτῷ ἔλεγεν· δέομαί σου, κύριε, σύ με βάπτισον. ὁ δὲ ἐκώλυσεν αὐτὸν λέγων· ἄφες, ὅτι οὕτως ἐστὶ πρέπον πληρωθῆναι πάντα" (*Pan.* 30.13.7-8).

74. A. Hilgenfeld, *Novum Testamentum extra Canonem Receptum*², 7.

(ἀνοίγω) of heaven corresponds to the same verb in Luke 3:21 and Matt 3:16, as opposed to Mark's use of σχίζω in the parallel passage. The entry of the Holy Spirit "into" Jesus (εἰς αὐτόν), however, is found only in Mark. The appendage of the divine pronouncement, "Today I have begotten you" (ἐγὼ σήμερον γεγέννηκά σε), a quotation of Ps 2:7, likewise occurs only in the Western text of Luke 3:22. The references to the bright light and the question "Who are you, Lord?" echo the account of the conversion of Paul in Acts (9:5; 22:8; 26:15). Nevertheless, the tradition of a light/fire at Jesus' baptism is very old and pervasive in early Christian tradition.[75]

The passage concludes, however, in correspondence with Matthew, specifically the divine address to Jesus in the third person singular in accordance with Matthew's baptismal narrative and the reference to Jesus overriding John's qualms about baptizing him (οὕτως ἐστὶ πρέπον πληρωθῆναι πάντα; Matt 3:15: οὕτως γὰρ πρέπον ἐστὶν ἡμῖν πληρῶσαι πᾶσαν δικαιοσύνην). The latter reference is reversed, however, for in Matthew it is John who attempts to prevent Jesus from being baptized, whereas according to the text quoted by Epiphanius it is Jesus who prevents John. The final quotation in this chapter of Jerome from *Against the Pelagians* 3.2 will likewise testify that in the Hebrew Gospel it was Jesus who attempted to prevent John from baptizing Jesus.

Panarion 30.14.3

The *Panarion* includes treatises on eighty sects and heresies, extending to three volumes in Karl Holl's edition.[76] *Against the Ebionites,* one of the longest treatments in the *Panarion,* is a rambling treatise with several digressions and repetitions. Epiphanius's fifth citation from a Hebrew Gospel is an example of such repetition, amplifying the third citation about John's baptism.

> For having removed the genealogies of Matthew, they begin, as I said earlier, by saying that "It came to pass in the days of Herod king of

---

75. See the extensive material gathered in E. B. Nicholson, *The Gospel according to the Hebrews,* 40-42.

76. Epiphanius, *Panarion,* ed. Karl Holl, 2d ed. Jürgen Dummer, 3 vols. (Berlin: Akademie, 1980).

Judea, when Caiaphas was chief priest, a certain man named John came baptizing a baptism of repentance in the Jordan river," etc.[77]

This quotation repeats *Panarion* 30.13.6 quoted above, and like it is related more distinctly to Luke than to the Synoptic parallels in Matt 3:1-2 and Mark 1:4. The wording ἐγένετο ἐν ταῖς ἡμέραις Ἡρώδου βασιλέως τῆς Ἰουδαίας again repeats verbatim the opening line of Luke's infancy narrative (1:5). The addition of the high priesthood of Caiaphas is also found only in Luke (3:2), and the reference to "the baptism of repentance in the Jordan river" is closer to Luke 3:3 than to its parallels in either Matt 3:1 or Mark 1:4. The repetition of this passage is significant, for according to its introduction by Epiphanius, the body of the Hebrew Gospel began with Luke 1:5, not with the birth of Jesus as recorded in Matt 1:18.

Panarion 30.14.5

A sixth snippet included from the Hebrew Gospel refers to Jesus' rebuff of his mother and brothers. Not only were the Ebionites guilty of compromising the deity of Jesus, according to the testimonies of Epiphanius and Irenaeus, but they also compromised his humanity, as the following passage indicates.

> Again, they deny that [Jesus] was a true man, surely from the word spoken by the Savior when it was announced to him, "Behold, your mother and your brothers are standing outside." The Savior's word was, "Who is my mother and who are my brothers?" And having stretched out his hand to the disciples, he said, "These are my brothers and my mother, those who are doing the desires of my Father."[78]

---

77. παρακόψαντες γὰρ τὰς παρὰ τῷ Ματθαίῳ γενεαλογίας ἄρχονται τὴν ἀρχὴν ποιεῖσθαι ὡς προείπομεν, λέγοντες ὅτι "ἐγένετο," φησίν, "ἐν ταῖς ἡμέραις Ἡρώδου βασιλέως τῆς Ἰουδαίας ἐπὶ ἀρχιερέως Καϊάφα, ἦλθέν τις Ἰωάννης ὀνόματι βαπτίζων βάπτισμα μετανοίας ἐν τῷ Ἰορδάνῃ ποταμῷ" καὶ τὰ ἑξῆς (*Pan.* 30.14.3).

78. πάλιν δὲ ἀρνοῦνται εἶναι αὐτὸν ἄνθρωπον, δῆθεν ἀπὸ τοῦ λόγου οὗ εἴρηκεν ὁ σωτὴρ ἐν τῷ ἀναγγελῆναι αὐτῷ ὅτι "ἰδοὺ ἡ μήτηρ σου καὶ οἱ ἀδελφοί σου ἔξω ἑστήκασιν," ὅτι "τίς μού ἐστι μήτηρ καὶ ἀδελφοί; καὶ ἐκτείνας τὴν χεῖρα ἐπὶ τοὺς μαθητὰς ἔφη· οὗτοί εἰσιν οἱ ἀδελφοί μου καὶ ἡ μήτηρ καὶ ἀδελφαὶ οἱ ποιοῦντες τὰ θελήματα τοῦ πατρός μου" (*Pan.* 30.14.5).

This is the second quotation in *Panarion* 30 that could be judged a harmony of the Synoptics, though again with preference for Matthew's and Luke's versions over Mark's. The one exception is the question, "Who is my mother and who are my brothers?" (τίς μου ἐστὶ μήτηρ καί μου ἀδελφοί;), which looks more like Mark 3:33 than either Matthew or Luke. Otherwise, the passage agrees with Matthew and Luke. The reference to Jesus stretching out his hand over the disciples (καὶ ἐκτείνας ἐπὶ τοὺς μαθητὰς τὴν χεῖρα) appears only in Matt 12:49 (although in different word order). In other respects the text correlates with Luke. Luke is the only Evangelist who uses the plural θελήματα, "desires," although in Acts 13:22 rather than in the Gospel. The word for "announced" (ἀναγγέλλω) repeats the same word found only in Luke 8:20. The final sentence, "These are my brothers and my mother, those who are doing the desires of my Father," shows closer agreement with 2 *Clement* 9:11 than with any of the Synoptics; but among the Synoptics the plural, "These are my brothers" (οὗτοί εἰσιν οἱ ἀδελφοί μου) parallels the wording (but not order) of Luke 8:21, as opposed to the singular ("This is . . .") in both Matthew and Mark.

Panarion 30.16.4-5

A seventh passage from Epiphanius is a maverick text with only one possible allusion to Matthew.

> But they claim that [Jesus] was not begotten from God the Father, but rather that he was created as one of the archangels, although greater than them. He rules over both angels and all things made by the Almighty, and he came and instructed, as their so-called Gospel relates, "I came to abolish the sacrifices, and unless you cease from sacrificing, the wrath [of God] will not cease from you."[79]

According to Epiphanius, the Ebionites denied that Christ was begotten of the Father, being an archangel of some sort who instructed his fol-

---

79. οὐ φάσκουσι δὲ ἐκ θεοῦ πατρὸς αὐτὸν γεγεννῆσθαι, ἀλλὰ κεκτίσθαι ὡς ἕνα τῶν ἀρχαγγέλων [καὶ ἔτι περισσοτέρως], αὐτὸν δὲ κυριεύειν καὶ ἀγγέλων καὶ πάντων <τῶν> ὑπὸ τοῦ παντοκράτορος πεποιημένων, καὶ ἐλθόντα καὶ ὑφηγησάμενον, ὡς τὸ παρ' αὐτοῖς εὐαγγέλιον καλούμενον περιέχει, ὅτι "ἦλθον καταλῦσαι τὰς θυσίας, καὶ ἐὰν μὴ παύσησθε τοῦ θύειν, οὐ παύσεται ἀφ' ὑμῶν ἡ ὀργή (*Pan.* 30.16.4-5).

lowers to "abolish the sacrifices." The phrase, "I came to abolish the sacrifices" (ἦλθον καταλῦσαι τὰς θυσίας) immediately suggests "I did not come to abolish the law" (οὐκ ἦλθον καταλῦσαι τὸν νόμον) of Matt 5:17. There indeed seems to be a relationship between the two sayings, but that relationship cannot be discerned without the quotation of yet a third related saying from the Talmud, which will be discussed in Chapter Seven. A resolution of this text must therefore be held in abeyance until then. For now I would simply say that the reference to abolishing *sacrifices* in 30.16.4 is not an error on Epiphanius's part, due perhaps to a slip of memory of Matt 5:17, for in a rebuttal of the Ebionites later in *Panarion* 30.27.2 Epiphanius correctly quotes Matt 5:17. Rather, as we shall see in Chapter Seven, this quotation apparently comes from a different written source than canonical Matthew.

Although I believe the quotation in *Panarion* 30.16.5 to be primarily related to the saying of Matt 5:17, it is possible that its wording has influenced two passages in the Third Gospel, for "I came to abolish the sacrifices" (ἦλθον καταλῦσαι τὰς θυσίας) correlates closely with two Lukan texts. A similar wording (εἰσῆλθεν καταλῦσαι) appears in Luke 19:7, although the reference to sacrifices is absent in the story of Zacchaeus. Likewise, Nicholson suggests that the pronouncement, "I came to abolish the sacrifices, and unless you cease from sacrificing, the wrath [of God] will not cease from you," fits closely with Luke 13:3, where Jesus says in response to Pilate's slaughter of the Galileans, "I tell you, unless you repent you shall all likewise perish."[80] Appendix II shows that Luke 19:7 and 13:3 both occur in Lukan sections rife with Semitisms.

Panarion 30.22.4

An eighth and final citation in *Against the Ebionites* also correlates distinctly with Luke. According to Epiphanius, the Ebionites attempted to justify their refusal to eat meat by falsifying a saying of Jesus from the Last Supper (see also *Pan.* 30.15.3-4). The saying under consideration is Luke 22:15: "I have truly desired to eat this Passover with you" ('Επιθυμίᾳ ἐπεθύμησα τοῦτο τὸ πάσχα φαγεῖν μεθ' ὑμῶν). Epiphanius quotes the falsified claim of the Ebionites as follows:

80. E. B. Nicholson, *The Gospel according to the Hebrews*, 77, 98.

[The Ebionites] changed the saying . . . and made the disciples to say, "Where do you wish for us to prepare the Passover feast for you?" And look what they make the Lord say, "I have not desired to eat meat in this Passover with you."[81]

The question where the disciples should celebrate the Passover meal is practically verbatim with Matt 26:17, although it is not substantially different from the parallels in Mark 14:12 and Luke 22:9. It thus appears again to be evangelical "public domain." The statement about "earnestly desiring [to eat] this Passover with you," however, occurs only in the Eucharistic words of institution in Luke 22:15. The reference to "earnestly desiring" (Ἐπιθυμίᾳ ἐπεθύμησα) is a literal rendering in Greek of the Hebrew infinitive absolute נכסף נכספתי (e.g., Gen 31:30). It is a classic Semitism.[82] Neither Greek nor Aramaic shows emphasis in this way, or if so only rarely, whereas the use of the infinitive absolute before a finite verb of the same root to show emphasis or decisiveness is standard in Hebrew and ubiquitous in the MT.[83] This construction is virtually incontrovertible evidence that an original Hebrew expression lay behind Luke's literal Greek rendering.[84]

Conclusions

As the foregoing analysis reveals, the Hebrew Gospel cited by Epiphanius is not, as is often assumed, a general harmony of the Synoptic Gospels. Nor again are Epiphanius's citations of the Hebrew Gospel default reproductions of Matthew, nor do they favor Matthew. A synopsis of the above evidence, divided between passages in the *Gospel of the Ebionites* that are ei-

81. ἤλλαξαν τὸ ῥητόν, . . . καὶ ἐποίησαν τοὺς μαθητὰς μὲν λέγοντας "ποῦ θέλεις ἑτοιμάσωμέν σοι τὸ Πάσχα φαγεῖν," καὶ αὐτὸν δῆθεν λέγοντα "μὴ ἐπιθυμίᾳ ἐπεθύμησα κρέας τοῦτο τὸ Πάσχα φαγεῖν μεθ' ὑμῶν (*Pan.* 30.22.4).

82. Elsewhere in Lukan writings, Acts 4:17 (ψ); 5:28; 23:14.

83. The custom of emphasizing the finite verb by the addition of its infinitive is frequent and characteristic of Hebrew but rare in Aramaic. See G. Dalman, *The Words of Jesus*, 34-35; J. H. Moulton and W. F. Howard, *A Grammar of New Testament Greek*, vol. 2 (Edinburgh: T. and T. Clark, 1930), 443; C. F. D. Moule, *An Idiom-Book of New Testament Greek* (Cambridge: Cambridge University Press, 1960), 178.

84. E. B. Nicholson, *The Gospel According to the Hebrews*, 98: "The verse in Luke's form may have been contained in the Gospel according to the Hebrews before the Ebionites corrupted it."

ther *clearly* or *possibly* related to the various Synoptic Gospels, reveals the following:

	Clearly	Possibly
Luke	13	14
Matthew	6	5
Mark	3	3

The Epiphanius citations show clear and repeated similarities to material unique to Luke.[85] A number of the Epiphanius citations are, to be sure, common to Matthew or Mark or both. There is of course nothing surprising in this. Our knowledge of the formation of the Synoptic tradition, which is far from exhaustive, allows us to posit a variety of sources for each of the Synoptics, whether from literary sources or perhaps more probably from oral influences. It would be unreasonable to exclude categorically a degree of influence from the Hebrew Gospel on Matthew and Mark. Of the number of above citations, however, a passage is twice as likely to show a preference for Matthew as it is for Mark. But even when Matthew and Mark are combined, their number is less than half the total number of references to the Synoptics in the Epiphanius citations. The remaining majority of citations is related to Luke, either clearly or possibly, and in most of these instances the citations are not merely a preference for Lukan texts over similar texts in Matthew or Mark, but citations of texts unique to Luke that are not paralleled in Matthew or Mark. Epiphanius's quotations from the Hebrew Gospel in *Panarion* 30 show a distinct correspondence with the Gospel of Luke rather than with either Matthew or Mark.

Jerome (345-419)

As noted in the previous chapter, the most numerous quotations from the Hebrew Gospel come from the pen of Jerome. Jerome's quotations are also the most problematic, and for two reasons. On the one hand, some of his references to the Hebrew Gospel seem to conflict with his normal testi-

---

85. So too R. Handmann, *Das Hebräer-Evangelium* 128: the Ebionite Gospel mentioned by Epiphanius shows "noch viel deutlicher lucanische Elemente."

mony to it. And more significantly, his reputation as a credible witness to the Hebrew Gospel has been bitterly attacked in some quarters. In this final battery of citations from the Hebrew Gospel, therefore, we must discuss both ancient texts and, not infrequently, modern criticism of Jerome's witness to them.

Epistle 20, "To Damasus" (c. 380)[86]

Damasus, who presided as pope 366-84, wrote briefly to Jerome in about 380 asking for his informed judgment on the phrase "Hosanna to the son of David," which was receiving conflicting interpretations in its various Greek and Latin translations. Damasus quotes the passage from "the Hebrews," which must mean the *Gospel of the Hebrews,* since it is not a reference to the OT but rather to Jesus and the NT.[87] In a return letter to Damasus, Jerome admits the plurality of views on the phrase, and in turn quotes from the Hebrew Gospel, to which Damasus himself has ostensibly referred.

> Further, Matthew, who wrote a Gospel in the Hebrew language, put it thus: *"osianna barrama,"* which means, "Hosanna in the highest," for when our Savior was born deliverance reached from heaven "on high," and peace reigned not only on earth but also in heaven.[88]

Nicholson ventures the suggestion that the quotation refers to the Feast of Dedication in 2 Macc 10:6-7, when Judas Maccabeus purified and rededicated the temple.[89] This is made unlikely, however, by the fact that Jerome's discussion of the quotation occurs in a long consideration of the Hebrew word "Hosanna" in the various recensions of Ps 118:24 in the Greek OT versions of Aquila, Symmachus, and Theodotion and the Septu-

---

86. Jerome's references are considered in the chronological order provided in Migne's *Patrologia Latina,* vols. 22-30.

87. "Osanna filio David," . . . quid se habeat apud Hebraeos (*Epist.* 19, *Dam. ad Hieron.*).

88. Denique Matheus, qui evangelium Hebraeo sermone conscripsit, ita posuit: *"osianna barrama,"* id est "osanna in excelsis," quod salvatore nascente salus in caelum usque, id est etiam ad excelsa, pervenerit pace facta non solum in terra, sed et in caelo *(Epist.* 20.5, *ad Dam.).*

89. E. B. Nicholson, *The Gospel According to the Hebrews,* 52.

agint, as well as in the citations of the Psalm in the triumphal entry of Jesus into Jerusalem (Matt 21:9; Mark 11:9-10; Luke 19:38; John 12:13).[90] "Hosanna in the highest" repeats verbatim the acclamation at Jesus' entry into Jerusalem in Matt 21:9 and Mark 11:10, but it also may recall "Glory in the highest" in Luke 2:14 and 19:38. "Osianna" is an exact transliteration of the Hebrew הושעה נא. "Barrama" is a less exact transliteration of the Hebrew במרומים, although we cannot be certain this was the exact form of the Hebrew word before Jerome. The phrase is Hebrew, not Aramaic; and it is equally Hebraic in form, for "glory in the highest," meaning "glory *to God* in the highest," is a circumlocution intended to avoid using the name of God.[91]

90. In his discussion of this text in *Die apokryph gewordenen Evangelien,* 249-50, D. Lührmann attacks Jerome's reputation as a translator. Because Jerome's Latin transliterations do not fully conform to the MT, Lührmann accuses Jerome of a sham mastery of Hebrew. Lührmann's denigration is unfair in more than one respect. As a translator, Jerome opted for dynamic rather than literal equivalency, and although consistency was his goal, it was not always his practice. Jerome never claimed to be a master exegete, "but what he does claim is that he has read as many different authors as possible . . . and that he has distilled their essence for the benefit of his readers" (H. F. D. Sparks, "Jerome as Biblical Scholar," in *The Cambridge History of the Bible,* ed. P. R. Ackroyd and C. F. Evans [Cambridge: Cambridge University Press, 1970], 1.35). *Epistle* 20 is a classic example of that claim. In *Epistle* 20, Jerome discusses the various OT Greek renderings of Aquila, Symmachus, Theodotion, and the LXX and cites a different Latin translation of Ps 118:24 from the Vulgate. Jerome is thus dealing with several textual traditions of Ps 118:24, none of which perfectly agrees with the MT. Lührmann makes no mention of the polyglot task before Jerome in *Epistle* 20. When we are able to check Jerome for certain, as we can in his translations of a half-dozen Hebrew words in the opening of the epistle, for example, his Latin is properly equivalent and indicates a very satisfactory knowledge of Hebrew. A. F. J. Klijn, *Jewish-Christian Gospel Tradition,* 121, correctly exonerates Jerome here: "The word *osianna* to which Jerome refers is, therefore, in agreement with the Hebrew expression."

91. Astonishingly, Klijn, *Jewish-Christian Gospel Tradition,* 121, rejects the source of this statement in the Hebrew Gospel "because we do not know of any Jewish-Christian Gospel in that language"! Whenever Jerome speaks of the language of the Hebrew Gospel, in every instance save one he identifies it as *Hebrew.* Klijn acknowledges the Hebrew background of this text (see previous footnote), but he rejects the explicit testimony of the citation because he is convinced the Jewish Christian Gospel was composed in Aramaic. A. Resch, *Agrapha. Aussercanonische Evangelienfragmente,* 338-39, by contrast, rightly recognizes the Hebraic roots of the saying.

Commentary on Ephesians (387-88)

Jerome's earliest datable reference to the Hebrew Gospel appears in his *Commentary on Ephesians:* "And also in the Hebrew Gospel we read of the Lord speaking to his disciples, 'Never be joyous unless you observe charity with your brother.'"[92] This saying is cited with reference to Eph 5:4, where Paul enjoins believers to avoid "obscenity, foolish speech, and crudity, which are not proper, but pursue rather thankfulness." No exact replica of Jerome's citation of the Hebrew Gospel exists in the canonical Gospels, but the dominical saying cited by Jerome does include three key verbs in Luke's Gospel — "rejoice" (εὐφραίνειν), "be glad" (χαίρειν), and "love" (ἀγαπᾶν). Klijn concludes that the phrase "observe charity" *(videritis in caritate)* "reveals an obvious Semitism."[93] The citation bears a correspondence to the words of the father to the older brother in the parable of the Prodigal Son and could be a summary of it: "The father said to [the older brother], 'Son, you are always with me and everything that is mine is yours. You should rejoice and be glad, for this your brother was dead and is alive, was lost and is found'" (Luke 15:30-31).

Lives of Illustrious Men 2 (392)

In the second chapter of Jerome's *Illustrious Men,* devoted to the apostle James, the following reference to the Hebrew Gospel appears:

> The Gospel also entitled "according to the Hebrews," which I lately translated into Greek and Latin and which Origen often quotes, contains the following narrative after the Resurrection: "Now the Lord, when he had given the cloth to the servant of the priest, went to James and appeared to him." For James had taken an oath that he would not eat bread from that hour on which he had drunk the cup of the Lord till he saw him risen from the dead. Again a little later the Lord said, "Bring a table and bread," and forthwith it is added: "He took bread and blessed

---

92. Ut in Hebraico quoque evangelio legimus dominum ad discipulos loquentem: "Et numquam," inquit, "laeti sitis, nisi cum fratrem vestrum videritis in caritate" (*Comm. Eph.* 5:4).

93. *Jewish-Christian Gospel Tradition,* 79.

and broke it and gave to James the Just and said to him, 'My brother, eat your bread, for the Son of Man is risen from those who sleep.'"[94]

This quotation begins with Jerome's testimony, made in several different epistles and contexts, of having translated the Hebrew Gospel into Greek and/or Latin. The mention of James, without distinguishing him from James the son of Zebedee and brother of John who died in 44, suggests that this account was composed after that date. James *the Just* also recalls the brother of Jesus rather than the son of Zebedee.[95] The James mentioned here must therefore be the bishop of Jerusalem (Gal 2:9, 13), also called the Lord's brother (Gal 1:19). The asceticism ascribed to James is typical of other stories in early church tradition in which the Lord's brother abstains from wine, meat, shaving, and so forth.[96] The resurrection narratives are among the most divergent narratives preserved in the Gospels, and, although they do not mention a resurrection appearance to James, it does not overtax our credibility — especially in light of the resurrection appearance to James in 1 Cor 15:7 — to imagine an appearance like the one recorded here. The phrase "again a little later" *(rursusque post paululum)* may in fact splice the record of such an appearance to this ac-

94. According to the translation in J. K. Elliott, *The Apocryphal New Testament,* 9-10. Jerome's original reads: Evangelium quoque quod appellatur secundum Hebraeos et a me nuper in Graecum sermonem Latinumque translatum est, quo et Origenes saepe utitur, post resurrectionem Salvatoris refert: "Dominus autem cum dedisset sindonem servo sacerdotis, ivit ad Iacobum et apparuit ei," iuraverat enim Iacobus se non comesurum panem ab illa hora qua biberat calicem Domini, donec videret eum resurgentem a dormientibus rursusque post paululum, "Adferte, ait Dominus, mensam et panem," statimque additur; "Tulit panem et benedixit et fregit et dedit Iacobo Iusto et dixit et: 'Frater mi, comede panem tuum, quia resurrexit Filius hominis a dormientibus'" (*Vir. ill.* 2). J. B. Lightfoot, *The Epistle of St. Paul to the Galatians* (Grand Rapids: Zondervan, 1971), 274, emends the text to "qua biberat calicem *Dominus,*" i.e., "on which the Lord has drunk the cup." Lightfoot explains the resurrection appearance to James as follows: "It is characteristic of a Judaic writer whose aim it would be to glorify the head of the church at all hazards, that an appearance, which seems in reality to have been vouchsafed to this James to win him over from his unbelief, should be represented as a reward for his devotion." For a positive assessment of "the cup" as a metaphor of death, see R. Handmann, *Das Hebräer-Evangelium,* 79-82.

95. Eusebius, *Hist. eccl.* 2.23: James was "named by all Just from the times of the Lord until our own times."

96. See the many references gathered by E. B. Nicholson, *The Gospel According to the Hebrews,* 61-65; and M. Hengel, *The Four Gospels and the One Gospel of Jesus Christ,* 276, n. 454.

count. The mention of the (chief) priest (rather than the Roman guard) seems to anchor this vignette to an early source related to the Sanhedrin.[97] Luke 22:4 (and its several textual variants) is the only Synoptic text suggesting a collusion of the chief priest and the (temple) guard in the arrest of Jesus. Matt 26:20 and Mark 14:17 both record that only the Twelve participated in the Lord's Supper; this would seem to exclude James, the brother of the Lord, who (although later counted among the "apostles") was not among the original Twelve. Luke 22:14, however, expands the Eucharistic guest list to include the "the apostles," which could include the brother of the Lord.

Jerome's account of a special postresurrection appearance of Jesus to James apparently spawned a series of similar accounts in late antiquity[98] and may be related to Jesus' appearance to Cleopas and a fellow disciple on the way to Emmaus in Luke 24:13-27.[99] In both stories the resurrected Lord serves a Eucharist-like meal *of bread only* to disciples, and in the same sequence of words: he took bread, blessed, broke, and gave.[100] The presence of bread alone suggests a very early date, which later traditions would have expanded to bread *and wine*. In both stories the meal enlightens previously noncomprehending disciples. The testimony of the Hebrew Gospel is close enough to the wording of Luke 24:30, in fact, to suggest that the mysterious companion of Cleopas may have been James, the brother of the Lord.[101]

Hans Waitz regards Jerome's account as an "autonomous legend" and rejects a relationship between it and the Emmaus story. The giving of the cloth to the servant of the priest is foreign to the Emmaus story, according to Waitz. In his opinion, that act is a conflation of the burial shroud of Jesus in Matt 27:59 and the servant of the high priest assigned as a guard at the

97. So R. Handmann, *Das Hebräer-Evangelium*, 78.

98. A. F. J. Klijn, *Jewish-Christian Gospel Tradition*, 80-83, cites a later Greek translation of *Vir. ill.* 2, as well as similar renditions in pseudo-Abdias, Gregory of Tours, the Irish Reference Bible, Sedulius Scottus, and Jacobus a Voragine.

99. Also recognized by P. Parker, "A Proto-Lukan Basis for the Gospel According to the Hebrews," 472-73.

100. Luke 24:30 (Vulg.): accepit panem et benedixit ac fregit et porrigebat illis; *Vir ill.* 2: Tulit panem et benedixit et fregit et dedit Iacobo Iusto. Both readings faithfully render the Greek of Luke 24:31: λαβὼν τὸν ἄρτον εὐλόγησεν καὶ κλάσας ἐπεδίδου αὐτοῖς.

101. Hegesippus, as quoted by Eusebius (*Hist. eccl.* 4.22.4), lists James, the brother of the Lord, and Symeon, his cousin, the son of Cleopas, as the first two bishops of Jerusalem. Nicephorus, *Chronographia Brevis* (6, Patriarchae Hierosolymitani), lists James and Symeon Cleopas, both brothers of the Lord, as the first two bishops of Jerusalem.

tomb of Jesus in the *Gospel of Peter.* Furthermore, Waitz sees a discrepancy between the unbelief of the disciples in the Emmaus story and James's faithful vow in Jerome's account.[102] Neither of Waitz's objections — nor both combined — seriously imperils the possible relation of the two accounts, however. The presence of the servant of the priest in the Hebrew Gospel would seem to root the account in the Sanhedrin — and thus attest its great antiquity. Luke 23:53 mentions a grave cloth similar to the cloth in the Hebrew Gospel cited by Jerome. It is not difficult to imagine that Jesus presented his grave cloth, along with his wounds (Luke 24:39), as material evidence to bewildered disciples after the resurrection. Moreover, the Emmaus story does not say the disciples were unbelieving, but that "their eyes were prevented from knowing him." James could have pledged himself to a vow of abstinence — which was not atypical of Jews in distress (e.g., Acts 23:12)[103] — prior to the revelation of the risen Jesus at the memorial meal.

A further reference to this event occurs in Sedulius Scottus, an itinerant Irish scholar and biblical critic. His *Collected Works on All the Epistles of Paul* (written between 855 and 859) reveal him to be a versatile and gifted theologian who was remarkably widely read. Scottus identifies the James of 1 Cor 15:7 as "the son of Alphaeus who vowed not to eat bread from the table of the Lord until he saw Christ rising again, as is read in the Gospel according to the Hebrews."[104] Scottus is probably indebted to Jerome, at least in part, for this quotation, since he was familiar with Jerome, having produced *Explanations of Jerome's Prefaces to the Gospels.* He also shares brief verbal agreements with Jerome's narrative.[105] Scottus does not claim to be quoting from Jerome in the note on 1 Cor 15:7, however, and his identification of James *the son of Alphaeus* is new, as is his reference to Jesus as the *Christ.* He may thus rely on additional sources, perhaps the Hebrew Gospel itself.[106]

---

102. "Neue Untersuchungen über die sogen. judenchristlichen Evangelien," 75-76.

103. On Jewish vows in distress, see Str-B 1.767.

104. Alphaei filio, qui se testatus est a coena Domini non comesurum panem usquequo videret Christum resurgentem: sicut in Evangelio secundum Hebraeos legitur (*Collectanea in Epistolam I ad Corinthios* 15:7; PL 103.158).

105. "Non comesurum panem," and "videret . . . resurgentem."

106. For a discussion of a story of Persian visitors to the manger of Jesus preserved by Sedulius Scottus (*Super Evangelium Mathei* 1:1–11:1), see A. F. J. Klijn, *Jewish-Christian Gospel Tradition,* 125-28. Due to its late date (tenth century) and remoteness from earlier reputable tradition, I am discounting it from consideration.

Jerome's *Commentary on Matthew* (398)

Jerome mentions the Hebrew Gospel several times in his *Commentary on Matthew.*

Matthew 2:5   The first occurs in Matthew 2:5 in connection with the spelling of the word "Judah."

> This is an error of the copyists; for we think the first edition of the evangelist [Matthew] read, as the Hebrew itself reads, "Judah," not "Judea."
> . . . For that reason, however, Judah is written, because there is also another Bethlehem in Galilee. . . . Again, in the same testimony found in the prophet Micah, it reads thus: "And you, Bethlehem, in the land of Judah."[107]

Matt 2:5 reads "Bethlehem of Judah," explains Jerome, in order to distinguish it from another Bethlehem in Galilee, mentioned in Josh 19:15. Jerome's precision with regard to the spelling of Judah evinces both an interest and accuracy regarding biblical place names. More important, however, is his reference to a "proto-Gospel" written in Hebrew. Like virtually all the fathers, Jerome affirmed that the first evangelical work of the apostle Matthew was a Hebrew Gospel intended for the use of Jewish Christians and for the conversion of Jews.

Matthew 6:11   In his commentary on the Lord's Prayer, Jerome renders a judgment on the meaning of *epiousion* (ἐπιούσιον, Matt 6:11; Luke 11:3), which occurs only in the NT, and which is variously translated as "daily" bread or "tomorrow's" bread. Jerome defers to the reading in the Hebrew Gospel to settle the matter. "In the Gospel called 'According to the Hebrews,'" he writes, "I found *mahar* with reference to the supernatural bread, which means 'tomorrow.'"[108] Jerome refers to the Hebrew Gospel on the same issue in his *Tractate on the Psalms,* although without reference

---

107. Librariorum hic error est; putamus enim ab evangelista primum editum, sicut in ipso Hebraico legimus "Iudae" non "Iudaeae." . . . Iudae autem idcirco scribitur, quia est et alia Bethleem in Galilaea. . . . Denique et in ipso testimonio, quod de Michaeae prophetia sumptum est, ita habetur: Et tu Bethleem terra Juda" *(Comm. Matt. 2.5).*

108. In evangelio quod appellatur secundum Hebraeos pro supersubstantiali pane reperi *mahar,* quod dicitur crastinum *(Comm. Matt. 6.11).*

to the Hebrew word. "In the Hebrew Gospel according to Matthew it has this: 'Give us today our bread for tomorrow'; that is, the bread that will be given to us in your kingdom, give us today."[109] In the ninth century, Sedulius Scottus quoted Jerome's *Commentary on Matthew* to this effect: "In the Gospel that is called According to the Hebrews instead of 'super-natural bread' I found *moar*, which means 'tomorrow's'. . . ."[110] Hebrew *mahar* (מהר), meaning "tomorrow," which Jerome found in the Lord's Prayer in the Hebrew Gospel, gave him the inspiration to interpret it as, "give us today what we will need for *tomorrow*." *Mahar* is Hebrew (Aramaic would be דמהר), and Jerome correctly renders it "tomorrow."[111] More importantly, Jerome's hermeneutical judgment is rendered on the basis of the Hebrew Gospel, as was Origen's above and Didymus's in the last chapter. In appealing to a noncanonical source in order to interpret a canonical text, all three fathers attest that, despite its unofficial status, the Hebrew Gospel possessed a *de facto* hermeneutical authority in the patristic period.[112]

Matthew 12:13 With reference to the healing of a man with a withered hand in Matt 12:13 (par. Mark 3:5; Luke 6:10), Jerome cites the following passage from the Hebrew Gospel:

> In the Gospel used by the Nazarenes and Ebionites, which we recently translated into Greek from the Hebrew language — and which many call the authentic Matthew — the man having a withered hand was a

109. In Hebraico evangelio secundum Matthaeum ita habet: Panem nostrum crastinum da nobis hodie, hoc est panem quem daturus es in regno tuo, da nobis hodie (*Tract. Ps.* 135).

110. In evangelio, quod appellatur 'Secundum Ebreos' pro 'supersubstantiali pane' 'moar' repperi, quod dicitur 'crastinum' . . . (*Super Evangelium Mathei;* cited in A. F. J. Klijn, *Jewish-Christian Gospel Tradition,* 87).

111. J. B. Lightfoot's exhaustive excursus on ἐπιούσιον in *A Fresh Revision of the English New Testament*[2] (London and New York: Macmillan, 1872), Appendix II, 195-242, supports Jerome's interpretation as "tomorrow." R. Handmann, *Das Hebräer-Evangelium,* 98, sees in *mahar* evidence of both Hebrew composition and antiquity: "So hat uns das H. E. den ursprünglichen Wortlaut aufbehalten, und wir haben hier einen deutlichen Beweis nicht nur seiner hebräischen Abfassung, sondern auch seines hohen Alters."

112. Note A. F. Findlay, *Byways in Early Christian Literature,* 53: "When we consider that Jerome was even morbidly apprehensive lest any suspicion of heresy should be attached to him, we may regard it as certain that he saw nothing in the [Hebrew] Gospel calculated to disturb the most orthodox."

mason who begged for help in the words, "I was a mason who worked with my hands for a living; I beg you, Jesus, restore me to health so that I may not have to shamefully beg for food."[113]

This citation of the Hebrew Gospel follows directly on the quotation of Matt 12:13 in Latin. Jerome's deference to the Hebrew Gospel without any introduction or apology implies that it was widely known and enjoyed a degree of hermeneutical authority. Several details relate the passage to the Third Gospel. Nowhere outside Luke 23:42 is "Jesus" used in direct address as here.[114] The Latin word *victum*, "livelihood," likely translates βίος, which is used four times by Luke, but only once by Mark among the other Evangelists. The idea of "shamefully begging for food" also recalls Luke 16:3. "Altogether we have reasons to suspect relations with Luke," declares Nicholson.[115]

New in the citation is the first person testimony of the man with the withered hand, who is identified as a stonemason. None of the canonical Gospels preserves the narrative in the first person or identifies the man as a mason. This is the third first person account ascribed to the Hebrew Gospel; the Hebrew Gospel evidently offered first person accounts of several events that appear in the Synoptic Gospels as third person narratives.[116] First person accounts may sound contrived to ears long accustomed to the third person narratives of the Gospels. Nevertheless, even in the four canonical Gospels first person testimonies can still be heard in the centurion from Capernaum (Luke 7:8; Matt 8:9), the plea of the father of the epileptic boy (Mark 9:17-18 par. Luke 9:38-39), John 19:35 and 21:24-25, and in authorial testimony in Luke 1:1-4. The plea of the mason is very reminiscent of the plea of blind Bartimaeus in Luke 18:41 par. Mark 10:51. Richard Bauckham makes a strong case for the likelihood that gospel sto-

---

113. In evangelio, quo utuntur Nazareni et Hebionitae, quod nuper in Graecum de Hebraeo sermone transtulimus et quod vocatur a plerisque Mathei authenticum, homo iste, qui aridam habet manum, caementarius scribitur, istiusmodi vocibus auxilium precans: "Caementarius eram, manibus victum quaeritans, precor te, Jesu, ut mihi restituas sanitatem ne turpiter mendicem cibos" (*Comm. Matt.* 12:13). This passage is cited practically verbatim early in the ninth century by Rabanus Maurus, *Commentary in Matthaeum* (PL 107.923B; cited from A. F. J. Klijn, *Jewish-Christian Gospel Tradition*, 88).

114. B. W. Bacon, "Papias and the Gospel according to the Hebrews," 174.

115. E. B. Nicholson, *The Gospel according to the Nazarenes*, 95.

116. Ignatius, *Smyrn.* 3.2 and Epiphanius, *Pan.* 30.13.2-3 are both preserved as first person narratives of the apostle Matthew.

ries with proper names in them — Jairus, Bartimaeus, Mary Magdalene, and others — were both transmitted and received into the canonical Gospels on the authority of their first person witnesses.[117] It is thus reasonable to suppose that the earliest accounts of such stories, of which the account of the stonemason in the Hebrew Gospel may be an example, would be narrated in the first person.

Many stories without proper names might also have originated as first person narratives, however. Gerd Theissen's theory of "protective anonymity" may also apply here. The names of individuals who were still alive and known when the Gospels were composed may have been obscured or removed in order to protect them from recriminations from Jewish authorities. The mason's name and occupation may have been expurgated from the canonical record if he were known to the Sanhedrin, for instance, and if his being so known might have endangered him.[118]

Matthew 23:35 We also read in Jerome's *Commentary on Matthew:* "In the Gospel that is used by the Nazarenes, we find 'son of Johoiada' in place of 'son of Barachias.'"[119] Jerome presumably implies the Hebrew Gospel here, for "the Gospel that is used by the Nazarenes" recalls similar references to the Hebrew Gospel in his writings. Zechariah was a common name throughout Israel's history, and the many Zechariahs were usually distinguished from one another by appending a father's name. Zechariah the prophet is identified as "the son of Barachias" in Zech 1:1, 7 (but see also Ezra 6:14; Neh 12:16), but he did not suffer the gruesome fate described in Matt 23:35 and Luke 11:51. The Zechariah who was slain in the court of priests in the temple was another Zechariah, "the son of Jehoiada" (2 Chron 24:20-21).

As for whether Matthew influenced the Hebrew Gospel or vice versa, plausible cases can be made for both. Since the reading cited by Jerome is the *lectio facilior,* it could be argued that the Hebrew Gospel altered the earlier and more difficult Matthew text.[120] In a full note on the question, Handmann concludes that it is impossible to pass a final judgment on

---

117. R. Bauckham, *Jesus and the Eyewitnesses*, 8, 45, 93.

118. See G. Theissen, *The Gospels in Context*, trans. L. Maloney (Minneapolis: Fortress, 1991), ch. 4; Bauckham, *Jesus and the Eyewitnesses*, 184-94.

119. In evangelio quo utuntur Nazaraeni pro filio Barachiae "filium Joiadae" reperimus scriptum (*Comm. Matt.* 23.35).

120. So A. F. J. Klijn, *Jewish-Christian Gospel Tradition*, 91.

which is earlier. Nevertheless, a relationship with the Zechariah of Chronicles poses the *fewest* problems, in his judgment. On this basis the reading of the Hebrew Gospel likely preserves the earliest reading, which also would account for its preservation by the church fathers.[121] In a similar vein, Nicholson offers the intriguing conjecture that the original form of the name was "Zechariah, son of Jehoiada," as written in the Hebrew Gospel, but that a copyist of Matthew's Gospel altered the name to his more famous namesake, "Zechariah, son of Barachias," thus introducing an error into canonical Matthew.[122]

"Son of Barachias" in Matt 23:35 is a *hapax legomenon* in the NT. Luke 11:51 also relates the story of the slaying of Zechariah, but without "son of Barachias." Luke preserves nine references to Zechariah, however. The first eight refer to the father of John the Baptist, and only the last in 11:51 refers to the Zechariah slain in 2 Chron 24:20-21. We should expect Luke to distinguish the two Zechariahs from one another, but he does not. The name of Zechariah is ingrained in readers of the Third Gospel by the time they get to 11:51. They could easily imagine — and perhaps not without intention on Luke's part — that the final fate of Zechariah, father of John the Baptist, is that of Zechariah the prophet. This is, of course, speculative, but Jerome also notes this interpretative possibility in his commentary on the passage. If this conjecture is correct, then the father of the Baptist, like the Baptist himself, is intended as a harbinger of the impending death of the Messiah.

Matthew 27:16 Another reference to the Hebrew Gospel in Jerome's *Commentary on Matthew* occurs with reference to the name of Barabbas in 27:16. "He [Barabbas] signifies 'the son of their teacher' in the Gospel that is written 'According to the Hebrews,' because he had been condemned for sedition and murder."[123] Barabbas's condemnation for sedition and murder, which Jerome cites from the Hebrew Gospel, is mentioned in Mark 15:7 and Luke 23:19, but not in Matthew. This is a further instance of a citation from the Hebrew Gospel lacking correspondence with Matthew but demonstrating correspondence with Luke (and in this instance also with

---

121. R. Handmann, *Das Hebräer-Evangelium,* 99-101.

122. E. B. Nicholson, *The Gospel According to the Hebrews,* 59; again, "The Nazarene Gospel keeps what must almost certainly have been the original reading" (97). This conjecture is further supported by the omission of υἱοῦ Βαραχίου in Sinaiticus.

123. Iste in evangelio quod scribitur iuxta Hebraeos filius magistri eorum interpretatur qui propter seditionem et homicidium fuerat condemnatus (*Comm. Matt.* 27.16).

Mark). Barabbas (בר אבא) is an Aramaic name meaning "son of the father," whereas "son of their teacher" would be בר רבן. The derivation of "son of their teacher" from "son of the father" could perhaps be explained by the fact that "father" is not infrequently used metonymically of priests, prophets, and teachers. In the NT (e.g., Matt 23:8-10) and early church words such as "abba," "abunah," "pater," "father" (e.g., "church fathers") became honorable forms of address for teachers, mentors, and doctors of learning. On lexical grounds "son of their teacher" can thus be related to "father," but that seems unlikely in Jerome's quotation because the expression is obviously not used honorifically. Rather, Jerome draws a causal inference between the name and Barabbas's *crime:* He was called "son of their teacher . . . *because* he had been condemned for sedition and murder." If there is a relationship with "father" it would appear to be a negative metonym in his instance, as it is in John 8:44 ("your father the devil"). The name of Barabbas in the Hebrew Gospel would appear to be a wordplay on the Aramaic homophone "Bar-Rabban"; that is, as a revolutionary and murderer, Barabbas was but a child of his Jewish teachers.

Matthew 27:51 Finally, in three instances Jerome preserves evidence of a tradition in the early church of the breaking of the Temple *lintel* rather than the tearing of the Temple curtain at the crucifixion of Jesus (Matt 27:51; Mark 15:38; Luke 23:45). "In the Gospel we often mention we read that the immense temple lintel fell and broke to pieces.'"[124] Again, "In the Gospel, however, which is composed in Hebrew, we read not that the Temple curtain was torn but that the Temple lintel of wondrous size fell."[125] A late Latin text (fourteenth century) cites Jerome's text and attributes it to the *Gospel of the Nazarenes:* "In like manner, the Gospel of the Nazarenes says that at the death of Christ the Temple lintel of great size was broken."[126] The last text identifies the source of the tradition as "the Gospel of the Nazarenes," but references in the first text to "the Gospel we often

---

124. In evangelio cuius saepe facimus mentionem superliminare templi infinitae magnitudinis fractum esse atque divisum legimus (*Comm. Matt.* 27:51).

125. In evangelio autem, quod Hebraicis litteris scriptum est, legimus non velum templi scissum, sed superliminare templi mirae magnitudinis conruisse (*Epist.* 120.8.2, *Ad Hedybiam*).

126. Item in ewangelio Nazareorum legitur superliminare templi infinite magnitudinis in morte Christi scissum (*Hist. pass. Dom.* f.65; cited from *Synopsis Quattuor Evangeliorum*[5], 489).

mention," and in the second to "the Gospel composed in Hebrew" relate the breaking of the temple lintel tradition implicitly to the Hebrew Gospel. I shall argue in Chapter Three that "the Gospel of the Nazarenes" is an ellipsis for "the [Hebrew] Gospel that is used by the Nazarenes," and thus identical with the Hebrew Gospel.

Attempts to harmonize the account in the canonical Gospels of the tearing of the Temple curtain with the account in the Hebrew Gospel of the breaking of the Temple lintel — perhaps by a confusion of two similar Hebrew words — are unsuccessful.[127] The mention of the earthquake in Matt 27:51 is noteworthy, however, for an earthquake is more likely to dislodge a stone lintel than to tear a curtain. On this basis, R. Handmann argues that the fallen lintel of the Hebrew Gospel is probably earlier and older than the image of the torn curtain in the canonical Gospels.[128] Jerome refrains from any attempt to harmonize or explain the two different traditions. Rather, in each citation he mentions an apocalyptic vision, related by Josephus, that prior to the destruction of the Temple by Titus heavenly powers hovered over the Temple and warned, "Leave this place."[129] The portents attending the destruction of the Temple by Titus were perhaps regarded by Jerome as fulfillments of the shaking of the foundations of the Temple in Isa 6:4.[130] Evidence for this conclusion can be found in his letter to Pope Damasus, written earlier in 378-80, where, commenting on Isa 6:1-8, Jerome wrote that "the removal of the lintel and filling of the Temple with smoke were signs of the razing of the Jewish Temple and incineration of all Jerusalem."[131] Jerome thus evidently cites the tradition of the collapse of the Temple lintel not as a rival tradition to the tearing of the Temple curtain, but simply as a supplementary attestation to the destruction of the Temple. At the death of Jesus, in other words, not only the Temple curtain but the whole *portal* was destroyed. The fall of the lintel and tearing of the Temple curtain thus signify the total destruction of the Temple. The citation of this incident indicates, as Lührmann rightly observes, that the Hebrew Gospel was not a collection of eclectic

---

127. See C. Schneider, καταπέτασμα, *TDNT* 3.630.

128. So R. Handmann, *Das Hebräer-Evangelium*, 76-77.

129. *J.W.* 6.290. In *J.W.* 6.288-315 Josephus recounts numerous marvelous omens that predicted the fall of the Temple, but none of a collapsed lintel.

130. So A. F. J. Klijn, "Jérome, Isaie 6 et l'Évangile de Nazoréens," *VC* 40 (1986), 245-50.

131. Quod autem sublatum est superliminare et domus inpleta est fumo, signum est temple Iudaici destruendi et incendii universae Hierusalem (*Epist.* 18.9 *ad Damasum*).

episodes or sayings, but rather a complete Gospel with a passion narrative included.[132] For Jerome, the overriding purpose of the various Temple calamities is to cause salvation to be brought to the Gentiles, as he says in his commentary on Matt 27:51, "so that all the deposits of the law might be delivered from their confinement and go forth to the Gentiles."

Commentary on Isaiah 11:1-2 (410)

In his commentary on Isa 11:1-2, Jerome twice mentions the Hebrew Gospel. He begins the exposition with a play on words: the "root" *(virga)* of Jesse is in truth the holy virgin *(virginem)* Mary; and the flower of the root is our Lord and Savior Jesus Christ. Jerome cites no fewer than sixteen biblical references in his two-page commentary on this passage.[133] The only noncanonical text cited — and cited twice — is from the Gospel of the Hebrews. The text reads *in toto:*

> But according to the Gospel that is written in the Hebrew language, the Nazarenes read: "the whole fountain of the Holy Spirit will descend on him." . . . Further, in the Gospel that we mentioned above, we find these words written: "It happened that when the Lord came up out of the water, the whole fountain of the Holy Spirit descended on him, and rested on him, and said to him, 'My Son, in all the prophets I awaited you, that you might come and that I might rest in you. For you are my rest, you are my firstborn Son, who reigns eternally.'"[134]

132. D. Lührmann, *Die apokryph gewordenen Evangelien,* 242.

133. Psalms (2x), Proverbs, Canticles, Isaiah, Zechariah, Malachi, Matthew (2x), John (2x), Romans, Colossians, 1 Corinthians, 2 Corinthians, 1 John.

134. Sed iuxta evangelium quod Hebraeo sermone conscriptum legunt Nazaraei: "Descendet super eum omnis fons Spiritus sancti." . . . Porro in evangelio, cuius supra fecimus mentionem, haec scripta reperimus: "Factum est autem cum ascendisset Dominus de aqua, descendit fons omnis Spiritus sancti, et requievit super eum, et dixit illi: 'Fili mi, in omnibus prophetis exspectabam te, ut venires, et requiescerem in te. Tu es enim requies mea, tu es filius meus primogenitus, qui regnas in sempiternum'" (*Comm. Isa.* 11:1-3). Contra J. K. Elliott, *The Apocryphal New Testament,* 10, and *Synopsis Quattuor Evangeliorum* 27, I take the words following "Spiritus sancti" (Dominus autem spiritus est, et ubi spiritus Domini, ibi libertas = "The Lord is the Spirit, and where the Spirit of the Lord is, there is liberty") to be a quotation of 2 Cor 3:17 and not part of the quotation from the Hebrew Gospel. Harnack, *Geschichte der altchristlichen Literatur bis Eusebius²,* 9, rightly omits the phrase.

According to Jerome the baptism of Jesus fulfilled Isa 11:2, and he appeals to the Hebrew Gospel to verify his understanding. The reference to the ascent out of the water corresponds to Matt 3:16 and Mark 1:10. But several details recall the Gospel of Luke, including "in all the prophets" (Luke 24:27); *factum est,* which reproduces the Semitism καὶ ἐγένετο (Hebrew ויהי) so prevalent in Luke; *filius primogenitus,* which likewise reproduces the Hebrew יחיד; and the reference to Jesus' eternal reign, which is mentioned in the Gospels only in Luke 1:33. The reference to Jesus as "Lord" may also recall Luke, who refers to Jesus as Lord more frequently than do the other Gospels. As in Luke (and Mark), the baptismal declaration is addressed to Jesus rather than to the bystanders.[135] The baptismal declaration as a first person testimony of the Holy Spirit recalls John 1:32-33, as does the statement of the Spirit resting on Jesus. The reference to "my firstborn Son" corresponds only with Exod 4:22. This citation from the Hebrew Gospel, in other words, does not correspond particularly closely with any one canonical Gospel narrative, but contains elements found in all of them — and in none of them. "The whole fountain of the Holy Spirit descending on Jesus," for instance, is not present in the Gospels, although it was characteristic of Judaism and early Christianity in general.[136] The Hebrew Gospel thus preserved a fuller baptismal narrative than any found in the four Gospels, but it was not a compilation of them. In the OT echoes and imagery in the Hebrew Gospel Handmann detects evidence of a very early baptismal account.[137] Overall, the narrative quoted by Jerome seems to combine the theology of John's baptismal narrative (1:32-33) with the language of Isa 11:1-2. With good reason Jerome cited the Hebrew Gospel in relation to Isa 11:1-2, for its version of the baptism is a veritable consummation of the prophetic text.

Commentary on Ezekiel (411-14)

In Jerome's *Commentary on Ezekiel* a passage from the Hebrew Gospel is cited with reference to the injunction in Ezek 18:7 not to wrong anyone. "In

135. Also noted in O. Holtzmann, *The Life of Jesus,* 47.

136. A. F. J. Klijn, *Jewish-Christian Gospel Tradition,* 99-100, cites Ps 36:10; Jer 2:13; 17:13; Rev 21:6; *2 Bar.* 3:12, and passages in Justin Martyr and Tertullian.

137. R. Handmann, *Das Hebräer-Evangelium,* 68-69: "Diese Taufgeschichte . . . steht aber den alttestamentlichen Vorstellungen viel näher . . . und trägt desshalb auch einen alterthümlicheren Charakter zur Schau. . . . Die Taufe Christi ist also im H.E. mit der ächt jüdischen Anschauung der Messiasweihe verbunden."

the Gospel according to the Hebrews that is common to the Nazarenes, among the greatest of wrongs is 'to grieve the spirit of one's brother.'"[138] The Latin word for "wrong," *contristare*, means "sadden" or "make sorrowful." Jerome's comment on Ezek 18:7 consists of a catena of prooftexts on *contristare*, including Eph 4:30, "Do not grieve [Latin *contristare*] the Holy Spirit of God," who "dwells in you" (Rom 8:9, 11; 1 Cor 3:16). He concludes by quoting the above passage from the Hebrew Gospel, which in the Latin translation again employs *contristare*. One wonders whether Jerome recalled the various uses of *contristare* from memory or utilized some form of concordance. If the former, this would attest to a prodigious recall of biblical terminology. Either way, the Hebrew Gospel was included in the retrieval system along with Scripture. The inclusion of the Hebrew Gospel — the only non-canonical text in his pool of sources — attests to its status not only in Jerome's estimation but also among his readership.

The reference in the Hebrew Gospel to the greatest of wrongs being a violation of one's brother must be related to Luke 17:1-2. There Jesus says that sin is inevitable, but that violations of one's brother must be avoided at all costs. Indeed, he warns, it would be better to be thrown into the sea with a millstone around one's neck than to cause "your brother" to stumble. The Luke 17 passage picks up the two foci of the Hebrew Gospel cited by Jerome — the gravest of wrongs, and grievance against a brother. Luke 17:1-2 is immediately followed in vv. 3-4 with a statement about rebuking and then forgiving a sinful brother. In Jerome's final quotation of the Hebrew Gospel in *Against the Pelagians* 3.2, we shall see a saying about forgiving a sinful brother seventy times seven. The passage on the gravity of sinning against a brother that Jerome here cites from the Hebrew Gospel must have immediately preceded the one cited in *Against the Pelagians*. Those two passages evidently formed a unit in the Hebrew Gospel, just as they do in Luke 17:1-4.[139]

Clement of Alexandria also cites a text about sin that repeats the

138. Et in evangelio quod iuxta Hebraeos Nazaraei legere consuerunt, inter maxima ponitur crimina: "qui fratris sui spiritum contristaverit" (*Comm. Ezech.* 18:7).

139. R. Handmann, *Das Hebräer-Evangelium*, 87, correctly notes the Lukan preservation of the originality of the Hebrew Gospel and the Matthean mutilation of it: "Die Ursprünglichkeit [der Lesung liegt] auf Seiten des H.E., wie uns auch Luc. 17,4 den Ausspruch Jesus vom siebenmaligen Vergeben an einem Tage richtig erhalten hat, freilich zusammengearbeitet mit anderen Sprüchen, wesshalb bei ihm der Dialog ganz weggefallen ist, während er bei Mtth. verstümmelt erscheint."

theme of the responsibility of the elect to be examples of virtue rather than stones of stumbling.

> For they say in the Traditions that Matthew the Apostle repeatedly said, "If the neighbor of an elect individual sins, the elect has sinned; for if [the elect] had conducted himself as the Word dictates, the neighbor would have venerated his life and not sinned."[140]

This passage may possibly derive in some form from the Hebrew Gospel, for elements of it correspond with the Third Gospel, as do elements of the Hebrew Gospel. Γείτων, ἁμαρτάνω, and βίος are all either unique or strongly characteristic of Luke; and ἐκλεκτός is used in Luke 18:7 much as it is in Clement's quotation. Nevertheless, in its present form it cannot be equated with the Hebrew Gospel, for Clement applies the saying to the Gnostics, whom he vigorously opposed. In *Stromata* 6.6.53 Clement uses the same word for "elect" (ἐκλεκτός) of the Gnostic Basilides, who was unanimously condemned by the church fathers.[141] Moreover, in *Stromata* 2.9.45 Clement expressly differentiates the Hebrew Gospel from "The Traditions of Matthew," which, as we shall see in the next chapter, was placed on an index of proscribed books throughout the patristic period. Thus, whatever the origin of the material in Clement's quotation, in its present form it cannot be considered part of the Hebrew Gospel.

Dialogue against the Pelagians 3.2 (416)

Jerome's *Dialogue against the Pelagians* 3.2 has just been mentioned, as well as in Chapter One.[142] The text quoted and discussed in Chapter One reads:

> In the Gospel according to the Hebrews, which is written in the Chaldean and Syrian language, but in Hebrew characters, and which is used

140. λέγουσι δὲ ἐν ταῖς παραδόσεσι Ματθίαν τὸν ἀπόστολον παρ' ἕκαστα εἰρηκέναι ὅτι ἐὰν ἐκλεκτοῦ γείτων ἁμαρτήσῃ, ἥμαρτεν ὁ ἐκλεκτός· εἰ γὰρ οὕτως ἑαυτὸν ἧγεν, ὡς ὁ λόγος ὑπαγορεύει, κατηδέσθη ἂν αὐτοῦ τὸν βίον καὶ ὁ γείτων εἰς τὸ μὴ ἁμαρτεῖν (*Strom.* 7.13).

141. Eusebius, *Hist. eccl.* 4.7.7; Irenaeus, *Haer.* 1.24.5; Clement of Alexandria, *Strom.* 3.1.1-4; Epiphanius, *Pan.* 24.3.7. For a further discussion of Clement's citation, see H.-C. Puech and B. Blatz, *New Testament Apocrypha*, 1.384.

142. Chapter 1, pp. 16, 32, 41.

to this day by the Nazarenes — [the Gospel] according to the Apostles, or, as many allege, [the Gospel] according to Matthew — which also is found in the library in Caesarea.[143]

In addition to this reference, Jerome immediately appends the following two citations from the Hebrew Gospel:

And behold, the mother of the Lord and his brothers were saying to him, "John the Baptist baptizes for the remission of sins; let us go and be baptized with him." He [Jesus] said to them, "What sin have I committed that I should go and be baptized by him? Unless in saying this I am in ignorance."[144] And in the same volume, he [Jesus] said: "If your brother would sin in word and would make restitution to you seven times in one day, receive him." His disciple Simon said to him, "Seven times in one day?" The Lord responded and said to him, "Even, I say to you, as many as seventy times seven. For even in the prophets this word about sin was found after they were anointed by the Holy Spirit."[145]

This quotation contains two sin texts from the Hebrew Gospel, the first from the baptism of Jesus and the second similar to the saying on forgiveness in Matt 18:21-22 and Luke 17:3-4. On a superficial level, both citations stand in closer relation to Matthew than to the other Gospels. "What sin have I committed that I should go and be baptized by him?" recalls Matt 3:15. But in Matthew's baptismal account, Jesus' self-presentation for baptism raises doubts in the Baptist, who attempts to dissuade Jesus from being baptized. In the Hebrew Gospel, however, the prospect of baptism pro-

---

143. In Euangelio iuxta Hebraeos, quod Chaldaico quidem Syroque sermone, sed Hebraicis litteris scriptum est, quo utuntur usque hodie Nazareni, secundum apostolos, sive, ut plerique autumant, iuxta Matthaeum, quod et in Caesariensi habetur bibliotheca (*Pelag.* 3.2).

144. This statement could also perhaps be translated: "Unless perhaps I said something in ignorance."

145. Et ecce mater Domini et fratres eius dicebant ei: "Iohannes Baptista baptizat in remissionem peccatorum; eamus et baptizemur ab eo." Dixit autem eis: "Quid peccavi, ut vadam et baptizer ab eo? Nisi forte hoc ipsum quod dixi, ignorantia est." Et in eodem volumine: "Si peccaverit," inquit, "frater tuus in verbo et satis tibi fecerit, septies in die suscipe eum." Dixit illi Simon discipulus eius: "Septies in die?" Respondit Dominus, et dixit ei: "Etiam, ego dico tibi, usque septuagies septies. Etenim in Prophetis quoque, postquam uncti sunt Spiritu sancto, inventus est sermo peccati" (*Pelag.* 3.2).

vokes a self-justifying defense on Jesus' part.[146] The two sayings are thus thematically related but different in content.

The saying on the forgiveness of sins depends on Lev 26:18-28, in which the Israelites are instructed on a sevenfold chastisement for their sins. In the Hebrew Gospel, however, as well as in Matthew and Luke, the sevenfold is applied not to chastisement but to forgiveness. The saying on unlimited forgiveness at first appears to be closer to Matt 18:21-22 than to its counterpart in Luke 17:3-4. The similarity to Matthew's version is suggested by the memorable refrain to forgive a brother "seventy times seven." But closer examination reveals a number of discrepancies from the Vulgate of Matthew. In the Hebrew Gospel it is Jesus who poses the question, whereas in Matthew, Peter poses the question. In the Hebrew Gospel the chief apostle is called "Simon," but he is "Peter" in Matthew. The Hebrew Gospel limits the sin to one of word only *(in verbo)*. In Matthew (and Luke) the word for "forgiveness" is *dimitto,* whereas in the Hebrew Gospel it is *suscipio*. Finally, the summary sentence about the prophets in the Hebrew Gospel is lacking in the NT. As in the preceding baptismal text, the account of the forgiveness of the sinful brother shares a thematic relationship to Matthew and Luke, but there are noticeable differences in details with the canonical Gospels.

Nevertheless, Jerome's citation of the Hebrew Gospel reveals several remarkable agreements with Luke 17:3-4. First, "remission of sins" is distinctively Lukan.[147] Further, in both the Hebrew Gospel and Luke 17:3-4 the initial question is put by Jesus — and in the same verb tense. The Vulgate translation of Luke and Jerome's Latin citation of the Hebrew Gospel also preserve two three-word sequences verbatim.[148] Moreover, the idea of sinning "in word" in Jerome's quotation seems curiously restrictive. One is tempted to see behind *verbo* the Hebrew דבר, which would result in the more plausible rendering, "If your brother would sin in any *thing*. . . ." Luke's vocabulary and syntax (ἐὰν ἁμάρτῃ ὁ ἀδελφός σου) allow for this

---

146. R. Dunkerley, "The Gospel According to the Hebrews," 442, appeals for the antiquity and veracity of this saying in the Hebrew Gospel. "The words of Jesus here appear to suit exactly what we may feel was His spiritual condition at this time. The canonical story of the baptism probably represents something of His own thought upon that matter, and it evidently indicates that it was not until then that He fully realized His Divine commission."

147. The phrase occurs once in Matt 26:28, twice in Mark 1:4 and 3:29, but thrice in Luke 1:77; 3:3; 24:47 and five times in Acts 2:38; 5:31; 10:43; 13:38; 26:18.

148. "peccaverit frater tuus"; "septies in die."

phrase, but Matthew's does not. The same point should be made about the final use of *sermo;* if it renders דבר, the preferable translation "any manner of sin was found" results. Finally, Luke alone of the Evangelists refers to the anointing of the Holy Spirit, in particular, "God anointed him with the Holy Spirit" (Acts 10:38; also Luke 4:18; Acts 4:27). Thus, although Luke's version of the saying on forgiveness is shorter than Matthew's, it agrees in important details more closely with the form of the saying cited by Jerome from the Hebrew Gospel. Perhaps more important than the particulars themselves is the fact that the commonalities between Luke and the Hebrew Gospel are *incidental.* That is, they are not the kind of anchor data that would be consciously remembered. This agreement of incidental particulars would seem to heighten the likelihood of a literary relationship between the Hebrew Gospel and Luke. Once again, a correspondence between the Hebrew Gospel and Luke seems likely, even if in this instance it is not certain.

CHAPTER THREE

Taking Stock of the Hebrew Gospel
in the Early Church

Chapters One and Two present all known references to and quotations from the Hebrew Gospel in the first nine centuries of the Christian era.[1] The data surveyed are profuse and diverse. For the sake of clarity and convenience, Appendix I provides a chronological inventory of the most important patristic data related to the Hebrew Gospel — including author and source, citation in its original language, English translation, and pages where each reference is discussed. Before proceeding with the investigation of the relationship of the Hebrew Gospel to the Gospel of Luke in the next chapter, it will be helpful to summarize the mass of detail in the first two chapters related to the Hebrew Gospel. But before the material witness *of* the Hebrew Gospel can be properly assessed, the preliminary question of the reliability of the patristic testimony *to* the Hebrew Gospel must be raised. Not infrequently the previous two chapters have mentioned modern challenges to patristic testimony to the Hebrew Gospel, particularly that of Jerome and Epiphanius. I have endeavored to address those challenges case by case, but it is important also to address the larger issue of the trustworthiness of patristic evidence in general, for patristic testimony is a factor of some importance in properly weighing the major conclusions of this chapter.

There is a long-standing bias among many scholars — and particularly German scholars — that the handling of the traditions related to the formation of the gospel tradition in the church fathers was uncritical. Conse-

---

1. With the exception of *Šabb.* 116, which is discussed in Chapter Seven.

quently, patristic evidence has often been ignored in investigations of the origins of the Synoptic tradition. Even when patristic evidence is admitted, it is not infrequently subjected, especially in the cases of Epiphanius and Jerome, to intense suspicion. As a result, consideration of the Synoptic Gospels is often limited primarily or even exclusively to literary data and internal evidence among the first three Gospels. The working hypothesis of much modern scholarship is that an erroneous judgment about the existence of an original Hebrew Gospel entered the bloodstream of the church as early as Papias and that veneration for ancient testimony caused the error to be transmitted and elaborated rather than rectified and uprooted.[2] This suspicion has resulted in the denigration of patristic evidence related to the formation of the gospel tradition and in an increased ignorance of that evidence. It is, of course, true that the fathers were *pre*-critical in the modern sense of that term, but were they *un*critical?

The formation of the gospel tradition comprises a major theme in the church fathers. It would, in fact, be difficult to overemphasize its significance in patristic literature. It is highly doubtful that a proper understanding of the Synoptic tradition, and perhaps even a resolution to its formation, can be achieved by either denigrating or ignoring patristic testimony, for the fathers devoted their consideration to the problem from a historical and cultural proximity much closer than ours. They were not, of course, post-Enlightenment critics, but they not uncritical of Christian origins. The Eusebian Canons, a tenfold system of tables showing parallels (or similarities) among the four Gospels, are the most distinguished example of comparative analysis of the Gospels in the early church. The Canons, which derived from the pioneering work of Ammonius Saccas (175-242), evince not only an awareness as early as the second century of the "problem" of a fourfold gospel tradition, but also a degree of precision in the analysis of that tradition that remains useful even today.

Nor were the fathers oblivious to questions that exercise modern critical scholars. For example, both Origen and Jerome were aware of the discrepancy in style between the book of Hebrews and the undisputed Pauline epistles. On the basis of similarities between Hebrews and *1 Clement*,

---

2. For a further elaboration of this idea, see A. F. Findlay, *Byways in Early Christian Literature*, 311 n. 51. Findlay argues that A. Schmidtke greatly influenced this idea by his argument that canonical Matthew was early translated into Aramaic. This version won the reputation of originality, especially by Papias, who subsequently injected it into the bloodstream of early Christianity.

both fathers entertained the possibility that Clement of Rome (or perhaps Luke, in Origen's case) played some role in the authorship of Hebrews.[3] Again, Eusebius's long discussion with Dionysius of Alexandria regarding whether John the son of Zebedee was the author of the book of Revelation is remarkably nuanced,[4] as is Augustine's discussion of the ages of people recorded in the primeval history of Genesis 1–11.[5] Epiphanius, often regarded as one of the least critical of the fathers, is also aware of challenges to the Johannine authorship of Revelation — and (like Eusebius) he sides with those who deny it.[6] An observation made in Chapter One provides explicit evidence for such critical awareness. The fact that Eusebius could disparage the intelligence of Papias and at the same time accept his testimony to a Hebrew Gospel composed by the apostle Matthew shows an ability on Eusebius's part to distinguish between the tradition relayed by Papias and Eusebius's personal estimation of him.[7]

It is especially necessary to say something about Jerome, whose historical trustworthiness has been vehemently contested.[8] Jerome's besetting sin, according to his detractors, is of claiming knowledge of texts with which he had no contact, and of claiming to have translated works that he did not translate. It is not necessary to defend Jerome's character with the same degree of passion with which his accusers revile him. It is important to remember, however, that Jerome, alone of western fathers, was in a unique position to make the claims that he did. As a young man he traveled to the East and, from 374 to 379, lived a semi-ascetic life in Chalcis in northern Syria. There he learned Hebrew from a Jewish

---

3. Eusebius, *Hist. eccl.* 6.25.11-14; Jerome, *Vir. ill.* 1.3; 5.10; 15.2.

4. *Hist. eccl.* 7.25.1-26.

5. *Civ.* 15.12-13.

6. *Pan.* 51.3.1-5; for Eusebius's judgment, see *Hist. eccl.* 3.39.6.

7. *Hist. eccl.* 3.39.13, 16. Hengel, *The Four Gospels and the One Gospel of Jesus Christ*, 76, argues that Eusebius "wrongly called Papias 'very weak-minded'" because, as a follower of Origen, Eusebius rejected Papias's millenarian convictions. Eusebius's criticism of Papias is in fact balanced by a further testimony that the latter did not accept everything he heard at face value, but weighed the truth of the testimony (*Hist. eccl.* 3.39.2-3).

8. A. Schmidtke's vilification in "Neue Fragmente und Untersuchungen zu den judenchristlichen Evangelien," 66-67, n. 1, is utterly uncontrolled: "[Jerome] was one of the most shameless and deceitful liars and exploiters that there ever was. There was no book that he had not read, offered expert opinion on, and quoted; no profound thought that he had not brought forth; no unusual inquiry that he had not pursued. He even wrote of the knowledge of texts that never existed."

Christian[9] and came into close contact with Jewish Christian sects and the books they read.[10] Jerome was a prodigious reader, transporting small libraries with him on his journeys. Like Origen, he employed scribes — often many at a time — to read, transcribe, and take dictation. He spent the last thirty-four years of his life in Bethlehem, where he became intimately acquainted with the beginnings of eastern monasticism. For decades he furthered his knowledge of Jewish Christian sects and texts in the great library of Caesarea, whose librarian, Pamphilus, he held in deep affection.[11] He was thus one of the few western fathers who was in a position to gain firsthand knowledge of such matters over an extended period of time.[12]

Anyone who thumbs through *Illustrious Men* will find that some 800 texts are *named* by Jerome. We cannot say for certain how many of these he had actually seen and read — nor does he claim to have read them all. But he must have read the majority of them because his descriptions correspond favorably with those of Eusebius, for example, who names many of the same texts. Moreover, Jerome is candid about works he has not seen or read, such as those of Triphylius, Phoebadius, or Dexter.[13] He also admits to not knowing Syriac and hence of having to read Bardesanes, Archelaus of Mesopotamia, and Ephrem the Syrian only in translation.[14] These disclosures make it reasonable to assume that Jerome had a working knowledge, at the very least, of the texts he names. He dedicated his life to the gathering of texts, and his bibliographies in *Illustrious Men,* for example, do not tax my credibility any more than do lengthy bibliographies of modern scholars. In my judgment, his honesty in admitting what he had *not* read enhances the credibility of his claims.

Jerome's abilities as a translator were both unrivaled and undisputed in the ancient world. As far as we know, no other father was capable of translating the Hebrew OT and the Greek NT into Latin. Given his facility with Hebrew, Greek, and Latin, there is nothing preposterous in his claim

---

9. *Epist.* 125.8, *ad Rustic.*

10. *Comm. Matt.* 27.9.

11. The writings of Pamphilus were embraced by Jerome "with such joy that I believe I am in possession of the riches of Croesus" (*Vir. ill.* 75.2).

12. See H. Waitz, "Neue Untersuchungen über die sogen. judenchristlichen Evangelien," 63-64. So too A. F. Findlay, *Byways in Early Christian Literature,* 52.

13. *Vir. ill.* 92.1; 108.1; and 132.1 respectively.

14. *Epist.* 7.2; 17.2; *Vir. ill.* 115.2.

to have translated a particular book of Didymus the Blind, "On the Holy Spirit," into Latin,[15] or the Hebrew Gospel into both Greek and Latin. Jerome's various references and allusions to the Hebrew Gospel account for nearly one-third of all the references and allusions to the Hebrew Gospel in patristic literature. His many references occur in different forms of literature over several decades, and they are addressed to different audiences. The discrepancies in his various references and allusions are neither alarming nor particularly significant, especially given the fact that the Hebrew Gospel circulated under several names and perhaps even versions by Jerome's day. *Ad hominem* attacks on Jerome have the wearisome effect of obscuring the real issue at stake in this study, which is the Hebrew Gospel. Jerome's personal history certainly distinguished him to make the claims he did, and nothing in his various claims about the Hebrew Gospel seems to me either nefarious or implausible.[16]

Jerome was not a naive or gullible textual critic. He rejected the story of Paul and Thecla as "nonsense,"[17] as well as the detail in the *Epistle of Aristeas* that the seventy translators of the Hebrew Bible into Greek, separated in seventy cells, each produced identical translations — an account, incidentally, that his contemporary Augustine accepted.[18] Jerome rejected the *Acts of Peter* and the *Gospel of Peter* as apocryphal,[19] and on the basis of stylistic differences he questioned the authorship of the James,[20] 2 Peter,[21] 2 and 3 John,[22] and at least two books ascribed to Theophilus, bishop of Antioch.[23]

---

15. *Vir. ill.* 109.2.

16. T. C. G. Thornton, "Jerome and the 'Hebrew Gospel According to Matthew,'" in *Studia Patristica* 28 (Leuven: Peeters, 1993), 118-22, argues that in his later writings Jerome ceased referring to the Hebrew Gospel because he realized he had made a blunder in supposing it to be an Aramaic version of the original Gospel of Matthew. There does not seem to be a blunder — at least on Jerome's part. As late as 415, in his lengthy note on the Hebrew Gospel in *Against the Pelagians,* Jerome 1) names "the Gospel According to the Hebrews," 2) ascribes it to the apostolic tradition and the original Gospel of Matthew, and 3) locates it in the library of Caesarea. This reference to the Hebrew Gospel only four years before Jerome's death is a rather robust refutation of Thornton's thesis.

17. "fabulam inter apocryphas scripturas" (*Vir. ill.* 7).

18. PL 28.150A; for Augustine's acceptance of the legend, see *Civ.* 18.42-43.

19. *Vir. ill.* 1.5.

20. *Vir. ill.* 2.2.

21. *Vir. ill.* 1.3.

22. *Vir. ill.* 18.3.

23. *Vir. ill.* 25.3.

These judgments are not uncritical or "unmodern." They anticipate critical contemporary scholarly judgments — and they could be multiplied by others in patristic literature. The fathers were as a rule not uncritical vis-à-vis the traditions they inherited. More to the point, their estimation of the Hebrew Gospel is far less ambivalent and skeptical than their estimation of the authorship of the book of Hebrews, for example, or of the book of Revelation or of the authenticity of the *Acts of Paul and Thecla*. The extensive, diverse, and until relatively modern times *unchallenged* testimony of the early church to an original Hebrew Gospel composed by Matthew argues in favor of a rehabilitation of that witness.

1. The Hebrew Gospel Was Widespread and Widely Known in Early Christianity

The widespread and enduring testimony in early Christianity to a Hebrew Gospel is the single most important conclusion of the first two chapters.[24] The evidence is more considerable than even specialists in the field often imagine. The tradition of an original Gospel written in Hebrew is attested by twenty church fathers — Ignatius, Papias, Irenaeus, Clement of Alexandria, Pantaenus, Hegesippus, Hippolytus,[25] Origen, Eusebius of Caesarea, Ephrem of Syria, Didymus of Alexandria, Epiphanius, John Chrysostom, Jerome, Theodoret, Marius Mercator, Philip Sidetes, the Venerable Bede, Nicephorus, and Sedulius Scottus. When references to the Hebrew Gospel by Pope Damasus, the Islamic Hadith, the scholia of Sinaiticus, and tractate *Šabbat* 116 in the Babylonian Talmud (see Chapter Seven) are added to this number, the list lengthens to over two dozen different witnesses. It is highly probable, moreover, that the scholia in Codex Sinaiticus derive from several sources rather than a single source. The Hebrew Gospel is therefore identified by name in at least two dozen patristic sources. Each

---

24. Contra A. Resch, *Agrapha. Aussercanonische Evangelienfragmente,* 324-26, who says the evidence for the Hebrew Gospel is "verhältnissmässig späte Ausbildung und eng begrenzte Verbreitung." M. Hengel, *The Four Gospels and the One Gospel of Jesus Christ,* 73, correctly declares that "The trace of a Jewish-Christian Gospel (or even several) in Aramaic (and afterwards in Greek) runs through the whole of the early church, beginning with Papias. . . ."

25. The authenticity of the Hippolytus reference is probable, but not certain; see Chapter One, pages 16-17.

source mentions it at least once, and most mention it several times. Jerome references the Hebrew Gospel twenty-two times. Combined, there are some seventy-five different attestations to the Hebrew Gospel, extending from the late first century to the early tenth century. Several of these references appear in Latin authors of late antiquity and the early Middle Ages, and this is significant, for "the period from roughly 550 to 750 was one of almost unrelieved gloom for the Latin classics on the continent; they virtually ceased being copied."[26] It is true that patristic and ecclesiastical texts fared better during this wintry interlude than did the Latin classics. Nevertheless, repeated references to the Hebrew Gospel from Latin authors of the period attest to the depth of its roots in ancient church tradition.

Specific witnesses to the Hebrew Gospel come from Lyons, Rome, Constantinople, Jerusalem, and Alexandria and as far east as India. Those points are roughly coextensive with the Roman Empire in the same centuries, with the exception of India, which was well beyond its eastern frontier. Twelve fathers attribute the Hebrew Gospel to the apostle Matthew, and eleven specify that it was written in Hebrew. No other noncanonical document occupied the "disputed" category in canonical deliberations in the early church as long and consistently as did the Hebrew Gospel. To my knowledge no other noncanonical text was cited as frequently and positively alongside canonical texts in early Christian exegesis. More important, witnesses to the Hebrew Gospel are as ancient as patristic witnesses to any of the four canonical Gospels.[27] The Hebrew Gospel was the most highly esteemed noncanonical document in the early church.[28]

26. L. D. Reynolds and N. G. Wilson, *Scribes and Scholars: A Guide to the Transmission of Greek and Latin Literature*[3] (Oxford: Clarendon, 1991), 85.

27. E. B. Nicholson, *The Gospel According to the Hebrews*, 110: "The reader who has not studied the history of the Canon will nevertheless assume that far more ancient witness can be brought for the authority and authorship of the canonical Gospels than for the authority and authorship of the Gospel according to the Hebrews. He will make a great mistake." Nicholson demonstrates that the second-century witness of Irenaeus, Hegesippus, and Papias to the Hebrew Gospel is not inferior, but in some cases superior, to testimony to the four canonical Gospels of the same period.

28. P. Parker, "A Proto-Lucan Basis for the Gospel According to the Hebrews," 471: "the Gospel according to the Hebrews was by far the most important aside from the canonical four"; E. Gla, *Die Originalsprache des Matthäusevangeliums*, 109: "Kein Apocryphum genoss in der Kirche solches Ansehen, wie die Hebräerurkunde"; E. B. Nicholson, *The Gospel According to the Hebrews*, 82: "The Fathers of the Church, while the Gospel according to the Hebrews was yet extant in its entirety, referred to it always with respect, often with rever-

Given the reputation of the Hebrew Gospel in the early church, why was it not canonized? No extant list of canonical works by any church father lists the Hebrew Gospel as canonical, and as far as we know no father attempted to argue for its inclusion in such a list. Why? An answer to this question must remain tentative, for the canonical classifications of Origen and Eusebius do not explain why given documents were placed in the accepted, disputed, and rejected categories. Rather, Origen and Eusebius simply report which documents the churches on the Mediterranean rim assigned to which categories, evidently confident that their assignment to such categories was sufficient indication of the will of the Holy Spirit operative through the various churches and over long periods of time. Throughout this process, the Hebrew Gospel was never accorded canonical status, although no church father, with the single exception of Philip Sidetes, who writes late and with only a marginal knowledge of the Hebrew Gospel, rejected it as heretical.[29]

The Hebrew Gospel occupied a unique status in the first Christian millennium, enjoying wide vestigial authority, but not canonicity. Its non-canonical status was almost certainly not the result of incompleteness. A fragmentary nature would surely have drawn comment from one or more fathers, none of whom notes such a defect. Epiphanius notes its "mutilation" by the Ebionites, but that was the result of additions or alterations rather than deficiencies.[30] The Hebrew Gospel comprised 2200 lines, according to Nicephorus, which would make it only slightly shorter than canonical Matthew.[31] It might be supposed that a Gospel in Hebrew would possess only "local" appeal and fail to achieve canonicity for want of ecumenical appeal. In the case of the Hebrew Gospel this, too, seems unlikely, for, as we have noted above, the Hebrew Gospel was widely known and valued throughout the broad geographical sweep of the early church for many centuries.

---

ence; some of them unhesitatingly accepted it as being what tradition affirmed it to be — the work of Matthew — and even those who have not put on record their expression of this opinion have not questioned it."

29. Addressing suspicions regarding either the existence or authority of the Hebrew Gospel, G. E. Lessing, *New Hypothesis on the Evangelists as Merely Human Historians* (§14), overstates the case only slightly in declaring, "Did any Church Father who mentions the gospel of the later Nazarenes ever express such a suspicion, or utter the least word to suggest it? — Never; not one of them."

30. Epiphanius, *Pan.* 30.13.2.

31. Nicephorus, *chron. Brev.*, Quae Scripturae Canonicae 2.a.

The one factor that did compromise the Hebrew Gospel in the eyes of the early church was its (often exclusive) use by Jewish Christian communities such as Ebionites, Nazarenes, and others. These groups were early and increasingly rejected by "normative" Gentile Christianity for their adherence to Jewish rites and customs, their rejection of the apostle Paul, their christological aberrations (primarily in denying the deity of Jesus and affirming adoptionism),[32] and for their resistance to integration into the larger Gentile church. Negative judgments of such groups cast an inevitable shadow on the Gospel used by them. Guilt by association was increased by claims of alterations of the text of that Gospel in accord with aberrant Jewish customs and theology, real or imagined. Among the known detriments of canonization — or reasonable inferences of such — the establishment of the Hebrew Gospel by Jewish Christians as a rival tradition to the emerging Greek canonical tradition of Matthew, Mark, Luke, and John certainly jeopardized the standing of the Hebrew Gospel in later Gentile Christianity, and almost certainly played a negative — and perhaps decisive — role in debarring it from inclusion in the NT canon.

2. The Hebrew Gospel Was Endowed with Unusual Authority in Early Christianity

The preeminence and pervasiveness of the Hebrew Gospel in the early church was due to a residual though unofficial authority with which it was endowed by early church testimony. No noncanonical text appears in patristic prooftexts as often and as favorably as does the Hebrew Gospel. The single most important evidence of this is that in their canonical deliberations both Origen and Eusebius place the Hebrew Gospel in a rare middle category of "disputed" works, along with the book of Revelation, James, 2 Peter, Jude, and 2-3 John. As late as the early ninth century Nicephorus continued to retain the Hebrew Gospel, along with the book of Revelation, the *Apocalypse of Peter,* and the *Epistle of Barnabas,* in the disputed category.[33] The placement of books into the recognized, disputed, and rejected

---

32. See the long list of patristic complaints against the Ebionites in n. 79 below.

33. *Chron. Brev.,* Quae Scripturae Canonicae 2.a. A later namesake of the above-mentioned Nicephorus, Nicephorus Callistus Xanthopulus, son of Michael Palaeologus and priest of Hagia Sophia, whose library he utilized, composed a *Historia ecclesiastica* in eigh-

categories was not due to the judgment of any single church father or even of a church council, but rather to the reception and use of a given document within confessing ecclesiastical communities. The various works, in other words, were declared either authentic or spurious on the basis of their homiletical, catechetical, and disciplinary usefulness in active churches. The placement of the Hebrew Gospel in the disputed category attests to the very considerable status that it possessed in widespread Christian communities over long periods of time.

Perhaps more important than the formal position of the Hebrew Gospel in the canonical taxonomy of the early church was its practical viability as an auxiliary resource in patristic hermeneutics. Clement's *Stromata* prefaces a quotation from the Hebrew Gospel with γέγραπται, "it is written," a *terminus technicus* for the written Word of God.[34] In seeking to demonstrate the superiority of the Christian revelation to Greek philosophy, Clement assigns greater authority to the Hebrew Gospel than to Plato![35] In his exegesis of Isa 11:1-2, Jerome quotes *sixteen* canonical texts; in the same exegesis there are only *two* noncanonical texts — and both come from the Hebrew Gospel. Origen, Didymus, and Jerome all appeal to the Hebrew Gospel to assert a proper interpretation (or correct a false interpretation) of sacred Scripture. They reference the Hebrew Gospel, in other words, as a *de facto* authority *over* Scripture.[36] Holtzmann overestimates the Hebrew Gospel when he says it "rank[ed] as equal to the Johannine Gospel in value," but he is nevertheless correct in acknowledging its functional (though unofficial) authority in early Christianity.[37] Findlay's assessment is closer to the mark when he observes that several fathers, Origen among them, felt compelled to show that their opinions did not conflict with the Hebrew Gospel.[38] That is a revealing observation, especially with regard to Origen, who in his *Homily on Luke* 1:1 declares that the church recognizes only four Gospels. Origen, in other words, espouses

---

teen volumes between 1332 and 1335, in which he too places *Barnabas,* the *Didache,* and the Hebrew Gospel in the disputed category (*Hist. eccl.* 2.46; PG 145.888).

34. *Strom.* 2.9.45.

35. *Strom.* 5.14.96.

36. G. E. Lessing, *New Hypothesis on the Evangelists as Merely Human Historians* (§16), speaks of the Fathers, and of Jerome in particular, using "various passages from it [the Hebrew Gospel] to elucidate the Greek text of the existing evangelists."

37. O. Holtzmann, *The Life of Jesus,* 46.

38. A. F. Findlay, *Byways in Early Christian Literature,* 50.

the Hebrew Gospel with the enthusiasm that he otherwise reserves for the four canonical Gospels.

3. The Hebrew Gospel Is Not a Compilation of the Synoptic Gospels, but Repeatedly and Distinctly Similar to Luke

Scholarly opinion has generally been — and continues to be — that the Hebrew Gospel is either an indiscriminate harmony of the Synoptics or derived from (usually a corruption of) canonical Greek Matthew.[39] The former judgment is the more common, and it may be helpful to rehearse the frequency and finality with which it continues to be held and expressed. W. L. Peterson says that the *Gospel of the Ebionites* "appears to have been harmonized, woven from traditions found in the Synoptic Gospels (Matthew, Mark, and Luke)."[40] Vielhauer and Strecker write that the "few fragments that have been preserved [of Gospel of the Hebrews] indicate no special relationship to one of the canonical Gospels, but contain syncretistic elements."[41] H. Koester believes that a harmony of the Gospels of Matthew and Luke "is not only in evidence in Justin and 2 Clement, but also in the *Gospel of the Ebionites*."[42] J. Elliott sees the *Gospel of the*

---

39. Scholars who see the Hebrew Gospel as derived from Matthew include Burton H. Throckmorton Jr., *Gospel Parallels: A Synopsis of the First Three Gospels*[2] (New York: Thomas Nelson, 1957), xviii, who references each passage in the *Gospel of the Ebionites* to the First Gospel. Likewise, R. Dunkerley, "The Gospel according to the Hebrews," 441, states as "fact" "that there is a greater similarity between 'Hebrews' and Matthew than between it and either of the other Synoptics." A. F. Findlay, *Byways in Early Christian Literature,* 44, states that "The Gospel of the Ebionites shows unmistakably that it was dependent on the Gospels which were in common use in the Church. Its greatest affinity is with St. Matthew. . . ." A. Resch, *Agrapha. Aussercanonische Evangelienfragmente,* 328, asserts: "Die Hauptquelle des Hebräerevangeliums war ohne Zweifel das erste canonische Evangelium." Most recently, C. Evans, "Jewish Christian Gospel Tradition," states that the Jewish Gospel tradition, and especially *Gos. Naz.* and *Gos. Eb.,* are based on canonical Matthew (245, 255).

40. "Ebionites, Gospel of the," *ABD* 2.262. Further, "The opening story [of *Gos. Eb.*] is similar to that in Mark, although harmonized from all three Synoptic Gospels"; again, "It is difficult to determine which if any of the canonical gospels provides the framework for the *Gospel of the Ebionites.*"

41. *New Testament Apocrypha,* 1.152.

42. *Ancient Christian Gospels: Their History and Development* (Philadelphia: Trinity, 1992), 334.

Ebionites as a generic harmony of the "synoptic type."[43] In a study devoted to the provenance of the *Gospel of the Ebionites,* D. A. Bertrand sees the latter as a harmony of the three Synoptics (though with slight preference for Matthew), which was a precursor to Tatian's *Diatessaron.*[44] The harmony theory was asserted years ago by A. Schmidtke, "The H[ebrew] G[ospel] exhibits a collage of the four canonical Gospels";[45] and it has been recently renewed by D. Lührmann, "In the Text [of the *Gospel of the Ebionites*] are found strains from all three Synoptic Gospels; . . . It is most probably a harmony of the Gospels."[46] In his monograph on Jewish Christian Gospels, A. F. J. Klijn writes that "the Gospel according to the Ebionites was composed with the help of the three synoptic Gospels."[47] Most recently, A. Gregory surmises that the Hebrew Gospel of the Ebionites represents "an early form of the synoptic tradition prior to that found in the later manuscript tradition of the Synoptic Gospel."[48]

The oft-repeated and widely held scholarly consensus that the Hebrew Gospel, particularly as cited by Epiphanius in his discussion of the Ebionites, derives from the Synoptic tradition and is in various degrees a corruption of it can no longer be maintained.[49] The evidence surveyed in Chapters One and Two repeatedly demonstrates that the quotations of the Hebrew Gospel are neither generic Synoptic harmonies nor primarily in agreement with the Gospel of Matthew.[50] One of the few scholars to have

---

43. Elliott, *The Apocryphal New Testament,* 6, claims only that *Gos. Eb.* is familiar "with the contents of the canonical Gospels." This is an overstatement, since *Gos. Eb.* contains no quotations in common with the Gospel of John.

44. D. A. Bertrand, "L'*Evangile des Ebionites:* Une Harmonie Evangelique Anterieure au *Diatessaron,*" 548-63.

45. A. Schmidtke, "Zum Hebräerevangelium," 24, 38. Schmidtke regards the Hebrew Gospel "nur als eine fictive Niederschrift des Mt. . . . Das ist völlig sichergestellt" (32).

46. *Fragmente apokryph gewordenen Evangelien in griechischer und lateinischer Sprache,* 32.

47. *Jewish-Christian Gospel Tradition,* 38.

48. "Prior or Posterior? The *Gospel of the Ebionites* and the Gospel of Luke," 354.

49. Nearly a century and a half ago R. Handmann, *Das Hebräer-Evangelium,* 128, warned: "Auch ist in der That das Verhältnis das H.E. [Hebräer-Evangelium] zum kanonischen Mtth. keineswegs ein so nahes und ausschliessliches, wie es die Tradition und später ein Theil der Kritik gemeint hat."

50. Even T. Zahn, *Geschichte des neutestamentlichen Kanons,* 1/2.776-77, whose mastery of the patristic tradition rivaled Harnack's, continued to maintain that the Hebrew Gospel was a work of harmless expansions and sagas of the Aramaic original that was the precursor of Matthew's Greek Gospel.

noted this fact is Pierson Parker, who in an article on the Hebrew Gospel of some seventy years ago wrote that ". . . it can be shown that . . . the Gospel according to the Hebrews is not Matthean, and is to be related to the non-Markan portions of Luke."[51] The most obvious refutation of the assumption that the Hebrew Gospel is a mere compilation of Synoptic pericopes is that virtually every quotation from the Hebrew Gospel surveyed in Chapter Two contains details of information not present in the Synoptics. If the Hebrew Gospel were held to be simply a later pastiche of the Synoptic Gospels, then a very convincing argument would be required to explain the presence of information in it that is different from and additional to what is found in the Synoptic Gospels.

The flaw in supposing the Hebrew Gospel to be a compilation of the Synoptic Gospels is made inescapably apparent when the Hebrew Gospel quotations are considered specifically and individually. A collation of all the quotations from the Hebrew Gospel surveyed in the first two chapters reveals an unmistakable affinity with the Gospel of Luke rather than with the first two Gospels. The evidence may be summarized as follows:

Synoptic Text Type. Four quotations from the Hebrew Gospel demonstrate general agreement with all three Synoptic Gospels, without particular preference for any one of them:

> Epiphanius, *Pan.* 30.13.7-8 = Matt 3:13-17 par. Mark 1:9-11; Luke 3:21-22
>
> Epiphanius, *Pan.* 30.14.5 = Matt 12:46-50 par. Mark 3:31-35; Luke 8:19-21
>
> Jerome, *Epistle* 20, *ad Dam.* = Matt 21:9 par. Mark 11:9; Luke 19:38
>
> Jerome, *Comm. Matt.* 12:13 = Matt 12:13 par. Mark 3:5; Luke 6:10

Mark Alone. No single quotation from the Hebrew Gospel shows an agreement with Mark over against Matthew and Luke. A given quotation of the Hebrew Gospel may of course replicate a word or phrase in Mark, or exhibit a thematic similarity to a Markan pericope; but when this is the case, a similar degree of similarity will also be seen with Matthew or Luke,

---

51. P. Parker, "A Proto-Lukan Basis for the Gospel According to the Hebrews," 472. Many scholars have recognized similarities between the Hebrew Gospel and Luke without pursuing them further; e.g., D. Gla, *Die Originalsprache des Matthäusevangeliums*, 86: "Mehrere Anklänge an das Lukasev. finden sich auch [im Hebräerevangelium]."

or both. In no instance does a quotation of the Hebrew Gospel agree exclusively with the Gospel of Mark.

Matthew Alone. In five instances a quotation from the Hebrew Gospel agrees with Matthew over against Mark and Luke. Again, a given quotation of the Hebrew Gospel may replicate a word or phrase in Matthew, or exhibit a thematic similarity to a Matthean pericope; but when this is the case, a similar degree of similarity will also be seen with Mark or Luke, or both. The only instances when a quotation of the Hebrew Gospel agrees exclusively with Matthew are:

> Origen, *Comm. Matt.* 15:14 = Matt 19:16
> Epiphanius, *Pan.* 30.16.4-5 = Matt 5:17
> Epiphanius, *Pan.* 30.13.7-8 = Matt 3:15
> Jerome, *Pelag.* 3.2 = Matt 3:15
> Jerome, *Comm. Matt.* 2: = Matt 2:5

Matthew and Luke. In four instances a quotation from the Hebrew Gospel agrees with both Matthew and Luke in roughly equal proportion, but not with Mark.

> Clement, *Strom.* 2.9.45 = Matt 7:7-8 par. Luke 11:9-10
> Clement, *Strom.* 5.14.96 = Matt 7:7-8 par. Luke 11:9-10
> Jerome, *Comm. Matt.* 6:11 = Matt 6:11 par. Luke 11:3
> Jerome, *Comm. Matt.* 23:35 = Matt 23:35 par. Luke 11:51

Luke Alone. In twenty-five instances a quotation from the Hebrew Gospel shows either an *explicit* parallel with the Gospel of Luke, or a close *thematic* parallel with it, but not with either Matthew or Mark. *Explicit* (=) parallels are:

> Ignatius, *Smyrn.* 3.2 = Luke 24:39
> Origen, *Princ.* Praefatio 8 = Luke 24:39
> Eusebius, *Hist. eccl.* 3.36.11 = Luke 24:39
> Epiphanius, *Pan.* 30.13.2-3 = Luke 3:23; 4:38; 6:15
> Epiphanius, *Pan.* 30.13.4-6 = Luke 1:5
> Epiphanius, *Pan.* 30.14.3 = Luke 1:5
> Epiphanius, *Pan.* 30.22.4 = Luke 22:15

Jerome, *Vir. ill.* 2 = Luke 24:30
Jerome, *Vir. ill.* 16 = Luke 24:39

Thematic (≈) parallels are:

Papias, in Eusebius, *Hist. eccl.* 3.39.17 ≈ Luke 7:47
Clement, *Strom.* 7.13 ≈ (see Chapter Two, p. 93)
Origen, *Hom. Jer.* 15.4 ≈ (see Chapter Two, pp. 55-57)
Origen, *Comm. Jo.* 2.12 ≈ (see Chapter Two, pp. 56-59)
Origen, *Comm. Matt.* 15.14 ≈ Luke 16:19-31
Eusebius, *Theoph.* 4.12 ≈ Luke 6:3
Eusebius, *Theoph.* 4.22 ≈ Luke 15:13, 30
Didymus, *Comm. Eccl.* 4.223.6-13 ≈ Luke 7:36-50
Didymus, *Pap.* 1224 ≈ Luke 5:27, 29; 19:1-10
Jerome, *Pelag.* 3.2 ≈ Luke 17:3-4
Jerome, *Comm. Eph.* 5:4 ≈ Luke 15:30-31
Jerome, *Comm. Ezech.* 16:13 ≈ (see Chapter Two, pp. 58-59)
Jerome, *Comm. Ezech.* 18:7 ≈ Luke 17:1-2
Jerome, *Comm. Isa.* 40:9 ≈ (see Chapter Two, pp. 57-59)
Jerome, *Comm. Matt.* 27:16 ≈ Luke 23:19
Jerome, *Comm. Mich.* 7:7 ≈ (see Chapter Two, pp. 58-59)

No Synoptic Parallels. Of the isolated details present in various quotations of the Hebrew Gospel that have no parallels or similarities with the Synoptic Gospels, the following three preserved by Jerome are the most significant:

Jerome, *Epist. 120.8 ad Hedy.*: Breaking of Temple lintel
Jerome, *Comm. Matt.* 27:51: Breaking of Temple lintel
Jerome, *Comm. Isa.* 11:1-2: Whole font of Holy Spirit resting on Jesus as baptism

The foregoing analysis shows the unusually strong correlation of the Hebrew Gospel and the Gospel of Luke. Of the 41 texts considered, 25 demonstrate an explicit or close thematic likeness to the Third Gospel. Three-fifths of the purported citations of the Hebrew Gospel, in other words, exhibit stronger agreement with Luke than with Matthew and/or Mark. Moreover, the texts cited with reference to Luke are, on the whole, longer excerpts of the Hebrew Gospel. Longer texts provide more comparative data, and multiple instances of longer texts constitute stronger evidence for relationships between two texts than do agreements of single words, short phrases, or isolated details, which may be coincidental. Patristic citations of the Hebrew Gospel are thus not of a "general Synoptic text type." On the contrary, they demonstrate a clear affinity with the Lukan text.[52]

4. The Hebrew Gospel Was Most Plausibly a Source of the Gospel of Luke

The repeated correlation between the Hebrew Gospel and the Gospel of Luke demonstrates a relationship between the two documents, but it does not explain whether one document influenced the other or both depended on a third source. We have noted that scholars typically assume that Hebrew Gospel quotations derive from the prior Synoptic tradition. The striking correspondence between Luke and the Hebrew Gospel, however, warrants a reconsideration of that assumption. No church father identifies the source of the Hebrew Gospel as the Synoptic tradition. On the contrary, the fathers often declare explicitly that they are quoting from an early Hebrew Gospel authored by the apostle Matthew.[53] No father who identifies the author of the Hebrew Gospel attributes it to anyone except Matthew. Epiphanius even concedes that the Cerinthians and Merinthians use the Hebrew Gospel authored by Matthew.[54] The favorable description of Hebrew Matthew in this context is remarkable, since Epiphanius re-

---

52. A point emphasized by R. Handmann, *Das Hebräer-Evangelium,* 128, and recognized but not argued by O. Holtzmann, *The Life of Jesus,* 51. Although A. Resch, *Agrapha. Aussercanonische Evangelienfragmente,* 328-29, believes the Hebrew Gospel was a later translation of canonical Greek Matthew, he recognizes in the Hebrew Gospel "echte Stoffe zu Grunde . . . mit Lucas" that goes back to an original gospel.

53. Epiphanius, in particular, identifies the Matthean authorship of the Hebrew Gospel on seven occasions: *Pan.* 29.9.4; 30.3.7; 30.6.9; 30.13.1, 2; 30.14.2, 3. In *Pan.* 46.2 Epiphanius makes an additional reference to the Hebrew Gospel in relation to Tatian's *Diatessaron:* λέγεται δὲ τὸ διὰ τεσσάρων εὐαγγέλιον ὑπ᾽ αὐτοῦ [= Tatian] γεγενῆσθαι, ὅπερ κατὰ Ἑβραίους τινὲς καλοῦσι ("Some call the Gospel that is reputed to have been produced by Tatian from the Four [Gospels] 'According to the Hebrews'").

54. "[The Ebionites] also accept the Gospel of Matthew, and they, like the Cerinthians and Merinthians, use it alone. They properly call it 'According to the Hebrews,' because Matthew alone made an exposition of the gospel and proclamation (κήρυγμα) of the new covenant in the Hebrew language and in Hebrew letters" (*Pan.* 30.3.7).

garded the Cerinthians and Merinthians as heretics. The fathers clearly imply that the Hebrew Gospel is independent of the canonical Gospels, and several, such as Origen and Jerome, leave the impression that it was written earlier than the canonical Gospels.

The church fathers, like the ancients in general, believed that antiquity was an important criterion of orthodoxy. What was older had stood the test of time and therefore had greater claim to truth than did innovation, which was often suspected of falsification.[55] This assumption is clearly evidenced in *Panarion* 30.13.2, where it is not the Hebrew Gospel itself but an incomplete, falsified, and distorted version of it that is disparaged by Epiphanius (οὐχ ὅλῳ δὲ πληρεστάτῳ, ἀλλὰ νενοθευμένῳ καὶ ἠκρωτηριασμένῳ).

This brings us to a critical juncture in the study of the Hebrew Gospel. How can the two manifest but apparently contradictory patristic conclusions with reference to the Hebrew Gospel be resolved? On the one hand, the material quoted from the Hebrew Gospel is preponderantly Lukan. On the other, the fathers categorically assign the Hebrew Gospel to Matthew. Predominantly *Lukan* material, in other words, is repeatedly assigned to the apostle *Matthew*. In no instance do the fathers ascribe the Hebrew Gospel to any source other than Matthew; neither do they ascribe the material to the Gospel of Luke or even mention Luke in relation to it.

Some scholars attribute this discrepancy to a blunder, especially on the part of Epiphanius.[56] Here it is necessary briefly to address the trustworthiness of Epiphanius, as we earlier addressed Jerome's, if his witness to the Hebrew Gospel is to be trusted. A confusion of Matthew and Luke on Epiphanius's part cannot be categorically eliminated, of course, but the likelihood of his having made the same mistake on six different occasions is highly improbable. Morton Enslin's abrupt dismissal of Epiphanius on this point seems unjustified, at any rate, for throughout *Panarion* 30 Epiphanius repeatedly quotes Scripture carefully and accurately in refuta-

---

55. In his dispute with Marcion, Tertullian, *Marc.* 4.4, appeals to this principle: "What is to settle the point for us [i.e., whether Marcion's version of Luke or Tertullian's version of Luke is the more authentic], except it be that principle *(ratio)* of time, which rules that the authority lies with that which shall be found to be more ancient."

56. Epiphanius and Jerome again take the brunt of abuse. Morton S. Enslin, "Ebionites, Gospel of the," *IDB* 2.5, for instance, says that "Epiphanius . . . vies with Jerome for the distinction of being the least to be trusted of the ancient fathers in such matters." R. Handmann, *Das Hebräer-Evangelium*, 40-44, asserts that the Gospel attributed to the Ebionites by Epiphanius is a "Bastardwerk" that has nothing to do with the Hebrew Gospel.

tion of the Ebionites' various claims. Epiphanius is polemical and sarcastic, to be sure, but he is not egregiously erroneous. His factual and historical descriptions of the Ebionites agree throughout with what we know from other ancient sources, particularly Irenaeus.[57] So it is not likely that he was in error — and repeatedly so — in referring to material that is predominantly Lukan as deriving from Matthew.

How, then, might the correlation of predominantly Lukan texts with a Matthean source be explained? The composite evidence points rather persuasively to the conclusion that the Hebrew Gospel is not, as commonly assumed, a compilation of the Synoptics, but rather one of the *sources* of the Gospel of Luke to which the author alludes in his prologue (Luke 1:1-4). The Hebrew Gospel authored by the apostle Matthew may have been translated into Greek quite early. Jerome mentions such a translation into Greek prior to his own, and given the pervasiveness of Greek in the Mediterranean world this is not at all surprising. At a somewhat later date the Hebrew Gospel evidently underwent textual alterations in accordance with the tenets of the Jewish Christian sects that used and copied it. Evidence of at least two such recensions appears in Epiphanius and Jerome. In the *Panarion* Epiphanius debunks the *Gospel of the Ebionites* as a falsification and distortion (νενοθευμένῳ καὶ ἠκρωτηριασμένῳ, 30.13.2) of an original Matthew that was issued in Hebrew (Ἑβραϊστὶ καὶ Ἑβραϊκοῖς γράμμασιν, 30.3.7).[58] Likewise, "now that the stream [of the Hebrew Gospel] is distributed into different channels," writes Jerome in his *Preface to the Four Gospels* to Pope Damasus in 383, "we must go back to the fountainhead."[59] Not surprisingly, the original Hebrew Gospel suffered changes at the hands of its host communities and interest groups.

It would be a mistake to overestimate the changes, however, for

---

57. Both Epiphanius (*Pan.* 30.24.6) and Irenaeus (*Haer.* 3.3.4), for example, attest that John the Apostle lived until the time of Trajan; and both relate the story of John the Apostle's fleeing from heresy in the bathhouse in Ephesus (*Pan.* 30.24.1-5; *Haer.* 3.3.4), with the exception that Irenaeus identifies the heretic as Cerinthus, but Epiphanius as Ebion. A. F. J. Klijn and G. J. Reinink, *Patristic Evidence for Jewish-Christian Sects,* 28-39, who believe that most of what Epiphanius "wrote about the Ebionites was drawn from written sources," are able to demonstrate Epiphanius's faithfulness to such sources.

58. In *Pan.* 29.9.4 Epiphanius says that the Nazoraeans ἔχουσιν δὲ τὸ κατὰ Ματθαῖον εὐαγγέλιον πληρέστατον Ἑβραϊστί. The word πληρέστατον seems to mean here not that the Nazoraeans possessed a fuller copy of Matthew but rather a less mutilated copy of the original Hebrew Matthew. See M.-J. Lagrange, "L'Évangile selon les Hébreux," 179.

59. See Chapter One, pp. 33-34.

Epiphanius, who seems intent on highlighting "mutilations" in the Hebrew Gospel used by the Ebionites, mentions only eight. Eight alterations — especially of the kind Epiphanius brings to light — in a text of 2200 lines (if Nicephorus's testimony to the length of the Hebrew Gospel is correct) does not constitute a major corruption of the *Urtext*. Moreover, as we have seen, quotations from the various traditions of the Hebrew Gospel cited by the fathers reveal a demonstrable affinity especially with the Gospel of Luke. The various recensions and traditions, in other words, seem to have been generally faithful to the "fountainhead," the original Hebrew Matthew. Why then does Epiphanius identify material that correlates with Luke as coming from Matthew? The answer appears to be that Epiphanius — along with other church fathers — is quoting from a corruption of an original Hebrew Matthew that was used as one of the sources of the Third Gospel.

Nearly a century ago M.-J. Lagrange asked the same question and came to virtually the same conclusion. "If the Gospel (of the Ebionites) is no nearer to Matthew than it is to Luke, why is it named for Matthew? It surprised Epiphanius that he could find no other cause than an original Hebrew Matthew. His thought was that the Gospel in question depended on a Hebrew writing."[60] In response to his own question Lagrange concluded that "[A]t the origin of the Gospel texts, as the source of Luke and of Matthew, one finds therefore Mark and the Gospel according to the Hebrews."[61]

At least four fathers who cite the Hebrew Gospel — Hegesippus, Origen,

---

60. M.-J. Lagrange, "L'Évangile selon les Hébreux," *RB* 31 (1922), 170.

61. "L'Évangile selon les Hébreux," 162. Marie Joseph Lagrange (1855-1938), a French Dominican, was writing at a time when the Catholic Church did not allow scholars to conclude otherwise than that canonical Greek Matthew was the first Gospel and the source of the other two Synoptics. Hence, Lagrange had to advance his hypothesis of a proto-Hebrew Matthew cautiously. Lagrange had personally experienced the power of the Church to proscribe unsanctioned scholarship. In 1907, having already founded both the École Biblique in Jerusalem and the prestigious *Revue Biblique,* Lagrange was forbidden by the Holy See from pursuing his work as a Semiticist and Old Testament scholar because of his sympathy with higher criticism. Thereafter he devoted his prodigious scholarship to the New Testament, and particularly to the Gospels. His expertise in Semitics and patristics (including the Hebrew Gospel) lends particular credibility to his conclusion that the source used by Epiphanius in *Panarion* 30 was not, as has been so often supposed, a compilation of the Synoptic Gospels, but rather the Hebrew Gospel of Matthew. Lagrange also knew, however, that the climate in the Catholic Church of his day did not allow him to assert such a conclusion with the confidence that it deserved — at least if he wished to avoid a second proscription.

Ephrem the Syrian, and Jerome — knew Hebrew. The full extent of Epiphanius's knowledge of Hebrew cannot be determined with certainty, but, like Hegesippus, he was of Jewish birth and knew at least some Hebrew, for in *Panarion* 30.31.1 he correctly cites the Hebrew word גלמי = Γολμη, of Ps 139:16 (see also *Pan.* 30.6.7). Although Epiphanius refers to the *Gospel of the Ebionites* as the "Hebrew Gospel" (e.g., 30.13.2), and twice says that it was originally written in Hebrew (30.3.7, 6.9), it is clear from his testimony that the document from which he quotes is a Greek document.[62] We know this not only from the foregoing synopsis, but specifically from *Panarion* 30.22.5, where he accuses the Ebionites of falsifying a dominical saying by a Greek addition, τὸ μῦ καὶ τὸ ἦτα. Thus, along with Hegesippus, Origen, Ephrem, and Jerome, all of whom knew Hebrew, Epiphanius knew enough Hebrew to explain Greek peculiarities in the *Gospel of the Ebionites* on the basis of its Hebrew original.

The most economical hypothesis that satisfies the foregoing evidence is that *the author of the Third Gospel utilized an early Hebrew Gospel (perhaps in Greek translation) as one of the sources to which he refers in his prologue (Luke 1:1-4)*. The proposal can be diagrammed thus:

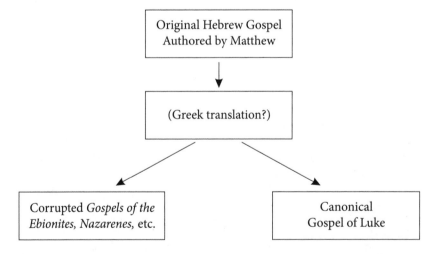

62. A. Hilgenfeld, *Novum Testamentum extra Canonem Receptum*[2], 35, and R. Handmann, *Das Hebräer-Evangelium*, 41, are in error in asserting that Epiphanius nowhere declares that the Gospel used by the Ebionites was written in Hebrew. Rather, Lagrange, "L'Évangile selon les Hébreux," 175, is correct to note that the Hebrew Gospel was a Greek translation of a Hebrew original, "sans perdre le contact avec un original hébreu."

This does not imply that an original Hebrew Gospel was the sole source of canonical Luke. I shall endeavor to demonstrate in the next chapter, however, that it was the chief source of the material unique to Luke, and thus one of the *main* sources to which he refers in his prologue.[63] This hypothesis will be verified by demonstrating that there is an increase in Hebraisms in Lukan material not derived from Mark or paralleled with Matthew. For the present, however, the above proposal satisfies the major problems that arise from a comparison of the Hebrew Gospel and the Gospel of Luke. First, it explains why the quotations of the Hebrew Gospel correspond predominantly to the Greek text of Luke, for the Hebrew Gospel used by the Ebionites or Nazarenes would be a copy with minor corruptions of the same Greek translation of the original Hebrew Gospel that Luke used as one of the sources of his Gospel. This Greek translation obviously cannot have been canonical Greek Matthew, for, as we have seen, quotations of the Hebrew Gospel show no unusual affinity with canonical Greek Matthew. More importantly, the proposal explains why quotations from the Hebrew Gospel considered in Chapter Two correspond predominantly with material unique to Luke. The correspondence is due to the reasonable inference that Luke's primary source for Special Luke is the original Hebrew Gospel itself. Finally, the proposal explains why the fathers refer to the author of the Hebrew Gospel as authored by Matthew rather than Luke, for the text they quote must be a Greek translation of an original Hebrew source, which they believed was written by the apostle Matthew.[64]

Ascription of the Hebrew Gospel to the apostle Matthew is very widespread in the fathers. No father attributes it to anyone other than Matthew. Most emphatically, Epiphanius asserts that Matthew the apostle both conceived (τὸ κατὰ Ματθαῖον εὐαγγέλιον Ἑβραϊκὸν φύσει ὄν, *Pan.* 30.6.9)

---

63. B. W. Bacon, "Papias and the Gospel according to the Hebrews," 174, writes that there is "no small amount of evidence for the exceptional dependence of our third and fourth evangelists on 'the Gospel according to the Hebrews.'" Bacon's inclusion of the Fourth Gospel is curious because he makes no mention of it in his article. He evidently includes it on the basis of H. J. Holtzmann, *Lehrbuch der historisch-kritischen Einleitung in das Neue Testament*[3] (Freiburg: Mohr, 1892), 441. The evidence Holtzmann gathers there is unrelated to the Hebrew Gospel, however.

64. The proposal further explains why the Ebionites believed that Jesus was the human son of Joseph who was subsequently adopted as Son of God, for only in Luke is Jesus called the supposed son of Joseph (Luke 3:23). Moreover, the Western text of Luke 3:22 (which, according to Epiphanius, was cited in the Hebrew Gospel of the Ebionites) is more suggestive of adoptionism than is any other baptismal narrative.

and wrote (30.3.7) his Gospel in Hebrew, not in Greek. Likewise, no father asserts that the Hebrew Gospel was a compilation of the Greek canonical Gospels. Worth mentioning in this regard is that Epiphanius tends to inform readers when a text is a translation. In *Panarion* 30.6.9 he states, for example, that the Gospel of John was later translated from Greek into Hebrew. This is an important datum of information, for although Epiphanius knows of the translation of Greek Gospels into Hebrew, in his several references to the Hebrew Gospel he never says that it was a translation from a Greek original. There is no patristic evidence that the Hebrew Gospel was a translation of a Greek document. Rather, as Epiphanius and a chorus of fathers maintain, it was conceived and written in Hebrew.[65]

5. The Relation of the Hebrew Gospel to Other "Jewish Christian Gospels"

The relationship of the Jewish Christian Gospels to one another is, in the words of Martin Hengel, "one of the greatest unresolved riddles of Gospel writing."[66] For some scholars it is not only an unresolved riddle, but exasperating, "the most irritating problem in the NT Apocrypha."[67] This closing note does not claim to be a final resolution of the riddle, but rather is an attempt to marshal three reasonably certain conclusions that clarify the status of the Hebrew Gospel in early Christianity.

First, two texts should be excluded from the discussion of the Hebrew Gospel. The first is "The Traditions of Matthias," which was unanimously proscribed throughout the patristic period. It is banned in Origen's index of heterodox books in his *Homilies on Luke*.[68] Eusebius likewise lists it in the rejected category in his canonical classifications.[69] Clement of Alexan-

---

65. See E. B. Nicholson, *The Gospel According to the Hebrews*, 10; and G. H. R. Horsley, "The Fiction of 'Jewish Greek,'" in *New Documents Illustrating Early Christianity*, vol. 5 (Macquarie: Ancient History Documentary Research Center, 1989), 33. In Chapter Eight the relationship of Hebrew Matthew and canonical Greek Matthew will be considered.

66. *The Four Gospels and the One Gospel of Jesus Christ*, 74.

67. William L. Peterson, "Ebionites, Gospel of the," *ABD* 2.261.

68. Along with the *Gospel of the Egyptians*, the *Gospel of the Twelve*, the *Gospel of Basilides*, the *Gospel of Thomas*, and "several more" (*Hom. Luc.* 1.1). Importantly, the Hebrew Gospel is *not* in Origen's list.

69. Several works circulating pseudonymously under apostolic names are rejected as

dria explicitly differentiates the Hebrew Gospel from "The Traditions of Matthias," associating the latter with the Gnostic Basilides.[70] "The Traditions," which could also be known as "The Gospel of Matthias," is mentioned unfavorably in passing by Ambrose, Jerome, and Bede and appears in two further indices of late antiquity, the Gelasian Decrees and the seventh-century Byzantine *Catalogue of the Sixty Canonical Books*.[71] The ubiquitous interdiction of "The Traditions/Gospel of Matthias" in the patristic period, which (with the single exception of Philip of Side) was never the fate of the Hebrew Gospel, distinguishes it from the Hebrew Gospel.[72] Along with the "Traditions," a second document referred to by Eusebius as the "Teachings (of the Apostles)" and by Origen as the "Gospel of the Twelve" is proscribed by both.[73] Neither "The Traditions" nor "The Teachings" should be confused with the Hebrew Gospel.

A second point can be made with equal confidence, namely, that the apostle Matthew published an original Gospel written in Hebrew that was occasionally called "The Gospel of Matthew," but was more frequently known as "the Gospel according to the Hebrews" or simply "the Hebrew Gospel." Four church fathers — Eusebius, Epiphanius, Jerome, and Theodoret of Cyrrhus — attest that the Hebrew Gospel was identical with this "Gospel of Matthew."[74] This Hebrew "Gospel of Matthew," as we have seen throughout the first two chapters, is not a Hebrew version of canonical Greek Matthew, nor closely related to canonical Matthew. Theodore of Mopsuestia's accusation that Jerome fabricated the Hebrew Gospel was the lone challenge to this tradition among the Fathers;[75] otherwise, the Mat-

---

spurious "writings which are put forward by heretics" (Eusebius, *Hist. eccl.* 3.25.6). Among these are the Gospels of Peter, Thomas, and Matthias and the Acts of Andrew and John.

70. *Strom.* 2.9.45; see also 3.4.6; 7.13.82; 7.7.108.

71. Decretum Gelasianum 3.1 (TU 38.4, p. 11); *Catalogue of Sixty Canonical Books* (T. Zahn, *Geschichte des neutestamentlichen Kanons*, 2/1.289-93; W. Schneemelcher, *New Testament Apocrypha*, 1.42-43).

72. See the evidence assembled in H.-C. Puech, rev. B. Beatte, *New Testament Apocrypha*, 1.382-85; J. K. Elliott, *The Apocryphal New Testament*, 19.

73. Eusebius, *Hist. eccl.* 3.25.6; Origen, *Hom. Luc.* 1:1. A Gospel "secundum XII apostolos" is likewise condemned as heretical by Ambrosius, *Proem. in Luc.;* Theophylact, *Prooem. in Luc.,* and by Jerome, *Comm. Matt.* (Praefatio).

74. Eusebius, *Hist. eccl.* 6.17.1; Epiphanius, *Pan.* 30.3.7; Jerome, *Pelag.* 3.2; Theodoret, *Haer. Fab.* 2.1.

75. Photius, *Bibliotheca* 177, τοῦτον (i.e., Jerome) δὲ πέμπτον εὐαγγέλιον προσανα-πλάσαι λέγει (i.e., Theodore of Mopsuestia), ἐν ταῖς Εὐσεβίου τοῦ Παλαιστίνου βιβλιο-

thean authorship of the Hebrew Gospel was affirmed by a dozen fathers and not challenged by any ancient writer. The above attestations of Eusebius, Epiphanius, Jerome, and Theodoret explicitly state what was generally and widely affirmed throughout the early church, that the *Gospel of the Hebrews* was originally composed in Hebrew by the apostle Matthew.

A third conclusion — more qualified but still reasonably certain — pertains to the relationship of the Hebrew Gospel to two other so-called Jewish Christian Gospels. Modern discussions tend to assign Jewish Christian Gospels to at least three textual traditions: the *Gospel of the Hebrews,* the *Gospel of the Ebionites,* and the *Gospel of the Nazarenes.*[76] These three divisions may aid in identifying the primary readers and host communities of the Hebrew Gospel, but a critical reading of the sources does not justify the conclusion that they refer to different texts by such names. The *Gospel according to the Hebrews* was widely attested in the early church, although it did not circulate under a fixed epithet.[77] As we have previously

---

θήκαις ὑποπλαττόμενον εὑρεῖν ("[Jerome] ascribed an additional fifth Gospel, he [Theodore] says, feigning to have found it in the library of Eusebius of Palestine"). Photius died in the late ninth century (ca. 890).

76. H. Waitz, "Neue Untersuchungen über die sogen. judenchristlichen Evangelien," 61-81, provides a list of the major German scholars who divide the Jewish Christian Gospels into these traditions, although Waitz himself argues for only two traditions — the Hebrew Gospel (which he believes was identical with the so-called *Gospel of the Ebionites* mentioned by Epiphanius) and the *Gospel of the Nazarenes.* Prior to Waitz, A. Resch, *Agrapha. Aussercanonische Evangelienfragmente,* 326-27, also limited the tradition to two recensions by the Nazarenes and Ebionites. The threefold tradition is advocated and expounded by P. Vielhauer and G. Strecker, "Jewish-Christian Gospels," in *New Testament Apocrypha,* 1.134-78; and J. K. Elliott, *The Apocryphal New Testament,* 3-16. A. F. J. Klijn's pronouncement on this matter is the most dogmatic: "Es ist heute unbestritten, dass von kirchlichen Schriftstellern mittelbar oder unmittelbar drei verschiedene judenchristliche Evangelien angeführt worden sind, nämlich das Hebräerevangelium, das Nazoräerevangelium und das Ebionitenevangelium" ("Das Hebräer- und das Nazoräerevangelium," *ANRW* 2.25.5, 3997; also, Klijn, *Jewish-Christian Gospel Tradition,* 29-36).

77. The Hebrew Gospel is referred to variously by the fathers — and even variously by a given father — as "the Gospel according to the Hebrews," "the Gospel existing among the Jews in the Hebrew language," "the Gospel that has come to us in Hebrew characters," "the Gospel according to Matthew," "the Hebrew Gospel," "the Gospel that is written in Hebrew letters," "the Gospel according to the Hebrews . . . according to the Apostles, or, as very many reckon, according to Matthew," "the Gospel that is written in Hebrew and read by the Nazarenes," "the Gospel that the Nazarenes and Ebionites use," "the Gospel that the Nazarenes use." For names and references, see A. Resch, *Agrapha. Aussercanonische Evangelienfragmente,* 322-23. The fact that the Hebrew Gospel was known by different names

noted, "The Gospel of the Ebionites" is a neologism of modern scholarship. This title is commonly associated with the Gospel that Epiphanius mentions in *Panarion* 29 and 30. Technically speaking, however, it is a misnomer, because the title "The Gospel of the Ebionites" never occurs in Epiphanius or any other ancient source.[78] Epiphanius speaks of "the Hebrew Gospel *used* by the Ebionites," but neither he nor any church father specifies a "Gospel of the Ebionites." The absence of the supposed title "The Gospel of the Ebionites" in patristic literature is quite significant. The aberrations of the Ebionites — major, minor, rumored, or imagined — were not left unpunished by the score of fathers who claimed to stand within and speak for the orthodox Christian tradition. Epiphanius, in particular, rehearses their aberrations with relish.[79] Had a separate "Gospel of the Ebionites" existed beyond the Hebrew Gospel, we can scarcely imagine that Irenaeus or Epiphanius — or any of the fathers — would have left it unmentioned.

A similar conclusion must also be drawn with respect to "the Gospel of

---

is scarcely an argument against either its existence or its identifiable content and text type. Criminologists as well as secret police in oppressive regimes (e.g., the Stasi in former East Germany) know that truth tellers often vary in their description of a factual matter, whereas liars formulate a fixed alibi and adhere to it without alteration.

78. A. Hilgenfeld, *Novum Testamentum extra Canonem Receptum*[2], 10, mistakes Theodoret's testimony in *Haer. Fab.* 2:1 to read τὸ κατὰ Ἐβιωναίους εὐαγγέλιον (the Gospel according to the Ebionites), whereas Theodoret's original in fact reads τὸ κατὰ Ἑβραίους εὐαγγέλιον (the Gospel according to the Hebrews).

79. According to Epiphanius, the errors of the Ebionites are legion. They use Clement's so-called Peregrinations of Peter (*Pan.* 30.15.1), reject celibacy and continence (30.2.6; 30.15.2), consider Jesus a human who was infused by the divine Christ (30.14.4; 30.16.4; 30.17.1; 30.18.6; 30.29.1) and engendered by human procreation (30.2.2), are unduly attached to the Jewish law, circumcision, and other Jewish and Samaritan observances (20.2.2), avoid touching Gentiles (30.2.3), require men to bathe after being with women (30.2.4), require frequent baptisms and washings (30.16.1), abhor Elijah, David, Samson, and all the prophets and accept the gospel over such figures (30.15.2; 30.18.4), do not eat meat (30.15.3-4), celebrate a Eucharist of bread and water only (30.16.1), deny the deity of Jesus (30.14.4), adhere to adoptionism (30.17.1), believing Jesus remained mere man (30.18.5-6; 30.29.3), follow James (30.16.7) and Peter (30.21.1), denigrate or reject Paul (30.16.8; Eusebius, *Hist. eccl.* 3.27.4), call on Elxai in emergencies (*Pan.* 30.17.4), consider the Holy Spirit female (30.17.6), marry children by compulsion (30.18.2), call their churches synagogues (30.18.2), allow divorce and remarriage (30.18.3), "have much to do with sex" (30.21.2), and deny the virgin birth (30.29.3). Finally, with specific reference to the Hebrew Gospel, Epiphanius says that they accept only the Gospel of Matthew that they call "According to the Hebrews" (30.3.7).

the Nazarenes."[80] The medieval *History of the Passion of the Lord* speaks of "the Gospel of the Nazarenes,"[81] but the latter is surely identical with Jerome's "Hebrew Gospel *used* by the Nazarenes." The vocabulary of the early church implies that "the Gospel of the Ebionites" and "the Gospel of the Nazarenes" were not different documents, but rather the Hebrew Gospel as it was used by the Ebionite and Nazarene communities. Jerome reinforces this equation by referring to the one Hebrew Gospel used by two Jewish Christian sects, "the Gospel used by the Nazarenes and Ebionites."[82] "It would appear," notes Klijn correctly, "that Jerome always speaks of one single Gospel but gives it various names."[83] This seems to be true throughout patristic literature. In his early fourth-century canonical classifications, Eusebius speaks of "the Gospel according to the Hebrews" as a single entity rather than as a family of Jewish Christian Gospels. Never in Eusebius's several references to the Hebrew Gospel does he designate it as "The Gospel of the Ebionites" or "The Gospel of the Nazarenes," or use such titles.[84] The testimony of the ancient sources implies that "the Gospel of the Ebionites" and "the Gospel of the Nazarenes" were either identical with the Hebrew Gospel of the apostle Matthew or clearly within its textual family.[85]

All the fathers who refer to the Hebrew Gospel, with the exception of Ignatius and Pantaenus, refer to it as either "the Gospel to the Hebrews" or

---

80. D. Lührmann, *Die apokryph gewordenen Evangelien*, 244-45, thinks the "Nazarenes" mentioned by Jerome hailed from the "sect of the Nazarenes" mentioned in Acts 24:5, 14. This could be true, but it is not certain. Particularly in the early patristic period the epithet "Nazarene" was used generically of followers of Jesus. It could (and probably did) refer to any number of groups in the intervening three and a half centuries between the writings of Luke and Jerome.

81. *Hist. pass. Dom.* f.65.

82. *Comm. Matt.* 12:13.

83. A. F. J. Klijn, *Jewish-Christian Gospel Tradition*, 18, 27.

84. G. Dorival, "Un Groupe Judéo-Chrétien Méconnu: Les Hébreux," 7-36; D. Lührmann, *Die apokryph gewordenen Evangelien*, 239.

85. This judgment is variously endorsed by G. E. Lessing, *New Hypothesis on the Evangelists as Merely Human Historians* (§21); A. F. Findlay, *Byways in Early Christian Literature*, 56-57; P. Parker, "A Proto-Lukan Basis for the Gospel According to the Hebrews," 471-72; P. F. Beatrice, "The 'Gospel According to the Hebrews' in the Apostolic Fathers," 190-91; G. Dorival, "Un Groupe Judéo-Chrétien Méconnu: Les Hébreux," 9-11; P. L. Schmidt, "'Und es war geschrieben auf Hebräisch, Griechisch und Lateinisch.' Hieronymus, das Hebräer-Evangelium und seine mittelalterliche Rezeption," *Filologia mediolatina* 5 (1998), 49-93. R. Dunkerley, "The Gospel According to the Hebrews," 438-39, equates the Hebrew Gospel and the *Gos. Naz.*, but accepts without evidence or argument *Gos. Eb.*

"the Gospel according to the Hebrews." With the single exception of Hegesippus, each of the fathers attributes the Hebrew Gospel to the apostle Matthew. All these fathers attest that the document was written as opposed to oral, a "published" text, to use Eusebius's term.[86] All the fathers with the exception of Clement of Alexandria say that the Gospel was written in Hebrew. This chorus of evidence suggests a single unified text. But, beginning with Hegesippus late in the second century, we hear of the division of the Hebrew *Urtext,* the "fountainhead" in Jerome's words, into various "channels." It is difficult to say for certain what the "channels" were, but passing references in patristic literature allow us to posit translations into Syriac and perhaps Aramaic and then later into Greek and Latin at the hands of Jerome. Certainly by Jerome's day, and perhaps already in the late second century, several translations, versions, and traditions of the Hebrew Gospel were in circulation. Among these "mutilations," to use Epiphanius's description, surely belonged copies of the Hebrew Gospel used by the Ebionites and perhaps also by the Nazarenes. The resultant changes in the Hebrew Gospel were not surprisingly abhorred and denounced by Epiphanius in particular, but also by other orthodox fathers. The Hebrew Gospel fell under a haze of suspicion in the orthodox church because it was increasingly perceived as a rival and renegade tradition in competition with the emergent Greek canon of the greater church. The extant evidence does not indicate alarming textual alterations in the Hebrew Gospel, however, and one suspects that the skepticism of the later fathers was due less to objectionable content in the Hebrew Gospel than to the disfavor of the Jewish Christian communities that used it.

Whatever the changes introduced into the Hebrew Gospel by the Ebionites and Nazarenes — and by other communities both unknown and unnamed — we can be fairly certain that it retained an identifiable text type in continuity with the original Hebrew Gospel of Matthew. This is not to imagine an "inerrant" or ossified text type, for a degree of fluidity in textual traditions, such as can now be seen in the various streams of biblical texts preserved at Qumran, for instance, had been accepted by Jewish communities for centuries. But to repeat and emphasize what has already been said, two observations allow us to be confident of a more or less unified textual tradition of the Hebrew Gospel. The first is Epiphanius's condemnation of the changes made by the Ebionites in the text of the Hebrew

---

86. *Hist. eccl.* 6.25.4.

Gospel. Epiphanius can only deplore such changes — some of which seem quite minor — because as late as 400 the text of the Hebrew Gospel was still well enough established for him to point out each particular aberration. Indeed, if the Hebrew Gospel consisted of some 2200 lines, as Nicephorus reports, then the eight changes documented by Epiphanius in *Panarion* 30 would suggest that the text of the Hebrew Gospel had not been egregiously altered.

The second proof is, of course, the evidence to which this book has been devoted up to this point. The various patristic citations of the Hebrew Gospel, and especially the latest and most numerous texts cited by Epiphanius and Jerome, continue to evince a pronounced correlation with the Gospel of Luke, as opposed to Matthew or Mark or the Synoptic tradition in general. Whatever "delta" effect the textual tradition of the Hebrew Gospel underwent, it appears to have remained integral enough to be referred to as "the Hebrew Gospel." It is with this or some similar epithet that Eusebius at the beginning of the fourth century continues to refer to it, as do Epiphanius and Jerome nearly a century later. The plenary evidence of the fathers justifies the conclusion that the original Hebrew Matthean Gospel and the "Hebrew Gospel" constituted a continuous and integral textual tradition.[87]

---

87. This conclusion is supported most recently by P. F. Beatrice, "The 'Gospel According to the Hebrews' in the Apostolic Fathers," 191, who argues that the Hebrew Gospel was composed "in the first century CE, [and was] not a document written by Greek-speaking Alexandrian Jewish-Christians in the first half of the second century, as many scholars habitually repeat treading in Walter Bauer's footsteps. Secondly, the existence of other Judaeo-Christian gospels, such as the *Gospel of the Nazoraeans* and the *Gospel of the Ebionites,* whatever their relationship may have been, appears to be at least improbable, and at any rate should be judged a superfluous hypothesis. Only one Judaeo-Christian gospel, the *Gospel of the Hebrews,* seems in fact to be sufficient to explain coherently and economically all the data supplied by the ancient sources, in as much as it gives a detailed account of the public life of Jesus from the baptism in the Jordan river and the call of the apostles in Capernaum until the final post-Resurrection appearance of the Lord." More than a century ago R. Handmann, *Das Hebräer-Evangelium,* 110-18, devoted a long discussion to the name of the Hebrew Gospel. He summarized the evidence thus: "Es wird wohl mit einer einmaligen Verarbeitung oder Umänderung sein Bewenden gehabt haben, die sich dann im Wesentlichen unverändert weiter erhalten hat, abgesehen freilich von einzelnen Correcturen und Missverständnissen der Abschreiber oder fehlerhafter Texte, wodurch ja alle Handschriften mehr oder weniger Varianten aufweisen" (109). He concluded: "Der allgemeinere Name εὐαγγέλιον καθ᾽ Ἑβραίους wird von Clems Alex. bis Nicephorus einstimmig bezeugt" (112).

CHAPTER FOUR

Semitisms in the Gospel of Luke

The first three chapters presented all the material in the church fathers relevant to the subject of the Hebrew Gospel. Chapters Two and Three especially demonstrate that when the Hebrew Gospel is quoted by the fathers, the quotations show stronger correspondence with canonical Luke than they do, as commonly supposed, with either canonical Matthew or Mark. The present chapter now shifts focus away from the patristic tradition to the New Testament itself, specifically to the Third Gospel, in order to investigate its possible relationship to the Hebrew Gospel. Since the conclusions of this chapter are essential to sustaining the thesis of this book, I shall begin by providing an overview of the substance of the argument.

The objective of this chapter is to test the validity of a hypothesis that is prompted by Epiphanius's repeated references to quotations from the Hebrew Gospel as coming from "the Gospel of Matthew," or having been written by the apostle Matthew. Not only Epiphanius's quotations but also those of other patristic writers correspond more closely with the Gospel of Luke than they do with canonical Matthew. I have already suggested that the best way to account for this fact is by supposing that the Gospel attributed to Matthew by Epiphanius was not canonical Greek Matthew but the Hebrew Gospel attributed to Matthew throughout the early church, and furthermore that this Hebrew Gospel of Matthew was utilized by Luke, in accordance with the testimony of his prologue, as one of the principal sources of the Third Gospel.

The hypothesis that Luke utilized a Hebrew source in the composition of his Gospel is the subject of this chapter. Scholars have long noted that the Third Gospel, for reasons that have never been adequately explained, contains an abnormally high number of Semitisms in comparison with Matthew and Mark. A very compelling explanation for this fact is that the Semitisms derive from an original Hebrew Gospel authored by the apostle Matthew. This hypothesis should be testable by the following proposal. If the individual Semitisms of Luke are charted verse by verse, they should occur — or occur in statistically greater numbers — in passages unique to Luke. If, as I believe, Mark was used as one source of Luke's Gospel, Luke's Greek should display approximately the same degree of Semitic influence in those parts of his Gospel dependent on Mark. Where Luke is dependent on Mark, in other words, we should not expect to find significantly greater Semitic influence than is present in Mark itself. On the other hand, if Luke utilized the Hebrew Gospel as a source, we should expect to see traces of it in those parts of the Third Gospel not dependent on Mark.

The data necessary to test this thesis is presented in Appendix II, which lists by chapter and verse every Semitism — some 700 — for which there is reasonable certainty in Luke. Appendix II clearly establishes both of the above hypotheses. When Lukan material parallels Matthew and/or Mark, it shows on the whole no greater Semitic influence than do Matthew and/or Mark. The overwhelming bulk of Luke's Semitisms occur rather in material unique to Luke. Indeed, we shall see that they occur nearly four times more often in Special Luke than in material shared in common with Matthew and/or Mark.

Luke's Semitic Vocabulary

Gustav Dalman writes that "Hebraisms proper are special characteristics of Luke. There is reason, therefore, for a closer scrutiny of the style of this evangelist with its wealth of Hebraisms."[1] Scholars have long noted the profusion of Lukan Semitisms, but until now they have failed to give a satisfactory explanation of them. In the introduction to his commentary on Luke, Joseph Fitzmyer speaks of the elusive nature of Semitisms in the Third Gospel. "For all its good Greek, Lukan style has always been noted for a significant amount of Semitisms."[2] Fitzmyer attributes the bulk of

---

1. G. Dalman, *The Words of Jesus*, 38.
2. J. Fitzmyer, *The Gospel According to Luke*, 1.113.

Luke's Semitisms not to reliance on Semitic sources, but to "Septuagint-isms," i.e., to an imitation of the style of the Septuagint. Fitzmyer follows earlier scholars such as Lagrange in this conclusion, and both are followed by more recent scholars. The Septuagint hypothesis will be considered in the next chapter, but suffice it to say at this point that the hypothesis is generally inadequate, for a number of Hebraic forms occur in Luke that find no counterpart in the LXX. Fitzmyer is aware of the inadequacy of the proposal. "There is no evidence that Luke knew any Hebrew," he continues, "hence the source of [the Hebraisms] is puzzling."[3] Fitzmyer's evidence for and discussion of Semitisms in Luke is among the best of recent scholars, yet he is not optimistic that a satisfactory explanation for Luke's Semitisms can be found. He concludes rather dejectedly that "it will undoubtedly remain a mystery" why Luke incorporated so many Semitisms in his Gospel.[4]

In this chapter I hope to dispel the skepticism of Fitzmyer and others like him. Several lines of evidence intersect in support of the proposal that the frequency and various concentrations of Semitisms in Luke are the result of Luke's use of the Hebrew Gospel that is frequently referred to by the fathers and ostensibly alluded to in the prologue of the Third Gospel.

The Nature of Semitisms

What are "Semitisms," and how may they be determined?[5] Languages are structured according to general rules that allow speakers and hearers to

---

3. Fitzmyer, *Gospel According to Luke*, 1.113-18; likewise, A. T. Robertson, *A Grammar of the Greek New Testament*, 107.

4. Fitzmyer, *Gospel According to Luke*, 109.

5. On Semitic influence especially on Luke, see W. H. Guillemard, *Hebraisms in the Greek New Testament*, 12-24; H. J. Cadbury, "Luke — Translator or Author," 436-55; M.-J. Lagrange, *Evangile selon Saint Luc*[2], xcvii-cx; J. M. Creed, *The Gospel According to St. Luke*, lxxvi-lxxxiv; R. H. Connolly, "Syriacisms in St Luke," 374-85; C. C. Torrey, *Our Translated Gospels: Some of the Evidence* (London: Hodder and Stoughton, 1937); H. F. D. Sparks, "The Semitisms of St. Luke's Gospel," 129-38; E. Schweizer, "Eine hebraisierende Sonderquelle des Lukas?" 161-85; A. Plummer, *A Critical and Exegetical Commentary on the Gospel According to S. Luke*[5] (Edinburgh: T. & T. Clark, 1956), xlviii-lxvii; K. Beyer, *Semitische Syntax im Neuen Testament*, vol. 1, Satzlehre Teil 1 (SUNT, Göttingen: Vandenhoeck & Ruprecht, 1961); Fitzmyer, *Gospel According to Luke,* 1.116-27; M. Wilcox, "Semitisms in the New Testament," 1019-21; L. T. Stuckenbruck, "An Approach to the New Testament through Aramaic Sources:

say and hear things according to predictable patterns. Hebrew and Aramaic are closely related linguistically, and they follow similar elementary rules. Greek follows a different and more complex set of rules. Nevertheless, the rules of a language — even the most structured language — are not inflexible laws. The rules governing language can be and often are broken, whether by accident or for effect. It is thus impossible to decide with absolute certainty in every instance whether a given word or expression is a Semitism, i.e., an alteration in conventional Koine Greek usage due to the influence or interference of either Hebrew or Aramaic.

Languages are complex, and the translation of one language into another can be affected by multiple factors that must be considered when deciding whether a given word or phrase in Greek Luke derives from a Hebrew or Aramaic original. Some terms and phrases in Luke that seem to be derived from a Semitic original are, to be sure, possible in conventional Greek. Likewise, a native speaker of Hebrew or Aramaic might write Greek in a Semitic style that could mistakenly suggest reliance on a Semitic *Vorlage*. In Luke's case this particular problem can probably be eliminated, however, for although Luke *may* have been able to translate Hebrew, he does not appear to have been a Jew, and it is unlikely that he thought in either Hebrew or Aramaic.[6] It is not impossible, however, that Luke used a Greek translation of a Semitic original as one of his sources. In this case, Semitisms would be more apparent in a formally equivalent translation than in a dynamically equivalent translation; i.e., a more literal translation would be expected to retain Semitic echoes or residue that a freer paraphrase would not. The problems of detecting Semitisms in a Greek translation are obviously compounded and complex. The LXX, however, generally leans in the direction of more literal rather than freer renderings, and thus exhibits a distinctively Semitic style. If other Greek translations of He-

---

The Recent Methodological Debate," *JSP* 8 (1991), 3-29; S. Olofsson, "Consistency as a Translation Technique," *SJOT* 6 (1992), 14-30; K. de Troyer, *Rewriting the Sacred Text: What the Old Greek Texts Tell Us about the Literary Growth of the Bible* (SBLTCS 4; Atlanta: Society of Biblical Literature, 2003); J. Davila, "(How) Can We Tell If a Greek Apocryphon or Pseudepigraphon Has Been Translated from Hebrew or Aramaic?" 3-61.

6. G. Dalman, *The Words of Jesus,* 40-41, attributes distinct Hebraic coloring in the Third Gospel to what modern linguists call "bilingual interference," i.e., to the author himself. Dalman's hypothesis raises the obvious question — which he does not attempt to answer — how a Greek Gentile like Luke, who was almost certainly not a native Hebrew speaker, could impose such a tongue, either knowingly or unknowingly, on his Gospel?

brew Scriptures followed this general principle — and a Greek translation of an original Hebrew Gospel might be expected to do so — then they too might display a similar penchant for literalness. If so, then it seems reasonable to assume that Semitisms would still be evident in a Greek rendering of the Hebrew Gospel used by Luke.[7]

The ability to determine Semitic influence on Greek texts, particularly in isolated instances, is thus far from certain. The one factor that can lower the degree of uncertainty and raise the probability of reliance on a Semitic prototype is the occurrence of *patterns*.[8] The chance of detecting such patterns in longer documents like the Third Gospel increases in proportion to the mass of data. When terms and phrases appear repeatedly, the likelihood increases that they are not isolated aberrations but the result of explicable influences. The case for Semitic influence is further strengthened when clusters of Semitisms occur in portions of a document that otherwise and in other portions is drafted in conventional Koine Greek. "If we found blocks of text containing a high density of Semitisms alongside blocks of good Greek," concludes Davila, "we could conclude that the writer was either incorporating translated Greek passages into the work or translating passages from a Semitic source in some places while writing in his or her normal style in others. This appears to be the case with Acts."[9] Davila's axiom is actually much truer of Luke than of Acts. Appendix II exhibits the distinct concentrations of Semitisms that occur in various sections of Luke. If Semitisms occurred in consistent proportion throughout the Third Gospel, this could suggest that the author was deliberately affecting a Semitic style, as

---

7. For a full discussion of the problems of detecting Semitisms in Greek texts, see J. Davila, "(How) Can We Tell If a Greek Apocryphon or Pseudepigraphon Has Been Translated from Hebrew or Aramaic?" Davila is aware of the complexity of Semitic interference in Greek texts and the lack of a methodology fully competent to detect such interference. He attempts to set forth "a fully rigorous methodology for establishing translational interference," but admits the difficulty "perhaps to the point of impossibility to apply [such a rigorous methodology] fully to a substantial Greek work" (57).

8. Davila, "(How) Can We Tell If a Greek Apocryphon or Pseudepigraphon Has Been Translated from Hebrew or Aramaic?" 42: "A single case would generally not be enough to establish with any confidence that a text was translated. Rather, what is needed is a pattern of several such features in a text that already scores a significant number of non-septuagintal Semitisms."

9. Davila, "(How) Can We Tell If a Greek Apocryphon or Pseudepigraphon Has Been Translated from Hebrew or Aramaic?" 38-39.

in the Septuagint.[10] But this is not the case. The ebbs and flows of Semitisms in Luke can be reasonably explained by the premise of a Semitic prototype for portions of Luke with high Semitic concentrations. We have reason to posit "Semitisms" when unusual or awkward words, phrases, idioms, and expressions appear with uncharacteristic frequency in an author who otherwise writes cultivated Greek, and when those linguistic abnormalities, which can range from the slightly unusual to the virtually impossible, can be plausibly explained as the result of normal linguistic conventions that regulate Hebrew and Aramaic. The likelihood of Lukan Semitic colorings and concentrations deriving from an original Semitic source is further strengthened by the observation, repeatedly demonstrated in the first three chapters, that patristic quotations of the Hebrew Gospel show more frequent and distinct correspondence with Luke than with either Matthew or Mark.[11]

In this chapter I refer to these alterations simply as "Semitisms," since my goal here is only to demonstrate changes in Luke's Greek due to general Semitic influence. In the next chapter, I shall press this question further and argue that there is more evidence for Luke's Semitisms being the result of Hebraic influence than of either Aramaic or Septuagintal influence. That conclusion is not decisive for the argument of this chapter, however. Much of the evidence adduced in this chapter is equally valid whether Luke is utilizing a Hebrew or Aramaic source, although Hebrew accounts for the evidence better than does Aramaic. Likewise, the conclusions of this chapter are equally valid whether Luke is translating from a Semitic document or utilizing translation Greek, i.e., a Semitic document already translated into fairly literal Greek. Semitisms are clustered in discernible concentrations in the Third Gospel. The following evidence intends to give the best possible explanation of them.

---

10. Davila, "(How) Can We Tell If a Greek Apocryphon or Pseudepigraphon Has Been Translated from Hebrew or Aramaic?" 39: "If an entire work was written in good idiomatic Greek apart from a high density of Semitisms, the most natural explanation is that the writer was deliberately composing in a biblical Greek style. The Semitisms would then be a stylistic affection, not a sign of a Semitic *Vorlage*."

11. M. Wilcox, *Semitisms in the New Testament*, 979-86, offers a long discussion on the detection of Semitic influence in the NT, although I am skeptical whether it is possible to determine "how far such Semitisms may point to written or oral sources, or bilingualism."

Semitisms Characteristic of the Gospel of Luke

The most obvious features of Lukan Greek that display Semitic influence, and that are not shared by either Matthew or Mark, include the following:

1. καὶ ἐγένετο occurs 37 times in Luke as a formula introducing important episodes and pericopes, and as such it repeats in Greek the same function that initial ויהי ("and it happened," or "it came to pass") does in Hebrew.[12] In another 12 instances Luke uses ἐγένετο δέ in virtually the same sense, doubtlessly also rendering the initial Hebrew ויהי.[13] In yet another 20 instances Luke preserves ἐγένετο alone, the majority of which likewise reproduce the effect of ויהי in Greek.[14] Altogether, there are 69 occurrences of καὶ ἐγένετο, ἐγένετο δέ, and ἐγένετο in the Third Gospel. In contrast to Luke's "monotonous" use of ἐγένετο, to quote Fitzmyer,[15] Matthew uses the combined expressions a total of 13 times (καὶ ἐγένετο 7x; ἐγένετο 6x, ἐγένετο δέ 0x), most notably καὶ ἐγένετο in each of the refrains concluding the five major divisions of the Gospel (Matt 7:28; 11:1; 13:53; 19:1; 26:1).[16] Mark uses the expressions a total of 17 times (καὶ ἐγένετο 8x; ἐγένετο 9x; ἐγένετο δέ 0x).[17] Ἐγένετο thus appears five times more often in Luke than in Matthew and roughly four times more often in Luke than in Mark. Of its 69 occurrences in Luke, only two are shared with Matthew and only five with Mark. Thirty-eight (= 55%) of Luke's uses of ἐγένετο occur in Special Luke. Twenty-four (= 35%) occur as Lukan additions to passages shared in common with Matthew and/or Mark. In 62 instances — i.e., in 90% of all occurrences — ἐγένετο appears in Lukan passages not shared by Matthew or Mark.

"Even in Biblical Aramaic," says Dalman, "[ויהי] is already unfamiliar, and in the post-biblical Jewish Aramaic it has entirely disappeared."[18] Καὶ ἐγένετο is thus almost certainly a Hebraism. So impressive is the evidence of a Hebrew *Vorlage* for καὶ ἐγένετο that Dalman — who himself rejects the theory of such a *Vorlage* — admits that "any one desiring to collect in-

---

12. 1:23, 41, 59, 65; 2:15, 46; 4:36; 5:12, 17; 6:49; 7:11; 8:1, 24; 9:18, 29, 33, 34, 35; 11:1; 13:19; 14:1; 17:11, 14, 26, 28; 19:15, 29; 20:1; 22:14, 44, 66; 23:44; 24:4, 15, 30, 31, 51.

13. 1:8; 2:1, 6; 8:22; 9:28, 37, 51; 11:14, 27; 16:22; 18:35; 22:24.

14. 1:5, 44; 2:2, 13, 42; 3:2, 21; 4:25; 5:1; 6:1, 6, 12, 13, 16; 10:21; 11:30; 14:14; 19:9; 24:19; 21.

15. Fitzmyer, *Gospel according to Luke*, 1.119.

16. Matthew: 7:28; 8:24, 26; 9:10; 11:1, 26; 13:53; 17:2; 19:1; 21:42; 26:1; 27:45; 28:2.

17. Mark: 1:4, 9, 11; 2:23, 27; 4:4, 10, 22, 39; 5:16; 6:14; 9:3, 7 (2x), 26; 11:19; 12:11; 15:33.

18. G. Dalman, *The Words of Jesus*, 32. Similarly, BDF §442 (5).

stances in favour of a Hebrew primitive gospel would have to name in the first rank this καὶ ἐγένετο."[19]

2. Ἐνώπιον occurs 22 times in the Gospel of Luke,[20] but never in Matthew or Mark and only once in John (20:30). Ἐνώπιον occurs some 540 times in the LXX, most frequently as a translation of לִפְנֵי.[21] Sixteen (= 73%) of the occurrences of ἐνώπιον in Luke occur in Special Luke. Of the remaining occurrences, three occur as Lukan additions to passages shared in common with Matthew, two in passages shared in common with both Matthew and Mark, and one in a passage shared in common with Mark. Every occurrence, in other words, is peculiar to Luke. The use of ἐνώπιον in pericopes shared in common with Matthew and/or Mark seems to indicate Luke's partiality for the Hebrew Gospel, allowing it to color the Synoptics. Lagrange notes that in one-third of its uses in Luke ἐνώπιον refers to passing "before" God or the Lord or an angel, which, in turn, is typical of the use of לִפְנֵי and ἐνώπιον in the MT and LXX, respectively, "because it opposes what happens before the face of a human being to what happens before the face of God."[22]

3. Luke's use of πρόσωπον resembles his use of ἐνώπιον,[23] which in various constructions functions like לִפְנֵי in the MT to mean "before." In four instances in Luke the construction is πρὸ προσώπου (1:76; 7:27; 9:52; 10:1), in another three ἐπὶ πρόσωπον (5:12; 17:16; 21:35), and in one instance κατὰ πρόσωπον (2:31). Additionally, Luke twice speaks of "setting or directing one's face [to Jerusalem]" (9:51, 53), and once of "prostrating one's face to the ground" (24:5).[24] When πρόσωπον occurs in these various forms it is a classic Hebraism.[25] Of the 11 total occurrences of πρόσωπον in

19. Dalman, *The Words of Jesus*, 32.

20. 1:15, 17, 19, 75, 76; 4:7; 5:18, 25; 8:47; 11:53; 12:6, 9; 13:26; 14:10; 15:10, 18, 21; 16:15 (2x); 23:14; 24:11, 43.

21. H. Krämer, ἐνώπιον, *EDNT* 1.462; A. Deissmann, *Neue Bibelstudien. Sprachgeschichtliche Beiträge, zumeist aus den Papyri und Inschriften, zur Erklärung des Neuen Testaments* (Marburg, 1897), 40.

22. *Évangile selon Saint Luc*², c.

23. The similarity between the two terms is demonstrated in Luke 1:76, where the apparatus of *NA*²⁷ shows an evenly divided textual tradition between ἐνώπιον and πρὸ προσώπου.

24. 9:51, (53), αὐτὸς τὸ πρόσωπον ἐστήρισεν τοῦ πορεύεσθαι = וַיָּשֶׂם אֶת־פָּנָיו לָלֶכֶת (see, e.g., Num 24:1); 24:5, κλινουσῶν τὰ πρόσωπα εἰς τὴν γῆν = וַתִּשְׁתַּחֲוֶינָה פְּנֵיהֶן אָרְצָה.

25. "A clear Hebraism," according to A. T. Robertson, *A Grammar of the Greek New Testament in the Light of Historical Research*, 94-95; "an obvious Hebraism," so G. Dalman, *The Words of Jesus*, 29; see BDF §217.

Luke, eight (= 73%) occur in Special Luke, with two (5:12; 24:5) as Lukan additions to Matthew and Mark, and one (7:27) in a quotation of Mal 3:1 (LXX) shared also by Matthew and Mark.

4. ἐν τῷ + infinitive, followed by the subject of the clause, occurs 28 times in Luke.[26] The articular infinitive is very rare in Matthew (thrice: 13:4, 25; 27:12), rarer yet in Mark (twice: 4:4; 6:48), and absent in John. Eighteen (= 64%) of Luke's uses of the articular infinitive occur in Special Luke, and nine (= 32%) occur as Lukan additions to passages shared with Matthew and/or Mark. These nine additions to Matthew and/or Mark again suggest Luke's privileging of the Hebrew Gospel over the Synoptic tradition. Only once does Luke share an articular infinitive in common with Matthew and Mark (Luke 8:5 par. Matt 13:4 par. Mark 4:4).

The articular infinitive is, of course, perfectly good Greek, especially in Greek historians until the end of the first century.[27] The prefacing of an initial ב to an infinitive is rare to nonexistent in Aramaic, however.[28] Attic Greek may occasionally use a preposition with the dative of the articular infinitive, but not nearly as frequently as Luke does.[29] Nevertheless, the articular infinitive occurs frequently in translation Greek, particularly in the LXX, as a translation of the Hebrew ב commonly prefaced to the infinitive construct.[30] Thus, the usage of the articular infinitive in standard Greek does not account for its high frequency in Luke over against Matthew and Mark, who employed the same Greek medium. The tenfold increase in the use of the articular infinitive in Luke over against Matthew and Mark should be explained rather as the result of Hebrew usage.[31]

---

26. 1:8, 21; 2:6, 27, 43; 3:21; 5:1, 12; 8:5; 9:18, 29, 33, 34, 36, 51; 10:35; 11:1, 27; 12:15; 14:1; 17:11, 14; 18:35; 19:15; 24:4, 15, 30, 51.

27. Lagrange, *Évangile selon Saint Luc*[2], xcix.

28. Dalman, *Words of Jesus*, 34-35; Fitzmyer, *Gospel of Luke*, 1.120; BDF §404; Gesenius-Kautzsch §114 (2).

29. BDF §404 may overstate the case in claiming that "Attic does not use ἐν τῷ [with the articular infinitive]." H. W. Smyth, *Greek Grammar*, rev. G. M. Messing (Cambridge, Mass.: Harvard University Press, 1984), §2033, provides a few examples of the construction in classical Greek.

30. BDF §404.

31. Here "Luke shows himself partial to Hebraising formulae" (G. Dalman, *The Words of Jesus*, 33-34); Lagrange, *Évangile selon Saint Luc*, c, also recognizes the Hebraism, although he attributes it to Luke's imitation of the LXX: "C'est un des cas où Luc a su le mieux fondre ensemble la tradition de la Bible et un usage délicat de la langue."

5. καὶ ἰδού occurs 26 times in Luke[32] and functions similarly to the ubiquitous וְהִנֵּה in Hebrew. Fitzmyer notes that καὶ ἰδού can also translate Aramaic וַאֲרוּ.[33] Although ἰδού alone is good Attic Greek, καὶ ἰδού is much less so, and Luke's excessive use of the expression is not explicable on the basis of the infrequently attested καὶ ἰδού in Greek.[34] On the other hand, וְהִנֵּה is so frequent and characteristic in the MT — and καὶ ἰδού likewise in the LXX — that Luke's repeated use of the expression is most reasonably explained as a Semitism. Of Luke's 26 uses of καὶ ἰδού, 17 (= 65%) occur in Special Luke, 5 (= 19%) occur in Lukan additions to Matthew, and four (= 15%) are shared in common with Matthew. Mark has no instances of καὶ ἰδου (ἰδού alone 8 times, however).[35] In Matthew, however, καὶ ἰδού appears 28 times,[36] of which four are shared with Luke (Luke 5:12 par. Matt 8:2; 5:18 par. Matt 9:2; 9:30 par. Matt 17:3; and 11:31 par. Matt 12:42).

6. καὶ αὐτός (αὐτή, αὐτοί) appears 40 times in Luke,[37] and only five times in Matthew and four times in Mark.[38] Of Luke's 40 occurrences, 29 (= 73%) occur in Special Luke. Not all these uses of καὶ αὐτός (αὐτή, αὐτοί) are definite Semitisms, however, for when the expression is used to show contrast or emphasis it reflects standard Greek usage. Nevertheless, when καὶ αὐτός (αὐτή, αὐτοί) are unstressed, i.e., when they are not intensive, they stand in contrast to Luke's more literary αὐτὸς δέ or αὐτοὶ δέ.[39] In these instances they appear to be Semitisms, functioning similarly to καὶ ἰδού, ostensibly as a rendering of Hebrew וְהִנֵּה.[40]

---

32. 1:20, 31, 36; 2:25; 5:12, 18; 7:12, 37; 8:41; 9:30, 38, 39; 10:25; 11:31, 32, 41; 13:11, 30; 14:2; 19:2; 23:14, 15, 50; 24:4, 13, 49.

33. *Gospel according to Luke* 1.121.

34. BDF §442 (7): "καὶ ἰδού is even more Semitic [than apodotic καί]." So too, P. Rolland, *L'Origine et la Date des Évangiles*, 79-80. R. H. Connolly, "Syriacisms in St Luke," 378-81, argues that simple ἰδού in Luke 13:7, 16 and 15:29 is an example of Syriac influence in using *ha*, "lo," before expressions of time in *direct speech*. Connolly's argument is mitigated, however, by the fact that 1) ἰδού alone is good Attic Greek, and 2) there are many cases of placing "lo" before numbers in Hebrew.

35. Mark 1:2; 3:32; 4:3; 10:28, 33; 13:23; 14:41, 42.

36. Matt 2:9; 3:16, 17; 4:11; 7:4; 8:2, 24, 29, 32, 34; 9:2, 3, 10, 20; 12:10, 41, 42; 15:22; 17:3, 5; 19:16; 20:30; 26:51; 27:51; 28:2, 7, 9, 20.

37. 1:17, 22, 36; 2:28, 37, 50; 3:23; 4:15; 5:1, 14, 17, 37; 6:20; 7:12; 8:1, 13, 22 (41), 42; 9:36, 51; 11:4, 46; 14:1, 12; 15:14; 16:24, 28; 17:11, 13, 16; 18:34; 22:23, 41; 24:14, 15, 25, 28, 31, 35, 52.

38. Matt 19:28; 20:10; 21:27; 25:44; 27:57; Mark 4:38; 8:29; 14:15; 15:43; (16:9).

39. Αὐτὸς δέ (4:30; 5:16; 6:8; 8:37, 54; 11:17, 28; 18:39; 23:9), αὐτοὶ δέ (6:11).

40. E. Schweizer, "Eine hebraisierende Sonderquelle des Lukas?" 163, counts 17 unstressed uses in Luke; BDF §277; Fitzmyer, *Gospel according to Luke*, 1.120-21.

7. ἐν μιᾷ τῶν . . . occurs five times in Luke in a manner that parallels the indefinite use of באחת in Hebrew, "in one of the. . . ."[41] The first day of the month or week is designated in the New Testament not by πρώτη but by μία, in accordance with Semitic usage.[42] Josephus draws attention to this fact in saying, "The day we call πρώτη, Moses called μία."[43] One of Luke's uses of ἐν μιᾷ τῶν . . . occurs in Special Luke and the other four in Lukan additions to Matthew and/or Mark. In the MT באחת is used variously to refer to one of the cities (Deut 13:13; 1 Sam 27:5; 2 Sam 2:1), pits (2 Sam 17:9), places (2 Sam 17:12), valleys (2 Kgs 2:16), hands (Neh 4:11), or eyes (Cant 4:9).

Joachim Jeremias recognizes the uniqueness of ἐν μιᾷ τῶν . . . , but he passes over it as merely a "peculiar characteristic" *(Eigentümlichkeit)* of Luke.[44] Connolly attempts to dismiss the construction as a Hebraism on the grounds that the MT nowhere reads "in one of those *days*," as Luke does in 5:17; 8:22; and 20:1.[45] This is a weak objection. Luke is entirely capable of employing Semitisms that do not occur in the MT. His use of this convention with reference to cities (5:12), synagogues (13:10), and days (5:17; 8:22; 20:1) appropriately parallels the calculated ambiguity of the Hebrew examples cited in the MT above. Indeed, ἐν μιᾷ τῶν . . . appears to be an example of a Hebraism that derives neither from the MT nor the LXX, but from faithfulness to the Hebrew Gospel itself. Fitzmyer's attempt to dismiss the convention as a Hebraism on the basis that unstressed εἰς is well attested in Classical and Hellenistic Greek is no more compelling.[46] Although unstressed εἰς alone is attested in Classical and Hellenistic Greek, the fuller expression ἐν μιᾷ τῶν . . . is less frequent and better explained as a Semitism.[47] The fact that other Semitisms appear in each of the five verses in which ἐν μιᾷ τῶν . . . occurs strengthens the likelihood of the Semitic provenance of ἐν μιᾷ τῶν . . .[48] Schweizer is correct in noting

41. Luke 5:12, 17; 8:22; 13:10; 20:1.

42. BDF §247.

43. *Ant.* 1.29.

44. *Die Sprache des Lukasevangeliums,* 228.

45. R. H. Connolly, "Syriacisms in St Luke," 381-83.

46. *Gospel according to Luke,* 1.121-22.

47. So M. Wilcox, "Semitisms in the New Testament," 1009, who notes that the phrase 1) occurs only in Luke, 2) appears in neither the MT nor the LXX, and 3) appears to be "Christian Palestinian Aramaic." The first two points are grounded on evidence, the third is a presupposition.

48. In 5:12, 3 Semitisms; in 5:17, 5 Semitisms; in 8:22, 3 Semitisms; in 13:10, 3 Semitisms; in 20:1, 2 Semitisms.

that when Luke is not influenced by a Semitic *Vorlage* he prefers to use τις rather than the Semitically flavored ἐν μιᾷ τῶν. . . .[49]

8. An undeniable Hebrew convention is the infinitive absolute in which the infinitive of a word is added to the same word in its finite verb form in order to show emphasis. The infinitive absolute is unique to Hebrew and has no parallel in any language besides Hebrew, whether Aramaic, Syriac, Greek, or Latin. "The Hebrew infinitive construct with a preposition is lacking in Aramaic," writes James Davila, "but is often reflected in Greek translations from Hebrew. It would be unlikely that a Greek translation with examples of this construction would have come from an Aramaic Vorlage."[50] Greek translations of the Hebrew infinitive absolute occur once in Luke 22:15 and three times in Jewish sections of Acts (4:17; 5:28; 23:14).[51] Select instances of the infinitive absolute occur in Matthew and Mark (and once additionally in Acts), but only in quotations of the LXX.[52] As quotations, they do not derive from the Evangelists or redactors. In Luke and Acts, however, we have four instances from the hand of Luke that surely derive from the Hebrew infinitive absolute. In Luke's Eucharistic words of institution, Jesus says ἐπιθυμίᾳ ἐπεθύμησα, "*I have greatly desired* to eat the Passover with you before I die" (22:15). This unconventional Greek redundancy is a literal rendering of Hebrew נכסף נכספתה. Two similar expressions, although not technically infinitive absolutes, occur in Luke 2:9 and 23:46, both in Special Luke sections.[53] Both the infinitive absolutes and these allied expressions surely preserve "une forte saveur hébraique," to quote Lagrange.[54] Luke 22:15 appears to preserve in Greek the *ipsissima verba Jesu*.

9. A further Lukan Hebraism occurs in the spelling of "Jerusalem." The normal NT spelling is Ἱεροσόλυμα, which Luke himself uses on four occa-

---

49. "Eine hebraisierende Sonderquelle des Lukas?" 163.

50. J. Davila, "(How) Can We Tell If a Greek Apocryphon or Pseudepigraphon Has Been Translated from Hebrew or Aramaic?" 43.

51. Acts 4:17 (ἀπειλῇ ἀπειλησώμεθα); 5:28 (παραγγελίᾳ παρηγγείλαμεν); and 23:14 (ἀναθέματι ἀνεθεματίσαμεν).

52. ἀκοῇ ἀκούσετε, βλέποντες βλέπετε (Matt 13:14 par. Mark 4:12); θανάτῳ τελευτάτω (Matt 15:4 par. Mark 7:10); ἰδὼν εἶδον (Acts 7:34).

53. Luke 2:9, ἐφοβήθησαν φόβον μέγαν; 23:46, φωνήσας φωνῇ μεγάλῃ (similar expressions also occur in Mark 4:41 and Matt 2:10). See Lagrange, *Évangile selon Saint Luc²*, ci; and G. Dalman, *The Words of Jesus*, 34.

54. *Évangile selon Saint Luc²*, ci; and G. Dalman, *The Words of Jesus*, 34.

sions (2:22; 13:22; 19:28; 23:37). Of the 31 references to Jerusalem in the Third Gospel, however, 27 spell it Ἰερουσαλήμ, which is the only way Jerusalem is spelled in the LXX (except in Tobit, Maccabees, and 1 and 2 Esdras). Ἰερουσαλήμ is a closer transliteration of Hebrew יְרוּשָׁלַ͏ם than is Ἰεροσόλυμα. Hebrews — the NT document most attentive to things Jewish — also spells "Jerusalem" Ἰερουσαλήμ (12:22). Ἰερουσαλήμ does not occur in either Mark or John (although Ἰεροσόλυμα occurs 10 times and 12 times respectively). Matthew uses Ἰερουσαλήμ only once in Jesus' lament, "Jerusalem, Jerusalem, you who kill the prophets . . ." (23:37) — a passage he shares verbatim with Luke 13:24; otherwise, Matthew too uses Ἰεροσόλυμα (11 times). Luke thus refers to Jerusalem roughly twice as often as do Matthew and Mark; and more importantly, 87% of Luke's spellings are "a pure Hebraic form" of Jerusalem, to quote Lagrange.[55] Of the 27 occurrences of Ἰερουσαλήμ in Luke, 21 (= 78%) appear in Special Luke. Only two of Luke's uses are shared with Matthew (in Jesus' lament over Jerusalem, Luke 13:34 par. Matt 23:37), another single use appears as a Lukan addition to a passage otherwise shared in common with Matthew (Luke 4:9), and three uses of Ἰερουσαλήμ appear as additions to Matthew and Mark (Luke 5:17; 6:17; 18:31). L. Hartman attempts to account for Luke's unique spelling of Jerusalem on the basis that Ἰεροσόλυμα "had a more common and neutral ring," whereas Ἰερουσαλήμ had "an archaizing or festive ring."[56] This baffling judgment lacks any material basis, for Luke's usage of Ἰερουσαλήμ displays nothing ostensibly archaic or festive. It is explicable, rather, as a derivative either from Hebrew יְרוּשָׁלַ͏ם or from the spelling of "Jerusalem" in the LXX.

The references to Jerusalem in Acts are of further relevance here. In the first seven chapters of Acts, where Jerusalem itself is the narrative point of reference, "Jerusalem" appears 10 times in the Hebraic spelling[57] and only once (1:4) in the Hellenistic spelling Ἰεροσόλυμα. From Acts 8 onward both spellings of the word occur in roughly equal numbers, "mixed without any perceptible consistency," according to Hartman.[58] Contrary to this dictum, however, a general pattern seems to emerge when the two spellings are examined in Acts 8–28. When Jerusalem is referred to from a Diaspora or Gentile point of view — specifically, narrative perspec-

---

55. "cette forme purement hébraïque," *Évangile selon Saint Luc,* cii.
56. Ἰεροσόλυμα, Ἰερουσαλήμ, *EDNT* 2.177.
57. Twelve times including textual variants in 2:42, 43.
58. Ἰερουσαλήμ 27x; Ἰεροσόλυμα 24x (*EDNT* 2.177).

tives from Samaria, Caesarea, Antioch, Asia Minor, Macedonia, Achaia, or Rome — the spelling is usually in the Hellenistic form Ἱεροσόλυμα. When the narrative point of reference is in Jerusalem or when the narrative is told from the perspective of Jerusalem, the spelling of the city is usually in the Hebraic form Ἱερουσαλήμ. This general rule is illustrated in Acts 25:1-3, where both spellings occur. When Jerusalem is referred to from the point of view of Festus in Caesarea in v. 1, the Hellenistic spelling appears. Two verses later, when Jerusalem is referred to from the perspective of the chief priests and Jewish leaders in Jerusalem, the Hebraic form appears. Thus, not only does Ἱερουσαλήμ appear in the Gospels exclusively in Luke (except for Matt 23:37) — and overwhelmingly in Special Luke — it also occurs predominantly in those sections of Acts that are set in Jerusalem or where Jerusalem is spoken of from a Jewish perspective.[59]

10. The expression "to glorify God" (δοξάζειν τὸν θεόν) is also an apparent Semitism in Luke, occurring eight times in the Third Gospel[60] and only once each in Matthew and Mark. Four of its occurrences in Luke appear in Special Luke, and in three more it appears in Lukan additions (5:25; 18:43; 23:47) to passages otherwise common to Matthew and Mark. In 88% of its uses it is unique to Luke. Only once is it shared in common with all three Synoptics (Matt 9:7; Mark 2:12; Luke 5:26). Δοξάζειν τὸν θεόν also occurs four times in Jewish contexts of Acts (4:21; 11:18; 13:48 [τὸν λόγον τοῦ κυρίου]; 21:20). Once (Acts 3:13) it refers to glorifying *Jesus,* which is the way it is also used in 15 of its 23 occurrences in the Gospel of John.

Lagrange says that δοξάζειν τὸν θεόν "est assurément biblique," i.e., a Septuagintism.[61] This is either an overstatement or erroneous. "The glory of God" is common in the OT,[62] but the verbal form "to glorify God" (δοξάζειν τὸν θεόν) and its Hebrew equivalent הללו־אלהים are very rare in the OT. Occasionally the variant הללו־אל occurs (Ps 150:1), but the Hebrew more commonly reads "praise the Lord," להלל ליהוה, or הללו יה,

---

59. The above analysis of Ἱερουσαλήμ in Acts is generally confirmed by Raymond A. Martin, *Syntactical Evidence of Semitic Sources in Greek Documents* (SBLSCS 3; Missoula: Society of Biblical Literature, 1974), 105-8. Martin subjects the Greek vocabulary and syntax of Acts to seventeen criteria that indicate Greek translation of Semitic originals. He concludes that Acts 1:1–15:36 contains statistical evidence of translation from Semitic originals, whereas Acts 15:36–28:31 does not.

60. 2:20; 5:25, 26; 7:16; 13:13; 17:15; 18:43; 23:47.

61. *Évangile selon Saint Luc,* ci.

62. G. Kittel, δόξα, *TWNT* 2.256.

which would be δοξάζειν τὸν κύριον, a phrase that does not appear in Luke. Even these latter forms are rare in the OT, occurring predominantly in Psalms and Chronicles. The evidence thus argues against Lagrange's opinion that it is a Septuagintism. Δοξάζειν τὸν κύριον would appear rather to reflect the living Hebrew idiom of the church.

11. Luke also preserves several instances of inner dialogues in which an individual admits something, intends to do something, makes an inner resolve, or "comes to his senses." The Lukan way of rendering these ruminations and resolves is by ἐν ἑαυτῷ (1:29 [D]; 7:39; 11:38 [D]; 12:17, 32 [D]; 16:3; 18:4), or by πρὸς ἑαυτόν (18:11) or εἰς ἑαυτόν/αὐτούς (7:30; 15:17; perhaps also ἐφ᾽ ἑαυτοῖς in 18:9). Each of these nine uses occurs in Special Luke. Two instances of this convention also occur in Jewish sections of Acts (10:17; 12:11). The only similar instance of this usage in the other Synoptics is Matt 9:21, where the hemorrhaging woman resolves to touch the hem of Jesus' garment. In the MT this identical process of speaking or thinking to oneself, which includes the realm of conceiving and planning up to the point of action, is characteristically expressed by בלבו, "in his heart."[63] In only one instance, however, is בלבו translated as ἐν ἑαυτῷ in the LXX (Esth 6:6). This argues against the hypothesis that Lukan Semitisms are mere Septuagintisms, for this example is virtually absent in the LXX. It looks like a free Greek rendering of a characteristic Hebraic expression.

12. A further Lukan Semitism is the use of καί to connect the main clause of a sentence to a preceding subordinate clause. The use of καί in such instances is not logically necessary, nor is it evident in Greek usage elsewhere except on rare occasions. The connection of a main clause to a preceding subordinate clause by "and" is very common in biblical Hebrew (though not in Aramaic), though as a conclusion to a prior condition.[64] William Most calls this convention "apodotic καί."[65] Luke employs apodotic καί in 17 instances, all in Special Luke.[66] Matthew and Mark never employ apodotic καί. Apodotic καί appears to be "a true hard-core Hebraism and a relatively frequent one" in Luke.[67]

---

63. H.-J. Fabry, לב, *TDOT* 7.424; Schlatter, *Das Evangelium des Lukas,* 713. See Gen 17:17; 27:41; 1 Kgs 12:26; Esth 6:6; Pss 10:6, 11, 13; 14:1; 53:2; Obad 1:3.

64. K. Beyer, *Semitische Syntax im Neuen Testament* (Göttingen: Vandenhoeck & Ruprecht, 1962), 1.66.

65. "Did St Luke Imitate the Septuagint?" 30-41.

66. 2:21, 27; 5:1, 12, 17; 7:12; 8:1, 22; 9:28, 51; 13:25; 14:1; 17:11; 19:1, 15; 24:4, 15.

67. W. Most, "Did St Luke Imitate the Septuagint?" 32.

13. In the LXX, ἀνθ' ὧν, generally translated "because (of which)," occurs 107 times broadly throughout the OT as a translation usually of the Hebrew אשר (תחת), but also of יען, על, עקב, or כי. These various Hebrew conjunctions express purpose, as does the somewhat awkward Greek rendering ἀνθ' ὧν. Ἀνθ' ὧν appears to be a true Hebraism. When the LXX is omitted from consideration, a *TLG* search reveals only 13 uses of the expression in Greek writers prior to the Christian era.[68] Ἀνθ' ὧν is thus not regular Greek idiom, but rather an example of a Hebrew expression translated into Greek. Despite its frequency in the LXX, ἀνθ' ὧν occurs only five times in the NT, four of which are in Luke-Acts (Luke 1:20; 12:3; 19:44; Acts 12:23; 2 Thess 2:10). Two of the three Lukan occurrences are in Special Luke (1:20; 19:44).

14. Finally, attention must be given to the use of the imperfect of the verb "to be" (either ἦν or ἦσαν) in conjunction with the participle in the Third Gospel. This construction also appears in Classical Greek for the purpose of periphrasis, i.e., to show continuous action (although primarily with the perfect or pluperfect participle).[69] Since it is permissible in Classical Greek, justification is required for the claim that it is a Semitism. Although εἶναι with the participle can occur in Classical Greek, its use decreased in the Hellenistic period. In contrast to its decreased employment in Koine Greek, however, εἶναι with the participle occurs with uncommon frequency in Luke and the first half of Acts.[70] There is much to be said for Dalman's explanation that the use of "to be" with the participle "is an established principle in regard to the Hebrew of the Old Testament that the union of היה with the participle is quite permissible, even where there is no question of the continuance of an action."[71] The attribution of εἶναι + participle to Hebraic influence by BDF and Dalman should be taken seriously, for the construction occurs only four times in Matthew, seven times in John, 18 times in Mark, but 50 times in Luke. Thirty-six instances of the construction occur in Special Luke,[72] another 10 in Lukan additions to the

---

68. I owe this search statistic to Professor Shane Berg.

69. BDF §352; H. W. Smyth, *Greek Grammar* (Cambridge, Mass.: Harvard University Press, 1984), §599.

70. BDF §353: "[T]his idiom, which is just possible in Greek, was at least strongly supported by the extensive Semitic use of such periphrases, especially in the imperfect."

71. *Words of Jesus*, 35.

72. 1:6, 7, 10, 21, 22; 2:8, 26, 33, 36, 51; 3:23; 4:16, 17, 20; 5:1, 17(3x), 18; 6:12; 8:2; 9:32, 53; 10:39; 11:14; 13:10, 11; 14:1; 15:1, 24; 18:2; 21:37; 23:8, 51; 24:13, 53.

Triple Tradition,[73] and three as Lukan additions to passages shared in common with Mark.[74] In only one instance (Luke 8:32 par. Matt 8:30; Mark 5:11) does the construction appear in the Triple Tradition. Thus, 72% of its occurrences appear in Special Luke, and a full 98% of its occurrences are due to the hand of Luke. Since εἶναι + participle occurs in similar proportion to other Semitisms in Special Luke, and since the construction can be explained by the common employment of the same construction in Hebrew but cannot be explained by its infrequency otherwise in Hellenistic Greek, it seems justifiable to attribute the Lukan penchant for εἶναι + participle to Semitic influence.

Summary of Evidence

The above list contains the most familiar words and expressions in the Gospel of Luke that are generally recognized as Semitic derivatives. They are only a fraction of the complete Semitisms in Luke, however. A thorough investigation of the vocabulary and phraseology characteristic of Luke results in a much fuller list of words and expressions. Such a list is supplied in Appendix II, where all of the above Semitisms and many more that do not fall into the above categories are set forth in a chart showing their occurrences by chapter and verse in the Third Gospel.

On the basis of Appendix II, four conclusions are evident. First, it is immediately apparent that *Semitisms are not isolated to the first two chapters of Luke,* as is often supposed. There is, to be sure, a steady flow of Semitisms in Luke 1–2, but the intermittent concentrations and dearths of Semitisms continue throughout the Third Gospel. Appendix II reveals particularly strong concentrations of Semitisms in 4:14-30; 5:1-12; ch. 7; the end of ch. 9; the latter half of ch. 10; and throughout chs. 13–19 and 24. The number and density of Semitisms in Luke 24, in fact, exceed their number and density in any other chapter in the Gospel.

Second, the large number of Semitisms in bold print reveals that the vast majority of Semitisms is unique to Luke and not shared in common with Matthew and/or Mark. There is a total of 703 Semitisms listed in Appendix II. Of this number, 653 are in bold print; that is, they are unique to Luke. They appear either in Special Luke or as Lukan additions to material

---

73. 4:38, 44; 5:16, 29; 8:40; 9:45; 18:34; 23:19, 53, 55.
74. 4:31, 33; 19:47.

shared in common with Matthew and/or Mark, in other words, but they do not appear in the other two Synoptics. In other words, 93% of the Semitisms in Luke — more than nine out of 10 Semitisms in the chart — are unique to Luke. Of all Luke's Semitisms, only 15 (= 2%) appear in common with both Matthew and Mark; only 26 (= 4%) appear in common with Matthew; and only nine (= 1%) appear in common with Mark. This profusion of Semitisms from the hand of Luke begs for explanation.

Third, and more importantly, Appendix II reveals that *Semitisms occur in much higher frequency in Special Luke than in passages that Luke shares in common with Matthew and/or Mark.*[75] The Gospel of Luke contains a total of 1151 verses, exactly half of which (574 verses) are Special Luke, having no parallel with Matthew and/or Mark. These 574 verses contain a total of 504 Semitisms. The 504 Semitisms in Special Luke account for 72% of the 703 total Semitisms in Luke; and they account for 77% — over three quarters — of the 653 Semitisms in bold print in Luke, i.e., Semitisms unique to the Third Gospel. This means that 72% of the total number of Semitisms in Luke occur in material unique to Luke. When one eliminates the Semitisms that Luke shares in common with Matthew and/or Mark and considers only those that derive from his hand, one discovers that 77% — again, over three-quarters — of the Semitisms in Special Luke occur in material unique to Luke. This second figure is the more important because it shows the Semitisms *chosen* by Luke. When we recalculate on the basis of the 653 Semitisms that Luke intentionally chose to include in his Gospel, we find that over three-quarters of them appear in Special Luke. Seventy-seven percent of the Semitisms in Luke appear in the 50% of the material unique to Luke. Semitisms appear in Special Luke, in other words, nearly four times as often as they appear in those sections of Luke that are shared in common with Matthew and/or Mark. That amounts to almost a 400% increase of Semitisms in Special Luke over Semitisms that Luke shares in common with Matthew and/or Mark.[76]

---

75. The specific pericopes where Semitisms are most conspicuous are 4:16-30; 4:38-39; 5:1-11; 7:11-17; 7:36-50; 9:51-56; 10:29-37; 11:37-54; 13:10-17; 14:1-6; 14:7-14; 14:25-33; 15:11-32; 16:1-9; 16:10-12; 16:14-15; 16:19-31; 17:11-19; 17:20-21; 18:1-14; 19:1-9; 19:11-27; 19:41-44; 21:34-36; 21:37-38; 22:15-18; 22:43-44; 23:6-12; 23:13-16; 23:27-32; 23:39-43; 23:50-51; 24:1-53.

76. Raymond A. Martin has also recognized the unusually high number of Semitisms in Special Luke. "Luke's special material is considerably more Semitic than any other Gospel material, having translation Greek net frequencies about 40% of the time; whereas Matthew's special material seldom has net frequencies characteristic of translation Greek" (*Syntax Criticism of the Synoptic Gospels*, 128).

A further statistic is relevant here. The discussion earlier in this chapter of the 14 most agreed Semitic words and phrases in Luke noted both their frequency of occurrence in Special Luke and their frequency throughout the Third Gospel as a whole in comparison with the other two Synoptics. Those statistics are repeated and summarized as follows:

Lukan Expression	Frequency in Special Luke	Frequency throughout the Gospel of Luke
1. καὶ ἐγένετο	55%	90%
2. ἐνώπιον	73%	100%
3. πρόσωπον	73%	66%
4. ἐν τῷ + infinitive	64%	96%
5. καὶ ἰδού	65%	84%
6. καὶ αὐτός	73%	85%
7. ἐν μιᾷ τῶν . . .	20%	100%
8. Infinitive absolute	100%	100%
9. Ἰερουσαλήμ	78%	90%
10. δοξάζειν τὸν θεόν	50%	88%
11. ἐν ἑαυτῷ	100%	100%
12. Apodotic καί	100%	100%
13. ἀνθ' ὧν	66%	100%
14. εἶναι + participle	72%	98%
Averages	71%	93%

71% of these 14 most commonly acknowledged Semitisms in Luke appear in Special Luke, and, in comparison with Matthew and/or Mark, 93% of them appear in the Third Gospel. On average, in other words, seven out of 10 of each of the above constructions will appear in Special Luke; and when compared with the Synoptics, over nine out of 10 will occur in the Gospel of Luke. These averages are important because they set a general standard to which *all* Semitisms in Appendix II may be compared. On the basis of the control group of 14 Semitisms in Luke, in other words, we have determined two fixed percentages to which the "softer" or more speculative Semitisms in Appendix II may be compared. Remarkably, the summary of Appendix II above shows virtually identical percentages. Seventy-two percent of the total number of Semitisms in Appendix II (as opposed to 71% in the control group of 14 Semitisms) appear in Special Luke; and in both charts exactly 93% of the total number of Semitisms in Appendix II appear in the Third Gospel. The composite data in Appendix II, in other words, agrees almost exactly with the control data based on the 14 most commonly acknowledged Semitisms in Luke.

An observation of Richard Bauckham is relevant in connection with this third point. Bauckham makes a credible case that individual names were remembered and preserved in the Gospels because they contributed, most often as eyewitnesses, to the gospel tradition.[77] A survey of named individuals in Luke reveals that nearly two-thirds (64%) appear in Special Luke. Of the 44 named individuals in the Gospel of Luke, 28 occur in Special Luke and 16 in Luke, Matthew, and Mark. Interestingly, no named individual is shared by Luke and Matthew or Luke and Mark alone. The high proportion of named individuals in the Third Gospel appearing in Special Luke is further suggestive of the early, eyewitness character of the Hebrew Gospel underlying Special Luke. But whereas named individuals appear with disproportionate high frequency in Special Luke, anonymous persons appear with disproportionate low frequency in Special Luke. Of the 45 anonymous persons in Luke, four (8%) appear also in Mark, six (13%) appear also in Matthew, 21 (47%) appear also in Matthew and Mark, and only 14 (31%) appear in Special Luke. *On the basis of this evidence, material in Special Luke appears to be more directly linked to named, eyewitness testimony, whereas material in the half of Luke shared in common with Matthew and Mark appears to derive more generally from anonymous tradition.* The evidence of named individuals in Special Luke thus corroborates the evidence of Semitisms in Special Luke. If the earliest gospel traditions rest on greater eyewitness testimony, then probability argues that the many proper names in Special Luke, like the Semitisms, derive from the *Hebrew Gospel of Matthew.*

The high frequency of Semitisms in Special Luke can best be attributed to a Hebrew source for the one-half of the Third Gospel not shared with Matthew and/or Mark. This is the most plausible explanation for the fact that in pericopes that Luke shares with Matthew and/or Mark, Semitic influence decreases or disappears altogether. The one-half of Luke's Gospel shared in common with Matthew and/or Mark demonstrates that its author wrote in a Koine style relatively free of Semitisms and not particularly dissimilar from the Greek of Matthew and Mark. But in the one-half of his

---

77. *Jesus and the Eyewitnesses: The Gospels as Eyewitness Testimony*, 58-60.

Gospel not paralleled by Matthew and/or Mark, Luke's Semitic vestiges show an almost 400% increase. Luke obviously did not attempt to camouflage the Semitisms in Special Luke or alter them to conventional Koine standards. Why would an intentional and able author — and Luke's prologue assures us of both — adhere to a style of Greek that is peppered with Semitisms in nearly half of the Gospel unless motivated to do so by extrinsic literary influence? In his prologue Luke informs Theophilus that his Gospel rests on the tradition of eyewitnesses and servants of the word (Luke 1:2), i.e., apostolic testimony. What source would be granted such influence by Luke unless it equally qualified with apostolic authority? The only such source known to us is the Hebrew Gospel attributed to the apostle Matthew. This Gospel was frequently attested in the patristic era, and quotations from it show an abnormally high correspondence with the Third Gospel. The frequent and conspicuous vestiges of Semitisms in Special Luke can most plausibly be explained by the inference that Luke was intent on *preserving* the flavor of this preeminent Hebrew source in the one-half of his Gospel not paralleled by Matthew and/or Mark.

Fourth and finally, Appendix II shows 19 **bold** verses, some with as many as a half-dozen Semitisms or more.[78] 5:12a, 17; 9:51; 17:11; and 21:34, in fact, are entirely Semitic. They beg to be translated back into standard biblical Hebrew. These hyper-Semitic verses share several things in common. First, they are not limited to one particular section of Luke, but occur intermittently throughout the Gospel. Second and more importantly, all but one of the verses stand at the beginning of Lukan pericopes. The only exception is 21:24, which stands within a pericope; all other hyper-Semitic verses introduce pericopes. In fourteen instances they stand at the beginning of bold pericopes in Special Luke.[79] In six instances they stand at the beginning of pericopes that Luke shares in common with both Matthew and Mark.[80] None of the nineteen verses introduces a pericope shared by Luke and Matthew alone or by Luke and Mark alone.

This would suggest that a Semitic source played a constitutive role in the composition of Luke's Gospel. The fact that hyper-Semitic verses introduce some twenty pericopes in Luke suggests that the subject of those

---

78. 1:5; 2:25; 4:16; 5:1; 5:12a; 5:17; 8:1; 8:22; 9:18; 9:28; 9:51; 11:27; 13:10; 14:1; 17:11; 21:24; 21:34; 23:27; 24:13.

79. 1:5; 2:25; 4:16; 5:1; 7:11; 8:1; 9:51; 11:27; 13:10; 14:1; 17:11; 21:34; 23:27; 24:13.

80. 5:12a; 5:17; 8:22; 9:18a; 9:28; 20:1.

pericopes, and perhaps also their sequence, is due to the influence of a prior Hebrew exemplar in Luke's hands. This is particularly true of the fourteen instances where the hyper-Semitic verses introduce pericopes in Special Luke. When Luke is not influenced by Mark, he ostensibly defers to a Hebrew exemplar in style, and perhaps also in sequence of events. Even in those parts of the Third Gospel paralleled by Matthew and Mark, however, the Hebrew exemplar appears to retain considerable influence, for in six instances it provides the opening verses of pericopes that Luke shares in common with Matthew and Mark. It is important to recall in this connection that Papias preferred the *order and sequence* of Hebrew Matthew to the Gospel of Mark. The above evidence likewise suggests that the *order and sequence* of the Hebrew Gospel was granted preference over Mark in the Third Gospel.[81] This Semitic source thus appears to have been a *primary* source, into which the author of Luke integrated supplementary material.[82]

81. A point recognized and affirmed by R. Bauckham, *Jesus and the Eyewitnesses,* 228: "The original Hebrew or Aramaic work written by the eyewitness Matthew himself must have had the accurate order Matthew would have been able to give it, but Papias thought this order had been disrupted by those who exercised considerable freedom in their rendering of the Gospel in Greek. These evaluations of the Gospels of Mark and Matthew make excellent sense once we realize that Papias valued above all the Gospel of John, which was directly written by an eyewitness and offered a much more precise chronological sequence of events. It was by comparison with John that Papias had to see the Gospels of Mark and Matthew as lacking order, but, not wishing to dismiss these Gospels, Papias set out to explain why they lacked order but were nevertheless of great value because of their closeness to eyewitness testimony."

82. This hypothesis has been anticipated and explained by several scholars. The earliest and also most precise is J. Vernon Bartlet, "The Sources of St. Luke's Gospel," who argued that a single source of unusual Semitic character (which he thought was a conflation of several earlier sources) played a primary role in the composition of Luke, both supplying the balance of material in the Third Gospel that was not found in Mark, and also influencing the form in which Mark's material was represented in Luke. "All these phenomena suggest the presence in various parts of Luke of *a source parallel with Mark even in sections which at first sight appear dependent on Mark alone:* and this result will be found to prove the best working hypothesis in every part of his Gospel" (p. 323, emphasis in original). Also in the nineteenth century in Germany, R. Handmann, *Das Hebräer-Evangelium,* 130-42, rightly recognized that the Hebrew Gospel was not a later compilation of the Synoptics, but rather an earlier independent Palestinian Christian Gospel, which, along with the Gospel of Mark, influenced the formation of Luke and Matthew.

The following four scholars followed the general lines of the above argument, although without identifying the special source on which Luke relied as *Semitic.* A. Schlatter, *Das*

I would like to conclude this discussion of Semitisms in Luke with an illustration. Semitisms in the Third Gospel remind one of the Frauen-kirche in Dresden. The distinctive landmark of Dresden, once known as "the Florence on the Elbe," was the 220-foot-high bell-shaped dome of the Frauenkirche, built in 1738. Along with the entire city of Dresden, the Frauenkirche was reduced to rubble by Allied bombing on the night of February 13, 1945. For sixty years the Frauenkirche remained a pile of stone, blackened by the 1800°F firestorm that engulfed Dresden. In 2005 the Frauenkirche was rebuilt and restored to its original splendor. If you go to Dresden today, you will see a beautiful honey-colored sandstone exterior peppered with charred stones, in some places more densely than others. The blackened stones — 8425 to be exact — were salvaged from the rubble and reset in the new church in the exact places they occupied in the original church. The present Frauenkirche, in other words, consists of remnants of original stones — even parts of them — now integrated into the fully reconstructed edifice. But the old stones have not been altered to

---

Evangelium des Lukas, 463-71, sought to demonstrate in his massive philological examination of Luke that the Third Evangelist began with a well-developed Gospel based on his special source, which Schlatter attributed to "Der neue Evangelist." Into this proto-Gospel (a term Schlatter did not use) Luke later integrated Markan material. This "new Evangelist" was 1) one of the Twelve, who 2) probably lived in Syria. In Schlatter's judgment, the "new Evangelist" possessed authority on a par with the apostle John. Schlatter did not equate the "new Evangelist" with the apostle Matthew (although he believed him to be "Palestinian"), but his conclusions and the evidence of this study clearly invite the equation. The hypothesis of a "proto-Luke" was popularized in English-speaking scholarship by B. H. Streeter, *The Four Gospels,* 199-222. Likewise, J. Jeremias, *The Eucharistic Words of Jesus,* trans. N. Perrin (New York: Scribner, 1966), 99, n. 1, writes: "It is my opinion that Luke has incorporated the Markan material into his own and not *vice versa.* For this hypothesis at least one reason may be mentioned here. Wherever Luke reports a story in a form different from that of Mark (e.g., the preaching at Nazareth, Luke 4.16-30; the call of Peter, 5.1-11; the anointing, 7.36-50; the greatest commandment, 10.25-28; the fig tree, 13.6-9, etc.), he has the relevant pericope in a context different from that in Mark (only the temptation story, 4.1-13, is in the same place as in Mark). In each of these cases Luke had the material before him in two different forms (the Markan and the divergent form in his own source), and in each case he prefers the form in his special source and abandons that of Mark. The striking thing in this is that Luke does not simply put his version in the place of the one in the text of Mark but rather brings it in at a quite different place. Since he is an enemy of rearrangement . . . this means *that the pericopes in question must already have had their fixed positions when he came to know the gospel of Mark*" (italics in original). Finally, P. Rolland, *L'Origine et la date des Évangiles,* 107-16, has recently argued that an original Hebrew document translated by Paul (!) was a base document for Luke.

conform to the new. They have been reset in the new structure in the condition in which they were found, in order to illustrate the elements of the original church that now constitute the new one. The Semitisms in Luke, as carefully collected and accounted for in Appendix II as the remnant stones of the Frauenkirche, pepper the fully complete edifice of the Third Gospel as do the original stones the modern edifice of the Frauenkirche. And like the charred stones in the Frauenkirche, the Semitisms in Luke have not been altered to conform to Luke's felicitous Greek. They, too, have been incorporated "as found," in order to honor the legacy of the source from which they came.

Luke's Prologue

I wish to conclude this chapter by considering the foregoing evidence in light of the prologue to the Gospel of Luke, which Birger Gerhardsson regards the most important item of information in the first century about the prehistory of the Gospels.[83] Luke is the only Evangelist in the NT who offers a formal *apologia* for his Gospel. What can be justifiably deduced from this prologue about the provenance of the Third Gospel, especially in relation to its unusual Semitic flavor? Jerome reminds us that "Luke was the most erudite Greek author among the Evangelists."[84] Why would an author craft a prologue in cultivated and literary Greek and then adhere to a style, particularly on the half of his Gospel not paralleled by Matthew and/or Mark, characterized by perceptible and sometimes awkward Semitisms?

In the prologue Luke clearly acknowledges his dependence on sources for the composition of his Gospel, although he does not name them. Luke reminds Theophilus, the dedicatee of the Gospel, that others before him have attempted to document the Jesus story (Luke 1:1). The Greek words ἀνατάξασθαι διήγησιν mean to organize a complete and orderly account, to make a coherent narrative. The aorist middle of the infinitive ἀνατάξασθαι would appear to intensify the endeavor, implying the personal investment

83. "The Gospel Tradition," in *The Interrelations of the Gospels: A Symposium Led by M.-E. Boismard, W. R. Farmer, F. Neirynck, Jerusalem 1984,* ed. D. Dungan (BETL 95; Leuven: Leuven University Press, 1990), 534-37.

84. *Epist.* 20, *ad Dam.*

and assiduousness of the "many" who contributed to the conversion of the oral testimony into a written tradition.[85] The noun διήγησις occurs in the NT only here, but its verbal form, a distinctive Lukan word, reinforces this meaning. Διηγέομαι occurs five times in Luke-Acts (Luke 8:39; 9:10; Acts 8:33; 9:27; 12:17; only three times elsewhere in the NT), in each instance meaning "recount a narrative."[86] These narratives or accounts were necessarily *written,* for διήγησις is a "historical-*literary* term which appears both in Jewish-Hellenistic literature and among Greek authors."[87] At any rate, the accounts to which Luke refers were known both to Theophilus and Luke, which would necessitate written sources.

There were, in fact, *many* (πολλοί) such narratives before Luke — indeed written from a closer perspective than Luke's, from "those who from the first were eyewitnesses and servants of the word" (Luke 1:2). The use of κἀμοὶ παρηκολουθηκότι in 1:3 — "also I have followed" — indicates that Luke was not a participant in the events described but rather that he has fully understood and faithfully transmitted eyewitness testimony.[88] "Servants of the word" refers to those who had been active in preaching and transmitting the gospel themselves. The description of "eyewitnesses and servants of the word" (αὐτόπται καὶ ὑπηρέται γενόμενοι τοῦ λόγου) designates "insiders" who were personally present and committed to the enterprise. This cannot refer to the Gospel of Mark, which, in the unanimous judgment of early Christian tradition, was not composed by an eyewitness.

---

85. G. Delling, ἀνατάσσω, *TWNT* 8.32-33.

86. A variant form of the word, ἐκδιηγέομαι, occurs in Acts 15:3 also with the meaning of setting forth a plenary narrative of events. G. E. Lessing, *New Hypothesis on the Evangelists as Merely Human Historians* (§§45-47), actually suggests that the name of the Hebrew Gospel is preserved in Luke's prologue. The title was: διήγησιν περὶ τῶν πεπληροφορημένων ἐν ἡμῖν πραγμάτων καθὼς παρέδοσαν ἡμῖν οἱ ἀπ᾽ ἀρχῆς αὐτόπται καὶ ὑπηρέται γενόμενοι τοῦ λόγου (Luke 1:1-2), "A Narrative of the Things That Have Been Fulfilled among Us, as Handed Down to Us by Those Who from the Beginning were Eyewitnesses and Ministers of the Word." The "many" who transmitted the witness in the Hebrew Gospel were the Twelve. Vv. 3-4 announce Luke's particular agency. Lessing concludes: "This much is certain: Luke himself had before him the Hebrew document, the Gospel of the Nazarenes, and he transferred if not all, at least most of it, into his gospel, only in a somewhat different order and in somewhat better language" (§48).

87. M. Hengel, *The Four Gospels and the One Gospel of Jesus Christ,* 100, 415; Delling, ἀνατάσσω, *TWNT* 8.32-33.

88. See A. Schlatter's analysis of Luke's prologue, *Das Evangelium des Lukas,* 14-23. Also, R. Bauckham, *Jesus and the Eyewitnesses,* 123.

Rather, "eyewitnesses and servants of the Lord" carries the same sense as Acts 1:21-22 and John 15:27, which refer specifically to the twelve apostles, although Luke may not intend to limit the reference to them. The tradition of the eyewitnesses contains a full account of events "from the beginning" (Luke 1:2). A similar phrase appears in Acts 1:22 with reference to the necessary credentials of an apostle, which extended "from the beginning of Jesus' baptism (ἀρξάμενος ἀπὸ τοῦ βαπτίσματος) by John until the day he was taken up from us." If ἀπ' ἀρχῆς carries a similar sense in Luke 1:2, it signifies the participation of the eyewitnesses in the complete earthly ministry of Jesus. The sense of a tradition rooted in personal contact with eyewitnesses is further conveyed by παρέδοσαν, which in general — and quite specifically here — denotes the authoritative tradents of a tradition.[89] The inescapable sense of Luke 1:2, in the words of Richard Bauckham, is "a claim that the eyewitnesses had been present throughout the events from the appropriate commencement of the author's history onward."[90]

The use of ἔδοξε in v. 3 certifies the authority of Luke's account. This particular word, which was widespread in honorary Hellenistic decrees and councils (e.g., ἔδοξεν τῆι βουλῆι καὶ τῶι δημῶι . . .) signifies the legitimacy of the body politic. Luke's use of the term would assure Theophilus, who was probably a Roman official, of the full authority of his Gospel. Luke presupposes his readers' familiarity with the saving story. Their familiarity allows Luke occasionally to telescope a given narrative, such as 3:19, for example, which is virtually nonunderstandable without knowing the events described in Mark 6:14-29. Luke writes to assure Theophilus of the veracity of these prior accounts, which were the source of Theophilus's initial knowledge of the gospel. More specifically, Luke's Gospel is written to assure Theophilus of a proper ordering of events (ἀκριβῶς καθεξῆς, 1:3). Exactly how literally this phrase should be taken is debatable.[91] It seems

89. "This personal link of the Jesus tradition with particular tradents, or more precisely their memory and missionary preaching, on which more or less emphasis is put, is historically undeniable" (M. Hengel, *The Four Gospels and the One Gospel of Jesus Christ*, 143).

90. *Jesus and the Eyewitnesses*, 119. Bauckham sees Luke's prologue as a functional equivalent of Josephus's testimony in *Contra Apion* 1.47, "I, on the contrary, have written a veracious account, at once comprehensive and detailed, of the war, having been present in person at all the events."

91. See J. V. Bartlet, "The Sources of St. Luke's Gospel," 354; I. H. Marshall, *Commentary on Luke* (NIGTC; Grand Rapids: Eerdmans, 1978), 43; E. Klostermann, *Das Lukasevangelium* (HNT 5; Tübingen: Mohr, 1975), 3.

significant, however, that Luke chooses a term — καθεξῆς — that signifies a proper narrative *sequence and order,* a term Luke again uses similarly in Acts 11:4. Luke's own working with respect to order corroborates the testimony of Papias to the same. It also corroborates the fourth and final conclusion above that at particular points Luke integrated Markan material into the sequence of a Semitic source. Luke's expression thus implies that his primary contribution to the foregoing tradition consists in matters of sequence and order more than in content and substance. In sum, Luke's prologue assures Theophilus 1) that his Gospel is the fruit of careful and competent utilization of an unspecified number of written narratives of the life of Jesus, 2) that these prior narratives were themselves based on eyewitnesses identifiable with the Twelve who had been present throughout the duration of the events narrated, and 3) that Luke ostensibly contributed to the tradition by setting forth an orderly account of events rather than in altering the substance of the events recorded.[92]

Our knowledge of the Hebrew Gospel from patristic testimony, and especially the comparisons of patristic quotations of the Hebrew Gospel with the text of Luke, fit like a mortise and tenon with these three conclusions. The clusters of Semitisms in Special Luke suggest intentional and undisguised utilization of a prior Hebrew or Semitic source. The virtual unanimity in the patristic tradition in ascribing the Hebrew Gospel to the apostle Matthew fully comports with and corroborates Luke's *apologia* to have based his Gospel on eyewitness and apostolic testimony. Finally, with regard to the question of Luke's ordering of source material, the discussion of Lukan Semitisms in this chapter has repeatedly demonstrated that Luke accorded his Semitic source high priority in the composition of his Gospel. Indeed, several linguistic splices indicate that he integrated *Markan* material into his Semitic source.

Eusebius understands the prologue of Luke to imply that his Gospel supersedes the accounts of his predecessors. Eusebius defends this judgment on the basis that the Third Gospel is undergirded by the authority of Paul, and also that the earlier Gospels alluded to in the prologue were "rashly" composed.[93] Eusebius probably came to this conclusion on the

92. On Luke's prologue as a whole, see L. Alexander, "Luke's Preface in the Context of Greek Preface Writing," in *The Composition of Luke's Gospel,* ed. D. E. Orton (Leiden: Brill, 1999), 90-116, who argues that, according to the genre of Greek prefaces to which Luke's prologue conforms, Luke claims a level of credibility that we would today call *scientific* accuracy.

93. *Hist. eccl.* 3.24.15.

basis of Origen's *Homily on Luke,* in which Origen interprets "taken in hand" in Luke 1:1 in the sense of producing spurious Gospels.[94] Origen then employs this interpretation to denounce the Gospels of the Egyptians, Twelve, Basilides, Thomas, Matthias, and "several more."[95] This interpretation of both Origen and Eusebius seems to be a careless understanding of the prologue. More precisely, it seems to be a tendentious interpretation used as a pretext for identifying and exposing heretical Gospels. On its own terms, Luke's prologue makes no mention of Paul, nor does it insinuate that the "many" earlier attempts were rashly composed, inferior, or spurious. To the contrary, their being "handed down to us by servants of the word who personally witnessed everything from the beginning" (Luke 1:2) implies the superior authority of the prototypes. Nor does Luke claim that his Gospel surpasses the prototypes. Rather, he implies that the credibility of his Gospel *depends* on the eyewitness value of the prototypes. Exactly why Luke assumes that Theophilus will receive his account rather than one of the predecessors we are not told. But he justifies the trustworthiness of his account to Theophilus on the grounds that it is rooted in eyewitness testimony that is fully credible and to which he has carefully attended.

Patristic testimony and deference to a Hebrew Gospel in the first three chapters of this book are nicely corroborated by internal evidence from the Gospel of Luke in this chapter. Semitic influence in Luke can be quantified as nearly four times higher in Special Luke than in those sections of Luke that are paralleled by Matthew and/or Mark. These flagrant Lukan Semitisms — long recognized and yet long unexplained — provide convincing material evidence that in the composition of Special Luke, in particular, the Third Evangelist relied on an earlier Hebrew Gospel. Luke's reliance on the Hebrew Gospel explains why, as we saw in the first three chapters, citations and quotations from the Hebrew Gospel in the patristic period show an abnormally high correspondence with Special Luke, in contrast to the Gospels of Matthew and Mark. The influence of this Hebrew Gospel is strongly and uniformly evident throughout Special Luke, whereas it decreases appreciably in material that Luke shares in common with Matthew

---

94. Origen may have interpreted ἐπιχειρέω in Luke 1:1 in the sense of "subterfuge," which is its sense in the only other two uses in the NT in Acts 9:29 and 19:13. In literary contexts, however, the word carries the sense of literary composition (BDAG 386).

95. W. Schneemelcher, *New Testament Apocrypha,* 1.44-45.

and/or Mark. This Semitic source apparently functioned as a primary source for Luke, into which other sources were integrated or to which they were supplemented according to Luke's overall purpose. That Luke did not try to expunge and blend his sources, and particularly his Semitic source, is indicated by stylistic differences in the Third Gospel, which are particularly evident in the high-caliber Greek of the prologue, the basic Koine in passages shared with Matthew and/or Mark, and the distinctly Semitically-flavored Greek of Special Luke. As suggested in the prologue, Luke endeavored to produce a full and final narrative while leaving vestiges of the sources that comprise it. The multiple lines of evidence traced in this chapter thus intersect at a conclusive point: the Hebrew Gospel, which was universally attributed to the apostle Matthew in the patristic period, and whose currency and distinction were such that it was classified among the "disputed" canonical books by Origen and Eusebius, was very likely one of the chief though unnamed sources of the Third Gospel to which Luke refers in the prologue.

CHAPTER FIVE

The Hebrew *Gospel*

The first four chapters have marshaled evidence and developed a chain of argumentation dedicated to establishing the thesis that the Hebrew Gospel was the primary source for Special Lukan material. Chapter One surveyed explicit references to a Hebrew Gospel in the patristic tradition, Chapter Two sharpened the focus to examine those references that purportedly *quote* from a Hebrew Gospel, and Chapter Three summarized the composite evidence in the first two chapters in six major conclusions. In Chapter Four I presented a range of philological data and argumentation that, in conjunction with the exhibit of Lukan Semitic vocabulary in Appendix II, showed a dramatic spike in Semitisms in the half of Luke not paralleled by Mark and/or Matthew. A striking number of these Hebraisms in Special Luke — and only in Special Luke — correspond to quotations from the Hebrew Gospel examined in Chapter Two. When internal evidence from Luke in Chapter Four is combined with the patristic testimony to the Hebrew Gospel in Chapter Two, a rather compelling case emerges that the Hebrew Gospel was the principal source used by Luke for the roughly one-half of his Gospel not shared in common with Matthew and/or Mark.

Now that the principal thesis has been established, the remainder of this book is devoted to several questions that have arisen in the course of the discussion but could not be considered earlier without detracting from the argument. It will be helpful at this point to survey the terrain still lying before us. This chapter considers the first question, namely, whether it is possible to determine the actual language of the "Semitic" source of Special Luke? Was it Aramaic or Hebrew, and how certain can we be? Chapter

Six will consider a second and more fundamental question that will have begged for explanation in the minds of readers to this point: if evidence for a Hebrew Gospel is as widespread and weighty as Chapters One and Two indicate, why is the Hebrew Gospel so neglected and virtually unknown in modern scholarship? Chapter Seven will deal with a question more specific to the guild of NT scholarship. Nothing has been said so far about the so-called "Q" document, the hypothetical sayings source common to Matthew and Luke. Could the Hebrew Gospel be the lost and enigmatic "Q" source behind Luke and Matthew? Or is the Hebrew Gospel a different source, and if so, what role (if any) can still be ascribed to "Q"? Finally, the last chapter will consider the question that more than any other has determined virtually all discussions of the Hebrew Gospel in the past two centuries and continues to beg for explanation today, namely, the relationship between the Hebrew Gospel and canonical Greek Matthew.

The Task

The task of this chapter is to attempt to define the "Semitic" source of Special Luke more closely. "Semitic" is a generic scholarly neologism identifying the family tree to which a number of languages and people groups belong. With regard to languages — and this chapter deals with Semitic languages rather than peoples — no one reads or writes or speaks in "Semitic." One does so in Akkadian, Phoenician, Hebrew, Aramaic, Syriac, Arabic, Amharic, or in other languages — all of which share linguistic characteristics that define "Semitic" languages. The Semitic source of Special Luke to which we have repeatedly referred can be only one of three Semitic languages — Hebrew, Aramaic, or Syriac. Syriac can be eliminated from consideration because its alphabet is unique and cannot be mistaken for any other. Moreover, there is no certain evidence of NT literature existing in Syriac before the end of the second century, which considerably postdates references to the Hebrew Gospel in Papias and Irenaeus.[1] The distinction between Hebrew and Aramaic, however, is more controversial. When Christian writers use the Greek word Ἑβραϊστί, they are sometimes supposed to refer to the *letters* or characters of a

---

1. See B. Metzger, *The Early Versions of the New Testament: Their Origin, Transmission, and Limitations* (Oxford: Oxford University Press, 1977), 8-10.

language. This opinion, which will be discussed later in the chapter, ignites a heated controversy whether the term means Hebrew or Aramaic, both of which share an identical alphabet. Or was it perhaps not a Semitic source at all but only a masquerade of "Septuagintisms," i.e., an attempt by Luke to enhance his credibility by composing a Gospel in the revered idiom of the Septuagint?

Thus, the three possible options in identifying "Semitic" are Hebrew, Aramaic, or Septuagintisms. On what evidence could a judgment be rendered? What does the linguistic landscape of first-century Palestine reveal about the use of Hebrew and Aramaic at the time when the Gospels were being composed? From what we know about the use of Hebrew and Aramaic in the first century, would an apostle such as Matthew, a Jewish Christian writing to Jews and Jewish Christians, be more likely to compose a Jesus-document in Hebrew or in Aramaic? As I noted in the discussion of Semitisms in the last chapter, given the complexity of languages, it is not always possible to render an absolute judgment on such matters — especially at a distance of two thousand years. But considering the available evidence as a whole, what is the most *reasonable* answer to the question?

The Septuagint Hypothesis

I wish to begin with the third option noted above, the hypothesis maintained by a number of scholars that Lukan Semitisms may not have derived from a Semitic source at all. Perhaps they are simply the result of Luke's imitation of the language and style of the Septuagint? According to this widely held theory, Semitic vestiges are present in the Third Gospel because Luke intentionally reproduced the style of the Septuagint, which, as a translation of the original Hebrew OT, is inevitably colored by Hebrew. The Septuagint hypothesis has been recently championed by Joseph Fitzmyer. "I am convinced," he says, "that Luke's dependence on the Greek OT — specifically the so-called LXX — is such that the Semitisms of Lukan Greek which are found in the LXX should be frankly labeled as 'Septuagintisms,' and only those that are not should be sorted out as true Aramaisms or Hebraisms."[2] Fitzmyer advocates a reductionist view of the

---

2. *The Gospel According to Luke*, 1.114. Earlier, M.-J. Lagrange, *Évangile selon Saint Luc*[2], xcix, argued similarly; as did H. F. D. Sparks, "The Semitisms of St. Luke's Gospel," 132.

problem: only those Semitic elements that are not paralleled in the LXX should be considered genuine Semitisms, whether Aramaic or Hebrew.

Fitzmyer's thesis is influenced by the criterion of dissimilarity that was employed in NT scholarship in the 1970s and 1980s. The criterion of dissimilarity is based on the assumption that analogy accounts for genealogy. Whenever a counterpart to a particular datum in the NT can also be found in the Jewish or Hellenistic milieu of the NT, the particular NT datum should be attributed to that milieu rather than to the originality of its author. Replication, in other words, indicates derivation; parallels account for origin. According to the criterion of dissimilarity, originality may only be presumed where there is uniqueness or distinctiveness from the surrounding milieu.

The criterion of dissimilarity is no longer riding the crest of popularity it enjoyed when it was first proposed, primarily because it applies over-exacting conditions of causality to states that could arise in several different ways. In assuming a mechanical consistency to which no author would aspire, or of which no author would perhaps even be capable, the criterion of dissimilarity fails to give due weight to the "human factor" in the production of texts. Luke's style, at any rate, is *not* consistently the same Koine style. With regard to the question of Semitisms in Luke, the criterion of dissimilarity is particularly arbitrary and inconclusive. Greek expressions in Luke that resemble Greek expressions in the LXX could of course be derived from the LXX. But such expressions can also be explained in the same way that Semitisms in the LXX are explained, i.e., as genuine translations of a Hebrew original into a Greek medium. Either possibility could account for Lukan Semitisms — and either possibility is equally difficult to prove. In any case, the criterion of dissimilarity is too arbitrary to decide the issue.[3]

When Lukan Semitisms are considered case by case, the weight of evidence in favor of the Septuagint hypothesis is not particularly compelling. In the last chapter I noted that Luke's signature Semitism, καὶ ἐγένετο, occurs with monotonous regularity. This expression could be a Septuagintism, since both καὶ ἐγένετο and plain ἐγένετο occur in roughly

---

3. As M. Wilcox, "Semiticisms in the NT," *ABD* 5.1081-82, correctly notes, the Septuagint hypothesis "is of little explanatory help." "The fact that Biblical Hebrew was in use in the NT period means that apparent 'septuagintisms' must be examined carefully, for they may indeed be genuine cases of Hebrew influence after all."

the same proportion in both Luke and the LXX. But the presence of the same form in Luke and the LXX proves nothing if the form is an obvious Greek rendering of a Hebrew original. Such is the case with καὶ ἐγένετο, which is the expected Greek rendering of the Hebrew וַיְהִי.[4] That καὶ ἐγένετο is a genuine Hebraism is indicated by the fact that this expression virtually disappears from those texts in the LXX that are not translated from Hebrew, i.e., Tobit, Judith, the additions to Esther, Wisdom, Sirach, and the books of the Maccabees. Likewise, in the Aramaic portions of the OT in Dan 2:4-28 and Ezra 7:11-26, καὶ ἐγένετο and ἐγένετο again fall off precipitously, occurring only twice. It can thus be asserted that καὶ ἐγένετο and plain ἐγένετο are genuine Hebraisms, for they predominate in those parts of the LXX dependent on a Hebrew prototype, but they diminish or disappear in those parts of the LXX that were either composed in Greek or are dependent on an Aramaic prototype. Thus, if καὶ ἐγένετο is a Septuagintism, it is a *qualified* Septuagintism, for it is an instance of Luke imitating *only those parts of the LXX dependent on a Hebrew Vorlage*. It is an *unqualified* Hebraism, however. Virtually all scholars who have considered the use of καὶ ἐγένετο in Luke conclude that it should be regarded as a true Hebraism. In fact, so impressive is the evidence of καὶ ἐγένετο for a Hebrew *Vorlage* of Luke that Dalman, who himself rejects the theory of such a *Vorlage,* admits that "any one desiring to collect instances in favour of a Hebrew primitive gospel would have to name in the first rank this καὶ ἐγένετο."[5]

Another example of a *qualified* Septuagintism but *unqualified* Hebraism applies to the spelling of "Jerusalem" as Ἰερουσαλήμ, which occurs in the Third Gospel in 27 instances over against four instances of the Hellenistic transliteration Ἱεροσόλυμα. The first is the only way Jerusalem is spelled *in those portions of the LXX dependent on a Hebrew Vorlage,* whereas in the Greek texts of Tobit, the books of the Maccabees, and 1 and 2 Esdras the latter Hellenistic form of the word appears. Once again, if Luke is following the LXX, he is choosing to follow only those parts of the LXX translated from Hebrew.

As noted in the last chapter, several other Lukan Semitisms are either difficult or impossible to explain as Septuagintisms. In the MT the process of

---

4. So Lagrange, *Évangile selon Saint Luc,* xcviii, who notes that the Greek γίγνομαι perfectly captures the movement of the Hebrew וַיְהִי.

5. *The Words of Jesus,* 32.

speaking or thinking to oneself is characteristically expressed by בלבו, "in his heart."[6] In only one instance is בלבו translated as ἐν ἑαυτῷ in the LXX (Esth 6:6). In order to maintain the Septuagint hypothesis in this instance, one would have to argue that Luke used an expression five times on the basis of *one* occurrence in all the LXX. That contradicts the definition of a "Septuagintism," which is the conscious imitation of a pattern or characteristic style in the LXX. But a single occurrence of a word in the LXX constitutes neither a pattern nor a characteristic style. It is perilous to argue that ἐν ἑαυτῷ is a Septuagintism. It is almost certainly an idiomatic rendering of a characteristic Hebraic expression that occurs but once in the LXX. Again, as noted in Chapter Four, the phrase "glorify the Lord" (δοξάζειν τὸν κύριον), which occurs eight times in Luke, is surprisingly rare in the LXX. Of course, it still *could* be an example of Luke borrowing from the LXX, but, like ἐν ἑαυτῷ, it would be an example of Luke developing something of a linguistic rule in his Gospel on the basis of a linguistic exception in the LXX.

A third example of this same phenomenon occurs in the Lukan expression ἐν μιᾷ τῶν . . . , which clearly seems to reflect the indefinite use of the Hebrew באחת. As we noted in the last chapter, Luke normally prefers to use the indefinite pronoun τις, whereas ἐν μιᾷ τῶν . . . appears to be the result of a Semitic *Vorlage*.[7] Moreover, ἐν μιᾷ τῶν . . . occurs only eight times in the LXX, whereas it occurs five times in Luke. Once again, in order to explain it as a Septuagintism one would have to argue that Luke chose a rare and nontypical use in the LXX and made it into a standard in his own Gospel. Again, these three examples refute the definition of a "Septuagintism," which is the conscious adoption in a receptor text of a *pattern* in the host text. The above examples either do not occur in the LXX or are so rare that they do not constitute imitable patterns.

In a different vein, I noted in the last chapter that ἀνθ᾽ ὧν, which occurs four times in Luke-Acts and only once again in the NT (2 Thess 2:10) is a virtually undisputed Hebraism, since it occurs only 13 times in Greek literature prior to the LXX. Of course, ϛανθ᾽ ὧν does occur in the LXX (107x), so one *might* argue that Luke derives it from the Septuagint. In order to sustain such an argument in this instance, however, one would have to suppose that Luke's knowledge of the subtleties of Septuagint vocabu-

---

6. H.-J. Fabry, לב, *TDOT* 7.424; Schlatter, *Das Evangelium des Lukas*, 713. See Gen 17:17; 27:41; 1 Kgs 12:26; Esth 6:6; Pss 10:6, 11, 13; 14:1; 53:2; Obad 1:3.

7. E. Schweizer, "Eine hebraisierende Sonderquelle des Lukas?" 163.

lary and grammar exceeded that of all other NT writers. That would be a most remarkable claim.

In further specific instances Lukan Semitisms fail to reflect the LXX. With regard to apodotic καί discussed in Chapter Four, Luke uses the expression in only 20-25% of the instances he would be expected to employ it if he were attempting to reproduce its usage and frequency in the LXX.[8] Again, Schlatter notes that if the phrase ὅταν . . . ἐκβάλωσιν τὸ ὄνομα ὑμῶν ὡς πονηρὸν in Luke 6:22 were a Septuagintism, it should read ἐξήνεγκεν, which would harmonize with the virtually identical phrase in Deut 22:19. Luke's use of ἐκβάλωσιν suggests that he is not imitating the LXX but freely translating the Hebrew הוֹצִיא. Yet again, in Luke 9:54, which produces a phrase nearly verbatim with 2 Kgs 1:10, Luke does not follow the LXX καταφάγεται but writes ἀναλῶσαι, which freely renders Hebrew תאכל.[9] Likewise, the expression "to set one's face" in the highly Semitic Luke 9:51 "has no parallel in the Septuagint" and should be reckoned a Hebraism.[10] Blass, Debrunner, and Funk observe that Luke departs from Septuagint usages in another respect, namely, that he introduces sayings "in contexts very different from those exhibiting Septuagintisms."[11] Examples of Lukan departures from standard LXX usage could be multiplied. All the above examples from the Third Gospel are at variance from LXX Greek. When one subjects the Septuagint hypothesis to close and particular scrutiny it fails to explain a significant number of Lukan Semitisms. Obviously, the greater the number of exceptions, the less compelling the Septuagint hypothesis becomes.

Perhaps the most fundamental obstacle to the Septuagint hypothesis is the intermittent character of Hebraisms in the Third Gospel. If Lukan Semitisms are attempts to imitate the LXX, why do they ebb and flow rather than appear evenly in the Third Gospel? As noted in the last chapter, Semitic influence is roughly four times more prevalent in Special Luke than it is in those parts of Luke that are paralleled by Matthew and/or Mark. Why are there clusters of Semitisms in some parts of Luke and dearths in others? Why would Luke seek to imitate the LXX only when he

8. W. Most, "Did St Luke Imitate the Septuagint?" 32-37, writes: "The sparse distribution of apodotic *kai* shows that [Luke] was not just imitating the LXX but was translating, and translating slavishly. He must have been translating Hebrew sources at certain points."

9. For these two examples, see A. Schlatter, *Das Lukasevangelium des Lukas*, 246, 273.

10. M. Wolter, *Das Evangelium* (HNT; Tübingen: Mohr Siebeck, 2008), 369-70.

11. BDF §245a (1).

is not following Matthew and/or Mark?[12] The Septuagint hypothesis has no answer for this fact. The Hebrew hypothesis, however, does: the differences in Lukan style are the result of different sources in the Third Gospel.

A. T. Robertson combs through the philological relationship of the LXX and NT in considerable detail, but he does not find direct or mechanistic influence of the LXX on particular NT grammatical forms and constructions. A large portion of NT words are of course found in the LXX, but this fact is not sufficient proof of borrowing on the part of NT authors since few of the words are found in the NT and LXX and nowhere else. As a rule the syntax of the LXX is far more "Hebraistic," to use Robertson's word, than is the syntax of the NT. OT quotations in the NT usually follow the LXX, but not always; there are a significant number of quotations that reflect the Hebrew more closely, not a few of which are in canonical Matthew.[13] Nowhere does Robertson single out Luke for special dependence on or likeness to the LXX. Among NT authors who quote from the LXX, Peter, James, Matthew, and Mark are cited by Robertson, but Luke is curiously omitted from his list and discussion of the matter. The caution exhibited in Robertson's discussion of Septuagintisms in the NT, and in Luke in particular, is doubly significant because he was writing at a time when Dalman's influence cast a long shadow over NT scholarship.[14]

---

12. W. Most, "Did St Luke Imitate the Septuagint?" 38: "What of the fact that Luke's style is so very different in different passages, i.e., that he does at times write a good quality of normal Greek? Could it be that Luke just *chose* to use different styles at different times? We must say no. For if it were just a *free choice* by Luke, we would have to ask: Why the choice? Writers do not normally shift style that way. Luke could hardly have chosen to imitate the LXX closely at times to provide a Biblical f[l]avor, and then without reason have dropped that imitation. We could not imagine what such a reason would be. But we can, on the contrary, see a very plausible reason for the variation if we take Luke at his word and affirm that he did use documents."

13. See R. F. Shedinger, "Must the Greek Text Always Be Preferred? Versional and Patristic Witnesses to the Text of Matthew 4:16," *JBL* 123 (2004), 449-66, who shows that Matthew's OT quotations frequently include combinations of Septuagint and Masoretic elements. Similar to exegetical and catechetical procedures evident in the Dead Sea Scrolls, the OT quotations in canonical Matthew, according to Shedinger, may reflect *gezerah shavah*, the rabbinic method of explaining one text by another when the two share a common word or phrase. According to M. J. J. Menken, *Matthew's Bible: The Old Testament Text of the Evangelist* (BETL 173; Leuven: Leuven University Press, 2004), Matthew used an OT text different from the LXX.

14. A. T. Robertson, *A Grammar of the Greek New Testament in Light of Historical Research*, 95-102. Robertson mentions in passing that the Semitic influence in Luke and Acts is

The NT arose in a bilingual environment and was influenced in a general way by the LXX. But for the most part that influence was formal rather than particular. The number of actual *words* in the NT that are generally agreed to derive from Hebrew and Aramaic are relatively few.[15] Direct influence of the LXX on the language of the NT — and this is also true of Luke — cannot be demonstrated to the degree presumed by advocates of the Septuagint hypothesis.[16] To be sure, most of the Semitisms noted in Chapter Four *could* be explained as Septuagintisms, but *all* of them can be *better* explained as Hebraisms. Proponents of the Septuagint hypothesis are unable to endorse it with the enthusiasm of a vital and persuasive option. When adhered to, it is inevitably given the reluctant adherence of a consolation hypothesis. It has persisted not because it is a necessary or particularly compelling hypothesis, but simply because of the lack of a better hypothesis.

The Aramaic Hypothesis

Other scholars posit a genuine Semitic source, albeit it in Aramaic, operative in an early stage of the development of the Synoptic tradition. We know that several languages — among them Hebrew, Aramaic, Greek, and to some extent Latin — were spoken in first-century Palestine. Of these, Aramaic and Greek were apparently the most common, although I shall make the case shortly that Hebrew probably played a larger role than has been acknowledged. The hypothesis that Aramaic permeated all levels of Jewish life in Palestine and was both the spoken and written medium of communication in Jewish Palestinian life, is so predominant and widespread that is it is scarcely questioned.[17] "The vernacular Hebrew in that

---

due, in Dalman's view, "to the LXX example" (104). Robertson remains undeclared on the matter, however, and offers no evidence in favor of Dalman's position.

15. Although the pattern of the LXX influenced NT writers, direct influence of the LXX on NT language was minimal. M. Silva, "Semantic Borrowings in the New Testament," *NTS* 22 (1976), 104-10, counts about 60 Hebraisms and 20 Aramaisms. M. Wilcox, "Semitisms in the New Testament," *ANRW* 25/2, counts only 20 Semitic words (both Hebrew and Aramaic); and G. Dalman, *Words of Jesus,* 17-42, lists only 15.

16. For a discussion of the limits of determining the "interference" of the LXX, see J. Davila, "(How) Can We Tell If a Greek Apocryphon or Pseudepigraphon Has Been Translated from Hebrew or Aramaic?" 31-37.

17. R. Handmann, *Das Hebräer-Evangelium,* 48, says that the Hebrew Gospel was composed in the Aramaic dialect, "welcher schon lange vor Christus das Hebräische aus dem

period was probably almost totally absorbed into Aramaic," declares J. Wanke.[18] That Aramaic was the predominant or even sole medium of communication among Jews in first-century Palestine has become virtually instinctual among many scholars — and, like the above quotation, there seems to be no need to substantiate it.[19] I wish to critique this widespread and enduring impression, first with reference to supposed Aramaisms in Luke, and second in the broader context of what we know of the use of Aramaic and Hebrew in first-century Palestine.

With regard to the Gospel of Luke, the several conclusions of Chapter Four point to the untenability of the Aramaic hypothesis. The hypothesis that Lukan Semitisms are the result of an Aramaic *Vorlage* finds even less support than does the Septuagint hypothesis. Luke's signature Hebraism καὶ ἐγένετο (plus ἐγένετο δέ and ἐγένετο) occurs 62 times in the Third Gospel, 90% of which appear in Lukan passages not shared in common with Matthew or Mark. We have noted the unlikelihood of this convention being a Septuagintism. Here we must note the virtual impossibility of its being an Aramaism, for as Dalman declares, "Even in Biblical Aramaic [ויהי] is already unfamiliar, and in the post-biblical Jewish Aramaic it has entirely disappeared."[20] Καὶ ἐγένετο is thus almost certainly a Hebraism. As we noted earlier in this chapter, so impressive is the evidence of a Hebrew *Vorlage* for καὶ ἐγένετο that Dalman — who himself rejects the theory of such a *Vorlage* — admits that "any one desiring to collect instances

---

Munde des Volkes verdrängt hatte." A. T. Robertson declares in *A Grammar of the Greek New Testament in Light of Historical Research,* 94, that "The Hebrew was not a living language any longer," although he acknowledges that Hebrew continued to be used for literary purposes. Vielhauer and Strecker, *New Testament Apocrypha* 1.138, simply assume that "The 'Hebrew tongue' is, as elsewhere in Eusebius, the Aramaic, the 'mother tongue' of the 'Hebrews.'"

18. Ἑβραῖος, *EDNT* 1.369.

19. What P. Rolland, *L'Origine et la date des Évangiles,* 78, says of one scholar ("Vaganay traitait indistinctement tous les sémitismes des évangiles comme des araméismes") could be said of scores of scholars. For instance, note the way A. F. J. Klijn's imposition of the Aramaic hypothesis leads to the imputation of error in Epiphanius: "We have no reason to doubt that Epiphanius knew something of a Christian sect with the name Nazoraeans. Their language was Aramaic. From this we may conclude that they also read the Gospel in Aramaic. But Epiphanius causes confusion when he writes that this Gospel is the original Hebrew Gospel of Matthew. It is clear that he does not know anything of its contents" (*Jewish-Chistian Gospel Tradition,* 14). Klijn simply pronounces that "the notion of an original Gospel of Matthew in Hebrew rests on a fallacy" (18).

20. G. Dalman, *The Words of Jesus,* 32. Similarly, BDF §442 (5).

in favour of a Hebrew primitive gospel would have to name in the first rank this καὶ ἐγένετο."[21]

Similarly, ἐν τῷ + infinitive, followed by the subject of the clause, occurs 28 times in Luke, but only thrice in Matthew and twice in Mark. The articular infinitive is thus strongly characteristic of Luke, and two-thirds of its usages occur in Special Luke. Although the articular infinitive is perfectly good Greek, especially in Greek historians until the end of the first century,[22] in comparison with other NT writers, Luke uses it inordinately frequently. Luke's preference for the construction can be — and almost certainly should be — explained as a Hebraism, i.e., as the prefacing of an initial ב to an infinitive. This construction is rare to nonexistent in Aramaic, however, thus severely reducing the possibility of its being an Aramaism.[23]

A further Lukan Hebraism is the use of καί to connect the main clause of a sentence to a preceding subordinate clause. All 17 instances of this convention in the Third Gospel occur in Special Luke. The connection of a main clause to a preceding subordinate clause by "and" is very common in biblical Hebrew as a conclusion to a prior condition.[24] It is not characteristic of Aramaic, however. "Apodotic καί," as William Most calls it, is "a true hard-core Hebraism."[25]

The strongest evidence for Lukan Hebraisms is found in the combining of the infinitive of a word with the same word in its finite verb form in order to show emphasis. The infinitive absolute is unique to Hebrew and has no parallel in any other language, including Aramaic and Syriac, both of which are Semitic languages. "The Hebrew infinitive construct with a preposition is lacking in Aramaic," writes James Davila, "but is often reflected in Greek translations from Hebrew. It would be unlikely that a Greek translation with examples of this construction would have come from an Aramaic Vorlage."[26] This is an extremely important conclusion, for, as Davila notes,

21. Dalman, *The Words of Jesus,* 32.

22. Lagrange, *Évangile selon Saint Luc*[2], xcix.

23. Dalman, *Words of Jesus,* 34-35; Fitzmyer, *Gospel of Luke,* 1.120; BDF §404 (1); Gesenius-Kautzsch §114 (2).

24. K. Beyer, *Semitische Syntax im Neuen Testament* (Göttingen: Vandenhoeck & Ruprecht, 1962), 1.66.

25. "Did St Luke Imitate the Septuagint?" 32.

26. J. Davila, "(How) Can We Tell If a Greek Apocryphon or Pseduepigraphon Has Been Translated from Hebrew or Aramaic?" 43.

"It is very difficult to distinguish translated Hebrew from translated Aramaic, since the vocabulary and grammar of the two languages are so similar."[27] Thus, at one of the few places where it is possible to distinguish translated Hebrew from translated Aramaic, the four occurrences in Luke-Acts of Greek translations of the Hebrew infinitive absolute indicate a definite derivation from the *Hebrew* infinitive absolute. In the words of M.-J. Lagrange, infinitive absolutes preserve "une forte saveur hébraïque."[28]

It should be recalled that Gustav Dalman, a foremost champion of the Aramaic hypothesis, saw much greater Hebrew influence in the Gospel of Luke than in Jewish religious literature as a whole. "Genuine Hebraisms are almost exclusively peculiarities of Luke's Gospel," he noted. Again, "Hebraisms proper are the special characteristics of Luke."[29] This is a revealing pronouncement coming from a scholar who championed the dominance of Aramaic in first-century Palestine. Dalman's overt defense of the influence of Hebrew in Luke was echoed with equal decisiveness by H. F. D. Sparks. Writing in the 1940s when Dalman's Aramaic hypothesis was still dominant, Sparks nevertheless noted that only two Lukan expressions are common in Aramaic — and even they are not exclusively Aramaic.[30] "But although hardly any of St. Luke's Semitisms are demonstrably derivable from Aramaic, there are several which can be traced without question to Biblical Hebrew."[31] Sparks concludes, "St. Luke has not Aramaized, but Hebraized."[32]

27. J. Davila, "(How) Can We Tell If a Greek Apocryphon or Pseduepigraphon Has Been Translated from Hebrew or Aramaic?" 43.

28. *Évangile selon Saint Luc*², ci; and G. Dalman, *The Words of Jesus,* 34.

29. *The Words of Jesus,* 37-38. Dalman later quotes F. Delitzsch's verdict that "The Shemitic woof of the N.T. Hellenism is Hebrew, not Aramaic" (42, n. 2).

30. "The Semitisms of St. Luke's Gospel," 131-32. The two possible Aramaisms in Luke are the use of the participle with the main verb, and the phrase "to begin to do something." As Sparks concedes, however, and as we noted in the last chapter, both phrases are typical of good Hebrew as well.

31. "Three of these," notes Sparks, "may be conveniently illustrated from one verse [Luke 5:12]: Καὶ ἐγένετο ἐν τῷ εἶναι αὐτὸν ἐν μιᾷ τῶν πόλεων καὶ ἰδοὺ ἀνὴρ πλήρης λέπρας· The opening phrase καὶ ἐγένετο, so frequent in St. Luke, is the familiar Old Testament 'and it came to pass'. Here, as often in the Old Testament, it is followed by 'in' with the infinitive and the personal pronoun. There is, furthermore, no main verb in the verse: instead, the graphic Hebraic 'and behold' leaves 'a man (in the nominative) full of leprosy' hanging in the air. The whole sentence just asks to be translated into Hebrew word for word" (Sparks, "The Semitisms of St. Luke's Gospel," 132).

32. Sparks, "The Semitisms of St. Luke's Gospel," 132.

By way of summary, there are, to be sure, some Semitisms in Luke that can be accounted for as Aramaisms. Nevertheless, the same conclusion may be invoked here — and indeed with greater applicability — that was earlier set forth with reference to Septuagintisms. Although *some* of Luke's Semitisms can be accounted for as Aramaisms, *all* of them may be accounted for as Hebraisms. With reference to the specific question of Lukan Semitisms, the hypothesis of Hebraisms has greater explanatory power than does the hypothesis of Aramaisms, and should be preferred.

The Use of Hebrew and Aramaic among Jews in First-Century Palestine

As noted above, the assumption that Aramaic had largely or entirely replaced Hebrew in first-century Palestine is a commonplace in NT studies. In order to test this assumption it is necessary to show not only that Lukan Semitisms are better accounted for as Hebraisms than as Aramaisms, but also to address the broader question of the use of Aramaic and Hebrew in the period in which the Hebrew Gospel was in circulation, particularly in the early centuries of the Christian era. I hope to adduce enough evidence to make a plausible case that the composition of a Gospel in Hebrew, both for the purposes of instruction of Jewish Christians and of witness to Jews, is precisely what we should *expect* given the linguistic lay of the land in first-century Palestine.

Since the latter half of the seventeenth century, it has been widely held that Aramaic was the predominant if not exclusive linguistic medium of first-century Palestinian Jews. The assurance with which this opinion is voiced is not matched by equal evidential support, however. We still possess very few Aramaic documents that are agreed to represent the spoken Aramaic of the first century. Equally problematic are the several dialects of Aramaic that evidently were spoken in the first century.[33] At the beginning of the twentieth century the Aramaic hypothesis was reaffirmed and given a reputable boost through the influence of Gustav Dalman. Dalman's stat-

---

33. K. Beyer, *Die Aramäischen Texte vom Toten Meer* (Göttingen: Vandenhoeck & Ruprecht, 1984), identifies *seven* dialects of Western Aramaic in Palestine and western Syria in Jesus' day. On the whole question of identifying Aramaic sources in Greek, see L. Stuckenbruck, "An Approach to the New Testament through Aramaic Sources: The Recent Methodological Debate," *JSP* 8 (1991), 3-29.

ure as a Hebraist and his dogmatism on the prevalence of Aramaic in first-century Palestine assumed almost canonical authority in subsequent scholarship. Dalman was generally (though not entirely) correct that the original words in the Gospels attributed to Jesus are Aramaic rather than Hebrew, as are the nicknames of the disciples.[34] From this and other evidence he concluded that the language of the Jewish people in the first century C.E. was Aramaic rather than Hebrew.[35] Dalman declared himself with equal certainty on the language of the "Hebrew" Gospel. Taking Jerome's sole statement to mean that the Gospel of the Jewish Christians was written in "Chaldean" (Aramaic),[36] Dalman concluded that "there is much to justify the view — unless decisive evidence to the contrary should be found in Church tradition or in the Gospels themselves — that a collection of the sayings of our Lord designated for 'Hebraists,' in other words, a primitive gospel (Urevangelium), was written in Aramaic."[37]

It would be a mistake to imagine that on this matter Dalman's views were the only ones of merit. At the same time that Dalman was popularizing the Aramaic hypothesis, Adolf Schlatter, a contemporary and arguably greater scholar, was demonstrating in his magisterial commentaries on John, Matthew, and Luke the affinities of the Gospels with rabbinic *Hebrew*.[38] That Dalman rather than Schlatter caught the ear of English-speaking scholarship was due to the fact that Dalman's work was translated into English, whereas Schlatter's was not (and is only now being translated).

I have no desire to deny that Aramaic played a significant linguistic role in first-century Palestine. It was apparently in wide use, especially in oral communication. What I wish to deny is that it had eclipsed Hebrew, which remained in use as a written language, and particularly in the writing of sacred texts. Dalman himself recognized such a distinction and freely admit-

34. Among Aramaic expressions attributed to Jesus in the Gospels are ταλιθα κουμ (Mark 5:41), εφφαθα (Mark 7:34), αββα (Mark 14:36), and ελωι ελωι λεμα σαβαχθανι (Mark 15:34; Matt 27:46). But some Hebrew expressions are also attributed to Jesus, including ωσαννα (Mark 14:9, 10; Matt 21:9; John 12:13; *Did* 10:6) and κορβαν (Mark 7:11), which may be either Hebrew or Aramaic.

35. G. Dalman, *The Words of Jesus,* 1; idem, *Jesus — Jeschua: Studies in the Gospels,* trans. P. Levertoff (New York: KTAV, 1971), 1-23.

36. See the discussion on this passage in Chapter One, pp. 31-34 above.

37. *The Words of Jesus,* 16.

38. *Die Sprache und Heimat des vierten Evangelisten* (1902); *Der Evangelist Matthäus. Seine Sprache, sein Ziel, seine Selbständigkeit* (1948); *Das Evangelium des Lukas. Aus seinen Quellen erklärt*[2] (1960).

ted what later scholars often forgot, that although Aramaic was the language of the marketplace in first-century Palestine, it was not the only language of writing, and especially not the language of sacred *written* texts. "As a 'holy language,'" he conceded, "Hebrew was still held to be the real language of Israel."[39] We should not be far wrong to imagine a situation analogous to German-speaking Switzerland, where Swiss German in its various dialects prevails in day-to-day verbal communication, but High German remains the language of published writing and formal communication. Dalman thus acknowledged that although first-century Jews spoke Aramaic, their sacred literature continued to be written in Hebrew. Hebrew, not Aramaic, he correctly noted, remained the written medium in all periods of Jewish history, as evidenced by the texts contained in the Apocrypha and Pseudepigrapha.[40] Even in Dalman's day it was well known that the Mishnah of the second century, the Tosefta, which predated the Mishnah, and the Talmuds of the fifth century were composed not in Aramaic but in Hebrew. That the *sancti fontes* of Judaism were written and transmitted in Hebrew rather than Aramaic is indisputable evidence of the continuing significance of Hebrew, at least in religious literature, in Second Temple Judaism.

As a result of the Babylonian exile in the sixth century B.C.E. Aramaic gained significant currency in Jewish life in Palestine. In the wake of Alexander's conquests in the late fourth century B.C.E. and the Roman occupation of Palestine beginning in the early first century B.C.E. Greek was also introduced as an important linguistic medium in Palestine. Nevertheless, it appears that Hebrew retained a privileged status in public prayers, religious instruction, and, as already noted, in the transmission of sacred texts.[41] The spectacular discoveries of Jewish texts in the Judean wilderness in the twentieth century have demonstrated that the linguistic medium of Jewish religious texts remained primarily Hebrew in the early Christian centuries.

---

39. *Jesus — Jeschua: Studies in the Gospels,* 27.

40. *The Words of Jesus,* 12-15. Dalman posited Hebrew originals for the *Assumption of Moses,* the *Apocalypse of Baruch, 2 Esdras, Jubilees,* 1 Maccabees, and the Jewish groundwork of the *Testament of the Twelve Patriarchs;* and he assumed Hebrew as the original language of composition of writings under the names of Enoch (*1 Enoch,* at least chs. 1–36), Noah, Abraham, Moses, Elijah, Isaiah, Baruch, and Ezra, and the *Psalms of Solomon.* Recently, K. De Troyer, *Rewriting the Sacred Text: What the Old Greek Texts Tell Us about the Literary Growth of the Bible* (SBLTCS 4; Atlanta: Society of Biblical Literature, 2003), 126, has argued that "The Greek 1 Esdras text is a witness to a lost Hebrew-Aramaic *Vorlage.*"

41. P. Rolland, *L'Origine et la Date des Évangiles,* 77-78.

About 75% of the Dead Sea Scrolls are written in Hebrew, with the remainder written in either Aramaic or, to a much lesser extent, in Greek. These general proportions also apply to the documents of Wadi Murabbaʿat, Nahal Hever, the Bar Kokhba letters, and Jewish ossuary inscriptions in Palestine. These discoveries corroborate the evidence of the Mishnah, which was compiled in Hebrew about 200 C.E., that Hebrew remained in widespread use in Second Temple Judaism, especially in religious and official literature, but perhaps also in some forms of spoken communication.

That Hebrew played a vital role in correspondence and communication among Jews in the early centuries of Christianity — at least in Palestine — is beyond question. According to the Gospel of John, the title over Jesus' cross was posted in Hebrew, Latin, and Greek (John 19:20). That Romans would list Hebrew in such an instance — and list it before Latin and Greek — is a revealing admission about the currency of Hebrew. Likewise, the surprise of the tribune when Paul addressed him in Greek after his arrest in the Temple suggests that the tribune was accustomed to hearing Hebrew or Aramaic among Jews (Acts 21:37). Particularly in schools and synagogues, Hebrew was used in Palestine in the early Christian centuries and was certainly read by many.[42] 4QMMT, the important Qumran missive to the Temple in Jerusalem, communicates its regulations regarding Temple sacrifices — the holiest part of the Temple cult — in Hebrew, not in Aramaic. The appropriate language in which to deliver and discuss sacred texts and tasks in Palestine was Hebrew, as indicated, among other things, by the fact that *Tephillin* texts were required to be written in Hebrew.[43] Greek was of course a living language among Jews as well, and by the time of the codification of the Mishnah around 200 it had assumed a status of "second among equals" with Hebrew.[44] But, as Mish-

---

42. Jerome's testimony that all the Jews of his time knew the Hebrew Old Testament must be seen as an exaggeration, but it nevertheless attests to the enduring use of Hebrew in synagogues of the fourth century. See A. T. Robertson, *A Grammar of the Greek New Testament in Light of Historical Research* (Nashville: Broadman), 103.

43. E. Schürer, *History of the Jewish People in the Age of Jesus Christ*, 2.23.

44. On the use of Greek by Jewish populations in the first century, see *Masada II: The Latin and Greek Documents,* ed. H. M. Cotton and J. Geiger, with contributions by J. D. Thomas (Jerusalem: Israel Exploration Society/The Hebrew University of Jerusalem, 1989); and *The Documents from the Bar-Kochba Period in the Cave of Letters: Greek Papyri,* ed. N. Lewis (Judean Desert Studies; Jerusalem: Israel Exploration Society/The Hebrew University of Jerusalem/The Shrine of the Book, 1989).

nah *Sotah* 7.2 admonishes, the most authoritative and holy portions of Scripture must be read in לשון הקדש, "the Holy Tongue," referring to Hebrew, not Aramaic.[45]

A ruling preserved in the Mishnah is most instructive on the relationship of Hebrew, Greek, and Aramaic in Second Temple Judaism. Both *Megillah* 1.8 and *Gittin* 9.6, 8 guaranteed the validity of Hebrew scriptural texts, including marriage and divorce certificates, that were translated into Greek. But, although both Hebrew and Greek were sanctioned for sacred use among Jews, Aramaic was not.[46] *Yadaim* 4.5 preserves a revealing ruling that an Aramaic text of a biblical document polluted the hands of a Jew. A Jew could read and hold an Aramaic text that was a translation of a Hebrew original without being defiled; and vice versa, a Jew could read and hold a Hebrew translation of an Aramaic original without being defiled. But an Aramaic text that was not translated into Hebrew or transliterated into ancient Hebrew characters — and this included the Aramaic portions of Ezra and Daniel, plus Jer 10:11 and Gen 31:47 — rendered the hands of a Jew unclean.[47] This point is reinforced in *Megillah* 4.4, 6, 10, where readings from the Scriptures, and especially Torah, are required to be read in Hebrew and "interpreted" in Aramaic only if time allows. In other words, Hebrew — even the archaic Hebrew script such as was found in the Siloam and Moabite inscriptions — linguistically cleansed an Aramaic text, which otherwise remained polluted.

Relevant terms in the OT attest to the continued vitality of Hebrew in Jewish life. The Hebrew word יהודית, for example, occurs six times in the OT and in each instance it appears to mean Hebrew as opposed to Aramaic.[48] The LXX consistently renders יהודית by Ἰουδαϊστί, which also

---

45. See the discussion of לשון הקדש and various rabbinic citations in Str-B 2.442-53, which declares: "In der Regel haben die Rabbinen das Hebräische als Sprache der Schrift mit der Bezeichnung "heilige Sprache" לשון הקדש geehrt" (443).

46. C. Rabin, "Hebrew and Aramaic in the First Century," in vol. 2 of *Jewish People in the First Century*, ed. S. Safrai and M. Stern (Compendiarum Rerum Judaicarum ad Novum Testamentum; Philadelphia: Fortress, 1976), 1/2.1033-37.

47. See the explanatory note in *The Mishnah*, trans. and ed. H. Danby (London: Oxford University Press, 1933), 784. Kurt Treu, "Die Bedeutung des griechischen für die Juden im Römischen Reich," *Kairos* 15 (1973), 133, notes that Greek was employed favorably alongside Hebrew among the Tannaim, but that Aramaic was generally regarded as inferior and vulgar.

48. 2 Kgs 18:26, 28; 2 Chron 32:18; Neh 13:24; Isa 36:11, 13. G. Lisowsky, *Konkordanz zum Hebräischen Alten Testament*[3] (Stuttgart: Deutsche Bibelgesellschaft, 1993), 581, likewise translates יהודית as "judäisch, Hebrew, hebraice."

means Hebrew. On the other hand, the Hebrew word for Aramaic, ארמית, which occurs four times in the OT, is translated in each instance by συριστί in the LXX.[49] Both the MT and LXX, in other words, are agreed in distinguishing between Hebrew and Aramaic. The distinction is made unmistakably clear in 2 Kgs 18:26 where, in the Rabshakeh's address to the people of Jerusalem, יהודית is specifically contrasted with ארמית. "Speak to your servants in Aramaic (ארמית)," pleads Eliakim to the Assyrian general, "and do not speak in Hebrew (יהודית)." Josephus's Greek reference to this passage in *Antiquities* 10.7-8, and later Gregory of Nazianzus's reference to the same passage, maintain the same distinction between Hebrew (= ἑβραϊστί) and Aramaic (= συριστί).[50] In Ezra 4:7 (LXX 4:8) the Hebrew word for Aramaic, ארמית, is likewise translated by συριστί in the LXX. There are, of course, instances where phrases like κατὰ τὴν Ἑβραίων διάλεκτον ("according to the Hebrew language"), τῇ πατρίῳ γλώσσῃ ("the ancestral language"), τῇ Ἑβραΐδι ("in Hebrew"), and Ἑβραϊστί ("in Hebrew") occasionally refer to Aramaic rather than Hebrew in Jewish Greek sources.[51] But these instances are exceptions. In the rabbinic writings עברי refers almost without exception to Hebrew, as opposed to ארמית, Aramaic. Likewise, in the Apocrypha and Pseudepigrapha, in Josephus and in coin inscriptions, עברי customarily denotes Hebrew ethnicity and language rather than Aramaic speech.[52] Even when Ἑβραι-roots refer to ethnicity rather than specifically to language, they should normally be understood to refer to the Jewish ancestral language of Hebrew as well, since Aramaic was not an exclusively Jewish language but was spoken by several ethnicities.[53] Thus, in both biblical and relevant extrabiblical texts, עברי/Ἑβραι-roots normally refer to Hebrew, as opposed to ארמי/συριστί-roots, which refer to Aramaic.[54]

The single most important boost to the use of Hebrew in Second Temple Judaism was the Maccabean Revolt, which not only reinforced Hebrew

---

49. 2 Kgs 18:26; Ezra 4:7; Isa 36:11; Dan 2:4. On Aramaic being referred to as "Syriac" (συριστί), see H. Birkeland, *The Language of Jesus* (Oslo: 1 Kommisjon Hos Jacob Dwbwad, 1954), 12-13.

50. Gregory of Nazianzus, *Or. Bas.* 4, *Contra Julianum* 1.110 (PG 35.648).

51. See Schürer, *History of the Jewish People in the Age of Jesus Christ*, 2.28, n. 118.

52. K. G. Kuhn, Ἑβραῖος, ἑβραϊκός, ἑβραῗς, ἑβραϊστί, *TWNT* 3.366-69.

53. J. W. van Henten, "The Ancestral Language of the Jews in 2 Maccabees," in *Hebrew Study from Ezra to Ben-Yehuda,* ed. W. Horbury (Edinburgh: T. & T. Clark, 1999), 65-68.

54. On the differentiation between Hebrew and Aramaic in rabbinic literature, see Str-B 3.444.

as the language of sacred texts, but also appears in the minds of many modern scholars to have sparked a renaissance in spoken Hebrew. The antipathy against Rome and Roman culture in the wake of the destruction of Jerusalem in 70 c.e. reinforced the Hebrew renaissance. "During the war of Vespasian they forbade . . . that a man should teach his son Greek," records the Mishnah.[55] J. T. Milik, the Qumran scholar whose experience with the Dead Sea Scrolls has perhaps exceeded that of any contemporary scholar, notes that the documents of Qumran were mainly written in an imitation of Biblical Hebrew, which he and others term "Mishnaic Hebrew." The literary and nationalistic fervor unleashed by the Maccabees resulted in a raft of translations into Hebrew of Aramaic documents that had fallen into disuse or oblivion because of their omission from the emerging Hebrew canon of the Bible.

The research of Milik and fellow scholars has confirmed what we have already suggested, that Mishnaic Hebrew was not confined merely to sacred texts or to written documents in general. Similar to the Hebrew of Qohelet, Mishnaic Hebrew is the same colloquial language that appears in the copper rolls from Cave III, in various Jewish contracts of the period, and in the Hebrew Bar Kokhba letters of the second century. This indicates that Hebrew was not only the genre of sacred religious texts of Second Temple Judaism, but evidently also a spoken language of the era. In Milik's words, the various forms of evidence "prove beyond reasonable doubt that Mishnaic [Hebrew] was the normal language of the Judaean population in the Roman period."[56]

Milik's judgment is echoed by a number of authorities.[57] Joshua Grintz argues that Hebrew was "the main vehicle of speech in Jerusalem and the surrounding country, as well as the language most used for literary purposes during this period."[58] Chaim Rabin agrees that as a living and spo-

---

55. *Sotah* 9.14.

56. J. T. Milik, *Ten Years of Discovery in the Wilderness of Judaea,* trans. J. Strugnell (SBT; Naperville: Allenson, 1959), 130. So too C. Rabin, "Hebrew and Aramaic in the First Century," 1033-37.

57. M. H. Segal, *A Grammar of Mishnaic Hebrew* (Oxford: Oxford University Press, 1927), 17; M. Wilcox, *The Semitisms of Acts* (Oxford: Clarendon, 1965), 14; M. Black, *An Aramaic Approach to the Gospels and Acts*[3] (Peabody: Hendrickson, 1998), 47; Birkeland, *The Language of Jesus,* 12-40.

58. "Hebrew as the Spoken Language and Written Language in the Last Days of the Second Temple," *JBL* 79 (1960), 32.

ken language in Judea, Hebrew was spoken until the third century.[59] Even when Greek became the *lingua franca* of Galilee, inscriptional evidence shows that Hebrew continued to outweigh Aramaic. Of the nearly 280 inscriptions at Beth Shearim — the burial site of the Sanhedrin — dating from the late second through early fourth centuries, 80% are in Greek, 16% in Hebrew, and the remaining 4% are in either Aramaic or Palmyrene.[60] Although Greek predominated over Hebrew, Aramaic did not. Prior to the ascendancy of Greek, however, Hebrew continued to be a vital linguistic medium in Judea at least until the Bar Kokhba Revolt in the second century. Between the Maccabean Revolt and the Bar Kokhba Revolt — a period of some 350 years — Hebrew was not on the wane, as is commonly supposed. It was revived. Only after the depopulation of Judea as a result of the failure of the Second Revolt in 135 was the force of colloquial Hebrew spent among Palestinian Jews. But by then a normative Hebrew style had emerged for Jewish religious texts. By comparing the various scripts of the Dead Sea Scrolls, Milik finds that Hebrew script evolved to the "Masoretic" style evident in the manuscripts of Wadi Murabbaʿat, at which point Hebrew script became more or less canonized. "Between the Murabbaʿat script and that of medieval manuscripts [in the Masoretic era], little change takes place."[61]

This survey provides enough evidence to dispel the fiction that Ara-

59. "Hebrew and Aramaic in the First Century," 1033-37.

60. L. I. Levine, "Beth Shearim," *Oxford Encyclopedia of Archaeology in the Near East,* ed. E. Meyers (New York: Oxford University Press, 1997), 1.309-11. The thoroughly Jewish character of Galilee in Jesus' day — and for several decades afterward — is evinced by the prevalence of stone (rather than earthen) vessels, imageless coinage, and *mikvoth* (Jewish ritual baths) in first-century Galilee. See M. Chancey, "How Jewish Was Jesus' Galilee?" *BAR* 33 (2007), 42-50, 76.

61. *Ten Years of Discovery in the Wilderness of Judea,* 29. Although Schürer maintains that Aramaic predominated in parlance at the time of Jesus, he admits that in the sphere of Temple worship sacred texts continued to be written and read in Hebrew. "Mishnaic or rabbinic Hebrew was also the learned language of schools and academies. It is the regular medium in the Mishnah and the Tosefta, and Aramaic the exception. Aramaic did not enter the domain of rabbinic literature until the Amoraim of the third and fourth centuries A.D." (*History of the Jewish People in the Age of Jesus Christ,* 23). Schürer even concedes the continued use of spoken Hebrew alongside Aramaic: "But mishnaic Hebrew served as an additional medium of oral communication. It was later also occasionally employed by scribes at Qumran, and more frequently by those of Simeon bar Kosiba during the A.D. 132-135 war, until it becomes the official tongue of the Galilean academies in the second half of the second century A.D." (28).

maic had eclipsed Hebrew in the time of Jesus and that Hebrew was either a dead or dormant language at the time of the composition of the Hebrew Gospel. There was important evidence already in Dalman's day — and much more since — indicating that Hebrew was the normative language of Jewish religious literature in Second Temple Judaism, and in the same time period still widely used, along with Aramaic, in written literature and common parlance as a whole.[62]

The Probability of a *Christian* Text like the Hebrew Gospel Being Written in Hebrew

Jesus was a Jew. He called disciples who were Jews; he lived, traveled, and died in Jewish Palestine under Roman rule; his primary *Auseinander-setzungen* — his contests and clashes — were with scribes and Pharisees, the gatekeepers of the rabbinic traditions; and he interpreted his mission in terms of Old Testament prototypes, especially Isaiah's Servant of the Lord. Although Jesus attracted at least some attention from non-Jews and even on occasion traveled beyond the confines of Jewish Palestine, his life was consciously identified with Judaism, as were the lives of his first followers. The Acts of the Apostles locates the early years of the fledgling Christian movement within the Jerusalem Temple precincts or its vicinity, during which the growing numbers of adherents to "the Way" were Jews (Acts 2:41, 47; 4:4; 5:14; 11:21), and some of them even Jewish priests (Acts 6:7). Even in the Gentile mission of the apostle Paul, Jewish and Hebraic roots of the gospel retained a privileged status. Writing to the Corinthians — scarcely a Jewish stronghold — some twenty-five years after the resurrection of Jesus, Paul refuted his apostolic detractors by appealing to his Jewish origins. "Are they Hebrews? So am I! Are they Israelites? So am I!" (2 Cor 11:22). Or, writing to the Philippians in Macedonia, Paul lists a half-dozen hallmarks of his Jewish heritage — circumcision, an Israelite of the tribe of Benjamin, a Pharisee, righteous in Torah — to remind his Greek readers that he is a "Hebrew of Hebrews" (Phil 3:3-6). Or yet again, in writ-

---

62. Paul Billerbeck, the great Hebraist who devoted his life to the monumental five-volume *Kommentar zum Neuen Testament aus Talmud und Midrasch,* declares that although Aramaic had superseded Hebrew in the post-exilic period, "das Hebräische . . . hörte es darum noch nicht auf, in bestimmten engeren Kreisen eine lebende Sprache zu sein" (Str-B 2.450).

ing to Ephesus, the capital of the Roman province of Asia where the emperor cult freely applied to itself divine epithets such as *divi filius, pontifex maximus,* υἱὸς τοῦ θεοῦ, αὐτοκράτωρ, the author speaks of being rescued from alien and godless existence in the world and being restored to "the citizenship of Israel" (Eph 2:12, 19). Early Christianity was deeply rooted in Jewish soil. It is of course true that no later than the beginning of the second century a widening gulf appeared between synagogue and church — a gulf about which our understanding today is still very imperfect. But it would be mistaken to imagine that the divide was either complete or unbridged. Christianity continued to be nourished by Jewish soil throughout its formative period.[63]

We noted earlier that in both OT and relevant extrabiblical texts עברי/ ʿεβραι-roots normally refer to Hebrew, as opposed to ארמי/συριστί-roots, which refer to Aramaic. It will be helpful at this point also to review the evidence for similar terms in the NT. The word "Hebrew" (Ἑβραῖος) occurs three times in the NT. In Acts 6:1 it occurs in the complaint of the Greek widows against the Jewish widows; in 2 Cor 11:22 Paul uses the term as a self-designation: "Are they Hebrews? So am I"; and in Phil 3:5 Paul again declares that he is "a Hebrew of Hebrews." Each of these uses of Ἑβραῖος refers more to ethnicity than to language, although in contrast to "Jew" (Ἰουδαῖος), which occurs 195 times in the NT, "Hebrew" may also connote language. But it would not indicate whether Aramaic or Hebrew, or both.

Somewhat more instructive is Ἑβραϊστί, which in its primary sense refers to Hebrew,[64] but which by NT times inevitably could refer to Aramaic as well. The word occurs seven times in the NT, five in John and two in Revelation. Six of the seven occurrences refer either to translations of proper nouns or place names. This complicates matters, however, because place names are often linguistic hybrids. The two instances in Rev 9:11 (Ἀβαδδών) and 16:16 (Ἁρμαγεδών) are Hebrew rather than Aramaic. The evidence in John is divided. In John 20:16 Ραββουνί is Aramaic; and Γολγοθά in 19:17 is closer to Aramaic than to Hebrew.[65] In John 19:13 Γαββαθά is probably Hebrew, since it is not the Aramaic equiv-

---

63. J. C. Vanderkam, *The Dead Sea Scrolls Today* (Grand Rapids: Eerdmans, 1994), 184. Also J. Charlesworth, "The Dead Sea Scrolls: Fifty Years of Discovery and Controversy," *PSB* 19 NS (1998), 131.

64. Str-B 2.442.

65. R. Brown, *The Gospel According to John* (AB 29; Garden City: Doubleday, 1970), 2.899.

alent of Λιθόστρατος.[66] The name of the pool in John 5:2 is especially difficult to judge because the Greek textual history is peppered with a half-dozen different spellings of the name.[67] Thus, the use of Ἑβραϊστί in the Fourth Gospel and Revelation is rather equally divided between Hebrew and Aramaic.

Perhaps the most relevant term is another word for "Hebrew," Ἑβραΐς, which occurs three times in Acts alone, and in each instance in the construction τῇ Ἑβραΐδι διαλέκτῳ, "in the Hebrew/Aramaic language." The last of the instances occurs in the third account of Paul's conversion, in which the heavenly voice addressed him τῇ Ἑβραΐδι διαλέκτῳ. The first two occur, however, in a speech that Paul attempted to deliver to the hostile Jewish crowd in the Temple immediately after his rescue by the Roman tribune and soldiers. Paul requested permission from the tribune to address the crowd. Luke informs readers that Paul then called out to the crowd τῇ Ἑβραΐδι διαλέκτῳ (Acts 21:40), and when the crowd heard him speak τῇ Ἑβραΐδι διαλέκτῳ (Acts 22:2) it granted him a hearing. Standard reference works on this passage again pronounce that Paul must have spoken in Aramaic.[68] But is this so certain? Paul was speaking in the Temple, the one place where Hebrew was dominant. He was intent to show that he was equally "zealous for God" (Acts 22:4) as were the Jews to whom he was speaking (e.g., Rom 10:2). One can imagine a man in his predicament — and in this place — demonstrating his zeal by delivering this momentous speech not in Aramaic but in Hebrew, a tongue he had mastered under the aegis of the learned Gamaliel. I am rather certain Paul would have considered these data relevant at the time. The unexpected hush of the crowd indicates that he did — and suggests that he spoke in *Hebrew.*

This concludes the specific evidence that the NT provides on the use of Hebrew and Aramaic. We have *not* seen — as so many modern scholars assume — that all references connote Aramaic. The evidence suggests that some connote Aramaic, but the same evidence suggests with the same force that roughly the same number connotes Hebrew. This generally corroborates, in other words, the larger picture that emerges from a wide

---

66. Brown, *The Gospel According to John,* 2.882.

67. See B. Metzger, *A Textual Commentary on the Greek New Testament* (London and New York: United Bible Societies, 1971), 208. Nevertheless, one of the most widely supported readings, Βηθεσδά, is a Hebraism for בית חסדא, "House of God's Mercy."

68. E.g., Ἑβραΐς, *EDNT* 1.370; W. Gutbrod, Ἑβραῖος, *TWNT* 3.391.

range of composite evidence: Aramaic had not "eclipsed" or "absorbed" Hebrew in the first Christian century. Particularly in the writing of sacred texts and in the parlance of the religious leadership, Hebrew maintained a privileged position in Second Temple Judaism.

This general conclusion seems to be corroborated by the fathers as well. Most frequently — especially in Irenaeus and Eusebius — the language of the Hebrew Gospel is called the Hebrew "dialect" (διάλεκτος).[69] Thus, when Eusebius recounts the list of OT books that Origen believed canonical — and for which Origen gave the *Hebrew* name — he twice refers to the people who produced them as Ἐβραῖοι — Hebrews.[70] When Theodoret of Cyrrhus, a fourth-century contemporary of Eusebius, refers to Symmachus's translation of the Hebrew OT into Greek, he writes ἐκ τῆς Ἐβραίων, which can only mean Hebrew.[71] BDAG gives as the only definition of διάλεκτος "the language of a nation or region," and English translations of patristic texts usually translate it "language." Other terms include στοιχεία, φωνή, and γλῶττα. The first term, στοιχεία, connoted the constitutive elements of a thing. It could be used to refer to the letters and alphabet as the fundamental principles of language. In philosophy στοιχεία provided both the vocabulary and intellectual constructs for the four elements of the world (earth, air, fire, water). Eusebius employs στοιχεία with reference to Origen's comprehensive knowledge and mastery of Hebrew.[72] The last two terms refer to the audible aspects of a language. Φωνή denotes "sound" or "noise," but when context dictates it means a verbal code or language. Γλῶττα, an Attic form of γλῶσσα, meaning "tongue," likewise connotes vocalization. Both Philo and Josephus use Ἐβραίων γλῶττα repeatedly to imply Hebrew rather than Aramaic.[73] A scholion on Plato's

---

69. Irenaeus, *Haer.* 3.1.1; Eusebius, *Eccl. hist.* 4.22.8; 5.8.3

70. Eusebius, *Hist. eccl.* 6.25.1-2. See G. Dorival, "Un groupe Judéo-Chrétien méconnu: les Hébreux," 26-34, for further uses of "Hebrew" in Origen with reference to the Hebrew language.

71. Σύμμαχος, ὁ τὴν παλαιὰν γραφὴν ἐκ τῆς Ἐβραίων μετατεθεικὼς εἰς τὴν Ἑλλάδα φωνήν (*Haer. fab.* 2.1).

72. *Hist. eccl.* 6.16.1.

73. Philo, *Conf.* 68; Josephus, *Ant.* 5.323; 1.36. All three references in Philo and Josephus refer to the description of *Hebrew* words in the OT. A fourth use of the term in Josephus in *J.W.* 6.96 refers to Josephus himself translating Caesar's speech into Hebrew for the benefit of the besieged populace of Jerusalem. Editors of a former era readily assumed that the term implied that Josephus was speaking in Aramaic. Given the widespread use of Hebrew at the time, however, and given the solemnity of the situation, one would rather expect Josephus to

Phaedrus speaks of a Hebrew Sibyl who "prophesied her prophecies in the Hebrew language."[74] The scholion begins by differentiating between "Chaldean" and "Hebrew," which justifies the assumption that the Sibyl prophesied in Hebrew rather than Aramaic. Like עברי/ʿεβραι-roots, the terms διάλεκτος, στοιχεῖα, φωνή, and γλῶττα that occur in Philo, Josephus, and a number of church fathers in the majority of instances refer to Hebrew rather than Aramaic.

Throughout the early centuries of the church, Christian luminaries continued to acknowledge the Hebraic roots of the gospel. In his polemic against Celsus, Origen (185-254) avowed that the roots of Christianity began not with Jesus but in "the Mosaic worship and the prophetic writings." Christians do not disrespect the Jewish Law, maintained Origen, but acknowledge that "the beginning of the Gospel is connected with the Jewish writings."[75] That Origen would defend Christianity before Celsus, a pagan skeptic, by appealing to its *Judaic* roots is particularly noteworthy. The greatest testimony to early Christian allegiance to its Jewish past was doubtlessly Origen's Hexapla, in which he endeavored to set Christian dialogue with Jews on a scientific basis by placing the four principal Greek versions of the Old Testament (Aquila, Symmachus, the Septuagint, and Theodotion) in parallel columns beside two Hebrew texts, one original and one transliterated into Greek. The purpose of this monumental undertaking was to demonstrate the faithfulness of the Greek versions to the original Hebrew.

Nearly two centuries after Origen, Augustine (354-430) held that the Septuagint and not the Hebrew Old Testament was the "preferred authority" of the church. Nevertheless, Augustine, who knew no Hebrew and Greek only moderately, defended textual expansions in the Septuagint and in Jerome's Vulgate on the grounds that they accorded with the spirit and intention of the Hebrew original. Since the apostles quote from both the Hebrew and Septuagint, "both should be used as authoritative, since both

---

speak in Hebrew — exactly as he says. On the question of Josephus's use of the term, see J. Grintz, "Hebrew as the Spoken and Written Language in the Last Days of the Second Temple," 32-47. On the basis of the use of the term in *Ant. Proem.* 5; *Ant.* 1.33, 34, 36, 333; 5.21; 10.2; 12.14-15; *J.W.* 6.93-110, 435-42, Grintz concludes that in each instance Josephus intends *Hebrew*, not Aramaic.

74. γλώσσῃ φασὶ τὰ χρησμῳδηθέντα τῇ Ἑβραΐδι, cited from *Greek and Latin Authors on the Jews and Judaism*, ed. M. Stern, 3.62.

75. *Cels.* 2.4.

are one and divine," concluded the Bishop of Hippo.[76] Indeed, in cases where differences between the Hebrew and LXX/Vulgate could not be reconciled, Augustine decreed that "we do well to believe in preference that language out of which the translation was made."[77] In those cases where a choice must be made between the Hebrew and the LXX, in other words, Augustine accorded primacy to the Hebrew. Augustine's practice in this regard seems to have been typical of the patristic period.[78]

Jerome surpassed both Origen and Augustine in his deference to Hebrew. To the best of our knowledge, Jerome's and Origen's mastery of Hebrew exceeded that of all the other fathers. Jerome attributes OT quotations in canonical Matthew to the Hebrew rather than to the Septuagint — and in so doing he implies their superiority to the LXX.[79] Jerome was virtually alone among the fathers in rejecting on critical grounds the pious legend that the LXX was inspired by seventy-two translators working independently in their cells.[80]

Above all, Jerome, like Origen, preferred the Hebrew Old Testament over its Greek translations. Jerome's decision to base his Latin translation on the Hebrew rather than the Greek OT was not met with universal approval. For some, like Rufinus, the Hebrew OT was tainted with Judaism.[81] Although Augustine himself affirmed the integrity of the Hebrew OT, including its reading in the church,[82] he advised Jerome on two grounds against basing his translation on it. First, by Augustine's day the LXX was clearly preferred over the Hebrew OT among the rank and file of the church. In *The City of God* he notes that discrepancies or contradictions in the LXX were regularly explained by his parishioners as the result of errors in the Hebrew original rather than as errors on the part of the LXX transla-

---

76. *Civ.* 18.43-44 (Marcus Dods translation).

77. *Civ.* 15.13 (Marcus Dods translation). On Augustine and the LXX, see M. Hengel, *The Septuagint as Christian Scripture,* trans. M. Biddle (Grand Rapids: Baker Academic, 2002), 51-54.

78. Kurt Treu, "Die Bedeutung des griechischen für die Juden im Römischen Reich," *Kairos* 15 (1973), 139: "Das Ergebnis: Die LXX wird von den christlichen Gelehrten nicht kritiklos übernommen, sondern am Original gemessen."

79. "Whenever the Evangelist, whether on his own account or in the person of our Lord the Savior, quotes the testimonies of the Old Testament, he does not follow the authority of the translators of the Septuagint, but the Hebrew" (*Vir. ill.* 3.3; trans. T. Halton).

80. M. Hengel, *The Septuagint as Christian Scripture,* 48.

81. Rufinus, *Apol. Hier.* 2.32-37.

82. *Epist.* 71.3-5; 82.35.

tors. His parishioners maintained that "[t]he Jews, envying us our translation of their Law and Prophets, have made alterations in their texts so as to undermine the authority of ours."[83] Augustine's second admonition, similarly, was based on the preference of the eastern churches for the LXX. Both warnings, in other words, were based on the fear that a translation based on the Hebrew would jeopardize its reception in the church — and in the case of the eastern churches drive a further wedge between them and the western churches.[84] Despite the political sagacity of Augustine's admonitions, Jerome translated the Vulgate, as it came to be known, from the Hebrew rather than the LXX.

An example from Josephus is instructive. In *The Jewish War*, Josephus recounts being sent by Titus, who was besieging Jerusalem, to parley with John of Gischala, the leader of the Jewish defenders of Jerusalem. Speaking of himself in the third person, he writes, "Josephus, standing so that his words might reach the ears not only of John but also of the multitude, delivered Caesar's message in Hebrew."[85] The LCL translator immediately asserts that by "Hebrew" Josephus means "Aramaic." But is this absolutely certain? Josephus surely knew that an appeal would be more effective — and less capable of being understood by the Romans — in Hebrew than in Aramaic. Moreover, in his own preface to *The Jewish War*, Josephus declares his rationale for writing in these words:

> I — Josephus, son of Matthias, a Hebrew by race, a native of Jerusalem and a priest, who at the opening of the war myself fought against the Romans and in the sequel was perforce an onlooker — propose to provide the subjects of the Roman Empire with a narrative of the facts, by translating into Greek the account which I previously composed in my vernacular tongue.[86]

Josephus describes his "vernacular tongue" — which indeed means "Aramaic" in this instance — by the phrase "father tongue."[87] In the one in-

83. *Civ.* 15.11.

84. H. F. D. Sparks, "Jerome as Biblical Translator," *The Cambridge History of the Bible: From the Beginnings to Jerome,* ed. P. R. Ackroyd and C. F. Evans (Cambridge: University Press, 1975), 521.

85. *J.W.* 6.96: διήγγελλεν ἑβραΐζων (trans. H. St.-J. Thackeray, LCL).

86. *J.W.* 1.3.

87. τῇ πατρίῳ συντάξας.

stance when we know Josephus means "Aramaic," he does not call it "Hebrew." Is it not probable that when he uses "Hebrew" he means Hebrew — especially when the benefit of using Hebrew over Aramaic is obvious?[88]

Tractate *Šabbat* 116 in the Babylonian Gemara deserves a special note here because it preserves an Aramaic quotation of a text that likely derives from the Hebrew Gospel.[89] This Aramaic quotation could be understood to confirm the view that the Hebrew Gospel was, as widely believed, an *Aramaic* Gospel. In fact, this Aramaic quotation says very little about the language of the Hebrew Gospel, because it appears in a satirical story narrated in Aramaic. It is thus an open question whether the *Šabbat* 116 quotation, which may echo Matt 5:17 or perhaps Luke 13:1-3, was *quoted* from Aramaic or *translated* into Aramaic so as to conform to the Aramaic story in which it occurs.

It should be apparent that the revival and reinforcement of Hebrew as a language of sacred literature would have set a natural precedent for Jewish Christians to follow when they first reduced the story of Jesus to writing. That the apostle Matthew composed an original Gospel in Hebrew is, as we have seen, widely attested among the church fathers. Its composition in *Hebrew* is exactly what we should expect in light of the authority enjoyed by Hebrew in sacred Jewish literature at the time. Let us recall Eusebius's report that the first fifteen bishops of Jerusalem down to the time of Hadrian (ruled 117-38) "were all Hebrews." Indeed, "the whole church at that time consisted of Hebrews," noted Eusebius.[90] By "whole church" Eusebius must mean the whole church in Jerusalem or perhaps in Palestine. If the apostle Matthew wrote the Hebrew Gospel to Jewish Christians and for the purpose of evangelizing Jews — and that is the consistent testimony of the early church — then, especially given the ongoing Hebrew complexion of the church in Palestine, we should expect him to

---

88. On Josephus's distinction between Hebrew and Aramaic, see Str-B 2.451-53. Billerbeck concludes "daß Josephus jedenfalls keinen Wert darauf gelegt hat, zwischen hebräisch u. aramäisch überall streng zu unterscheiden." Despite this ambiguous conclusion, the majority of examples Billerbeck cites shows that Josephus preferred to use Ἑβραϊστί for Hebrew!

89. See Chapter Six, pp. 228-33 below.

90. *Eccl. hist.* 4.5.1-2. Theodor Zahn, *Geschichte des neutestamentlichen Kanons,* 1/2.774-75, speaks of the predomination of Jews in a mixed Palestinian church of Jews and Gentiles (including mixed languages) until Hadrian's eradication of Jews from Jerusalem and Palestine following the Bar Kokhba revolt.

have written in the medium in which Jewish sacred texts were composed and received. That language was Hebrew.

One further point is worthy of remembrance: Hebrew was the mother-tongue of the Scriptures that birthed the Christian church. That mother-tongue, moreover, was not expunged in translation into Greek but allowed to retain its "voice," even showcased.[91] That same mother-tongue would have been the obvious medium of composition for a Gospel intended for Jews.[92] Nearly a century ago Lagrange recognized that the truth of the gospel with which Jewish Christians wished to impress Jews would have been virtually dependent on its being transmitted in Hebrew.[93] Schonfield concurs: "In the first and second centuries no Jewish book professing even a measure of divine inspiration would have been composed in Aramaic."[94] Finally, it is worth recalling an observation made over two hundred years ago by G. E. Lessing: "the unanimous testimony of the Church Fathers maintain[s] that the original language of Matthew's Gospel was Hebrew."[95] The evidence is substantial and compelling in favor of the conclusion that a Jewish Christian apostle would have chosen Hebrew in which to compose a Gospel intended for the propagation of the gospel among Jews.

Luke's Use of a Hebrew Source

Between the Maccabean Revolt in 168 B.C.E. and the Second Revolt against Rome in 132-35 — the era of concern for our purposes — Hebrew remained in widespread use, and particularly for sacred Jewish literature and worship. The refrain in the early church from the second through the eighth centuries that the apostle Matthew produced the first Gospel in He-

91. K. De Troyer, *Rewriting the Sacred Text,* 88, notes a tendency to correct Greek and Latin manuscripts of the book of Esther toward the Hebrew text.

92. So C. Tresmontant, *The Hebrew Christ: Language in the Age of the Gospels.*

93. "L'Évangile selon les Hébreux," 175: "un original hébreu qui pouvait se conserver ailleurs, de sorte que tous les vrais chrétiens d'origine juive pouvaient se croire en possession du meme évangile."

94. H. Schonfield, *According to the Hebrews,* 241.

95. *New Hypothesis on the Evangelists as Merely Human Historians* (§30). It was Lessing's opinion that the original Hebrew Gospel was used by all three Synoptists in the composition of their Gospels.

brew to evangelize Jews is thus consonant with our knowledge of Hebrew at the time — a knowledge that has been vastly enhanced by twentieth-century discoveries in the Judean desert. This Hebrew source circulated widely in the early church and was held in sufficient esteem to qualify for the "disputed" category in Origen's and Eusebius's canonical classifications. The notable increase of Semitisms in those portions of Luke that are not paralleled by Matthew and/or Mark suggest rather persuasively that the Hebrew Gospel of Matthew was one of the two chief sources of the Third Gospel.

This raises the question whether Luke knew Hebrew, and, if so, to what extent? Modern scholars who express themselves on the subject are few and, for the most part, doubtful. "Luke knows no Hebrew," declares Jeremias.[96] Fitzmyer agrees that "[t]here is no evidence that Luke knew any Hebrew; hence the source of [his so-called Hebraisms] is puzzling."[97] I suggest that they are puzzling only if one assumes in advance that Luke was a stranger to Hebrew. For the ancient church, which stood far closer to such matters than we do today, Luke's ignorance of Hebrew was by no means an assumed fact. Both Clement of Alexandria and Eusebius of Caesarea, in fact, declare themselves positively on the question. Eusebius's *Ecclesiastical History* was of course written in the early fourth century, but in it he quotes Clement's *Hypotyposeis,* written two centuries earlier and therefore of greater historical value, with reference to Luke's knowledge of Hebrew. The occasion of his pronouncement was the perplexing question of the authorship of Hebrews. "As for the Epistle to the Hebrews," writes Eusebius, "[Clement] says indeed that it is Paul's, but that it was written for Hebrews in the Hebrew tongue, and that Luke, having carefully translated it, published it for the Greeks."[98] In Eusebius's mind this explanation accounts for the fact that Hebrews bears the same stylistic complexion as the book of Acts. Whether Clement and Eusebius were correct in this matter is perhaps not the most important aspect of their testimony. What is remarkable for our discussion is that Luke's knowledge of Hebrew is for both Clement and Eusebius not only a received tradition, but a common-

---

96. *New Testament Theology: The Proclamation of Jesus,* trans. J. Bowden (New York: Scribner, 1971), 294.

97. *Gospel According to Luke* 1.118.

98. *Hist. eccl.* 6.14.2 (trans. J. E. L. Oulton, LCL). An eleventh-century minuscule manuscript (104) includes the following subscript to the book of Hebrews: "Written in Hebrew (Ἑβραϊστί) from Italy anonymously (ἀνονύμως) through Timothy."

place requiring no explanation. That is a highly unlikely assumption to make about the only Gentile author in Scripture — unless, in fact, Luke were known to possess proficiency to translate a difficult Hebrew text into high-caliber Greek. This is precisely what Eusebius and Clement maintain.

A related comment in the *Ecclesiastical History* may enhance the credibility of Eusebius's testimony on this matter. In connection with Luke's knowledge of Hebrew, Eusebius recalls Origen's knowledge of Hebrew — and makes a passing comment that leaves our post-Qumran jaws hanging. Noting the thoroughness of Origen's knowledge of Hebrew and his equally thorough quest for Hebrew texts to include in his Hexapla, Eusebius says that Origen found "certain other" Hebrew documents hidden in a jar in the recesses near Jericho.[99] This is the vicinity where, seventeen centuries after Eusebius, the Dead Sea Scrolls were discovered. A GPS device could scarcely have pinpointed Qumran's textual trove more precisely. With *Eccl. Hist.* 6.16 in hand and a sturdy pair of walking shoes under foot one could have found the Dead Sea Scrolls long before their chance discovery in 1947. The spectacular accuracy of Eusebius's memory of *rerum Hebraicorum* in relation to Origen should caution us against hastily dismissing his testimony of Luke's knowledge of Hebrew.

Of course, the thesis that a Hebrew Gospel was a primary source for the Third Gospel is not entirely dependent on Luke's knowledge of Hebrew. As we saw in Chapter Two, Epiphanius knew the Hebrew Gospel of the Ebionites in a Greek translation. We have no information about when the translation was made, but given the rapidity with which the early Christian mission penetrated the Gentile world and the early church's widespread acquaintance with the Hebrew Gospel of Matthew, it was likely translated into Greek quite early.[100] It is entirely possible that Matthew's Hebrew Gospel could have been known to Luke in a Greek translation literal enough to preserve the Hebraisms that we observed in Chapter Three.

What does not seem disputable, however, is that an unusually high number of Semitisms occur in Special Luke, and that they are most satisfactorily explained as Hebraisms. These Hebraisms include:

---

99. *Hist. eccl.* 6.16. The term for "jar" (πίθος) describes the kind of large wine jars in which the Dead Sea Scrolls were discovered, as opposed to smaller portable jars mentioned in the NT (ὑδρία, John 2:6, 7; 4:28; κεράμιον, Mark 14:13; Luke 22:10).

100. So A. Harnack, *Geschichte der altchristlichen Literatur bis Eusebius*², 1/1.7.

1. The adding of the infinitive of a word to the same word in its finite verb form in order to show emphasis. This convention, known as the infinitive absolute, is characteristic of Hebrew but not of Aramaic, Syriac, Latin, or Greek.
2. Multiple instances of the use of ἐν τῷ plus the infinitive, which is the acceptable Greek equivalent of an initial ⲃ prefaced to a Hebrew infinitive. This convention is rare to nonexistent in Aramaic.
3. The use of πρόσωπον, which, as we saw in the last chapter, is a classic Hebraism.
4. The ubiquitous initial καὶ ἐγένετο in Luke, which is also the acceptable Greek equivalent of the Hebrew ויהי, but which is obsolete in first-century Aramaic.
5. The use of εἰ as a negative, "a strong Hebraism" in the judgment of BDF, consonant with the Hebrew use of אם.[101]
6. The use of pleonastic personal pronouns.[102]
7. The use of apodotic καί to connect main clauses of sentences to preceding subordinate clauses.
8. The use of periphrastic tenses — pairing the participle with the verb "to be" to represent continuous aspect. Although this construction is known in Greek, it is not a major feature of Hellenistic Greek, and it is quite unusual in Aramaic. It is, however, typical of Hebrew.[103]
9. The use of ἀνθ' ὧν, a Hebraism that is virtually absent in Greek until the translation of the LXX from Hebrew, and that appears with one exception in the NT only in Special Luke.

A number of these constructions are poorly explained as either Aramaisms or Septuagintisms, but they are all legitimate and recognized Hebraisms. They all occur in the Gospel of Luke, and predominantly in Special Luke. The most obvious and compelling explanation for them is that Luke was not borrowing from an Aramaic source or imitating the LXX, but translating conscientiously from the Hebrew Gospel or preserving the translation Greek of a Greek version of the same for the roughly one-half of his Gospel not shared in common with Matthew and Mark. The most satisfactory hypothesis for Hebraic influence on Luke's Greek is

---

101. BDF §372 (4).
102. BDF §297.
103. M. Wilcox, "Semiticisms in the NT," *ABD* 5.1083.

that Luke, who was demonstrably capable of writing high-caliber Greek prose, introduced Hebraic conventions into his Gospel out of esteem for and deference to an original Hebrew Gospel of Matthew. The language of that Gospel, as Hugh Schonfield and Rudolf Handmann recognized, was most probably Hebrew.[104]

104. H. Schonfield, *According to the Hebrews*, 241: "The original language of the Gospel was Hebrew." R. Handmann, *Das Hebräer-Evangelium*, 117: "Weil es [das Hebräerevangelium] ursprünglich eine hebräische Schrift war und von den hebräisch redenden, paläs-tinensischen Judenchristen stammte, so nannte man es, da es selbst keinen Namen an die Hand gab, zum Unterschied von den übrigen griechischen Evangelien das εὐαγγέλιον καθ' Ἑβραίους." This fact explains the long-noted observation of Robert Lindsey, *New Approach to the Synoptic Gospels* (Jerusalem: Dugith, 1971), 14-15, that Luke, unique among the Gospels, is universally easy to translate back into Hebrew. "Back of our Gospels," says Lindsey, "lie Greek texts which have been literally translated from Hebrew." I am quite skeptical that this is true of the Gospels in general, but the evidence for its truth regarding Special Luke seems to me overwhelming.

CHAPTER SIX

The Neglect of the Hebrew Gospel in Christian Tradition

Given the substantial testimony to the Hebrew Gospel in early Christianity, why has it by and large been neglected in modern Christian scholarship? The weight of evidence in support of the Hebrew Gospel, both in the testimony of the church fathers and in philology of the Third Gospel, makes this question urgent and inescapable. The twentieth century witnessed an investigative explosion into the history of religions and Christian origins, but the Hebrew Gospel remains virtually unknown. Many New Testament scholars are not aware of the widespread and enduring testimony to the Hebrew Gospel in the early church. A recent example of this neglect appears in Helmut Koester's *Ancient Christian Gospels*. "For practical reasons," declares Koester, "I am excluding from this treatment some of the later gospels which show dependence upon the canonical gospel literature, including the Jewish-Christian gospels."[1] In one comment — a footnote, no less — Koester dismisses a wealth of evidence related to the Hebrew Gospel. Likewise, in a book on the Synoptic problem in a respected commentary series, David Dungan makes a staggering error in his judgment of the Hebrew Gospel:

> Where is this original "Hebrew" Matthew? No trace of such a writing has survived; no Hebrew fragments found in caves along the Dead Sea, no mention by scholars of the second century (such as Origen) or fourth century (such as Jerome) saying that they had seen copies of the original

---

1. H. Koester, *Ancient Christian Gospels* (Philadelphia: Trinity, 1992), 46-47.

Hebrew Matthew, nothing apart from this one statement of Papias. The absence of any other solid evidence for an original Hebrew Matthew is so complete that some modern scholars conclude that this report of Papias must be erroneous.[2]

Although extreme, judgments such as these are not atypical of NT scholarship.

Even when the Hebrew Gospel is not summarily dismissed, it often strikes readers rather like the Shroud of Turin, as something wildly speculative or pseudo-scholarly. New Testament scholarship is of course not immune or adverse to speculation. The "Q" hypothesis (which I shall discuss in the next chapter) and the hypothesis that the Gospels were products of anonymous communities, to mention but two examples, have enjoyed wide support, despite a dearth of evidence in the historical record for either. Historical evidence in support of the existence of the Hebrew Gospel is considerably stronger than is evidence for either of those theories.

Why, then, has this evidence by and large failed to engage recent New Testament scholarship? The answer lies in several factors. Until late in the twentieth century interest in Christian origins beyond the first century remained at a fairly low ebb in Protestant New Testament scholarship. This perpetuated a general ignorance of the patristic testimony to the Hebrew Gospel, and ignorance of that testimony inevitably handicapped study of the Hebrew Gospel. Nineteenth-century scholarship, by contrast, was generally more interested in and better informed about the patristic period and, as a review of the titles in the Selected Bibliography reveals, produced not a few seminal studies and monographs related to the Hebrew Gospel.

But the failure of the Hebrew Gospel to be accorded scholarly legitimacy is not simply the result of ignorance. Oversight has played a role, but its relegation to scholarly limbo has also been due to at least two factors, both of which are the subjects of this chapter. The first is a simple fact: the lack of an extant copy of the Hebrew Gospel has deprived the Hebrew Gospel of the critical examination it otherwise would have received. In conjunction with this fact we need to consider *why* there is no extant copy of the Hebrew Gospel. The second factor is more complex, and more uncomfortable: post-Enlightenment investigation of the origin of the Gospels has

2. D. Duncan, *A History of the Synoptic Problem* (AB Reference Library; New York: Doubleday, 1999), 26.

focused on Greek rather than on non-Greek sources. On the one hand, that is largely explainable — and justifiable — on the grounds that the earliest and best sources of the Gospels *are* in Greek. Nevertheless, many of our extant Greek sources derived from Jews and Jewish communities that spoke Aramaic and certainly utilized Hebrew sacred texts, perhaps the Hebrew Gospel among them. Hebraic influences on the provenance of the gospel tradition have received less scholarly attention than they deserve. In part, of course, that is due to the paucity of Hebraic sources. But, as I shall seek to demonstrate in the latter half of this chapter, scholarly negligence with respect to the Hebrew Gospel is also the result of resistance to a primary Hebrew influence in the Synoptic tradition.

Why Is There No Extant Copy of Hebrew Matthew?

The first factor militating against investigations into the Hebrew Gospel is that there is simply no known copy of the Hebrew Gospel in existence. By all canons of historical investigation, the Hebrew Gospel *did exist,* but according to all modern means of verification it is *no longer extant.* This latter reality is not only regrettable. It has resulted in a virtually insurmountable scholarly disadvantage with respect to study of the Hebrew Gospel. Modern biblical scholarship is a child of the Enlightenment, and the Enlightenment, which birthed the scientific method, endowed *material* evidence with a higher degree of authority than historical testimony. It is worth recalling that Western scholarship regarded the *Iliad* more or less as historical fiction until Schliemann's excavations actually unearthed Troy beginning in 1871. Likewise, the existence of the Essenes is attested in a half-dozen ancient authors, including Philo, Josephus, Pliny, Dio, Hippolytus, and Epiphanius, but until the discoveries of the Dead Sea Scrolls in 1947 the Essenes played a marginal role, at best, in the sociology of Second Temple Judaism and early Christianity. To date the Hebrew Gospel has not enjoyed verification like the discovery of a Troy or a Qumran. No copy of the Hebrew Gospel is extant — not even a fragment that conceivably could be traced to it. As we saw in Chapters One and Two, quotations of the Hebrew Gospel do exist, but only in references from various church fathers. To the best of our knowledge, the Hebrew Gospel has been missing for roughly the past millennium. Although it may be hoped that a copy of the Hebrew Gospel will be found, it is possible if not probable that it has been lost forever. In an age when "hard evidence" is conclusive evidence — whether the results of DNA, carbon 14, or manuscript finds — the hypothesis of a Hebrew Gospel without an extant copy of the Hebrew Gospel is swimming against a current of evidential incredibility. Martin Dibelius distilled the consensus of thinking on this matter when he said that further "enlightenment will not come from new hypotheses, but rather only from new discoveries."[3]

If, as many church fathers attest, there was a Hebrew Gospel, and if, as our analysis has indicated, Luke evidently used it in the composition of his Gospel, why is there no trace of it in Christian tradition? Of the thousands of NT manuscripts, why is there no surviving copy in Hebrew? There are to date over 5,300 Greek manuscripts that contain all or part of the NT, and there are an additional 2,200 Greek lectionary manuscripts. In addition to the plethora of Greek manuscripts of the NT, there is a much smaller number of early versions of the NT extant in Latin, Syriac, Coptic, Armenian, Georgian, and Ethiopic and occasional manuscripts in Arabic, Nubian, Persian, Sogdian, Gothic, Anglo-Saxon, and Old High German. But there is neither shred nor sherd of a Hebrew copy of the NT. This yawning absence seems to be the result of something more than the normal ravages of time.

Manuscripts disappear from history for many reasons. By definition, manuscripts are hand-written documents, and hand-written documents are both costly and painstaking to produce, which in principle limits the number of copies of a given document. The fewer the copies, the more vulnerable they are to extinction. Manuscripts of the Hebrew Gospel, which were not counted among the Christian canon, were copied less frequently than canonical texts were. The invention of new scribal technologies such as the transition from the scroll to the codex, or changes in style from majuscules (printed upper case) to minuscules (cursive lower case), further endangered marginal documents. Ancient texts that failed to make the transition from an older to a newer form tended to fall into further disuse. Disuse was only one step away from disappearance.[4] If a single copy of a document existed in a library and the library burned — as did the famous

---

3. *Geschichte der urchristlichen Literatur* 1 (Berlin and Leipzig: de Gruyter, 1926), 55: "Aufklärung ist nicht von neuen Hypothesen, sondern nur von neuen Funden zu erwarten."

4. See R. Netz and W. Noel, *The Archimedes Codex: How a Medieval Prayer Book Is Revealing the True Genius of Antiquity's Greatest Scientist* (Philadelphia: Da Capo, 2007), 70-74.

library of Alexandria — or was plundered — as were Mar Saba, Hagia Sophia, and countless other repositories of ancient books — the document vanished in an instant and forever. These and many other factors threatened the existence of every ancient document.

But the Hebrew Gospel was imperiled by more than the normal vagaries of history. Ironically, it eventually fell victim to both Jews and Christians, the two groups for whom it was originally intended. On the Jewish side, the reason is more obvious. As the Christian gospel made inroads in the Mediterranean world, the church became in the eyes of the synagogue an increasing threat to its faith and existence. As the roots of the church deepened and expanded in early antiquity, so did the need, from the Jewish perspective, of minimizing its influence on the synagogue. In *Against Celsus,* Origen recounts in detail the Jewish theological polemic against Christianity that existed at the end of the second century and in the first half of the third century.[5] By the fourth century this sentiment had become an official policy and was reinforced by the authority of both Tosefta and Talmud. The policy, at least as promulgated in official decrees, was uncompromising. Tosefta *Šabbat* 13.5 decrees that "one does not keep the *Gilyonim* and the books of the heretics, but has them and the divine name contained in them burned on the spot." The Babylonian Talmud preserves similar decrees. "The books of those who write in the margins and the schismatics,"[6] i.e., heretics and Christians, according to Tractate *Šabbat,* should not be rescued from a fire. Rabbis Meir and Yohanan referred to the *Siphre Minim* — the books of Jewish Christians or Christians in general — as "sin pages." "By the life of my son," wrote Rabbi Tarphon, "should they (the books of Jewish Christians) come into my hand I would burn them together with the names of God which they contained. Were I pursued, I would rather take refuge in a temple of idols than in their houses."[7] Likewise, Rabbi Nahum declared that "we have been taught that a Torah book written by a heretic should be burned."[8] In these decrees, "heretic," if not always a circumlocution for "Christian," certainly included Christians. A Christian account of Jesus circulating in the Hebrew language was especially vulnerable to such machinations, for

---

5. *Cels.* 1.2; 2.1; 5.2; 8.69; see the material gathered in M. Stern, *Greek and Latin Authors on the Jews,* 2.224-305.

6. הגליונין דספרי מינין, *b. Šabb.* 116a-b.

7. The above quotations are from *b. Šabb.* 116a-b.

8. *b. Giṭ.* 45b.

in the eyes of the synagogue it presented the most reprehensible ideas in the most trusted medium. The interdict of the Hebrew Gospel sealed its fate in the Jewish synagogue.[9]

At the same time, but for different reasons, a Hebrew Christian Gospel fell into increasing disfavor with normative Christianity of the late patristic period. Already in the second century a number of Jewish Christian sects, the Ebionites and Nazarenes among them, were adhering exclusively to the Hebrew Gospel of Matthew rather than embracing the emergent Greek canon of the church. It was the widespread opinion of the Gentile church that these same sects were introducing into the Hebrew Gospel textual changes that, although consonant with sectarian interests, were regarded as aberrant and heretical. Irenaeus in the second century and more especially Epiphanius in the fourth century produced teeth-gnashing catalogues of theological errors being perpetuated and disseminated by the Ebionites and Nazaroeans via the Hebrew Gospel. These idiosyncrasies and errors included Sabbatarianism, vegetarianism, insistence on circumcision, and strict Torah observance rather than faith in Christ. Above all, they included defective christologies and a rejection of Paul. These tenets were more than irritations in the eyes of the Greek and Latin churches. They were increasingly viewed as corrupt and as intractable, like the sects that zealously clung to them. From Irenaeus onward, the fathers pronounced harsh judgments against them.

We cannot judge these Jewish Christian communities entirely fairly since they did not survive beyond late antiquity and are known to us only through the testimony, often polemical, of Gentile Christianity. But in the perspective of Gentile Christianity, the theological truculence of Jewish Christian sects warranted condemnation. By the third century, at the latest, Jewish Christian sects that resisted assimilation into the greater Gentile church fell under the suspicions and increasing polemics of Greek and Latin Christianity. In general, the Hebrew Gospel escaped the gravest suspicions — or it fell under such suspicions to a lesser extent — that otherwise befell Jewish Christian sects. Nevertheless, jealous use of the Hebrew Gospel by proscribed Jewish Christian communities such as the Ebionites and Nazarenes made it vulnerable to suppression. The precise chain of events that led to its demise is unknown, but its inevitable fate is not. In the

---

9. See M. Hengel, *The Septuagint as Christian Scripture: Its Prehistory and the Problem of the Canon*, trans. M. Biddle (Grand Rapids: Baker Academic, 2002), 43-47.

words of Rudolf Handmann, "The Hebrew Gospel came to an end with Jewish Christianity."[10]

The Hebrew Gospel, which according to Eusebius came into existence as a consolation for Jewish Christian believers and as a medium of Jewish evangelization, was caught in a deadly crossfire from the two communions it sought to reconcile. Ever since, it has been missing in action and presumed dead.[11] It is, of course, possible, and certainly to be hoped, that a copy may be found. Hugh Schonfield finds it extraordinary, in fact, "that the work should have so completely disappeared"; and Rendel Harris that the Hebrew Gospel "has eluded us so long."[12] The Hebrew Gospel could still be preserved in the sands of the Middle East, as were the Dead Sea

---

10. *Das Hebräer-Evangelium*, 118.

11. I am skeptical that the (in)famous *Toldoth Jeshu*, "The Generations of Jesus," a polemical, medieval, Jewish pseudo-history of Jesus, is either directly or otherwise derivatively related to the Hebrew Gospel. The various versions of the *Toldoth Jeshu*, of which there are some dozen; its various titles, of which there are nearly as many; and the disparities in its supposed origin, which range over the better part of a millennium display so many differences that one can scarcely attribute them to a single author or tradition (see G. Schlichting, *Ein jüdisches Leben Jesu* [WUNT 24; Tübingen: Mohr/Siebeck, 1982], 1-21). The *Toldoth* portrays Mary in a generally favorable light, but Jesus' father (variously named) is portrayed as a wicked man, and Jesus himself is depicted as a bastard who in his youth (as in the *Infancy Gospel of Thomas*) was insolent toward elders and wisdom. As a consequence of having stolen the ineffable name from the Temple in his adult years, Jesus became a magician, which enabled him to work miracles, declare his divine, messianic status, and predict his impending death and resurrection (see H. Schonfield, *According to the Hebrews*, 35-61; G. Schlichting, *Ein jüdisches Leben Jesu*, 53-187). The extant versions of the *Toldoth Jeshu* do not exhibit any particular agreement with quotations from the Hebrew Gospel preserved in the fathers. Rather, the *Toldoth* develops the nascent anti-Christian polemic that is already evident in the exaggerations and absurdities that Celsus attributes to Christians (e.g., *Cels.* 3.55; 5.62) and that also appear sporadically in the Talmud (*b. Sotah* 47a; *b. Sanh.* 43a, 107b). The names of Jesus' disciples in the *Toldoth* (Mathai, Naki, Buni, Netser), for example, are taken directly from the Talmud. Shem Tob's version of the *Toldoth Jeshu* (see G. Howard, *The Gospel of Matthew according to a Primitive Hebrew Text* [Macon: Mercer University Press, 1987]; rev. ed. *Hebrew Gospel of Matthew* [Macon: Mercer University Press, 1995]; idem, "The Pseudo-Clementine Writings and Shem-Tob's Hebrew Matthew," *NTS* 40 [1994], 622-28; idem, "The Textual Nature of Shem-Tob's Hebrew Matthew," *JBL* 108 [1989], 239-57) is in fact a point-by-point refutation of canonical Greek Matthew rather than related in any apparent way to the Hebrew Gospel under discussion in this volume (so too C. Evans, "The Jewish Christian Gospel Tradition," 267-70).

12. Schonfield, *According to the Hebrews*, 17; Harris, *Sidelights on New Testament Research* (London: James Clarke, 1908), 100.

Scrolls and Nag Hammadi texts. Its preservation is more likely, perhaps, in an eastern library — most probably a monastic library like Mar Saba, whence a codex containing three lost treatises of Archimedes recently appeared at auction by Christies. And, like the Archimedes Codex, the Hebrew Gospel may exist only as a faint palimpsest concealed under the text of a later document. But ancient texts are fragile, and some are lost forever. Given the specificity with which it was suppressed, it is not surprising that the Hebrew Gospel is no longer extant.[13]

Resistance to a Hebrew Ancestor in the Family

A second factor militating against investigations into the Hebrew Gospel, and particularly against its influence in the Christian tradition, is a prejudice against "a Hebrew ancestor in the family," to quote Hugh Schonfield.[14] This is a subtler factor, but it is no less significant than want of an extant copy of the Hebrew. Whereas the material factor has exerted its influence for the past three centuries since the Enlightenment, the resistance to a primary Hebrew influence in the Christian Gospel tradition has been evident in various forms from the patristic period to the present. In various times and ways the church has failed to be Christian — and at worst has been anti-Christian — in its treatment of Jews.[15] The disparagement of the Hebrew Gospel over the centuries is an example of the church's reluctance to entertain a direct and formative Hebrew influence on the gospel tradition.

Twice in its history the Christian church has devoted intense consideration to the formation of the gospel tradition, and in both instances the chemistry of the consideration has been influenced by anti-Jewish senti-

---

13. I have inquired about the Hebrew Gospel at the Hebrew University, the Firkovich Library in St. Petersburg, and St. Catherine's Monastery. I have personally visited the monasteries of Mount Athos and Mar Saba, the Schloss Friedenstein Bibliothek in Gotha (Germany), and the Staatsbibliothek zu Berlin on the same errand. If such a manuscript still exists, I could imagine Tiberias to be a possible location, since a long tradition of rabbinic literature, including the Palestinian Talmud, is associated with Tiberias. Epiphanius also associates the Hebrew Gospel with Tiberias.

14. *According to the Hebrews*, 247.

15. G. Steiner, *The Idea of Europe* (Tilburg: Nexus Library, 2004), 33: "[T]he isolation, the hounding, the social and political humiliation of the Jew has been integral to the Christian presence, which has been axiomatic, in Europe's grandeur and abjection."

ment. The first was the patristic era and the second the post-Enlightenment era. The patristic period was intensely interested in the four Gospels, not only in the fact that there were four rather than one, but also in their respective provenances. Chapter One traced the tradition of the Hebrew Gospel through the patristic period, a tradition which is but a rivulet in comparison with the major current of consideration devoted to the four canonical Gospels. Interest in and quotations from the Gospels of Matthew and John far outnumber those from Luke, and especially Mark, in the patristic period. This was due to the fact that Matthew, like John, was believed to derive from the hand of the apostle for whom it was named. Mark and Luke, on the other hand, were not apostles, but the early church invested the Gospels bearing their names with the authority of Peter and Paul, respectively, to whom both Evangelists were believed indebted. All four Gospels were thus theoretically accorded equal authority, because all four depended on and preserved the ἀπομνημονεύματα — the faithful memoirs — of apostles. The major currents of both Greek and Latin Christianity, which increasingly defined Christian orthodoxy, defined and defended these four Gospels against sectarian interests, including, as we have seen, Jewish Christian communities that persisted in using the Hebrew Gospel to the exclusion of the four Greek canonical Gospels. The patristic consensus on the four canonical Gospels prevailed from late antiquity through the Middle Ages and the Reformation.[16]

Not until the Enlightenment did debate on gospel traditions reopen on a scale equal to the patristic era. The Enlightenment reoriented the intellectual compass of the Western world, and it would also reorient approaches to the Gospels. With regard to NT studies, the primary interest of the Enlightenment was in recovering the sources of the Gospels and in charting their relationships to one another. This approach differed from the patristic approach, but it would again result in an accentuation of Hellenic influences and minimizing or neglect of Hebraic roots. This was due to several factors, perhaps the most important of which was the application of modern literary and historical theories to the study of the Synoptic Gospels. Those theories were built on assumptions about the *past* and *evolutionary development* that affected conclusions about the Gospels.

One of the many hallmarks of the Enlightenment was its reappraisal of the past. Until the time of the Enlightenment, the ideal past had been seen

16. See B. Orchard and H. Riley, *The Order of the Synoptics: Why Three Synoptic Gospels?*

as something to emulate. Dante's divine and celestial hierarchy was fashioned after a medieval feudal model. The Renaissance rediscovered the golden age of the classical world, and in so doing sought to recover the apogee of human achievement. The Reformation returned *ad fontes* — to the original sources of the Bible and the church fathers — in order to restore the proper theological foundations of Christianity. Until the Enlightenment, the past provided the most important hermeneutical resource for framing and resolving problems.

The Enlightenment lowered the past in its hierarchy of values, and this tended to discount patristic testimony with regard to the gospel tradition in favor of what could be deduced about the provenance of the Gospels from *internal evidence* among them. The most well-known result of the criterion of internal evidence was the rejection of the theory of Matthean priority. Matthean priority continued to be taught and maintained as dogma by the Roman Catholic Church, of course, but in Protestant scholarship — and in the nineteenth and early twentieth centuries Protestant scholarship pioneered the major academic approaches to the Gospels — the theory of Markan priority replaced Matthean priority. Reliance on internal evidence as the most important methodological criterion in Gospels research had a second consequence as well. Although less well known, the result is more important for this study, for in devaluing and neglecting patristic evidence, post-Enlightenment approaches to the Gospels also effectively eliminated the Hebrew Gospel as a potential source of the gospel tradition.

The Enlightenment also introduced new standards of historical judgments based on theories of biological evolution and human progress. Henceforth, the past would be investigated in terms of theories of growth — the development of ideas and institutions from primitive to advanced states. Earlier was considered primitive; later, higher and more sophisticated. The theory of things evolving from inferior to superior states was inevitably applied to Scripture as to other fields of investigation. Scripture too needed to be explained and defended on scientific grounds, and scientific grounds were controlled by theories of biological evolution. If life developed from simpler to more complex forms, then it seemed reasonable to think of the development of historical texts similarly, which became viewed in terms of literary genealogies and pedigrees. In OT scholarship the most celebrated example of this methodology was the Documentary Hypothesis, which posited four literary building blocks — J, P, E, and D —

in the Pentateuch. In NT scholarship the most celebrated example was the theory that Mark (or even Ur-Markus) and "Q" were the building blocks of Matthew and Luke. Once the earliest components had been determined, texts could be hypothetically reconstructed according to the chronological strata of materials.[17]

A curious paradox has resulted, however, when this methodology was applied to the Hebrew Gospel. In the cases of the Pentateuch or Synoptic research, the earliest constitutive literary building blocks were generally accorded a high degree of historical integrity. Generally speaking, the greater their antiquity, the greater their historical value. A text's reliability increased in proportion to its proximity to recorded events. But this equation failed with regard to the Hebrew Gospel. Some scholars, myself included, believe the Hebrew Gospel derived from the hand of the apostle Matthew around the middle of the first century, perhaps even earlier than the Gospel of Mark. Virtually no scholar, however, assigns it a date later than mid-second century. Despite its uncontested antiquity, the Hebrew Gospel regularly remains under a cloud of suspicion in Christian scholarship. The "primitive" nature of "J" or "P" in the Documentary Hypothesis, or of Mark and "Q" in the two-source theory of the Synoptic problem, is valued positively. But the "primitive" nature of the Hebrew Gospel was viewed pejoratively, as though it was unworthy to participate in and contribute to the Greek Christian tradition. A Hebrew source of the gospel tradition was not something to be recovered but to be *superseded* in the Greek gospel tradition.

Take the Jesus Seminar, for example. Organized in 1985, the Seminar is a North American manifestation of the quest of the historical Jesus, dedicated to the "momentous enterprise" of determining the degree of authenticity of Jesus' words and deeds.[18] The Seminar views the *Gospel of Thomas* as a virtual "Fifth Gospel."[19] The Seminar also views "Q" as the earliest and most authentic witness to Jesus, in comparison with which the canonical Gospels are in various ways bastardized accounts. Few scholars would date the Hebrew Gospel later than the *Gospel of Thomas* — and it may well have been composed in the same time frame assigned to the hypothetical "Q"

---

17. See W. Farmer, "State *Interesse* and Marcan Primacy," 22-23.

18. http://www.westarinstitute.org/Jesus_Seminar.html.

19. R. W. Funk et al., *The Five Gospels: The Search for the Authentic Words of Jesus, A New Translation and Commentary* (New York: Macmillan, 1993).

document. But neither the Jesus Seminar nor any modern Gentile authority of whom I am aware invests the Hebrew Gospel with authenticity and authority commensurate with its antiquity. How is this apparent double standard to be explained?

In order to pursue this question it may be helpful to consider the somewhat analogous case of Gotthold Ephraim Lessing (1729-1781), the guiding star and polymath of the German Enlightenment, who posited the Hebrew Gospel as the *prototype* of Matthew, Mark, and Luke. In 1778, Lessing, who had devoted "many years" to the investigation of the gospel tradition and was the first modern scholar to devote an entire work to the Hebrew Gospel, published an essay of sixty-eight lean hypotheses entitled *A New Hypothesis on the Evangelists as Merely Human Historians,*[20] in which he argued that the Synoptic Gospels all derive from an original Hebrew Gospel.[21] Lessing relied on two quotations from Eusebius, the first being the Papias quotation and the second Eusebius's statement that Matthew "having first preached to the Jews, and when he was about to depart from them, transmitted in writing in his native language the Gospel according to himself."[22] Lessing took "native language" to mean Greek, and concluded that Matthew was the first to translate the Hebrew original, which had been composed by an unknown author, into Greek, thereby producing the first Gospel that has survived. In subsequent Enlightenment theories, Lessing would be a rare exception in acknowledging the contribution of a Hebrew original to the formation of the Synoptic tradition. Nevertheless — and this is the point I wish to make in citing Lessing — although Lessing believed the Hebrew Gospel to be the *source* of the Synoptic Gospels, *he did not believe it important.* Indeed, he proceeded to argue that, despite both its antiquity and primacy, the original Hebrew Gospel — and the Gospels of Matthew, Mark, and Luke that flowed from

20. In G. E. Lessing, *Philosophical and Theological Writings,* trans. and ed. H. B. Nisbit (Cambridge Texts in the History of Philosophy; Cambridge: Cambridge University Press, 2005), 148-71.

21. The bias against Hebrew is evident even in reference works. Lessing specifically stated that the earliest Gospel was written in *Hebrew,* but the entry on Lessing in *The Oxford Dictionary of the Christian Church*[3], ed. F. L. Cross and E. A. Livingstone (Oxford: Oxford University Press, 1997), 973 reads: "[Lessing] argued that an *Aramaic* original underlay St. Matthew's Gospel" (emphasis added).

22. Both quotations were discussed in Chapter One. See Eusebius, *Hist. eccl.* 3.39.16 and 3.24.5-6 respectively.

it — gave "a completely false conception" about the person of Christ. Only a true Greek source could rectify the error and establish Christianity apart from Judaism.

> In a word: both orthodox and sectarians either had no conception at all of the divine person of Christ or a completely false conception, as long as no other gospel was available except the Hebrew document of Matthew or the Greek gospels derived from it (§61). Thus, if Christianity was not to become dormant again and disappear among the Jews as a mere Jewish sect, and if it was to survive among the Gentiles as a distinct and independent religion, John had to intervene and write his Gospel (§62). His Gospel alone gave the Christian religion its true identity. We have only his Gospel to thank if the Christian religion, despite all attacks, still survives in this definitive form and will presumably last as long as there are human beings who think they require a mediator between themselves and the deity; that is, *for ever* (§63).[23]

Only John's Greek contribution established the autonomous integrity of the Christian gospel and rescued it from remaining "a mere Jewish sect." It is surely easier to see the cultural biases in Lessing than it is in more recent counterparts such as the Jesus Seminar, or the judgments of scholars like Koester and Dungan. Lessing's testimony represents, in my judgment, a brilliant literary and historical insight and a remarkable breakthrough on the role of the Hebrew Gospel in the Synoptic tradition. But no less remarkable is its cultural triumphalism and anti-Jewish sentiments that relativize — indeed debase — the tradition represented by the Hebrew Gospel. The more recent examples of neglect and disparagement of the Hebrew Gospel that I have mentioned in this chapter are not as explicitly culturally hegemonic — perhaps not even consciously so — but they continue to accord the Greco-Roman tradition with a decided handicap over other traditions. In the case of the Hebrew Gospel, it appears that other-

---

23. This essential position was articulated a century later by the Roman Catholic scholar J. N. Sepp, *Das Hebräer-Evangelium oder die Markus- und Matthäusfrage und ihre friedliche Lösung,* 79-80. Like Lessing, Sepp also wrote a book on the Hebrew Gospel (though with much less sympathy toward it) in which he declared, "Alle drei Synoptiker sind bloss Sammler von Begebenheiten und Lehrvorträgen ohne selbsteigene Kunde von Zeit und Ort, nur Johannes tritt als Geschichtschreiber auf, der das Geschehene historisch schichtet und ordnet."

wise impartial methodological criteria are subordinated to pro-Hellenic and anti-Jewish biases.

It has been axiomatic in the West to understand the Western world as a development of the Greco-Roman world. The roots of the Western intellectual tradition certainly derive primarily, although not exclusively by any means, from the Greeks and Romans. The gravitational pull of the Greek tradition in Western scholarship is, of course, not something that has been formally defined or officially instituted. It simply belongs to a long-held, deeply ingrained cultural assumption that the Western world is an outgrowth of the Greco-Roman tradition. A majority of Western scholars follows this assumption, and scholars are not considered to be prejudiced or misinformed in doing so. They are (if I may use a mountaineering metaphor) simply following the most obvious line of ascent from their vantage point. The Western roots of European culture have seldom been contested; indeed, until the past few decades it was seldom thought necessary to contest them. It was thus practically axiomatic that the higher-critical method, like other Western historical intellectual expeditions, would return to Athens rather than to Jerusalem — or at least return *first* to Greco-Roman theories and sources before considering other sources, including Semitic sources.

An experience I had in Berlin illustrates this reality. In January 2005 I visited the *Orientalabteilung* of the *Staatsbibliothek* — the Oriental Section of the Berlin Library — inquiring about Hebrew manuscripts. I was told that a number of manuscripts had been deposited in the library under more or less clandestine circumstances during the Nazi and Communist years and had remained unidentified and uncatalogued since. In May 2006 I returned to the *Staatsbibliothek* and spent two weeks examining and identifying the cache of salvaged Hebrew manuscripts.[24] The actual

---

24. The acquisitions ledger of the *Orientalabteilung,* which comprises the years 1919 to 1995, bears eloquent testimony to the effects of political ideologies on scholarly achievements. The 13 years between World War I and the Nazi accession (1919-32) record the acquisition of 2772 manuscripts — an average of 213 manuscripts per year. The same number of years during the Nazi dictatorship (1933-45) records the acquisition of 500 manuscripts — an average of 38 manuscripts per year. The next 50 years (1946-95), most of it under Communist dictatorship, records a total acquisition of 139 manuscripts — fewer than *three* manuscripts per year. The Nazi years, obviously, decimated the vigorous acquisitions program of the *Orientalabteilung* of the *Staatsbibliothek* — but far more calamitous were the Communist years, which reduced the acquisitions to *one percent* of the level in the 1920s!

number of cryptic manuscripts, as it turned out, was fewer than the library staff had supposed, of which most were medieval (or later) liturgical texts rather than biblical texts. In my two weeks in the *Staatsbibliothek,* the small Oriental reading room, in which Hebrew and Arabic manuscripts and materials are housed, was unoccupied apart from an Islamic scholar and myself. During the same two-week period, by contrast, the much larger Hellenistic reading room, in which Greco-Roman manuscripts and materials are housed, was packed with scholars from morning until night. It should not be supposed that the scarcity of scholars in the Oriental section was due to inferiority of materials. Although the Hellenistic collection of the *Staatsbibliothek* is good, it is not outstanding, as is the Oriental division, which possesses 600 Hebrew manuscripts. In Europe, only the National Gallery in London possesses more Semitic materials than does Berlin's *Staatsbibliothek.* The superiority of the Semitic collection at the Staatsbibliothek does not equate to greater utilization, however.

Even in the fields of ethnicity and linguistics the Western ethos is granted superiority. The source of Indo-European languages has historically been located in an original tongue called "Aryan," from which a family of peoples and languages stemmed, who, like the word *aryas* itself, were "noble," of "the highest caliber." History was henceforth rehearsed as a march of progress leading to great accomplishments and ideas and civilizations. In the West the family tree was defined by Celts, Romans, Latins, Greeks, Byzantines, Gauls, Anglo-Saxons, and, above all, Germanic tribes and peoples. The physiognomies, cultures, and languages of such peoples were likewise thought to define the human and historical ideal. What is omitted from such paradigms of progress is equally instructive. Despite uncontested contributions made by Jews in so many fields of human endeavor, it is a rare work that acknowledges their contributions to the development of civilizations.[25]

The effect of such anti-Jewish predispositions in theology has historically resulted in downplaying, and sometimes attempting to deny, the Jewishness of Jesus. In France, Ernest Renan's vivid *Life of Jesus* created a sensation in Europe as well as in England and America. In a discreet effort to declare that Jesus' Jewishness was irrelevant to his importance, Renan stressed that Galilee, where Jesus was born and raised, was a region of

---

25. See J. Barzun, *From Dawn to Decadence: 500 Years of Western Cultural Life, 1500 to the Present* (New York: HarperCollins, 2000), 502-3.

mixed ethnicity, "thus making it impossible to raise the issue of race and to know what kind of blood ran through the veins of the one who did so much to efface from humanity the distinctions of blood."[26] In England William Ramsay recognized and decried "the tendency in modern times, especially in [Britain], to consider that the Oriental and the European mind are absolutely contrary to each other and to regard it as an impossibility that Asiatic and European should mix in a stable and contented common society." "The so-called irreconcilability of Asiatic and European" was, in the mind of Ramsay, an "entirely modern product."[27]

Germany, in particular, employed the artificial antipathy of Occident and Orient in order to diminish and sometimes reject the OT and its influence on Jesus, the NT, and the Christian church. In his *Christian Faith,* published in 1821, Schleiermacher summarily dismissed the OT as "superfluous," "too Jewish." "Everything in the Old Testament is but the husk and wrapping of its prophecy; whatever is most definitely Jewish has least value."[28] The precedent for Schleiermacher's views was already supplied in both the Reformation and Reformed traditions, which typically rejected the OT cultic, ceremonial, and civil laws and maintained only its moral laws. But in Schleiermacher and others, this principle was applied to *Jesus* as well. Jesus, too, was stripped of his Jewish identity and citizenship in Israel. That which was most essential about Jesus had nothing in common with Judaism; "so from the very beginning He [Jesus] must have been free from every influence of earlier generations."[29] So great was the divide between the Hebrew and Hellenic souls that Hermann von Soden in his *History of Early Christian Literature* spoke of the attempt of early Christians to express Hebraic ideas in Greek words as an offense against the Greek tongue and genius.[30] Perhaps most startling was Adolf von Harnack, a figure cited frequently in Chapters One and Two and one of the most erudite and respected scholars of the early twentieth century. Harnack braved the thesis that Protestantism should at last follow in the steps of Marcion and reject the OT; indeed, averred Harnack, Luther's boldness in freeing the faith

---

26. *The Life of Jesus* (New York: A. L. Burt, n.d.), 83.

27. *The Cities of St. Paul: Their Influence on His Life and Thought* (London: Hodder and Stoughton, 1907), 44.

28. *The Christian Faith*[2], trans. H. R. Macintosh and J. S. Stewart (Edinburgh: T. & T. Clark, 1928), 62.

29. *The Christian Faith*[2], 388.

30. Cited in A. T. Robertson, *A Grammar of the Greek New Testament,* 93.

from its "Babylonian Captivity" to Roman Catholicism failed him when it came to rejecting the canonical status of the OT.[31] Likewise, Moshe Weinfeld has recently documented the prejudice against Judaism that underlay Julius Wellhausen's analysis of Torah, a prejudice that Weinfeld describes as "Wellhausen's willful ignorance of Jewish sources."[32]

The banishment of Jesus from his Jewish culture has not been uncommon in church history, and it was not uncommon in the post-Enlightenment world. But something new was afoot in the nineteenth century. The names of Renan and Schleiermacher, von Soden, Harnack, Wellhausen, Bousset, and Schürer were not simply additional voices in a chorus of racial and cultural prejudice. Schleiermacher and Harnack, in particular, were lions of the discipline; they were the church fathers of nineteenth-century theology. Whole generations and institutions and theological traditions oriented and aligned themselves according to their judgments.

A Jew can perhaps see and express the profound intellectual and moral offense in such tendencies more appropriately than can a Gentile. In his own study of the Hebrew Gospel, Hugh Schonfield decries the jaundiced perspectives of modern Gospel scholars.

> It is quite extraordinary to find in tome after tome of modern Gospel origins studies the labour which is expended in trying to prove that our Matthew was true blue or Greek from the start. A Hebrew ancestor in the family was something of which to be ashamed. But there the unfortunate semite was, who dared to call himself Matthew. What could be done with him? By inspiration Hebrew *Matthew* . . . was declared to be a

31. A. Harnack, *Marcion: The Gospel of the Alien God,* trans. J. E. Steely and L. D. Bierma (Durham: Labyrinth, 1990), 134: "The rejection of the Old Testament in the second century was a mistake which the great church rightly avoided; to maintain it in the sixteenth century was a fate from which the Reformation was not yet able to escape; but still to preserve it in Protestantism as a canonical document since the nineteenth century is the consequence of a religious and ecclesiastical crippling." In his *Acts of the Apostles,* trans. J. Wilkinson (NTS 3; London: Williams and Norgate, 1909), xxiv-xxv, Harnack writes: "The Jew is in a sense the villain in this dramatic history, yet not — as in the Gospel of St John and the Apocalypse — the Jew in the abstract who has almost become an incarnation of the evil principle, but the real Jew . . . in his manifold gradations of Pharisee, Sadducee, aristocrat, Jews of Palestine or of the Dispersion."

32. *The Place of the Law in the Religion of Ancient Israel* (VTSup 100; Leiden: Brill, 2004).

targum of the Greek for the benefit of converted Jews. In fact this text was rather like a converted Jew, allowed by courtesy to bear his august sponsor's name.

It is rather difficult not to write with levity, and a little bitterness, about this scholarly anti-semitism, which has done so much to sidetrack investigators, and to hinder a true historical analysis of primitive Christian traditions.[33]

Chapters One and Two are a veritable commentary on Schonfield's dictum. In the discussion of quotations from the Hebrew Gospel it was not uncommon for scholars to slight the Hebrew Gospel with the assumption — neither proven nor argued — that it was a "late" second-century work, the product of a discredited Jewish brand of Christianity that was fated to wane and die.

A more virulent strain of anti-Semitism preyed on virtually all aspects of German scholarship during the Nazi period. "German Christians" — a movement that in the Nazi era numbered three out of every four German pastors — were swept up in the theological alchemy of attempting to construct a "heroic" Aryan faith by the eradication from Christianity of every possible vestige of Judaism. Several premier German theologians — Gerhard Kittel, Paul Althaus, and Emanuel Hirsch among them — attempted to justify anti-Semitism on theological grounds.[34] Entire institutes were formed — one thinks of the Institute for Research into and Elimination of Jewish Influence in German Church Life in Jena, whose research division was directed by the leading NT scholar Walter Grundmann — whose chief scholarly objective was to uncircumcise Jesus, so to speak, to place him on an ethnic dialysis machine that would cleanse his blood of the pernicious stains of Judaism and preserve him for the Aryan cause.[35]

---

33. *According to the Hebrews*, 247.

34. See R. P. Ericksen, *Theologians under Hitler: Gerhard Kittel, Paul Althaus, and Emanuel Hirsch* (New Haven: Yale University Press, 1985); L. Siegele-Wenschkewitz, *Neutestamentliche Wissenschaft vor der Judenfrage. Gerhard Kittels theologische Arbeit im Wandel deutscher Geschichte* (Munich: Christian Kaiser, 1980); K. Scholder, *A Requiem for Hitler and Other New Perspectives on the German Church Struggle*, trans. J. Bowman (Philadelphia: Trinity, 1989); idem, *The Churches and the Third Reich*, 2 vols., trans. J. Bowden (Philadelphia: Fortress Press, 1988).

35. See D. L. Bergen, *Twisted Cross: The German Christian Movement in the Third Reich* (Chapel Hill: University of North Carolina Press, 1996), 149.

The beginnings of such absurd and nefarious ideas were already present in nineteenth-century Germany. The Third Reich did not invent anti-Semitism; it harvested it. Already in 1922 Paul Billerbeck had to begin his massive five-volume commentary on the NT from the Talmud and Midrash with an opening line *defending* Jesus' Jewishness.[36] Thus, before the formation of the Nazi Party, before the publication of *Mein Kampf,* and still a decade before the takeover of the Third Reich, scholars like Billerbeck already needed to expose the utter groundlessness of books published in the first two decades of the twentieth century dedicated to showing that Jesus was an Aryan. Nor should it be imagined that such anti-Jewish sentiment was isolated to Germany. In his "Anti-Judaism in the Critical Studies of the Gospels," Joseph Tyson rightly rejects the claim that critical NT scholarship is responsible for the Holocaust, but he nevertheless rightly insists that "the tendencies in this tradition to portray Judaism with unrelieved negativity almost certainly contributed toward the shaping of a culture that harbored sentiments against Jews and provided a justification for widespread anti-Judaic concepts."[37]

One would hope that the Holocaust would have awakened and chastised scholars to the dangers inherent in such prejudices, but that hope has not been entirely realized. We need only recall the original team of eight scholars assembled under the auspices of the Jordanian government to examine the Dead Sea Scrolls. The initial team was intentionally chosen to be international, interconfessional, and aided by a variety of national universities and institutes. And in one further respect it was intentional — in the exclusion of Jews.[38] The prohibition of granting Jews

36. Billerbeck's footnote on the first sentence of Str-B 1.v reads: "Theod. Fritsch (Beweismaterial gegen Jahwe, 3. Aufl., Leipzig 1913), Paul Haupt-Baltimore (Orientalistische Literaturzeitung, Mai 1908), Friedrich Delitzsch (Die grosse Täuschung, Berlin 1920), Friedrich Döllinger (Baldur und Bibel, Nürnberg 1920) und, ihnen folgend, viele andre wollen zwar glauben machen, Jesus sei ein Arier gewesen; ihre Behauptungen sind aber völlig haltlos."

37. In *Anti-Judaism and the Gospels,* ed. W. R. Farmer (Harrisburg: Trinity, 1999), 216-64. For further exposes of anti-Judaism in Christian scholarship, see E. P. Sanders, *Jesus and Judaism* (Philadelphia: Fortress, 1985), 23-52; G. Vermes, "Jewish Studies and New Testament Interpretation," *JJS* 31 (1980), 1-17; C. Klein, *Anti-Judaism in Christian Theology,* trans. E. Quinn (Philadelphia: Fortress, 1978).

38. "The only rule that was imposed was that the group must be *Judenrein* (free of Jews)," writes Hershel Shanks (H. Shanks, J. C. Vanderkam, P. K. McCarter Jr., and J. A. Sanders, *The Dead Sea Scrolls after Forty Years* [Washington: Biblical Archaeology Society, 1992], 8). Also, J. Vanderkam, *The Dead Sea Scrolls Today* (Grand Rapids: Eerdmans, 1994), 189.

access to documents that were produced by their own forebears, prized by their own people, and preserved in their historic homeland raises serious moral questions. The initial exclusion of Jews from the Dead Sea Scrolls team was, to be sure, dictated by the Jordanian government. It would be wrong to blame the scandal of debarring Jews from the Dead Sea Scrolls committee on Jordan alone, however. After the Six Day War in 1967, Israel took control of all territories west of the Jordan River formerly held by Jordan. It was not until 1980, however, that the first Jew (Emanuel Tov) was added to the Scrolls committee, and not until 1990 that the Scrolls project in Israel was fully entrusted to Israelis. The Dead Sea Scrolls committee, in other words, maintained the *de facto* anti-Jewish policy of the Jordanian government for a full two decades after Jordan's authority in such matters lapsed.

Offensive as it was, the exclusion of Jews from the early editorial committee of the Scrolls was more than an ethnic injustice. It also symbolized — perhaps somewhat unconsciously — the types of questions and purposes that governed the early investigations of the Scrolls. Prior to the inclusion of Jews in Scrolls research, the Dead Sea Scrolls tended to be viewed primarily as proto-Christian documents. Similar perhaps to the way that Philo and Josephus were preserved and valued by Christians over the centuries, the Scrolls were initially valued for what they could teach about nascent Christianity. Although the community that produced the Scrolls was recognized as Jewish, it attracted special interest because it appeared to represent a community on the periphery of Judaism, or even an example of a tradition in transition away from Judaism. Questions at the forefront of early Scrolls research included the relationship of Jesus and the Teacher of Righteousness, whether John the Baptist had been a member of the Essene community, or the relationship between lustrations in the Manual of Discipline and early Christian baptism. The Scrolls were initially valued for what they might teach about *Christian* origins.

Inclusion of Jewish scholars in the editorial committee after 1980, not surprisingly, began to reorient Scrolls research. Lawrence Schiffman describes the effect in terms of "re-Judaizing" the Scrolls.[39] Earlier questions were not abandoned, of course, but the Scrolls were opened to wider perspectives. The second half-life of Scrolls research has viewed and valued them as a testimony to the religious ferment within Second Temple Juda-

---

39. L. H. Schiffman, "Re-Judaizing the Scrolls," *BAR* 33 (2007), 58-61.

ism and has awakened Christian scholars to the Jewish roots of many early Christian teachings and customs. I would like to think that this subtle but important shift in Scrolls research might be a morning star of renewed interest on the role of the Hebrew Gospel in the Synoptic tradition.

The above discussion is not intended as a survey of anti-Semitism *per se*. "Anti-Semitism" is a concept too broad and certainly too political to serve the question at hand. Nor have I desired to chart the sweep, however briefly, of anti-Semitism in the Christian tradition. Rather, I have been interested in showing that in the post-Enlightenment period — the period in which the major theories regarding the formation of the Synoptic tradition were formulated — the Jewish tradition has generally been viewed pejoratively and judged inferior. Whether consciously or unconsciously, whether openly or subtly, Hebraic influences on the formation of early Christianity and early Christian literature have been either minimized or neglected.

In my judgment, it would be a mistake to think of this phenomenon primarily in terms of a "campaign," i.e., as something planned or intentional. There were, to be sure, planned aspects of it in Bismarck's *Kulturkampf* of the 1870s, in the writings of given scholars (as noted in this chapter), and above all in the agenda of the *Deutsche Christen* in the Third Reich. But the "tendency" to disparage the Jewish tradition within Western culture is broader and deeper than these particularly ugly expressions of it. The investiture of Occidental as positive and Oriental (and Jewish) as negative produced a cultural climate that in turn begot a cultural mind-set, a phrenic landscape, that views and values things in a given way. The resultant ideologies, dogmas, and *theologoumena* were often the unconscious harvesting of a cultural inheritance in the Western intellectual tradition.[40] Herbert Danby, a Jewish Christian who in 1933 produced the authoritative English edition of the *Mishnah* and served as canon of St. George's Cathedral in Jerusalem, speaks of "the age-long, inbred, instinctive Jew-hatred" of the West. "Centuries of Christianity of a kind have made it a Christian instinct to loathe the Jew."[41] "Instincts" are difficult to document. Virtually all New Testament scholars are aware, however, that the shape of the discipline has been influenced by deep-seated cultural and intellectual biases

---

40. On the function of such cultural dogmas and "ideological needs" and their influence on biblical interpretation, see W. Farmer, "State *Interesse* and Marcan Primacy."

41. H. Danby, *The Jew and Christianity* (London: Sheldon, 1927), 55.

that have disparaged Judaism.[42] Post-Enlightenment Christian scholarship has by and large endeavored to accentuate the distinctiveness — and superiority — of Christianity over against Judaism.

In this historic ethos of disparagement and divorce from Judaism there was virtually no incentive to investigate or incorporate a Hebrew source as foundational to the gospel tradition. Indeed, as Schonfield has said, a Hebrew source was a cause of shame rather than pride in the family tree. How ironic, therefore, that this earnest quest to maintain the Hellenic pedigree of the gospel tradition is confounded by the Gospel of Luke. According to virtually all ancient tradition, Luke was written by a Greek Gentile, and the Third Gospel is the only Gospel expressly addressed to Theophilus, a Gentile bearing a Greek name. Yet this most expressly Greek Evangelist, who at last promises to fulfill the Western cultural hunger for a uniquely Greek Christianity, includes the highest number of Semitisms. These Semitisms, as we have seen in the last chapter, cannot be attributed to Septuagintisms or Aramaisms, but rather must derive from a *Hebrew* original — perhaps the *earliest* written source in the gospel tradition. What Luke appears to have included by necessity, later Gentile Christianity invariably excluded — as if by equal necessity.

Any change from the status quo would require a fundamental shift of attitude regarding Christian origins and the relationship of Christianity and Judaism. A Hebrew ancestor in the Synoptic family of Gospels would require the church — and not only the church but the synagogue as well — to acknowledge the contribution of the Hebraic speech and conceptual world to the NT, and to what eventually became a Hellenic understanding of Gentile Christianity. As a further consequence, it would require a reconception of the mutual existence of Jews and Christians no longer in terms of divorce but rather in terms of a positive indebtedness to the Hebraic origins of the Gospels that remain in the Christian canon to this day.

---

42. To illustrate a particular facet of this phenomenon, see C. Kavin Rowe's assessment of a plethora of contemporary New Testament theologies, all of which, in contrast to earlier New Testament theologies, stress the importance of the Old Testament *en toto* for a proper understanding and interpretation of the New Testament ("A Review of Recent Contributions to the Field," *JBL* 125 [2006], 406).

CHAPTER SEVEN

Adieu to "Q"

The Gospel of Mark and the Hebrew Gospel account for the vast majority of the Gospel of Luke, but they do not account for all of it. There still remains a comparatively small remnant of material in Luke — 177 verses according to Appendix II — that cannot be explained by Mark and the Hebrew Gospel. This remnant is also shared in common with Matthew but not with Mark and thus comprises material commonly attributed to "Q." The purpose of this chapter is to consider this body of material. Since this material apparently cannot be explained by either Mark or Luke's Hebrew source, the most obvious and pressing question is whether it could be accounted for by the traditional "Q" hypothesis?

The traditional two-source hypothesis argues that Mark and a special sayings source, code-named "Q," are the two identifiable sources that were used in the composition of Matthew and Luke. Mark and "Q" do not account for all the material in Matthew and Luke, however. When Mark and "Q" are subtracted from the First and Third Gospels, some 350 verses still remain unaccounted for in Matthew, and over 500 in Luke. Considerably more verses remain to be accounted for, in other words, than are accounted for in the fewer than 200 verses attributed to "Q." The material assigned to "Q" thus comprises a comparatively small amount of material.

For the first century and a half of its existence, the "Q" hypothesis assumed modest proportions: it was commonly held to be a written source (probably in Greek) of Jesus' sayings, a "partial Gospel" as opposed to a full Gospel, that helped explain the roughly 200 verses shared in common by

Matthew and Luke but not with Mark.[1] Beginning in the 1980s, however, the hypothesis began to undergo extravagant mutations. The nearly 600-page *Critical Edition of Q*, an outgrowth of the International Q Project, no longer sees "Q" as an elementary sayings source but rather as an evolutionary literary phenomenon with a complex compositional history involving as many as three redactional stages.[2] Layers of hypotheses are piled on the hypothetical "Q" source, including theologies of the various "Q" strata and the natures of the communities that produced them.[3] For the Jesus Seminar, "Q" has become the first legitimate "Gospel," pristine and unadulterated, in contrast to "later" canonical Gospels that present portraits of Jesus embellished with unhistorical and legendary accretions. "Q" has become a subdiscipline in NT studies, generating an enormous body of literature. It has also been elevated beyond proportion to both reason and evidence, and this has recently caused other scholars to find the whole concept of "Q" problematic. Interdisciplinary studies from the fields of anthropology, ethnography, political science, and oral cultures are challenging virtually every assumption about "Q" — including its form, content, and indeed its very existence.[4] Some scholars wish to abandon "Q" on the grounds that it suggests a single definable document, for which there is no historical evidence. They favor a more objective description — "the double tradition," for example — which describes the actual material shared by Matthew and Luke rather than the characteristics of an unknown document.[5]

1. The 1962 *Interpreter's Dictionary of the Bible* describes the "Q" hypothesis in a brief, two-paragraph entry (D. T. Rowlingson, "Q," *IDB* K-Q, 973). Thirty years later a successor reference work, *The Anchor Bible Dictionary,* required six pages for the same entry (C. M. Tuckett, "Q (Gospel Source)," *ABD* 5.567-72). Likewise, U. Schnelle, *Einleitung in das Neue Testament* (Göttingen: Vandenhoeck & Ruprecht, 1994), 220-30.

2. *The Critical Edition of Q,* ed. J. M. Robinson, P. Hoffmann, and J. Kloppenborg (Minneapolis: Fortress, 2000).

3. So too D. Lührmann, *Die Redaktion der Logienquelle* (WMANT 33; Neukirchen-Vluyn: Neukirchener Verlag, 1969), who ascribes a long redactional history to "Q," which is seen to be independent of gospel narratives. The lack of control and consensus over ever-multiplying "Q" hypotheses is bemoaned by T. Bergemann, *Q auf dem Prüfstand* (Göttingen: Vandenhoeck & Ruprecht, 1993), 59: "Diese Beobachtungen wirken deprimierend; sie sind mit dem, was ich mir unter einer sinnvollen Q-Hypothese vorstellen kann, nur zu vereinbaren, wenn die Differenzen zu einem weit überwiegended Teil auf redaktionelle Eingriffe der Evangelisten Mt und Lk zurückgeführt werden können."

4. R. Horsley, ed., *Oral Performance, Popular Tradition, and Hidden Transcript in Q* (Semeia Studies 60; Atlanta: SBL, 2006).

5. So S. Hultgren, *Narrative Elements in the Double Tradition,* 60; similarly, J. D. G. Dunn,

It is impossible in a single chapter to rehearse and critique the present state of an academic industry such as "Q." My purpose here is not to trace the ripple effect of contemporary "Q" studies in ever-widening circles, but rather to focus on specific aspects of "Q" that are of special relevance to the central thesis of this book. In particular, I wish to examine whether the traditional "Q" hypothesis contributes to a further understanding of the Gospel of Luke presented in Chapter Three, or whether the results of Chapter Three and this chapter argue against the "Q" hypothesis.

The Challenge

Martin Hengel closes his important study on the four Gospels with this admonition:

> Anyone who wants to maintain the existence of "Q" in the form that has been conjectured hitherto must produce stringent proof that in principle Matthew cannot be dependent on Luke, say because Luke was composed later or at best at the same time. I doubt whether this will be possible. However, in all these questions we are not helped by merely literary-critical hypotheses. We have had more than enough of those. Only convincing historical and philological arguments will take us further.[6]

I wish to take Hengel's challenge to ground "Q" in convincing historical and philological data as my starting point. Although "Q" persists as a well-known landmark in European, British, and American NT scholarship, its moorings are not as firm as its life span — now going on two centuries — might suggest. The "Q" hypothesis is a complex literary theory, and a critique of it — at least publicly or in print — requires a substantial degree of expertise. Lack of overt opposition is thus not an indication of support for "Q." It is my impression that many NT scholars are willing to accept "Q" as a useful hypothesis to explain common material between Matthew and Luke, but that fewer endorse it keenly. For many lay people

---

"Jesus in Oral Memory: The Initial Stages of the Jesus Tradition," in *Jesus: A Colloquium in the Holy Land,* ed. D. Donnelly (New York: Continuum, 2001), 134, proposes "q" for the material common to Matthew and Luke, and "Q" for the hypothetical document from which the material common to Matthew and Luke was drawn.

6. *The Four Gospels and the One Gospel of Jesus Christ,* 207.

and scholars, "Q" remains a conundrum or irritant. The problem is not simply that, according to modern scholarship, the hypothetical "Q" document is non-extant (even if material common to Matthew and Luke may be attributed to "Q"). Rather, as I shall demonstrate in this chapter, no patristic testimony mentions a source like the hypothetical "Q" document. Hengel's discontent with the state of affairs regarding "Q" is a constructive challenge to move the discussion from ideology to a more scientific discourse based on objective factors. What kind of historical and philological data would substantiate the "Q" hypothesis — or lay it to rest? An answer to this question will "take us further" regarding the question of "Q."

History and philology are thus the twin poles of this chapter. I wish to begin with an examination of how the "Q" theory was first developed. Who proposed it, and why? On what specific evidence was it based, and what questions or problems did it intend to solve? What historical, cultural, or political factors contributed to its proposal, development, and reception? To what evidence from the early church, if any, does it appeal? Answers to such questions can help to explain why "Q" has grown from an academic theory into its dogmatic status in the discipline. With the genesis of "Q" in mind, it will be possible to consider the second aspect of Hengel's admonition. The philological pole of the "Q" hypothesis is the more important of the two admonitions, for in the final analysis a theory must be judged not simply on its origin but on its ability to explain objective data. The second half of the chapter will thus focus on the claims of "Q" in relation to the findings of Chapter Three.

The Genesis of "Q"

Reference works typically give little or no attention to the genesis of the "Q" hypothesis. That would be the more understandable if the beginnings of "Q" were shrouded in mystery, or if it emerged from obscure beginnings. But this is not the case. "Q" has an exact point of conception, and its story plays a spectacular role in nineteenth-century intellectual history. If "Q," like the combatants at Troy, were to trace its patronage to the Greek pantheon, it would have to claim Athena; for like Athena, who sprang to life from the head of Zeus, "Q" was birthed nearly fully grown by Friedrich Daniel Ernst Schleiermacher (1768-1834).

Schleiermacher first proposed what would become the "Q" hypothesis in 1832 in an article entitled "The Testimony of Papias to Our First Two Gospels."[7] From the first sentence of his article, Schleiermacher bases his study on Papias's famous testimony that "Matthew wrote the 'logia' in the Hebrew language, and each interpreted them as he was able."[8] Unlike later scholars who frequently disparaged Papias, Schleiermacher vigorously defends Papias's historical reliability, and he finds the controversial τὰ λόγια expression to be the key to Papias's testimony. Schleiermacher quotes two occurrences — one in Justin and one in Photius — where τὰ λόγια clearly means "Gospel" in early Christian literature, but he rejects that meaning in favor of "a collection of sayings" *(Reden)*, which he defends on the basis of Acts 7:38 and Rom 3:2. Schleiermacher attributes this compendium of Jesus' teachings, pronouncements, and sayings — some shorter, some longer — to the apostle Matthew. The compendium was not narrative, but only sayings; "Papias' sentence can mean nothing other," he declares.

He then proceeds to ask why there is no further record of the sayings in the early church. Schleiermacher could not imagine that a trove of dominical sayings would simply vanish from the church's legacy. Indeed, he argues, the sayings were not lost, but rather preserved in canonical Greek Matthew.

> I have no intention of giving an exact analysis of the Gospel [of Matthew], . . . but rather provisionally to advance both of these points, first, that we have no reason to deny what such an ancient and qualified correspondent [i.e., Papias] reports, namely, that the apostle Matthew drew up a collection of the sayings and remarks of Christ in the Palestinian dialect, which many others — each in his own way — later reworked. Our Gospel of Matthew is, in fact, one of its reworkings, and even its name, "According to Matthew," rests on that document of Matthew [the apostle].[9]

This was the first proposal of what has become the "Q" hypothesis. Schleiermacher proceeds to attribute the teachings of Jesus in canonical

---

7. F. Schleiermacher, "Papias Zeugnisse von unsern beiden ersten Evangelien," *ThStKr* 5 (1832) 735-68. This article is reprinted in *Friedrich Daniel Ernst Schleiermacher. Kritische Gesamtausgabe*, Abteilung 1: Schriften und Entwürfe, vol. 8: Exegetische Schriften, ed. H. Patsch and D. Schmid (Berlin: Walter de Gruyter, 2001), 227-54.

8. Preserved in Eusebius, *Hist. eccl.* 3.39.16. See discussion of the text in Chapter One, pp. 2-10 above.

9. Schleiermacher, "Papias Zeugnisse von unsern beiden ersten Evangelien," 745-46.

Matthew 5–7, 10, 13, 18, and 24–25 to the putative collection of sayings mentioned by Papias. Matthew signifies the conclusion of each unit of sayings, in Schleiermacher's judgment, with the formula, "When Jesus finished these words . . ." (7:28; 11:1; 13:53; 19:1; 26:1). Schleiermacher refers throughout to the collection as a *Quelle* ("source") or a *Sammlung* ("collection"), although he does not refer to it explicitly as *the Quelle,* or "Q," as it subsequently became known. According to Schleiermacher, the sayings collection utilized by the author of canonical Matthew in chs. 5–25 does not extend to Matthew's virgin birth narrative or to his account of the passion and resurrection of Jesus. Although the compendium exceeded Matthew's quotation of it, it was never a narrative Gospel but only a collection of sayings. Hence, the earliest sources behind our canonical Gospels (and Schleiermacher believes this is also true of Mark) are disparate collections of kerygmatic sayings of Jesus severed from their original contexts.

In only two respects did Schleiermacher's original proposal fall short of the mature "Q" hypothesis current today. The first was that he isolated the sayings collection to the Gospel of Matthew alone, and made no reference to its possible relation to Luke. And second, he continued to regard the Gospel of Mark as a later redaction of the Gospel of Matthew. But in the critical points noted above, Schleiermacher's article was as prophetic for subsequent Gospels research as was Einstein's theory of general relativity for subsequent physics.[10] Few things could have been more ironic than Papias, "a man of very little intelligence," to quote Eusebius,[11] becoming the chief source of one of the most influential intellectual theories in biblical studies of the nineteenth century. Never had the star of the supposedly hapless Papias shone so brightly.

Once Schleiermacher launched the maiden voyage of what would become the "Q" hypothesis, other scholars quickly trimmed its sails. Within three years Karl Lachmann, a distinguished NT textual critic, weighed in favorably with Schleiermacher's proposal.[12] Within six years C. H. Weisse modified two aspects of Schleiermacher's hypothesis by extending it to include Luke as well as Matthew and by arguing for the priority of Mark. With Mark and the "Sayings Collection" posited as the two constitutive sources for Matthew and Luke, Weisse became the first to explicate the

---

10. "Die Grundlagen der Allgemeinen Relativitätstheorie," 1916.

11. *Hist. eccl.* 3.39.13.

12. "De ordine narrationum in evangeliis synopticis," *ThStKr* 8 (1935), 577.

two-source theory.[13] By 1838 that theory, the polestar of modern Gospels research, was firmly established. Only a name for the epic-making theory was still outstanding. Schleiermacher never referred to the putative sayings source as other than *Quelle* ("source") or *Sammlung* ("collection"). The cipher "Q" probably derives from Johannes Weiss in the late nineteenth century.[14]

Schleiermacher quotes Papias as follows: Ματθαῖος μὲν οὖν Ἑβραΐδι διαλέκτῳ τὰ λόγια συνεγράψατο, ἡρμήνευσε δ' αὐτὰ ὡς ἠδύνατο ἕκαστος ("Matthew wrote the sayings in the Hebrew dialect, and each interpreted them as he was able"). Schleiermacher's translation and exegesis of the Papias text rest on three assumptions. First, as we have seen, Schleiermacher understands τὰ λόγια to mean "a compendium of revealed teachings" of Jesus. Although Schleiermacher is aware that τὰ λόγια can mean a "reminiscence" or "Gospel" — as the very word appears to mean in Papias's five Λογίων κυριακῶν ἐξηγήσεως — he defines it as a source of sayings without biographical narrative. It is relevant to note that when Eusebius, who reports the Papias testimony, wants to convey the idea of combining and collecting a series of things he does not use τὰ λόγια, as Schleiermacher supposes, but rather a form of the verb συνάγω, which is common Greek usage.[15] I have offered further evidence in the discussion of τὰ λόγια in Chapter One that the expression — and particularly in Eusebius — does not mean "sayings," but rather a narrative entity, a Gospel. Moreover, even the International Q Project, which unambiguously champions the "Q" hypothesis, is agreed that Schleiermacher was in error in imagining Papias's τὰ λόγια to mean "a compendium of sayings."[16]

Second, Schleiermacher argues that the word ἡρμήνευσε cannot mean "translated." Schleiermacher reasons that translations of the *ipsissima verba Jesu* would have been highly prized by the early church and not easily lost. On the other hand, if ἡρμήνευσε meant "provided *Erläuterungen* ('explana-

---

13. *Die evangelische Geschichte, kritisch und philosophisch bearbeitet*, 2 vols. (Leipzig: Breitkopf und Härtel, 1938), 1.83.

14. F. Neirynck, "The Symbol Q (= Quelle)," *ETL* 54 (1978), 119-25.

15. Thus, in describing the compilation of the Diatessaron, Eusebius (*Hist. eccl.* 4.29.6) writes that "Tatian composed *in some way a combination and collection* (συνάφειάν τινα καὶ συναγωγὴν) of the Gospels, and gave this the name of *The Diatessaron*." Theodoret, *Haer. fab. comp.* 1.20, uses συναγωγή similarly in describing his gathering together the many copies of Tatian's *Diatessaron* in his diocese. In the NT, see a similar usage in Luke 11:23.

16. *The Critical Edition of Q*, xx-xxxii.

tions' or 'explanatory notes')," then their loss could be more easily explained, since a set of explanations or glosses would not have been as highly prized and carefully preserved as authentic sayings of Jesus. Schleiermacher therefore adopts the interpretation "provide *Erläuterungen*," which he believes to be a permissible rendering of ἡρμήνευσε.

Finally, Schleiermacher's interpretation of the Papias text is derived from a different text than the modern critical text of Eusebius's *Ecclesiastical History* followed by Kirsopp Lake in the Loeb series. Specifically, Schleiermacher's text reads συνεγράψατο in place of συνετάξατο in the Loeb text. This is a point curiously overlooked by some "Q" scholars.[17] Συγγράφω generally means "collect" or perhaps "collate." But συντάσσω, from which the word "syntax" is derived, means "arrange an account," even "write a book." On the basis of a defective Greek text and the two hermeneutical judgments related to τὰ λόγια and ἡμήνευσε above, Schleiermacher concludes that "Matthew collected the sayings of Jesus in the Palestinian dialect, and each explained them as he was able." On that foundation the "Q" edifice was first raised.

All three of Schleiermacher's conclusions depart from the discussion of the Papias testimony in Chapter One. The first two are the result of poor exegetical judgments, and the third is the result of a defective text. Their combined effect necessitates the abandonment of Schleiermacher's conclusions. With regard to the first point, had Schleiermacher examined the specific use of τὰ λόγια in Eusebius he should have concluded that it was a circumlocution for "memoirs" or "gospel account" rather than a reference to a collection of sayings.[18] With regard to the second point, Schleiermacher's decision to translate ἡρμήνευσε as "explain" or "apply" is open to even greater doubt. A standard lexical definition of ἑρμηνεύειν is "interpret" or "translate," a definition that is supported by its context in Papias. Schleiermacher's translation imposes an alien sense to the term. No one who reads Theodor Zahn's convincing discussion of this term should

17. *The Critical Edition of Q*, xx, assumes that Schleiermacher used the same text as that reproduced in the Loeb series. Even S. Hultgren, *Narrative Elements in the Double Tradition*, 9, who critiques Q scholarship, fails to note the different text on which Schleiermacher based his hypothesis.

18. See the discussion of this term on pp. 3-5. S. Hultgren, *Narrative Elements in the Double Tradition*, 12-18, rightly notes that Schleiermacher chose contrary to evidence to translate λόγια as "sayings"; indeed, that "Schleiermacher's interpretation of Papias was wrong." See his critique of the development of the "Q" hypothesis, pp. 4-57.

doubt that by the use of ἡρμήνευσε, Papias referred to an original *Hebrew* document that needed translating into Greek.[19] In a long discussion of the word, Dietrich Gla "decisively rejects [Schleiermacher's] translation." "One cannot find a single example, either in the Biblical or classical Greek world, where ἑρμηνεύειν means 'to apply.'"[20] Finally, with regard to the third point, Schleiermacher's interpretation is the result of working from a different *Grundtext.* The Greek recension on which Schleiermacher relied appears to have been that of Henricus Valesius, first published in Paris in 1659. The superior recension of Eduard Schwartz appeared in 1903 — seventy years after Schleiermacher's article appeared — and rendered earlier recensions of Eusebius obsolete. The Schwartz recension has become the rightful textual basis of Eusebius, as followed by Kirsopp Lake in the Loeb series.[21]

To summarize the discussion of Papias in Chapter One, the best understanding of his testimony is that "Matthew organized (or structured) the account in the Hebrew language, and each translated it as he was able." Schleiermacher interpreted Papias to be describing a collection of Jesus' sayings. According to the most reasonable and defensible exegetical judgments, however, Papias was actually describing the first Hebrew edition of Matthew's reminiscences of Jesus. The genesis of the "Q" hypothesis thus rests on two erroneous exegetical judgments and on one defective textual reading. Despite these weaknesses, Schleiermacher's article had an enormous impact. The subtitle of the journal in which Schleiermacher's article appeared was "A Journal for the Entire Spectrum of Theology." His article

19. *Geschichte des neutestamentlichen Kanons,* 1/2.890-94. In a sharp critique of Schleiermacher's entire thesis, Zahn writes on p. 892: "Wenn die innere Kritik unserer kanonischen Evv. zu dem Ergebnis führt, das eine der verloren gegangenen Quellenschriften, aus welchen diese erwachsen sind, wesentlich eine Sammlung von Reden Jesu gewesen sei, so sollte die Kritik auch den Muth haben, auf eigenen Füssen zu stehen, statt aus dem Zeugnis des Papias eine Krücke zu machen; und sie sollte ihrer eigenen Entdeckung auch einen eigenen Namen geben, statt durch Misbrauch des beiläufig einmal von Papias gebrauchten, ausserhalb des Zusammenhangs aber sinnlos unvollständigen Ausdrucks τὰ λόγια den Schein zu erwecken, als ob das der überlieferte Titel einer alten Schrift wäre."

20. *Die Originalsprache des Matthäusevangeliums,* 49: "Es lässt sich auch nicht in einziges Beispiel, weder aus der biblischen noch klassischen Gräcität, beibringen, wo ἑρμηνεύειν = 'anwenden' wäre."

21. See K. Lake, *Eusebius: The Ecclesiastical History* (London: Heinemann; New York: Putnam, 1926), xxvii-xxxiii.

brilliantly accomplished that purpose, for it has influenced a great spectrum of theology in the last century and a half.

Exegesis does not exist in a vacuum. Different eras and generations bring their own questions to texts, and the questions influence, at least to some extent, not only the information that the texts yield, but also the way such information functions within the host cultural milieu. This is particularly true of biblical texts. Eugen Rosenstock-Huessy has noted the inordinate cultural influence of nineteenth-century Germany in biblical scholarship. "Something happened [in German academic history] during the nineteenth century," declares Rosenstock-Huessy, "that had served to distort the twentieth century voice of Jesus."[22] Schleiermacher's 1832 article was a prime example of such an influence. Its compatibility with Enlightenment ideals in nineteenth-century Germany ensured that his theory would have the prevailing cultural winds at its back.

One of those Enlightenment ideals was Schleiermacher's Romantic individualism. Schleiermacher was a multifaceted *universal Mensch*. His *Life of Jesus* played a role in inaugurating the nineteenth-century quest of the historical Jesus. His exhortation for a "reformed" and assimilated Jewry sowed the seeds of what would become the Reform branch of Judaism later in the nineteenth century. His translation of Plato became the standard text of Plato used in nineteenth-century German pedagogy. His writings on scientific subjects and his participation in the intellectual salons of early nineteenth-century Berlin enhanced his reputation and extended his influence. Above all, his sermons and theological writings helped reinterpret Christianity to the Enlightenment and the Enlightenment to Christianity. In all these respects Schleiermacher was a preeminent Enlightenment intellectual. But in one significant respect Schleiermacher broke rank with the lockstep of Enlightenment ideas, and that was in its reduction of religion to mere rational and moral phenomena. Schleiermacher strove to emancipate the human spirit from the dull conformity of modern life, from the straitjacket of the human individual viewed solely as *homo sapiens,* as only a *knowing* creature. He found relief from Kant's arid psychology of human rationality by appealing to the genius of human individuality, to *homo sentiens,* a creature capable of experience and feeling. Such experiences and feelings belong to the essential uniqueness of what it

---

22. From a personal interview of W. Farmer with Rosenstock-Huessy in 1965, cited from W. Farmer, "State *Interesse* and Markan Primacy: 1870-1914," 15.

means to be human. They are nonquantifiable, and as such they are unmeasurable by rational standards.[23]

Schleiermacher believed that the same individualism that typified the essence of human beings also typified the communities, ethnicities, and cultures formed by human beings. The stories that give expression to the ethos of a given culture provide front-row seats into the soul of the culture. Each community or ethnic group tells its story in a unique fashion. The tendency within Romanticism was to reject the concept that such idiomatic myths and sagas could be written *for* a community by a single individual. Romantics, rather, were fond of ascribing "authorship" to spontaneous genesis from within a community or people-group. Myths like the Mesopotamian *Gilgamesh Epic,* the German *Nibelungenlied,* or the Anglo-Saxon *Beowulf* began in the subliminal ethnic past like scattered vines, which only at a later time grew together and intertwined into a united and prolific vineyard. The tendency to view myths, sagas, legends, and epic traditions in terms of the coalescence of initially disparate fragments had more than a century of steam behind it by the time Schleiermacher suggested that Matthew's "sayings source" was a collection of sayings dismembered from its historic context in Jesus' ministry. Indeed, his 1832 article appropriated a theory of literature that had been developed with reference to pagan and ethnic classics and already applied to the Pentateuch and the book of Isaiah. It was not surprising — indeed, it was quite predictable — that Schleiermacher would apply to the Gospels an approach that had proven serviceable in explaining the origin of myths and sagas in general.[24]

New theories of literary formation were not the only winds blowing in favor of Schleiermacher's proposal. The fierce *Kulturkampf* was a second factor that favored the acceptance of a theory like the "Q" hypothesis. One of the essential planks in Otto von Bismarck's platform was to bolster the power of the newly established German Empire by curbing the power of

---

23. See F. Schleiermacher, *On Religion: Speeches to Its Cultured Despisers,* trans. and ed. R. Crouter (Cambridge Texts in the History of Philosophy; Cambridge: Cambridge University Press, 1996), xxx.

24. Karl Lachmann, Schleiermacher's younger Berlin contemporary and fellow textual critic, regarded the *Nibelungenlied* and the *Iliad* as mosaics of short and autonomous ballads, heroic songs, and so forth that were later combined into the classics we know them as today. Lachmann was also among the first to follow Schleiermacher's lead in supposing the Gospels to be the end products of a long process of anonymous communal shaping. See B. Knox, *The Odyssey,* trans. R. Fagles (New York: Penguin, 1996), 7-8.

the Vatican. In reaction to Vatican I in 1868, the Iron Chancellor threw up a defensive maneuver against Pope Pius IX, his doctrine of papal infallibility, and Vatican influence in Germany in general. In order to undergird his own command of the German Reich against claims of papal supremacy in Germany, Bismarck locked into a take-no-prisoners ideological struggle against Catholicism. By its climax in 1875, he had closed down 40 Catholic newspapers, arrested and expelled nearly 140 Catholic editors, and imprisoned nearly a thousand Catholic priests in Prussian parishes. Bismarck was not unaware of the dividends that theological factors could pay in his strategy of containment. He was shrewd enough to realize that the theory of Markan priority, then coming of age in German academia, dealt a grave blow to claims of papal supremacy, since the famous "keys to the kingdom" passage in Matt 16:19, so dreaded by Bismarck, was not found in the earlier and more "genuine" Gospel of Mark. The leverage that Bismarck applied to seat professors in prestigious chairs of NT who advocated Markan priority, particularly in the appointment of H. J. Holtzmann to the University of Strasbourg, enhanced the theory of Markan priority while diminishing papal influence in German public and political life.[25]

In comparison to the theory of Markan priority, the theory of an original source of Jesus' sayings proposed by Schleiermacher played but a minor role in the *Kulturkampf*. But it too could be rallied, if only in an auxiliary fashion, to arrest papal supremacy in the German Reich. The assignment of a late date of composition — and disparate sources — to the Gospel of Matthew was at least a small victory against the claim that Peter's successor was endowed *in perpetuity* with papal supremacy. Coupled with the claim of Markan priority, Schleiermacher's theory on the formation of Matthew helped Bismarck ensure that the locks in Germany could not be opened

---

25. See W. Farmer, "State *Interesse* and Markan Primacy: 1870-1914"; H. H. Stoldt, *History and Criticism of the Markan Hypothesis*, trans. D. L. Niewyk (Macon: Mercer University Press, 1980), 47-131; D. L. Dungan, *A History of the Synoptic Problem* (New York: Doubleday, 1999), 302-41; *Beyond the Q Impasse: Luke's Use of Matthew*, ed. A. McNicol, D. Dungan, and D. Peabody (Valley Forge: Trinity, 1996), 7. It would be a mistake to assume, however, as Farmer in particular comes close to suggesting, that Bismarck's endorsement of Markan priority was the main or only reason for its predominance in the scholarly guild. The theory of Markan priority has long outlived Bismarck's intrigues. Without reference to or influence from the *Kulturkampf*, Markan priority has been adopted and defended by a majority of scholars in the past century and a half on grounds of internal evidence among the Synoptic Gospels.

by Peter's keys. Although it would be a mistake to overestimate the role of the *Kulturkampf* in German biblical criticism, it would also be foolish to ignore it.

No scholar documented nineteenth-century German biblical scholarship more comprehensively or authoritatively than Albert Schweitzer. At the outset of his *Quest of the Historical Jesus,* Schweitzer reminds readers that historical criticism of the NT was not developed or employed disinterestedly. Rather, it was "as an ally in the struggle against the tyranny of dogma."[26] Historical criticism of the NT, in other words, was serviceable in the Enlightenment and Romantic program of emancipating individuals from political and ecclesiastical autocracy. The theory of a source of Jesus' moral teachings abstracted from his biography was a particularly useful tool in that project.

In addition to Schleiermacher's Romanticism and Bismarck's *Kulturkampf,* there was yet a third and much more important way in which the sails of Schleiermacher's "sayings source," once unfurled, swelled with the winds of the Enlightenment, carrying the Jesus produced by the new historical criticism without tack or slack to the shores of modernity. With respect to religion, the Enlightenment sought to emancipate individuals from external authorities of church and dogma and to purge the Bible of all elements offensive to human reason. In the study of the Gospels, the most offending elements were the miraculous — not only the virgin birth and resurrection, but also accounts of Jesus' healings and power over nature. Schweitzer's *Quest of the Historical Jesus* bears eloquent and repeated testimony to the nineteenth-century obsession with providing rational explanations, however far-fetched, for the miraculous in Jesus' life and ministry. Equally offensive, and equally in need of purging, were theories of

26. *The Quest of the Historical Jesus,* trans. W. Montgomery (New York: Macmillan, 1968), 4. Schweitzer's full development of the idea is illuminating, not the least for the note about the influence of the Order of the Illuminati a full two centuries before Dan Brown's *Da Vinci Code.* "The historical investigation of the life of Jesus did not take its rise from a purely historical interest; it turned to the Jesus of history as an ally in the struggle against the tyranny of dogma. Afterwards when it was freed from this πάθος it sought to present the historic Jesus in a form intelligible to its own time. For Bahrdt and Venturini He was the tool of a secret order. They wrote under the impression of the immense influence exercised by the Order of the Illuminati at the end of the eighteenth century. For Reinhard, Hess, Paulus, and the rest of the rationalist writers He is the admirable revealer of true virtue which is coincident with right reason. Thus, each successive epoch of theology found its own thoughts in Jesus; that was, indeed, the only way in which it could make Him alive."

the atoning significance of the crucifixion. The Enlightenment was again convinced that Jesus' death on the cross could not and did not exonerate humanity of moral responsibility. What was *not* objectionable in the life of Jesus, however, were his moral teachings and example. Indeed, these were essential to outfit humanity morally and politically in an age of waning autocracies and emerging democracies. In this regard, Schleiermacher's proposal of an early "sayings source" was particularly advantageous. Whether Schleiermacher intentionally misinterpreted Papias I cannot say, but the stage had been so set by the Enlightenment that Schleiermacher was encouraged to act upon it in the way he did. Indeed, had he not done so, someone else surely would have. The provision of a body of moral propositions shorn of miracle and dogma was the realization of an Enlightenment dream. To provide such was the least that Christianity — long accused of mischief and magic, witch hunts and obstruction of "progress" — should do to make itself worthy to play a role in the social and political cause of human emancipation. Schleiermacher never justified his proposal of a "sayings source," which appeared two years before his death, on the above grounds, but his study of Papias nevertheless matches the blood-type of his whole theological legacy, which was to make an *apologia* for religion on grounds acceptable to the Enlightenment. In his article on Papias he indeed hints at the inviolable importance of Jesus as a moral teacher. While admitting that the original Hebrew Gospel of Matthew must have contained a fuller account of Jesus, Schleiermacher concludes that Papias's extraction of only the sayings must imply that they were the most important aspect of the Gospel.[27]

What is implicit in Schleiermacher becomes explicit and indisputable in the tradition following him. Hengel can say without qualification that the chief attraction of the "Q" hypothesis is its offer of a Jesus who is simply a moral teacher and preacher. "The main champion of 'Q', Adolf von Harnack, was already interested in such an undogmatic, primarily ethical, picture of Jesus."[28] For Harnack, like nearly all liberal post-Enlightenment theologians, the essential core behind and beneath the cultural husk of Christianity is its morality. In *What Is Christianity?*, Harnack unsuccessfully searches for a direct relation between Jesus and "the Greek spirit," whether in Plato or Stoicism. Nevertheless, the "higher righteousness"

---

27. F. Schleiermacher, "Papias Zeugnisse von unsern beiden ersten Evangelien," 752.
28. *The Four Gospels and the One Gospel of Jesus Christ*, 68-70, 172.

preached and lived by Jesus was for Harnack independent of and superior to anything in the OT or Judaism. Safely rescued from Judaism — indeed, seemingly abstracted from any cultural context — Jesus "defined the sphere of the ethical in a way no one before him had ever defined it." Harnack reduced religion to morality, and morality to religion; both of these were personified *par excellence* in Jesus. "Jesus combined religion and morality, and in this sense religion may be called the soul of morality, and morality the body of religion." The love of neighbor was but the practical side of the love of God. The Beatitudes and the Sermon on the Mount "contain [Jesus'] ethics and his religion, united at the root, and freed from all external and particularistic elements."[29] For Harnack and nineteenth-century liberalism, the teachings of Jesus became the epitome of the most sublime and enduring moral aspirations of the human race. The degree to which cultural factors determined such judgments may be illustrated by comparing Harnack's views of Jesus with those of his older contemporary Abraham Geiger, one of the first Jews in the modern era to write a book on Jesus. At the same time that Harnack saw nothing Jewish in Jesus and everything new in him, Geiger saw everything Jewish in Jesus and nothing new in him.[30] That a learned Christian and a learned Jew could find in Jesus nothing other than reflections of their respective cultures is an acid reminder of the power of culture to influence scholarship.

The adoption of a theory like "Q" was particularly well-suited to the intellectual climate of nineteenth-century Enlightenment Europe. Indeed, the "Q" hypothesis found a handsome escort in nineteenth-century German liberalism. Schleiermacher's choice to interpret Papias's words as referring to a compendium of Jesus' sayings and moral teachings was exegetically strained at the time, and it appears even more so in retrospect. Its scholarly shortcomings were but minor losses, however, compared to the generous gains bestowed on it by the disposition of the Enlightenment. "Q" — or something like it — was clearly encouraged by an anti-dogma, anti-clerical, and anti-papal *Zeitgeist*. The "Q" hypothesis was like a modern farm chemical that contained an herbicide capable of killing the weeds of miracle and dogma, and also a fertilizer capable of nourishing the ethical core of Jesus' message.

---

29. *What Is Christianity?*[2], trans. T. B. Saunders (New York: Putnam, 1901), Lecture IV.

30. A. Geiger, *Das Judentum und seine Geschichte*[2] (Breslau: Schletter, 1865), 116-37; H. Danby, *The Jew and Christianity* (London: Sheldon, 1927), 71.

Is There a Precedent for "Q" in Early Christianity?

The ruling assumption behind "Q" is that the early church gathered the teachings and sayings of Jesus into a wisdom collection before producing a full-fledged Gospel of Jesus. This assumption produced both a step forward and a step backward. The step forward consisted in the preservation of an anthology of Jesus' teachings, which, according to the theory, were the most unique and important aspect of Jesus' ministry. But there was also a step backward, for in compiling the anthology, the historical contexts of the constituent sayings were forgotten forever. These detached and orphaned sayings, the theory continues, were later appropriated to augment the editorial needs of the authors of Matthew and Luke. Having said this, an obvious question arises: is there any evidence in the NT or from the early church of this putative sayings collection? Or, if the specific collection cannot be documented, are there indications of other such collections that could offer precedents for a "Q" collection? Is the gathering of a series of Jesus' sayings into a compendium, in other words, the kind of thing the early church did, or could be expected to have done? A positive answer to one or both of these questions would help establish the plausibility of "Q," since a theory based upon a historically validated source or practice is preferable to a hypothesis lacking any historical attestation.

The NT offers occasional clues — e.g., John 5:39; Acts 8:35; 17:11; 18:28 — to the existence of underlying documentary layers. In those four passages, however, the source is almost certainly the writings of the OT rather than a collection of Jesus' sayings. Beyond these verses, references in the NT to anything approximating "Q" are rare to nonexistent. This observation should not be overemphasized, however, for virtually all scholars concede that similarities among the Synoptic Gospels are due, in part, to their use of one another, although none of them (Luke's prologue?) admits to doing so. Is there, however, a *precedent* for a document like "Q"? Are there early Christian collections of Jesus' sayings — or intimations of such — from which "Q" could be postulated? John Kloppenborg concludes *The Formation of Q* with an in-depth survey of ancient sayings collections.[31] He assembles copious data on genres of instructional literature extant in first-century Egyptian, Sumerian, Akkadian, Babylonian, Hellenistic, and

---

31. *The Formation of Q: Trajectories in Ancient Wisdom Collections* (Harrisburg: Trinity, 1987), 263-316.

Greco-Roman traditions. Some of these collections are instructions of kings to their subjects, others of fathers or teachers to youth, still others of proverbial wisdom in general. The question is not whether such sayings collections existed. They did — and Kloppenborg has examined the breadth and depth of the various genres. The question is whether any of these various moral, didactic, hortatory, or wisdom collections resembles the putative "Q" source closely enough to provide either a parallel or precedent for it? It is precisely this lack of analogy that strikes the reader of Kloppenborg's extensive survey. Except for the OT Proverbs and the Sayings of the Fathers in the Mishnah and Talmud, nearly all the traditions surveyed by Kloppenborg come from cultures outside — and some alien to — the Jewish tradition in which Jesus participated. The attempt to demonstrate parallels between such traditions and the teachings of Jesus in the NT rehearses a similar agenda — and results in a similar impasse — to that of the early form critics who attempted to explain Jesus and the Gospels by "parallels" to the Greco-Roman world. The worlds were too far apart and too dissimilar. The "parallels" explained little, if anything. Kloppenborg's survey seems to be no more relevant.[32]

Kloppenborg seems to be aware of this problem, for he nowhere presents a "case for Q" on the basis of the traditions he cites. The closest he comes to doing so, not surprisingly, is with the *Gospel of Thomas,* which he claims is "a good example of a sayings collection which functioned presumably as an instrument of instruction."[33] *Thomas* thus apparently becomes his closest analogy — although even here Kloppenborg refrains from claiming an analogy to "Q." The case of the *Gospel of Thomas* is important to consider, however, because Gospels like *Thomas* that consist ex-

---

32. J. N. Sepp, *Das Hebräer-Evangelium oder die Markus- und Matthäusfrage und ihre friedlich Lösung,* 104-7, argues for the certainty of a sayings source preserved in canonical Matthew on the basis of other known sayings sources. He draws attention to teachings preserved in the Talmud, Zoroastrian sagas preserved in the Avestas, the collection of Muhammad's teachings that were written on strips of leather, shards, leaves, and dried bones; and the ἱεροὶ λόγοι, the mysteries of the Ophites, Eleusinians, and Samothracians. Sepp assumes that Schleiermacher's theory of a sayings source is proved by such "parallels." But he has not shown that *Christians* gathered such sayings. The sole Christian testimony he alludes to is Eusebius, *Hist. eccl.* 3.39. As demonstrated in Chapter One, however, it is clearly contrary to Eusebius's intentions to imagine that his references to Papias, Polycarp, the Gospel of Mark, or the traditions of Aristion and John the Elder are to collections of sayings. Sepp is guilty of assuming what he wishes to prove.

33. *The Formation of Q: Trajectories in Ancient Wisdom Collections,* 301.

clusively of Jesus' sayings and teaching are often suggested as analogies for "Q." This suggestion amounts to a curious paradox, however, for most people I know who read the *Gospel of Thomas* are struck by how *unlike* the canonical Gospels it is. In my NT courses, I regularly assign comparison/contrast papers on the *Gospel of Thomas* and the Gospel of Mark. Without fail, students find it difficult to draw meaningful comparisons between the two, but no difficulty in finding distinct differences. It is not simply that the *Gospel of Thomas* contains no miracles, healings, or travels of Jesus, no Passion, Eucharist, cross, death, and resurrection — elements that normative Christianity believed essential to a Gospel. Even in his sayings and teachings, the Jesus of *Thomas* is unlike the canonical Gospels and the NT. A number of his teachings are nonunderstandable, or practically so,[34] and many are characterized by a Platonic and Gnostic dualism that is alien to the NT.[35] The early church recognized these and other differences, for whenever the *Gospel of Thomas* or other Gnostic Gospels are mentioned in early canonical lists they are without exception consigned to the rejected category. *Thomas* reduces Jesus to a "talking head," and the early church did not find the reduction a "good example" of wisdom instruction.

With the rejection of the *Gospel of Thomas* and Gnostic Gospels like it as analogies of early Christian wisdom anthologies, the well of viable parallels to a putative "Q" source dries up quickly. If there was a collection of Jesus' sayings, how do we explain the fact — and it is a fact — that the patristic tradition as a whole is ignorant of it? Unless an adequate answer can be given to this question, the existence of a "Q" source becomes highly improbable. Since Jesus' words were highly treasured from the earliest time, the likelihood of a collection of dominical sayings existing, yet being unmentioned by any of the fathers, seems next to impossible. The fathers refer to any number of books and letters deriving from the early Christian era, many of which still exist, although some have been lost. What does not appear among them, however, is the very thing the "Q" hypothesis assumes — the existence of an independent source of sayings of the historical Jesus. Nowhere in the patristic reservoir is there a witness to this chief cornerstone of the "Q" hypothesis.

The significance of this point can best be illustrated by considering Jerome's *On Illustrious Men*. Written in 386, *Illustrious Men* at first impres-

---

34. E.g., sayings 3, 7, 37, 42, 51, 70, 114!
35. E.g., sayings 18, 22, 29, 30.

sion appears to be a collection of brief biographical sketches of 135 leaders (all men) of the early church, beginning with Simon Peter in the first century and ending with Jerome himself in the early fifth century. Although biographical in format, *Illustrious Men* is in reality *bibliographical* in content, for it is a catalog of nearly 800 authors and works in early Christianity. In addition, Jerome names 36 works of Philo and 31 of Josephus. The inclusion of Philo and Josephus indicates Jerome's intent to give a complete survey of Christian literature — and Jewish literature pertaining to it — in the early church. Of the nearly 800 works named by Jerome, 770 are Christian works that are either known to us from other authors (many from Eusebius's *Ecclesiastical History*) or that remain extant in whole or in part. Jerome also names some 25 works that are either lost or unknown. The works named by Jerome vary in size from single letters to encyclopedic volumes such as Epiphanius's *Panarion,* which extends to three large volumes in Karl Holl's modern edition. This plethora of works does not exhaust Jerome's knowledge of early Christian literature, however. He leaves Origen's impressive bibliography of works unnamed, and not infrequently he notes that so-and-so wrote "many volumes," or that "countless other epistles could be added to the list." These latter works are left unnamed (and untallied in the nearly 800 works), either because Jerome does not have access to them, or because for various reasons he judges them unworthy of mention.

What is most significant for our purposes is that none of the works named in *Illustrious Men* corresponds in any recognizable degree to the hypothetical profile of "Q." This is more than a stumbling block for the acceptance of the "Q" hypothesis. It is a major barrier, since 95% of the named works in *Illustrious Men* — a total of 770 texts — are identifiable. None of them, however, resembles "Q." This difficulty is accentuated by the fact that "[a]fter the third century it becomes more and more uncommon to find any educated man showing knowledge of the texts that have not come down to the modern world."[36] It is unlikely, in other words, that a "Q"-like text has escaped Jerome's eye — especially since in *Illustrious Men* he aims to give a complete account of early Christian literature. Of the remaining five percent of works mentioned by Jerome (i.e., the 25 otherwise unknown and non-extant), we obviously cannot be certain, because they

---

36. L. D. Reynolds and N. G. Wilson, *Scribes and Scholars: A Guide to the Transmission of Greek and Latin Literature* (Oxford: Clarendon, 1991), 53.

no longer exist. But in description none of them *suggests* "Q." Moreover, I think it safe to assume that a collection of Jesus' sayings would scarcely be relegated to such a marginal category. If Jerome had access to the greatest repository of Christian books at the Caesarea library, and if he utilized that library and his prodigious compilation of "the first history of Christian theological literature,"[37] and if this Jerome makes no mention of a document resembling "Q," then the historian cannot but doubt its existence. The teachings of Jesus were assigned the highest importance in the early church. Had such a collection of teachings existed, we should expect it to have played a prominent, even preeminent, role in a catalog of early Christian works. Had such a collection of teachings existed, it seems inconceivable that Jerome would leave it unmentioned. But there is no mention of it — and his silence on the matter is momentous. This is an instance when an argument from silence seems virtually conclusive.

Rather than concluding with what is absent from *Illustrious Men,* however, let me conclude with what is *present.* Where we should expect mention of a dominical sayings source (had one existed), we find instead mention of *the Hebrew Gospel.* The first two major chapters of *Illustrious Men* are on James (2) and Matthew (3). The last third of the chapter on James — the longest in *Illustrious Men* — is devoted to the Hebrew Gospel, and the entirety of the next chapter on Matthew is devoted to the Hebrew Gospel as well. This seems to me of inestimable importance. The *first* seminal document that Jerome deals with in the Christian tradition, in other words, is not "Q." It is the Hebrew Gospel! The place of honor that should be accorded to the phantom "Q" document is accorded rather to the *actual* Hebrew Gospel.

Thus, the *Gospel of Thomas,* the only example of a "Q"-like document suggested (but not asserted) by Kloppenborg, is not a viable candidate for a collection of dominical sayings. Nor is there a known example of a collection of dominical sayings in early Christianity. To my knowledge only one further possibility of a "Q"-like document has been suggested, and it is found in the Babylonian Gemara. William Horbury sees *Šabbat* 116a-b as evidence — evidently the lone evidence — of a collection of Jesus-sayings in early Christianity.[38] The quotation he cites appears in a satirical story

---

37. J. Quasten, *Patrology: The Beginnings of Patristic Literature* (Westminster, Md.: Christian Classics. 1992), 1.1.

38. "The Hebrew Matthew and Hebrew Study," in *Hebrew Study from Ezra to Ben-Yehuda,* ed. W. Horbury (Edinburgh: T. & T. Clark, 1999), 130.

from the Talmud involving Imma Shalom, wife of Rabbi Eliezer and sister of Rabban Gamaliel II — the grandson of the Gamaliel mentioned in Acts 5:34, under whom the apostle Paul claims to study in Acts 22:3. A certain "philosopher" of high moral standing lives in their neighborhood. Shalom and Gamaliel hatch a plot to bribe him with a golden lamp to secure a favorable verdict from him and thus tarnish his reputation.

> Imma Shalom, R. Eliezer's wife, was R. Gamaliel's sister. Now a certain philosopher lived in his vicinity, and he bore a reputation that he did not accept bribes. They wished to expose him, so she brought him a gold lamp, went before him, and said to him, "I desire that a share be given me in my [deceased] father's estate." "Divide," ordered he. [R. Gamaliel] said to him, "It is decreed for us, Where there is a son, a daughter does not inherit." [The philosopher replied], "Since the day that you were exiled from your land the Law of Moses has been superseded and another book [= gospel, עון גליון] given, where it is written, 'A son and daughter inherit equally.'" The next day [R. Gamaliel] brought him a Libyan ass. [The philosopher] said to them, "Look at the end of the book, wherein it is written, 'I came not to diminish the Law of Moses nor to add to the law of Moses, and it is written therein, 'A daughter does not inherit where there is a son.'" [Imma Shalom] said to him, "Let thy light shine forth like a lamp." [R. Gamaliel] to him, "An ass came and knocked the lamp over."[39]

39. The Aramaic text (*b. Šabb.* 116a-b) reads:

אימא שלום דביתהו דרבי אליעזר אחתיה דרבן גמליאל הואי: הוה ההוא
פילוספא בשבבותיה דהוה שקיל שמא דלא מקבל שוחדא בעו לאחוכי: ביה
אעיילא ליה שרגא דדהבא ואזול לקמיה אמרה ליה בעינא דניפלגי לי בנכסי
דבי נשי אמר להו פלוגו אמר ליה כתיב לן במקום ברא ברתא לא תירות אמר
להו מן יומא דגליתון מארעכון איתנטלית אורייתא דמשה ואיתיהיבת עון גליון
וכתיב ביה ברא וברתא ירתון למחר הדר עייל ליה איהו חמרא לובא אמר להו
שפילית לסיפיה דעון גליון וכתיב ביה אנא עון גליון לא למיפחת מן אורייתא
דמשה אתיתי אלא לאוספי על אורייתא דמשה אתיתי וכתב ביה במקום ברא
ברתא לא תירות אמרה ליה נהור נהוריך כשרגא אמר ליה רבן גמליאל אתא
חמרא ובטש לשרגא

Cited (with slight changes) from to the *Hebrew-English Edition of the Babylonian Talmud,* ed. I. Epstein (London: Soncino, 1972). On this particular text, see especially B. L. Visotzky, *Fathers of the World: Essay in Rabbinic and Patristic Literature* (Tübingen: Mohr-Siebeck, 1995), 81; and W. D. Davies and D. Allison Jr., *The Gospel According to Saint Matthew* (ICC; London/New York: T. & T. Clark, 1988), 84-485.

Rabbi Eliezer was one of the most famous rabbis of his day. According to the Talmud, he was charged before a Roman governor with Christian leanings. In order to counteract Eliezer's Christian sympathies, his wife and brother-in-law conspire to bribe the "philosopher" in the story. The story is a clever anti-Christian parody, beginning with the reference to the gospel as עון גליון. The phrase technically means "sin pages," but its vocalization, *awen gilyon*, is an unmistakable homophone for the Greek *euaggelion*, "gospel."[40] Šabbat 116 does not mention the name of Jesus Christ, but substitutes instead the "gospel" as a personification of Jesus. Both Jewish and Christian interpreters are correct in taking the "philosopher" to be a Christian (spokesman), since he renders a decision based on the gospel. The lampoon ends with the light (= gospel) overturned by a donkey and placed under a bushel, which appears to be a reference to and mockery of the motif of the lamp/light in Matt 5:14-16. The image of a donkey overturning a lamp became a later rabbinic proverb.[41] The point of the satire is to provide a legitimate Jewish response to the claims of Christians, as if to say: Whatever Jesus did, he neither added to nor subtracted from the Torah.[42]

The polemic satire of the Imma Shalom story obviously rests on an intimate acquaintance with Christianity.[43] Billerbeck identifies it as one of the few passages in rabbinic literature that expressly quotes from the NT.[44] But is it evidence of a "Q"-like source, as Horbury suggests? That is to say, does anything in the story say or intimate that the NT quotation comes

40. Rightly perceived by P. Billerbeck, Str-B 1.241.

41. Str-B 1.242.

42. See the insightful discussion of the passage in L. Wallach, "The Textual History of an Aramaic Proverb (Traces of the Ebionean Gospel)," *JBL* 60 (1941), 408. Likewise, R. T. Herford, *Christianity in Talmud and Midrash* (New York: KTAV, 1903), 154-55: "The rectitude of the Jew has been corrupted by the spirit of Christianity, the light of the true religion had been extinguished by a mischievous heresy." The editors of the *Hebrew-English Edition of the Babylonian Talmud*, 116b, n. B, maintain without justification that "[Herford's] conjecture that the story ends with a covert jibe at Christianity is hardly substantiated."

43. The various versions of the saying have been attributed to mutations resulting from the process of oral transmission or to inaccuracies of memory. G. Dalman, *Jesus Christ in the Talmud, Midrash, Zohar, and the Liturgy of the Synagogue* (New York: Arno, 1973), 66-70, attributes the changes to the former; and L. Wallach, "The Textual History of an Aramaic Proverb," 407-9, suspects an interpolation on the basis that Matt 5:17 interrupts the teachings on inheritance in Deut. 27:36 and Num 27:1-8 that precede and follow it.

44. Str-B 1.241.

from a sayings source? In answer to this, the only hard evidence in the story is provided in עון גליון, which as noted above is a homophone for *"euaggelion,"* the gospel. Should that "gospel" be understood as a collection of sayings? It would appear not, for immediately before the Imma Shalom satire, *Šabbat* 116 addresses the problem of the books read by the Minim, which is usually an allusion to Christian literature. *Šabbat* 116 appears to give clues to the identification of this Christian literature, for the references to "the Books of *Be Abedan*" and *"Be Nizrefe"* seem to reference the Ebionites and Nazarenes respectively. If so, then the "gospel" referenced in the subsequent Imma Shalom story would appear to be the Hebrew Gospel. No other gospel is introduced, and the context leads one to conclude that the gospel of the *"Abedan"* and *"Nizrefe,"* mentioned immediately before, is the gospel referred to in *Šabbat* 116, and the source of the citation from it. These clues suggest that *Šabbat* 116 is not generic anti-Christian polemic, but directed rather to two Jewish-Christian sects, the Ebionites and Nazarenes, and to the *Sifre Minim,* the Hebrew Gospel they read.

But what about the quotation, "I did not come to diminish the Torah of Moses, (nor/but [textual variant] to add"? Is not this, along with the reference to the lamp, a reference to Matt 5:15-17? The verbal and thematic agreements seem strong enough to assume so. But here again, it is at least possible that the reference could come from the Hebrew Gospel. In Chapter Two we noted a related saying reported by Epiphanius, "I came to destroy the sacrifices."[45] We can imagine such a saying being altered by the authors of *Šabbat* 116 in order to reflect the wording of Deut 4:2, "Do not *add* to the words I have commanded you and do not *subtract* from them." The Aramaic word למיפחת means "to lessen or diminish" as opposed to "to dissolve or destroy" in the Epiphanius wording. By harmonizing Epiphanius's quotation from the Hebrew Gospel with Deut 4:2, the offense of the quotation from the Hebrew Gospel would be effectively removed. The result would be — as evinced in *Šabbat* 116 — that whatever the gospel does, it does not alter the final authority of the Torah.[46] This possibility is supported by earlier allusion to the Ebionites and Nazarenes, and the "Gospel" they read, which ostensibly is the Hebrew Gospel.[47]

---

45. *Pan.* 30.16.5. See pp. 73-74 above.

46. I am indebted to the insights of Shane Berg in this alternative explanation.

47. There is no further reference in Christian literature to the additional quotation, "Where there is a son, the daughter may not inherit." This quotation is not found in the Gos-

We cannot be certain of the dating of the satire in *Šabbat* 116. K. G. Kuhn assigns the composition to the third century.[48] The actual *logion* on which the satire is built appears to be much earlier, however. R. T. Herford argues for the historicity of the Talmudic story, at least in substance, by placing it in the early 70s.[49] If this date is correct — and the dates of Rabbis Eliezer and Gamaliel II and the reference to the fall of Jerusalem in 70 C.E. all corroborate it — then the saying, "I came not to diminish the Law of Moses," could date to the late first century.[50] Whether or not it pre-dates canonical Matthew is not clear, but if it does, then the "Gospel" referred to would doubtlessly be the Hebrew Gospel — the same Hebrew Gospel mentioned just prior to the satirical story. If this is the case, then the quotation in *Šabbat* 116 is not only another independent witness to the Hebrew Gospel, but by far the earliest reference to it.

It seems highly unlikely, therefore, that the source of the saying resembling Matt 5:17 is a "Q"-like collection of Jesus sayings, as Horbury suggests. Rather, the strongest internal evidence in *Šabbat* 116 points to *the Hebrew Gospel* in use among Ebionite and Nazarene Christians. *Šabbat* 116 bears this out, for, as we noted, it is not generic anti-Christian polemic. It was deftly crafted to mock the Hebrew Gospel that preserved such sayings in the medium most dangerous to Jews — Hebrew. The saying preserved in *Šabbat* 116, therefore, appears to be no better candidate for a "Q"-like document than the *Gospel of Thomas*. Its context within a discussion of the Ebionites and Nazarenes, and its resemblance to a similar version found in the Hebrew Gospel as cited by Epiphanius, argue that its most plausible source is the Hebrew Gospel.[51]

---

pel of Matthew, but it could conceivably come from the Hebrew Gospel, although there is no secondary corroboration of it.

48. K. G. Kuhn, "Giljonim und sifre minim," ed. W. Eltester, *Judentum, Urchristentum, Kirche*[2] (BZNW 26; Berlin: W. de Gruyter, 1964), 24-61.

49. *Christianity in Talmud and Midrash* (New York: KTAV, 1903), 149. E. B. Nicholson, *The Gospel according to the Hebrews*, 147, offers further evidence of its essential historicity on the grounds that 1) from 82 C.E. until his death in 123, Rabban Gamaliel was president of the synagogue, and it seems unlikely that he would compromise the dignity of that office by the unseemly behavior reported in the satire, and 2) he did not succeed his father until the latter's death in 70; Nicholson thus concludes that 3) the event most plausibly falls between 70 and 82 C.E., immediately following the fall of Jerusalem.

50. See J. Jeremias, *New Testament Theology*, trans. J. Bowden (New York: Scribner, 1971), 83.

51. L. Wallach, "The Textual History of an Aramaic Proverb," 404, cites Markus Jost,

A survey of ancient literature leaves the "Q" hypothesis in a precarious position. The examples of the instructional or wisdom genre of literature marshaled by John Kloppenborg do not seem to belong to the same family of literature envisioned by "Q" proponents. A plethora of Greco-Roman examples in Kloppenborg's study, which are scarcely analogous to the "Q" hypothesis, is augmented by a paucity of Jewish sayings collections, which are no closer in analogy. I find it significant that Kloppenborg, a leading proponent and architect of the critical study of "Q," refrains from making a case for "Q" on the basis of either genre, including the *Gospel of Thomas*. Thus, proponents of "Q" do not advance a genuine example of a "Q"-like collection in the early church. Moreover, the lack of reference to a "Q"-like document in Jerome's *On Illustrious Men* is of utmost significance. It is scarcely imaginable that a source of dominical sayings would have escaped the notice of the early church, and especially of Jerome, who wrote *Illustrious Men* for the express purpose of providing a comprehensive catalog of Christian literature of the first four centuries. The complete silence of Jerome on a "Q"-like document — and his emphasis, by contrast, on the Hebrew Gospel — makes it highly doubtful that such a document ever existed. Proponents of "Q" cannot evade the force of Alfred Hilgenfeld's summary judgment: "In all of Christian antiquity there is no knowledge of a mere collection of Christ's sayings."[52]

"Q" and Luke

The foregoing discussion makes two things clear: first, the development of "Q" served the intellectual, political, and social persuasions of Enlightenment Europe, and second, no document approximating "Q" remains from the written memory of early Christianity. From a historical perspective therefore — and that is Hengel's first criterion necessary to advance the discussion — the "Q" hypothesis is not viable. That does not sound the death knell of "Q," however. Despite its bad pedigree, "Q" could still be

---

Geschichte des Judentums und seiner Sekten, 1858; and Leopold Loew, *Hehaluz, Wissenschaftliche Abhandlungen über Jüdische Geschichte,* 1853, who likewise attribute the quotation in *b. Šabb.* 116 to the Hebrew Gospel.

52. A. Hilgenfeld, *Historisch-Kritische Einleitung in das Neue Testament* (Leipzig: Fues, 1875), 456-57: "Eine blosse Sammlung von Christusreden kennt aber das ganze christliche Alterthum nicht."

correct. Unusual things occasionally happen in history. "Q" could be one of them. Virtually no one predicted the fall of the Berlin Wall, and even today no one can fully explain how the whole Soviet world imploded not by World War III, but by nothing more than a bloody nose here and there. But no one denies that the Wall — and the Soviet Union — did fall. Likewise, for reasons beyond our imagination, "Q" could in fact still preserve a voice of the early church. But if so, it must make a better showing on the basis of internal evidence among the Synoptic Gospels than it did with regard to its historical existence in early Christianity.

The final avenue remaining to be pursued with regard to the "Q" hypothesis pertains to internal evidence within the Synoptic Gospels. If "Q" could explain a body of material in Luke and Matthew in such a way that it is the only explanation — or clearly the strongest explanation — then it might be maintained as a necessary inference, despite the problems surrounding its inception and lack of historical attestation. In this regard, a small body of Lukan material needs to be considered that was not discussed in Chapter Three. This material consists of a remnant of 177 verses, according to the divisions of Luke in Appendix II, which remains when both Mark and Special Luke have been considered. These 177 verses are also shared in some form by Matthew; hence, they qualify as traditional "Q" material. The 177 verses, in other words, are shared by Matthew and Luke, but not by Mark. At this point I shall refer to these verses as "the double tradition" rather than "Q," since the "Q" hypothesis is freighted with connotations that may cloud an objective consideration of the verses alone.

In order to consider these options, the verses need to be identified and briefly analyzed. The 177 verses in the double tradition are contained in the following 33 pericopes:

1. Luke 3:7-9	Matt 3:7-9	Preaching of repentance by John the Baptist
2. Luke 3:17	Matt 3:12	Preaching of repentance by John the Baptist
3. Luke 4:1-13	Matt 4:2b-11	Temptation of Jesus
4. Luke 6:20b-23	Matt 5:3-12	Beatitudes
5. Luke 6:27-49	Matt 5:38-48; 7:1-5, 15-20, 21-27	On love of enemies; on judging others

6. Luke 7:6b-10	Matt 8:7-13	Jesus heals a centurion's son in Capernaum
7. Luke 7:18-28	Matt 11:2-11	Emissaries from John the Baptist to Jesus
8. Luke 7:31-35	Matt 11:16-19	Contrast between John the Baptist and the Son of Man
9. Luke 9:57-60	Matt 8:18-22	On Following Jesus
10. Luke 10:2-16	Matt 9:37-38; 10:7-16; 11:20-24; 10:40	Commissioning of the Seventy-two; woes to cities in Galilee; rejection of Jesus equals rejection of God
11. Luke 10:21-24	Matt 11:25-27; 13:16-17	All things given to Jesus by the Father
12. Luke 11:2-4	Matt 6:9-13	Lord's Prayer
13. Luke 11:9-13	Matt 7:7-11	"Ask and you will receive . . ."
14. Luke 11:23-26	Matt 12:30, 43-45	Return of the unclean spirit
15. Luke 11:29-35	Matt 12:38-42; 5:15; 6:22-23	The sign of Jonah
16. Luke 12:2-9	Matt 10:26-33	Exhortation to fearless confession
17. Luke 12:22-31	Matt 6:25-34	Anxieties about earthly things
18. Luke 12:33-34	Matt 6:19-21	Treasures in heaven
19. Luke 12:39-46	Matt 12:42-51	The watchful and faithful servant
20. Luke 12:53	Matt 10:35	Jesus the cause of divisions in households
21. Luke 12:54-59	Matt 16:2-3; 5:25-26	Interpreting the times
22. Luke 13:20-21	Matt 13:33	Parable of the Leaven
23. Luke 13:24	Matt 7:13	The narrow gate
24. Luke 13:26-30	Matt 7:22-23; 8:12; 8:11; 19:30	The great assize
25. Luke 13:34-35	Matt 23:37-38	Lament over Jerusalem
26. Luke 14:16-18	Matt 22:1-6	Parable of the Great Supper
27. Luke 14:21-24	Matt 22:7-10	Parable of the Great Supper
28. Luke 16:13	Matt 6:24	On serving two masters

29. Luke 16:16-17	Matt 11:12-13; 5:18	On the law
30. Luke 17:3b-4	Matt 18:15, 21-22	On forgiveness
31. Luke 17:23-27	Matt 24:23, 26-27, 37-39	The Day of the Son of Man
32. Luke 17:33-37	Matt 10:39; 24:28, 40-41	Sayings on the end times
33. Luke 22:28-30	Matt 19:28	Eating with Jesus at the heavenly banquet.[53]

With one exception, Luke 22:28-30, the above material is set in Jesus' public ministry in Galilee and on the journey to Jerusalem. Two clues, however, suggest that the double tradition was not limited to Jesus' pre-Passion ministry. The first is 22:28-30, which occurs in Luke's Passion material (but not in Matthew's). Virtually all "Q" scholars consider this a legitimate "Q" text, and its placement in Luke's Passion materials suggests a Passion narrative as its source. The second clue is saying #25, the lament over Jerusalem. This saying occurs in Luke 13:34-35, long before Jesus arrives in Jerusalem, but its placement there seems "out of place." It would appear that Luke transposed a saying from Jesus' final week in Jerusalem to a location early in the travel narrative. If this is correct, we have a second clue that the source from which the 177 verses were gleaned extended from the commencement of Jesus' ministry in Galilee into Passion week in Jerusalem.[54]

Twenty-eight of the 33 pericopes consist of teachings, parables, exhor-

53. The precise limits of "Q" are not entirely agreed. The Eusebian Canons, for example, identify 82 units of material shared by Matthew and Luke, which exceeds the conventional "Q" material. My list of 177 verses, on the other hand, is slightly less than conventional "Q" material. C. M. Tuckett includes 66 additional verses in his reckoning of "Q" ("Q [Gospel Source]," *ABD* 5.567): 7:1-5; 11:14-20, 39-52; 12:10-12, 51-52; 13:18-19, 23, 25; 14:19-20, 26-27, 34-35; 15:4-7; 16:18; 17:6, 28-30; 18:14; 19:12-17. Most of the additions occur in relation to the same blocks of material I list above. My list includes four verses not listed by Tuckett: 12:54-56 and 17:25.

54. S. Hultgren, *Narrative Elements in the Double Tradition*, 310, summarizes his entire study of the double tradition thus: "The single most important conclusion that arises from this study may be summarized in two sentences: Before any of our canonical gospels were written, there existed in the gospel tradition a common, coherent, and primitive narrative-kerygmatic framework that ran from the baptism of Jesus to his passion, death, and resurrection. The narrative elements in the Double Tradition were not only fully embedded in this narrative-kerygmatic framework from the beginning of the gospel tradition, but they were in part constituent of that framework."

tations, and didactic material, most of which are dominical sayings. Nevertheless, the teachings are not disembodied abstractions of wisdom as one finds, say, in the sayings of the Buddha in the *Dhammapada* or in *The Meditations* of Marcus Aurelius. The rudiments of a narrative structure are still preserved in the material, as evinced, for example, by the healing of the centurion's son in Capernaum (#6). Jesus' temptation in the wilderness (#3) is also itself a narrative unit.[55] There seems to be some awareness of the Passion already in the temptation narrative, and particularly in Luke's version, which climaxes in Jerusalem. Nor is the sayings material associated exclusively with Jesus. John the Baptist figures heavily in the early material, first in his wilderness calls for repentance (#s 1 and 2), and later in his sending emissaries to Jesus from prison (#s 7 and 8).[56] The narrative structure also includes Peter (#19). The stage on which the 177 verses are performed is thus not simply a readers' theater of Jesus' teachings, for scene changes and plot developments are still discernible in the background of several of the teachings. To change the metaphor, not all the narrative mortar has eroded from among the didactic bricks. The 33 pericopes preserve rudiments of a narrative framework that extends from the commencement of Jesus' Galilean ministry to its consummation in Jerusalem. The sayings are ostensibly excerpted from a larger διήγησις (Luke 1:1), a written account, that contained both narrative and didactic material.

What can be said of the origin of the double tradition? The double tradition does not occur in the Gospel of Mark, and Mark therefore can be eliminated as a possible source for it. That leaves three remaining possibilities: 1) the double tradition derives from the Hebrew Gospel, or 2) it derives from additional material in the same source that Mark used, or 3) it derives from yet a third source, which could lead to the revival of the "Q" hypothesis in some form. The final task of this chapter is to examine the

---

55. Already in 1888 R. Handmann, *Das Hebräer-Evangelium,* 138, recognized that these two stories indicated more than a sayings source: "Diese zweite Quelle kann nicht eine blosse Spruchsammlung gewesen sein, sondern eine Art Evangelium . . . , welches also auch geschichtliche Stücke enthielt."

56. For detailed discussions of the temptation of Jesus (#3) and John's emissaries to Jesus (#7), see S. Hultgren, *Narrative Elements in the Double Tradition,* 62-127, who confirms the narrative structure of both. E.g., "The double-tradition material in Matt 11.2-11//Luke 7.18-28 reflects a thoroughgoing *narrative* interest in the relationship between John the Baptist and Jesus that is fully congruent with the gospel tradition as a whole and with the narrative framework of the canonical gospels" (p. 92).

double tradition in light of these options. Unfortunately, the task is rendered virtually impossible to decide with any degree of certainty, because each of the three options claims suggestive evidence, but none claims conclusive evidence.

With regard to the first option — that the double tradition derives from the Hebrew Gospel — there is evidence pro and con. An intriguing datum of evidence favoring a source in the Hebrew Gospel occurs with reference to the spelling of "Jerusalem." We noted in Chapter Four that of the 31 references to Jerusalem in Luke, 27 spell the name not Ἱεροσόλυμα (the normal spelling of the name in the NT), but Ἱερουσαλήμ, which is closer to the Hebrew form of the word and the only way Jerusalem is spelled in the LXX (except for Tobit, Maccabees, and 1 and 2 Esdras). The Gospel of Matthew, by contrast, refers to "Jerusalem" 13 times, all but once spelled Ἱεροσόλυμα. The single exception is Matt 23:37, the lament of Jesus over Jerusalem — which is also double tradition (see #25 above). In this instance the spelling of Jerusalem is not Ἱεροσόλυμα, but rather Ἱερουσαλήμ. Since Matt 23:37 is double tradition, and since the spelling of Jerusalem follows the *Lukan* form rather than the otherwise consistent Matthean form, it seems reasonable to conclude that Matthew 23:37-38 derives from Luke 13:34-35. The spelling of Jerusalem in Luke's version of the saying indicates a source in the Hebrew Gospel. It therefore seems further justified to conclude that the spelling of "Jerusalem" in Matt 23:37 probably derives from the Hebrew Gospel, as transmitted through Luke. This suggests that the earlier form of saying #25 above is found in Luke; and that Matthew derives saying #25 from Luke.

Would it be possible, then, to hypothesize that *all* double tradition material in Matthew derives from Luke?[57] The evidence is insufficient to make such a judgment, and may even argue against it. The 177 verses under consideration exhibit, on average, no higher Hebraic influence than material that Luke shares in common with Mark. According to Appendix II, the 177 verses shared in common by Luke and Matthew contain 55 Hebraisms. That amounts to a 31% likelihood that a Hebraism will occur in the double tradition. By comparison, Appendix II shows that Luke shares

---

57. E. Schweizer, "Eine hebraisierende Sonderquelle des Lukas?" 173-76, makes a modified version of this claim in arguing that Hebraic elements in Luke are found in Special Luke and in two blocks of material shared in common with Matt 16:13–17:23 and Matt 8:1–9:34. I do not find the same Hebraic influence in the two Matthean blocks that Schweizer does.

377 verses in common with the triple tradition (Matthew and Mark). These 377 verses contain 159 Hebraisms, which amounts to a 42% likelihood that a Hebraism will occur in the triple tradition. The 177 verses that Luke and Matthew share in common in the double tradition thus exhibit statistically lower Semitic content than the 377 verses that Luke shares in common with Matthew and Mark in the triple tradition. The fact that the double tradition material has the *lowest* Hebraic content seems to argue against the Hebrew Gospel as a possible source of it. Option #1 thus claims evidence pro and con, and is inconclusive.

If the double tradition does not derive from Luke's Hebrew source, another source must be considered. That source, according to the second option listed above, could have been additional material from the source(s) that fed the Gospel of Mark. Stephen Hultgren is inclined to regard the double tradition as additional material in the source from which Mark drew for the composition of his Gospel.[58] In principle, this is possible, but there is no way to verify such a hypothesis, since nothing is known of the source or sources of Mark, other than the generally accepted patristic opinion of a Petrine influence in Mark. An observation that would argue against option #2 is that the double tradition shows a slightly lower number of Semitisms than does material that Matthew and Luke must have derived from Mark. I noted above that the double tradition exhibits 11 percent fewer Semitisms than does the triple tradition. That is not a major difference, but it is noticeable. It may suggest that the double tradition does not come from the same source as Mark.

This brings us to the third option, the positing of a third source for Luke. In itself that poses no inherent problem, for in his prologue Luke acknowledges that "many" (πολλοί) put their hands to the task of writing narratives of Jesus. The block of 177 verses could thus derive from another narrative to which Luke alludes in 1:1-4. It could be argued that an 11 percent drop in Semitic influence in the double tradition in comparison with the triple tradition is evidence of an additional source of the Gospel of Luke, and perhaps also of Matthew. That is a tentatively defensible hypothesis, but it is very conjectural, and few scholars will be willing to place

---

58. S. Hultgren, *Narrative Elements in the Double Tradition,* 325-50, believes that so-called "Q" material and Markan material both appear to derive from the same primitive narrative-kerygmatic source(s). "There is absolutely no evidence that the Double Tradition forms a separate Jesus tradition from that which we find in the triple tradition" (325).

much weight on it. Even if this option were chosen, it would not imply the acceptance of the traditional "Q" hypothesis, for, as we have seen, the material in the double tradition preserves the rudiments of a narrative framework, indicating that it was part of a narrative structure rather than a simple anthology of sayings, as "Q" supposes. This means that the double tradition is not, as the "Q" hypothesis posits, detached teachings and sayings, but part of a narrative framework.[59]

It is impossible to decide among the above three options with anything approaching certainty. The best we can do is to make inferences to the best explanation, and each of the three most plausible explanations claim arguments pro and con. Whatever the source of the double tradition, it has covered its tracks well. All three options bring us to a fork in the road, and ultimately to an impasse. The third "Q"-like option *could* be correct, but it cannot claim the strongest support, and may not be as strong as the first option. There is not enough evidence to assert with confidence any of the three options.

Adieu to "Q"

On the grounds of internal evidence among the Synoptics, the "Q" hypothesis *could* explain the double tradition, but it is by no means a *necessary* inference. "Q", in other words, is no stronger or more compelling than the first and second options. It is therefore impossible to affirm the "Q" hypothesis on the one remaining ground which could justify its existence. On historical and philological grounds, the traditional hypothesis of "Q" as a sayings source is unnecessary and indefensible. No theory is conceived in a perfect state of objective equilibrium, but one suspects genetic engineering in the case of "Q" in order to fulfill the Enlightenment pledge of enhancing Jesus' theologically desirable traits (as moral example and teacher), and eliminating his undesirable ones (the miraculous). Nor is a survey of ancient Christian literature successful in producing either a parallel or precedent for a "Q"-like document of dominical sayings. Finally, with regard to internal evidence among the Synoptics, the hypothesis of a

---

59. Contrary to H. Koester, *Ancient Christian Gospels* (Philadelphia: Trinity, 1992), 45, who says, "The Synoptic Sayings Source, used by the Gospels of Matthew and Luke, was a collection of wisdom sayings and apocalyptic prophecies; it never contained a passion narrative."

source of detached dominical sayings is not a particularly close fit with the double tradition shared in common by Luke and Matthew; nor is it either the only or best explanation for the verses in question. From a scientific point of view, the vital signs of "Q" have never been strong — and they have not improved with time. With regard to history and philology — the two grounds on which Martin Hengel requires convincing evidence — the "Q" hypothesis is suffering from a state of entropy.

Several scholars have recently joined the chorus of evidence against "Q" that is presented in this chapter. P. F. Beatrice believes the whole gospel tradition can be traced back to the *Gospel of the Hebrews* and Mark. "If this is true," he concludes, "what sense would still be there in talking about the source Q, the collection of the sayings of Jesus? . . . Q seems to be condemned to remain a 'bodiless demon,' or more simply an optical illusion."[60] With less flair but no less substance, S. Hultgren declares, "It seems to me, then, that the Q hypothesis must either be abandoned or radically redefined."[61] H. Philip West Jr. maintains, "But for all the assumptions about its origin, contents or history, Q has remained a literary ghost. Continued study has produced increasing uncertainty as to the precise form and content of Q. Many scholars have been reduced to using 'Q' purely as a symbol for the non-Markan material common to Matthew and Luke."[62] Most perceptive, perhaps, is Joshua Grintz: "[I]t is hardly credible that there ever existed a separate collection of Sayings and Parables only. Jesus was not a wise man (in the sense of Ben Sira). The extraordinary value attributed to him by his disciples derived from his personal deeds and death; these betokened to them his genius."[63] These admonitions rescue us from a fog of "Q" speculation and set our feet on the only solid ground available, namely, that the comparatively small amount of material common to Matthew and Luke can be accounted for in several ways, none of which is conclusive. Although we cannot be certain of the exact content and provenance of the double tradition, we can be fairly certain what it was *not*. It was not a mere *Redesammlung*, a compendium of sayings and teachings abstracted from and divorced from a narrative of Jesus' life. To be sure, the double tradition contained sayings, but they

---

60. "The Gospel according to the Hebrews," 194.

61. *Narrative Elements in the Double Tradition,* 329,

62. "A Primitive Version of Luke in the Composition of Matthew," 78.

63. "Hebrew as the Spoken and Written Language in the Last Days of the Second Temple," 41.

were evidently part of a larger διήγησις, i.e., one of the narrative accounts to which Luke refers in his prologue.

The need to think of this source as a full narrative account rather than as just a sayings source should not surprise us. In the canonical Gospels and, so far as we can tell, in their sources Jesus was not regarded as a mere sage, according to the fashion of a Ben Sira or Socrates. A proper witness to the gospel required a certain type of proclamation and literary form. The kerygmatic forms preserved in the book of Acts, in the early Hebrew Gospel, and of course in the canonical Gospels all *narrate* the story of Jesus. We have no evidence in "normative" early Christianity of the gospel being reduced to a compendium of instruction, even moral instruction, as the "Q" hypothesis supposes. The extrapolation of the wisdom of Jesus seems to have been foreign to the interests of the early church. The gospel could not be merely taught as a formula or rational truth could be taught. The gospel had to be *told*. The earliest description of the Gospel of Mark speaks of it as an account "of the things *said* and *done* by the Lord."[64] The teachings of Jesus, in other words, were set within the context of his life. The evidence suggests that already in the earliest Christian proclamations the Incarnation — or what would become the doctrine — determined the Jesus story from the most primitive forms until the fourfold Gospel tradition. A collection of Jesus' sayings was less than the gospel, and there is no evidence in the early church that such a collection contributed to the formation of the four Gospels.

---

64. Eusebius, *Hist. eccl.* 3.39.15: τὰ ὑπὸ τοῦ κυρίου ἢ λεχθέντα ἢ πραχθέντα.

CHAPTER EIGHT

The Hebrew Gospel and the Gospel of Matthew

The foremost objectives of this book have been to survey the diverse and widespread attestation to the Hebrew Gospel in the patristic tradition and to demonstrate that the disproportionately high number of Hebraisms in Special Luke are due to Luke's reliance on the Hebrew Gospel for the one-half of his Gospel not shared in common with Matthew and/or Mark. There are, of course, other sources of Luke, some more certain than others, that have not been considered in equal detail. A virtually certain source, in my judgment, is the Gospel of Mark. I have not felt a similar burden to argue the case of Markan priority, because that case has been sufficiently demonstrated and long embraced by the majority of NT scholars.[1] It is, at

---

1. B. H. Streeter, *The Four Gospels,* 151-52, offers five reasons for accepting the priority of Mark:

1. Matthew reproduces 90% of Mark in language largely identical with that of Mark; Luke does the same for more than half of Mark.
2. In an average section occurring in all three Synoptics, "the majority of the actual words used by Mark are reproduced by Matthew and Luke, either alternately or both together."
3. The relative order of incidents or sections in Mark is generally supported by both Matthew and Luke; when one deviates from Mark, the other usually also does so.
4. Mark's more primitive character is demonstrated by offensive words or phrases usually omitted or toned down in Matthew and Luke, roughness of style and grammar, and preservation of Aramaic words.
5. The way in which Markan material is distributed in Matthew and Luke looks as if each had before him Markan material *in a single document* (italics Streeter's).

The fifth reason is the most subjective, but the first four (and especially #4) incline the vast majority of modern scholars in favor of Markan priority.

any rate, a position I find both compelling and defensible, and I have assumed on the basis of a considerable and consistent body of scholarly data that the Gospel of Mark was a second source of the Gospel of Luke. A third though less certain source of both Luke and Matthew is the double tradition, which, as discussed in the last chapter, could be explained in various ways, none of them conclusive. I have suggested on the basis of limited evidence available that the double tradition may have been an additional source.

What can be said about the Gospel of Matthew, however, which has not yet been specifically considered in the discussion of the Hebrew Gospel? The early chapters demonstrated that the Hebraisms which strongly characterize Special Luke appear much less frequently and distinctively in canonical Greek Matthew. In the last chapter we saw that fewer Hebraisms appear in the double tradition — and perhaps even slightly fewer in the Matthean versions of it. Canonical Greek Matthew, in other words, seems to represent a textual tradition independent of the Hebrew Gospel. Nevertheless, as the title of this book indicates, I wish to advance a global hypothesis of the development of the Synoptic tradition, and this must obviously include an account of the Gospel of Matthew. "Q" scholars generally hold that Matthew is the *earlier* purveyor of the double tradition, and that the Gospel of Matthew may even have been one of the written sources on which Luke relied.[2] I wish to contest this assumption. Internal evidence within Matthew and Luke seems to point fairly clearly to Matthew as the final and consummate Gospel in the Synoptic flowchart. "Q" scholarship may at least *suspect* the same, for it designates "Q" units according to Lukan priority, since "Q" material is generally united in Luke, but scattered throughout Matthew. In this final chapter, I wish, first of all, to set forth a basic and straightforward case for Matthean posteriority. This case is not directly related to the Hebrew Gospel, and thus it is less essential to the thesis of this book. I shall make the case for Matthean posteriority, therefore, with less interaction with secondary literature. Finally, I shall conclude by considering the question, which was first adumbrated in the discussion of Epiphanius in Chapter Two, of the *naming* of the First Gospel. On the basis of textual relatedness, the Third Gospel should bear the name "Matthew," since its most distinctive portions ostensibly derive from the

---

2. For arguments and evidence against this view, see J. Fitzmyer, *To Advance the Gospel*[2] (Grand Rapids: Eerdmans, 1998), 16-18.

Hebrew Gospel of Matthew. Why, despite its textual unrelatedness, does the First Gospel bear Matthew's name?

Matthean Posteriority

"Posteriority," a rarely used antonym of "priority," needs a word of interpretation. The historical-critical method endeavored to uncover or recover the oldest and earliest forms of a given tradition. "Earlier" connoted (more) genuine, whereas "later" was regarded as derivative and less authoritative. On this scale of values, "posterior" is at least slightly denigrating. In the current discussion, however, I wish, if possible, to free "posterior" of any pejorative connotations, for the Gospel of Matthew is not a lesser and redundant work. Throughout the history of the church, the Gospel of Matthew, along with the Gospel of John, has been held in special esteem as one of the two most important Gospels. Readings for Sundays and holy days have traditionally been taken from Matthew, and only from other Gospels where Matthew was thought to be deficient. At least until modern times, Matthew has always been regarded as the "primary" Gospel among the Synoptics. If Matthew was not primary in terms of chronology, from a historical perspective it rightly claims a primacy in terms of *definitiveness*.[3]

But exactly how is Matthew definitive? Certainly, it is definitive in terms of structure. None of the other Gospels exhibits the symmetry of the First Gospel. They display basic structures, to be sure, even elementary symmetrical structures. Both Mark and John devote roughly the first halves of their Gospels to Jesus' initial ministry in Galilee, and the second halves to his concluding ministry in Judea and Jerusalem. The Third Gospel adds a lengthy travel narrative in 9:51–18:14 between the Galilean and Jerusalem ministries of Jesus, creating a three-part structure. But none of the three Gospels exhibits the complex design and proportion of the First Gospel, which begins with two chapters of infancy prologue and ends with two chapters of Passion narrative. In between, the body of Matthew consists of five major divisions, each consisting of three subdivisions, contain-

---

3. G. A. Blair, *The Synoptic Gospels Compared*, 311: "Matthew was called the 'first' Gospel . . . because [it] was the most important of the Gospels, the 'definitive Gospel' (at least with respect to the three Synoptics)."

ing a block of narrative material, followed by a block of didactic material, and concluding with a summary refrain, "When Jesus had finished all these things. . . ."[4] The Gospel of Matthew displays greater design, balance, proportion, and order than any of the other three Gospels.

Perhaps the most distinctive aspect of the Gospel of Matthew is the Sermon on the Mount. The material in Matthew's Sermon, gathered in chs. 5–7, is also present in Luke, but in Luke the material is dispersed throughout chs. 6, 8, 11, 12, 13, 14, and 16, where it is intermingled with Jesus' travels and healings and parables. The same material is decidedly less distinctive and accessible in Luke. Matthew's Sermon on the Mount, on the contrary, presents readers with an arranged manual of Jesus' teaching delimited by subjects and presented in formulaic refrains (e.g., "You have heard it said of old . . . but I say to you"), a catechetical handbook that can be memorized, taught, and transmitted.

To somewhat lesser degrees the blocks of didactic material elsewhere in Matthew follow similar canons of arrangement. The instructions to disciples in Matthew 10, for example, or the unit on parables in Matthew 13, the litany of woes against Pharisees in Matthew 23, and the eschatological discourse in Matthew 24, all display similar editorial intent and design. None of the other gospels orders material into the clearly defined categories that are evident in Matthew.[5]

---

4. Division I: narrative, 3:1–4:25; teaching, 5:1–7:27; summary refrain, 7:28;
     Division II: narrative, 7:28–9:38; teaching, 10:1-42; summary refrain, 11:1;
     Division III: narrative, 11:2–12:50; teaching, 13:1-52, summary refrain, 13:53;
     Division IV: narrative, 13:54–17:27; teaching, 18:1-35; summary refrain, 19:1;
     Division V: narrative, 19:2–22:46; teaching, 23:1-25:46; summary refrain, 26:1.

5. M. Hengel, *The Four Gospels and the One Gospel of Jesus Christ*, 176-77, summarizes the above situation as follows: "[Matthew's] five great discourse complexes are predominantly fashioned by this [marked theological concern]. Luke has little to set over against this overarching skill in composition. . . . Luke's 'Sermon on the Plain' is itself a mere 'shadow' of the Sermon on the Mount. Therefore, it is utterly improbable that, for example, Luke reshaped a Matthean original. He would not have torn apart discourses which have been worked out so masterfully, but integrated them into his work. One could make a Sermon on the Mount out of a 'Sermon on the Plain,' but not vice versa. Therefore, Luke cannot be dependent on Matthew, as is consistently asserted." See also pp. 186-207 in the same volume. Similarly, H. P. West Jr., "A Primitive Version of Luke in the Composition of Matthew," 91: "it is incredible to think that the Sermon on the Plain comes from the Sermon on the Mount. To argue that Luke has so abridged Matthew's sermon is to accuse him of using Matthew in a way utterly different from his use of Mark. We remember that Luke nowhere selectively abridges a Marcan block in this way."

The same attention to symmetry and formulaic harmony is evident in Matthew's version of the Lord's Prayer. Luke's prayer in 11:2-4 seems truncated and incomplete compared to Matthew's prayer in 6:9-13. In Luke, God is addressed simply as "Father," and two brief ascriptions of praise ("hallowed be your name; your kingdom come") are followed by three petitions (for bread, forgiveness, and deliverance from temptation). Matthew's version of the Lord's Prayer, by contrast, is perfectly crafted and balanced: three formulaic ascriptions of praise to God are complemented by three subsequent petitions, the whole of which is prefaced and concluded (at least in a large portion of the textual tradition) with liturgical formulas. Few literary critics will doubt that Matthew's version represents the full flowering of an earlier version of Luke's prayer.[6]

Another illustration of the same developmental flow occurs in the NT accounts of the Lord's Supper. All three Synoptics preserve a generally fixed Eucharistic form in which Jesus first institutes the bread and then the cup (Matt 26:26-29; Mark 14:22-25; Luke 22:19-20). The Eucharistic liturgy of the early church antedated (e.g., 1 Cor 11:23-26) and undoubtedly influenced the earliest gospel accounts of the Lord's Supper. But Luke is unique among the canonical Gospels, and other early Christian Eucharistic texts preserved in the *Didache,* for example, in prefacing the words of institution with a preliminary cup attended by eschatological sayings. This produces a Lukan Eucharist sequence of cup-bread-cup. The only other early Christian Eucharistic account known to include the Lukan preface to the Lord's Supper is the Hebrew Gospel as quoted by Epiphanius. On form-critical grounds scholars have long suspected that Luke 22:15-18 preserves the earliest authentic Eucharistic words of Jesus.[7] The agreement of this material with the wording of the Hebrew Gospel not only confirms that suspicion but makes it highly probable that the source of Luke 22:15-18 is the Hebrew Gospel itself. In contrast to Luke's longer and complex account of the Lord's Supper, Matthew (and Mark also) presents a concise account of the words of institution, evenly proportioned between bread and cup. Matthew's account is close to Paul's account of the same in 1 Cor 11:23-26, and appears to preserve the ultimate ecclesiastical consensus on the Eucharist.

---

6. On Luke's preservation of a more primitive form of the Lord's Prayer, see S. Hultgren, *Narrative Elements in the Double Tradition,* 290-309.

7. Str-B 4.75; J. Jeremias, *The Eucharistic Words of Jesus,* trans. N. Perrin (New York: Scribner, 1966), 97-100, 164; L. Goppelt, ποτήριον, *TDNT* 6.153-54.

The Greek of the First Gospel must also be mentioned in regard to its dating. Although the Gospel of Mark exhibits dramatic structural features by sandwiching a defining narrative into the midst of a host narrative,[8] or signaling a relationship between two texts by placing them side-by-side (e.g., Mark 4:35–5:20), the Greek of the Second Gospel can be and often is less than felicitous. Luke's Greek is technically superior to Mark's but is generally more complex, not the least because of its Hebraisms. Matthew's Greek, on the other hand, is clean and consistent, and his style and wording rarely need to be (or can be) improved. The Gospel of Matthew appears to have passed through many editorial filters. The result is a Gospel that affords memorization and is eminently suitable for public reading.

Matthew also presents a more developed christology than does Mark or Luke. This is especially true of *titular* christology, as evinced by Matthew's (frequent) use of such terms as Son of Abraham, Son of David, Son of God, Emmanuel, Prophet, Christ, Son of Man, and the Coming One. These titles appear in greater frequency in Matthew than they do in Mark and Luke. If Matthew were the source of the Synoptic tradition or double tradition, it is difficult to explain why such terms would be reduced or eliminated in Mark and/or Luke. Matthew also exhibits a sophisticated implicit christology, an example of which appears in the use of προσέρχομαι, which occurs 52 times in Matthew, but only 5 times in Mark and 10 times in Luke. In the Pentateuch, προσέρχομαι bears unmistakable cultic connotations, indicating an approach to God (or a representative of God in priest, altar, tabernacle, etc.). In Matthew, *Jesus* is overwhelmingly made the object of this verb, thus implicitly transferring divine status to him.[9] Luke, in particular, knew the LXX too well to have missed the significance of Matthew's achievement with προσέρχομαι. It seems inexplicable why Luke, who otherwise showcases Hebraisms in his Gospel, would omit such a term if he were drawing on canonical Matthew as one of his written sources.

The above evidence of Matthean posteriority can be illustrated and augmented by considering, briefly, a number of specific Matthean texts that are best explained as developments of earlier Lukan texts.

8. See J. R. Edwards, "Markan Sandwiches: The Significance of Interpolations in Markan Narratives," *NovT* 31 (1989), 193-216, reprinted in *The Composition of Mark's Gospel* (Brill's Readers in Biblical Studies 3, compiled by D. Orton; Leiden: Brill, 1999), 192-215.

9. See J. R. Edwards, "The Use of προσέρχεσθαι in the Gospel of Matthew," *JBL* 106 (1987), 65-74.

- Luke's first beatitude in 6:20, "Blessed are the poor," is expanded into a spiritual virtue in Matt 5:3, "Blessed are the poor *in spirit.*"
- Jesus' teaching about turning the other cheek in Luke 6:29 is further specified as the *right* cheek in Matt 5:39.
- The metaphor in Luke 6:43 that "a good tree cannot make bad fruit" is developed into a moral maxim (that compromises the metaphor) in Matt 12:33, "Do the good tree and its fruit. . . ."
- In the story of the father who brings his demon-possessed boy to Jesus for healing, Luke 9:39 ascribes the possession primitively to "a spirit," whereas Matt 17:15 provides a rational explanation as "epilepsy."
- Luke's metaphor of Jesus casting out demons by the "finger of God" (11:20) is changed in Matt 12:28 into the less Hebraic "spirit of God."
- Jesus' lament over Jerusalem, which in Luke 13:34-35 is uttered five chapters before he arrives in Jerusalem, is relocated more reasonably in Matt 23:37-39 to Jerusalem itself.
- The same text clearly signals a Lukan origin of the saying, for Matthew's spelling of Jerusalem follows the Lukan spelling of the city (Ἰερουσαλήμ) rather than the normal Matthean spelling (Ἰεροσόλυμα).
- Luke omits the controversy with the scribes and Pharisees over clean and unclean in Mark 7:11, whereas Matt 15:5 Hellenizes Mark's "Corban," leaving the simple Greek "gift" (δῶρον) in its place.
- In Mark 10:17-18 and Luke 18:18-19 the rich man addresses Jesus as "good teacher," to which Jesus responds, "Why do you call me good?" Matt 19:16-17 alleviates the offense of Jesus questioning his own goodness by changing the rich man's question to, "What good *thing* must I do to inherit eternal life?"
- The perplexing parable of Luke 19:11-27, seemingly a composite of two parables (a parable of a king and his rebellious subjects, and another of pounds), has been stripped of the first parable and groomed into a coherent Parable of the Pounds in Matt 25:14-30.
- In the same parable, Luke 19:13 speaks of ten servants who were summoned, only three of whom were given money; Matt 25:14 eliminates the superfluous servants and regulates the story to three servants and three loans.
- Luke 23:33 inexplicably omits "Golgotha" from the crucifixion account, whereas Matt 27:33 restores "Golgotha" on the basis of Mark 15:22.

• Matt 28:9-15 is unique in the Gospels in offering an explanation for the Jewish failure to respond to the proclamation of the gospel. That explanation indicates a period late in the first century when the breach between church and synagogue appeared to be final, and such an explanation was needed.

These examples — and more could be added — can be satisfactorily explained on the assumption that the Matthean form of the material is a later development of a more primitive Lukan form. The examples can be less satisfactorily explained, however, on the assumption that Luke has reworked earlier Matthean material.[10] The comparative data point to the more primitive nature of the Lukan material, which was later developed by Matthew.[11]

This conclusion appears to be corroborated in a study of textual transmission, in which Robert McIver and Marie Carroll argue that *"[a]ny sequence of exactly the same 16 or more words that is not an aphorism, poetry, or words to a song is almost certain to have been copied from a written document."*[12] McIver and Carroll note 46 passages, each consisting of 16 or more words, that two of the Synoptic Gospels have in common. In no case do all three Synoptics share a text of 16 or more words in common. Luke and Mark have three passages in common,[13] and Luke and Matthew have 11 passages in common.[14] In addition to the three passages that Mark has in common with Luke, Mark has nine passages in common with Matthew.[15] Of the 46 passages, 14 appear in Luke, 12 appear in Mark, and 20

10. See the discussion of the very considerable difficulties in assuming that Luke followed Matthew in S. Hultgren, *Narrative Elements in the Double Tradition*, 329-35.

11. So M. Hengel, *The Four Gospels and the One Gospel of Jesus Christ*, 69-70: ". . . as a rule the more original version is attributed to Q-Luke as opposed to Q-Matthew."

12. "Experiments to Develop Criteria for Determining the Existence of Written Sources, and Their Potential Implications for the Synoptic Problem," *JBL* 121 (2002), 680 (italics in original).

13. Luke 18:15-17 par. Mark 10:13-16; Luke 4:31-37 par. Mark 1:21-28; Luke 20:45-47 par. Mark 12:38-40.

14. Luke 10:21-24 par. Matt 11:25-30; Luke 12:41-48 par. Matt 24:45-51; Luke 16:10-13 par. Matt 6:24; Luke 3:1-20 par. Matt 3:1-12; Luke 11:9-13 par. Matt 7:7-12; Luke 9:57-62 par. Matt 8:18-22; Luke 11:29-32 par. Matt 12:38-42; Luke 7:18-35 par. Matt 11:1-19; Luke 7:1-10 par. Matt 8:5-13; Luke 5:12-16 par. Matt 8:1-4; Luke 9:21-27 par. Matt 16:21-28.

15. Mark 13:3-13 par. Matt 10:16-25; Mark 8:31–9:1 par. Matt 16:21-28; Mark 13:14-23 par. Matt 24:15-28; Mark 14:12-21 par. Matt 26:17-25; Mark 7:1-23 par. Matt 15:1-20; Mark 12:35-37

appear in Matthew. Of a total of 23 pairs shared by Luke and Mark, or Luke and Matthew, or Mark and Matthew, Matthew shares 20 of them. Matthew, in other words, is almost twice as likely to share material in common with Mark, or in common with Luke, as either Luke or Mark is to share material in common with the other. This statistic suggests that Matthew is either the *source* of material for Mark and Luke; or, conversely, that Matthew is the *recipient* of material from either Mark or Luke. The theory of Markan priority supplies solid and repeated evidence for the assumption that Matthew has been the recipient of Markan material. The foregoing arguments, and especially the list of examples on pages 249-50 above, argue the same, that Matthew is the recipient of Lukan material. The work of McIver and Carroll seems to supply further statistical evidence that Matthew concludes and consummates the Synoptic tradition.

Already in 1838, Christian Gottlob Wilke argued that the similarities between Luke and Matthew could best be explained by Matthew's use of Luke.[16] The Gospel of Matthew appears to represent positions on women, sinners, tax collectors, lawless people, wealth, and possessions that reflect a time period later than the Gospel of Luke.[17] Detailed literary analyses of the relationship between Matthew and Luke are offered by Ronald Huggins and George Blair. Huggins argues that the problem of the relationship between Matthew and Luke is reasonably and satisfactorily resolved on the supposition that Matthew used Mark as his main source, which he supplemented by the use of Luke.[18] In a thorough and minute comparison of Matthew and Luke, Blair sets forth the similar thesis that Mark was the first Gospel, Luke a revision of Mark with additions, and Matthew was a revision of both.[19]

---

par. Matt 22:41-46; Mark 10:35-45 par. Matt 20:20-28; Mark 8:1-10 par. Matt 15:32-39; Mark 13:24-31 par. Matt 24:29-35. For a chart of all 46 passages and their relationships among the Synoptics, see McIver, "Experiments to Develop Criteria for Determining the Existence of Written Sources, and Their Potential Implications for the Synoptic Problem," 681.

16. C. G. Wilke, *Der Urevangelist oder kritische Untersuchung über das Verwandtschaftsverhältnis der drei ersten Evangelien,* 685-93. On pages 460-62 Wilke specifically argues this case for Matt 3:1-12; 10:1-14; 12:9-14; 12:22-32; and 13:1-35.

17. H. P. West Jr., "A Primitive Version of Luke in the Composition of Matthew," 80-88.

18. R. Huggins, "Matthean Posteriority: A Preliminary Proposal." Likewise, G. D. Kilpatrick, *The Origins of the Gospel According to St. Matthew* (Oxford: Oxford University Press, 1946), 7, 140.

19. G. A. Blair, *The Synoptic Gospels Compared,* esp. 307-12.

The posteriority of Matthew can also be advocated on historical grounds. Martin Hengel argues that Luke stands closer to the catastrophic fall of Jerusalem in 70 than does Matthew, and that he displays better knowledge of Judaism prior to it. Hengel further argues that the divide between the Christian movement and the Roman state is less critical in Luke than in later Matthew, and that Matthew presupposes the consolidation of Judaism under later rabbinic programs. Hengel's arguments that the gospels named for apostles are *later* than those named for non-apostles are also well known.[20]

From both a global and detailed perspective, the Gospel of Matthew looks like the terminus of a long process of kerygmatic incubation in the early church. If Matthew were prior to the other two Synoptics, it would be difficult to conceive why its symmetry, practical design, topical organization, and structural felicity would be dismembered and parceled into more pedestrian roles in both Mark and Luke.[21] According to generally accepted standards of literary creativity and development, the design and content of canonical Matthew suggest a later provenance in the Synoptic birth order.

The Authorship of Canonical Matthew

Nearly two centuries of work on the Hebrew Gospel have repeatedly come to an impasse on the mistaken presumption that the Hebrew Gospel, which was attributed to the apostle Matthew from Papias onward, is a Semitic precursor of later canonical Greek Matthew. This was an easy error to make — and not only for Roman Catholics whose ecclesiastical tradi-

20. See *The Four Gospels and the One Gospel of Jesus Christ*, 169-79, 254-55, and 303-5 (nn. 663-70). In a personal letter to me (May 24, 1998), Hengel succinctly summarizes the same: "Dass Lk früher ist als Mt ergibt sich 1. aus seiner grösseren Nähe zur Katastrophe von 70, 2. aus seiner besseren Kenntnis der Verhältnisse vor 70, 3. aus der Tatsache, dass die den Apostelschülern zugeschriebenen Evangelien älter sind als die angeblich von Aposteln verfassten, 4. dass Mt schon die Konsolidierung des Judentums unter rabbinischer Führung voraussetzt und 5. dass Lk noch denkt, dass ein Kompromiss mit dem römischen Staat möglich ist, d.h. er gehört in die frühere Flavierzeit."

21. S. Hultgren, *Narrative Elements in the Double Tradition*, 333: "In general it has been thought more likely that Matthew grouped disparate sayings material into a few great speeches than that Luke broke up Matthew's well-constructed speeches and scattered the sayings throughout his gospel. This argument is compelling, and it makes it that much less likely that Luke is dependent on Matthew in the double tradition."

tion and official pronouncements declared canonical Matthew the earliest Gospel. The error was made by Protestants as well, though for different reasons. And it was made repeatedly. The "Matthew" named by the fathers as the author of the Hebrew Gospel was inevitably associated with the canonical Gospel of the same name, and both Matthews were collapsed into one and the same person. Rarely was the assumption challenged — or thought necessary to be challenged. Eusebius, after all, had spoken of Matthew having first proclaimed the gospel in Hebrew, after which he intended to reduce it to writing when he left the Jewish Christians to whom he had been ministering.[22] According to the reading of the patristic evidence documented in the first three chapters, this written version of Matthew's legacy was the original Hebrew Gospel. But many in the early church — and afterwards — took it to be a precursor of canonical Greek Matthew.

It was fairly common, after all, in a bilingual culture like first-century Palestine and the early Christian centuries that followed for an author to make a first draft of a work in his native language and later to translate the work — and usually expand it in the process — into a second language. This process of translation and expansion often required the aid of native speakers of the receptor language. Eusebius reports that Tertullian's *Apology* was first written in Latin and later translated into Greek.[23] Bardesanes's Syriac refutations of the Marcionites was likewise translated into Greek.[24] Hebrew and Aramaic texts, in particular, needed to be brought into the common vernaculars — usually Greek but sometimes Latin — if they were to extend their influence beyond Judaism and increase their chances of survival. A celebrated example of a Semitic document translated into Greek is the *Jewish War*, first written by Josephus in Aramaic and later expanded and translated into Greek — again with the help of native Greek speakers.[25] Naturally, other Semitic texts were translated as well. At Qumran, five copies of Tobit — four in Aramaic and one in Hebrew — have been found, all of which agree with the longer Greek text of Tobit. These manuscripts preserve the Semitic original from which the Greek text of Tobit was translated. Likewise, *Jubilees* was originally writ-

---

22. *Hist. eccl.* 3.24.6.
23. Eusebius, *Hist. eccl.* 2.2.4.
24. *Hist. eccl.* 4.30.1.
25. *J. W.* 1.3; *Ant.* 1.7; *C. Ap.* 1.50; Eusebius, *Hist. eccl.* 3.9.3.

ten in Hebrew and later translated into Greek, after which the Hebrew originals vanished. A dozen and a half lost Hebrew copies of *Jubilees* were discovered among the Dead Sea Scrolls. Likewise, at Cave 4 — the bonanza cache at Qumran — several Aramaic manuscripts of *1 Enoch* were found. Until the discovery of the Scrolls, *1 Enoch* was known only in an Ethiopic translation of a Greek rendering of lost Semitic originals. Yet another example is the Wisdom of Jesus Ben Sira, which was composed in Hebrew and translated into Greek by the author's grandson, who added a preface explaining the provenance of the work.[26] The translation of Hebrew into Greek was common enough that many in the early church and since assumed — but again mistakenly — that canonical Greek Matthew was a translation of an earlier Hebrew version of the Gospel written by the apostle Matthew.

Despite the reasonableness of this assumption, it was fatally flawed, for canonical Greek Matthew exhibits no particular signs, as does Special Luke, of having been indebted to a Hebrew original. Special Luke flows naturally back into Hebrew, but rendering Matthew into Hebrew is like trying to place two magnets together. The quest for the Hebrew Gospel, particularly in the nineteenth century, inevitably ran around on this linguistic reef. The error was smartly exposed in 1879 by E. B. Nicholson:

> I think we may assume without hesitation that, believing in an Aramaic original of the Greek Matthew and finding an Aramaic Gospel (ascribed to him [Matthew] by the tradition of centuries) bearing much substantial and even verbal agreement with the Greek Gospel, they over hastily jumped to the conclusion that the Aramaic must be *somehow* the original of the Greek.[27]

Nicholson's description applies to modern scholarship no less than to the early church. The hope of recovering a Hebrew or Aramaic *Vorlage* of canonical Matthew launched repeated quests for the Hebrew Gospel. But scholars who undertook the quest soon encountered the inevitable disparities between the Hebrew Gospel and canonical Greek Matthew. In an attempt to salvage their theories, they often concocted fanciful hypotheses

---

26. On these translations from Hebrew and Aramaic into Greek, see J. Vanderkam, *The Dead Sea Scrolls Today* (Grand Rapids: Eerdmans, 1994), 35-40.

27. *The Gospel according to the Hebrews*, 108.

for which there was little or no historical and linguistic evidence. A common proposal was that the Hebrew Gospel was a second-century translation of canonical Greek Matthew *into* Hebrew.[28] But critics of such proposals usually had the last word; and in the rare instance where they did not, the irresolvable disparities between the Hebrew Gospel of Matthew and canonical Greek Matthew did. Research into the Hebrew Gospel succumbed to a pattern of ebbs and flows. Fascination with the Hebrew Gospel gave birth to revived interests and new theories (or attempts to revive old ones). But this initially promising step was too often and too quickly followed by a misstep. Many scholars who tackled the Hebrew Gospel assumed that the apostle Matthew with whom it was associated in patristic tradition was the same Matthew to whom the first canonical Gospel was assigned. Unless repented of, this mistake always led to the same dead-end. And it was seldom repented of. The disparities between the Hebrew Gospel and canonical Matthew inexorably asserted themselves, and research into the Hebrew Gospel was followed by seasons of abandonment. Most of the twentieth century was a long and barren season. From the 1930s to the end of the century an occasional article on the Hebrew Gospel made a timid appearance, but without garnering support or sparking discussion. Nearly a century of NT scholarship was educated in virtual ignorance of the Hebrew Gospel. Had scholars doubted their presupposition of a relationship between the Hebrew Gospel and canonical Matthew rather than the Hebrew Gospel itself, the quest could have recovered from its fatal misstep.[29] Some scholars, of course, did doubt the mistaken presupposition, and some of those also rightly detected the relationship between the Hebrew Gospel and Luke. But no scholar investigated that relationship to the degree it deserved.

Who, then, authored canonical Matthew? It might be imagined that Matthew the apostle authored the canonical Gospel in the same process by which many ancient authors, including Josephus, produced texts, by a first draft in a Semitic tongue, followed by a translation and expansion into Greek. But this suggestion amounts to a contradiction rather than explanation, for the First Gospel omits all the material in Special Luke that de-

---

28. Argued already in 1870 by J. N. Sepp, *Das Hebräer-Evangelium oder die Markus-und Matthäusfrage und ihre friedliche Lösung*, v, and not infrequently subsequently.

29. L. Vaganay, *Le problème Synoptique. Une hypothèse de travail* (Tournai: Desclée, 1952), shows that of the fourteen major attempts to solve the Synoptic Problem, Luke is presupposed as the final stage of tradition in all of them.

rived from the Hebrew Gospel. It is scarcely to be imagined that in a second draft of a work an author would omit material that was most constitutive in the first draft. The only reasonable explanation for the absence of material from the Hebrew Gospel in canonical Matthew is that, unlike Luke, the author of canonical Matthew did not have the Hebrew Gospel at his disposal. This virtually eliminates the possibility of the apostle Matthew being the author of canonical Greek Matthew.

But perhaps canonical Greek Matthew, although not authored by the apostle Matthew, was named for him because of the apostle Matthew's founding contribution to the Synoptic tradition in the composition of the Hebrew Gospel. This was Lessing's original hypothesis in 1778. The Synoptic problem, according to Lessing, could be explained by supposing that Matthew, Mark, and Luke wrote the Gospels bearing their names by drawing on the same unnamed original Hebrew Gospel. The first to draw on the Hebrew Gospel was the apostle Matthew, who subsequently bequeathed his name in Christian tradition to the Hebrew Gospel.[30] This seemingly plausible proposal is plagued (although to a lesser degree) by the same objection noted above: why would the author of canonical Greek Matthew omit material essential to the original Hebrew Gospel? Once again, the most compelling answer to this question seems to be that the author of canonical Greek Matthew did not know of or possess the Hebrew Gospel. If so, then Lessing's hypothesis on the naming of canonical Matthew seems highly doubtful.

A more probable theory, in my opinion, posits that the First Gospel derived its name *in honor of Matthew,* who authored the Hebrew Gospel referred to by Papias. It is Martin Hengel's view that an unknown Jewish Christian author, who was a member of the mainstream church, named his Gospel in honor of Matthew, who was the author of the first and seminal Gospel in Christian tradition.[31] Rendering a final judgment on this matter is impossible, of course, because of the paucity of relevant historical data. Nevertheless, I wish to conclude by noting two long historical traditions that support the honorary hypothesis. First, the early church consistently maintained a relationship between canonical Greek Matthew and Matthew the apostle, who throughout the patristic period was reputed to be the author of the Hebrew Gospel. The early church does not seem fully to have

---

30. *New Hypothesis on the Evangelists as Merely Human Historians,* §37.
31. *The Four Gospels and the One Gospel of Jesus Christ,* 77.

understood the relationship between the Hebrew Gospel and canonical Greek Matthew, but the "Matthew" who is firmly anchored to the tradition of the Hebrew Gospel in patristic memory and testimony seems to be the same individual whose name is associated with canonical Greek Matthew. We have fully acknowledged that whatever the relationship is, it is *not* that of a translation of the original Hebrew Gospel into canonical Greek Matthew.[32] Too many voyages into the waters of the Hebrew Gospel have run aground on that hidden and adamant reef. But that acknowledgement does not exhaust the explanations for the association of one and the same Matthew with both the Hebrew Gospel and canonical Greek Matthew, which enjoyed a virtually uncontested affirmation in the early church.

If canonical Greek Matthew is not a translation of the Hebrew Gospel, or even directly indebted to the content of the Hebrew Gospel, it could be associated with the author of the Hebrew Gospel because of a *common audience.* This is the second point on which tradition agrees, that both the Hebrew Gospel and canonical Greek Matthew were *composed for and addressed to Jewish-Christian communities.* Canonical Greek Matthew would not derive its name, therefore, because it originally shared the Hebrew language in common with the Hebrew Gospel. It did not. Canonical Greek Matthew was almost certainly a Greek document from its inception. Nor did canonical Greek Matthew derive its name because it used the Hebrew Gospel as a source for its content. Again, it did not. The only Gospel to contain content similar to that of the Hebrew Gospel is Luke, not Matthew. Matthew cannot have used the Hebrew Gospel as a source for its content because the quotations of the Hebrew Gospel in the church fathers show no particular correlation with canonical Matthew. Moreover, none of Luke's content from the Hebrew Gospel is also present in canonical Matthew. The one thing, rather, that the Hebrew Gospel and canonical Greek Matthew share specifically and historically in common is not the language or common content but rather, simply and basically, that both were composed for and addressed to Jewish Christian communities. Perhaps they were even addressed to Jewish Christian communities with different pur-

32. R. Bauckham, *Jesus and the Eyewitnesses,* 111-12, is altogether too tentative when he says, "The most plausible explanation of the occurrence of the name Matthew in [Matt] 9:9 is that the author of this Gospel, knowing that Matthew was a tax collector and wishing to narrate the call of Matthew in the Gospel that was associated with him, but not knowing a story of Matthew's call, transferred Mark's story from Levi to Matthew." Bauckham does not deal with the crucial question *why* the First Gospel was associated with this Matthew.

poses in mind.[33] Both were addressed to the special interests and problems of Jewish Christian communities, however, and the importance of that mission was sufficient, whatever else their differences, to endow them with the name of "Matthew."

33. So P. F. Beatrice, "The Gospel according to the Hebrews," 183-85, who maintains that canonical Greek Matthew intends to *correct* errors of Jewish Christians who were nurtured on the Hebrew Gospel alone.

Summary Theses

The essential conclusions of this book can be summarized in 23 theses, one for each letter of the Hebrew alphabet.

א (1) The tradition of the Hebrew Gospel extends from the late first century to the early tenth century. Within this period, the Hebrew Gospel is attested by twenty church fathers — Ignatius, Papias, Irenaeus, Clement of Alexandria, Pantaenus, Hegesippus, Hippolytus, Origen, Eusebius of Caesarea, Ephrem of Syria, Didymus of Alexandria, Epiphanius, John Chrysostom, Jerome, Theodoret, Marius Mercator, Philip Sidetes, the Venerable Bede, Nicephorus, and Sedulius Scottus. When references to the Hebrew Gospel by Pope Damasus, the Islamic Hadith, the scholia in Sinaiticus, and tractate *Šabbat* 116 in the Babylonian Talmud are added to this number, the list lengthens to over two dozen different witnesses. The Hebrew Gospel is therefore identified by name in at least two dozen patristic sources. Combined, there are some 75 different attestations to the Hebrew Gospel in ancient Christianity.

ב (2) The geographical locations of the ancient witnesses range from Lyons and Rome in the west, to Alexandria and North Africa in the south, to India in the east, and to Jerusalem and Constantinople in between.

ג (3) Specific *quotations* from the Hebrew Gospel occur in Ignatius of Antioch, Clement of Alexandria, Origen, Didymus of Alexandria, Eusebius, Epiphanius, Jerome, Sedulius Scottus, and perhaps the

Talmud. The most numerous references or citations of the Hebrew Gospel come from Jerome, who cites it 22 times.

ד (4) Witnesses to the Hebrew Gospel are transmitted primarily in Greek and Latin, although one occurs in Arabic in the Islamic Hadith, and perhaps the earliest appears in Aramaic in the Babylonian Talmud.

ה (5) One dozen ancient witnesses attribute the Hebrew Gospel to the apostle Matthew. No father or ancient source attributes the Hebrew Gospel to anyone other than the apostle Matthew.

ו (6) Eleven ancient witnesses specify that the Hebrew Gospel was written in Hebrew. "Hebrew" does not appear to be a circumlocution for "Aramaic," as is commonly supposed, but rather to designate genuine biblical Hebrew, perhaps with some Mishnaic influence.

ז (7) The Hebrew Gospel occupied the "disputed" category of a select six or eight books throughout early Christianity, and is cited more frequently and positively alongside canonical texts than is any other noncanonical document of which I am aware.

ח (8) The Hebrew Gospel enjoyed wide circulation and esteem in early Christianity. No noncanonical text appears in patristic prooftexts as often and as favorably as does the Hebrew Gospel.

ט (9) Neither "The Traditions (or Gospel) of Matthias" nor the "Teachings (of the Apostles)" should be confused with the Hebrew Gospel. On the other hand, the testimony of the ancient sources implies that "the Gospel of the Ebionites" and "the Gospel of the Nazarenes" were either identical with the Hebrew Gospel of the apostle Matthew, or clearly within its textual family.

י (10) Patristic quotations from the Hebrew Gospel exhibit a stronger correlation with the Gospel of Luke, and especially material in Special Luke, than they do with either Matthew or Mark.

כ (11) The Hebrew Gospel was most plausibly a source of the Gospel of Luke, and specifically either the primary or sole source of Special Luke.

ל (12) The Semitisms in Luke cannot be properly explained as "Septuagintisms," i.e., as imitations of the language and style of the LXX. Nor can they be explained as reliance on an Aramaic spoken *Vorlage*. Semitisms in Luke are most plausibly explained by reliance on the Hebrew language of the original Hebrew Gospel.

מ (13) The Hebrew Gospel was not a compilation of the Synoptic Gospels, but repeatedly and distinctly similar to Luke.

נ (14) Semitisms appear in Special Luke nearly four times as often as they appear in those sections of Luke that are shared in common with Matthew and/or Mark.

ס (15) The distinct and unusually high number of Semitisms in Special Luke is most plausibly explained by Luke's reliance on the Hebrew Gospel for those parts of his Gospel not shared in common with Matthew and/or Mark.

ע (16) The Hebrew Gospel, although not specified, is most probably one of the eyewitness sources that Luke used as a source of the Third Gospel and to which he refers in the prologue.

פ (17) It appears that the Hebrew Gospel, at least in order and sequence, forms the *Grundtext* of the Gospel of Luke, into which Luke integrated material from Mark.

צ (18) The Hebrew Gospel has been neglected in post-Enlightenment NT scholarship because it is no longer extant and because of anti-Jewish biases in Christian scholarship.

ק (19) The "Q" hypothesis is not defensible on the basis of scholarly evidence, and should be abandoned. Schleiermacher's original proposal of what became the "Q" hypothesis was based on faulty scholarly conclusions, and there is no evidence, as "Q" maintains, of a written compendium of Jesus' sayings in early Christianity.

ר (20) A sum of 177 verses in Luke does not appear to derive either from the Hebrew Gospel or from Mark. These verses, which are present in one form or another also in Matthew, could be accounted for in various ways, none of which is conclusive. The verses, which I refer to as the double tradition, do not appear to have derived from a hypothetical sayings source, however, and thus cannot be explained or associated with the traditional "Q" hypothesis.

ש (21) A plethora of evidence, including factors related to the design, style, vocabulary, and historical allusions in canonical Matthew, argue for Matthean posteriority, i.e., that the First Gospel was the final and consummate Gospel in the Synoptic tradition.

שׂ (22) Canonical Greek Matthew represents a separate and independent tradition from the Hebrew Gospel and cannot be explained as a Greek translation of the Hebrew Gospel. Canonical Greek Matthew and the Hebrew Gospel most probably share the name "Matthew" because both were written for and addressed to Jewish Christian audiences.

ת (23) On the basis of this evidence, the Synoptic tradition can properly be diagrammed thus:[1]

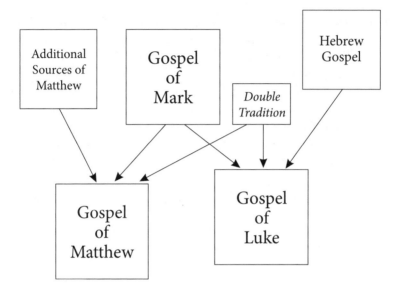

---

1. Normal font indicates high degree of certainty; *italics indicate some doubt about source.*

References to the Hebrew Gospel
in the First Nine Centuries[1]

First Century

Talmud

Šabb. 116a-b (see pp. 228-32)

אימא שלום דביתהו דרבי אליעזר אחתיה דרבן גמליאל הואי: הוה
ההוא פילוספא בשבבותיה דהוה שקיל שמא דלא מקבל שוחדא בעו
לאחוכי: ביה אעיילא ליה שרגא דדהבא ואזול לקמיה אמרה ליה
בעינא דניפלגי לי בנכסי דבי נשי אמר להו פלוגו אמר ליה כתיב לן
במקום ברא ברתא לא תירות אמר להו מן יומא דגליתון מארעכון
איתנטלית אורייתא דמשה ואיתיהיבת עון גליון וכתיב ביה ברא
וברתא ירתון למחר הדר עייל ליה איהו חמרא לובא אמר להו
שפילית לסיפיה דעון גליון וכתיב ביה אנא עון גליון לא למיפחת מן
אורייתא דמשה אתיתי אלא לאוספי על אורייתא דמשה אתיתי וכתב
ביה במקום ברא ברתא לא תירות אמרה ליה ברא נהור ליה נהורך כשרגא
אמר ליה רבן גמליאל אתא חמרא ובטש לשרגא:

[Imma Shalom] brought a gold lamp to [the philosopher] when she
came before him. She said, "I wish to divide my father's estate [so that I
might claim a share for myself]." [The philosopher] said, "Divide."

---

1. Centuries refer to the putative *origin* of sources rather than when they were written
down.

[Gamaliel] responded, "It is written in the Torah, 'Where there is a son, a daughter may not inherit.'" The philosopher answered, "From the day that you were exiled from your land, the Torah of Moses was taken away, and the Gospel (עון גליון) given in its place. There it is written, 'Son and daughter as one shall inherit.'" The next day Rabban Gamaliel came back and brought the philosopher a Libyan donkey. The philosopher then said, "Let us turn to the end of the Gospel, for there it is written, 'I came not to diminish the Torah of Moses, (nor/but [textual variant]) to add.' And there it is written, 'Where there is a son, a daughter may not inherit.'" [Imma Shalom] reminded him, "May your light shine forth like a lamp." But Rabban Gamaliel noted, "The donkey has come and overturned the lamp" (according to the translation [with slight variations] of B. L. Visotzky, *Fathers of the World: Essays in Rabbinic and Patristic Literatures* [Tübingen: Mohr-Siebeck, 1995] 81).

Second Century

Papias

Eusebius, *Hist. eccl.* 3.39.16 (see pp. 3-7)

Ματθαῖος μὲν οὖν Ἑβραΐδι διαλέκτῳ τὰ λόγια συνετάξατο, ἡρμήνευσεν δ' αὐτὰ ὡς ἦν δυνατὸς ἕκαστος,

"Matthew organized the oracles (of Jesus) in the Hebrew language, and each interpreted them as he was able."

Eusebius, *Hist. eccl.* 3.39.17 (see pp. 7-10)

κέχρηται δ' ὁ αὐτὸς [ὁ Παπίας] μαρτυρίαις ἀπὸ τῆς Ἰωάννου προτέρας ἐπιστολῆς καὶ ἀπὸ τῆς Πέτρου ὁμοίως, ἐκτέθειται δὲ καὶ ἄλλην ἱστορίαν περὶ γυναικὸς ἐπὶ πολλαῖς ἁμαρτίαις διαβληθείσης ἐπὶ τοῦ κυρίου, ἣν τὸ καθ' Ἑβραίους εὐαγγέλιον περιέχει.

"The same writer [Papias] has used testimonies from the First Epistle of John and likewise from Peter, and he has also set forth another account about a woman who was accused before the Lord of many sins, which is found in the Gospel according to the Hebrews."

Ignatius

Smyrn. 3.1-2 (see pp. 45-54)

> ἐγὼ γὰρ καὶ μετὰ τὴν ἀνάστασιν ἐν σαρκὶ αὐτὸν οἶδα καὶ πιστεύω ὄντα. καὶ ὅτε πρὸς τοὺς περὶ Πέτρον ἦλθεν, ἔφη αὐτοῖς· λάβετε, ψηλαφήσατέ με καὶ ἴδετε, ὅτι οὐκ εἰμὶ δαιμόνιον ἀσώματον. καὶ εὐθὺς αὐτοῦ ἥψαντο καὶ ἐπίστευσαν.

> "For I know and believe that he was in the flesh even after the resurrection. And when he [Jesus] came to those with Peter he said to them, 'Take, touch me and see that I am not a disembodied ghost.' And immediately they touched him and believed."

Irenaeus

Haer. 1.26.2 (see pp. 10-12)

> Solo autem eo quod est secundum Matthaeum evangelio utuntur (Ebionaei) et apostolum Paulum recusant apostatam eum legis dicentes.

> "(The Ebionites) use only the Gospel according to Matthew, and repudiate the Apostle Paul, maintaining that he was an apostate from the law."

Haer. 3.1.1; Eusebius, *Hist. eccl.* 5.8.2 (see pp. 10-12)

> ὁ μὲν δὴ Ματθαῖος ἐν τοῖς Ἑβραίοις τῇ ἰδίᾳ αὐτῶν διαλέκτῳ καὶ γραφὴν ἐξήνεγκεν εὐαγγελίου, τοῦ Πέτρου καὶ τοῦ Παύλου ἐν Ῥώμῃ εὐαγγελιζομένων καὶ θεμελιούντων τὴν ἐκκλησίαν.

> "Matthew also published among the Hebrews a written gospel in their own language, while Peter and Paul were preaching and founding the church in Rome."

Appendix I

Pantaenus

Eusebius, *Hist. eccl.* 5.10.3 (see p. 12)

> ὧν εἷς γενόμενος καὶ ὁ Πάνταινος, καὶ εἰς Ἰνδοὺς ἐλθεῖν λέγεται, ἔνθα λόγος εὑρεῖν αὐτὸν προφθάσαν τὴν αὐτοῦ παρουσίαν τὸ κατὰ Ματθαῖον εὐαγγέλιον παρά τισιν αὐτόθι τὸν Χριστὸν ἐπεγνωκόσιν, οἷς Βαρθολομαῖον τῶν ἀποστόλων ἕνα κηρῦξαι αὐτοῖς τε Ἑβραίων γράμμασι τὴν τοῦ Ματθαίου καταλεῖψαι γραφήν.

> "One of these was Pantaenus, and it is said that he went to the Indians, and the tradition is that he found there that among some of those there who had known Christ the Gospel according to Matthew had preceded his coming; for Bartholomew, one of the apostles, had preached to them and had left them the writing of Matthew in Hebrew letters, which was preserved until the time mentioned" (trans. K. Lake, Loeb).

Clement of Alexandria

Strom. 2.9.45 (see pp. 12-15)

> κἂν τῷ καθ᾽ Ἑβραίους εὐαγγελίῳ ὁ θαυμάσας βασιλεύσει γέγραπται καὶ ὁ βασιλεύσας ἀναπαήσεται.

> "And in the Gospel according to the Hebrews it is written, 'The one who wonders will reign, and reigning he will rest.'"

Strom. 5.14.96 (see pp. 12-15)

> ἴσον γὰρ τούτοις ἐκεῖνα δύναται. οὐ παύσεται ὁ ζητῶν, ἕως ἂν εὕρῃ· εὑρὼν δὲ θαμβηθήσεται, θαμβηθεὶς δὲ βασιλεύσει, βασιλεύσας δὲ ἐπαναπαήσεται.

> "Equal to these words [from the *Timaeus* immediately preceding] are the following: 'The one who seeks will not cease until he finds; and having found he will be amazed, and being amazed he will reign, and reigning he will rest.'"

?*Strom.* 7.13.1 (see pp. 93, 111, 119)

> λέγεται δὲ ἐν ταῖς παραδόσεσι Ματθίαν τὸν ἀπότολον παρ' ἔκαστα εἰρηκέναι ὅτι ἐὰν ἐκλεκτοῦ γείτων ἁμαρτήσῃ, ἥμαρτεν ὁ ἐκλεκτός· εἰ γὰρ οὕτως ἑαυτὸν ἦγεν ὡς ὁ λόγος ὑπαγορεύει, κατηδέσθη ἂν αὐτοῦ τὸν βίον καὶ ὁ γείτων εἰς τὸ μὴ ἁμαρτεῖν.

> "They say in the traditions that Matthew the apostle constantly said that 'if the neighbor of an elect man sin, the elect man has sinned. For had he conducted himself as the Word prescribes, his neighbor also would have been filled with such reverence for the life he led as not to sin'" (trans. *ANF* 2).

Hegesippus

Eusebius, *Hist. eccl.* 4.22.8 (see pp. 15-16)

> ἔκ τε τοῦ καθ' Ἑβραίους εὐαγγελίου καὶ τοῦ Συριακοῦ καὶ ἰδίως ἐκ τῆς Ἑβραΐδος διαλέκτου.

> "[Hegesippus made extracts] from the Gospel according to the Hebrews and from the Syriac, and especially from the Hebrew language."

Third Century

?Hippolytus

De Duodecim Apostolis (see pp. 16-17)

> Ματθαῖος δὲ, τὸ εὐαγγέλιον Ἑβραϊστὶ γράψας, δέδωκεν ἐν Ἱερουσα-λήμ, καὶ ἐκοιμήθη ἐν Ἱερέει τῆς Παρθείας.

> "Matthew, having written the Gospel in Hebrew, published it in Jerusalem, and slept in Hierae of Parthia."

Origen

Eusebius, *Hist. eccl.* 6.25.4 (see p. 18)

πρῶτον μὲν γέγραπται τὸ κατὰ τόν ποτε τελώνην ὕστερον δὲ
ἀπόστολον Ἰησοῦ Χριστοῦ Ματθαῖον, ἐκδεδωκότα αὐτὸ τοῖς ἀπὸ
Ἰουδαϊσμοῦ πιστεύσασιν, γράμμασιν Ἑβραϊκοῖς συντεταγμένον.

"[The first Gospel] was written by Matthew, who once had been a tax
collector but later became an apostle of Jesus Christ, having published it
for believers from Judaism, composed in Hebrew script."

Hom. Jer. 15.4 (See pp. 17, 56)

εἰ δέ τις παραδέχεται τὸ Ἄρτι ἔλαβέ με ἡ μήτηρ μου, τὸ ἅγιον πνεῦμα,
καὶ ἀπήνεγκέ με εἰς τὸ ὄρος τὸ μέγα Θαβώρ. καὶ τὰ ἑξῆς, δύναται αὐτοῦ
ἰδεῖν τὴν μητέρα.

"If anyone receives the [word], 'Just now my mother, the Holy Spirit,
took me and bore me to great Mount Tabor,' etc., he can see his mother."

Comm. Jo. 2.12 (see pp. 56-59)

ἐὰν δὲ προσιῆταί τις τὸ καθ' Ἑβραίους εὐαγγέλιον, ἔνθα αὐτὸς ὁ σωτήρ
φησίν; Ἄρτι ἔλαβέ με ἡ μήτηρ μου, τὸ ἅγιον πνεῦμα, ἐν μιᾷ τῶν τριχῶν
μου καὶ ἀπήνεγκέ με εἰς τὸ ὄρος τὸ μέγα Θαβώρ, ἐπαπορήσει πῶς
μήτηρ Χριστοῦ τὸ διὰ τοῦ λόγου γεγενημένον πνεῦμα ἅγιον εἶναι
δύναται. ταῦτα δὲ καὶ τούτῳ οὐ χαλεπὸν ἑρμηνεῦσαι.

"Whoever accepts the Gospel according to the Hebrews, where the Savior himself says, 'Just now my mother, the Holy Spirit, took me by a lock
of hair and lifted me up to great Mount Tabor,' raises a new question
how the Holy Spirit coming through the Word is able to be the mother
of Christ."

Comm. Matt. 15.14 (see pp. 17, 59-62)

Scriptum est in evangelio quodam, quod dicitur secundum Hebraeos (sit
tamen plac et suscipere illud, non ad auctoritatem, sed ad manifestationem propositae quaestionis): Dixit, "inquit ad eum alter divitum:

magister, quid bonum faciens vivam? dixit ei: homo, legem et prophetas fac. respondit ad eum: feci. dixit ei: vade, vende omnia quae possides et divide pauperibus, et veni, sequere me. coepit autem dives scalpere caput suum, et non placuit ei. et dixit ad eum Dominus, "Quomodo dicis 'legem feci et prophetas'? quoniam scriptum est in lege: diliges proximum tuum sicut teipsum, et ecce multi fraters tui filii Abahae amicti sunt stercore, morientes prae fame, etdomus tua plena est multis bonis, et non egreditur omnino aliquid ex ea ad eos. et conversus dixit Simoni discipulo suo sedenti apud se: Simon, fili Jonae, facilius est camelum intrare per foramen acus quam divitem in regnum coelorum.

"It is written in that Gospel, which is called 'According to the Hebrews' (if it pleases one to receive it, not as an authority, but as an example of the proposed question): 'Another rich man,' it says, 'inquired, 'Master, what good must I do to live?' He said to him, 'Man, do the law and prophets.' He responded to him, 'I have done (so).' He said to him, 'Go, sell all you possess and distribute it among the poor, and come, follow me.' The rich man began to scratch his head in displeasure. The Lord said to him, 'How can you say, 'I have done the law and prophets,' since it is written in the law: Love your neighbor as yourself; and behold, your many brothers, who are sons of Abraham, are covered in dung, dying from hunger, while your house is filled with many good things, and not one of the good things goes out to them.' And [Jesus] turned to Simon, his disciple sitting with him, 'Simon, son of John, it is easier for a camel to go through the eye of a needle, than for a rich man to enter the kingdom of heaven.'"

Princ. Praefatio 8 (see p. 48)

Si vero qui velit nobis proferre ex illo libello, qui Petri Doctrina appellatur, ubi salvator videtur ad discipulos dicere: Non sum daemonium incorporeum, primo respondendum est ei quoniam liber ipse inter libros ecclesiasticos non habetur, et ostendendum quia neque Petrus est ipsa scriptura neque alterius cuiusquam, qui spiritu dei fuerit inspiratus.

"But if any would produce to us from that book which is called 'The Doctrine of Peter,' the passage where the Savior is represented as saying to the disciples: 'I am not a bodiless demon,' he must be answered in the first place that that book is not reckoned among the books of the church, for we can show that it was not composed by Peter or by any other person inspired by the Spirit of God."

Fourth Century

Eusebius

Hist. eccl. 3.24.6 (see p. 19)

Ματθαῖός τε γὰρ πρότερον Ἑβραίοις κηρύξας, ὡς ἤμελλεν καὶ ἐφ' ἑτέρους ἰέναι, πατρίῳ γλώττῃ γραφῇ παραδοὺς τὸ κατ' αὐτὸν εὐαγγέλιον, τὸ λεῖπον τῇ αὐτοῦ παρουσίᾳ τούτοις ἀφ' ὧν ἐστέλλετο, διὰ τῆς γραφῆς ἀπεπλήρου.

Matthew had first preached to Hebrews, and when he was on the point of going to others he transmitted in writing in his native language the Gospel according to himself, and thus supplied by writing the lack of his own presence to those from whom he was sent (trans. K. Lake, Loeb).

Hist. eccl. 3.25.5 (see pp. 18-21)

τινὲς καὶ τὸ καθ' Ἑβραίους εὐαγγέλιον κατέλεξαν, ᾧ μάλιστα Ἑβραίων οἱ τὸν Χριστὸν παραδεξάμενοι χαίρουσιν.

"Some have also counted the Gospel according to the Hebrews in which those of the Hebrews who have accepted Christ take a special pleasure" (trans. K. Lake, Loeb).

Hist. eccl. 3.27.4 (see p. 18)

οὗτοι δὲ τοῦ μὲν ἀποστόλου πάμπαν τὰς ἐπιστολὰς ἀρνητέας ἡγοῦντο εἶναι δεῖν, ἀποστάτην ἀποκαλοῦντες αὐτὸν τοῦ νόμου, εὐαγγελίῳ δὲ μόνῳ τῷ καθ' Ἑβραίους λεγομένῳ χρώμενοι, τῶν λοιπῶν σμικρὸν ἐποιοῦντο λόγον.

"[The Ebionites] thought that the letters of the Apostle [Paul] ought to be wholly rejected and called him an apostate from the law. They used only the Gospel called according to the Hebrews and made little account of the remaining (Gospels?)."

Hist. eccl. 3.36.11 (see pp. 45-55)

ὁ δ' αὐτὸς Σμυρναίοις γράφων, οὐκ οἶδ' ὁπόθεν ῥητοῖς ὁπόθεν ῥητοῖς συγκέχρηται, τοιαῦτά τινα περὶ τοῦ Χριστοῦ διεξιών· ἐγὼ δὲ καὶ μετὰ τὴν ἀνάστασιν ἐν σαρκὶ αὐτὸν οἶδα καὶ πιστεύω ὄντὰ καὶ ὅτε πρὸς τοὺς περὶ Πέτρον ἐλήλυθεν, ἔφη αὐτοῖς· λάβετε, ψηλαψήσατέ με καὶ ἴδετε ὅτι οὐκ εἰμὶ δαιμόνιον ἀσώματον· καὶ εὐθὺς αὐτοῦ ἥψαντο καὶ ἐπίστευσαν.

"He [Ignatius] also wrote to the Smyrnaeans quoting words from I know not what source and discoursing thus about Christ: 'For I know and believe that he was in the flesh even after the Resurrection. And when he came to those with Peter he said to them: "Take, handle me and see that I am not a phantom without a body." And they immediately touched him and believed'" (trans. K. Lake, Loeb)

Theoph. 4.12 (see pp. 18-19, 62-63)

(Extant only in Syriac)

The cause therefore of the divisions of souls that take place in houses Christ himself taught, as we have found in a place in the Gospel existing among the Jews in the Hebrew language, in which it is said: "I will choose for myself the best which my Father in heaven has given me (cited from A. Harnack, *Geschichte der altchristlichen Literatur bis Eusebius*, 7; and J. K. Elliott, *The Apocryphal New Testament*, 11).

Theoph. 4.22 (see pp. 63-65)

ἐπὶ δὲ τὸ εἰς ἡμᾶς ἦκον ἑβραϊκοῖς χαρακτῆρσιν εὐαγγέλιον τὴν ἀπειλὴν οὐ κατὰ τοῦ ἀποκρύψαντος ἐπῆγεν, ἀλλὰ κατὰ τοῦ ἀσώτως ἐζηκότος· τρεῖς γὰρ δούλους περιεῖχε, τὸν μὲν καταφαγόντα τὴν ὕπαρξιν τοῦ δεσπότου μετὰ πορνῶν καὶ αὐλητρίδων, τὸν δὲ πολλαπλασιάσαντα τὴν ἐργασίαν, τὸν δὲ κατακρύψαντα τὸ τάλαντον· εἶτα τὸν μὲν ἀποδεχ-

θῆναι, τὸν δὲ μεμφθῆναι μόνον, τὸν δὲ συγκλεισθῆναι δεσμωτηρίῳ·
ἐφίστημι μήποτε κατὰ τὸν Ματθαῖον, μετὰ τὴν συμπλήρωσιν τοῦ λόγου
τοῦ κατὰ τοῦ μηδὲν ἐργασαμένου, ἡ ἑξῆς ἐπιλεγομένη ἀπειλή, οὐ περὶ
αὐτοῦ ἀλλὰ περὶ τοῦ προτέρου κατ᾽ ἐπανάληψιν λέλεκται τοῦ ἐσθίοντος καὶ πίνοντος μετὰ τῶν μεθυόντων.

"For the Gospel that has come to us in Hebrew characters does not bring
condemnation on the man who hid [the money], but on the man who
lived dissolutely. For he had three servants: the one who squandered the
wealth of the master with prostitutes and flute-players; the one who
greatly increased the principal sum; and the one who hid the talent. One
of them was praised; another was merely rebuked; the other was locked
up in prison. As for the last condemnation of the servant who earned
nothing, I wonder if Matthew repeated it not with him in mind but
rather with reference to the servant who caroused with the drunks."

Ephem the Syrian

Comm. on Tatian's Diatessaron (see p. 23)

Matthaeus hebraice scripsit id (i.e., evangelium), et deinde translatum
est in graecum.

"Matthew wrote his Gospel in Hebrew, and it was then translated into
Greek."

Didymus (the Blind) of Alexandria

Comm. Ps. 34.1 (see pp. 23-26)

καὶ πολλαὶ γέ εἰσιν τοιαῦται ὁμωνυμίαι. τὸν Ματθαῖον δοκεῖ ἐν τῷ κατὰ
Λουκᾶν Λευὶν ὀνομάζειν. οὔκ ἐστιν δὲ αὐτός, ἀλλὰ ὁ κατασταθεὶς ἀντὶ
τοῦ Ἰούδα ὁ Ματθίας καὶ ὁ Λευίς εἷς διώνυμός εἰσιν ἐν τῷ καθ᾽
Ἑβραίους εὐαγγελίῳ τοῦτο φαίνεται.

There are many such name changes. Matthew appears in the [Gospel]
According to Luke under the name of Levi. He is not the same person,

but rather the Matthew who was appointed [apostle] in place of Judas; he and Levi are the same person under two different names. This is made apparent in the Hebrew Gospel.

Comm. Eccl. 4.223.6-13 (see pp. 9-10)

φέρομεν οὖν ἔν τισιν εὐαγγελίοις; γυνή, φησίν, κατεκρίθη ὑπὸ τῶν Ἰουδ[αί]ων ἐπὶ ἁμαρτίᾳ καὶ ἀπεστέλλετο λιθοβοληθῆναι εἰς τὸν τόπον, ὅπου εἰώθει γίν[εσθ]αι. ὁ σωτήρ, φησίν, ἑωρακὼς αὐτὴν καὶ θεωρήσας ὅτι ἕτοιμοί εἰσιν πρὸς τὸ λιθ[οβολ]ῆσαι αὐτήν, τοῖς μέλλουσιν αὐτὴν καταβαλεῖν λίθοις εἶπεν· ὅς οὐκ ἥμαρτεν, αἰ[ρέ]τω λίθον καὶ βαλέτω αὐτόν. εἴ τις σύνοιδεν ἑαυτῷ τὸ μὴ ἡμαρτηκέναι, λαβὼν λίθον παισάτω αὐτήν. καὶ οὐδεὶς ἐτόλμησεν. ἐπιστήσαντες ἑαυτοῖς καὶ γνόντες, ὅτι καὶ αὐτοὶ ὑπε[ύθυ]νοί εἰσίν τισιν, οὐκ ἐτόλμησαν ‹καταπταῖσαι› ἐκείνην (quoted from D. Lührmann, *Die apokryph gewordenen Evangelien*, 192).

"We report in certain gospels: they say a woman was condemned by the Jews for a sin and was sent to be stoned in the place where it was the custom for such things to be done. They say the Savior, seeing her and beholding that they were ready to stone her, said to those who were about to stone her: 'Let the one who has not sinned take a stone and smite her. Whoever knows himself to be free from sin, take a stone and hurl it at her.' And no one dared. Smitten by the knowledge of their own shortcomings in various matters, they no longer had the nerve to stone her."

Pap. 1224 (see p. 25)

οἱ δὲ γραμματεῖς κα[ὶ φαρισσαῖ]οι καὶ ἱερεῖς θεασάμ[ενοι αὐ]τὸν ἠγανάκτουν [ὅτι σὺν ἁμαρ]τωλοῖς ἀνὰ μέ[σον κεῖται. ὁ δὲ] Ἰησοῦς ἀκούσας [εἶ]πεν· οὐ χρείαν [ἔχ]ουσιν οἱ ὑ[γιαίνοντες ἰατροῦ] . . . (according to the reconstruction of D. Lührmann, *Die apokryph gewordenen Evangelien*, 186).

When the scribes and Pharisees and priests saw [Jesus] they were indignant because he was reclining in the midst of sinners. But when Jesus heard this, he said, "It is not the well who need a physician. . . ."

Appendix I

Epiphanius

Pan. 29.9.4 (see pp. 26-27)

ἔχουσι δὲ τὸ κατὰ Ματθαῖον εὐαγγέλιον πληρέστατον Ἑβραϊστί. παρ᾽ αὐτοῖς γὰρ σαφῶς τοῦτο, καθὼς ἐξ ἀρχῆς ἐγράφη, Ἑβραϊκοῖς γράμμασιν ἔτι σῴζεται.

"[the Nazoreans] have the Gospel according to Matthew complete in Hebrew. For it is still distinctly preserved among them, as it was originally written, in Hebrew script."

Pan. 30.3.7 (see pp. 26-27)

καλοῦσι δὲ αὐτὸ κατὰ Ἑβραίους, ὡς τὰ ἀληθῆ ἔστιν εἰπεῖν, ὅτι Ματθαῖος μόνος Ἑβραϊστὶ καὶ Ἑβραϊκοῖς γράμμασιν ἐν τῇ καινῇ διαθήκῃ ἐποιήσατο τὴν τοῦ εὐαγγελίου ἔκθεσίν τε καὶ κήρυγμα.

"They [the Cerinthians, Merinthians, and Ebionites who used only the Gospel of Matthew] call it, however, According to the Hebrews, which it truly is, for only Matthew put the exposition and proclamation of the Gospel in the Hebrew and in Hebrew script in the New Testament."

Pan. 30.6.9 (see pp. 16-18)

ἀλλὰ καὶ τὸ κατὰ Ματθαῖον εὐαγγέλιον, Ἑβραϊκὸν φύσει ὄν.

"But also the Gospel of Matthew, which is Hebrew in character."

Pan. 30.13.2-3 (see pp. 66-68)

ἐν τῷ γοῦν παρ᾽ αὐτοῖς εὐαγγελίῳ κατὰ Ματθαῖον ὀνομαζομένῳ, οὐχ ὅλῳ δὲ πληρεστάτῳ, ἀλλὰ νενοθευμένῳ καὶ ἠκρωτηριασμένῳ (Ἑβραϊκὸν δὲ τοῦτο καλοῦσιν) ἐμφέρεται ὅτι "ἐγένετό τις ἀνὴρ ὀνόματι Ἰησοῦς, καὶ αὐτὸς ὡς ἐτῶν τριάκοντα, ὃς ἐξελέξατο ἡμᾶς. καὶ ἐλθὼν εἰς Καφαρναούμ εἰσῆλθεν εἰς τὴν οἰκίαν Σίμωνος τοῦ ἐπικληθέντος Πέτρου καὶ ἀνοίξας τὸ στόμα αὐτοῦ εἶπεν· παρερχόμενος παρὰ τὴν λίμνην Τιβεριάδος ἐξελεξάμην Ἰωάννην καὶ Ἰάκωβον, υἱοὺς

Ζεβεδαίου, καὶ Σίμωνα καὶ Ἀνδρέαν καὶ Θαδδαῖον καὶ Σίμωνα τὸν ζηλωτὴν καὶ Ἰούδαν τὸν Ἰσκαριώτην, καὶ σὲ τὸν Ματθαῖον καθεζόμενον ἐπὶ τοῦ τελωνίου ἐκάλεσα καὶ ἠκολούθησάς μοι. ὑμᾶς οὖν βούλομαι εἶναι δεκαδύο ἀποστόλους εἰς μαρτύριον τοῦ Ἰσραήλ.

"In what they (i.e., the Ebionites) then call the Gospel according to Matthew, which however is not complete but forged and mutilated — they call it the Hebrew Gospel — it is reported: 'There appeared a certain man by the name of Jesus, about thirty years of age, who chose us. And having come to Capernaum, he entered the house of Simon who was called Peter, and having opened his mouth, said, "As I passed beside the Lake of Tiberias, I chose John and James the sons of Zebedee, and Simon and Andrew and Thaddaeus and Simon the Zealot and Judas the Iscariot, and you, Matthew, I called while you were sitting at the tax table, and you followed me. You therefore I desire to be twelve apostles for a witness to Israel."'"

Pan. 30.13.4-6 (see pp. 68-69)

καὶ "ἐγένετο Ἰωάννης βαπτίζων, καὶ ἐξῆλθον πρὸς αὐτὸν φαρισσαῖοι καὶ ἐβαπτίσθησαν καὶ πᾶσα Ἱεροσόλυμα. καὶ εἶχεν ὁ Ἰωάννης ἔνδυμα ἀπὸ τριχῶν καμήλου καὶ ζώνην δερματίνην περὶ τὴν ὀσφὺν αὐτοῦ. καὶ τὸ βρῶμα αὐτοῦ, φησί, μέλι ἄγριον, οὗ ἡ γεῦσις ἡ τοῦ μάννα, ὡς ἐγκρὶς ἐν ἐλαίῳ." ἵνα δῆθεν μεταστρέψωσι τὸν τῆς ἀληθείας λόγον εἰς ψεῦδος καὶ ἀντὶ ἀκρίδων ποιήσωσιν ἐγκρίδα ἐν μέλιτι. ἡ δὲ ἀρχὴ τοῦ παρ' αὐτοῖς εὐαγγελίου ἔχει ὅτι "ἐγένετο ἐν ταῖς ἡμέραις Ἡρῴδου βασιλέως τῆς Ἰουδαίας <ἐπὶ ἀρχιερέως Καϊάφα>, ἦλθεν <τις> Ἰωάννης <ὀνόματι> βαπτίζων βάπτισμα μετανοίας ἐν τῷ Ἰορδάνῃ ποταμῷ, ὃς ἐλέγετο εἶναι ἐκ γένους Ἀαρὼν τοῦ ἱερέως παῖς Ζαχαρίου καὶ Ἐλισάβετ, καὶ ἐξήρχοντο πρὸς αὐτόν πάντες."

"And John came baptizing, and Pharisees went out to him, and they and all Jerusalem were baptized. And John had clothing made of camel hair and a leather belt around his waist; and his food, it is said, was wild honey, the taste of which was that of manna, as a cake dipped in oil. Thus they were resolved to pervert the word of truth to a lie, and they replace grasshoppers with a honey cake. The beginning of their Gospel has this, 'In the days when Herod was king of Judaea <when Caiaphas

was high priest>, <a certain> John <by name> came baptizing a baptism of repentance in the Jordan River. John, it was said, was of the line of Aaron the priest, a child of Zechariah and Elisabeth, and all were going out to him.'"

Pan. 30.13.7-8 (see pp. 69-71)

καὶ μετὰ τὸ εἰπεῖν πολλὰ ἐπιφέρει ὅτι "τοῦ λαοῦ βαπτισθέντος ἦλθεν καὶ Ἰησοῦς καὶ ἐβαπτίσθη ὑπὸ τοῦ Ἰωάννου. καὶ ὡς ἀνῆλθεν ἀπὸ τοῦ ὕδατος, ἠνοίγησαν οἱ οὐρανοὶ καὶ εἶδεν τὸ πνεῦμα ὁ ἅγιον ἐν εἴδει περιστερᾶς, κατελθούσης καὶ εἰσελθούσης εἰς αὐτόν. καὶ φωνὴ ἐκ τοῦ οὐρανοῦ λέγουσα· σύ μου εἶ ὁ υἱὸς ὁ ἀγαπητός, ἐν σοὶ ηὐδόκησα, καὶ πάλιν· ἐγὼ σήμερον γεγέννηκά σε. καὶ εὐθὺς περιέλαμψε τὸν τόπον φῶς μέγα. ὃ ἰδών, φησίν, ὁ Ἰωάννης λέγει αὐτῷ· σὺ τίς εἶ, κύριε; καὶ πάλιν φωνὴ ἐξ οὐρανοῦ πρὸς αὐτόν· οὗτός ἐστιν ὁ υἱός μου ὁ ἀγαπητός, ἐφ᾽ ὃν ηὐδόκησα. καὶ τότε, φησίν, ὁ Ἰωάννης προσπεσὼν αὐτῷ ἔλεγεν· δέομαί σου, κύριε, σύ με βάπτισον. ὁ δὲ ἐκώλυσεν αὐτὸν λέγων· ἄφες, ὅτι οὕτως ἐστὶ πρέπον πληρωθῆναι πάντα."

After many things had been said, it continues, "When the people had been baptized, Jesus also came and was baptized by John. And as he arose from the water, the heavens were opened, and he saw the Holy Spirit of God in the form of a dove descending and entering into him. And a voice came from heaven, saying, 'You are my beloved Son, in you I am pleased'; and again, 'Today I have begotten you.' And immediately a great light shone on the place. When John saw it, it is recorded that he said to [Jesus], 'Who are you, Lord?' And again a voice from heaven came to him, 'This is my beloved Son, on whom my pleasure rests.' And then, it is reported, John fell before him saying, 'I beg you, Lord, to baptize me.' But he prevented it, saying, 'Let it be, for in this way it is necessary for all things to be fulfilled.'"

Pan. 30.14.3 (see pp. 71-72)

παρακόψαντες γὰρ τὰς παρὰ τῷ Ματθαίῳ γενεαλογίας ἄρχονται τὴν ἀρχὴν ποιεῖσθαι ὡς προείπομεν, λέγοντες ὅτι "ἐγένετο," φησίν, "ἐν ταῖς ἡμέραις Ἡρῴδου βασιλέως τῆς Ἰουδαίας ἐπὶ ἀρχιερέως Καϊάφα, ἦλθέν τις Ἰωάννης ὀνόματι βαπτίζων βάπτισμα μετανοίας ἐν τῷ Ἰορδάνῃ ποταμῷ" καὶ τὰ ἑξῆς.

For having removed the genealogies of Matthew, they begin, as I said earlier, by saying that "It came to pass in the days of Herod king of Judaea, when Caiaphas was chief priest, a certain man named John came baptizing a baptism of repentance in the Jordan River," etc.

Pan. 30.14.5 (see pp. 72-73)

πάλιν δὲ ἀρνοῦνται εἶναι αὐτὸν ἄνθρωπον, δῆθεν ἀπὸ τοῦ λόγου οὗ εἴρηκεν ὁ σωτὴρ ἐν τῷ ἀναγγελῆναι αὐτῷ ὅτι "ἰδοὺ ἡ μήτηρ σου καὶ οἱ ἀδελφοί σου ἔξω ἑστήκασιν," ὅτι "τίς μού ἐστι μήτηρ καὶ ἀδελφοί; καὶ ἐκτείνας τὴν χεῖρα ἐπὶ τοὺς μαθητὰς ἔφη· οὗτοί εἰσιν οἱ ἀδελφοί μου καὶ ἡ μήτηρ καὶ ἀδελφαὶ οἱ ποιοῦντες τὰ θελήματα τοῦ πατρός μου."

"Again, they deny that [Jesus] was a true man, surely from the word spoken by the Savior when it was announced to him, 'Behold, your mother and your brothers are standing outside.' The Savior's word was, 'Who is my mother and who are my brothers?' And having stretched out his hand to the disciples, he said, 'These are my brothers and my mother, those who are doing the desires of my Father.'"

Pan. 30.16.4-5 (see pp. 73-74)

οὐ φάσκουσι δὲ ἐκ θεοῦ πατρὸς αὐτὸν γεγεννῆσθαι, ἀλλὰ κεκτίσθαι ὡς ἕνα τῶν ἀρχαγγέλων [καὶ ἔτι περισσοτέρως], αὐτὸν δὲ κυριεύειν καὶ ἀγγέλων καὶ πάντων <τῶν> ὑπὸ τοῦ παντοκράτορος πεποιημένων, καὶ ἐλθόντα καὶ ὑφηγησάμενον, ὡς τὸ παρ' αὐτοῖς εὐαγγέλιον καλούμενον περιέχει, ὅτι "ἦλθον καταλῦσαι τὰς θυσίας, καὶ ἐὰν μὴ παύσησθε τοῦ θύειν, οὐ παύσεται ἀφ' ὑμῶν ἡ ὀργή.

But they claim that [Jesus] was not begotten from God the Father, but rather that he was created as one of the archangels, although greater than them. He rules over both angels and all things made by the Almighty, and he came and instructed, as their so-called Gospel relates, "I came to abolish the sacrifices, and unless you cease from sacrificing, the wrath [of God] will not cease from you."

Appendix I

Pan. 30.22.4 (see pp. 74-75)

> ἤλλαξαν τὸ ῥητόν, . . . καὶ ἐποίησαν τοὺς μαθητὰς μὲν λέγοντας "ποῦ θέλεις ἑτοιμάσωμέν σοι τὸ Πάσχαφαγεῖν," καὶ αὐτὸν δῆθεν λέγοντα "μη ἐπιθυμίᾳ ἐπεθύμησα κρέας τοῦτο τὸ Πάσχα φαγεῖν μεθ' ὑμῶν.

> [The Ebionites] changed the saying . . . and made the disciples to say, "Where do you wish for us to prepare the Passover feast for you?" And look what they make the Lord say, "I have not desired to eat meat in this Passover with you."

Pan. 46.1.2 (see p. 23)

> λέγεται δὲ τὸ διὰ τεσσάρων εὐαγγελίων ὑπ' αὐτοῦ γεγενῆσθαι, ὅπερ κατὰ Ἑβραίους τινές καλοῦσι.

> "It is said that from [Tatian] comes the Diatessaron, which certain call the Gospel according to the Hebrews."

Pan. 51.5.3 (see p. 26)

> καὶ οὗτος μὲν οὖν ὁ Ματθαῖος Ἑβραϊκοῖς γράμμασι γράφει τὸ εὐαγγέλιον καὶ κηρύττει.

> "Now this is the same Matthew who writes the gospel in Hebrew script and preaches."

John Chrysostom

Hom. Matt. 1.3 (see p. 28)

> λέγεται δὲ καὶ Ματθαῖος, τῶν ἐξ Ἰουδαίων πιστευσάντων προσελθόντων αὐτῷ καὶ παρακαλεσάντων, ἅπερ εἶπε διὰ ῥημάτων, ταῦτα ἀφεῖναι συνθεῖναι διὰ γραμμάτων αὐτοῖς, καὶ τῇ τῶν Ἑβραίων φωνῇ συνθεῖναιτὸ εὐαγγέλιον.

> "And of Matthew it is said, when Jews who believed approached him and asked him to reduce his spoken words into writing for them, he brought forth the Gospel in the Hebrew language."

Jerome

Epist. 19, *Dam. ad Hieron.* (see p. 77)

> Quid se habeat apud Hebraeos (Osanna filio David).

> "Which the [Gospel] of the Hebrews reads: Hosanna to the Son of David."

Epist. 20, *ad Dam.* (see pp. 77-78)

> Denique Matheus, qui evangelium Hebraeo sermone conscripsit, ita posuit: *"osianna barrama,"* id est "osanna in excelsis," quod salvatore nascente salus in caelum usque, id est etiam ad excelsa, pervenerit pace facta non solum in terra, sed et in caelo.

> "Further, Matthew, who wrote a Gospel in the Hebrew language, put it thus: 'osianna barrama,' which means, 'Hosanna in the highest,' for when our Savior was born deliverance reached from heaven 'on high,' and peace reigned not only on earth but also in heaven."

Comm. Eph 5.4 (see pp. 28, 79)

> Ut in Hebraico quoque evangelio legimus dominum ad discipulos loquentem: "Et numquam," inquit, "laeti sitis, nisi cum fratrem vestrum videritis in caritate."

> "And also in the Hebrew Gospel we read of the Lord speaking to his disciples, 'Never be joyous unless you observe charity with your brother.'"

Vir. ill. 2 (see pp. 35, 79-82)

> Evangelium quoque quod appellatur secundum Hebraeos et a me nuper in Graecum sermonem Latinumque translatum est, quo et Origenes saepe utitur, post resurrectionem Salvatoris refert: "Dominus autem cum dedisset sindonem servo sacerdotis, ivit ad Iacobum et apparuit ei," iuraverat enim Iacobus se non comesurum panem ab illa hora qua biberat calicem Domini, donec videret eum resurgentem a dormien-

tibus rursusque post paululum, "Adferte, ait Dominus, mensam et panem," statimque additur; "Tulit panem et benedixit et fregit et dedit Iacobo Iusto et dixit et: 'Frater mi, comede paem tuum, quia resurrexit Filius hominis a dormientibus.'"

"The Gospel also entitled 'according to the Hebrews' which I lately translated into Greek and Latin, and which Origen often quotes, contains the following narrative after the Resurrection: 'Now the Lord, when he had given the cloth to the servant of the priest, went to James and appeared to him.' For James had taken an oath that he would not eat bread from that hour on which he had drunk the cup of the Lord till he saw him risen from the dead. Again a little later the Lord said, 'Bring a table and bread,' and forthwith it is added: 'He took bread and blessed and broke it and gave to James the Just and said to him, "My brother, eat your bread, for the Son of Man is risen from those who sleep."'"[2] (according to the translation in J. K. Elliott, *The Apocryphal New Testament*, 9-10).

Vir. ill. 3 (see pp. 29-30)

Matthaeus qui et Levi, ex publicano apostolus, primus in Iudaea, propter eos qui ex circumcisione crediderunt, Evangelium Christi Hebraeis litteris verbisque composuit, quod quis postea in Graecum

---

2. According to the translation in J. K. Elliott, *The Apocryphal New Testament*, 9-10. Jerome's original Latin reads: Evangelium quoque quod appellatur secundum Hebraeos et a me nuper in Graecum sermonem Latinumque translatum est, quo et Origenes saepe utitur, post resurrectionem Salvatoris refert: "Dominus autem cum dedisset sindonem servo sacerdotis, ivit ad Iacobum et apparuit ei," iuraverat enim Iacobus se non comesurum panem ab illa hora qua biberat calicem Domini, donec videret eum resurgentem a dormientibus rursusque post paululum, "Adferte, ait Dominus, mensam et panem," statimque additur; "Tulit panem et benedixit et fregit et dedit Iacobo Iusto et dixit et: 'Frater mi, comede paem tuum, quia resurrexit Filius hominis a dormientibus'" (*Vir. ill.* 2). J. B. Lightfoot, *The Epistle of St. Paul to the Galatians* (reprint Grand Rapids: Zondervan, 1971), 274, emends the text to "qua biberat calicem *Dominus*," i.e., "on which the Lord has drunk the cup." Lightfoot explains the resurrection appearance to James as follows: "It is characteristic of a Judaic writer whose aim it would be to glorify the head of the church at all hazards, that an appearance, which seems in reality to have been vouchsafed to his James to win him over from his unbelief, should be represented as a reward for his devotion." For a positive assessment of "the cup" as a metaphor of death, see R. Handmann, *Das Hebräer-Evangelium*, 79-82.

transtulerit, non satis certum est. Porro ipsum Hebraicum habetur usque hodie in Caesariensi bibliotheca, quam Pamphilus martyr studiosissime confecit. Mihi quoque a Nazaraeis qui in Beroea, urbe Syriae, hoc volumine utuntur, describendi facultas fuit. In quo animadvertendum quo ubicumque evangelista, sive ex persona sua sive ex Domini Salvatoris veteris scripturae testimoniis abutitur, non sequatur Septuaginta translatorum auctoritatem, sed Hebraicam. E quibus illa duo sunt: "Ex Aegypto vocavi Filium meum," et "Quoniam Nazaraeus vocabitur."

"Matthew, also known as Levi, a tax-collector who became an apostle, was the first in Judea to compose a Gospel of Christ in Hebrew letters and words, on whose account those of the circumcision believed, although it is not certain who later translated the Gospel into Greek. Indeed, the Hebrew itself was diligently brought out by Pamphilus the Martyr and is still to this day in the library of Caesarea. I have actually had opportunity to have the volume described to me by people who use it, the Nazarenes of Beroea, a city in Syria. It should be noted that wherever the Evangelist, whether by his own person or by the Lord our Savior, quotes testimonies from the Old Testament he does not follow the authority of the translators of the Septuagint, but rather the Hebrew, from which these two forms exist: 'Out of Egypt I have called my son,' and 'For he shall be called a Nazarene.'"

Vir. ill. 16 (see pp. 45-55)

Ignatius . . . scripsit . . . ad Smyrnaeos et proprie ad Polycarpum . . . in qua et de evangelio, quod nuper a me translatum est, super persona Christi ponit testimonium dicens: Ego vero et post resurrectionem in carne eum vidi et credo, qui sit; et quando venit ad Petrum et ad eos qui cum Petro errant, dixit eis: Ecce palpate me et videte, quia non sum daemonium incorporale. Et statim tetigerunt eum et crediderunt.

"Ignatius . . . wrote . . . to the Smyrnaeans and separately to Polycarp . . . in which he bore witness also to the Gospel which I have recently translated, in respect of the person of Christ stating: I indeed saw him in the flesh after the resurrection and I believe that it was he and when he came to Peter and those who were with Peter, he said to them: Behold, touch me and see how I am not a demon without a body, and straight-way they touched him and believed" (trans. A. F. J. Klijn, *Jewish-Christian Gospel Tradition*, 122).

Vir. ill. 36.2 (see pp. 12, 17)

> Ubi repperit Bartholomeum de duodecim apostolis adventum Domini Jesu iuxta Matthaei Evangelium praedicasse, quod Hebraicis litteris scriptum, revertens Alexandriam secum detulit.

> "And there he [Pantaenus] found that Bartholomew of the twelve apos-tles had preached the coming of the Lord Jesus according to the Gsopel of Matthew, written in Hebrew letters, he brought back with him on his return to Alexandria" (trans. T. P. Halton, *The Fathers of the Church*, 59).

Comm. Matt. Praefatio (see p. 29)

> Primus omnium Mattheus est publicanus cognomento Levi, qui evangelium in Judaea hebreo sermone edidit, ob eorum vel maxime causam qui in Iesum crediderant ex Iudaeis et nequaquam legis umbra succedente evangelii veritatem servabant.

> The first evangelist was Matthew, a tax-collector, surnamed Levi, who edited a Gospel in Judea in the Hebrew language chiefly for the sake of Jews who believed in Jesus but were serving in vain the shadow of the law after the true Gospel had come.

Comm. Matt. 2.5 (see p. 83)

> Librariorum hic error est; putamus enim ab evangelista primum editum, sicut in ipso Hebraico legimus "Iudae" non "Iudaeae" . . . Iudae autem idcirco scribitur, quia est et alia Bethleem in Galilaea. . . . Denique et in ipso testimonio, quod de Michaeae prophetia sumptum est, ita habetur: Et tu Bethleem terra Juda."

> "This is an error of the copyists; for we think the first edition of the evangelist [Matthew] read, as the Hebrew itself reads, 'Judah,' not 'Judaea.' . . . For that reason, however, Judah is written, because there is

also another Bethlehem in Galilee. . . . Again, in the same testimony found in the prophet Micah, it reads thus: 'And you, Bethlehem, in the land of Judah.'"

Comm. Matt. 6.11 (see pp. 29, 83-84)

In evangelio quod appellatur secundum Hebraeos pro supersubstantiali pane reperi *mahar,* quod dicitur crastinum.

"In the Gospel called 'According to the Hebrews,' he writes, 'I found *mahar* with reference to the supernatural bread, which means 'tomorrow.'"

Comm. Matt. 12.13 (see pp. 35, 84-86)

In evangelio, quo utuntur Nazareni et Hebionitae, quod nuper in Graecum de Hebraeo sermone transtulimus et quod vocatur a plerisque Mathei authenticum, homo iste, qui aridam habet manum, caementarius scribitur, istiusmodi vocibus auxilium precans: "Caementarius eram, manibus victum quaeritans, precor te, Jesu, ut mihi restituas sanitatem ne turpiter mendicem cibos."

"In the Gospel used by the Nazarenes and Ebionites, which we recently translated into Greek from the Hebrew language — and which many call the authentic Matthew — the man having a withered hand was a mason who begged for help in the words, 'I was a mason who worked with my hands for a living; I beg you, Jesus, restore me to health so that I may not have to shamefully beg for food.'"

Comm. Matt. 23.35 (see pp. 29, 86-87)

In evangelio quo utuntur Nazaraeni pro filio Barachiae "filium Joiadae" reperimus scriptum.

"In the Gospel that is used by the Nazarenes, we find 'son of Johoiada' in place of 'son of Barachias.'"

Comm. Matt. 27.16 (see pp. 87-88)

Iste in evangelio quod scribitur iuxta Hebraeos filius magistri eorum interpretatur qui propter seditionem et homicidium fuerat condemnatus.

"He [Barabbas] signifies 'the son of their teacher' in the Gospel that is written 'According to the Hebrews,' because he had been condemned for sedition and murder."

Comm. Matt. 27.51 (see pp. 29, 88-90)

In evangelio cuius saepe facimus mentionem superliminare templi infinitae magnitudinis fractum esse atque divisum legimus.

"In the Gospel we often mention we read that the immense temple lintel fell and broke to pieces."

Tract. Ps. 135 (see pp. 83-84)

In Hebraico evangelio secundum Matthaeum ita habet: Panem nostrum crastinum da nobis hodie, hoc est panem quem daturus es nobis in regno tuo, da nobis hodie.

"In the Hebrew Gospel according to Matthew it has this: 'Give us today our bread for tomorrow'; that is, the bread that will be given to us in your kingdom, give us today."

Comm. Isa. Praefatio 18 (see p. 29)

Cum enim apostoli eum putarent spiritum vel iuxta evangelium, quod Hebraeorum lectitant Nazaraei "incorporale daemonium," dixit eis . . .

"For since the apostles supposed him to be a spirit or, according to the Gospel which is of the Hebrews and is read by the Nazoraeans, a demon without a body, he said to them . . ." (trans. A. F. J. Klijn, *Jewish-Christian Gospel Tradition,* 122).

Comm. Isa. 11.1-3 (see pp. 29, 90-91)

> Sed iuxta evangelium quod Hebraeo sermone conscriptum legunt Nazaraei: "Descendet super eum omnis fons Spiritus sancti." . . . Porro in evangelio, cuius supra fecimus mentionem, haec scripta reperimus: "Factum est autem cum ascendisset Dominus de aqua, descendit fons omnis Spiritus sancti, et requievit super eum, et dixit illi: 'Fili mi, in omnibus prophetis exspectabam te, ut venires, et requiescerem in te. Tu es enim requies mea, tu es filius meus primogenitus, qui regnas in sempiternum.'"

> "But according to the Gospel that is written in the Hebrew language, the Nazarenes read: 'the whole fountain of the Holy Spirit will descend on him.' . . . Further, in the Gospel that we mentioned above, we find these words written: 'It happened that when the Lord came up out of the water, the whole fountain of the Holy Spirit descended on him, and rested on him, and said to him, 'My Son, in all the prophets I awaited you, that you might come and that I might rest in you. For you are my rest, you are my first-born Son, who reigns eternally.'"

Comm. Isa. 40.9 (see p. 58)

> Sed et in Evangelio quod iuxta Hebraeos scriptum Nazaraei lectitant, Dominus loquitur: "Modo me tulit mater mea, Sanctus Spiritus.

> "But in the Gospel written according to the Hebrews the Nazarenes read, the Lord says, 'My mother, the Holy Spirit, once took me.'"

Comm. Ezech. 16.13 (see pp. 29, 58)

> In evangelio quoque quod Hebraeorum lectitant Nazaraei, Salvator inducitur loquens: Modo me arripuit Mater mea, Spiritus sanctus. . . .

> "Also in the Gospel of the Hebrews that is read by the Nazaraeans, the Savior is introduced saying, 'Just now my mother, the Holy Spirit, seized me. . . .'"

Appendix I

Comm. Ezek. 18.7 (see pp. 29, 91-93)

Et in evangelio quod iuxta Hebraeos Nazaraei legere consuerunt, inter maxima ponitur crimina: "qui fratris sui spiritum contristaverit."

"In the Gospel according to the Hebrews that is common to the Nazarenes, among the greatest of wrongs is 'to grieve the spirit of one's brother.'"

Comm. Mich. 7.5-7 (see pp. 34-35, 58)

Sed qui legerit Canticum canticorum, et sponsum animae, Dei sermonem intellexerit, credideritque Evangelio, quod secundum Hebraeos editum nuper transtulimus, in quo ex persona Salvatoris dicitur: "Modo tulit me mater mea, Sanctus Spiritus in uno capillorum meorum."

"But whoever makes the Song of Songs the spouse of his soul will come to know the word of God and believe the Gospel, the Hebrew edition of which we recently translated (in which it is said of the person of the Savior, 'My mother, the Holy Spirit, once took me by a lock of hair')."

Praefatio in Quattuor Evangeliorum (see pp. 33-34)

De novo nunc loquor Testamento: quod Graecum esse non dubium est, excepto apostolo Matthaeo, qui primus in Judaea Evangelium Christi Hebraicis litteris edidit. Hoc certe cum in nostro sermone discordat, et diversos rivulorum tramites ducit: uno de fonte quaerendum est.

"I will now speak of the New Testament, which was undoubtedly composed in Greek, with the exception of the Apostle Matthew, who was the first in Judea to produce a Gospel of Christ in Hebrew letters. We must confess that as we have it in our language it is marked by discrepancies, and now that the stream is distributed into different channels we must go back to the fountainhead."

Epist. 120.8.2, *ad Hedy.* (see pp. 37, 88-90)

In evangelio autem, quod Hebraicis litteris scriptum est, legimus non velum templi scissum, sed superliminare templi mirae magnitudinis conruisse.

"In the Gospel, however, which is composed in Hebrew, we read not that the temple curtain was torn but that the lintel of wondrous size of the temple fell."

Pelag. 3.2 (see pp. 30-33, 93-96)

In Euangelio iuxta Hebraeos, quod Chaldaico quidem Syroque sermone, sed Hebraicis litteris scriptum est, quo utuntur usque hodie Nazareni, secundum apostolos, sive, ut plerique autumant, iuxta Matthaeum, quod et in Caesariensi habetur bibliotheca. Et ecce mater Domini et fratres eius dicebant ei: "Iohannes Baptista baptizat in remissionem peccatorum; eamus et baptizemur dixi, ignorantia est." Et in eodem volumine: "Si peccaverit," inquit, "frater tuus in verbo et satis tibi fecerit, septies in die suscipe eum." Dixit illi Simon discipulus eius: "Septies in die?" Respondit Dominus, et dixit ei: "Etiam, ego dico tibi, usque septuagies septies. Etenim in Prophetis quoque, postquam uncti sunt Spiritu sancto, inventus est sermo peccati."

"In the Gospel according to the Hebrews, which is written in the Chaldean and Syrian language, but in Hebrew characters, and which is used to this day by the Nazarenes — [the Gospel] according to the Apostles, or as many allege, [the Gospel] according to Matthew — which also is found in the library in Caesarea. And behold, the mother of the Lord and his brothers were saying to him, 'John the Baptist baptizes for the remission of sins; let us go and be baptized with him.' He [Jesus] said to them, 'What sin have I committed that I should go and be baptized by him? Unless in saying this I am in ignorance.'[3] And in the same volume, he [Jesus] said: 'If your brother would sin in word and would make restitution to you seven times in one day, receive him.' His disciple Simon

---

3. This statement could also perhaps be translated: "Unless perhaps I said something in ignorance."

said to him, 'Seven times in one day?' The Lord responded and said to him, 'Even, I say to you, as many as seventy times seven. For even in the prophets this word about sin was found after they were anointed by the Holy Spirit.'"

Fifth Century

Theodoret of Cyrrhus

Haer. Fab. Comp. 2.1 (see p. 38)

μόνον δὲ τὸ καθ' Ἑβραίους εὐαγγέλιον δέχονται, τὸν δὲ ἀπόστολον ἀποστάτην καλοῦσι. A subsequent passage notes that the Ebionites εὐαγγελίῳ δὲ τῷ κατὰ Ματθαῖον κέχρηνται μόνῳ.

"[The Ebionites] alone accept the Gospel according to the Hebrews, and regard the Apostle [Paul] as apostate."

Marius Mercator

De Haeresi et Libris Hestorii 4.2 (PL 48.1127-28) (see pp. 38-39)

Solum hi [the Ebionites] Evangelium secundum Hebraeos recipient, Apostolum vero apostatam vocant . . . Evangelio autem secundum Matthaeium solo utuntur.

"The followers of Ebion receive only the Gospel according to the Hebrews, they call the Apostle (Paul) an apostate . . . they make use of the Gospel according to Matthew alone."

Philip Sidetes

From C. de Boor, *Neue Fragmente des Papias, Hegesippus und Pierius: in bisher unbekannten Excerpten aus der Kirchengeschichte des Philippus*

Sidetes, in *Die Abfassungszeit der Schriften Tertullians,* ed. E. Noeldechen (Leipzig: J. C. Hinrichs, 1888) (see p. 39)

τὸ δὲ καθ᾽ Ἑβραίους εὐαγγέλιον καὶ τὸ λεγόμενον Πέτρου καὶ Θωμᾶ τελείως ἀπέβαλλον [the ancients] αἱρετικῶν ταῦτα συγγράμματα λέγοντες.

"The Gospel according to the Hebrews and the Gospel attributed to Peter and Thomas were wholly repudiated (by the ancients), who asserted that they were jointly written by heretics."

Eighth Century

Venerable Bede

In Lucae Evangelium Expositio 1.1-4 (see p. 40)

Inter quae notandum quod dicitur euangelium iuxta Hebraeos non inter apocriphas sed inter ecclesiasticas numerandum historias. Nam et ipsi sacrae scripturae interpreti Hieronimo pleraque ex eo testimonia usurpare, et ipsum in Latinum Graecumque visum est transferre sermonem.

"Here it must be noted that the Gospel according to the Hebrews, as it is called, is not to be reckoned among apocryphal but among ecclesiastical histories; for it seemed good even to the translator of Holy Scripture himself, Jerome, to cite many testimonies from it, and to translate it into the Latin and Greek language."

Islamic Hadith

Sahih al-Bukhari 1.3 (see p. 42)

"Khadija then accompanied [Muhammed] to her cousin Waraqa ibn Naufal ibn Asad ibn ʿabdul ʿUzza, who, during the Pre-Islamic Period became a Christian and used to write the writing with Hebrew letters. He would write from the Gospel in Hebrew as much as Allah wished him to write."

Appendix I

Ninth Century

Nicephorus

Chron. Brev. (see pp. 21-22, 104-5)

καὶ ὅσαι τῆς Νέας ἀντιλέγονται;
α′ Ἀποκάλυψις Ἰωάννου στίχος ‚αυ′
β′ Ἀποκάλυψις Πέτρου στίχοι ‚τ′
γ′ Βαρνάβα ἐπιστολὴ στίχοι ‚ατξ′
δ′ Εὐαγγέλιον κατὰ Ἑβραίους στίχοι ‚βσ′

And these are the [writings] of the New Testament that are disputed:
1. The Revelation of John, 1400 lines;
2. The Revelation of Peter, 300 lines;
3. The Epistle of Barnabas, 1360 lines;
4. The Gospel according to the Hebrews, 2200 lines.

Sedulius Scottus

Collectanea in Epistolam I ad Corinthios 15:7 (PL 103.158) (see p. 82)

> Deinde Jacobo, Alphaei filio, qui se testatus est a coena Domini non comesurum panem usquequo videret Christum resurgentem: sicut in Evangelio secundum Hebraeos legitur.

> "Then James, the son of Alphaeus, vowed not to eat bread from the table of the Lord until he saw Christ rising again, as is read in the Gospel according to the Hebrews."

Super Evangelium Mathei (A. F. J. Klijn, *Jewish-Christian Gospel Tradition*, 87) (see p. 84)

> In evangelio, quod appellatur "Secundum Ebreos" pro "super-substantiali pane" "moar" repperi, quod dicitur "crastinum."

> "In the Gospel that is calledaccoridng to the Hebrews instead of 'supernatural bread' I found *moar*, which means 'tomorrow's.'"

Scholia in Codex Sinaiticus

A. Harnack, *Geschichte der urchristlichen Literatur bis Eusebius,* 1/1.10 (see pp. 40-42)

At Matt 4:5

τὸ ἰουδαϊκὸν οὐκ ἔχει Εἰς τὴν ἁγίαν πόλιν, ἀλλ᾽ Ἐν Ἰερουσαλήμ.

"The Jewish [Gospel] does not read 'into the holy city,' but 'in Jerusalem.'"

At Matt 16:17

τὸ ἰουδαϊκόν. Υἱὲ Ἰωάννου.

"The Jewish [Gospel]. 'Son of John.'"

At Matt 18:22

τὸ ἰουδαϊκὸν ἐξῆς ἔχει μετὰ τὸ ἑβδομηκοντάκις ἑπτά· Καὶ γὰρ ἐν τοῖς προφήταις μετὰ τὸ χρισθῆναι αὐτοὺς ἐν πνεύματι ἁγίῳ εὑρίσκετο ἐν αὐτοῖς λόγος ἁμαρτίας.

"Following the reference to 'seventy times seven' the Jewish [Gospel] reads: 'For also among the prophets sin was found in them even after they had been anointed by the Holy Spirit.'"

At Matt 26:74

τὸ ἰουδαϊκόν. Καὶ ἠρνάσατα καὶ ὤμοσεν καὶ κατηράσαντο.

"The Jewish [Gospel]. 'And he denied and swore and cursed.'"[4]

4. In this final footnote of Appendix I, I wish to pay respect to the high level of literacy evidenced by earlier scholars, and particularly nineteenth-century scholars, with regard to the patristic tradition. In my own research into patristic testimony to the Hebrew Gospel, I postponed utilizing computer resources until I had assembled all known references to the Hebrew Gospel found in scholarly works from Lessing to the present. Only then did I resort to the powerful *Thesaurus linguae graecae* and *Patrologia latina* search engines, which contain the sum of all Greek and Latin literature, respectively, in their data banks. The thorough acquaintance of nineteenth-century scholars with the patristic literature, which in the *Patrologia latina* extends to 225 folio volumes and in the *Patrologia graecae* to 161 folio volumes, is evidenced by the fact that modern computer search capabilities retrieved only *two* references to the Hebrew Gospel (one in Chrysostom and the other in Marius Mercator) that had not been found by nineteenth-century scholars.

Chart of Semitisms in the Gospel of Luke

The following chart attempts to list by chapter and verse every Lukan Semitism for which there is reasonable scholarly evidence. Three general explanations will help make this list understandable. First, a number in parentheses following a word or phrase refers to one of the fourteen explanatory paragraphs in Chapter Four in which Luke's primary Semitisms are discussed (pp. 131-41 above). Second, each additional word or phrase without a number in parentheses is, in my best judgment, a Semitism of reasonable certainty. In thus adding to the list I have followed a cautious methodology, leaving out doubtful words or phrases. Third, as a rule I have listed no words or phrases on the basis of my judgment alone. Virtually all Semitisms are listed on the basis of at least one other corroborating authority, named in footnotes. In rare instances where a second authority is not cited, I have supplied either the most reasonable Hebrew form from which the Lukan form is derived or have provided explanatory justification in a footnote.

Several Semitic constructions in Luke do not appear in the list.

- Quotations from or allusions to the LXX are not included, since a quoted source does not in itself show influence on the diction of the author.
- Similarities in Lukan Greek to Josephus's Greek, painstakingly demonstrated in Schlatter's *Das Evangelium des Lukas,* are omitted since these do not clearly indicate a common Semitic source.
- Greek descriptions of Hebrew customs (e.g., fasting twice on the Sab-

bath, Luke 18:12) are excluded unless the phrasing expressly reflects Semitic usage.

- The chart does not account for several elements of Semitic style such as syntax (aspect, verb, subject, indirect object, direct object), chiasmus, *parallelismus membrorum,* anacolutha, ellipsis of the verb, and so forth, which, though they may have influenced Lukan Greek at places, cannot be quantified or codified in a chart.

On occasion, an entire verse listed as a single Semitism contains several different Semitic constructions. Thus, Semitic influence in the Third Gospel almost certainly exceeds the data in this Appendix.

Not all proposed Semitisms listed here, of course, claim equal degrees of certitiude. Some, like the fourteen discussed in Chapter Four, are "hard" Semitisms affirmed by virtually all scholars who have attended to the question of Semitic influences on Lukan Greek. Others are in varying degrees "softer" Semitisms. "Softer" should not be understood as "imaginary," however. Harder Semitisms may claim fuller agreement, but, as stated above, all Semitisms proposed here claim reasonable scholarly evidence or the support of at least two authorities. A "quality control" employed in Chapter Four is worthy of being repeated in this regard. Even softer or more speculative Semitisms appear in roughly equal proportions with widely acknowledged Semitisms in Special Luke.[1] Thus, despite the varying degrees of certainty for the proposed Semitisms listed here, their remarkable concentrations in Special Luke constitute a powerful mass of evidence in favor of Luke's reliance on a Semitic source for the half of his Gospel not shared in common with Matthew and/or Mark.

The evidence is divided into four groups, which are indicated typographically:

- Material in **boldface** is **unique to Luke (Special Luke).**
- Material in *italics* is shared in common by *Luke and Matthew.*
- <u>Underlined</u> material is shared in common by <u>Luke and Mark</u>.
- Normal type indicates material shared by all three Synoptics.

1. Of further relevance is the comprehensive study of Lukan vocabulary by J. Jeremias, *Die Sprache des Lukasevangeliums.* Jeremias limits his consideration to tradition versus redaction rather than to pre-Lukan sources. His study nevertheless recognizes the uniqueness or peculiarity of a vast number of the words and expressions identified as Semitisms in Appendix II, nearly all of which he assigns to "redaction" (i.e., to non-Markan sources).

Appendix II

Semitisms in the Gospel of Luke

1:1-4

1:5-20

5   ἐγένετο (1); ἐν ταῖς ἡμέραις[2] (בימי)

6   ἦσαν . . . πορευόμενοι[3] (14)

7   ἐν ταῖς ἡμέραις[4]; ἦσαν προβεβηκότες[5] (14)

8   ἐγένετο δὲ (1); ἐν τῷ ἱερατεύειν (4)

10 ἦν προσευχόμενον[6] (14)

11 ὤφθη αὐτῷ ἄγγελος κυρίου[7]

13 εἰσηκούσθη ἡ δέησίς σου[8]; καλέσεις τὸ ὄνομα αὐτοῦ Ἰωάννην[9]

15 ἐνώπιον (2); οἶνον καὶ σίκερα (שכרה)[10]

17 ἐνώπιον (2); καὶ αὐτός (6); ἐν φρονήσει[11] (בתבונת)

18 κατὰ τί[12] (במה); ἐν ταῖς ἡμέραις[13]

19 ὁ παρεστηκὼς ἐνώπιον τοῦ θεοῦ[14] (2); ἀποκριθεὶς . . . εἶπεν[15]

20 καὶ ἰδού (5); εἰς τὸν καιρὸν αὐτῶν[16] (במועדם); ἀνθ' ὧν[17] (13); ἄχρι ἧς ἡμέρας[18]

---

2. Guillemard, *Hebraisms in the New Testament*, 12.

3. Guillemard, *Hebraisms in the New Testament*, 12; G. Dalman, *The Words of Jesus*, 36.

4. Guillemard, *Hebraisms in the New Testament*, 12; Schlatter, *Evangelium des Lukas*, 715.

5. Dalman, *Words of Jesus*, 32; Schlatter, *Evangelium des Lukas*, 715.

6. Dalman, *Words of Jesus*, 32.

7. Schlatter, *Evangelium des Lukas*, 711.

8. Schlatter, *Evangelium des Lukas*, 157.

9. BDF §157 (2); Schlatter, *Evangelium des Lukas*, 716.

10. Schlatter, *Evangelium des Lukas*, 158.

11. Guillemard, *Hebraisms in the New Testament*, 12.

12. Guillemard, *Hebraisms in the New Testament*, 12; Schlatter, *Evangelium des Lukas*, 712.

13. See n. 4 above.

14. Schlatter, *Evangelium des Lukas*, 159.

15. Fitzmyer, *Gospel According to Luke*, 1.114.

16. Guillemard, *Hebraisms in the New Testament*, 12.

17. Guillemard, *Hebraisms in the New Testament*, 12; Schlatter, *Evangelium des Lukas*, 711.

18. BDF §294 (5).

1:21-25

21   ἦν . . . προσδοκῶν[19] (14); ἐν τῷ χρονίζειν (4),

22   καὶ αὐτός (6); ἦν διανεύων[20] (14)

23   καὶ ἐγένετο (1)

25   ἀφελεῖν ὄνειδός μου[21]

1:26-38

29   ἐπὶ τῷ λόγῳ[22]

30   εὗρες γὰρ χάριν παρὰ τῷ θεῷ[23]

31   καὶ ἰδού (5); καλέσεις τὸ ὄνομα αὐτοῦ Ἰησοῦν[24]

32   οὗτος ἔσται μέγας καὶ υἱὸς ὑψίστου κληθήσεται[25]

33   βασιλεύσει ἐπὶ τόν (מלך על)[26]; εἰς τοὺς αἰῶνας[27]

34   ἄνδρα οὐ γινώσκω[28]

35   κληθήσεται υἱὸς θεοῦ[29]

36   καὶ ἰδού (5)

37   οὐκ ἀδυνατήσει παρὰ τοῦ θεοῦ πᾶν[30]; ῥῆμα (meaning "thing")[31]

1:39-45

39   ἀναστᾶσα . . . ἐπορεύθη[32]; εἰς πόλιν Ἰούδα[33]

41   καὶ ἐγένετο (1); ἐσκίρτησεν τὸ βρέφος ἐν τῇ κοιλίᾳ[34]

19. Dalman, *Words of Jesus*, 32.

20. Dalman, *Words of Jesus*, 32.

21. Schlatter, *Evangelium des Lukas*, 159.

22. Guillemard, *Hebraisms in the New Testament*, 12.

23. Schlatter, *Evangelium des Lukas*, 166.

24. BDF §157 (2).

25. See 4Q246 2:1; Fitzmyer, *Gospel According to Luke*, 1.117; Guillemard, *Hebraisms in the New Testament*, 12.

26. BDF §177.

27. BDF §141.

28. Guillemard, *Hebraisms in the New Testament*, 12; Schlatter, *Evangelium des Lukas*, 711.

29. See 4Q246 2:1; Fitzmyer, *Gospel According to Luke*, 1.117.

30. Guillemard, *Hebraisms in the New Testament*, 12; BDF §302, reflecting Hebrew לֹא . . . כֹּל; Schlatter, *Evangelium des Lukas*, 711 (see Gen 18:14 in Hebrew).

31. H. F. D. Sparks, "The Semitisms of St. Luke's Gospel," 133.

32. Dalman, *Words of Jesus*, 23; Schlatter, *Evangelium des Lukas*, 711.

33. M. Wilcox, "Semiticisms in the NT," *ABD* 5.1083, offers the suggestion that the unexpected rendering "to the city of Judah" could derive from the Hebrew מדינה, which can mean either "province" or "city."

34. Schlatter, *Evangelium des Lukas*, 170.

42 εὐλογημένη σὺ ἐν γυναιξίν[35]

44 ἐγένετο (1); ἐν ἀγαλλιάσει[36] (בְּשִׂמְחָה)

1:46-56[37]

49 ὁ δυνατός[38] (שַׁדַּי); καὶ ἅγιον τὸ ὄνομα αὐτοῦ[39]

50 εἰς γενεὰς καὶ γενεάς[40]

51 ποιεῖν κράτος[41]; ἐν βραχίονι αὐτοῦ[42] (בִּזְרֹעַ); διεσκόρπισεν ὑπερηφάνους διανοίᾳ καρδίας αὐτῶν[43]

54 Ἰσραὴλ παιδὸς αὐτοῦ[44]; μνησθῆναι ἐλέους[45]

1:57-66

58 μεγαλύνειν ἔλεος μετᾶ[46]

59 καὶ ἐγένετο (1); ἐκάλουν αὐτὸ ἐπὶ τῷ ὀνόματι τοῦ πατρὸς αὐτοῦ Ζαχαρίαν[47]

60 ἀποκριθεῖσα . . . εἶπεν[48]; εἶπεν οὐχὶ[49]

63 ἔγραψεν λέγων[50]

64 ἀνεῴχθη τὸ στόμα αὐτοῦ[51]

65 καὶ ἐγένετο (1); πάντα τὰ ῥήματα ταῦτα (כָּל-הַדְּבָרִים הָאֵלֶּה).

66 ἔθεντο . . . ἐν τῇ καρδίᾳ[52]

35. BDF §245.

36. Guillemard, *Hebraisms in the New Testament,* 12.

37. BDF §333 (2) attributes the eleven Greek aorists in the Magnificat to the Hebrew perfect; as a reflection of the perfect (= timeless acts), the aorists imply a future sense.

38. Guillemard, *Hebraisms in the New Testament,* 12.

39. BDF §442 (6); Schlatter, *Evangelium des Lukas,* 711.

40. BDF §493 (2).

41. Lagrange, *Évangile selon Saint Luc,* ci; Schlatter, *Evangelium des Lukas,* 717.

42. Guillemard, *Hebraisms in the New Testament,* 12; BDF §259 (3); Schlatter, *Evangelium des Lukas,* 712.

43. M.-J. Lagrange, *Évangile selon Saint Luc,* ci; BDF §259 (3); Schlatter, *Evangelium des Lukas,* 713, 172-173.

44. Lagrange, *Évangile selon Saint Luc,* cii; Schlatter, *Evangelium des Lukas,* 719.

45. BDF §391 (4), calls this an "infinitive of result," due to the Hebrew use of לְ; Schlatter, *Evangelium des Lukas,* 714.

46. Lagrange, *Évangile selon Saint Luc,* ci.

47. BDF §157 (2); Schlatter, *Evangelium des Lukas,* 716.

48. Dalman, *Words of Jesus,* 25.

49. Schlatter, *Evangelium des Lukas,* 179.

50. BDF §420 (1): "entirely Semitic."

51. Schlatter, *Evangelium des Lukas,* 711.

52. Fitzmyer, *Gospel According to Luke,* 1.115.

1:67-79

68 ἐπεσκέψατο (פקד)

69 κέρας σωτηρίας[53] (קרן ישׁועה); ἐν οἴκῳ Δαυὶδ παιδὸς αὐτοῦ[54]

70 διὰ στόματος[55] (בפי)

71 σωτηρίαν ἐξ ἐχθρῶν ἡμῶν καὶ ἐκ χειρὸς πάντων τῶν μισούντων ἡμᾶς[56]

72 ποιεῖν ἔλεος μετά; διαθήκης ἁγίας αὐτοῦ[57]

73 ὅρκον ὃν ὤμοσεν πρὸς Ἀβραὰμ τὸν πατέρα ἡμῶν[58]

74 ἐκ χειρὸς ἐχθρῶν ῥυσθέντας[59]

75 ἐνώπιον (2)

76 ἐνώπιον (2) or πρὸ προσώπου (3)

77 ἐν ἀφέσει[60] (בסליחת)

78 διὰ σπλάγχνα ἐλέους θεοῦ[61]; ἐπισκέψεται ἡμᾶς ἀνατολὴ ἐξ ὕψους[62]

79 τοῦ κατευθῦναι τοὺς πόδας ἡμῶν εἰς ὁδὸν εἰρήνης[63]

1:80 ἐκραταιοῦτο πνεύματι[64]; ἡμέρας ἀναδείξεως[65]

2:1-7

1 ἐγένετο δέ (1)

2 ἐγένετο (1)

6 ἐγένετο δέ (1); ἐν τῷ εἶναι (4); αἱ ἡμέραι[66] (ימיה)

---

53. Guillemard, *Hebraisms in the New Testament*, 12; Schlatter, *Evangelium des Lukas*, 716.

54. Lagrange, *Évangile selon Saint Luc*, cii; BDF §259 (3).

55. Dalman, *Words of Jesus*, 38.

56. Lagrange, *Évangile selon Saint Luc*, cii; BDF §259 (3); Schlatter, *Evangelium des Lukas*, 179.

57. Lagrange, *Évangile selon Saint Luc*, ci, cii; BDF §206 (3); §259 (3); Schlatter, *Evangelium des Lukas*, 179-80.

58. BDF §295; Schlatter, *Evangelium des Lukas*, 180.

59. Schlatter, *Evangelium des Lukas*, 180.

60. Guillemard, *Hebraisms in the New Testament*, 12.

61. Lagrange, *Évangile selon Saint Luc*, cii-ciii; BDF §259 (3).

62. Dalman, *Words of Jesus*, 38-39; Sparks, "Semitisms of St. Luke's Gospel," 133; Schlatter, *Evangelium des Lukas*, 711.

63. Schlatter, *Evangelium des Lukas*, 181.

64. Schlatter, *Evangelium des Lukas*, 181.

65. BDF §165: "the Hebraistic ἡμέρα = χρόνος is to be noted."

66. Guillemard, *Hebraisms in the New Testament*, 13.

2:8-20

8 ἦσαν . . . ἀγραυλοῦντες[67] (14)

9 ἐφοβήθησαν φόβον μέγαν[68]

10 παντὶ τῷ λατῷ[69] (לְכָל־הָעָם)

12 καὶ τοῦτο ὑμῖν τὸ σημεῖον[70]

13 ἐγένετο (1)

14 ἐν ὑψίστοις[71] (בַּמְּרֹמִים); ἐν ἀνθρώποις εὐδοκίας[72]

15 καὶ ἐγένετο (1); ῥῆμα[73]

20 δοξάζειν τὸν θεόν (10)

2:21

21 apodotic καί (12)

2:22-38

22 καὶ ὅτε ἐπλήσθησαν αἱ ἡμέραι τοῦ καθαρισμοῦ αὐτῶν[74]

23 καθὼς γέγραπται ἐν νόμῳ κυρίου[75]

25 καὶ ἰδού (5); Ἰερουσαλήμ (9); πνεῦμα ἦν ἅγιον ἐπ' αὐτόν[76];
   παράκλησιν τοῦ Ἰσραήλ[77]

26 ἦν . . . κεχρηματισμένον[78] (14)

27 ἐν τῷ εἰσαγαγεῖν (4); apodotic καί (12)

28 καὶ αὐτός (6)

31 κατὰ πρόσωπον (3)

32 εἰς ἀποκάλυψιν ἐθνῶν καὶ δόξαν λαοῦ σου Ἰσραήλ[79]

33 ἦν . . . θαυμάζοντες[80] (14)

34 ἰδοὺ οὗτος κεῖται εἰς[81] (הִנֵּה־זֶה מוּסָד לְ־)

---

67. Dalman, *Words of Jesus*, 32.

68. Lagrange, *Évangile selon Saint Luc*, ci; Fitzmyer, *Gospel According to Luke*, 1.116.

69. Guillemard, *Hebraisms in the New Testament*, 13.

70. Schlatter, *Evangelium des Lukas*, 190.

71. Guillemard, *Hebraisms in the New Testament*, 13.

72. BDF §165; Schlatter, *Evangelium des Lukas*, 715.

73. Sparks, "Semitisms of St. Luke's Gospel," 133.

74. Schlatter, *Evangelium des Lukas*, 197.

75. Schlatter, *Evangelium des Lukas*, 197.

76. Schlatter, *Evangelium des Lukas*, 711.

77. Schlatter, *Evangelium des Lukas*, 198.

78. Dalman, *Words of Jesus*, 32.

79. Lagrange, *Évangile selon Saint Luc*, ciii; BDF §259 (3).

80. Lagrange, *Évangile selon Saint Luc*, ciii.

81. Guillemard, *Hebraisms in the New Testament*, 13.

36   ἦν . . . προβεβηκυῖα[82] (14)

38   καὶ αὐτῇ τῇ ὥρᾳ[83]; ἀνθωμολογεῖτο τῷ θεῷ[84]
        (ותגש להדות ליהוה); Ἰερουσαλήμ (9)

2:39-40

2:41-52

41   Ἰερουσαλήμ (9)

42   ἐγένετο (1)

43   ἐν τῷ ὑποστρέφειν (4); Ἰερουσαλήμ (9)

44   ἡμέρας ὁδόν[85]

45   Ἰερουσαλήμ (9)

46   καὶ ἐγένετο (1)

48   τί ἐποίησας ἡμῖν οὕτως[86]

51   ἦν ὑποτασσόμενος[87] (14); διετήρει πάντα τὰ ῥήματα[88]

3:1-2

2   ἐγένετο (1); Ἰωάννην τὸν Ζαχαρίου υἱόν[89]

3:3-4   ἐν βίβλῳ λόγων Ἠσαΐου[90]

3:5-6

5   ἔσται τὰ σκολιὰ εἰς εὐθείαν[91]

3:7-9

7   *φυγεῖν ἀπό*[92]

---

82. Dalman, *Words of Jesus*, 32.
83. Fitzmyer, *Gospel According to Luke*, 1.117.
84. Guillemard, *Hebraisms in the New Testament*, 13.
85. Schlatter, *Evangelium des Lukas*, 205.
86. Schlatter, *Evangelium des Lukas*, 718.
87. Dalman, *Words of Jesus*, 32.
88. Fitzmyer, *Gospel According to Luke*, 1.115; Schlatter, *Evangelium des Lukas*, 713.
89. BDF §162 (1): "[the] addition of υἱός is not Attic but Semitic."
90. Fitzmyer, *Gospel According to Luke*, 1.117; 1QapGen 19:25.
91. BDF §145 (1).
92. BDF §149.

3:10-14

11   ὁμοίως ποιείτω[93]

3:15-16a

16a   ἀπεκρίνατο λέγων[94]

3:16b

3:17   *οὗ τὸ πτύον ἐν τῇ χειρὶ αὐτοῦ*[95]

3:19-20

3:21-22

21   ἐν τῷ βαπτισθῆναι (4)

3:23-38

23   καὶ αὐτός (6); ἦν . . . ἀρχόμενος[96] (14)

4:1-2a

4:2b-13

7   ἐνώπιον (2)

9   Ἰερουσαλήμ (9)

4:14a

4:14b-15

15   καὶ αὐτός (6)

4:16-30

16   ἦν τεθραμμένος[97] (14); κατὰ τὸ εἰωθὸς αὐτῷ[98]; τῇ ἡμέρᾳ τῶν σαββάτων[99]; ἀνέστη ἀναγνῶναι[100]

---

93. Schlatter, *Evangelium des Lukas*, 215.
94. Dalman, *Words of Jesus*, 24.
95. BDF §297.
96. Dalman, *Words of Jesus*, 35-36.
97. Dalman, *Words of Jesus*, 35-36.
98. Schlatter, *Evangelium des Lukas*, 226.
99. Schlatter, *Evangelium des Lukas*, 226.
100. Schlatter, *Evangelium des Lukas*, 711.

17 ἦν γεγραμμένον[101] (14)

20 ἦσαν ἀτενίζοντες[102] (14)

21 ἤρξατο δὲ λέγειν πρὸς αὐτούς[103] (ויחל ויאמר אליהם)

22 ἐπὶ τοῖς λόγοις τῆς χάριτος[104] (על־דברי הן); τοῖς ἐκπορευομένοις ἐκ τοῦ στόματος αὐτοῦ[105]

24 ἀμήν (אמן)

25 ἐπ᾿ ἀληθείας[106] (ואמת); ὅτε ἐκλείσθη ὁ οὐρανός[107]; ὡς ἐγένετο λιμὸς μέγας ἐπὶ πᾶσαν τὴν γῆν[108]

26 εἰ μή[109]

27 εἰ μή[110]

28 καὶ ἐπλήσθησαν πάντες θυμοῦ[111]

29 ἀναστάντες ἐξέβαλον[112]

30 διὰ μέσου αὐτῶν (בתוך)[113]

4:31-32

31 ἦν διδάσκων[114] (14)

4:33-37

33 ἦν . . . ἔχων[115] (14)

34 τί ἡμῖν καὶ σοί[116] (מה־לנו ולך)

36 καὶ ἐγένετο (1); τίς ὁ λόγος οὗτος;[117]

101. Dalman, *Words of Jesus*, 35-36.

102. Dalman, *Words of Jesus*, 35-36.

103. Fitzmyer, *Gospel According to Luke*, 1.117.

104. Guillemard, *Hebraisms in the Greek New Testament*, 13; Fitzmyer, *Gospel According to Luke*, 1.124.

105. BDF §217 (3); Schlatter, *Evangelium des Lukas*, 714.

106. Guillemard, *Hebraisms in the Greek New Testament*, 13; Fitzmyer, *Gospel According to Luke*, 1.117; 1QapGen 2:5.

107. Schlatter, *Evangelium des Lukas*, 227.

108. Schlatter, *Evangelium des Lukas*, 227.

109. BDF §448 (8): use of εἰ μή for ἀλλά is an Aramaism.

110. BDF §448 (8): use of εἰ μή for ἀλλά is an Aramaism.

111. Schlatter, *Evangelium des Lukas*, 227-28.

112. Dalman, *Words of Jesus*, 23.

113. BDF §215 (3).

114. Dalman, *Words of Jesus*, 35-36.

115. Dalman, *Words of Jesus*, 35-36.

116. Guillemard, *Hebraisms in the Greek New Testament*, 13.

117. Schlatter, *Evangelium des Lukas*, 50.

4:38-39

38   ἀναστὰς . . . εἰσῆλθεν; ἦν συνεχομένη[118] (14)

39   καὶ ἐπιστὰς ἐπάνω αὐτῆς[119]; ἀναστᾶσα διηκόνει[120]

4:40-41

4:42-43

   4:44   ἦν κηρύσσων[121] (14)

5:1-11

1   ἐγένετο (1); ἐν τῷ . . . ἐπικεῖσθαι (4); καὶ αὐτός (6); apodotic καί (12); ἦν ἑστώς[122] (14)

3   καθίσας . . . ἐδίδασκεν[123]

4   ὡς δὲ ἐπαύσατο λαλῶν[124]

5   ἀποκριθεὶς . . . εἶπεν[125]

7   κατένευσαν . . . τοῦ ἐλθόντας[126]

5:12a   καὶ ἐγένετο (1); ἐν τῷ εἶναι (4); ἐν μιᾷ τῶν πόλεων[127] (7); *καὶ ἰδοῦ;* apodotic καί; ἐπὶ πρόσωπον (3)

5:12b-16

14   καὶ αὐτός (6)

16   ἦν ὑποχωρῶν[128] (14)

5:17   καὶ ἐγένετο (1); ἐν μιᾷ τῶν ἡμερῶν[129] (7); καὶ αὐτός (6); ἦν διδάσκων / ἦσαν καθήμενοι / ἦσαν ἐληλυθότες[130] (14); Ἰερουσαλήμ (9); δύναμις κυρίου[131]; apodotic καί (12);

---

118. Both attested by Dalman, *Words of Jesus,* 23 and 35-36 respectively.

119. Schlatter, *Evangelium des Lukas,* 50.

120. Dalman, *Words of Jesus,* 23.

121. Dalman, *Words of Jesus,* 35-36.

122. Dalman, *Words of Jesus,* 35-36.

123. Dalman, *Words of Jesus,* 22.

124. Schlatter, *Evangelium des Lukas,* 233.

125. Fitzmyer, *Gospel According to Luke,* 1.114.

126. BDF §400 (7).

127. Fitzmyer, *Gospel According to Luke,* 1.121-22; Schlatter, *Evangelium des Lukas,* 714.

128. Dalman, *Words of Jesus,* 35-36.

129. Fitzmyer, *Gospel According to Luke,* 1.121-22.

130. Dalman, *Words of Jesus,* 35-36.

131. Guillemard, *Hebraisms in the New Testament,* 14.

5:18-26

18   καὶ ἰδού (5); ἦν παραλελυμένος[132] (14); ἐνώπιον (2)

19   ἀναβάντες ἐπὶ τὸ δῶμα[133]

21   ἤρξαντο διαλογίζεσθαι . . . λέγοντες[134]

25   ἐνώπιον (2); δοξάζων τὸν θεόν (10)

26   ἐδόξαζον τὸν θεόν (10)

5:27-32

28   ἀναστὰς ἠκολούθει[135]

29   ἐποίησεν δοχὴν μεγάλην . . . αὐτῷ;[136] ἦσαν . . . κατακείμενοι[137]
    (14)

5:33-38

34   υἱοὺς τοῦ νυμφῶνος[138]

37   **καὶ αὐτός (6)**

5:39   **entire verse[139]**

6:1-5

1   <u>ἐγένετο</u> (1)

4   τοὺς ἄρτους τῆς προθέσεως[140]

6:6-11

6   **ἐγένετο (1)**

8   <u>εἰς τὸ μέσον</u>[141] (בְּתוֹךְ); ἀναστὰς ἔστη[142]

132. Dalman, *Words of Jesus,* 35-36.
133. Schlatter, *Evangelium des Lukas,* 58.
134. BDF §420 (2); Schlatter, *Evangelium des Lukas,* 713.
135. Dalman, *Words of Jesus,* 23.
136. Schlatter, *Evangelium des Lukas,* 61.
137. Dalman, *Words of Jesus,* 35-36.
138. Guillemard, *Hebraisms in the New Testament,* 14.
139. Schlatter, *Evangelium des Lukas,* 236-37.
140. Guillemard, *Hebraisms in the New Testament,* 14.
141. Guillemard, *Hebraisms in the New Testament,* 14.
142. Fitzmyer, *Gospel According to Luke,* 1.114.

6:12-13

12   ἐγένετο δὲ ἐν ταῖς ἡμέραις ταύταις[143]; ἦν διανυκτερεύων[144] (14)

13   ἐγένετο (1); ἐκλεξάμενος ἀπ' αὐτῶν δώδεκα[145]

6:14-16

16   ἐγένετο (1)

6:17-20a

17   Ἰερουσαλήμ (9)

20a   καὶ αὐτός (6); ἐπάρας τοὺς ὀφθαλμούς[146]

6:20b-23

22   ὅταν . . . ἐκβάλωσιν τὸ ὄνομα ὑμῶν ὡς πονηρόν[147]

23   σκιρτήσατε[148]; ὁ μισθὸς ὑμῶν πολύς[149]

6:24-26

25   πενθήσετε καὶ κλαύσετε[150]

6:27-36

29   μὴ κωλύσῃς[151]

35   υἱοὶ ὑψίστου[152] (בני עליון);

36   οἰκτίρμονες . . . οἰκτίρμων[153]

6:37-42

38   δώσουσιν εἰς τὸν κόλπον ὑμῶν[154]; ᾧ γὰρ μέτρῳ μετρεῖτε
      ἀντιμετρηθήσεται ὑμῖν[155]

---

143. Guillemard, *Hebraisms in the New Testament*, 14.

144. Dalman, *Words of Jesus*, 35-36.

145. Schlatter, *Evangelium des Lukas*, 71.

146. Fitzmyer, *Gospel According to Luke*, 1.114.

147. Schlatter, *Evangelium des Lukas*, 246.

148. Schlatter, *Evangelium des Lukas*, 246-47.

149. Schlatter, *Evangelium des Lukas*, 247.

150. Schlatter, *Evangelium des Lukas*, 247.

151. BDF §180 (1): "Hebraizing as in LXX Gen 23:6."

152. Guillemard, *Hebraisms in the New Testament*, 14.

153. Schlatter, *Evangelium des Lukas*, 247.

154. Schlatter, *Evangelium des Lukas*, 247.

155. Schlatter, *Evangelium des Lukas*, 247.

6:43-45

6:46-49

    49   καὶ ἐγένετο (1)

7:1-6a

    6   ἤδη δὲ αὐτοῦ οὐ μακρὰν ἀπέχοντος ἀπὸ τῆς οἰκίας[156]

7:6b-10

7:11-17

    11   καὶ ἐγένετο (1); ἐν τῷ ἑξῆς[157]

    12   καὶ ἰδού (5); apodotic καί (12)

    16   ἐδόξαζον τὸν θεόν (10); ἐπεσκέψατο ὁ θεὸς τὸν λαὸν αὐτοῦ[158]

7:18-23

    22   ἀποκριθεὶς . . . εἶπεν[159]

    23   μὴ σκανδαλισθῇ ἐν ἐμοί[160] (לֹא־יִצָּשֵׁל בִּי)

7:24-26

    25   ἐν μαλακοῖς **ἱματίοις** ἠμφιεσμένον[161]

7:27   πρὸ προσώπου σου (3)

7:28

7:29-30

    29   ἐδικαίωσαν τὸν θεόν[162]

    30   ἠθέτησαν εἰς ἑαυτούς[163] (11)

---

156. Schlatter, *Evangelium des Lukas*, 252.

157. Guillemard, *Hebraisms in the New Testament*, 15.

158. Schlatter, *Evangelium des Lukas*, 254.

159. Fitzmyer, *Gospel According to Luke*, 1.114.

160. Guillemard, *Hebraisms in the New Testament*, 15.

161. BDF §159 (1).

162. Schlatter, *Evangelium des Lukas*, 256.

163. BDF §192; Schlatter, *Evangelium des Lukas*, 256.

7:31-35

33   μήτε ἐσθίων ἄρτον μήτε πίνων **οἶνον**[164]

7:36-50

37   καὶ ἰδού (5)

39   ἐν ἑαυτῷ (11)

42   μὴ ἐχόντων αὐτῶν ἀποδοῦναι[165]; πλεῖον ἀγαπήσει[166]

47   ἠγάπησεν πολύ[167]

50   πορεύου εἰς εἰρήνην[168] (לֵךְ לְשָׁלוֹם)

8:1-3

1   καὶ ἐγένετο (1); ἐν τῇ καθεξῆς[169]; καὶ αὐτός (6); apodotic καί (12)

2   ἦσαν τεθεραπευμέναι[170] (14); ἐξεληλύθει[171]

8:4-8

5   ἐν τῷ σπείρειν (4)

7   ἐν μέσῳ (בְּתוֹךְ)[172]

8   λέγων[173]; ὁ ἔχων ὦτα ἀκούειν ἀκουέτω[174]

8:9-10

8:11-15

8:16-18

17   ὃ οὐ φανερὸν γενήσεται[175]

8:19-21

---

164. Schlatter, *Evangelium des Lukas*, 496.
165. Schlatter, *Evangelium des Lukas*, 712, 265.
166. Schlatter, *Evangelium des Lukas*, 711.
167. Schlatter, *Evangelium des Lukas*, 711.
168. Guillemard, *Hebraisms in the New Testament* 15; BDF §206.
169. Guillemard, *Hebraisms in the New Testament*, 15.
170. Dalman, *Words of Jesus*, 35-36.
171. BDF §315: Aramaism for ἐξεβέβλητο.
172. BDF §215 (3).
173. Fitzmyer, *Gospel According to Luke*, 1.115.
174. Guillemard, *Hebraisms in the New Testament*, 15.
175. BDF §448 (8).

8:22-25

   22   **ἐγένετο δὲ (1); ἐν μιᾷ τῶν ἡμερῶν**[176] **(7); καὶ αὐτός (6); apodotic καί (12)**

   24   καὶ ἐγένετο (1)

8:26-39

   28   **ἀνακράξας . . . εἶπεν**[177]**; τί ἐμοὶ καὶ σοί**[178] (מה לי ולך)

   32   ἦν . . . βοσκομένη[179] (14)

8:40-56

   40   **ἐν δὲ τῷ ὑποστρέφειν (4); ἦσαν . . . προσδοκῶντες**[180] **(14)**

   41   **καὶ ἰδοῦ (5);**

   42   θυγάτηρ **μονογενὴς ἦν αὐτῷ**[181]

   43   <u>οὖσα ἐν ῥύσει αἵματος</u>[182]

   47   **ἐνώπιον παντὸς τοῦ λαοῦ**[183]

   48   θυγάτηρ[184]**; πορεύου εἰς εἰρήνην** (לך לשלום)[185]

   54   **ἡ παῖς, ἔγειρε**[186]

9:1-6

9:7-9

9:10a

9:10b-11

9:12   **ἡ δὲ ἡμέρα ἤρξατο κλίνειν**[187]

176. Fitzmyer, *Gospel According to Luke,* 1.121-22.
177. BDF §420 (2).
178. Guillemard, *Hebraisms in the New Testament,* 15.
179. Dalman, *Words of Jesus,* 35-36.
180. Dalman, *Words of Jesus,* 35-36.
181. Schlatter, *Evangelium des Lukas,* 87.
182. BDF §219 (4).
183. Dalman, *Words of Jesus,* 31.
184. BDF §147 (3), omission of vocative ὧ because of Semitic influence.
185. BDF §206.
186. BDF § 147 (3): use of nominative instead of vocative because of Semitic influence.
187. Schlatter, *Evangelium des Lukas,* 716.

9:13-17

15   καὶ ἐποίησαν οὕτως[188]

9:18a   καὶ ἐγένετο (1); ἐν τῷ εἶναι (4); αὐτὸν προσευχόμενον κατὰ μόνας συνῆσαν[189]

9:18b-21

9:22

9:23-27

9:28-30

28   ἐγένετο δέ (1); apodotic καί (12); μετὰ τοὺς λόγους τούτους[190] (אחרי הדברים האלה)

29   καὶ ἐγένετο (1); ἐν τῷ προσεύχεσθαι (4); προσώπου (3)

30   καὶ ἰδού (5)

9:31-32

31   Ἰερουσαλήμ (9)

32   ἦσαν βεβαρημένοι[191] (14)

9:33-36

33   καὶ ἐγένετο (1); ἐν τῷ διαχωρίζεσθαι (4)

34   ἐν τῷ εἰσελθεῖν (4)

35   <u>καὶ . . . ἐγένετο</u> (1); ὁ ἐκλελεγμένος[192]

36   ἐν τῷ γενέσθαι (4)

9:37-43a

37   ἐγένετο δέ (1)

38   ἐβόησεν λέγων[193] (זעק לאמר)

39   καὶ ἰδού (5)

188. Schlatter, *Evangelium des Lukas*, 94.
189. Guillemard, *Hebraisms in the New Testament*, 15; BDF §241 (6).
190. Dalman, *Words of Jesus*, 38, calls this a "quite un-Aramaic phrase."
191. Dalman, *Words of Jesus*, 35-36.
192. Schlatter, *Evangelium des Lukas*, 100.
193. Schlatter, *Evangelium des Lukas*, 712.

41   γενεὰ ἄπιστος καὶ διεστραμμένη[194]; ἕως πότε ἔσομαι πρὸς ὑμᾶς[195]

9:43b-44a

44a   θέσθε ὑμεῖς εἰς τὰ ὦτα ὑμῶν[196] (שִׂימוּ אַתֶּם בְּאָזְנֵיכֶם)

9:44b-45

45   ἦν παρακεκαλυμμένον ἀπ᾽ αὐτῶν[197]

9:46-48a

9:48b   ὁ γὰρ μικρότερος ἐν πᾶσιν ὑμῖν ὑπάρχων[198]

9:49-50

9:51   ἐγένετο δέ (1); ἐν τῷ συμπληροῦσθαι (4); τὰς ἡμέρας τῆς ἀναλήμψεως (יְמֵי הֵעָלוֹתוֹ); καὶ αὐτός (6); τὸ πρόσωπον ἐστήρισεν[199] (3); τοῦ πορεύεσθαι[200]; Ἰερουσαλήμ (9); apodotic καί (12);

9:52-56

52   ἀπέστειλεν . . . πρὸ προσώπου αὐτοῦ[201] (3); εἰς κώμην Σαμαριτῶν[202]

53   πρόσωπον (3); ἦν πορευόμενον[203] (14); Ἰερουσαλήμ (9)

54   πῦρ καταβῆναι ἀπὸ τοῦ οὐρανοῦ καὶ ἀναλῶσαι αὐτούς[204]

9:57-60

57   καὶ πορευομένων αὐτῶν ἐν τῇ ὁδῷ[205]

194. Schlatter, *Das Evangelium des Lukas*, 711, 104 (see Deut 32:5, 20).

195. Guillemard, *Hebraisms in the New Testament*, 15; A. Schlatter, *Der Evangelist Matthäus*, 533; BDF §146.

196. Schlatter, *Evangelium des Lukas*, 718.

197. Dalman, *Words of Jesus*, 35-36; BDF §155 (3).

198. Schlatter, *Evangelium des Lukas*, 108.

199. Dalman, *Words of Jesus*, 30.

200. BDF §400 (7).

201. Dalman, *Words of Jesus*, 29; BDF §217 (1); Schlatter, *Evangelium des Lukas*, 712.

202. BDF §262 (3).

203. Dalman, *Words of Jesus*, 35-36.

204. Schlatter, *Evangelium des Lukas*, 273.

205. Schlatter, *Evangelium des Lukas*, 500.

9:61-62

62   βλέπων εἰς τὰ ὀπίσω[206]

10:1   ἀνὰ δύο δύο[207]; πρὸ προσώπου αὐτοῦ[208] (3)

10:2-12

3   ἐν μέσῳ (בְּתוֹךְ)[209]

6   υἱὸς εἰρήνης[210]

9   ἐξελθόντες εἰς τὰς πλατείας[211] (וִיצָאתֶם אֶל־רְחוֹבוֹת)

10:13-15

10:16

10:17-20

18   σατανᾶς (שָׂטָן)

19   τοῦ πατεῖν ἐπάνω ὄφεων καὶ σκορπίων[212]

20   τὰ ὀνόματα ὑμῶν ἐγγέγραπται ἐν τοῖς οὐρανοῖς[213]

10:21-24

21   ἐν αὐτῇ τῇ ὥρᾳ[214]; οὕτως εὐδοκία ἐγένετο ἔμπροσθέν σου[215]

10:25-28

25   καὶ ἰδού (5); ἀνέστη ἐκπειράζων[216]

26   πῶς ἀναγινώσκεις[217] (מָה אַתָּה קוֹרֵא)

---

206. Schlatter, *Evangelium des Lukas*, 712, 273.

207. BDF §248.

208. Dalman, *Words of Jesus*, 29.

209. BDF §215 (3).

210. Fitzmyer, *Gospel According to Luke*, 1.115.

211. Guillemard, *Hebraisms in the New Testament*, 16.

212. Schlatter, *Evangelium des Lukas*, 281.

213. BDF §141 (1); Schlatter, *Evangelium des Lukas*, 281.

214. BDF §288 (2); Fitzmyer, *Gospel According to Luke*, 1.117.

215. Guillemard, *Hebraisms in the New Testament*, 16; Schlatter, *Der Evangelist Matthäus*, 383.

216. Dalman, *Words of Jesus*, 23.

217. Schlatter, *Evangelium des Lukas*, 711.

10:29-37

29 Ἰερουσαλήμ (9)

35 ἐν τῷ ἐπανέρχεσθαι (4)

37 ὁ ποιήσας τὸ ἔλεος μετ᾽ αὐτοῦ[218]; πορεύου καὶ σὺ ποίει ὁμοίως[219]

10:38-42

38 ἐν ... τῷ πορεύεσθαι (4)

39 καὶ τῇδε ἦν ἀδελφή καλουμένη[220] (14)

42 τὴν ἀγαθὴν μερίδα[221]

11:1 καὶ ἐγένετο (1); ἐν τῷ εἶναι (4); δίδαξον ἡμᾶς[222]

11:2-4 ἐν τοῖς οὐρανοῖς[223] (בשמים)

11:5-8

5 μεσονυκτίου[224] (חצות הלילה)

7 ἀποκριθεὶς εἴπῃ[225]; εἰς τὴν κοίτην εἰσίν[226]

11:9-13

11 τίνα δὲ ἐξ ὑμῶν τὸν πατέρα αἰτήσει ὁ υἱός[227]

11:14 ἦν ἐκβάλλων[228] (14); ἐγένετο δέ (1)

11:15-22

18 σατανᾶς (שטן)

20 ἐν δακτύλῳ θεοῦ[229]

---

218. Lagrange, *Évangile selon Saint Luc*, ci; Guillemard, *Hebraisms in the New Testament*, 16; BDF §206 (3).

219. Schlatter, *Evangelium des Lukas*, 291.

220. BDF §289.

221. Schlatter, *Evangelium des Lukas*, 294.

222. Schlatter, *Evangelium des Lukas*, 299.

223. BDF §141 (1).

224. Schlatter, *Evangelium des Lukas*, 299.

225. Dalman, *Words of Jesus*, 24.

226. Guillemard, *Hebraisms in the New Testament*, 17.

227. BDF §469.

228. Dalman, *Words of Jesus*, 35-36.

229. BDF §259.

11:23-26

25   ἐλθὸν εὑρίσκει[230]

11:27-28

27   ἐγένετο δέ (1); ἐν τῷ λέγειν (4); μακαρία ἡ κοιλία[231]; καὶ μαστοὶ οὓς ἐθήλασας[232]

28   μακάριοι οἱ ἀκούοντες[233]; φυλάσσοντες[234]

11:29-35

30   ἐγένετο (1)

31   καὶ ἰδού (5)

32   καὶ ἰδού (5); μετενόησαν εἰς τὸ κήρυγμα Ἰωνᾶ[235]

33   εἰς κρύπτην[236]

11:36-54

38   ἐν ἑαυτῷ [D] (11)

41   καὶ ἰδού (5)

49   ἐξ αὐτῶν ἀποκτενοῦσιν[237]

50   ἵνα ἐκζητηθῇ τὸ αἷμα[238]

54   ἐνεδρεύοντες αὐτὸν θηρεῦσαί τι ἐκ τοῦ στόματος αὐτοῦ[239]

12:1a

12:1b   προσέχετε . . . ἀπό[240]

---

230. Dalman, *Words of Jesus,* 21.

231. Schlatter, *Evangelium des Lukas,* 302.

232. Schlatter, *Evangelium des Lukas,* 302.

233. Schlatter, *Evangelium des Lukas,* 302.

234. Schlatter, *Evangelium des Lukas,* 302.

235. Guillemard, *Hebraisms in the New Testament,* 17; Schlatter, *Der Evangelist Matthäus,* 418.

236. BDF §132 (2): "the exact equivalent of Aram[aic]."

237. BDF §164 (2): the partitive genitive is quite rare in Classical, "but common in Semitic languages."

238. Schlatter, *Evangelium des Lukas,* 711.

239. Sparks, "The Semitisms in St. Luke's Gospel," 129; BDF §217 (3).

240. BDF §147.

12:2-9

3   ἀνθ᾽ ὧν (13)
4   φοβηθῆτε ἀπὸ τῶν ἀποκτεινόντων τὸ σῶμα[241]
5   γέενναν (גיהנם)
6   ἐνώπιον (2)
8   ἐν ἐμοί . . . ἐν αὐτῷ[242]
9   ἐνώπιον (2)

12:10   εἰς τὸν υἱὸν τοῦ ἀνθρώπου[243]

12:11-12

12   ἐν αὐτῇ τῇ ὥρᾳ[244]

12:13-15

13   μερίσασθαι μετ᾽ ἐμοῦ τὴν κληρονομίαν[245]
14   ἄνθρωπε[246]; τίς με κατέστησεν κριτὴν . . . ἐφ᾽ ὑμᾶς[247]
15   φυλάσσεσθε ἀπό[248]; ἐν τῷ περισσεύειν (4)

12:16-21

17   διελογίζετο ἐν ἑαυτῷ (בלבו; 11); λέγων[249]
19   τῇ ψυχῇ μου (לנפשי); φάγε, πίε, εὐφραίνου[250]
20   ἃ . . . ἡτοίμασας, τίνι ἔσται[251]

12:22-31

29   μετεωρίζεσθε[252]
30   τὰ ἔθνη τοῦ κόσμου[253]

---

241. Sparks, "Semitisms in St. Luke's Gospel," 130; Guillemard, *Hebraisms in the New Testament*, 17; Schlatter, *Der Evangelist Matthäus*, 345.

242. BDF §220.

243. Guillemard, *Hebraisms in the New Testament*, 17.

244. BDF 288 (2); Fitzmyer, *Gospel According to Luke*, 1.117.

245. Schlatter, *Evangelium des Lukas*, 317.

246. BDF §146: Semitic omission of the vocative ὦ.

247. Schlatter, *Evangelium des Lukas*, 317.

248. BDF §149.

249. Fitzmyer, *Gospel According to Luke*, 1.115.

250. Schlatter, *Evangelium des Lukas*, 317.

251. BDF §189 (2).

252. Schlatter, *Evangelium des Lukas*, 534.

253. Schlatter, *Evangelium des Lukas*, 534.

12:32   τὸ μικρὸν ποίμνιον[254]; ἐν ἑαυτῷ [D] (11)

12:33-34   ἐν τοῖς οὐρανοῖς[255] (בשמים)

12:35-38
35   ἔστωσαν ὑμῶν αἱ ὀσφύες περιεζωσμέναι[256]
37   μακάριοι (אַשׁרי); ἀμήν (אמן)

12:39-46
39   οἰκοδεσπότης (בעל הבית)
42   ὅν καταστήσει ὁ κύριος ἐπὶ τῆς θεραπείας αὐτοῦ τοῦ διδόναι ἐν
     καιρῷ σιτομέτριον (אשר יפקידהו האדון על־עבדיו לתת
     את־ארחתם בעתו)

12:47-48
47   δαρήσεται πολλὰς . . . ὀλίγας[257]
48   παντὶ δὲ ᾧ[258]

12:49-52
49   τί θέλω (מה)[259]

12:53

12:54-56
56   πρόσωπον (3); τὸν καιρὸν δὲ τοῦτον[260]

12:57-59
59   ἕως καὶ τὸ ἔσχατον λεπτὸν ἀποδῷς[261]

---

254. BDF § 147 (3), use of nominative instead of vocative because of Semitic influence.
255. BDF §141 (1).
256. Schlatter, *Evangelium des Lukas*, 318.
257. BDF §241 (6).
258. BDF §293 (1).
259. BDF §299 (4). R. H. Connolly, "Syriacisms in St. Luke," 376-78, asserts that the enigmatic Greek clause in Luke 12:49, καὶ τί θέλω εἰ ἤδη ἀνήφθη, corresponds word-for-word with the Curetonian Syriac *(C)* and is best explained by it. It can, however, also be translated (albeit ambiguously) by the Hebrew ומה־חששתי כי כבר בערה.
260. BDF §292.
261. Schlatter, *Evangelium des Lukas*, 712, 541.

13:1-9

1   ἐν αὐτῷ τῷ καιρῷ[262]

2   παρὰ πάντας[263]; ἐγένοντο (1)

4   Σιλωάμ (שִׁלֹחַ); ὀφειλέται[264]; ἐγένοντο (1); παρὰ πάντας[265];
     Ἰερουσαλήμ (9)

13:10-17

10   ἦν δὲ διδάσκων[266] (14); ἐν μιᾷ τῶν[267] (7)

11   καὶ ἰδού (5); πνεῦμα ἔχουσα ἀσθενείας[268]; ἦν συγκύπτουσα[269]
     (14)

13   ἐδόξαζεν τὸν θεόν (10)

14   ἀποκριθεὶς . . . ἔλεγεν[270]

16   σατανᾶς (שָׂטָן)

13:18-19

19   καὶ ἐγένετο (1)

13:20-21

13:22-23

13:24

13:25   apodotic καί (12); ἀφ’ οὗ . . . ἀποκλείσῃ τὴν θύραν[271]; ἀποκριθεὶς
            ἐρεῖ[272]

---

262. BDF §288 (1); Fitzmyer, *Gospel According to Luke*, 1.118.

263. BDF §245.

264. Fitzmyer, *Gospel According to Luke*, 1.117.

265. BDF §245.

266. Dalman, *Words of Jesus*, 35-36.

267. Fitzmyer, *Gospel According to Luke*, 1.121-22.

268. Fitzmyer, *Gospel According to Luke*, 1.117; see 1QapGen 20:26, 16.

269. Dalman, *Words of Jesus*, 35-36.

270. Dalman, *Words of Jesus*, 25.

271. Schlatter, *Evangelium des Lukas*, 711; 329.

272. Dalman, *Words of Jesus*, 24.

13:26-30

26   ἐνώπιον (2)

27   ἐργάται ἀδικίας[273]

30   καὶ ἰδού (5)

13:31-33

31   ἐν αὐτῇ τῇ ὥρᾳ[274]

32   πορευθέντες εἴπατε[275]; ἀλώπηξ (שׁוּעָל)[276]

33   Ἰερουσαλήμ (9)

13:34-35

34   Ἰερουσαλήμ (9)

14:1-6

1   καὶ ἐγένετο (1); ἐν τῷ ἐλθεῖν (4); apodotic καί (12) ἦσαν παρατηρούμενοι[277] (14)

2   καὶ ἰδού (5)

3   ἀποκριθεὶς . . . εἶπεν[278]

5   τίνος ὑμῶν υἱὸς ἢ βοῦς εἰς φρέαρ πεσεῖται[279]

14:7-14

10   ἐνώπιον (2)

12   ?ποιῇς ἄριστον[280]

14:15   μακάριος ὅστις (אַשְׁרֵי הָאִישׁ אֲשֶׁר)[281]

14:16-18

18   ἀπὸ μιᾶς[282]

---

273. Schlatter, *Evangelium des Lukas*, 711.

274. Fitzmyer, *Gospel According to Luke*, 1.117.

275. Schlatter, *Evangelium des Lukas*, 332.

276. Schlatter, *Evangelium des Lukas*, 711.

277. Schlatter, *Evangelium des Lukas*, 35-36; Guillemard, *Hebraisms in the New Testament*, 18.

278. Dalman, *Words of Jesus*, 25.

279. BDF §471 (2); Schlatter, *Evangelium des Lukas*, 712.

280. Schlatter, *Der Evangelist Matthäus*, 634.

281. Hauck, μακάριος, *TWNT* 4.370.

282. BDF §241 (6). For possible Syriac influence in the wording, see R. H. Connolly, "Syriacisms in St Luke," 378.

14:19-20

14:21-23

14:24-33

26	τὴν ψυχὴν ἑαυτοῦ[283]
28	καθίσας ψηφίζει[284]
30	καθίσας . . . βουλεύσεται[285]; ἐν δέκα χιλιάσιν[286] (בעשרת אלפים)
31	ἔτι αὐτοῦ πόρρω ὄντος[287]
33	πᾶς . . . ὅς[288]

14:34-35

34	μωρανθῇ ἐν τίνι ἀρτυθήσεται[289]
35	ὁ ἔχων ὦτα ἀκούειν ἀκουέτω[290]

15:1-7

1	ἦσαν δὲ αὐτῷ ἐγγίζοντες[291] (14)
7	χαρὰ ἐν τῷ οὐρανῷ ἔσται[292]

15:8-10

10	ἐνώπιον τῶν ἀγγέλων τοῦ θεοῦ (2)[293]

15:11-32

12	μέρος τῆς οὐσίας[294]
14	ἐγένετο λιμὸς ἰσχυρά[295]; καὶ αὐτός (6)

---

283. Schlatter, *Evangelium des Lukas,* 345.
284. Dalman, *Words of Jesus,* 22.
285. Dalman, *Words of Jesus,* 22.
286. Guillemard, *Hebraisms in the New Testament,* 18; BDF §195 (1).
287. Schlatter, *Evangelium des Lukas,* 345.
288. BDF §293 (1).
289. Guillemard, *Hebraisms in the New Testament,* 18; Schlatter, *Der Evangelist Matthäus,* 147.
290. Guillemard, *Hebraisms in the New Testament,* 18.
291. Dalman, *Words of Jesus,* 35-36; Schlatter, *Evangelium des Lukas,* 713.
292. Schlatter, *Evangelium des Lukas,* 351.
293. Dalman, *Words of Jesus,* 31.
294. Schlatter, *Evangelium des Lukas,* 358.
295. Schlatter, *Evangelium des Lukas,* 359.

15 πορευθεὶς ἐκολλήθη[296]

16 γεμίσαι τὴν κοιλίαν (11)[297]

17 εἰς ἑαυτὸν δὲ ἐλθών[298] (וַיָּשָׁב אֶל־לִבּוֹ; 11); χαρὰ ἔσται . . . ἤ[299]

18 ἀναστὰς πορεύσομαι[300]; ἥμαρτον εἰς τὸν οὐρανὸν[301]; ἐνώπιον (2)

20 ἀναστὰς ἦλθεν[302]; ἐπέπεσεν ἐπὶ τὸν τράχηλον αὐτοῦ καὶ κατεφίλησεν αὐτὸν[303]

21 ἐνώπιον (2); ἥμαρτον εἰς τὸν οὐρανὸν

22 δότε δακτύλιον εἰς τὴν χεῖρα αὐτοῦ[304]

23 τὸν μόσχον τὸν σιτευτόν[305]

24 ἦν ἀπολωλώς[306] (14)

29 ἀποκριθεὶς εἶπεν[307]

31 καὶ πάντα τὰ ἐμὰ σά ἐστιν[308]

16:1-9

3 εἶπεν δὲ ἐν ἑαυτῷ[309] (וַיֹּאמֶר בְּלִבּוֹ; 11)

5 πόσον ὀφείλεις τῷ κυρίῳ μου;[310]

6 καθίσας . . . γράψον[311]

7 κόρους[312]

8 τὸν οἰκονόμον τῆς ἀδικίας[313]; οἱ υἱοὶ τοῦ αἰῶνος τούτου . . . τοὺς υἱοὺς τοῦ φωτός[314]

296. Dalman, *Words of Jesus*, 21; Schlatter, *Evangelium des Lukas*, 716.

297. Schlatter, *Evangelium des Lukas*, 359.

298. Schlatter, *Evangelium des Lukas*, 359.

299. BDF §245.

300. Dalman, *Words of Jesus*, 23.

301. Guillemard, *Hebraisms in the New Testament*, 19; Schlatter, *Evangelium des Lukas*, 359: use of the ב prefix in sense of "against."

302. Dalman, *Words of Jesus*, 23.

303. Schlatter, *Evangelium des Lukas*, 360.

304. Schlatter, *Evangelium des Lukas*, 713, 360.

305. Schlatter, *Evangelium des Lukas*, 360.

306. Dalman, *Words of Jesus*, 35-36.

307. Dalman, *Words of Jesus*, 24.

308. Schlatter, *Evangelium des Lukas*, 360 (see 1 Kgs 20:4).

309. Schlatter, *Evangelium des Lukas*, 713.

310. Schlatter, *Evangelium des Lukas*, 371.

311. Dalman, *Words of Jesus*, 22.

312. Lagrange, *Évangile selon Saint Luc*, ci; Fitzmyer, *Gospel According to Luke*, 1.113.

313. Fitzmyer, *Gospel According to Luke*, 1.124; BDF §165.

314. Guillemard, *Hebraisms of the New Testament*, 19; BDF §176 (1).

9 μαμωνᾶ τῆς ἀδικίας[315]

16:10-12

11 ἐν τῷ ἀδίκῳ μαμωνᾷ[316]

16:13 μαμωνᾷ[317]

16:14-15

15 ἐνώπιον (twice, 2); βδέλυγμα[318]

16:16-17 ?βιάζεται (בְּיָד חֲזָקָה)

16:18

16:19-31

19 βύσσος (בּוּץ)
22 ἐγένετο (1); εἰς τὸν κόλπον Ἀβραάμ[319]
23 ἐπάρας τοὺς ὀφθαλμούς[320]
24 καὶ αὐτός (6)
25 νῦν δὲ ὧδε[321]
26 ἐστήρικται[322]

17:1-3a

2 λυσιτελεῖ . . . ἤ[323]
3 προσέχετε ἑαυτοῖς[324]

---

315. Guillemard, *Hebraisms of the New Testament,* 19; BDF §165: "Hebrew usage is thus reflected."

316. Guillemard, *Hebraisms of the New Testament,* 19; M. Black, *An Aramaic Approach to the Gospels and Acts*[3], 139-40.

317. Fitzmyer, *Gospel According to Luke,* 1.113.

318. BDAG 172; Schlatter, *Evangelium des Lukas,* 712, 379.

319. Schlatter, *Evangelium des Lukas,* 380.

320. Fitzmyer, *Gospel According to Luke,* 1.114.

321. BDF §289.

322. Guillemard, *Hebraisms in the New Testament,* 19.

323. BDF §245 (3).

324. Schlatter, *Evangelium des Lukas,* 384.

17:3b-4

4   ?ἀφήσεις[325]; εἰς σέ[326]

17:5-6

6   συκάμινος (שׁקמה)

17:7-10

10   ὃ ὠφείλομεν ποιῆσαι[327]

17:11-19

11   καὶ ἐγένετο (1); ἐν τῷ πορεύεσθαι (4); Ἰερουσαλήμ (9); καὶ
        αὐτός (6); μέσον Σαμαρείας καὶ Γαλιλαίας[328]; apodotic καί (12);

11   καὶ αὐτοὶ ἦραν φωνὴν λέγοντες[329]

12   πορευθέντες ἐπιδείξατε[330]; καὶ ἐγένετο (1); λιμὸς ἰσχυρά[331]; ἐν τῷ
        ὑπάγειν (4);

13   ὑπέστρεψεν μετὰ φωνῆς μεγάλης[332]; δοξάζων τὸν θεόν (10)

14   ἐπὶ πρόσωπον (3); καὶ αὐτὸς ἦν Σαμαρίτης[333]

18   δοῦναι δόξαν τῷ θεῷ[334]

19   ἀναστὰς πορεύου[335]

17:20-22

20   ἀπεκρίθη αὐτοῖς καὶ εἶπεν[336]

21   ἐντὸς ὑμῶν (בקרבכם)

---

325. Guillemard, *Hebraisms in the New Testament,* 19. The second person singular in-dicative is often used in Hebrew rather than the imperative, as here.

326. Use of the ב prefix in the sense of "against."

327. Schlatter, *Evangelium des Lukas,* 388.

328. BDF §261 (4).

329. Sparks, "The Semitisms in St. Luke's Gospel," 137; Schlatter, *Evangelium des Lukas,* 711.

330. Sparks, "The Semitisms in St. Luke's Gospel," 137.

331. Schlatter, *Evangelium des Lukas,* 359.

332. Sparks, "The Semitisms in St. Luke's Gospel," 137.

333. Sparks, "The Semitisms in St. Luke's Gospel," 137.

334. Schlatter, *Evangelium des Lukas,* 390.

335. Dalman, *Words of Jesus,* 23; Schlatter, *Evangelium des Lukas,* 711.

336. BDF §420 (1).

17:23-27

   26   καὶ . . . ἐγένετο (1)

17:28-30

   28   ἐγένετο (1)

17:31

17:32

17:33-37

18:1-8

   1   πρὸς τὸ δεῖν . . . προσεύχεσθαι[337]
   2   ἦν . . . φοβούμενος[338] (14)
   4   εἶπεν ἐν ἑαυτῷ (אמר בלבו or אמר בנפשו; 11)
   6   ὁ κριτὴς τῆς ἀδικίας[339]
   8   ἐν τάχει[340]

18:9-14a

   9   τοὺς πεποιθότας ἐφ' ἑαυτοῖς[341] (בטחים בנפשם)
   10   πρὸς ἑαυτόν (11)
   11   σταθεὶς . . . προσηύχετο[342]; πρὸς ἑαυτόν (לבדו); ὁ θεός[343]; οἱ λοιποὶ τῶν ἀνθρώπων[344] (כיתר האדם)
   13   μακρόθεν ἑστώς[345]; τοὺς ὀφθαλμοὺς ἐπᾶραι εἰς τὸν οὐρανόν[346]
   14a   παρ' ἐκεῖνον[347]

---

337. BDF §402 (5).

338. Dalman, *Words of Jesus*, 35-36.

339. Guillemard, *Hebraisms in the New Testament*, 20.

340. BDF §219.

341. Schlatter, *Evangelium des Lukas*, 719.

342. Dalman, *Words of Jesus*, 23.

343. BDF §147 (3): use of nominative instead of vocative because of Semitic influence; Fitzmyer, *Gospel According to Luke*, 1.115.

344. Schlatter, *Evangelium des Lukas*, 711.

345. Schlatter, *Evangelium des Lukas*, 401.

346. Fitzmyer, *Gospel According to Luke*, 1.114; Schlatter, *Evangelium des Lukas*, 717.

347. BDF §§245, 245a.

18:14b

18:15-17

   17   <u>ἀμήν</u> (אמן)

18:18-23

   19   The omission of the divine name ὁ θεός by B* and א* (so too Matt 19:17) is predictable in Hebrew.

   22   ἐν τοῖς οὐρανοῖς[348] (בשמים)

18:24-30

   29   ἀμήν (אמן)

   30   <u>ἐν τῷ καιρῷ τούτῳ</u>[349]

18:31-34

   31   Ἰερουσαλήμ (9)

   34   ἦν . . . κεκρυμμένον ἀπ᾽ αὐτῶν[350] (14)

18:35-43

   35   ἐγένετο δέ (1); ἐν τῷ ἐγγίζειν (4)

   43   δοξάζων τὸν θεόν (10); καὶ πᾶς ὁ λαὸς ἰδὼν ἔδωκεν αἶνον τῷ θεῷ[351]

19:1-9

   1   apodotic καί (12)

   2   καὶ ἰδού (5); καὶ αὐτός (twice, 6)

   3   οὐκ ἠδύνατο ἀπὸ τοῦ ὄχλου[352] (ולא יכל מפני העם)

   5   σπεύσας κατάβηθι[353]

   8   ἀποδίδωμι τετραπλοῦν[354]

   9   ἐγένετο (1); καὶ αὐτός (6)

---

348. BDF §141 (1).

349. BDF §292.

350. Dalman, *Words of Jesus*, 35-36; BDF §155 (3); Schlatter, *Evangelium des Lukas*, 717.

351. Guillemard, *Hebraisms in the New Testament*, 20; Schlatter, *Evangelium des Lukas*, 711.

352. Guillemard, *Hebraisms in the New Testament*, 21.

353. Schlatter, *Das Evangelium des Lukas*, 404.

354. Schlatter, *Das Evangelium des Lukas*, 712, 404 (see 2 Sam 12:6).

19:10

19:11-27

11	προσθεὶς εἶπεν[355] (וַיֹּסֶף וַיְדַבֵּר); Ἰερουσαλήμ (9)
14	βασιλεῦσαι ἐφ' (מֶלֶךְ עַל)[356]
15	καὶ ἐγένετο (1); ἐν τῷ ἐπανελθεῖν (4); apodotic καί (12)
22	ἐκ τοῦ στόματός σου κρινῶ σε[357]
27	βασιλεῦσαι ἐπ' (מֶלֶךְ עַל)[358]

19:28-40

29	καὶ ἐγένετο (1)
37	πασῶν ὧν εἶδον δυνάμεων[359] (הַגְּבוּרֹת)
38	ἐν ὑψίστοις[360] (בַּמְּרוֹמִים)

19:41-44

42	ἐκρύβη[361]; ἀπὸ ὀφθαλμῶν σου[362]
43	ἥξουσιν ἡμέραι ἐπὶ σέ[363] (יָמִים בָּמִים עָלַיִךְ)
44	ἀνθ' ὧν (13); οὐκ ἔγνως τὸν καιρὸν τῆς ἐπισκοπῆς σου[364]

19:45-46

<u>19:47-48</u>

    <u>47</u> ἦν διδάσκων[365]

20:1-8

| 1 | καὶ ἐγένετο (1); ἐν μιᾷ τῶν ἡμερῶν[366] (7) |

355. Fitzmyer, *Gospel According to Luke,* 1.115.

356. BDF §177.

357. Schlatter, *Evangelium des Lukas,* 407.

358. BDF §177.

359. Guillemard, *Hebraisms in the New Testament,* 21; BDF §294 (5).

360. Guillemard, *Hebraisms in the New Testament,* 21; Schlatter, *Der Evangelist Matthäus,* 610.

361. BDF §155 (3); Schlatter, *Evangelium des Lukas,* 717.

362. BDF §259.

363. Guillemard, *Hebraisms in the New Testament,* 21.

364. Schlatter, *Evangelium des Lukas,* 411; M. Wilcox, "Semiticisms in the NT," *ABD* 5.1083.

365. Guillemard, *Hebraisms in the New Testament,* 35-36.

366. Fitzmyer, *Gospel According to Luke,* 121-22.

20:9-19

10   ἐξαπέστειλαν . . . κενόν[367]

11   προσέθετο ἕτερον πέμψαι[368] (וַיֹּסֶף ל)

12   καὶ προσέθετο τρίτον πέμψαι[369]

13   ἴσως[370]

19   ἐν αὐτῇ τῇ ὥρᾳ[371]

20:20-26

20   ὑποκρινομένους ἑαυτοὺς δικαίους[372]

21   οὐ λαμβάνεις πρόσωπον (לֹא־תִשָּׂא פָנִים)[373]

20:27-40

34   οἱ υἱοὶ τοῦ αἰῶνος τούτου[374]

35   τοῦ αἰῶνος ἐκείνου[375]

36   καὶ υἱοί εἰσιν θεοῦ τῆς ἀναστάσεως υἱοὶ ὄντες[376]

39   καλῶς εἶπας[377]

20:41-44

20:45-47

46   προσέχετε ἀπὸ τῶν γραμματέων[378]

21:1-4

21:5-6

367. Schlatter, *Evangelium des Lukas*, 119.
368. Sparks, "The Semitisms of St. Luke's Gospel," 130; BDF §435 (a).
369. Sparks, "The Semitisms of St. Luke's Gospel," 130.
370. Schlatter, *Evangelium des Lukas*, 120.
371. Fitzmyer, *Gospel According to Luke*, 1.117; Schlatter, *Evangelium des Lukas*, 712.
372. BDF §157 (2).
373. Fitzmyer, *Gospel According to Luke*, 1.115; Schlatter, *Evangelium des Lukas*, 717.
374. Fitzmyer, *Gospel According to Luke*, 1.115.
375. BDF §292; Schlatter, *Evangelium des Lukas*, 711.
376. Guillemard, *Hebraisms in the New Testament*, 21.
377. Schlatter, *Evangelium des Lukas*, 123.
378. Guillemard, *Hebraisms in the New Testament*, 21.

21:7-11

    11   λιμοὶ καὶ λοιμοὶ ἔσονται[379]

21:12-19

    14   θέτε οὖν ἐν ταῖς καρδίαις ὑμῶν[380]

    16   θανατώσουσιν ἐξ ὑμῶν[381]

21:20-21a

    20   Ἰερουσαλήμ (9)

21:21b-22

    21b   ἐν μέσῳ (בְּתוֹךְ)[382]

    22   ἡμέραι ἐκδικήσεως[383]

    21:24   στόματι μαχαίρης[384]; καὶ Ἰερουσαλήμ (9) ἔσται πατουμένη ὑπὸ ἐθνῶν;[385] ἄχρι οὗ πληρωθῶσιν καιροὶ ἐθνῶν[386]

21:25-28

    26   τῶν οὐρανῶν[387] (בְּשָׁמַיִם)

21:29-33

    32   ἀμήν (אָמֵן)

21:34-36

    34   entire verse[388]

    35   ὡς παγίς, ἐπεισελεύσεται γὰρ ἐπὶ πάντας τοὺς καθημένους ἐπὶ πρόσωπον πάσης τῆς γῆς[389] (3)

---

379. Schlatter, *Evangelium des Lukas*, 131.

380. BDF §392 (3); Schlatter, *Evangelium des Lukas*, 716.

381. BDF §164 (2): the partitive genitive is quite rare in Classical, "but common in Semitic languages."

382. BDF §215 (3); Schlatter, *Evangelium des Lukas*, 418 (see Num 17:10).

383. Schlatter, *Evangelium des Lukas*, 418.

384. BDF §195 (1); Schlatter, *Evangelium des Lukas*, 717.

385. Schlatter, *Evangelium des Lukas*, 418.

386. Schlatter, *Evangelium des Lukas*, 418.

387. BDF §141 (1).

388. Sparks, "The Semitisms of St. Luke's Gospel," 129.

389. Sparks, "The Semitisms of St. Luke's Gospel," 129; Dalman, *Words of Jesus*, 29-30; Schlatter, *Evangelium des Lukas*, 418.

21:37-38

37 ἦν . . . διδάσκων³⁹⁰ (14)

38 ὤρθριζεν πρὸς αὐτόν³⁹¹

22:1-2

22:3-6

3 σατανᾶς (שָׂטָן)

22:7-14

14 καὶ . . . ἐγένετο (1)

22:15-18

15 ἐπιθυμίᾳ ἐπεθύμησα (8);

22:19-20

22:21-22

22:23

22:24-27

24 ἐγένετο δέ (1)

26 ὑμεῖς δὲ οὐχ οὕτως³⁹²

22:28-30

30 ἐπὶ τῆς τραπέζης μου³⁹³; καθήσεσθε . . . κρίνοντες³⁹⁴

22:31-32

31 σατανᾶς (שָׂטָן)

22:33-34

---

390. Dalman, *Words of Jesus*, 35-36.
391. Schlatter, *Evangelium des Lukas*, 131.
392. Schlatter, *Evangelium des Lukas*, 429.
393. Schlatter, *Evangelium des Lukas*, 429.
394. Dalman, *Words of Jesus*, 22.

22:35-38

    37   μετὰ ἀνόμων ἐλογίσθη[395]

22:39-42

    41   καὶ αὐτός (6); ἀπεσπάσθη ἀπ' αὐτῶν ὡσεὶ λίθου βολήν[396]

22:43-44

    43   ἐνισχύων αὐτόν[397]

    44   καὶ ἐγένετο (1)

22:46-47

22:48-52a

    49   εἰ πατάξομεν ἐν μαχαίρῃ[398]

22:52b-53a

    53a   οὐκ ἐξετείνατε τὰς χεῖρας ἐπ' ἐμέ[399]

22:53b   αὕτη ἐστὶν ὑμῶν ἡ ὥρα καὶ ἡ ἐξουσία τοῦ σκότους[400]

22:54-64

    55   ἐν μέσῳ (בְּתוֹךְ)[401]

    57   γύναι[402]

    58   ἄνθρωπε[403]

    60   ἄνθρωπε[404]

---

395. BDF §145 (2).

396. BDF §161 (1): "a Hebraistic acc[usative] of place"; Schlatter, *Evangelium des Lukas,* 712.

397. Schlatter, *Evangelium des Lukas,* 435.

398. Guillemard, *Hebraisms in the New Testament,* 22; BDF §195 (1).

399. Schlatter, *Evangelium des Lukas,* 139.

400. Guillemard, *Hebraisms in the New Testament,* 22.

401. BDF §215 (3).

402. BDF §146: Semitic omission of the vocative ὦ.

403. BDF §146: Semitic omission of the vocative ὦ.

404. BDF §146: Semitic omission of the vocative ὦ.

22:65-71

65   βλασφημοῦντες . . . εἰς αὐτόν[405]

66   καὶ . . . ἐγένετο (1)

68   ἐὰν δὲ ἐρωτήσω, οὐ μὴ ἀποκριθῆτε[406]

71   ἠκούσαμεν ἀπὸ τοῦ στόματος αὐτοῦ[407]

23:1   ἀναστὰν . . . ἤγαγον[408]

23:2

23:3

23:4-5

5   ἀρξάμενος ἀπό[409]

23:6-12

8   ἦν. . . θέλων[410] (14)

10   εἱστήκεισαν . . . κατηγοροῦντες[411]

12   ἐν αὐτῇ τῇ ἡμέρᾳ[412]

23:13-16

14   καὶ ἰδού (5); ἐνώπιον (2)

15   καὶ ἰδού (5)

23:17-23

19   ἦν . . . βληθείς[413] (14)

23:24-25

---

405. Use of the ב prefix in the sense of "against."

406. Schlatter, *Evangelium des Lukas,* 712, 438 (see Isa 41:28).

407. BDF §217 (3); Schlatter, *Evangelium des Lukas,* 711.

408. Dalman, *Words of Jesus,* 23.

409. Black, *An Aramaic Approach to the Gospels and Acts,* 299.

410. Dalman, *Words of Jesus,* 35-36.

411. Dalman, *Words of Jesus,* 23.

412. Fitzmyer, *Gospel According to Luke,* 1.118.

413. Dalman, *Words of Jesus,* 35-36.

23:26

23:27-32

28   θυγατέρες Ἰερουσαλήμ (בנות ירושלים); ἐπ' ἐμέ . . . ἐπὶ τὰ τέκνα
       ὑμῶν[414]; ἐφ' ἑαυτὰς κλαίετε[415]

29   ὅτι ἰδοὺ ἔρχονται ἡμέραι[416]

31   Verse follows pattern of Jewish argument *a minore ad maius.*[417]

23:33-34

23:35-38

35   εἱστήκει . . . θεωρῶν[418]; ὁ ἐκλεκτός[419]

23:39-43

42   μνήσθητί μου[420]

43   ἀμήν (אמן); ἐν τῷ παραδείσῳ[421] (פרדס)

23:44-45

44   καὶ . . . ἐγένετο (1)

23:46   φωνήσας φωνῇ μεγάλῃ[422]

23:47   ἐδόξαζεν τὸν θεόν[423]

23:48

23:49   εἱστήκεισαν . . . ἀπὸ μακρόθεν[424]

---

414. Guillemard, *Hebraisms in the New Testament,* 23.
415. Schlatter, *Evangelium des Lukas,* 449.
416. Schlatter, *Evangelium des Lukas,* 449.
417. Guillemard, *Hebraisms in the New Testament,* 23.
418. Dalman, *Words of Jesus,* 23.
419. Schlatter, *Evangelium des Lukas,* 449.
420. Schlatter, *Evangelium des Lukas,* 449.
421. Guillemard, *Hebraisms in the New Testament,* 23; Schlatter, *Evangelium des Lukas,* 719.
422. Lagrange, *Évangile selon Saint Luc,* ci.
423. Lagrange, *Évangile selon Saint Luc,* ci.
424. Schlatter, *Evangelium des Lukas,* 450.

23:50-51

50 καὶ ἰδού (5)

51 ἦν συγκατατεθειμένος[425]

23:52-56a

53 ἦν . . . κείμενος[426] (14)

55 ἦσαν συνεληλυθυῖαι[427] (14)

23:56b

24:1-8

1 τῇ δὲ μιᾷ τῶν[428] (7); φέρουσαι ἃ ἡτοίμασαν[429]

4 καὶ ἐγένετο (1); ἐν τῷ ἀπορεῖσθαι (4); καὶ ἰδού (5); apodotic καί (12); ἐν ἐσθῆτι ἀστραπτούσῃ[430]

5 κλινουσῶν τὰ πρόσωπα εἰς τὴν γῆν (3)

6-7 ἐλάλησεν . . . λέγων[431]

7 εἰς χεῖρας ἀνθρώπων ἁμαρτωλῶν[432] (לידי אנשים חטאים)

24:9-12

11 ἐφάνησαν . . . ὡσεὶ λῆρος[433]; ἐνώπιον (2)

12 ἀναστὰς ἔδραμεν[434]

24:13-35

13 καὶ ἰδού (5); ἐν αὐτῇ τῇ ἡμέρᾳ[435]; ἦσαν πορευόμενοι[436] (14); ἀπέχουσαν σταδίους; ἑξήκοντα ἀπό[437]; Ἰερουσαλήμ (9)

---

425. Dalman, *Words of Jesus,* 35-36.

426. Dalman, *Words of Jesus,* 35-36.

427. Dalman, *Words of Jesus,* 35-36.

428. Guillemard, *Hebraisms in the New Testament,* 23; BDF §247 (1).

429. BDF 294 (5).

430. Guillemard, *Hebraisms in the New Testament,* 23.

431. Dalman, *Words of Jesus,* 25-26.

432. Schlatter, *Evangelium des Lukas,* 711.

433. BDF §157 (5).

434. Dalman, *Words of Jesus,* 35-36.

435. Fitzmyer, *Gospel According to Luke,* 1.118.

436. Dalman, *Words of Jesus,* 35-36; BDF §353 (1).

437. BDF §161 (1): "a Hebraistic acc[usative] of place."

15 καὶ ἐγένετο (1); ἐν τῷ ὁμιλεῖν (4); καὶ αὐτός (6); apodotic καί (12)

16 οἱ δὲ ὀφθαλμοὶ αὐτῶν ἐκρατοῦντο[438] (ועיניהם אחוזות)

18 Ἰερουσαλήμ (9)

19 ἐγένετο (1); ἀνὴρ προφήτης[439] (איש נביא); δυνατὸς ἐν ἔργῳ καὶ λόγῳ[440]

20 εἰς κρίμα θανάτου[441]

21 ἐγένετο (1)

25 καὶ αὐτός (6)

27 ἀρξάμενος ἀπό[442]

28 καὶ αὐτός (6); προσεποιήσατο[443]

30 καὶ ἐγένετο (1); ἐν τῷ κατακλιθῆναι (4)

31 καὶ αὐτός (6); ἄφαντος . . . ἀπ’ αὐτῶν[444]; καὶ . . . ἐγένετο (1)

32 καιομένη ἦν[445]; ὡς διήνοιγεν ἡμῖν τὰς γραφάς[446]

33 ἀναστάντες . . . ὑπέστρεψαν[447]; αὐτῇ τῇ ὥρᾳ[448]; Ἰερουσαλήμ (9);

34 ὤφθη[449]

24:36-43

36 εἰρήνη ὑμῖν (שלום לכם)

38 διαλογισμοὶ ἀναβαίνουσιν ἐν τῇ καρδίᾳ[450]

43 ἐνώπιον (2)

24:44-53

44 πάντα τὰ γεγραμμένα ἐν τῷ νόμῳ[451]

---

438. Schlatter, *Evangelium des Lukas*, 717; Bartlet, "The Sources of St. Luke's Gospel," 322.

439. Schlatter, *Evangelium des Lukas*, 711.

440. Schlatter, *Evangelium des Lukas*, 458.

441. Schlatter, *Evangelium des Lukas*, 458.

442. Black, *An Aramaic Approach to the Gospels and Acts*, 299.

443. BDF §392 (2).

444. BDF §211.

445. BDF §211; Dalman, *Words of Jesus*, 35-36.

446. Schlatter, *Evangelium des Lukas*, 459.

447. Schlatter, *Evangelium des Lukas*, 459; Dalman, *Words of Jesus*, 23.

448. Fitzmyer, *Gospel According to Luke*, 1.117.

449. Fitzmyer, *Gospel According to Luke*, 1.117.

450. Schlatter, *Evangelium des Lukas*, 711.

451. Schlatter, *Evangelium des Lukas*, 459.

47   ἀρξάμενοι ἀπό[452]; Ἰερουσαλήμ (9);

49   καὶ ἰδού (5); ὑμεῖς δὲ καθίσατε ἐν τῇ πόλει ἕως οὗ ἐνδύσησθε ἐξ
     ὕψους δύναμιν[453]

51   καὶ ἐγένετο (1); ἐν τῷ εὐλογεῖν (4)

52   Ἰερουσαλήμ (9)

53   ἦσαν . . . εὐλογοῦντες[454] (14)

A total of 703 Semitisms are listed above.

> 505 occur in **Special Luke.**
> 148 occur as **Lukan additions to Matthew and/or Mark.**
> Thus, a total of 653 (505 + 148) are **unique to Luke.**
> 15 occur in the triple tradition.
> 26 are shared by *Luke and Matthew.*
> 9 are shared by Luke and Mark.

---

452. Black, *An Aramaic Approach to the Gospels and Acts,* 299.

453. Guillemard, *Hebraisms in the New Testament,* 23; Sparks, "The Semitisms of St.
Luke's Gospel," 129.

454. Dalman, *Words of Jesus,* 35-36.

Luke 6:5 (D)

Codex Bezae (D) places Luke 6:5 ("And [Jesus] said to them, 'The Son of Man is the lord of the Sabbath'") after v. 10, and in its place reads: τῇ αὐτῇ ἡμέρᾳ θεασάμενός τινα ἐργαζόμενον τῷ σαββάτῳ εἶπεν αὐτῷ, Ἄνθρωπε, εἰ μὲν οἶδας τί ποιεῖς, μαράριος εἶ· εἰ δὲ μὴ οἶδας, ἐπικατάρατος καὶ παραβάτης εἶ τοῦ μόμου ("On the same day he [Jesus] saw a certain man working on the Sabbath and said to him, 'Man, if you know what you are doing, you are blessed; but if you do not know, you are accursed and a transgressor of the law'"). This verse appears in no other Gospel and is often ascribed to an apocryphal piece of "floating tradition" in the early church. Its effect in Codex Bezae is to concatenate three Sabbath episodes in Luke 6:1-10, all of which are concluded by the pronouncement of the sovereignty of the Son of Man over the Sabbath.[1]

Most scholars are dubious that the tradition preserved by Codex Bezae either derived from the historical Jesus or was originally part of the Gospel of Luke. Some consider it "inconceivable" that a Jew in Jesus' day would be found working on the Sabbath.[2] More commonly, the Bezae addition is regarded as a post-Easter tradition that developed in response to the question of Sabbath observance in Hellenistic Christian congrega-

---

1. B. M. Metzger, *A Textual Commentary on the Greek New Testament* (New York: United Bible Societies, 1971), 140.

2. E. Lohse, σάββατον, *TWNT* 7.24; followed by H. Klein, *Das Lukasevangelium* (KEK 1/3; Göttingen: Vandenhoeck & Ruprecht, 2006), 232. Against the objection, the preoccupation of the rabbinic tradition with what constituted Sabbath-breaking surely indicates that it *was* a concern in first-century Judaism.

tions.[3] There are, however, arguments in favor of its authenticity or antiquity. Plummer finds "nothing incredible in Christ's having seen a man working (not necessarily in public) on the Sabbath."[4] Several details also suggest a Palestinian *Sitz im Leben* and/or conformity with Lukan style: Jesus does not rescind the Sabbath ordinance; the contrast between blessings and curses is not unlike the contrast between new and old in 6:36-39; and the word of Jesus redefines and supersedes a Torah commandment. These particulars support the picture of Jesus in the canonical Gospels.[5] On the basis of such evidence, the case cannot be considered closed against the authenticity or antiquity of the episode.

Further light may be shed on the Bezae addition in 6:5 by considering its philological particulars, which bear curious similarities to both Luke and the Hebrew Gospel. Most notably, the vocative ἄνθρωπε is unique to Luke (5:20 [D]; 12:14; 22:58, 60) among the Gospels.[6] Lukan style likewise shows a proclivity for names, and particularly "father," in the vocative.[7] The accusative indefinite pronoun τινα is also strongly Lukan, as is μακάριος.[8] These verbal particulars are especially evident in Special Luke, which, as we have seen, bears a distinctive similarity with patristic quotations attributed to the Hebrew Gospel. The unusual form of Jesus addressing an individual as "man" in the vocative is also preserved in the Hebrew Gospel, as cited by Origen in his *Commentary on Matthew* 15.14, "[Jesus]

---

3. R. Bultmann, *The History of the Synoptic Tradition,* rev. ed., trans. J. Marsh (New York: Harper & Row, 1972), 25; H. Klein, *Das Lukasevangelium,* 231-32; M. Wolter, *Das Lukasevangelium* (HNT 5: Tubingen: Mohr Siebeck, 2008), 235.

4. A. Plummer, *The Gospel According to S. Luke*[5] (Edinburgh: T. & T. Clark, 1981), 168. Plummer is tentatively followed by M.-J. Lagrange, *Évangile selon Saint Luc,* 177, in suggesting that the Bezae tradition influenced Paul, who in Romans 2 mentions παραβάτης νόμου (2x) and ἄνθρωπε (2x), both of which occur in the verse in question.

5. W. Grundmann, *Das Evangelium nach Lukas* (Berlin: Evangelische Verlagsanstalt, 1974), 136, concludes that the episode "conforms to Luke's presentation of Jesus and has its place in the history of Jesus." J. Jeremias, *Unbekannte Jesusworte* (Gütersloh, 1980), 61-64; and E. Bammel, "The Cambridge Pericope: The Addition to Luke 6.4 in Codex Bezae," *NTS* 32 (1986), 404-26, also advocate the originality of the episode.

6. The form of the word occurs only 16x in the Greek Bible: Kings (5x), Psalms (1x), Micah (1x), Luke (4x), Romans (3x), 1 Timothy (1x), James (1x).

7. Πάτερ occurs 11x in Luke, but only 3x in Matthew, 0x in Mark, 9x in John. For other forms of address in the vocative, see Luke 8:48, 49; 16:24, 27, 30; 19:5; 22:5.

8. Τινα: Luke (11x; 19x in Acts); Matthew (6x); Mark (4x); John (8x). Μακάριος: Luke (15x); Matthew (13x); Mark (0x); John (2x).

said to him, 'Man, do the law and prophets.'"[9] This similarity appears to me far stronger than the alleged similarity of the Bezae addition with *Gospel of Thomas* 3 and 14.[10] The similarities of the Bezae addition with both Lukan style and the Hebrew Gospel make the authenticity of this verse less improbable than it may otherwise appear. Even if the verse is not original with Luke, its inclusion in the Third Gospel can be plausibly explained as the result of a scribe or copyist who held the Hebrew Gospel in high esteem and recognized the appropriateness of the verse in question within the context of Luke 6:1-10.

---

9. Discussed on pp. 60-62 above.
10. So J. Fitzmyer, *The Gospel According to Luke I–IX,* 610.

Selected Bibliography

Books

Bauckham, Richard, *Jesus and the Eyewitnesses: The Gospels as Eyewitness Testimony.* Grand Rapids: Eerdmans, 2006.

Bauer, W., F. W. Danker, W. F. Arndt, and F. W. Gingrich, *A Greek-English Lexicon of the New Testament and Other Early Christian Literature*[3]. Chicago: University of Chicago Press, 2000 (cited in footnotes as BDAG).

Beyond the Q Impasse: Luke's Use of Matthew, ed. A. McNicol, D. Dungan, and D. Peabody. Valley Forge: Trinity Press International, 1996.

Bivin, David, and Roy Blizzard Jr., *Understanding the Difficult Words of Jesus: New Insights from a Hebraic Perspective.* Austin: Center for Judaic-Christian Studies, 1983.

Black, Matthew, *An Aramaic Approach to the Gospels and Acts*[3]. Peabody: Hendrickson Publishers, 1998.

Blair, George A., *The Synoptic Gospels Compared.* Studies in the Bible and Early Christianity, Vol. 55, Lewiston; Edwin Mellen Press, 2003.

Blass, F., A. Debrunner, and R. Funk, *A Greek Grammar of the New Testament and Other Early Christian Literature,* a translation and revision of the ninth-tenth German edition incorporating supplementary notes of A. Debrunner by R. Funk. Chicago: University of Chicago Press, 1967 (cited in footnotes as BDF).

Creed, John Martin, *The Gospel According to St. Luke.* London: Macmillan, 1930.

The Critical Edition of Q, ed. J. M. Robinson, P. Hoffmann, and J. S. Kloppenborg. Minneapolis: Fortress Press, 2000.

Dalman, Gustaf, *The Words of Jesus,* trans. D. M. Kay. Edinburgh: T. & T. Clark, 1909.

Dos Santos, Elmar Camillo, and Robert L. Lindsey, *A Comparative Greek Concordance of the Synoptic Gospels.* Jerusalem: Dugith Publishers.

Dupont, Jacques, *Études sur Les Évangiles Synoptiques,* Vol. 1. BETL 70A, Leuven: University Press, 1985.

Elliott, J. K., *The Apocryphal New Testament: A Collection of Apocryphal Christian Literature in an English Translation.* Oxford: Clarendon Press, 2004.

Farmer, William, *The Gospel of Jesus: The Pastoral Relevance of the Synoptic Problem.* Louisville: Westminster John Knox, 1994.

————, *The Synoptic Problem: A Critical Analysis.* Dillsboro, N.C.: Western North Carolina Press, 1976.

Farris, Stephen, *The Hymns of Luke's Infancy Narratives: Their Origin, Meaning and Significance.* JSNTSup 9, Sheffield: JSOT Press, 1985.

Findlay, Adam Fyfe, *Byways in Early Christian Literature: Studies in the Uncanonical Gospels and Acts,* Chapter Two. Edinburgh: T. & T. Clark, 1923.

Fitzmyer, Joseph A., S.J., *The Gospel According to Luke (I-IX).* AB 28, Garden City: Doubleday & Company, 1981.

The Four Gospels 1992: Festschrift Frans Neirynck, ed. F. Segbroeck, C. Tuckett, G. Van Belle, and J. Verheyden, Vol. 3. BETL C, Leuven: University Press, 1992.

Gla, Dietrich, *Die Originalsprache des Matthäusevangeliums.* Paderborn: Schöningh, 1887.

Guillemard, William Henry, *Hebraisms in the Greek New Testament.* Cambridge and London: Bell, 1879.

Halton, Thomas P., "Saint Jerome, On Illustrious Men," in *The Fathers of the Church,* Vol. 100. Washington, D.C.: Catholic University Press of America Press, 1999.

Handmann, Rudolf, *Das Hebräer-Evangelium. Ein Beitrag zur Geschichte und Kritik des hebräischen Matthäus.* Leipzig: J. C. Hinrichs, 1888.

Harnack, Adolf, *Geschichte der altchristlichen Literatur bis Eusebius*[2], 4 vols. Leipzig: J. C. Hinrichs, 1958.

Hengel, Martin, *The Four Gospels and the One Gospel of Jesus Christ,* trans. J. Bowden. Harrisburg: Trinity Press International, 2000.

Hilgenfeld, Adolf, *Novum Testamentum extra Canonem Receptum*[2]. Leipzig: T. O. Weigel, 1866.

Holtzmann, Oskar, *The Life of Jesus,* trans. J. T. Bealby and M. A. Canney. London: Adam and Charles Black, 1904.

Hultgren, Stephen, *Narrative Elements in the Double Tradition: A Study of Their Place within the Framework of the Gospel Narrative.* BZNW 113, Berlin/New York: de Gruyter, 2002.

The Interrelations of the Gospels, A Symposium Led by M.-E. Boismard, W. R. Farmer, F. Neirynck, Jerusalem 1984, ed. D. Dungan. BETL 95, Leuven: University Press, 1990.

James, M. R. *The Apocryphal New Testament.* Oxford: Clarendon Press, 1924.

Jeremias, Joachim, *Die Sprache des Lukasevangeliums. Redaktion und Tradition im Nicht-Markusstoff des dritten Evangeliums.* KEK Sonderband, Göttingen: Vandenhoeck & Ruprecht, 1980.

Klijn, A. F. J., *Jewish-Christian Gospel Tradition.* VCSup 17, Leiden: E. J. Brill, 1992.

Selected Bibliography

Klijn, A. F. J., and G. J. Reinink, *Patristic Evidence for Jewish-Christian Sects*. NovTSup 36, Leiden: Brill, 1973.

Lagrange, M.-J., *Évangile selon Saint Luc²*. Paris: J. Gabalda, 1921.

Lindsey, Robert L., *A Hebrew Translation of the Gospel of Mark*. Jerusalem: Dugith, 1973.

Linnemann, Eta, *Is There a Synoptic Problem? Rethinking the Literary Dependence of the First Three Gospels*, trans. R. Yarbrough. Grand Rapids: Baker Book House, 1992.

Lührmann, Dieter, *Die apokryph gewordenen Evangelien. Studien zu neuen Texten und zu neuen Fragen*. NovTSup 112, Leiden/Boston: Brill, 2004.

Lummis, E. W., *How Luke Was Written*. Cambridge: University Press, 1915.

Martin, Raymond, *Syntax Criticism of the Synoptic Gospels*. SBEC 10, Lewiston: Edwin Mellen Press, 1987.

Metzger, Bruce M., *The Canon of the New Testament: Its Origin, Development, and Significance*. Oxford: Oxford University Press, 1997.

Milik, J. T., *Ten Years of Discovery in the Wilderness of Judea*, trans. J. Strugnell. London: SCM, 1959.

Moulton, James Hope, and Wilbert Francis Howard, *A Grammar of New Testament Greek* Edinburgh: T. & T. Clark.

Neirynck, Frans, *Evangelica II. 1982-1991: Collected Essays*, ed. F. Segbroeck. Leuven: University Press, 1991.

———, *Q-Synopsis: The Double Tradition Passages in Greek*. SNTA 13, Leuven: University Press, 1988.

Neville, David J., *Argument from Order in Synoptic Source Criticism*. NGS 7, Mercer: Peters, 1993.

New Synoptic Studies, ed. W. Farmer. Macon: Mercer University Press, 1983.

Nicholson, Edward Byron, *The Gospel according to the Hebrews: Its Fragments Translated and Annotated with a Critical Analysis of the External and Internal Evidence Relating to It*. London: Kegan Paul, 1879.

Orchard, Bernard, and Harold Riley, *The Order of the Synoptics: Why Three Synoptic Gospels*. Macon: Mercer University Press, 1987.

Quasten, Johannes, *Patrology*, 3 vols. Westminster, Md.: Christian Classics, 1992.

Resch, Alfred, *Agrapha. Aussercanonische Evangelienfragmente*. Leipzig: J. C. Hinrichs, 1889.

Robertson, A. T., *A Grammar of the Greek New Testament in the Light of Historical Research*. Nashville: Broadman, 1923.

Rolland, Philippe, *L'Origine et la Date des Évangiles. Les témoins oculaires de Jésus*. Paris: Saint-Paul, 1994.

Sanders, E. P., and Margaret Davies, *Studying the Synoptic Gospels*. London: SCM and Philadelphia: Trinity Press International, 1989.

Schenke, Hans-Martin, *Das Matthäus-Evangelium im mittelägyptischen Dialekt des Koptischen (Codex Schøyen)*. Oslo: Hermes Academic, 2001.

Schlatter, Adolf, *Der Evangelist Matthäus, seine Sprache, sein Ziel, seine Selbständigkeit*. Stuttgart: Calwer, 1948.

————, *Das Evangelium des Lukas. Aus seinen Quellen erklärt*[2]. Stuttgart: Calwer, 1960.

Schmidtke, Alfred, "Neue Fragmente und Untersuchungen zu den judenchristlichen Evangelien," in *Texte und Untersuchungen* 3/7. Leipzig: J. C. Hinrichs, 1911.

Schonfield, Hugh J., *According to the Hebrews*. London: Duckworth, 1937.

Schürer, Emil, *The History of the Jewish People in the Age of Jesus Christ*, rev. and ed. by G. Vermes, F. Millar, and M. Black, 4 vols. Edinburgh: T. & T. Clark, 1979.

Sepp, Johann Nepomuk, *Das Hebräer-Evangelium oder die Markus- und Matthäusfrage und ihre friedliche Lösung*. Munich: J. J. Lentner, 1870.

Stern, Menachem, *Greek and Latin Authors on Jews and Judaism*, 3 vols. Jerusalem: The Israel Academy of Sciences and Humanities, 1974.

Stoldt, Hans-Herbert, *History and Criticism of the Marcan Hypothesis*, trans. and ed. D. L. Niewyk. Macon: Mercer University Press, 1980.

Streeter, Burnett Hillman, *The Four Gospels: A Study of Origins*. London: Macmillan, 1936.

Synopsis Quattuor Evangeliorum[5], ed. K. Aland. Stuttgart: Würtembergische Bibelanstalt, 1968.

The Synoptic Gospels: Source Criticism and the New Literary Criticism, ed. Camille Focant. BETL 90, Leuven: University Press, 1993.

Tresmonant, Claude, *The Hebrew Christ: Language in the Age of the Gospels*, trans. K. Whitehead. Chicago: Franciscan Herald, 1989.

The Two Source Hypothesis: A Critical Appraisal, ed. A. J. Bellinzoni Jr. Mercer: Mercer University Press, 1985.

Vaganay, L., *Le problème Synoptique. Une hypothèse de travail*. Tournai: Desclee, 1952.

Wenham, John, *Redating Matthew, Mark and Luke*. Downers Grove: InterVarsity, 1992.

White, H. G. E., *The Sayings of Jesus from Oxyrhynchus*. Cambridge: Cambridge University Press, 1920.

Wilke, Christian Gottlob, *Der Urevangelist*. Dresden und Leipzig: Gerhard Fleischer, 1838.

Zahn, Theodor, *Geschichte des neutestamentlichen Kanons*, 4 vols. Erlangen: A. Deichert, 1888.

————, *Grundriss der Einleitung in das Neue Testament*. Leipzig: A. Deichert, 1928.

Articles

Amphoux, Christian-Bernard, "L'Évangile selon les Hébreux. Sources de L'Évangile de Luc," *Apocrypha* 6 (1995), 67-77.

Bacon, B. W., "Papias and the Gospel According to the Hebrews," *Exp.* 11 (1905), 161-77.

Barnes, A. S., "The Gospel According to the Hebrews," *JTS* 6 (1905), 356-71.

Bartlet, J. Vernon, "The Sources of St. Luke's Gospel," in *Studies in the Synoptic Problem*, ed. W. Sanday (Oxford: Clarendon, 1911), 313-63.

Beatrice, Pier Franco, "The 'Gospel According to the Hebrews' in the Apostolic Fathers," *NovT* 48/2 (2006), 147-95.

Bertrand, D., "L'*Évangile des Ebionites:* Une Harmonie Evangelique Anterieure au *Diatessaron*," *NTS* 26/4 (1980), 548-63.

Brock, Sebastian, "A New Testimonium to the 'Gospel According to the Hebrews,'" *NTS* 18 (1971), 220-22.

Burch, Vacher, "The Gospel According to the Hebrews: Some New Matter Chiefly from Coptic Sources," *JTS* 21 (1920), 310-15.

Cadbury, Henry J., "Luke — Translator or Author?" *AJT* 24 (1920), 436-55.

Connolly, R. H., "Syriacisms in St Luke," *JTS* 37 (1936), 374-85.

Davila, James R., "(How) Can We Tell If a Greek Apocryphon or Pseudepigraphon Has Been Translated from Hebrew or Aramaic?" *JSP* 15 (2005), 3-61.

Dorival, Gilles, "Un Groupe Judéo-Chrétien Méconnu: les Hébreux," *Apocrypha* 11 (2000), 7-36.

Dunkerley, Roderic, "The Gospel according to the Hebrews," *ExpT* 39 (1927-28), 437-42, 490-95.

Edwards, James R., "The *Gospel of the Ebionites* and the Gospel of Luke," *NTS* 48 (2002), 568-86.

Evans, Craig, "The Jewish Christian Gospel Tradition," in *Jewish Believers in Jesus: The Early Centuries,* ed. O. Skarsaune and R. Hvalvik, Peabody: Hendrickson, 2007.

Farmer, William, "State *Interesse* and Markan Primacy: 1870-1914," in *Biblical Studies and the Shifting of Paradigms, 1850-1914,* ed. H. G. Reventlow and W. Farmer (JSOTSup 192; Sheffield: Sheffield Academic, 1995), 15-49.

Farrer, Austin, "On Dispensing with Q," in *Studies in the Gospels: Essays in Memory of R. H. Lightfoot,* ed. D. E. Nineham (Oxford: Basil Blackwell, 1955), 55-88.

Goulder, Michael D., "Farrer on Q," *Theology* 83 (1980) 190-95.

Gregory, Andrew, "Prior or Posterior? The *Gospel of the Ebionites* and the Gospel of Luke," *NTS* 51 (2005), 344-60.

Grintz, Jehoshua, "Hebrew as the Spoken and Written Language in the Last Days of the Second Temple," *JBL* 79 (1960), 32-47.

Hill, Charles E., "What Papias Said about John (and Luke): A 'New' Papian Fragment," *JTS* 49 (1998), 582-629.

Horbury, William, "The Hebrew Matthew and Hebrew Study" in *Hebrew Study from Ezra to Ben-Yehuda,* ed. W. Horbury (Edinburgh: T. & T. Clark, 1999), 122-31.

Huggins, Ronald V., "Matthean Posteriority: A Priliminary Proposal," *NovT* 34 (1992), 1-22.

Klinghardt, Matthias, "Markion vs. Lukas. Plädoyer für die Wiederaufnahme eines alten Falles," *NTS* 52 (2006), 484-513.

Lagrange, M.-J., "L'Évangile selon Les Hébreux," *RB* 31 (1922), 161-81.

Lessing, Gotthold Ephraim, "New Hypothesis on the Evangelists as Merely Human Historians," in *Philosophical and Theological Writings,* trans. and ed. H. B. Nisbet (Cambridge Texts in the History of Philosophy, Cambridge: Cambridge University Press, 2005), 148-71.

Most, William G., "Did St Luke Imitate the Septuagint," *JSNT* 15 (1982), 30-41.

Mussies, Gerard, "The Use of Hebrew and Aramaic in the Greek New Testament," *NTS* 30 (1984), 416-32.

Parker, Pierson, "A Proto-Lukan Basis for the Gospel According to the Hebrews," *JBL* 59 (1940), 471-78.

Peterson, William L., "The *Vorlage* of Shem-Tob's 'Hebrew Matthew,'" *NTS* 44 (1998), 490-512.

Schleiermacher, David Friedrich, "Ueber die Zeugnisse des Papias von unseren beiden ersten Evangelien," *ThStKr* 5 (1832), 735-68.

Schmidtke, Alfred, "Zum Hebräerevangelium," *ZNW* 35 (1936), 24-44.

Schmithals, Walter, "Vom Ursprung der synoptischen Tradition," *ZTK* 94 (1950), 288-316.

Schweizer, Eduard, "Eine hebraisierende Sonderquelle des Lukas?" *TZ* 6 (1950), 161-85.

Silva, Moises, "Semantic Borrowings in the New Testament," *NTS* 22 (1976), 104-10.

Sparks, H. F. D., "The Semitisms of St. Luke's Gospel," *JTS* 44 (1943), 137-38.

————, "The Semitisms of the Acts," *JTS* New Series 1 (1950), 16-28.

Stegner, W. R., "The Priority of Luke: An Exposition of Robert Lindsey's Solution to the Synoptic Problem," *BR* 27 (1982), 26-38.

Surkau, H. W., "Hebräerevangelium," *RGG*[3], 2.109.

Thornton, Timothy C. G., "Jerome and the 'Hebrew Gospel according to Matthew,'" in *Studia Patristica* 28 (Leuven: Peeters, 1993), 118-22.

Waitz, Hans, "Neue Untersuchungen über die sogen. judenchristlichen Evangelien," *ZNW* 36 (1937), 60-81.

Wallach, Luitpold, "The Textual History of an Aramaic Proverb (Traces of the Ebionean Gospel)," *JBL* 60 (1941), 403-15.

West, H. Philip, Jr., "A Primitive Version of Luke in the Composition of Matthew," *NTS* 14 (1967-68), 75-95.

Wilcox, Max, "Semitisms in the New Testament," *ANRW* 25/2 (1984), 978-1029.

Wilson, B. E., "The Two Notebook Hypothesis: An Explanation of Seven Synoptic Patterns," *ExpT* 108 (1997), 265-68.

Winter, Paul, "Two Notes on Luke 1–2 with Regard to the Theory of 'Imitation Hebraisms,'" *ST* 7 (1953), 158-65.

Index of Modern Authors

Alexander, L., 151
Allison, D., 229
Althaus, P., 204
Amphoux, C.-B., xxxiii, 10, 21, 46, 55
Anger, xxvi

Bacon, B. W., xxxi, 8, 59, 62, 85, 117
Bammel, E., 334
Barnes, A. S., 3
Bartlet, J. V., xxxi, 146, 150, 331
Barzun, J., 201
Bauckham, R., 85, 86, 144, 146, 149, 150, 257
Bauer, W., 124
Baumstark, W., 55
Baur, F. C., xxv
BDF (= F. Blass, A. Debrunner, R. W. Funk), 131, 132, 133, 135, 140, 160, 163, 164, 185, 294-307, 309-25, 237-328, 330-31
Beatrice, P. F., xxxiii, 4, 46, 52, 53, 54, 55, 122, 124, 241, 258
Berg, S., 140, 231
Bergemann, T., 210
Bergen, D., 204
Bertrand, D., 67, 69, 108
Beyer, K., 127, 164, 166
Birkeland, H., 171, 172
Black, M., 172, 319, 328, 331, 332

Blair, G. A., 245, 251
Blatz, B., 93
Bleek, F., xxv
Bockmuehl, M., 47
Bousset, W., 203
Brock, S., 24, 26
Brown, D., 221
Brown, R., 175, 176
Bultmann, R., 333
Burch, V., 59

Cadbury, H. J., 127
Carroll, M., 250
Chancey, M., 173
Charlesworth, J., 175
Connolly, R. H., 127, 134, 135, 314, 316
Credner, K. A., xxiv
Creed, J. M., 127, 139

Dalman, G., 75, 126, 128, 131, 132, 133, 136, 140, 158, 162, 163, 164, 165, 166, 167, 168, 230, 294-304, 306-12, 315-18, 320-22, 325-26, 328-32
Danby, H., 207, 223
Daniélou, J., 55
Davies, W. D., 229
Davila, J., 128, 129, 130, 136, 162, 164, 165
Deissmann, A., 132
Delitzsch, F., xxv, 165

342

Delling, G., 149
Dibelius, M., 190
Dobschütz, E., 47
Dorival, G., 21, 24, 55, 60, 122, 177
Dungan, D. L., 187, 188, 220
Dunkerley, R., xxxi, 15, 47, 95, 107, 122
Dunn, J. D. G., 210-11

Ebrard, J., xxv
Edwards, J. R., 66, 248
Eichhorn, G., xxiii
Elliott, J. K., xxx, 48, 63, 80, 90, 107, 108, 119, 120, 280
Enslin, M. S., 113
Ericksen, R. P., 204
Evans, C. A., 61, 107, 193
Ewald, G. H. A., xxv

Fabricius J. A., xxiii
Fabry, H.-J., 139, 159
Farmer, W., 197, 207, 218, 220
Findlay, A. F., 84, 98, 100, 106, 107, 122
Fitzmyer, J., 126, 127, 131, 133, 134, 135, 156, 164, 183, 244, 294-96, 299, 301-7, 310, 313, 315, 316, 318, 319, 321, 323-24, 328, 330-31
Flusser, D., xxxii
Frank, xxv
Frend, W. H. C., 17
Funk, R., 197

Geiger, A., 223
Gerhardsson, B., 148
Gesenius, W., and E. Kautzsch, 133, 164
Gieseler, J., xxiii, xxviii
Gla, D., xxiii, xxvi, xxvii, 1, 2, 7, 11, 15, 103, 109, 217
Goppelt, L., 247
Grabe, J. E., xxiii
Gregory, A., 46, 66, 108
Grintz, J., 172, 178, 241
Grundmann, W., 204, 334
Guillemard, W. H., 127, 294-99, 301-13, 316-24, 327, 329, 330, 332
Gutbrod, W., 176

Handmann, R., xxvii, xxviii, xxxi, 7, 13, 15, 16, 30, 49, 51, 53, 57, 61, 62, 63, 64, 76, 81, 84, 86, 87, 89, 91, 92, 108, 112, 113, 116, 124, 146, 162, 186, 193, 237, 280
Harnack, A. von, xxviii, 11, 13, 21, 22, 28, 33, 63, 90, 91, 184, 202, 203, 222-23
Harris, R., 193
Hartman, L., 137, 138
Hauck, F., 316
Hengel, M., 5, 6, 12, 80, 99, 102, 118, 149, 150, 179, 192, 211, 222, 246, 250, 252, 256
Herford, R. T., 230, 232
Hilgenfeld, A., xxvii, xxviii, 33, 56, 70, 116, 121, 233
Hill, C. E., 4, 5, 18
Hirsch, E., 204
Hoffmann, P., 210
Holl, K., 72, 227
Holtzmann, H. J., xxvi, 117
Holtzmann, O., 91, 106, 112
Horbury, W., 228, 232
Horsley, G. H. R., 118, 210
Howard, G., 193
Howard, W. F., 75
Hug, J., xxiii
Huggins, R., 251
Hultgren, S., 210-11, 216, 236, 237, 239, 241, 247, 250, 252

Inge, W. R., 55

Jeremias, J., xxxii, 61, 135, 147, 183, 232, 247, 293, 334
Jost, M., 232, 233

Keim, K. T., xxvi
Kilpatrick, G. D., 251
Kittel, G., 138, 204
Klein, C., 205
Klein, H., 333
Klijn, A. F. J., xxvii, xxx, 5, 6, 9, 11, 14, 15, 37, 51, 57, 58, 62, 63, 65, 68, 78, 79, 81, 82, 84, 85, 86, 89, 91, 108, 114, 120, 122, 163

Kloppenborg, J., 210, 224-25, 233
Klostermann, E., 150
Knox, B., 218
Koester, H., 47, 107, 187, 240
Kraft, R., 5
Krämer, H., 132
Kuhn, K. G., 171, 232
Kürzinger, J., 4

Lachmann, K., 214, 219
Lagrange, M.-J., xxix, 8, 11, 15, 17, 19, 21, 22, 33, 38, 39, 55, 57, 114, 115, 116, 127, 132, 133, 136, 137, 138, 139, 156, 158, 164, 165, 182, 296-98, 311, 318, 329, 334
Lake, K., 217
Lessing, G. E., xxii, xxiii, xxxi, 104, 106, 122, 149, 182, 198, 199, 256
Levine, L. L., 173
Lightfoot, J. B., 84, 280
Lindsey, R., xxxii, 186
Lisowsky, G., 170
Loew, L., 233
Lohse, E., 333
Lührmann, D., xxx, 6, 8, 9, 24, 25, 26, 78, 89, 90, 108, 122, 210

Marshall, I. H., 150
Martin, R., 138, 142
McCarter, K. P., 205
McIver, R., 250
Menken, M. J. J., 161
Metzger, B. M., 8, 13, 15, 21, 22, 155, 176, 333
Milik, J. T., 172, 173
Most, W., 139, 160, 161, 164
Moule, C. F. D., 75
Moulton, J. H., 75

Neirynck, F., 215
Netz, R., 190
Nicholson, E. B., xxvii, xxviii, 7, 15, 36, 46, 51-52, 56, 61, 71, 74, 75, 77, 80, 85, 87, 103, 104, 118, 232, 254
Noel, W., 190

Olofsson, S., 128
Olshausen, H., xxiv
Orchard, B., 2, 3, 195

Parker, P., xxxii, 61, 81, 103, 109, 122
Paulsen, H., 47
Peterson, W. L., 107, 118
Plummer, A., 127, 334
Puech, H.-C., 93, 119

Quasten, J., 228
Quispel, G., 55

Rabin, C., 170, 172, 173
Ramsay, W., 202
Reinink, G. J., 65, 114
Renan, E., 201
Resch, A., xxviii, 8, 78, 102, 107, 112, 120
Reuss, E. G. E., xxvi
Reynolds, L. D., 103, 227
Riley, H., 195
Rilliet, F., 23
Roberts, C. H., 5
Robertson, A. T., 132, 161, 162, 163, 169, 202
Robinson, J. M., 210
Rolland, P., xxxii, xxxiii, 134, 147, 163, 168
Rosenstock-Huessy, E., 218
Rowe, K., 208
Rowlingson, D. T., 210

Sanders, E. P., 205
Sanders, J. A., 205
Schenke, H.-M., xxxiii
Schiffman, L. H., 206
Schlatter, A., xxxi, 139, 146, 147, 149, 159, 160, 167, 294-331
Schleiermacher, F. D. E., xxiii, 202, 203, 212-23
Schlichting, G., 193
Schmidt, P. L., 54, 122
Schmidt, W., 12
Schmidtke, A., xxix, xxx, 33, 49, 57, 59, 98, 99, 108

Schneckenburger, M., xxiv
Schneemelcher, W., 152
Schneider, C., 89
Schneider, G., 3
Schoedel, W. R., 47
Scholder, K., 204
Schonfield, H. J., xxxii, 11, 23, 69, 182, 186, 193, 194, 203, 204, 208
Schürer, E., 171, 173, 203
Schwartz, E., 11, 217
Schwegler, F. C. A., xxv
Schweitzer, A., 221-22
Schweizer, E., xxxii, 127, 134, 136, 159, 238
Segal, M. H., 172
Sepp, J., xxvi, 199, 225, 255
Shanks, H., 205
Shedinger, R. F., 161
Siegele-Wenschkewitz, L., 204
Silva, M., 162
Simon, R., xxiii
Soden, H. von, 202, 203
Smyth, H. W., 133, 140
Sparks, H. F. D., 32, 78, 127, 156, 165, 180, 295, 298, 312, 313, 320, 324, 325, 332
Steiner, G., 194
Stoldt, H.-H., xvii, 220
Stern, M., 191
Strack and Billerbeck, 82, 170, 171, 174, 175, 181, 205, 230, 247
Strauss, D. F., xxvi
Strecker, G., xxx, 15, 27, 30, 33, 34, 49-52, 107, 120, 163
Streeter, B. H., 147, 243
Stuckenbruck, L. T., 128, 166
Sychowski, S. von, 30

Theissen, G., 86
Thiersch, H. W., xxv

Thornton, C. J., 12
Thornton, T. C. G., 101
Throckmorton, B. H., 107
Torrey, C. C., 127
Tov, E., 206
Tresmontant, C., 182
de Troyer, K., 128, 182
Tuckett, C. M., 210, 236
Tyson, J., 205

Vaganay, L., 255
Valesius, H., 217
Vanderkam, J., 175, 205, 254
Van Henten, J. W., 171
Vermes, G., 205
Vielhauer, P., xxx, 15, 27, 30, 33, 34, 49-52, 107, 120, 163
Visotzky, B. L., 229
Volkmar, xxvi

Waitz, H., xxix, xxx, 81, 82, 100, 120
Waitz, J., 55
Wallach, L., 232
Wanke, J., 163
Weber, xxiii
Weinfeld, M., 203
Weiss, J., 215
Weisse, C. H., 214-15
Weizsäcker, K. H., xxvi
Wellhausen, J., 203
West, H. P., 241, 246, 251
White, H. G. E., 13, 14
Wilcox, M., 128, 130, 135, 157, 162, 172, 185, 295
Wilke, C. G., xxvi, xxxi, 251
Wilson, N. G., 103, 227
Wolter, M., 160, 333

Zahn, T., xxviii, xxix, 5, 13, 21, 25, 33, 49, 108, 181, 216-17

Index of Subjects

Anti-Semitism, 207
Apelles, 40
Aramaic, use of in first-century Palestine, 166-74
Aramaic hypothesis, 162-66

Bardesanes, 254
Bartholomew (apostle), 12
Basilides, 22, 40, 119
Beowulf, 219
Bismarck, Otto von, 219-20

Cerinthians, 112-13
Clement of Rome, 2
Cyril of Jerusalem, 58-59

Damasus, Pope, 77
Dead Sea Scrolls, 205-6
Demons, 52-53
Dhammapada, 237
Didymus of Alexandria, 23-26
Disputed Canonical Books, 19-22
Documentary Hypothesis, 196-97
Double Tradition, 234-40

Early Christian Polemic against Judaism, 192-93
Early Jewish Polemic against Christianity, 191-92

Ebionites, 18, 19, 26, 27, 107-8, 121
Ebionites, Gospel of, 120-24
Enlightenment, 195-204, 221-22
1 Enoch, 254
Ephrem the Syrian, 23
Epiphanius, 26-27, 113-14
Essenes, 189
Eusebian Canons, 98, 236
Eusebius, 18-22

Frauenkirche, Dresden, 147

Geiger, Abraham, 223
"German Christians," 204, 205
Gilgamesh Epic, 219
Greek Manuscripts, 190

Harnack, Adolf von, 222-23
Hebraisms in Luke, 184-86
Hebrew, xviii, xix
Hebrew, use of in first-century Palestine, 166-74
Hebrew Gospel, 120-24
Hebrews, Epistle of, 98-99
Hegesippus, 15, 16
Hippolytus, 16, 18
Holtzmann, H. J., 220
Holy Spirit, 56-59

Ignatius of Antioch, 2, 35, 48, 49
Iliad, 219
Illuminati, Order of, 221
Irenaeus, 114

James, brother of Jesus, 79-82
Jerome, 28-37, 51-52, 99-102
Jerusalem, 136-38, 238
Jesus Seminar, 197-98
Jewish Gospel, 40-42
John Chrysostom, 28
Josephus, 253
Jubilees, 253-54
Julian the Pelagian, 36

Kulturkampf, 207, 219-21

Lagrange, M.-J., 115
Lessing, G. E., 198, 199
Luke, Gospel of, xx, 76

Maccabeus, Judas, 77
Marcion, 113, 202, 203
Marius Mercator, 38-39
Markan priority, xviii, 196-97, 220
Matthean priority, 196-97
Matthew (apostle), 29-30
Matthew, Gospel of, 245-58
Matthias, 24, 25
Matthias, Gospel of (see also *Traditions of Matthias/Matthew*), 22, 118-19
Meditations of Marcus Aurelius, 237
Merinthians, 112-13

Nazarenes, 26-27, 29
Nazarenes, Gospel of, 120-24
Nibelungenlied, 219
Nicephorus (Patriarch of Constantinople), 21, 22
Nicephorus Callistus Xanthopulus, 15
Nineteenth-century scholarship, xxii, xxix

On Illustrious Men, 100, 226-28
Origen, 17, 18, 34

Palimpsest, xix
Pamphilus, 30
Pantaenus, 12, 18
Papias, xxiii, 2-10, 11
Patristic testimony to the Hebrew Gospel, 97-102
Peter, Gospel of, 82
Photius, Patriarch of Constantinople, 36
Polycarp, 2

Q-Hypothesis, xviii, 209-42

Recognized Canonical Books, 19-22
Rejected Canonical Books, 19-22
Revelation, Book of, 99
Rufinus, 6, 7, 52

Saccas, Ammonius, 98
Schleiermacher, F. D. E., 218-19, 222
Scholia in Codex Sinaiticus, 40-42
Schweitzer, A., 221-22
Semitisms in the Gospel of Luke, xix, xx, 126-30, 131-48
Septuagintisms, xxi, 126, 127, 157-62
Synoptic Problem, xvii, 1

Teachings (of the Apostles), 119
Tertullian, 253
Theaetetus, 15
Theodore of Mopsuestia, 36, 119
Theodoret of Cyrrhus, 38
Thomas, Gospel of, 225-26
Timaeus, 13, 15
Tobit, 253
Toldoth Jeshu, 193
Traditions of Matthew (or *Matthias*), 13, 22, 118-19
Troy, 189
Tübingen School, xxv
Twelve, Gospel of the, 119

Vatican I, 219-20
Venerable Bede, 40

Wisdom of Jesus ben Sira, 254

Index of Scripture References

Genesis

17:17	139, 159
27:41	139, 159
31:30	75
31:47	170

Exodus

4:22	91
16:31	69

Leviticus

8:26	69
26:18-28	95

Numbers

11:8	69
17:10	325
24:1	132
27:1-8	230

Deuteronomy

4:2	231
13:13	135
22:19	160
27:36	230

Joshua

19:15	83

1 Samuel

27:5	135

2 Samuel

2:1	135
17:9	135
17:12	135

1 Kings

12:26	139, 159
18:12	57

2 Kings

1:10	160
2:16	57, 135
18:26	170, 171
18:28	170

2 Chronicles

24:20-21	86, 87
32:18	170

Ezra

4:7	171
6:14	86
7:11-26	158

Nehemiah

4:11	135
12:16	86
13:24	170

Esther

6:6	139, 159

Psalms

10:6	139, 159
10:11	139, 159
10:13	139, 159
14:1	139, 159
53:2	139, 159
118:24	77, 78
139:16	27, 116
150:1	138

Song of Songs

4:9	135

Isaiah

6:1-8	89
6:4	89
36:11	170, 171
36:13	170
41:28	328
61:1	58

Jeremiah
10:11   170

Ezekiel
8:3   57
18:7   91-93

Daniel
2:4   171
2:4-28   158

Obadiah
1:3   139, 159

Zechariah
1:1   86
1:7   86

Malachi
3:1   133

Bel and the Dragon
5:36   57

2 Maccabees
10:6-7   77

Matthew
1:18   57, 72
2:5   110
2:9   134
2:10   136
3:1-2   72
3:1-12   250
3:1–4:25   246
3:4   69
3:7-9   234
3:12   234
3:13-17   109
3:15   71, 94, 110
3:16   71, 91, 134
3:17   134
4:2b-11   234
4:5   40, 41

4:11   134
4:18   61
5–7   214, 246
5–25   214
5:2   68
5:3   249
5:3-12   234
5:14-16   230
5:15   235
5:17   74, 110, 110, 181, 230, 231, 232
5:18   236
5:25-26   235
5:38-48   234
5:39   249
6:9-13   235, 247
6:11   83
6:19-21   235
6:22-23   235
6:24   235, 250
6:25-34   235
6:33   14
7:1-5   234
7:4   134
7:7-8   14, 110
7:7-11   235
7:7-12   250
7:13   235
7:15-20   234
7:21-27   234
7:22-23   235
7:28   131, 214, 246
7:29–9:38   246
8:1-4   250
8:1–9:34   238
8:2   134
8:5-13   250
8:7-13   235
8:9   85
8:11   235
8:12   235
8:18-22   61, 235, 150
8:24   131, 134
8:26   131

8:28   61
8:29   134
8:30   141
8:32   134
8:34   134
9:2   134
9:3   134
9:7   138
9:9   24, 25, 68, 257
9:10   131, 134
9:11   25
9:17-18   85
9:20   134
9:27   61
9:37-38   235
10   214, 246
10:2   67
10:4   68
10:7-16   235
10:16-25   250
10:26-33   235
10:34-36   63
10:35   235
10:39   236
10:40   235
11:1   131, 214, 246
11:1-19   250
11:2-11   235, 237
11:2–22:50   246
11:12-13   236
11:16-19   235
11:20-24   235
11:25-27   235
11:25-30   250
11:26   131
11:28-29   14
12:10   134
12:13   84-86, 109
12:28   249
12:30   235
12:33   249
12:38-42   235, 250
12:41   134
12:42   134

12:42-51	235	20:20-28	251	28:9	134
12:43-45	235	20:30	61, 134	28:9-15	250
12:46-50	109	21:1-2	61	28:20	134
12:47	57	21:9	78, 109, 167		
12:49	73	21:27	134	**Mark**	
12:50	57	21:42	131	1:2	134
13	214	22:1-6	235	1:4	72, 95, 131
13:1-52	246	22:4-46	251	1:5-6	69
13:4	133	22:7-10	235	1:9-11	109, 131
13:14	136	23–25	246	1:10	91
13:16-17	235	23:8-10	88	1:21-28	250
13:25	133	23:35	86, 87, 110	2:12	138
13:33	235	23:37	137, 138	2:13-17	25
13:44	14	23:37-38	235, 238, 249	2:14	24
13:53	131, 214, 246	23:39	249	2:16-17	25
13:54–17:27	246	24–25	214	2:23	131
15:1-20	250	24:15-28	250	2:27	131
15:4	136	24:23	236	3:5	84, 109
15:5	249	24:26-27	236	3:16	67
15:22	134	24:28	236	3:29	95
15:31	14	24:29-35	251	3:31-35	109
15:32-39	251	24:37-39	236	3:32	134
16:2-3	235	24:40-41	236	3:33	73
16:7	40	24:45-51	250	3:35	57
16:13–17:23	238	25:14-30	64, 249	4:3	134
16:19	220	25:44	134	4:4	131, 133
16:21-28	250	26:1	131, 214, 246	4:12	136
17:2	131	26:17	75	4:19	131
17:3	134	26:17-25	150	4:22	131
17:5	134, 249	26:20	81	4:35–5:20	248
17:27	68	26:26	47	4:38	134
18	214, 246	26:26-29	247	4:39	131
18:15	236	26:28	95	4:41	136
18:21-22	40, 41, 94-96,	26:51	134	5:11	141
	236	26:74	40	5:16	131
19:1	131, 214, 246	27:12	133	5:41	167
19:2–22:46	246	27:33	249	6:14	131
19:16	110, 134	27:45	131	6:14-29	150
19:16-17	249	27:46	167	6:48	133
19:16-22	59-62	27:51	88, 89, 134	7:1-23	250
19:17	322	27:57	134	7:10	136
19:28	134, 236	27:59	81	7:11	167, 249
19:30	235	28:2	131, 134	7:34	167
20:10	134	28:7	134	7:37	14

8:1-10	251	**Luke**		2:26	140
8:29	134	1:1	148, 237	2:27	133, 139
8:31–9:1	250	1:1-4	5, 7, 40, 41, 85,	2:28	134
9:3	131		114, 116, 148-53,	2:31	132
9:7	131		239	2:33	140
9:26	131	1:2	145	2:36	140
10:17-18	249	1:5	67, 69, 72, 110,	2:37	134
10:17-22	59-62		131, 145	2:42	131
10:28	134	1:6	140	2:43	133
10:33	134	1:7	140	2:46	131
10:35-45	251	1:8	131, 133	2:50	134
10:51	85	1:10	140	2:51	140
11:9	109	1:15	132	3:1-20	250
11:9-10	78	1:17	132, 134	3:2	69, 72
11:19	131	1:19	132	3:3	72, 95
12:11	131	1:20	134, 140	3:7-9	234
12:35-37	250	1:21	133, 140	3:17	234
12:38-50	250	1:22	134, 140	3:19	150
13:3-13	250	1:23	131	3:21-22	70, 71, 109, 117,
13:14-23	250	1:29	139		133
13:23	134	1:31	134	3:23	67, 110, 117, 134,
13:24-31	251	1:33	91		140
14:9	167	1:35	57, 58	4:1-13	147, 234
14:10	167	1:36	134, 134	4:7	132
14:12	75	1:41	131	4:9	137
14:12-21	250	1:44	131	4:15	134
14:15	134	1:59	131	4:16	140, 145
14:17	81	1:64	68	4:16-30	142, 147
14:22	47	1:65	131	4:17	140
14:22-25	247	1:75	132	4:18	58, 96
14:30	184	1:76	132	4:20	140
14:36	167	1:77	95	4:25	131
14:41	134	2:1	131	4:30	134
14:42	134	2:2	131	4:31	67, 141
15:7	87	2:6	131, 133	4:31-37	250
15:22	249	2:8	140	4:33	141
15:33	131	2:9	136	4:36	131
15:34	167	2:13	131	4:38	67, 110, 141
15:38	88	2:14	78	4:38-39	142
15:43	134	2:15	131	4:44	141
16:5	14	2:20	138	5:1	131, 133, 134, 139,
16:9	134	2:21	139		140, 145
16:12	55	2:22	137	5:1-11	142, 147
		2:25	134, 145	5:9	14

5:12	131, 132, 133, 134, 135, 139, 145, 165	7:18-28	235, 237	9:45	141
5:12-16	250	7:18-35	250	9:51	131, 132, 133, 134, 139, 145
5:14	134	7:27	132, 133		
5:16	134, 141	7:30	139	9:51-56	142
5:17	131, 134, 135, 137, 139, 140, 145	7:31-35	235	9:52	132
		7:36-50	8, 111, 142, 147	9:53	132, 140
5:18	132, 134, 140	7:37	134	9:54	160
5:20	333	7:39	139	9:57-60	235
5:25	132, 138	7:47	111	9:57-62	61, 250
5:26	138	8:1	41, 131, 134, 139, 145	10:1	132
5:27	24, 111			10:2-16	235
5:27-32	25	8:2	140	10:21	131
5:29	24, 111, 141	8:5	133	10:21-24	235, 250
5:30-31	25	8:13	134	10:25	134
5:37	134	8:19-21	109	10:25-28	147
6:1	131	8:20	73	10:28	62
6:1-10	333, 335	8:21	57, 73	10:29-37	142
6:5	333-35	8:22	131, 134, 135, 139, 145	10:35	133
6:6	131			10:39	140
6:8	134	8:24	131	10:42	67
6:10	84, 109	8:32	141	11:1	131, 133
6:11	134	8:37	134	11:2-4	235, 247
6:12	131, 140	8:39	149	11:3	83, 110
6:13	63, 67, 131	8:40	141	11:4	134
6:14	67	8:41	134, 134	11:9-10	14, 110
6:15	67, 110	8:42	134	11:9-13	235, 250
6:16	68, 131	8:47	132	11:14	131, 140
6:17	137	8:48	334	11:17	134
6:20	134, 249	8:49	334	11:20	249
6:20-23	234	8:54	134	11:23	215
6:22	160	9:10	149	11:23-26	235
6:27-49	234	9:18	131, 133, 145	11:27	131, 133, 145
6:29	249	9:21-27	250	11:28	134
6:36-39	333	9:28	131, 139, 145	11:29-35	235, 250
6:43	249	9:29	131, 133	11:30	131
6:49	131	9:30	134	11:31	134
7:1-10	250	9:32	140	11:32	134
7:6-10	235	9:33	131, 133	11:37-54	142
7:8	85	9:34	131, 133	11:41	134
7:11	41, 131	9:35	67, 131	11:46	134
7:11-17	142	9:36	133, 134	11:51	86, 87, 110
7:12	134, 139	9:37	41, 131	11:53	132
7:16	138	9:38-39	85, 134	11:58	139
		9:39	249	12:2-9	235

12:3	140	14:21-24	235	18:7	93
12:6	132	14:25-33	142	18:9	139
12:9	132	15:1	140	18:11	139
12:14	62, 334	15:10	132	18:15-17	250
12:15	133	15:11-32	142	18:18-23	59-62
12:17	139	15:13	65, 111	18:18-29	249
12:22-31	235	15:14	134	18:31	137
12:32	139	15:17	139	18:34	134, 141
12:33-34	235	15:18	132	18:35	131, 133
12:39-46	235	15:21	132	18:39	134
12:41-48	250	15:24	140	18:41	85
12:51-53	63	15:29	134	18:43	138
12:53	235	15:30-31	65, 79, 111	19:1	139
12:54-56	236	16:1-9	142	19:1-9	142
12:54-59	235	16:3	85, 111, 139	19:1-10	25, 26, 111
13:1-3	181	16:10-12	142, 250	19:2	134
13:3	74	16:13	235, 250	19:5	334
13:6-9	147	16:14-15	142	19:7	74
13:7	134	16:15	132	19:9	62
13:10	135, 140, 145	16:16-17	236	19:11-27	64, 142, 249
13:10-17	142	16:19-31	61, 111, 142	19:15	131, 133, 139
13:11	134, 140	16:22	131	19:19	131
13:13	138	16:24	134, 334	19:28	137
13:16	62, 134	16:27	334	19:29	131
13:19	131	16:28	134	19:38	78, 109
13:20-21	235	17:1-2	92-93	19:41-44	142
13:22	137	17:3-4	92, 94-96, 111, 236	19:44	140
13:24	137, 235	17:11	131, 133, 134, 139, 145	19:47	141
13:25	139			20:1	131, 135
13:26	132	17:11-19	142	20:45-47	250
13:26-30	235	17:13	134	21:24	145
13:30	134	17:14	131, 133	21:34	145
13:34-35	235, 236, 238, 249	17:15	138	21:34-36	142
		17:16	132, 134	21:34-38	8
14:1	131, 133, 134, 139, 140, 145	17:20-21	142	21:35	132
		17:23-27	236	21:37	140
14:1-6	142	17:25	236	21:37-38	142
14:2	134	17:26	131	22:4	81
14:7	67	17:28	131	22:5	334
14:7-14	142	17:33-37	236	22:9	75
14:10	132	18:1-14	142	22:10	184
14:12	134	18:2	140	22:14	81, 131
14:14	131	18:4	139	22:15	74, 110, 136
14:16-18	235			22:15-18	142, 247

22:19-20	147	24:28	134	4:27	96
22:23	134	24:30	81, 111, 131, 133	5:14	174
22:24	131	24:31	81, 131, 134	5:28	75, 136
22:28-30	236	24:35	134	5:31	95
22:41	134	24:39	36, 46-54, 82,	5:34	229
22:43-44	142		110, 111	6:1	175
22:44	131	24:43	132	6:7	174
22:58	62, 334	24:47	95	7:34	136
22:60	62	24:49	134	7:38	4, 213
22:66	131	24:51	131, 133	8:33	149
23:6-12	142	24:52	134	8:35	224
23:8	140	24:53	140	8:39-40	57
23:9	134			9:5	71
23:13-16	142	**John**		9:27	149
23:13-27	81	1:32-33	91	9:29	152
23:14	132, 134	2:6-7	184	10:17	139
23:15	134	4:28	184	10:38	96
23:19	87, 111, 141	5:2	176	10:43	95
23:27	145	5:20	14	11:4	41, 151
23:27-32	142	5:39	224	11:18	138
23:33	249	6:37	63	11:21	174
23:34	37	7:53–8:12	7-10	12:11	139
23:37	137	8:44	88	12:17	149
23:39-43	142	12:13	78, 167	12:23	140
23:42	85	15:27	150	13:22	73
23:44	131	19:13	175, 176	13:38	95
23:45	88	19:17	175	13:48	138
23:46	136	19:35	85	15:3	149
23:47	138	20:16	175	17:11	224
23:50	134, 142	21:24-25	85	18:23	41
23:51	140, 142			18:28	224
23:53	82, 141	**Acts**		19:13	152
23:55	141	1:13	67	21:1	41
24:1-53	142	1:21-22	150	21:20	138
24:4	131, 133, 134, 139	1:23	24	21:37	169
24:5	132, 133	1:26	24	21:40	176
24:11	132	2:38	95	22:2	176
24:13	134, 140, 145	2:41	174	22:3	62
24:14	134	2:47	174	22:4	176
24:15	131, 133, 134, 139	3:13	138	22:8	71
24:19	131	3:24	41	22:30	229
24:21	131	4:4	174	23:12	82
24:25	134	4:17	75, 136	23:14	75, 136
24:27	91	4:21	138	24:5	122

24:14	122	15:7	80, 82	**Philippians**	
25:1-3	137			3:3-6	174, 175
25:17	41	**2 Corinthians**			
26:15	71	3:17	90	**2 Thessalonians**	
26:18	95	11:22	174, 175	2:10	140, 159
27:18	41				
		Galatians		**Hebrews**	
Romans		2:9	80	5:12	4
2	334	2:13	80	12:22	137
3:2	4, 213	2:19	80		
8:9-11	92			**1 Peter**	
10:2	176	**Ephesians**		4:11	4
		2:12	175		
1 Corinthians		2:19	175	**Revelation**	
3:16	92	4:30	92	9:11	175
11:23-26	247	5:4	29, 79	16:16	175

Index of Other Ancient Writings

Ambrosius

Proem. in Luc.   119

2 Apocalypse of James

56.2-6   14

Augustine

Civ.

15.11   180
15.12-13   99, 179
18.42-43   101
18.43-44   178, 179

Epist.

71.3-5   179
82.35   179

2 Baruch

6:3   57

1 Clement

13:6   4
53:1   4

2 Clement

9:11   73
13:3   4

Clement of Alexandria

Strom.

2.9.45   13, 22, 93, 106,
          110, 118-19, 266
3.1.1-4   93
3.4.6   119
3.9.63   13
4.35.2   25
5.14.96   13, 106, 110,
          266
6.6.53   93
7.7.108   119
7.13   93, 111, 119, 266

Clementine Homilies

18.3   61
18:17   61

Decretum Gelasianum

3.1   119

Didache

10.6   167

Didymus of Alexandria

Comm. Eccl.

4.223.6-13   9-10, 111, 273

Comm. Ps.

34.1   23-26, 272-73

Ephrem the Syrian

*Comm. on Tatian's
Diatessaron*   23, 272

Epiphanius

Pan.

20.2.2   121
24.3.7   93
29.9.4   26, 27, 114, 274
30.2.2   121
30.2.3   121
30.2.4   121
30.2.6   121
30.3.7   26, 27, 112, 116,
          118, 119, 121, 274
30.3.8-9   27
30.6.7   116
30.6.9   26, 116, 117, 118,
          274
30.13.1   26
30.13.2-3   26, 66-68, 85,
          104, 110, 113, 114,
          116, 274-75
30.13.4-6   68-69, 72, 110,
          275-76

30.13.7-8	69-71, 109, 110, 114, 276
30.14.2	26
30.14.3	26, 27, 71-72, 110, 276-77
30.14.4	121
30.14.5	72-73, 109, 277
30.15.1	121
30.15.2	121
30.15.3-4	74, 121
30.16.1	121
30.16.4-5	73-74, 110, 121, 231, 277
30.16.7	121
30.16.8	121
30.17.1	121
30.17.4	121
30.17.6	121
30.18.2	121
30.18.3	121
30.18.4	121
30.18.5-6	121
30.18.6	121
30.21.1	121
30.21.2	121
30.22.4	74-75, 110, 278
30.22.5	116
30.24.1-5	114
30.24.6	114
30.27.2	74
30.29.1	121
30.29.3	121
30.31.1	27, 116
46.1	23, 278
51.3.1-5	99
51.5.3	26, 278

Eusebius
Hist. eccl.

1.9.3	5
1.12.3	22
2.1.1	22
2.2.4	253
2.15.1	5
2.23	80
3.9.3	253
3.24.5	5
3.24.5-6	19, 28, 29, 198, 253, 270
3.24.5-13	5
3.24.7	5
3.24.8	5
3.24.10	5
3.24.11	5
3.24.12	5
3.24.13	5
3:24.15	151
3.25	19-22
3.25.5	18
3.25.6	118-19
3.27.4	10, 18, 38, 65, 121, 270
3.29.4	22
3.36.10-11	50, 51, 52, 110, 271
3.37.4	2
3.38.1	2
3.39.1-3	2, 99
3.39.4	2-3, 5
3.39.6	99
3.39.9-10	2, 22
3.39.13	99, 214
3.39.14	5, 7
3.39.15	4, 5, 242
3.39.16	3, 6, 7, 99, 198, 213, 264
3.39.17	7-10, 111, 264
4.5.1-2	181
4.7.7	93
4.22.4	81
4.22.8	7, 15, 177, 266
4.29.6	215
4.30.1	253
5.8.2	10, 12, 265
5.8.3	177
5.10.3	12, 266
5.24.5	5
5.33.4	11
6.6.1	18
6.14.2	183
6.14.5-7	5
6.16	184
6.16.1	177
6.17.1	10, 11, 119
6.25.1-2	55, 56, 177
6.25.4	18, 55, 123, 268
6.25.11-14	99
7.25.1-26	99
9.5.1	5
9.7.1	5

Theoph.

4.12	18, 19, 62-63, 111, 271
4.22	63-65, 111, 271-72

Genesis Rabbah   53

Gos. Pet.

5.19	59

Gos. Thom.

2	13
3	226, 335
7	226
14	335
18	226
22	226
29	226
30	226
37	226
41	64
42	226
51	226
70	226
114	226

Gregory of Nazianzus
Or. Bas.

4	171

Hadith, Islamic
Sahih al-Bukhari   42,
     289-90

Haimo Halberstensis
Comm. Isa. 53:13   37

Hippolytus
De Duodecim
Apostolis   12, 17, 266

Historia passionis Do-
mini
65   88, 122
551   37

Hugo of St. Cher
Libr. Isa.   37

Ignatius
Smyrn.
2.1   54
3.1-2   45-54, 67, 85, 110,
     265
3.3   51

Irenaeus
Haer.
1.8.1   4
1.24.5   93
1.26.1   11
1.26.2   10, 265
3.1.1   10, 12, 177, 265
3.3.4   114
3.11.7   10
3.15.1   10

Jerome
Comm. Eph.
5.4   29, 79, 111, 279

Comm. Ezech.
16.13   29, 57, 58, 111,
     285-86

18.7   29, 91-93, 111,
     286

Comm. Isa.
Praefatio   29, 35, 49,
     284-85
11.1-3   29, 90-91, 106,
     111, 285
18   53
40.9-11   29, 57, 58, 111,
     285

Comm. Matt.
Praefatio   29, 119, 282
2.5   34, 83, 110, 282-
     83
6.11   29, 83-84, 110,
     283
12.13   35, 39, 46, 84-86,
     109, 122, 283
23.35   29, 86-87, 110,
     283-84
27.9   100
27.16   29, 87-88, 111,
     284
27.51   29, 88-90, 111,
     284

Comm. Micah
7.5-7   34, 35, 46, 49, 58,
     111, 286

Epist.
7.2   100
17.2   100
18.9, *ad Dam.*   89
19, *Dam. ad*
Hieron.   77, 279
20, *ad Dam.*   29, 77-78,
     109, 148, 279
120.8-9, *ad Hedy.*   29, 37,
     88-90, 111, 287
125.8, *ad Rustic.*   100

Pelag.
3.2   16, 32, 41, 62, 71,

     92, 93-96, 110,
     119, 287-88

Praefatio in Quattuor
Evangeliorum 33-34, 286

Praefatio in Librum
Tobiae   32

Tract. Ps.
135   83-84, 284

Vir. ill.
1.3   99, 101
1.5   101
2   30, 34-35, 46, 49,
     56, 79-82, 111,
     279-80
2.2   101
3   29-30, 280-81
3.3   179
5.10   99
7   101
15.2   99
16   35-37, 46, 48, 49,
     50, 52, 54, 111,
     281-82
18.3   101
25.3   101
36.2   12, 17, 282
61   16
75.2   100
92.1   100
108.1   100
109.2   101
115.2   100
132.1   100

John Chrysostom
Hom. Matt.
1.3   28, 278

Josephus
Ant.
Proem. 5   178
1.7   253

1.29   135
1.33   178
1.34   178
1.36   177, 178
1.333   178
5.21   178
5.323   177
10.7-8   171, 178
12.14-15   178

Contra Apion
1.47   150

J.W.
1.3   6, 180, 253
1.133-37   62
6.93-110   178
6.96   177, 180
6.288   89
6.290   89
6.435-42   178

Justin Martyr
1 Apol.
66.3   5

Dial.
100.4   5

Marius Mercator
*De Haeresi et Libris
Nestorii*
4.2   39, 288

Mishnah
Gittin
9.6-8   170

Megillah
1.8   170
4.4-10   170

Sotah
7.2   170
9.14   172

Yadaim
4.5   170

Nicephorus
Chron. Brev.   104, 105,
                        290

Origen
Cels.
1.2   191
1.9.3   5
2.1   191
2.4   178
3.55   193
5.2   191
5.62   193
8.69   191

Comm. John
2.12   17, 55, 56-59, 111,
                        268

Comm. Matt.
5.19   4
15.14   17, 55, 110, 111,
            268-69, 334-35
19.13   4

Hom. Jer.
10.1   4
15.4   17, 55-57, 111, 268

Hom. Luc.
1.1   106, 118, 119, 152

Princ.
Praefatio 8   48, 53, 110,
                    269-70

Oxyrhynchus Papyri
654   13
1224   25, 111, 273

Philip Sidetes   39, 104,
                        288

Philo
Conf.
68   177

Vit. Mos.
2.26   32
2.31   32
2.38   32
2.40   32

Photius
Bibl.
177   36, 119

Polycarp
Phil.
1.7   4

Rufinus
Apol. Hier.
2.32-37   179

**Scholia in Codex
Sinaiticus**   40-42, 291

Sedulius Scottus
*Collectanea in Epistolam
I ad Corinthios*   82, 290

*Super Evangelium
Mathei*   84, 290

Talmud
Gittin
45b   191

Šabbat
116   181, 191, 228-32,
                     263-64

Sanhedrin
43a   193
107b   193

Sotah
47a   193

359

Tertullian
Marc.
4.4   61, 113

Theodoret of Cyrrhus
Haer. Fab. Comp.
1.20   215

2.1   38, 119, 121, 177,
                                    288

Theophylact
Proem. in Luc.   119

Thom. Cont.
145.12-14   14

Venerable Bede
*In Lucae Evangelium
Expositio*
1.1-4   40, 289